Birds

Birds is the first book to examine bird remains in archaeology and anthropology. Providing a thorough review of the literature on this topic, it also serves as a guide to the methods of study of bird remains from the past. It covers a wide range of topics, including anatomy and osteology, taphonomy, eggs, feathers, and bone tools. It examines the myriad ways in which people have interacted with birds in the past. The volume also includes discussion on the consumption of wild birds, the domestication of birds, cockfighting and falconry, birds in ritual and religion, and the role of birds in ecological reconstruction, providing an up-to-date survey of current knowledge on these topics. *Birds* will be an invaluable resource for undergraduate and graduate students interested in zooarchaeology and human–animal relations, as well as professional zooarchaeologists, archaeologists, and anthropologists interested in birds and people of the past.

Dale Serjeantson is a Research Fellow in Archaeology in the School of Humanities, University of Southampton, UK. She is the co-author, with Alan Cohen, of *Manual for the Identification of Bird Bones from Archaeological Sites* and has contributed papers on birds and other zooarchaeological topics in journals and popular magazines. She is associate editor of the *International Journal of Osteoarchaeology* and a member of the Institute of Field Archaeologists, the Society of Antiquaries of Scotland, the Association for Environmental Archaeology, and L'Homme et l'Animal: Sociétié de Recherche Interdisciplinaire.

Dedicated to Alistair Thomson, for his forbearance during the past four years

Cambridge Manuals in Archaeology

General Editor
Graeme Barker, *University of Cambridge*

Advisory Editors
Elizabeth Slater, *University of Liverpool*
Peter Bogucki, *Princeton University*

Cambridge Manuals in Archaeology is a series of reference handbooks designed for an international audience of upper-level undergraduate and graduate students and professional archaeologists and archaeological scientists in universities, museums, research laboratories, and field units. Each book includes a survey of current archaeological practice alongside essential reference material on contemporary techniques and methodology.

Books in the series
Pottery in Archaeology, CLIVE ORTON, PAUL TYERS, and ALAN VINCE
Vertebrate Taphonomy, R. LEE LYMAN
Photography in Archaeology and Conservation, 2nd edition, PETER G. DORRELL
Alluvial Geoarchaeology, A. G. BROWN
Shells, CHERYL CLAASEN
Sampling in Archaeology, CLIVE ORTON
Excavation, STEVE ROSKAMS
Teeth, 2nd edition, SIMON HILLSON
Lithics, 2nd edition, WILLIAM ANDREFSKY, JR.
Geographical Information Systems in Archaeology, JAMES CONOLLY and MARK LAKE
Demography in Archaeology, ANDREW CHAMBERLAIN
Analytical Chemistry in Archaeology, A. M. POLLARD, C. M. BATT, B. STERN, and S. M. M. YOUNG
Zooarchaeology, 2nd edition, ELIZABETH J. REITZ and ELIZABETH S. WING
Quantitative Paleozoology, R. LEE LYMAN

Birds

Dale Serjeantson *University of Southampton*

 CAMBRIDGE
UNIVERSITY PRESS

CAMBRIDGE UNIVERSITY PRESS
Cambridge, New York, Melbourne, Madrid, Cape Town, Singapore, São Paulo, Delhi

Cambridge University Press
32 Avenue of the Americas, New York, NY 10013-2473, USA

www.cambridge.org
Information on this title: www.cambridge.org/9780521758581

© Dale Serjeantson 2009

This publication is in copyright. Subject to statutory exception
and to the provisions of relevant collective licensing agreements,
no reproduction of any part may take place without the written
permission of Cambridge University Press.

First published 2009

Printed in the United States of America

A catalog record for this publication is available from the British Library.

Library of Congress Cataloging in Publication data

Serjeantson, D. (Dale)
Birds / Dale Serjeantson.
  p. cm. – (Cambridge manuals in archaeology)
Includes bibliographical references and index.
ISBN 978-0-521-86617-0 (hardback) – ISBN 978-0-521-75858-1 (pbk.)   1. Bird
remains (Archaeology)   2. Human-animal relationships – History.   3. Birds – History.
I. Title.   II. Series.
CC79.5.B57S47   2009
930.1 – dc22   2009000905

ISBN 978-0-521-86617-0 hardback
ISBN 978-0-521-75858-1 paperback

Cambridge University Press has no responsibility for the persistence or
accuracy of URLs for external or third-party Internet Web sites referred to in
this publication and does not guarantee that any content on such Web sites is,
or will remain, accurate or appropriate. Information regarding prices, travel
timetables, and other factual information given in this work are correct at
the time of first printing, but Cambridge University Press does not guarantee
the accuracy of such information thereafter.

CONTENTS

Figures	*page* xi
Tables	xix
Preface	xxiii
Acknowledgments	xxv

1.	**Introduction**	1
	Aims and Scope	2
	Zooarchaeology or Palaeontology	3
	Taxonomy and Classification	4
	History of the Study of Bird Remains	5
	Bird Remains: The Questions	7
2.	**Biology, Behaviour, and Anatomy**	8
	Bird Biology and Behaviour	8
	Skeletal Anatomy	15
	Individual Bones	21
	Gizzard Stones	32
	Conclusion	34
3.	**Ageing, Sexing, and Pathology**	35
	Age at Death	36
	Sexing	47
	Pathology *by Tony Waldron*	55
	Conclusion	61
4.	**Identification, Recording, and Quantification**	63
	Identification	63
	Recording	78

Quantification	85
Conclusion	97

5. Natural Taphonomy and Recovery — 99
Recovery — 100
Natural Accumulations — 104
Natural Damage and Decay — 109
Element Survival — 124
Conclusions — 128

6. Taphonomy: Human Modifications and Element Survival — 130
Cut Marks — 131
Chop Marks — 140
Butchery without Tools — 144
Human Chewing — 146
Burning — 149
Differential Disposal — 153
Fragmentation — 154
Recording Modifications — 155
Element Presence or Absence and Bone Density — 155
Conclusions — 162

7. Eggs and Eggshell — 165
Ethnography and History of Egg-Collecting and Production — 166
Survival and Recovery of Eggshell — 169
Eggshell Structure — 170
Identification and Quantification of Eggshell — 171
Eggshell from Archaeological Sites — 176
Ostrich Eggshell — 179
Discussion and Conclusions — 181

8. Feathers, Skins, and Other Products — 184
Feathers: Introductory Comments — 184
Anthropological Feather Use — 185
Feather Types and Structure — 189
Feather Identification — 193
Archaeological Finds — 193
Taphonomy — 197
Feathers as a Secondary Product — 197
Proxy Evidence for Feather Use — 199

	Feathered Skins	203
	Sinew and Oil	205
	Discussion	206
9.	**Tools and Ornaments**	209
	Manufacture of Tools	209
	Types of Tools, Flutes, and Beads	213
	Decorative Objects	224
	Conclusions	228
10.	**Wild Birds as Food**	230
	The Economics of Bird Capture	230
	Technology and Fowling Methods	238
	Birds: A Major or Minor Food Resource?	250
	Major Resource	251
	Minor Resource	255
	Supplementary and Rare Resources	256
	Birds as Indicators of Seasonal Occupation	256
	Preservation of Wild Birds for Food	259
	Prehistory of Bird Capture	260
	Discussion	265
11.	**The Domestic Chicken**	267
	Wild Ancestor	268
	History	269
	Early Archaeological Records	270
	Changes Following Domestication	273
	Discussion	283
12.	**Other Domestic Birds**	287
	Turkey	287
	Geese	292
	Ducks	299
	Pigeon	304
	Minor Domestic Birds	310
	General Discussion	314
13.	**Sport and Pleasure**	316
	Hawking	316
	Cockfighting	325
	Hunting and Other Sports	331

Birds for Pleasure	332
Conclusion	334
14. Birds in Symbol and Ritual	**335**
Divine and Totem Animals	336
Beliefs about Birds	337
Birds in Graves	340
Bird Burials	348
Temple Sacrifices, Feasting, and Rites	349
Medicine Bundles and Talismans	355
Sky Burial	358
Special Deposits and Ritual Refuse	360
Pre-Eminent Species	361
Discussion and Conclusion	364
15. Birds in the Environment	**365**
Birds as Environmental Indicators	365
Pleistocene and Holocene Climate Change	371
Introductions and Range Increases	374
Diminished Ranges	378
Extinctions	380
Discussion and Conclusions	392
16. Conclusions and Outstanding Questions	**393**
Why Are Bird Remains Scarce?	393
Ancient Bird Bones and Environmental Conservation	394
Unresolved Questions of Methodology	396
Outstanding Questions about Bird Domestication	399
Birds in Human Prehistory	399
Appendix 1. List of Scientific and English Names of Species Referred to in the Text	**403**
Appendix 2. Illustrations and Definitions of Bone Zones	**412**
Definitions of Zones	412
Appendix 3. Organisations and Internet Resources	**419**
Bibliography	423
Index	465

FIGURES

1.1.	Tarsometatarsi of various species of moa, Dinornithiformes.	*page* 6
2.1.	Relationship of the incubation period to the fledging period in seabirds.	10
2.2.	Relationship between body and egg weight in raptors.	13
2.3.	Microstructure of chicken bone, showing Haversian canals and absence of osteons.	17
2.4.	Cross section of an avian long bone.	17
2.5.	Splinter of a long bone of one of the moa, showing the thickness of the bone wall and the interior structure.	18
2.6.	Longitudinal section and exterior view through the proximal end of a chicken humerus.	19
2.7.	Examples of pneumatised bones: coracoid, humerus, and femur.	20
2.8.	Skull bones: cranium, mandible, tongue skeleton, and quadrate.	22
2.9.	Vertebrae of mute swan.	23
2.10.	Axial skeleton: notarium, synsacrum, pelvis, and ribs.	24
2.11.	Sterna of various birds.	25
2.12.	Pectoral girdle: furcula, scapula, and coracoid.	26
2.13.	Proximal wing: humerus, radius, ulna, and radial and ulnar carpal.	27
2.14.	Distal wing: carpometacarpus and distal phalanx of major wing digit.	28
2.15.	Proximal leg: femur and tibiotarsus.	30
2.16.	Distal leg: tarsometatarsus and foot phalanges.	31
2.17.	Gizzard stones of a domestic chicken.	33
3.1.	Humerus, scapula, and coracoid of adult and newly fledged gannet.	37
3.2.	Unfused bones of a crane from Haddenham.	41
3.3.	Transverse sections of the mandibles of house martin showing lines of arrested growth.	42

3.4.	Cortical cross section of a femur of a moa, *Euryapteryx geranoides*, showing lines of arrested growth.	42
3.5.	Size of adult and immature chicken femora from the Romano-British temple at Uley.	44
3.6.	Humeri of immature gulls from Nipisat I, Greenland.	45
3.7.	Stages in the development of the spur in the Galliformes.	48
3.8.	Tarsometatarsi of a modern hen with spurs and an unfused spur from Kalaureia.	49
3.9.	Medullary bone: cross section of a long bone; cross sections through femora; and a longitudinally sectioned femora.	50
3.10.	Percentage of chicken elements with medullary bone at Roman port of Berenike.	52
3.11.	Size of long bones of whooper swan and coracoid of the extinct California turkey showing sexual dimorphism.	54
3.12.	Fractured humerus of a goose healed with angulation from medieval York.	57
3.13.	Humerus of a chicken with avian osteopetrosis from medieval Lincoln.	61
4.1.	'Science is Measurement', 1878, by Henry Stacy Marks.	70
4.2.	Distinctions in the humerus and ulna of the domestic chicken, willow grouse, and black grouse.	71
4.3.	Size of tarsometatarsi of willow grouse and ptarmigan from Brillenhöhle.	72
4.4.	Sterna of wild turkey and domestic turkey.	73
4.5.	Size of humerus of ducks from Tell Mureybet compared with ranges for recent ducks.	75
4.6.	Identification of pigeon species: proximal ulna and proximal tarsometatarsus.	76
4.7.	Furcula and sternum of swans, *Cygnus olor* and *C. cygnus*.	77
4.8.	Scatter diagram of femur measurements of carrion crow and rook.	78
4.9.	Scale of usefulness for identification, most diagnostic elements, and most frequent elements in Spanish assemblages.	80
4.10.	Birds from Mesolithic site of Ølby Ling: rank order × log abundance of species.	86
4.11.	Birds from Mesolithic site of Ertebølle: rank order × log abundance of species.	87

4.12.	Number of identified specimens and minimum number of elements of chickens from Carisbrooke Castle.	90
4.13.	Numbers and bone weight of the bird remains from Schipluiden.	91
4.14.	Biomass of birds at Túnel VII.	92
4.15.	Comparison of kilocalories and meat weight of mammals, birds, fish, and molluscs at Túnel VII.	96
5.1.	Percentage of bird bones from sieved and unsieved deposits at Haddenham.	103
5.2.	Bones on the floor of Moa Cave, Honeycomb Hill Cave system.	105
5.3.	Carcass of a manx shearwater killed by a great black-backed gull.	107
5.4.	Element survival in American coots in bird- and mammal-scavenged carcasses.	108
5.5.	Element survival in manx shearwaters killed by gulls on Skomer Island.	108
5.6.	Weathering on the proximal femur of a pigeon after ten months on a cave floor.	112
5.7.	Schematic drawings of tunnels made by bioeroding organisms on the bone surface.	114
5.8.	Pellets of a bald eagle showing bone fragments in the feather matrix.	117
5.9.	Beak impact of an eagle owl on the humeri of pigeons.	118
5.10.	Humeri of pigeons, showing the beak impact of a peregrine falcon.	118
5.11.	Furcula and sternum of a manx shearwater, showing beak damage from a great black-backed gull.	119
5.12.	Pelvis of a moa, showing a notch made by the beak of a Haast's eagle.	119
5.13.	Bones of grouse from the pellets of a gyrfalcon, showing evidence of digestion.	120
5.14.	Marks of gnawing of bird bones by mammals.	123
5.15.	Sequence of gnawing damage, probably by dogs, on tarsometatarsi of domestic geese from medieval Dublin.	124
5.16.	Proportion of wing to leg bones in pellets and in uneaten food remains.	126
5.17.	Proportion of core to limb bones in pellets and in uneaten food remains.	127
6.1.	Cut marks on humeri from Grotta Romanelli and zones where cut marks were recorded.	132
6.2.	Location of disarticulation and filleting cuts on the skeleton of grouse from La Vache.	134
6.3.	Location and number of cut marks on humeri at Taï 2.	135

6.4.	Location of cut marks on bones of snowy owl from Bois-Ragot.	137
6.5.	Location of cut marks on phalanges of snowy owl from Bois-Ragot.	140
6.6.	Distal tibiotarsus of a great auk with a cut mark on the condyle.	141
6.7.	Peacock tarsometatarsus from Carisbrooke Castle with cut marks round the distal condyles.	141
6.8.	Butchered coracoid of a great auk from Hornish, showing surface marks and final chop.	142
6.9.	Butchered synsacra of domestic geese from medieval Dublin, chopped transversely.	144
6.10.	Notches and perforations in the olecranon fossa of humeri of grouse, made by overextending the joint.	145
6.11.	'Peeling' marks on the proximal and distal articulations of a left ulna of a snowy owl.	145
6.12.	Snapped-off wing bones of thrushes from the house of Amarantus, Pompeii.	146
6.13.	Oval holes, probably human bite marks, on humeri of grouse from La Vache.	147
6.14.	Humeri and ulnae of gulls from Greenland sites, apparently chewed by humans.	148
6.15.	Location of traces of charring on bird bones from La Vache.	151
6.16.	Charring on distal humeri of male and female great bustards from Klisoura Cave.	152
6.17.	Elements of thrushes and other passerines from the refectory and kitchen of St Gregory's Priory.	153
6.18.	Percentages of dry and fresh fractures on the bird bones from Ajvide.	154
6.19.	Frequency of wing elements of aquatic birds from British Camp, San Juan Islands.	158
6.20.	Regression of bulk density to cortical wall thickness for 65 ducks and grebes.	160
6.21.	Relationship between number of elements and bone density of duck remains from the Yerba Buena shellmound.	161
7.1.	Gathering eggs from the sea cliffs in Orkney, nineteenth century.	166
7.2.	Scanning electron micrographs of a cross section through eggshell of a turkey and greater flamingo.	171
7.3.	Diagrammatic radial cross section through eggshell of Cygninae, Anserinae, and Anatinae.	172

7.4.	Scanning electron micrograph of a cross section through eggshell of a guillemot, penetrated by a pore canal.	173
7.5.	Thickness of eggshell fragments from Roman and medieval deposits at Causeway Lane, Leicester.	175
7.6.	Reconstructed moa egg, from Shag Mouth, and fetal bones.	180
7.7.	Manufacture of beads of ostrich eggshell from archaeological sites in the Western Cape.	182
8.1.	Nuchanulth cloak decorated with appliquéd feathers of the bald eagle.	187
8.2.	Wing feathers of the domestic Poitou goose, showing the different names given to the feathers and their specialised uses.	190
8.3.	Topography of a contour feather, showing calamus, rachis, vane, barbs, and barbules.	191
8.4.	Wing showing the primary and secondary flight feathers and the skeletal elements to which they are attached.	192
8.5.	Bunch of feathers, probably of chicken, from the Roman quarry camp at Mons Claudianus.	194
8.6.	Types of damage to feathers by avian and mammalian predators.	197
8.7.	Cut or notched feather of a white-tailed ptarmigan from the Yukon.	198
8.8.	Elements present of geese, crane, partridges, and griffon vulture at Jerf el Ahmar.	201
8.9.	Bones from the left wing of a white-tailed sea eagle from The Farm Beneath the Sand, probably collected for feathers or used as a brush.	202
8.10.	Preparation and sewing of clothes from feathered skins of eider ducks.	205
9.1.	Neolithic bird bone tools from Aartswoud, the Netherlands.	211
9.2.	Bird bone awls from New Zealand.	214
9.3.	Neolithic bird bone point from De Bruin, the Netherlands.	215
9.4.	Needle manufacture and bird bone needles from Amaknak, Aleutian Islands.	216
9.5.	Pipes (flutes) from Isturitz Cave, made on the ulnae of black vultures.	219
9.6.	Flute with worn fingerholes from Visegrad, made on the ulna of an eagle.	220
9.7.	Five pieces of Islamic bird bone musical instruments from Mértola, Portugal.	220
9.8.	Method of manufacture of annular beads at Qumran Cave using the ulna of a corvid.	222
9.9.	Maxilla cut from the skull of a spoonbill from a Hungarian Iron Age site.	223

9.10.	Fishhooks and offcuts of moa bone from Archaic sites in New Zealand showing method of manufacture.	224
9.11.	Perforated claw of an eagle owl from Palaeolithic Tibocoaia Cave.	225
9.12.	Engraved proximal phalanges of a snowy owl from Bois-Ragot.	228
10.1.	Birds from Tell Mureybet shown in aggregation classes.	236
10.2.	Magellanic penguins at the breeding site by the Skyring Sea, Patagonia.	238
10.3.	Mesolithic bone arrowheads from the Upper Volga region, probably used for hunting birds.	242
10.4.	Snare with 21 loops, used by the Ona of Patagonia for catching ducks.	244
10.5.	Underwater net for catching ducks and coots, recently in use in Perpignan.	245
10.6.	Implements for catching puffins on the Faroe Islands, early twentieth century.	246
10.7.	Late nineteenth-century wildfowlers on Orkney with puffins and guillemots.	247
10.8.	Fixed decoy for capturing ducks in Borough Fen, Lincolnshire.	249
10.9.	Relative intensity of Mesolithic and Neolithic wildfowling in northern Europe and the Baltic region.	251
10.10.	Numbers (NISP) of mammal, bird, and fish remains from High Arctic sites.	254
10.11.	Numbers (NISP) of marine mammals, terrestrial mammals, birds, and fish from Ponsonby.	255
10.12.	Season of occupation of Nipisat I, based on the presence of medullary bone and immature birds.	259
10.13.	Remains of preserved songthrushes in a pottery vessel from a Roman settlement at Nijmegen.	260
10.14.	Relative frequencies of slow or sessile prey versus birds and lagomorphs in Palaeolithic assemblages.	262
11.1.	Examples of chicken tarsometatarsi from the Roman castellum at Velsen.	275
11.2.	Distribution of length of spurred and unspurred chicken tarsometatarsi from Roman sites in northern France.	277
11.3.	Distribution of length of chicken tarsometatarsi from Sagalassos, showing the presence of two types or breeds.	278
11.4.	Size of tarsometatarsi of chickens from the Roman castellum at Velsen, suggesting a single type or breed.	278

11.5.	Size change in chickens from northern France over time, in relation to reference chickens.	280
11.6.	Seasonal consumption of capons, chickens, and eggs in the medieval Suffolk household of Alice de Bryene.	282
11.7.	Comparison of the percentage of juvenile domestic chickens and geese from medieval Norwich.	283
12.1.	Relative numbers of artiodactyl, lagomorph, and turkey at two Pueblo sites.	290
12.2.	Goose bones from Tell el-Maskhuta compared with modern geese.	294
12.3.	Relative percentages of goose and duck from Saxon sites in southern England.	295
12.4.	Length and means of carpometacarpi of domestic geese from medieval Winchester.	296
12.5.	Seasonal consumption of domestic geese and pigeons in the medieval household of Alice de Bryene.	298
12.6.	Feral Muscovy ducks with mixed plumage from Ecuador.	303
12.7.	Dovecot from the sixteenth century AD at the Château de Puyguilhem.	309
12.8.	Skull of a guineafowl from medieval Genoa.	312
13.1.	Method of capturing hawks in the Netherlands in the nineteenth century AD.	319
13.2.	Hittite engravings of the first millennium BC, showing hawking equipment.	320
13.3.	Tail feather of a Korean hawk with identity tag and bell.	322
13.4.	Relative numbers of wild birds from the Slavonic stronghold at Oldenburg.	324
13.5.	Circular brick cockpit in the Welsh National History Museum, St Fagans.	328
13.6.	Modified spurs: cock with artificial metal spurs, and tarsometatarsus with spur sawn off.	328
13.7.	Carpometacarpus and coracoid of a parrot, from Norwich, seventeenth century AD.	333
14.1.	Bas relief on a pillar at Göbekli Tepe, showing two cranes, lines depicting snakes, and pictograms.	337
14.2.	Rock engraving of a 'Bird-Man', a human figure with the head of a bird, from Rapa Nui or Easter Island.	339

14.3.	Frequency of mammals and domestic chicken in Roman-period settlements and cemeteries compared with references in cookery books.	341
14.4.	Grave gifts on dishes from a cemetery in Nijmegen, fourth century AD.	341
14.5.	Grave of a Roman soldier from Aquincum-Testverhegy buried with a chicken and a young pig.	342
14.6.	Map of Sweden, showing graves with raptor burials, sixth to eleventh century AD.	346
14.7.	Burnt chicken bones from domestic sacrifices at the house and bar of Amarantus at Pompeii.	350
14.8.	Mummified saker falcon from Saqqara, Egypt: external view and X-ray view.	353
14.9.	Cut marks on the radius and ulna of a crane from Catal Höyük, suggesting the wing had been worn or suspended.	355
14.10.	Temporal bone of the skull of a griffon vulture from Jerf el Ahmar, with cut marks from scalping.	359
15.1.	Map showing records of grouse in Europe from Isotope Stages 5a–5d.	370
15.2.	Environmental conditions at Ain Mallaha in the eleventh to ninth millennia BC, inferred from breeding, resident, and migratory species.	372
15.3.	Flightless cormorant on the Galapagos Islands.	383
15.4.	Decline in numbers of great auk as a percentage of all birds at two sites on the island of Sanday, Orkney.	385
15.5.	Hypothesised decline to extinction in New Zealand of Finsch's duck.	386
15.6.	Decline in numbers of bones and species of native landbirds on Mangaia, Cook Islands.	389
15.7.	Hypothetical example of how cultural factors affected the number of avian extinctions on Pacific oceanic islands.	390
15.8.	Size of carpometacarpus of crane from Late Pleistocene and Holocene Europe.	391
16.1.	Pathways by which bird and other animal remains become incorporated into settlement refuse.	394
Appendix figure 1.	Bone zones: humerus, coracoid, scapula, ulna, radius, carpometacarpus, furcula, and sternum.	417
Appendix figure 2.	Bone zones: pelvis, synsacrum, femur, tibiotarsus, and tarsometatarsus.	418

TABLES

2.1.	Developmental states at hatching	*page* 11
2.2.	Scientific and anglicised names of bird bones	16
2.3.	Phalanges of the foot	32
3.1.	Bones which fuse after hatching	39
3.2.	Age of fusion in bones of domestic chicken	39
3.3.	Evidence of age in skeletons of four immature domestic geese	40
3.4.	Spur lengths in domestic chicken and turkey at different ages	44
3.5.	Age classes and bone length of the sacred ibis, from Tuna el-Gebel	46
3.6.	Four age categories for recording excavated bird bones	46
3.7.	Presence of medullary bone in the different elements of chicken from sites in England	52
4.1.	Bone length range of male and female wild turkeys	74
4.2.	Definitions of zones on avian limb bones	81
4.3.	Size categories used for recording bird bones	82
4.4.	Identified and unidentified bird remains from Eynsham Abbey by size class	83
4.5.	Database for chicken tibiotarsi from Carisbrooke Castle, showing bone zones	89
4.6.	Percentage NISP of domestic fowl compared with sheep/goat on Romano-British sites	93
4.7.	Percentage bone in the carcass weight of seven mammals and ten birds	94
4.8.	Weight and number of bones of food animals, horses, and dogs from the Mithraic temple at Deggendorf	95

4.9.	Ranking of elements to be recorded	98
5.1.	Disarticulation sequence in ice-trapped American coots, birds of various species in a field, and manx shearwaters	106
5.2.	Dispersal sequences for bones of rock dove in a flume	111
5.3.	Weathering categories for bird bones, correlated with stages for large mammals and microfauna	113
5.4.	Survival of pigeon long bones in pellets of eagle owl and in food remains of peregrine falcon	125
6.1.	Criteria to consider when identifying whether an assemblage is natural or anthropogenic	131
6.2.	Location of disarticulation and filleting cuts produced in experimental butchering of grey partridge	133
6.3.	Percentage of major elements with cut marks from eight Late Upper Palaeolithic sites	136
6.4.	Number and per cent of cut marks on remains of snowy owl from Bois-Ragot	139
6.5.	Number and location of chop marks observed on bird bones from St Gregory's Priory	143
6.6.	Incidence of damaged articular ends of radii and ulnae of gulls from Tofts Ness	149
6.7.	Ratio of anterior to posterior elements from Lovelock Cave and Humboldt Lakebed Site	157
6.8.	Average bulk density for five skeletal elements of weak and strong flyers	159
7.1.	Thickness range and other characteristics of eggshell of some common families	172
7.2.	Eggshell thickness of selected domestic and wild species	174
7.3.	Criteria to be taken into account in identifying flasks of ostrich eggshell at archaeological sites	181
8.1.	Identification, description, and date of ancient feathers associated with artefacts recovered from ice patches in the Yukon	196
9.1.	Bird species represented in artefacts and food remains at Dutch Neolithic sites	210
9.2.	Element distribution of griffon vulture, *Gyps fulvus*, from Jerf el Ahmar, Syria	227

10.1.	Weights of selected birds in approximate size classes	232
10.2.	Nutritional value (kilocalories, protein, and fat) of some domestic and wild birds	234
10.3.	Number of identified specimens of birds and mammals from Skyring Sea sites in Patagonia	235
10.4.	Species and age classes of birds from the Paternoster site	240
10.5.	Species with more than 500 identified bones from Upper Palaeolithic levels at Grotta Romanelli, Italy	262
10.6.	Birds and mammals from Magdalenian and Azilian levels at Taï 2	264
11.1.	Some of the names given to chickens of different ages and sexes	268
11.2.	Condition of tarsometatarsus and spur in domestic chickens, showing interpretations of the presence and absence of a spur or spur scar	274
11.3.	Incidence of medullary bone in chicken femora from Roman and medieval sites in southern Britain	284
12.1.	Domesticated and possible domesticated birds	288
12.2.	Plumage characteristics of some subspecies of turkey, *Meleagris gallopavo*	291
12.3.	Biometric and molecular identification of ancient goose bones from sites in England	297
12.4.	Archaeological finds of domestic pigeon from Central Europe and Scandinavia in the Late Iron Age and Roman period	307
13.1.	Raptors used for hawking in Europe and main prey species	318
14.1.	Burials of scarlet macaw, military macaw, and thick-billed parrot from Mimbres sites in New Mexico	347
14.2.	Element distribution of red-tailed hawks from a pit in the settlement of La Playa, Sonora, Mexico	357
14.3.	Ritual refuse: wild birds from a D-shaped structure at Sand Canyon Pueblo	361
14.4.	Worldwide beliefs about the raven, *Corvus corax*	363
15.1.	Bird species from four Late Pleistocene cave deposits on Gibraltar with positive evidence of breeding	368
15.2.	Birds from an Early to Mid Holocene lakebed in the Erg of Murzuq	373
15.3.	Some Holocene records of the house sparrow in Europe	377

15.4. Numbers of extinct Holocene birds by family — 382
15.5. Summary of the vertebrate fauna from Tangatatau Rockshelter — 388
16.1. Summary of the anatomical elements which give the best information on identification, ageing, sex distinctions, butchery, and other uses — 398

PREFACE

When I started studying bird remains from archaeological sites in Scotland and England in the 1980s, I would have been very grateful for a book which contained guidance on how to set about it and some ideas on how the bones might be interpreted. Later, when teaching the zooarchaeology of bird remains, I would also have found such a book very useful, so eventually I decided to write it myself. The literature on birds in archaeology has expanded greatly in the past 25 years, but it is not easily available except to specialists, as it is scattered in journals and collections of papers which have been published all over the world. This is my attempt to bring the scattered material together. It is intended as a guide to the subject, a synthesis of current research, and a basis for research in the future.

The early chapters are the practical ones. The later chapters contain surveys of the literature on capturing wild birds and their place in diet, the history and process of domestication, and the role of birds in religion, ritual, sport, and pleasure. One chapter is concerned with the role of bird remains in reconstructing past environments: the ways in which birds have been affected by human predation and environmental and climate change. The non-specialist reader who is more interested in birds and people in the past than in the minutiae of analysis may prefer to read the later chapters first. Conscious of the fact that the general reader will be interested in the history of the interactions between people and birds, I have included a very brief summary of the role of birds in early human history in Chapter 10. Otherwise, topics rather than geography and time have dictated the organisation of chapters.

The names of the birds provided the first challenge. In the end, I settled on using the vernacular English name and on using the lower case rather than the upper case in bird names, to conform to common and archaeological usage rather than to scientific ornithological usage. Where a species is found on both sides of the Atlantic, I have used the American or English vernacular name as appropriate. A list of the

English and scientific names used in the text is given in Appendix 1. So far as the domestic chicken is concerned, although it is historically correct to refer to it as 'domestic fowl' in scientific writing, I have used 'chicken', as in colloquial English usage.

Measurements quoted are metric, but imperial measurements are quoted and the conversion to metric added when research by scholars from the United States is discussed. I have used BC and AD (rather than BCE) and BP (Before Present) according to which is relevant for the area and date in question. Radiocarbon dates, if calibrated, follow the calibration of the original authors.

ACKNOWLEDGMENTS

Many colleagues have contributed to this book, and I am very grateful to them all. I particularly thank Tony Waldron, who wrote the section on pathology in Chapter 3 and commented on some other chapters. I owe a great debt to the long-suffering colleagues who read and commented on various chapters: Umberto Albarella, Zbigniew Bochenski, Jo Cooper, Carla Dove, Erica Gál, Véronique Laroulandie, Roel Lauwerier, Christine Lefèvre, Adrienne Powell, Wietske Prummel, Alice Storey, Naomi Sykes, and Derek Yalden.

I also heartily thank those colleagues and friends who have supplied offprints, suggestions, and photographs. As well as the people already mentioned, this group includes Atholl Anderson, Don Brothwell, Alan Cohen, Janet Davidson, Francesco D'Errico, Angela von den Driesch, Jonathan Driver, Inge Bodker Enghoff, Jordi Estevez, Marta Moreno Garcia, Gitte Gotfredsen, Lionel Gourichon, Yannis Hamilakis, Sheila Hamilton-Dyer, Rachel Hutton-MacDonald, Andrew Kandel, Foss Leach, Alison Locker, Kevin MacDonald, Kristin Mannermaa, Tom McGovern, Konstantin Mikhailov, Arturo Morales, Natalie Munro, Dimitra Mylona, Jill Oakes, Terry O'Connor, Joris Peters, Adrienne Powell, Rick Riewe, Peter Rowley-Conwy, Nerissa Russell, Jane Sidell, Alessandra Spinetti, David Stone, Antonio Tagliocozzo, Samuel Turvey, Tommy Tyrberg, Wim Van Neer, Barbara West, Becky Wigen, Loes van Wijngaarden-Bakker, Trevor Worthy, Andrew Yeoman, and Jorn Zeiler.

I also warmly thank Humphrey Serjeantson and Deirdre Serjeantson for editorial help and Hella Oliver for assistance with German translation. Finally, my most grateful thanks go to Penny Copeland, who drew or redrew many of the illustrations, including all those not otherwise acknowledged.

The following institutions have kindly given permission for the reproduction of photographs and illustrations: the University of California Press, Cambridge University Press, the Canterbury Archaeological Trust, Chicago University Press, the

Deutsches Archäologisches Institut of Berlin, the Institute of Systematics and Evolution of Animals of the Polish Acadamy of Sciences, the Orkney Library and Archive, the Natural History Museum, London, the Staatssammlung für Anthropologie und Paläoanatomie, Munich, and Winchester Museums.

1

Introduction

This book is about the study of bird remains from archaeological sites: how to study them and what information they provide about human prehistory and early history. Today we eat chicken and eggs in quantities which would have astonished the first people to domesticate the chicken in China or the Indian subcontinent, and we use feathers for pillows and occasionally for decoration. Otherwise, birds impinge little on modern life, though they have come back into prominence for their association with diseases which can be transmitted to humans, especially avian flu, and for the role they play as markers of environmental and climate change.

People were much more interested in birds in the past for non-material as well as material reasons. People admired and read significance into their flight, their colour, and their song. In flying, they could carry messages and even the human spirit to the heavens. Birds, like people, have excellent vision, which includes the ability to see in colour and in three dimensions. They seem to be communicating to us with their song or voice: indeed, parrots, ravens, and crows do communicate with us. Like humans, birds have a relatively poor sense of smell and, except for a few nocturnal species, limited hearing. This is unlike other mammals, most of which depend on a sense of smell and hearing and see only in black and white. The balance in the senses is much closer to that of humans (Morales 1993b), and it must be part of the reason why humans feel an affinity with birds. It certainly helps to explain why so many people in advanced industrial societies become birdwatchers (Barnes 2005).

In the past, both hunters and farmers were surely aware of the seasonal changes in the range of birds around them, even if they could not explain them. They must have watched and listened each year for the arrival of seasonal migrants such as cuckoos and cranes. Even the Palaeolithic hunters who shared a cave with nesting swallows and martins must have watched for their arrival as a sign of spring and their departure as a sign of approaching winter (Eastham 1997). In the days before compasses, mariners depended on birds for navigation: the flight patterns of seabirds returning to land in the evening were used by the Polynesian colonists in the Pacific, the Vikings, and even by Columbus (Hornell 1946). The calls of certain birds alerted the hunter to the presence of game (Driver 1999).

The domestication of birds was later than that of mammals – at least as far as we know, because the antiquity of the domestication of chickens and ducks is still uncertain. Several species seem to have been domesticated because the bird or its feathers played a part in religious or ritual activities; other birds such as the sacred ibis and the scarlet macaw were kept in captivity in the prehistoric past in surprisingly large numbers for the same reason. Birds play a part in myths and legends out of all proportion to the numbers in which their remains are found. In the context of medicine bundles of the Plains Indians (see Chapter 14), Ubelekar and Wedel (1975) wrote 'The ethnographic specimens are believed to identify the archaeological remains as to function; conversely, the archaeological materials add important time perspectives to native use of the ritual items in museum collections and in the documentary record'.

We are acutely aware today of how bird distributions are influenced by changes in the environment and by climate change. Remains from archaeological sites provide evidence for the major distribution changes which took place at the end of the last Ice Age. Butchered bones provide poignant evidence of how human colonisation of new areas brought about the extinction of species such as the moa in New Zealand and the great auk in the North Atlantic.

AIMS AND SCOPE

The first part of this book is concerned with methods of studying skeletal remains: anatomy, biology, ageing, sexing, pathology, quantification, and natural and human modifications. It is not an identification manual, though it does include protocols for setting about bird bone identification in Chapter 4. In the context of taphonomy I shall discuss some problems peculiar to birds, but I do not rehearse the taphonomic problems common to bone in general, as these have been fully explored in earlier volumes in this series (Lyman 1994; Reitz & Wing 1999). The central section of the book discusses eggs and eggshell, feathers and skins, and bird bone tools and ornaments, all subjects on which research has been relatively limited, despite the fact that bird bone flutes or pipes were probably the earliest musical instruments used, going back to the evolution of human culture in the Palaeolithic period. The last section of the book is concerned with the nature of the interactions between people and birds: hunting wild bird for food, the process and history of the domestication of birds, species kept for sport and pleasure, and those whose roles in the human past were symbolic rather than material. The discussion throughout focuses sharply on human actions as revealed by bird remains; accounts of bird bone assemblages where human activity is incidental are mainly found in Chapter 15, which is concerned with the environment and on birds themselves in the past. The case studies discussed come from all over the world. While most are from the Americas, Europe, and Oceania, some examples are included from Western and Eastern Asia and also Africa. The species differ, but people often chose birds of the same families for food, feathers, or as ritual offerings.

The study of bird remains in archaeology combines avian osteology with ornithology, economic and social history, and anthropology. The raw material is not only skeletal remains but also includes gizzard stones, feathers, eggshell, and even excrement. Historical records, illustrations, and archaeological material such as dovecots (Chapter 12) and hawking gear (Chapter 13) are also relevant. In the absence of archaeological material from the early millennia, ancient records and depictions are particularly useful for understanding the history of domestic birds in both the Old and New World. Following Clark (1948, 1952), I shall show how ethnographic analogy is invaluable for interpreting wildfowling; ethnography and ancient history are also important for discerning the ritual and symbolic significance of birds in the past.

ZOOARCHAEOLOGY OR PALAEONTOLOGY

The science of the analysis of bird bones from archaeological sites has no name which is universally recognized. 'Avian palaeontology', as Morales (1993b) has pointed out, focuses on the birds themselves, while this book is concerned with the relationships between humans and birds in the past. By analogy with 'palaeoethnobotany', we might coin a new term, 'palaeoethno-ornithology', but that is cumbersome and has never been used. Morales used the term 'archaeornithology', literally, the science of ancient birds, but this suggests the study of birds in their relations to humans, rather than vice versa. 'Ornithoarchaeology', literally the archaeology of birds, is more exact and closer to the focus of this book, but in fact I have chosen to refer to avian zooarchaeology or the zooarchaeology of birds, which emphasises that the book is about birds in contexts connected with human activities in the past.

There is a distinction between the palaeontologist and the zooarchaeologist with a research interest in ancient bird bones. Even though in practice these are sometimes one and the same individual, the goal of palaeontological research, discussed in

Chapter 15, is knowledge of the distribution and behaviour of avian species and climatic fluctuations in the past, while the aim of zooarchaeological research is to understand past human activities. As discussed in Chapter 4, this is even reflected in the approaches to the identification of archaeological bird remains. However, regardless of the research goal, both disciplines rely equally on knowledge of avian biology, behaviour, and taxonomy.

TAXONOMY AND CLASSIFICATION

Birds evolved from therapod dinosaurs in the Late Cretaceous era (Feduccia 1999) and are distinguished from other vertebrates by the presence of feathers. As all birds evolved from flying ancestors, they retain the pattern of wings and legs even when they have lost the capability for flight. At one time, most speciation was thought to have taken place in the Pleistocene era as glaciers came and went, but recent molecular studies suggest that lineages go back to the Pliocene, and that the Pleistocene merely accelerated trends which started earlier (Blondel & Mourer-Chauviré 1998). Birds belong to the phylum Cordata, the subphylum Vertebrata, and the class Aves. Within the Aves class, they are classified into orders, families, and genera. There are about 30 orders of birds, about 180 families, and about 2,000 genera (Hoyo et al. 1992; Dickinson 2003).

The Linnean classification established in the nineteenth century was based on morphology; it underwent minor changes, but it remained basically the same until the 1980s when cladistics and DNA analysis indicated some drastic changes in the accepted relationships between families (Monroe & Sibley 1997; Cracraft et al. 2003). Most of the research discussed here was reported in terms of the old taxonomy (e.g., Snow & Perrins 1998), but the revised taxonomy (Appendix 3) is increasingly being used.

It is worth bearing in mind, however, that the prehistoric and early historic peoples with whom we are concerned here classified birds in ways other than the Linnean system. The birds in North America were given names by the colonists with little regard for scientific equivalence. For example, the North American robin is a thrush that is different in size and habits from the European robin, with which it shares only a reddish breast. Gould (1980) has investigated the extent to which folk taxonomies and scientific taxonomy agree in New Guinea and Mexico: he found that there was a high correspondence at the species level, though some problems arose at the higher level. Against this, the various members of the thrush family (Turdidae) were not distinguished in England until the seventeenth century (Fisher 1966, 300–338). The bird depicted on the wall of the Palaeolithic cave of Grotte Cosquer has been claimed as a great auk but it could be a razorbill, and Palaeolithic food-gatherers may even not have distinguished the two (Eastham & Eastham 1995). To understand former distributions it is important to know which species of cormorants (Phalacrocoracidae) were present in Patagonia in prehistoric times (Causey & Lefèvre 2007), but it probably did not matter to the people who ate them. In the Western Isles of Scotland the people, who used to eat them until 60 years ago, said of the two species found there, the great cormorant and the shag, 'we juist call them all cormorants'.

HISTORY OF THE STUDY OF BIRD REMAINS

Avian anatomy has been the subject of study from the eighteenth century onwards by naturalists such as Brisson in France, but it was only in the mid-nineteenth century that scientists turned their attention to the whole skeleton rather than just the beak, claws, and skins. At that time, any work on archaeological as well as natural fossil bird bone assemblages was carried out by avian palaeontologists such as Alphonse Milne-Edwards in Paris and Richard Owen at the Natural History Museum (Olson 2003). Their primary interests were the evolution, distribution, and extinction of birds. When Owen was sent some limb bones of the extinct moa from New Zealand (Figure 1.1), he was certainly more interested in the birds themselves than the colonists from Polynesia who had killed them off. Darwin (1868) studied the origin and development of domestic chickens and pigeons by using contemporary comparative skeletons but was not concerned with ancient skeletal material, which is not surprising since very little was available at the time. However, it is notable that, of the palaeontologists working on fossil material, Milne-Edwards (1875) did observe and comment on cut marks on the bones of the avifauna from French cave sites, recognising that some were present in the caves because early humans had carried them there.

It was only in the twentieth century that bird bones began to be used to answer archaeological questions. In the 1920s Hildegard Howard, after working on the Rancho La Brea avifauna, which was uninfluenced by human intervention, went on to study the bird remains from the Emeryville shellmound on the shores of San Francisco Bay. In her book, she pointed out the significance of the remains for understanding the season during which the site was occupied (Howard 1929), a subject of continued interest in the archaeology of hunter-gatherers, as we see in Chapter 10. This publication also fixed the terminology for the skeletal elements for bird bone research in North America.

Graham Clark (1948, 1952) was the first archaeologist to summarise what was known about prehistoric relationships of people and birds in Europe. He drew on the

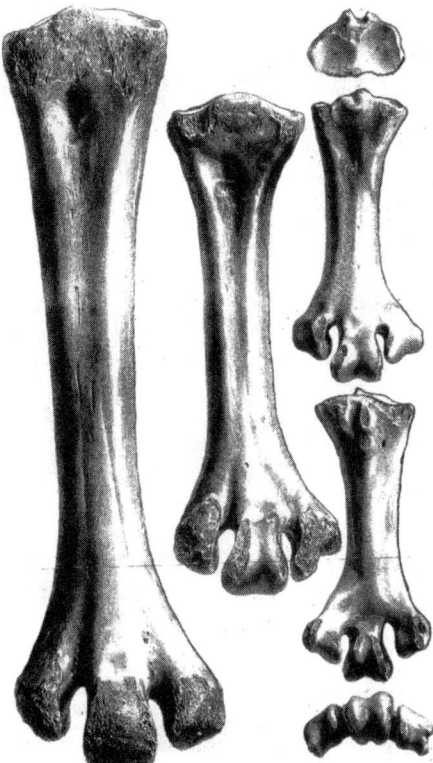

FIGURE 1.1. Tarsometatarsi of various species of moa, Dinornithiformes, sent from New Zealand to Richard Owen at the Natural History Museum, London, in the 1840s (from Owen 1879, pl. 27).

many classic nineteenth-century ethnographic and historic accounts of wildfowling to interpret the significance of bird remains for human prehistory. A comprehensive worldwide survey published ten years later includes references to only about 200 publications on bird remains from archaeological sites (Dawson 1969). That figure today has expanded tremendously.

One of the most important developments since the 1960s has been the creation of skeleton reference collections in institutions other than natural history museums. This gave a strong impetus to the study of bird remains in archaeology in Germany, with the methodological and zooarchaeological research carried out in Munich by Boessneck and von den Driesch. In England, the first substantial collection outside a museum was created by Jennie Coy at the University of Southampton. The subject came of age in the early 1990s with the recognition that a forum was needed for those concerned with archaeological as well as palaeontological reconstruction. The Bird Working Group of the International Council for Archaeozoology was founded in Madrid in 1991. It has now met five times and published four collections of papers (Morales 1993a; Serjeantson 1997; Bochenski 2002; Peters & Grupe 2005). From the beginning, it has been concerned both with methods of analysis and with interpretation.

Several of the archaeological bird bone assemblages discussed in this book feature in more than one chapter. Some of the key research includes innovative methodology as well as new insights into the significance of the bird remains. Where an assemblage is referred to more than once, there is a reference to the first time that the assemblage is discussed.

BIRD REMAINS: THE QUESTIONS

With bird remains, even more than with those of mammals and fish, it is important to consider whether they were actually associated with people or whether they accumulated naturally. If anthropogenic, were they killed for reasons other than for food? Were the birds killed – or perhaps scavenged – for feathers or for tools? Are the remains of domestic or wild birds? This is not a problem with a species such as the chicken when remains are found out of context, but it is a real – and unsolved – problem with pigeons, geese, and ducks over much of their range, as discussed in Chapter 12. Why were some birds given special burial or special treatment? Interpretation is not made easier by the fact that the remains are often meagre, small, and fragmentary and consequently sometimes given little attention by archaeologists.

The basic data are the same as in all zooarchaeological analysis: the identified and the unidentified bones, the parts of the body present, and the size, age, sex, and skeletal health of the bird. Natural modifications and the butchery are equally important. Above all, knowing the context in which the bones were found and the associated finds are essential for answering some of the more complex questions. For this, close collaboration between the zooarchaeologist and the excavation team is crucial. Together, all these data suggest the significance of archaeological bird bones, and each of these topics is discussed in the chapters which follow.

2

Biology, Behaviour, and Anatomy

To interpret the remains of birds from ancient sites, it is as important to understand their behaviour as it is to understand their anatomy. This chapter deals with both topics. The account of bird behaviour focuses on those aspects which are particularly relevant to the zooarchaeologist. The descriptions of the characteristics of bird bone and the individual bones which follow highlight the characteristics of avian osteology which differ from those of mammals, and they point out some of the features of the skeletal elements which may be valuable for the identification to family or species.

BIRD BIOLOGY AND BEHAVIOUR

Flight and Flightlessness

Birds as a class are defined by the presence of feathers. The majority of birds can fly and use flight as their main means of locomotion, but some have lost the use of their wings and some spend more time swimming than flying. Those families which are flightless today, the ratites, evolved from birds which originally flew but lost the ability to do so, rather than from ancestral species which failed to develop flight at an early stage in their evolution (Feduccia 1999). Some landbirds lost the ability to fly after they found themselves on islands on which there were no ground predators. Some became very large. The best known extinct large bird is the dodo from the island of Mauritius, but many oceanic islands formerly had populations of smaller species such as flightless rails which have become extinct, as discussed in Chapter 15. A few seabirds which live by swimming and catching fish have also lost the use of their wings for flying and instead use them for swimming: these include the flightless cormorant of the Galapagos Islands (see Figure 15.3), the larger penguins (Spheniscidae), of the southern hemisphere (see Figure 10.2), and the single flightless species of the northern hemisphere, the now extinct great auk. The ancestor of the ostrich, which lives in Africa, abandoned flight for a different reason. The wings adapted as an aid to running faster, rather like a kite or a sail (Cramp 1977, 1980; Hoyo et al. 1992).

Even some species which can fly spend a lot of time either on the ground or in the water. Galliformes such as the turkey, the peafowl, and the junglefowl are poor flyers, as they obtain most of their food on the ground or the forest floor. The auks (Alcidae), which obtain their food (fish) by swimming and diving, are also poor flyers. Some domestic birds fly with difficulty: one of the effects of domestication has been that body size grows so large that they can no longer fly, as discussed in Chapter 12.

Size

There is a maximum size which a species can attain while still retaining the ability to fly, which is dictated by the wing size. Consequently, the size range in flying birds is not as great as in mammals and fish. The wing increases only as the square of bone length, while body mass increases with the cube of those lengths (Worthy & Holdaway 2002). A few recent species seem to have approached this maximum, including the female Haast's eagle, *Harpagornis moorei*. This extinct giant eagle of New Zealand had a wing span of 2.4 m and a mass of up to 12.5 kg (Worthy & Holdaway 2002, tab. 8.16). Other species close to the maximum are the marabou, the Andean condor, and the black vulture. The ostrich, the southern cassowary, and the emu are the largest flightless birds, but they were exceeded in size by some of the dozen or so species of extinct moa, Dinornithiformes, of New Zealand (see Table 10.1; also see Worthy & Holdaway 2002). The largest moa, *Dinornis giganteus*, may have weighed as much as 240 kg (Worthy & Holdaway 2002, tab. 5.3). The smallest birds are in the hummingbird family; the smallest, the bee hummingbird, weighs less than 2 g. Hunters in general have been more interested in killing large rather than small birds for food (Chapter 10), but where feathers, especially decorative feathers, are concerned, small birds are sometimes just as significant if they have striking colours (Chapter 8).

Nesting and Breeding

Most birds make a nest of some sort, but a few, mainly cliff-nesting, seabirds, do not make any kind of nest (O'Connor 1984, 18). The rock dove and some species within families such as the swallows and choughs breed within caves and their remains

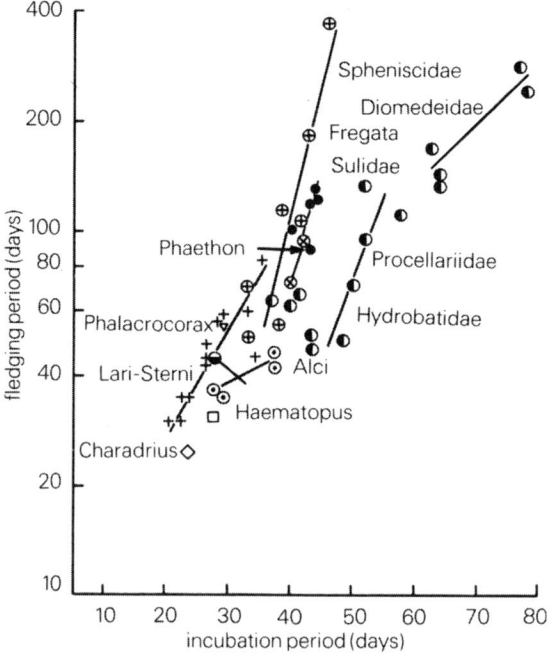

FIGURE 2.1. Relationship of the incubation period to the fledging period (days) in seabirds (redrawn from Nelson 1980, 146). Waders, gulls, and auks have a relatively short fledging and incubation period; frigate birds, penguins, gannets, boobies, and albatrosses have a lengthy fledging period; the latter two families also have a lengthy incubation period.

can potentially be confused with human prey brought to a cave as food (Chapter 5). Birds in seasonal environments nearly always breed in summer but some seabirds are an exception to this rule; being fish-eaters, they are less constrained by a dearth of food in winter. Nearer the tropics, nesting can take place at any time of year. Some birds space their nests and breeding sites within individual territories, but many breed in colonies. This is especially typical of seabirds, a habit which makes them more vulnerable to predation by humans than solitary nesters, as many of the studies discussed later in this book show.

The number of eggs is very varied, from clutches of more than a dozen (this is found particularly with the Galliformes) to those of a single egg (see Chapter 7). When they first hatch, chicks are described as 'hatchlings', then, until they leave the nest, as 'nestlings'. 'Fledglings' refers to birds before they are fully fledged, that is in full feather, which usually also coincides with the time when they cease to be fed by the parents. In ornithology, 'juveniles' describes birds in immature plumage before they have started to breed. This period lasts several years in long-lived species, but it should be noted that, unlike mammals, birds are skeletally mature at a much earlier age (Chapter 3) and these terms are not always appropriate for skeletal remains.

Table 2.1. *Developmental states at hatching*

State	Definition	Examples
Superprecocial	Independent of parents	Megapodidae
Precocial	Leave nest when siblings have hatched and natal down is dry	Anatidae, Phasianidae
Hypoprecocial	Require substantial period of continuous initial brooding	Gavidae, Synthliboramphidae
Quasi-precocial	Able to walk but remain at breeding place until body feathers and wing coverts grown	*Uria aalge, U. lomvia, Alca torda*
Semi-precocial	Able to walk but remain in nest until fledging	Laridae, Sterninae
Lower altricial	Eyes open or closed, down covered, unable to leave nest	Ardeidae, Falconiformes, Strigidae
Higher altricial	Eyes closed, little or no down, unable to leave nest	Passeriformes

Source: Data are from Gaskell (2004).

In general, birds construct a nest, lay the eggs, raise the chicks, and leave within a few weeks, but in a few species the sequence takes up to six months or longer. The length of time which the chick spends on the nest after hatching is surprisingly variable, with some leaving the nesting site after a few hours and others remaining on the nest or at the breeding site for several months until they are fully fledged (Figure 2.1). Indeed, some have to be ready to make a long migration almost as soon as they have fledged. The different strategies which are adopted in feeding and looking after the young divide broadly into 'precocial', in which hatchlings are to a greater or lesser degree independent of the parents, and 'altricial', in which the period of dependency on the parents is extended (Starck 1994; Gaskell 2004). The age at which the hatchlings become independent depends on their degree of motoneural control and the extent to which they are capable of regulating their own body temperature, as well as the ossification of the skeleton. The states have been subdivided: Starck defined four, and Gaskell identified five different precocial states (Table 2.1).

The Australasian megapodes are most independent of all. The chicks fend for themselves as soon as they have hatched, the parent birds being absent. Chicks of precocial species such as the pheasants (Phasianidae) can walk and feed themselves shortly after they have hatched, and some are capable of flight after as little as a week or two. The auks and gulls are examples of semi-precocial species: young guillemots fledge when they are approximately one third of the size of the adults. They launch themselves from a cliff near the breeding site into the sea, but they then swim around in nurseries or crèches and are fed by the parents for up to two months before becoming fully independent. This strategy is only possible because the auks forage for food at sea (Nelson 1980, 112–114). The lower or semi-altricial species include the Procellariformes, but within these the manx shearwater spends a long time on the nest. The higher altricial species include all the Passeriformes, the parrots (Psittaciformes) and certain seabirds such as the boobies and gannets (Sulidae), and the cormorants (Phalacrocoracidae) (Figure 2.1). The chicks of altricial birds are fully dependent on the parents for a relatively long time, but then they are able to fly and feed themselves as soon as they leave the nest (Nelson 1980; Snow & Perrins 1998). Gannets and boobies abandon their chicks as soon as they are fully fledged, and they play no further part in feeding them; by this time the fledglings are larger than the parents. The manx shearwater chick can weigh up to twice as much as the parent, the additional weight comprising mainly fat, which was highly sought after by human hunters. Precocial chicks are in greater danger from predation by small mammals but altricial species are in more danger from human predation. The skeletons of the two types develop slightly differently, as discussed later in the chapter. It is thought that different activities selected for differing growth patterns, with predation, a limited food supply, and sibling rivalry selecting for rapid growth (Starck 1994).

There is a general relationship between the size of a bird and its eggs: small species lay smaller eggs than large species, but they lay larger eggs relative to their body size. The relationship between the body weight of female raptors and the weight of the egg is shown in Figure 2.2; the relationship is constant except in some species at the upper end of the size range. Within these limits, precocial species generally lay relatively larger eggs than altricial species and also have a larger brood size (O'Connor 1984, 4–9), whereas with the raptors, the larger the egg, the smaller the clutch size. Occasionally the eggs laid last are smaller than those laid earlier (Newton 1979, 112).

Feather Growth and Moulting

As discussed in Chapter 8, feathers are renewed in a regular pattern of growth and moulting. The feathers are of highest quality at the start of the breeding season, and later become worn (Brown et al. 1999, 143). In some species the seasonal cycle has been significant for hunters because the moult is a time when some wildfowl are easily caught for food. Some species flock together at the time of moult, another factor which makes them tempting for hunters.

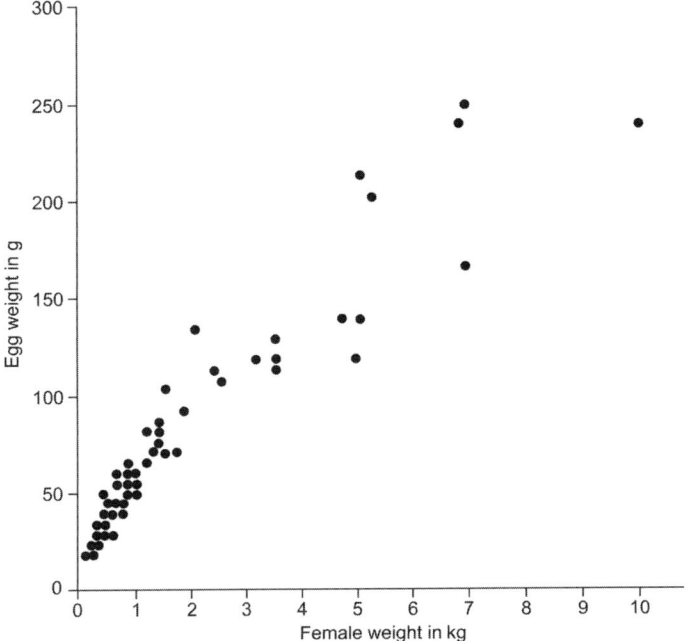

FIGURE 2.2. Relationship between body and egg weight in raptors (after Newton 1979, fig. 19).

Feeding

Feeding encompasses the whole range of strategies: birds are carnivores, omnivores, and herbivores, and they have distinct habits within those categories. Some top predators among the birds feed on the flesh of animals they have killed themselves – the Aquiline eagles, for instance, kill and eat small- and medium-sized mammals. Several predatory species are fish eaters, including the pelicans (Pelecaniformes), the majority of seabirds, some of the ducks, and the osprey among the raptorial birds. Some are scavengers of carrion; vultures are the best known example. Gulls and other species which feed on carrion have benefited from the expansion of human fishing and pastoralism, as discussed in Chapter 15. Small birds are particularly specialised in eating insects, since they can pursue insects on the wing as well as find them on trees and tall vegetation. Omnivorous birds eat small vertebrates, insects, seeds, and other plant foods. The adaptable members of the crow family are omnivorous: they consume small animals (including fledglings of other species), seeds, fruit, and also carrion, which allows them to live in a wide range of different environments, including within and around human settlements. Those species which are more specialised in feeding on certain plants, seeds, or fruit are more restricted in the environment in which they can live, and so are often diagnostic of their environment (Chapter 15). The digestive system in birds is fairly simple, so the herbivorous and graminivorous species in particular have to ingest small stones known as gizzard stones, which help to break up the plant food and make it digestible. The birds with the simplest diet are the hummingbirds; as they feed on nectar, a foodstuff which is rapidly converted into energy, they have a simplified digestive system.

Migration and Seasonal Movements

Birds are regarded as resident when they spend all year in the same area, and migratory if they move seasonally between the breeding and non-breeding areas. Most birds of the tropics and some temperate species are resident, but many mid-latitude species, and most which breed in high latitudes, are migratory. The most common reason for an annual migration is to allow the bird to occupy a part of the world which provides food at only one time of year. In continental North America and Eurasia, insects are available only in summer in boreal regions, so insect-eating birds migrate south in winter. Other reasons for migration include the weather, which becomes too cold or too wet at certain times of year, and competition from other species for food or nest sites. Nearly all migratory species are from the northern hemisphere, partly because seasons there are more marked than in the southern hemisphere. Current migration patterns of northern hemisphere birds have evolved only in the past 10,000 to 5,000 years, since the end of the last Ice Age. They are thought to have been preceded in the Pleistocene by shorter migrations because the temperate climatic zone at that time was more compressed (Alerstam et al. 2003; Cooper 2005).

Many of the waders and waterfowl today breed in the tundra of northern Eurasia, northern Canada and Alaska, Iceland, and Greenland, where the vegetation and insect life can support the birds during what is quite a brief breeding season. Geese, which breed up to the edge of the Arctic, migrate south in winter to escape frozen water; they remain in the northern hemisphere, but in milder countries. For example, the brant (brent goose) in North America migrates from Alaska and Northern Canada to the Pacific and the Atlantic coast and in Eurasia migrates from Siberia to the coasts around Western Europe. Many of the plovers follow a similar strategy, breeding inland and north, but returning to more southerly latitudes and to coastal locations in winter. Birds of these families are most easily caught on migration or in winter. Migration in seabirds takes a different form. Many come to land to breed but spend the rest of their life cycle at sea. The arctic tern breeds around the Arctic Circle in the northern summer and flies to Antarctica in the winter, a migration which is generally accepted as the longest of any species.

Even birds which do not migrate change their social behaviour in winter. Many of the species which congregate and breed colonially become solitary in winter and occupy a single territory. Others congregate in flocks at that time. They also become more mobile, and both are adaptations to less predictable food supplies: a tree which may be full of berries one winter may have few or none the next. As we shall see in Chapter 10, hunters often target flocks rather than solitary birds, so fowling is often a winter activity. Some species may be both migratory and sedentary. The woodcock, for instance, has a sedentary British population which is enhanced in winter by migrants from Scandinavia.

From the point of view of humans who live in one place, certain birds are present in one season only, either in summer to breed or in winter, or they appear for a short time in spring and autumn, passage migrants making temporary stops to feed and rest while en route between summer and winter territories. Migratory birds can be a reliable seasonal source of food for people because they return each year at a predictable time but then leave, thus preventing numbers from being reduced too far by predation. In the main, migration routes are fairly fixed. For instance, many ducks follow the shoreline, and other species follow major rivers. Some avoid crossing wide expanses of water, so they concentrate at narrow crossing points such as Gibraltar at the entrance to the Mediterranean and Falsterbö at the mouth of the Baltic. Migrating birds store fat reserves under the skin, an adaptation to the journey to be taken, so many are at their most desirable from the point of view of human hunters as they start the migration. The implications of the behavioural traits summarised here are explored more fully in Chapter 10, where patterns of wildfowling are discussed.

SKELETAL ANATOMY

Many of the behavioural adaptations just described are reflected in the avian skeleton, but – in spite of their very different lifestyles – the basic anatomy of birds is quite similar within the class. There are of course variations which reflect evolution and behaviour, some of which are subtle and some obvious. The account of the skeletal elements which follows highlights some of the features of the bird skeleton which are relevant to the interpretation of bird remains in archaeology, together with some comments on the more obvious or unusual variations. Details of avian musculature are outside the scope of this book, but they are described in some veterinary and ornithological textbooks (Harvey et al. 1921; Getty 1975; Baumel et al. 1993).

The terminology for the skeleton of birds has never been standardised, either in Latin or English, partly because anatomists originally used the terminology devised

Table 2.2. *Scientific and anglicised names of bird bones*

Baumel	Anglicised
Cranium	Skull, cranium
Maxilla	Maxilla
Quadratum	Quadrate
Mandibula	Mandible
Larynx	Larynx
Syrinx	Syrinx
Apparatus hyobranchialis	Tongue skeleton
Cartt. Tracheales	Tracheal rings
Atlas	Atlas
Axis	Axis
Vertebrae cervicales	Cervical vertebrae
Vertebrae thoracicae	Thoracic vertebrae
Notarium	Notarium
Synsacrum	Synsacrum
Vertebrae caudales	Caudal vertebrae
Pygostylus	Pygostyle
Costae (vertebralis, sternalis)	Ribs (vertebral, sternal)
Sternum	Sternum
Clavicula (Furcula)	Furcula
Scapula	Scapula
Coracoideum	Coracoid
Humerus	Humerus
Ulna	Ulna
Radius	Radius
Os carpi radiale	Radial carpal
Os carpi ulnare	Ulnar carpal
Carpometacarpus	Carpometacarpus
Phalanx digiti alulae	Wing (alular) digit (I/II)
Phalanx proximalis digiti majoris	Major digit (III), proximal phalanx
Phalanx distalis digiti majoris	Major digit (III), distal phalanx
Phalanx digiti minoris	Minor digit (IV)
Os coxae	Pelvis
Ilium	Ilium
Ischium	Ischium
Pubis	Pubis
Femur	Femur
Patella	Patella
Tibiotarsus	Tibiotarsus
Fibula	Fibula
Tarsometatarsus	Tarsometatarsus
Hallux	Medial digit (I)
Digitus secundus	Digit II
Digitus tertius	Digit III
Digitus quartus	Lateral digit (IV)
Phalanx proximalis	Proximal phalanx
Phalanx distalis (Phalanx ungularis)	Distal (terminal/ungual) phalanx

Source: Scientific names are from Baumel and Witmer (1993).

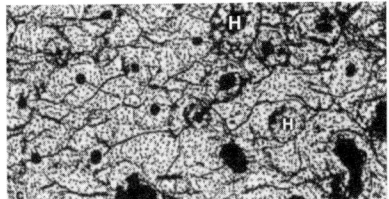

FIGURE 2.3. Microstructure of chicken bone (Strott 2005, fig. 1), showing Haversian canals (H); unlike mammals, bird bones lack osteons.

for the human skeleton. In North America, authors usually follow the terms fixed by Howard (1929) for the Emeryville fauna, referred to in Chapter 1. The terms used here are those which were assembled for the *Nomina Anatomica Avium* (Baumel 1979). This compilation set out to standardise Latin names, but it gives many alternatives and does not always indicate a preference between rival terms for the different elements. Here I have selected those which seem to be most commonly used, and I have anglicised them to conform to current American and English usage (Table 2.2).

Bird Bone Structure

Bird bone differs from mammal bone in having Haversian canals but no osteons (Figure 2.3). This limits the potential for separating species by their bone structure (Strott 2005). A more significant distinction is that, unlike those of mammals, the long bones of birds do not have a growing point between the epiphysis and diaphysis; rather, they grow by apposition from the shaft to the end (Figure 2.4). However some elements which are separate at hatching unite later as the bird matures (see Chapter 3). Other distinctive features of bird bones are the thinning and lightening of

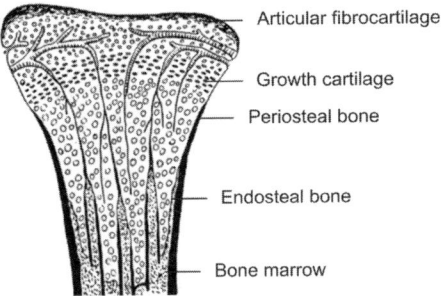

FIGURE 2.4. Cross section of an avian long bone (redrawn from Bellairs & Jenkin 1960, fig. 21), showing the bone structure and growth zone of cartilage cells, periosteal and endosteal bone, and bone marrow.

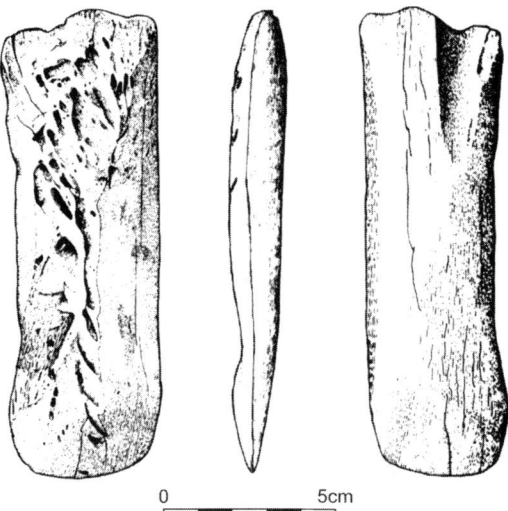

FIGURE 2.5. Splinter of a long bone of one of the moa, showing the thickness of the bone wall and the interior structure (Anderson 1989b, fig. 11.6). The bone has been fashioned into a chisel.

the bone cortex, the pneumatisation of certain elements, and the absence of teeth, all adaptations to flight. Because the fore and hind limbs are adapted for two different types of locomotion, the wings for flying and the legs for walking, the bones of the wing are very distinct from those of the posterior limb and are more distinguished from their homologues in mammals (Young 1950). All these features of the skeleton allow fragments of bird bone to be distinguished from those of mammals and fish, even if the element cannot be identified further. The bones of the wing are flattened in cross section in those species in which the wings are used for swimming. Some ratites retain vestigial wing bones, but these are completely lacking in the moa (Worthy & Holdaway 2002, 95).

Bird bones achieve their strength with trabeculae, thin struts which develop at angles to the bone wall in response to the mechanical loading on the bone. The bone wall is thickened in the large flightless ground-dwelling birds: in these it may be as thick as the bone wall in a mammal of equivalent size (Figure 2.5), but bird bones retain the characteristic trabeculae.

Bone Marrow

Bird bones contain marrow (Figure 2.4) which, as in mammals, fulfils the function of production of red and some white blood cells. The quantity of marrow is greater in

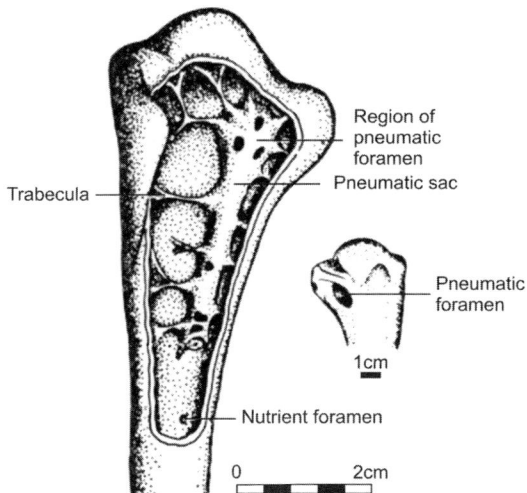

FIGURE 2.6. Longitudinal section (left) through the proximal end of a chicken humerus (after Bellairs & Jenkin 1960), showing bone trabeculae, the pneumatic sac, and a nutrient foramen; also shown (right) is an exterior view of the pneumatic foramen.

immature birds than adults. Immature birds have more haemopoietic tissue or 'red marrow' than adult birds; in adults it is replaced with more fat. Marrow also varies along the bone shaft; the midshaft area has more marrow, and the axial portion has more fat (Baumel et al. 1993, 81, n. 6; Starck 1994). The variation in the quantity of marrow between different elements has been analysed for the skeleton of a double-crested cormorant. Differences were found between the limb bones: the femur and tibiotarsus contained thick marrow that filled the bone cavity; the marrow in the coracoid and tarsometatarsus filled the cavity but was thinner in consistency; in the radius and ulna it was variable and thinner; and marrow was absent from the humerus (Higgins 1999).

Pneumatisation

The bodies of birds are pneumatised, that is, they contain hollow sacs or diverticula filled with air (Figure 2.6). The air sacs originate in the lungs and surround or penetrate many of the bones and organs. The skeletal elements which are pneumatised have foramina which allow for the entry of the air sacs, which should not be confused with nutrient foramina which are also present in bird bones and which are the entry points for the blood vessels which supply the bone marrow (Bellairs & Jenkin 1960; Hamlet & Fisher 1967; Hogg 1980).

20　BIRDS

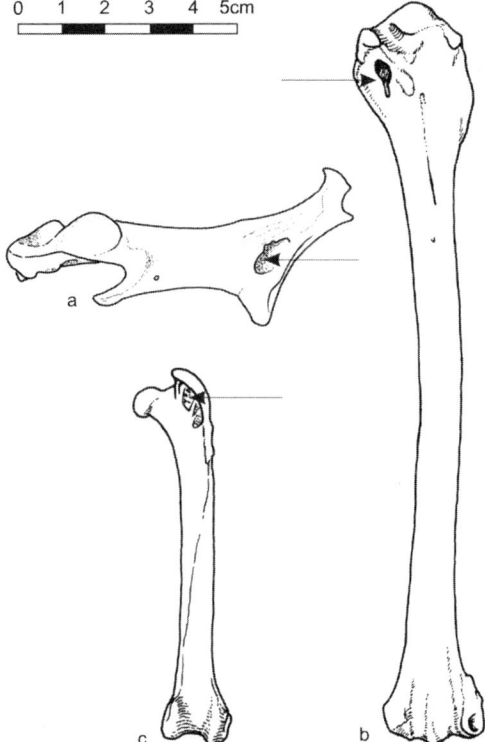

FIGURE 2.7. Examples of pneumatised bones: a, coracoid of crane, *Grus grus*; b, humerus of grey heron, *Ardea cinerea*; c, femur of pheasant, *Phasianus colchicus* (Cohen & Serjeantson 1996, 19, 63, 29). Arrows point to pneumatic foramina.

Pneumatisation is extensive in eagles, albatrosses (Diomedeidae), and the gannet family, but families with skeletons adapted to submerged swimming, such as penguins and auks, are scarcely pneumatised (Gilbert et al. 1981, 11). Pneumatisation is also minimal in most petrels, shearwaters (Procellariidae), loons, grebes, cormorants, anhingas, some ducks, most waders, rails (Rallidae), and even some passerines (Baumel et al. 1993, 98). Though pneumatisation is clearly related to weight reduction, the full reason for pneumatisation is not entirely clear, as it has not been shown to be directly related to size or even to how active a bird is in flying (Bellairs & Jenkin 1960). A pneumatic foramen in the humerus is characteristic of all flying birds (Figure 2.7), but it is absent from birds specialised in swimming such as the auks. Other elements which are usually pneumatised to a greater or lesser degree are the skull, coracoid, pelvis, sternum, and the vertebrae other than the atlas. The femur and scapula are also usually pneumatised (Koch & Rossa 1973, 46). The presence of pneumatic foramina in bird bones can help to differentiate bird bones from those of other classes of animals, and the location and their presence or absence is a useful marker for identification between species.

There are approximately 100 bones in the bird skeleton (Coy 1982). There is no agreement about directional terminology for the avian skeleton. 'Proximal' and 'distal' are used in relation to the midline, but otherwise, some sources refer to 'dorsal' and 'plantar' views; Howard (1929, 6) refers to 'anconal' and 'palmar' views; and Baumel (1993) and von den Driesch (1976, 116) refer to 'ventral' and 'dorsal' views.

INDIVIDUAL BONES

The brief descriptions of individual elements which follow are based on diverse sources, including zoological literature (Baumel et al. 1993), veterinary textbooks (Bellairs & Jenkin 1960; Getty 1975; King & McLelland 1984), and recent works compiled specifically for the analysis of archaeological bird remains (Olsen 1968; Gilbert et al. 1981; Cohen & Serjeantson 1996; Tomek & Bochenski 2000; Bochenski & Campbell 2005).

Skull

The skull (Figure 2.8a) is thin walled and hollow with large orbits and an interorbital septum. The elements are fully fused at the time of hatching. The premaxilla is fused to the skull from the time of hatching. The premaxilla and mandible (Figure 2.8b) are covered in keratin, which only exceptionally survives in archaeological deposits. The skull bones, particularly the premaxilla and mandible, are the elements that are the most distinct between different species, but, unfortunately for the zooarchaeologist, they do not survive as well as the bones of the axial skeleton. The palatine bone (Olsen 1979, 58) has been a very important feature in the classification of birds but is rarely useful to the zooarchaeologist. There is a 'tongue skeleton' (as in the mammalian hyoid) made up of four elements, some of which are not ossified (Figure 2.8c). Birds have a pterygoid and a quadrate bone (Figure 2.8d) from which the mandible is suspended; these two small bones are sometimes found separately.

In some species the cartilaginous trachea is partly ossified; where survival and recovery are exceptionally good, this is found as a series of thin, fragile, poorly ossified rings. The syrinx, an organ found at the bifurcation of the trachea in some waterfowl, is a delicate, hollow globular bone which is also part of the ossified tracheal cartilage.

22 BIRDS

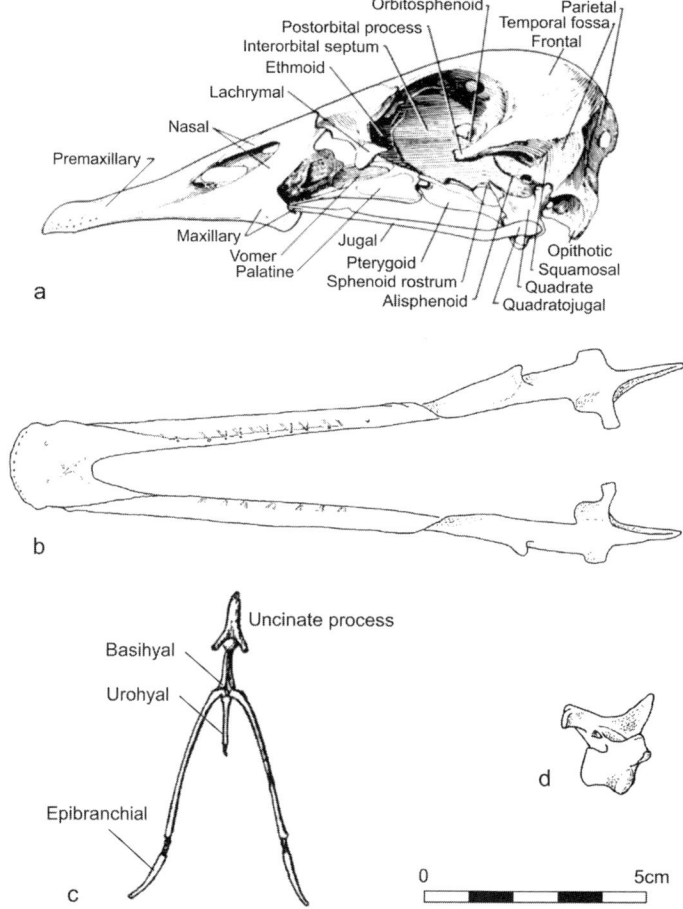

FIGURE 2.8. Skull bones: a, cranium of snow goose, *Anser (Chen) caerulescens* (after Howard 1929); b, mandible of mute swan, *Cygnus olor* (Cohen & Serjeantson 1996, 204); c, tongue skeleton of turkey, *Meleagris gallopavo* (after Olsen 1968, 123); d, quadrate of mute swan, *Cygnus olor* (Cohen & Serjeantson 1996, 104).

Axial Skeleton

The vertebral body in birds is saddle shaped (Figure 2.9), a feature which distinguishes the vertebrae from those of mammals. The number of vertebrae is very variable – from fewer than 40 in pigeons (Columbidae) (Darwin 1868) to more than 60 in swans (Whittow 2000). In moa the number ranged from 47 to 60 (Worthy & Holdaway 2002, 118). Avian anatomists do not agree over which vertebrae correspond with equivalents in the mammalian skeleton, nor over the total numbers. Whittow (2000) quotes a total of 51 for ostrich and Worthy and Holdaway (tab. 4.1) quote 56. Cervical vertebrae vary in number from 8 to 25 and thoracic from 5 to 10. The vertebral column

BIOLOGY, BEHAVIOUR, AND ANATOMY 23

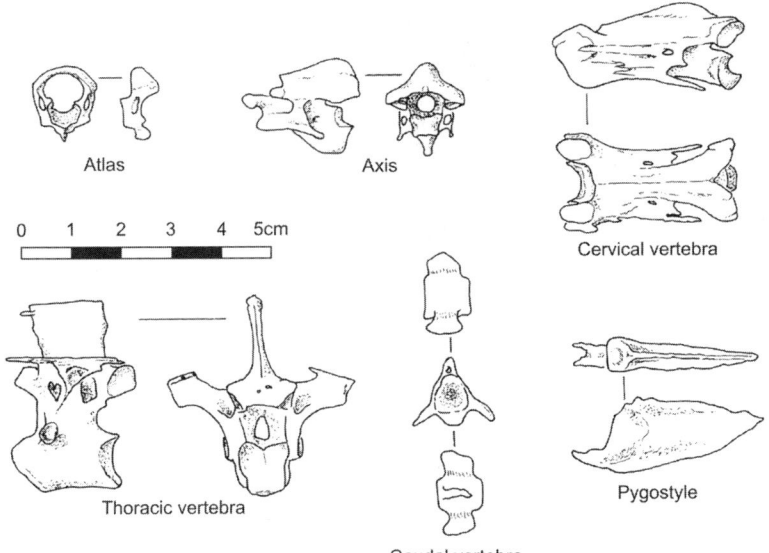

FIGURE 2.9. Vertebrae of mute swan, *Cygnus olor* (Cohen & Serjeantson 1996, 105).

includes two sections which fuse in the adult bird: the notarium and the synsacrum. In the turkey, for instance, the first thoracic vertebra is separate and the second to fifth fuse to form a rigid notarium (Figure 2.10a). The synsacrum (Figure 2.10b) is formed from the posterior thoracic, the lumbar, the sacral, and the anterior caudal vertebrae. The vertebral column terminates with the pygostyle (Figure 2.9), the last segment of the coccygeal vertebrae, to which the tail feathers are attached. In birds both the thoracic and sternal ribs (Figure 2.10d) are ossified. The thoracic ribs have a backward-pointing uncinate process, a feature which immediately distinguishes them from mammal ribs. The pelvis (os coxae) is made up of the ilium, ischium, and pubis. These are separate at hatching (see Figure 7.6 in Chapter 7) but later fuse at the acetabulum, which is perforated, unlike the acetabulum in mammals. The pelvis becomes attached to the synsacrum in the mature bird (Figures 2.10b and 2.10c).

The sternum (Figure 2.11), also often used in classification, is a triangular bone. The sternum of flying birds has a keel which acts as an anchor for the wing muscles, which is absent in ratites (Figure 2.11b). The size of the keel is an index of wing power (Bellairs & Jenkin 1960). The most robust area of the sternum is the groove for the articulation with the coracoid. This part of the bone is valuable for identification: though normally bilaterally symmetrical, it is asymmetrical in a few families such as the raptors (Figure 2.11c) and the herons (Ardeidae).

The pectoral girdle is composed of the clavicles, which unite to form the furcula, together with the scapula and the coracoid. The furcula is a bilaterally symmetrical

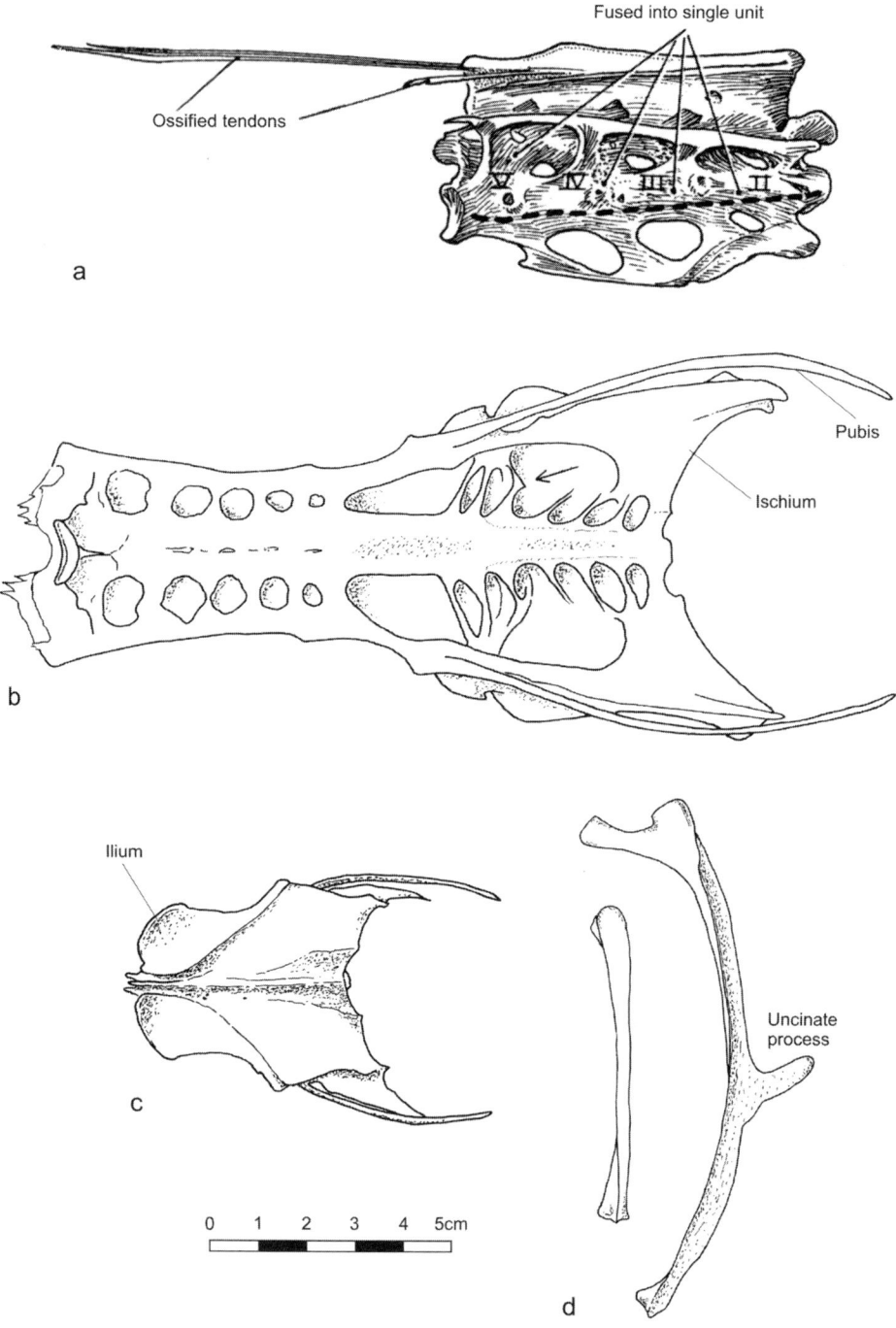

FIGURE 2.10. Axial skeleton: a, notarium of turkey, *Meleagris gallopavo* (after Olsen 1968, fig. 5); b, synsacrum of crane, *Grus grus*, ventral view; c, pelvis of woodpigeon, *Columba palumbus*; d, ribs of mute swan, *Cygnus olor* (Cohen & Serjeantson 1996, 91, 89, 105).

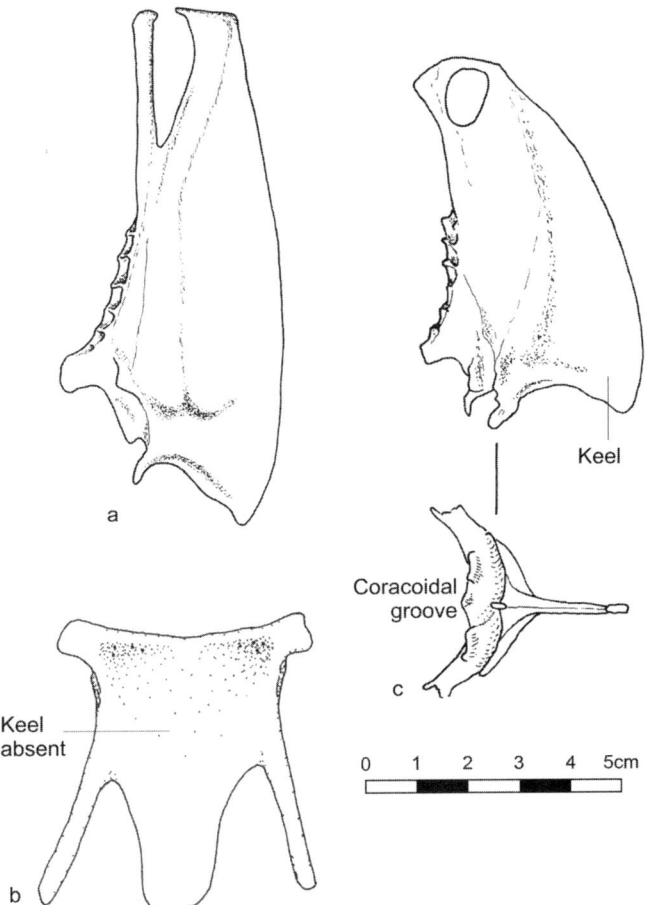

FIGURE 2.11. Sterna of a, mallard, *Anas platyrhynchos* (Cohen & Serjeantson 1996, 94); b, one of the moa, *Emeus* sp. (after Worthy & Holdaway 2002, 96); c, peregrine falcon, *Falco peregrinus*, with an asymmetrical coracoidal groove (Cohen & Serjeantson 1996, 99).

bone, in which the most robust and distinctive feature is the symphysis (Figure 2.12a). In the pelicans the furcula fuses to the sternum; in the parrots and owls, Strigiformes, the two elements do not unite but remain joined by cartilage. The scapula (Figures 2.12b and 2.12c) has a single articulation with the humerus – this facet, together with the acromion process, is its most distinctive feature. The body of the scapula is rounded near the articulation but flattened along most of its length. The coracoid is robust and approximately triangular in shape (Figures 2.12d and 2.12e; see also Figure 2.7). The apex of the triangle is made up of the articulation with the sternum. The shape of the coracoid is distinctive between families, as the apex is broad in some such as waders and the Procellariidae but narrow in families such

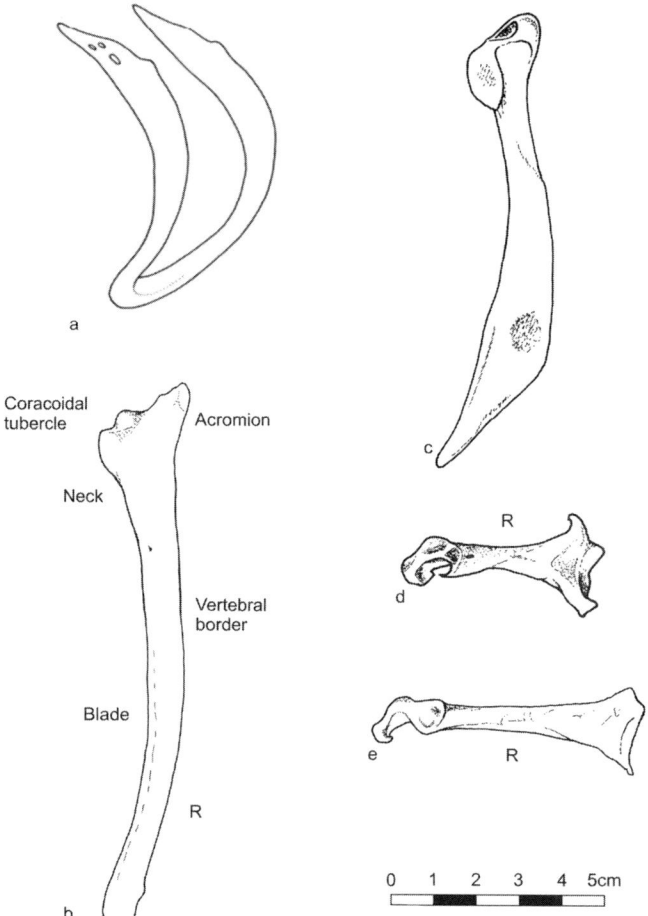

FIGURE 2.12. Pectoral girdle: a, furcula of white-fronted goose, *Anser albifrons*, with pneumatic foramen (after Gotfredsen 2002); b, scapula of mute swan, *Cygnus olor*; c, scapula of white-tailed sea eagle, *Haliaeetus albicilla*; d, coracoid of herring gull, *Larus argentatus*; e, coracoid of chicken, *Gallus gallus* (Cohen & Serjeantson 1996, 20, 26, 16, 15).

as the Galliformes (Figure 2.12e) and the passerines. It is one of the elements most superficially distinct from mammal bones. Some of the moa lack both scapula and coracoid, and some have a single fused bone (Worthy & Holdaway 2002, fig. 4.13).

The Wing

The wing comprises the humerus, radius, ulna, two carpal bones (Figure 2.13), a carpometacarpus, and the wing digits (Figure 2.14; see also Figure 8.4 in Chapter 8).

BIOLOGY, BEHAVIOUR, AND ANATOMY 27

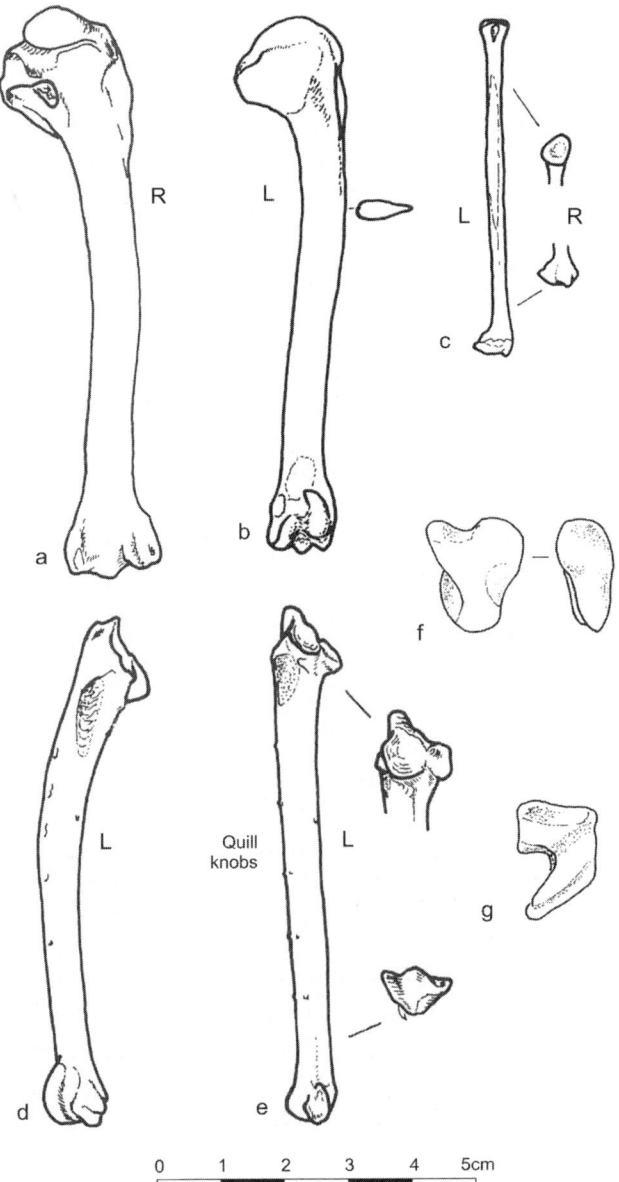

FIGURE 2.13. Elements of the proximal wing: a, humerus of mallard, *Anas platyrhynchos*; b, humerus of guillemot, *Uria aalge*, with flattened cross section; c, radius of willow grouse, *Lagopus lagopus*; d, ulna of chicken, *Gallus gallus*; e, ulna of carrion crow, *Corvus corone*; f, radial carpal and g, ulnar carpal of mute swan, *Cygnus olor* (Cohen & Serjeantson, 1996, 30, 32, 47, 39, 43, 104).

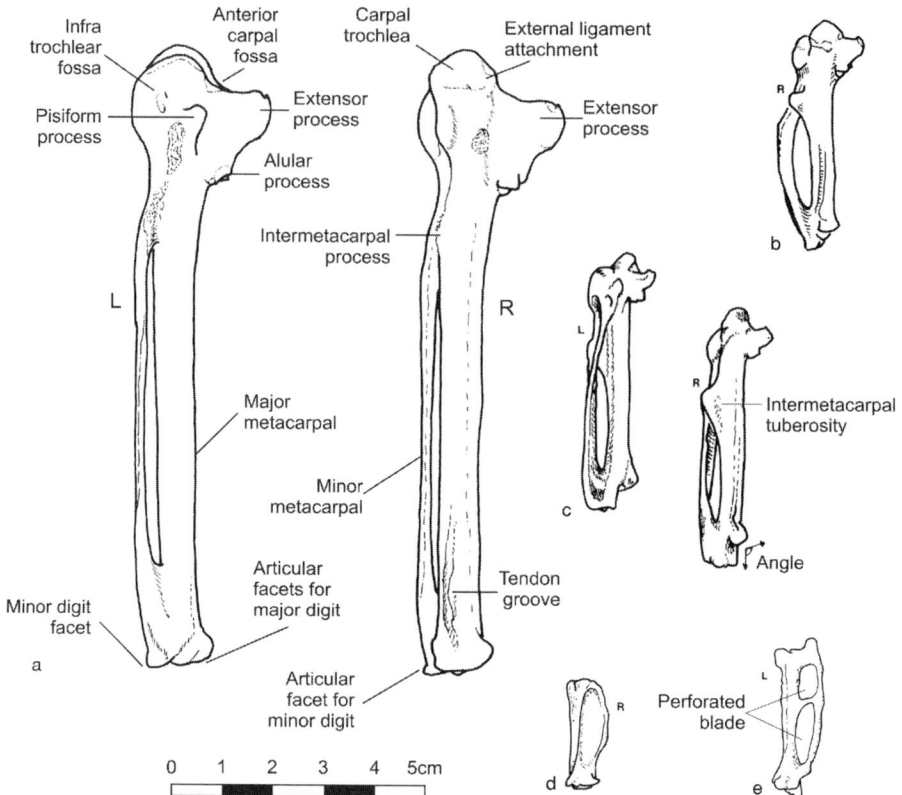

FIGURE 2.14. Elements of the distal wing. Carpometacarpus: a, mute swan, *Cygnus olor*; b, chicken, *Gallus gallus*; c, carrion crow, *Corvus corone*. Distal phalanx of the major wing digit: d, carrion crow; e, herring gull, *Larus argentatus* (Cohen & Serjeantson 1996, 52, 55, 59, 103, 102).

Though the cross section is normally round, in diving birds such as penguins and auks it is flattened (Figure 2.14b). The broad proximal articulation with pneumatic foramen (Figure 2.7) and the characteristic distal condyles distinguish it from a mammal bone. The radius is an elongated tubular bone, narrow in diameter (Figure 2.13c). The shape of the proximal articulation is probably its most distinctive feature but the radius is one of the most difficult of the limb bones to differentiate between species. The ulna is stouter, with a distinctive triangular cross section to the distal shaft. It is straight in most birds (Figure 2.13e) but curved in the Galliformes (Figure 2.13d). There is a series of small knobs on the bone shaft, the *papillae ulnare* or quill knobs, to which the flight feathers attach. These can be very pronounced or almost absent, depending on species. As with the humerus, in diving birds the ulna is flat in cross section. There are two carpals, the radial or scapholunar and the ulnar or cuneiform (Figures 2.13f and 2.13g).

The carpometacarpus (Figure 2.14) is made up of a major and a minor metacarpal (metacarpal II and metacarpal III), which are fused in the adult bird but separate in those still skeletally immature. In some species metacarpal II is square in cross section, while metacarpal II is thinner and flatter. The minor metacarpal is curved in the Galliformes (Figure 2.14b) but more or less straight in most other families. The extensor process on the proximal articulation is a robust process which is distinctive and usually survives in archaeological material. In Galliformes and also in the corvids (Figure 2.14c) there is a process on the shaft of metacarpal III, the intermetacarpal tuberosity. The distal end of the bone, with articular facets for the wing digits, is straight in many species but stepped in the passerines (Figure 2.14c). This feature distinguishes the corvids from other families in the same size range as well and the passerines from any other small and very small birds in an assemblage. In most species there are three wing digits – the major, minor, and alular. The major digit of the wing is a flat D-shaped bone (Figures 2.14d and 2.14e), more or less elongated. In the gulls and some owls the blade is penetrated with holes (Figure 2.14e). The two minor digits are elongated triangular elements with an articular surface at the proximal end.

The Leg

The femur (Figure 2.15a) is basically similar in shape to the mammal femur. The femoral head has a small depression, the *fovea capitis*, for attachment of the round ligament which attaches the head to the acetabulum. The distal lateral (fibular) trochlea is grooved, which is a reliable distinction from the mammalian femur. There is a patella in the groove between the epicondyles, more or less triangular in shape. The tibiotarsus (Figures 2.15b and 2.15c) is made up of the tibia and the proximal row of tarsal bones. It has a flattened proximal articulation, and in some species a cnemial crest extends above the articulation, which is very elongated in the loons (Gaviiformes). Unfortunately, in ancient material the crest is often broken off. There is a flattened flange or process, the fibular crest, on the proximal part of the shaft where the fibula attaches. The length and prominence varies between families. The distal end of the tibiotarsus has a pair of condyles, above which is the supratendinal bridge, an ossified bridge of bone covering the tendon which runs between the condyles (Figure 2.15b); this bridge is absent in owls and parrots and in all immature birds (Figure 2.15c). The relative size and shape of the distal condyles is distinctive between species, as is the angle and extent of the supratendinal bridge. The fibula is a reduced splint-like bone in many species.

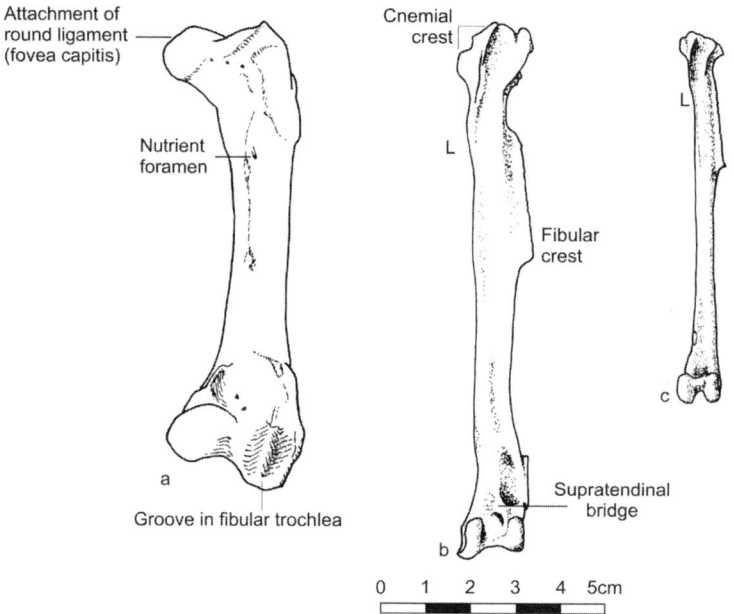

FIGURE 2.15. Elements of the proximal leg. Left: femur of mute swan, *Cygnus olor*; centre: tibiotarsus of cormorant, *Phalacrocorax carbo*, with a pronounced fibular crest; right: tibiotarsus of tawny owl, *Strix aluco*, lacking the supratendinal bridge (Cohen & Serjeantson 1996, 60, 69, 74).

The tarsometatarsus (Figure 2.16) is made up of the distal tarsal bones and three metatarsals (II, III, and IV). The tarsal elements are unfused or cartilaginous in immature birds and become fully fused with the metatarsals only in the adult bird (see Chapter 3). The length-to-breadth ratio of the tarsometatarsus is highly variable. At the proximal end some species have a backward projection, the hypotarsal ridge, which may surround the tendinal canals; the number can be diagnostic of family or species. The shaft is approximately square in cross section in most species, but in the loons and auks it is rectangular and laterally compressed. In the New World vultures it is compressed in the dorsoplantar direction; it is triangular with a flat plantar aspect in hawks and triangular with a flat dorsal aspect in pelicans. In owls the plantar face is concave (Baumel et al. 1993, 106, n. 292). The distal end has three trochleas which articulate with digits 2–4; the woodpeckers, the Picinae, are an exception in having four. In parrots, cuckoos (Cuculiformes), and some other species there is an accessory trochlea on the fourth metatarsal. The tarsometatarsus of some of the Galliformes, the domestic chicken, the pheasants, some francolins, and some partridges have a spur, the *processus calcaris*, attached to the medial part of the shaft; its formation and development is described in the next chapter. One

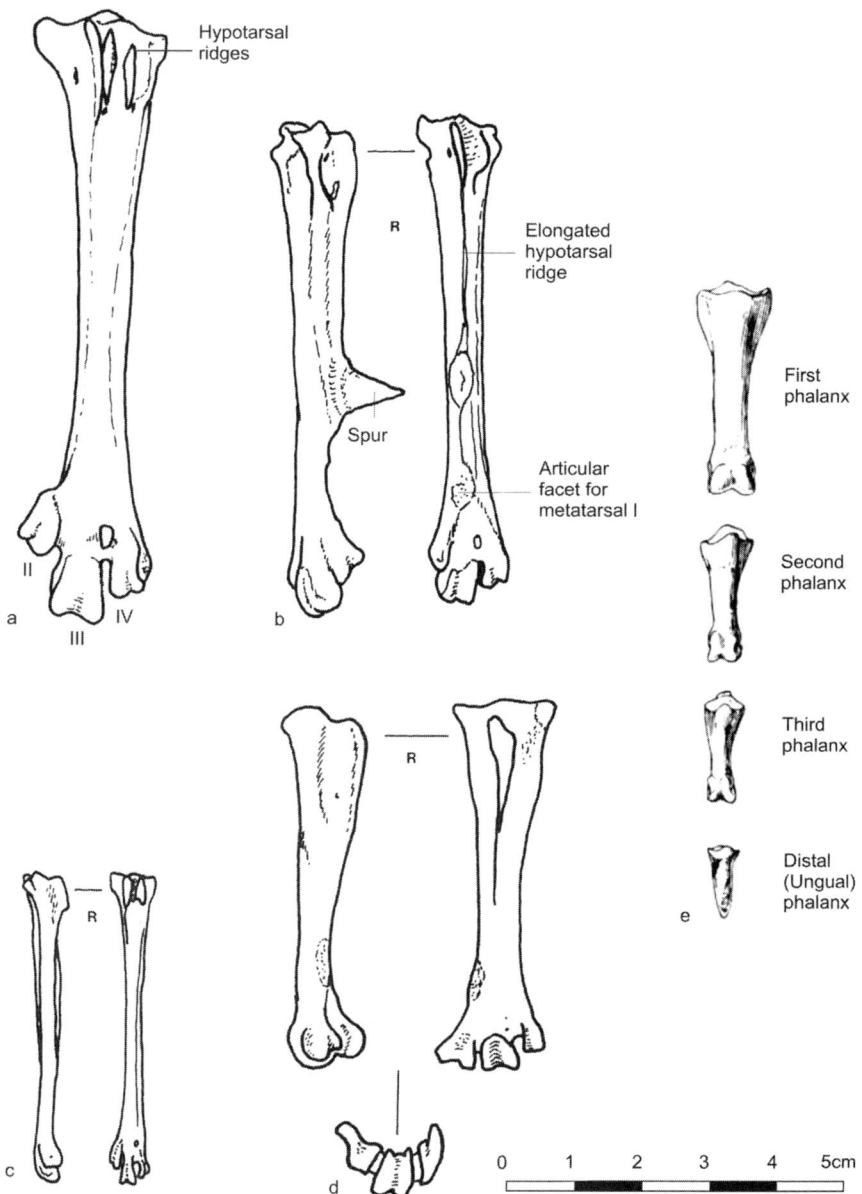

FIGURE 2.16. Elements of the distal leg. Tarsometatarsus: a, greylag goose, *Anser anser* (II, III, and IV indicate trochleas for metatarsi II, III, and IV); b, male pheasant, *Phasianus colchicus*, with spur and hypotarsal ridge; c, manx shearwater, *Puffinus puffinus*, with flattened cross section; d, tawny owl, *Strix aluco*, with strongly curved distal articulation (Cohen & Serjeantson 1996, 78, 79, 80, 82); e, foot phalanges of greylag goose (after Howard 1929).

Table 2.3. *Phalanges of the foot*

Digit	Latin name	No. of phalanges
I	Hallux	2
II	Secundus	3
III	Tertius	4
IV	Quartus	5

Source: Data are from Baumel et al. (1993).

species of francolin, the double-spurred, normally develops two or even more spurs; domestic turkeys occasionally do the same (Steadman 1980). The tendons of the hind limb ossify in some species and are found as long splint-like heterotopic ossifications. These occasionally survive in the ground, and their presence with the tarsometatarsus has been taken to indicate that the bird – or its complete leg – was buried in the flesh (Lyman 1994, 446).

The formula for the numbers of toes is set out in Table 2.3. In the majority of birds, phalanges II, III, and IV articulate with the trochleas of the tarsometatarsus and point forward, and phalanx I points backwards, but in owls, parrots, and cuckoos two phalanges point forward and two backwards. Most extant flightless birds lack the first phalanx; the ostrich also lacks the fourth. Phalanx III is the longest and phalanx I (the hallux) the shortest. The ungual (distal) phalanx on each digit is the bony core of the claw, which, in birds as in mammals, is made of keratin. The individual phalanges (Figure 2.16e) are superficially similar to those of mammals. The phalanges are elongated in birds which walk on the surface of water, such as bitterns (Botaurinae). Each phalanx can be distinguished in some of the raptors: each individual toe bone including the ungual phalanges was distinguished in the snowy owl (see Figure 6.5 in Chapter 6). They have often been used as pendants or in necklaces (Chapter 9).

GIZZARD STONES

The stones which birds ingest as an aid to digestion in place of teeth are known as gizzard stones, gizzard grit, or gastroliths (Figure 2.17). The term 'gizzard stones' is used here as the alternative, gastroliths, also refers to stony structures associated with other classes of animals as well as birds (Reitz & Wing 1999, 65; Wings 2004). Foodstuffs, especially seeds and other hard-to-assimilate plant food, are ground to pulp through the action of the muscles of the gizzard (crop) assisted by the gizzard

FIGURE 2.17. Gizzard stones of a domestic chicken. The crop also contained some seeds (scale bar is in cms). (Photograph by S. Hamilton-Dyer.)

stones. The stones are larger in birds which eat fibrous plant material and small or absent in carnivorous birds. The largest gizzard stones, not surprisingly, are those found in the large flightless birds such as the ostrich and the moa. Gizzard stones have even been used in traditional medicine, as discussed in Chapter 14.

Young birds swallow small stones soon after they start to feed for themselves, and as they get larger, the size of the stones ingested gets larger. Sharp, angular stones are picked up in spring and summer; as the year progresses, the stones become more rounded. Some gizzard stones develop a polished surface from the chemical action and the physical grinding up of food (Davis 1980). Other objects sometimes replace stones; researchers found that some pigeons had hawthorn fruit stones in the stomach 'in all stadia of abrasion' (Bottema 1975). In the recent past, swans and ducks have suffered lead poisoning because they ingested lead shot from hunters' pellets. One mute swan, found dead in Scotland, contained 944 gunshot pellets (Thom 1986, 93).

Gizzard stones have been recognised on archaeological excavations. Those of moa were first recognised in the nineteenth century when found within a crop. 'The stones were found to be closely compacted together in a ball-shaped mass, (as large as a man's head) and were of all sizes, from those of less than a pea to those larger than a pigeon's egg'. The crop also contained fibrous plant material (Worthy & Holdaway 2002, 200). The gizzard of *Dinornis* could contain 5 kg of pebbles. Thirty-four discrete patches of gizzard stones were found at the moa-hunting site of Glenaray in South Island, several in front of each temporary hut (Anderson 1989b, 77, 147–148). Each must represent one episode of butchery of an individual bird, and their presence implies that the birds were carried back whole to the camp. Gizzard stones may give clues to migration and movement. Bottema refers to stones of black lava that have been found in recent times in the stomachs of whooper swans and pink-footed geese in Scotland. The geological origin of the stones was Iceland, where the birds breed. The gizzard stones of moa were found to derive from the local geological outcrops, which implies that the home range of moa was restricted (Anderson 1989b, 77–78).

An excavator finding a group of smooth polished stones of approximately uniform size might be tempted to interpret them as culturally modified or collected for some purpose. The alternative possibility, that they are gizzard stones, should be borne in mind. When they are present, it is evidence that the bird was gutted and eaten on the site.

CONCLUSION

In the period of time with which we are concerned in this book, basic biological constraints such as breeding and feeding have remained unchanged but some aspects of behaviour have changed. Distributions, migration patterns, and breeding sites have certainly changed in the past 30,000 years, as we shall see in the chapters which follow.

So far as the skeleton itself is concerned, the identification of significant distinctions between species on which the zooarchaeology of birds depends rests on a basis of the important work carried out in the nineteenth century, when skeletal differences were the basis for avian taxonomy. Today the minutiae of the skeleton continue to be of importance in the research of palaeontologists and zooarchaeologists working with bird remains, but zoologists have turned their attention to the microstructure and biochemistry of bone. Research on these topics is going to have great importance for solving identification problems in the future. The study of the ancient DNA of bird bones has up to now been restricted (see Chapters 4, 11, and 12) but will one day complement the routine identification of excavated bones. Skeletal studies up to now have also left many questions unanswered on the growth and maturation of the avian skeleton, the subject to which we turn in the next chapter.

3

Ageing, Sexing, and Pathology

Recognising the changes in the skeleton which characterise ageing, differences between the sexes, disease, and trauma are basic data for interpreting skeletal remains, just as with mammals and fish (Reitz & Wing 1999, 256–261).

The avian skeleton reaches maturity relatively earlier than the mammalian skeleton. It is mature well before the bird develops breeding plumage and reaches sexual maturity. This rapid maturation – and also the absence of teeth – means that the study of immature bird bones has less potential than that of immature mammal bones (Serjeantson 2002), but it does nevertheless provide important insights into poultry husbandry and hunting. The presence of immature birds can be evidence for the season of occupation of a site, and its incidence is informative about both the selection of wild birds as prey (Chapter 10) and the husbandry of domestic birds (Chapters 11 and 12). In some cases even a single immature specimen can be significant: a humerus of an approximately four-week-old hawk recovered in Early Medieval levels at Tell Hesban in Jordan (see Chapter 13) suggested that a nestling had been taken from the nest to be trained for hawking (LaBianca & von den Driesch 1995). The presence of an immature bird also indicates that the species bred locally in the past (Chapter 15). The ability to age birds is potentially useful in wildlife management and research, including analyses of 'wrecks' (birds found dead), studies of the age structure of populations culled for conservation purposes, and studies of pollutant levels in relation to age (Klomp & Furness 1992). Bones of immature as well as mature domestic chickens and pigeons are often found on archaeological sites. Among wild birds it is rarer to find immature bones in quantity, though there are exceptions to this generalisation, discussed here and in later chapters.

The most visible distinction between the sexes in birds is, of course, the plumage. Birds have few secondary sexual characteristics in the skeleton, but the spur on the tarsometatarsus in the cocks of many species of Galliformes, including the domestic chicken, is a fortunate exception to this generalisation. In some species there are size differences between the sexes which follow similar principles to those in mammals. As in mammals, these are useful for establishing the ratio of males and females. Castrated male birds (see Chapter 11) can often be recognised in a population from bone size and from the condition of the spur. Otherwise, females can be distinguished from males only when medullary bone, the calcium within the marrow cavity released for the production of eggshell, is present. The presence of medullary bone is valuable in research into hunter-forager sites as it indicates the season of occupation, as discussed in Chapter 10. It also identifies the past breeding distribution of a species, which is significant if that is different from the present or historic past (Chapter 15). In domestic birds, especially chickens, a high percentage with medullary bone identifies a flock kept for eggs, discussed in Chapters 7 and 11.

Birds are subject to the same wide spectrum of disease as other animals (Brothwell 1993), even if relatively few affect the skeleton. Pathological changes in the bone are more often seen in chickens and geese, where husbandry in the past has allowed injured and diseased birds to survive, than in wild birds. Since it is difficult for a seriously injured or diseased bird to survive in the wild, the presence of healed fractures or other changes is potentially evidence for human intervention. For instance, a healed fracture on the ulna of a macaw (Brothwell 1993, fig. 2A) was evidence that macaws were kept in captivity in the Southwestern United States (see Chapter 12), and bone changes in hawks, as discussed in Chapter 13, suggest that birds were trained for falconry.

AGE AT DEATH

The techniques for ageing bird bones are based on bone growth and fusion, and, to a lesser degree, on incremental layers. Not much is known about the sequence and timing of skeletal development in wild birds, though deFrance found that 'the skeletons ossify completely soon after fledging', which in cormorants and pelicans is about 70 days (deFrance 2005). The sacred ibis, discussed in Chapter 14, does not reach skeletal maturity until at least 70 and probably as many as 90 days after hatching (von den Driesch et al. 2005). In the newly fledged gannet (known locally as a *guga*) the bones are adult size and the only traces of immaturity are some porosity in the proximal humerus and a less strongly developed articular surface on the coracoid (Figure 3.1). Maturation at the time of fledging is probably the general pattern, though there are differences between families. In the Galliformes the skeleton matures slowly relative to most other families (Ricklefs 1973; O'Connor 1984, 90; Starck 1994), which means that it is possible to identify domestic chickens killed at different ages. The

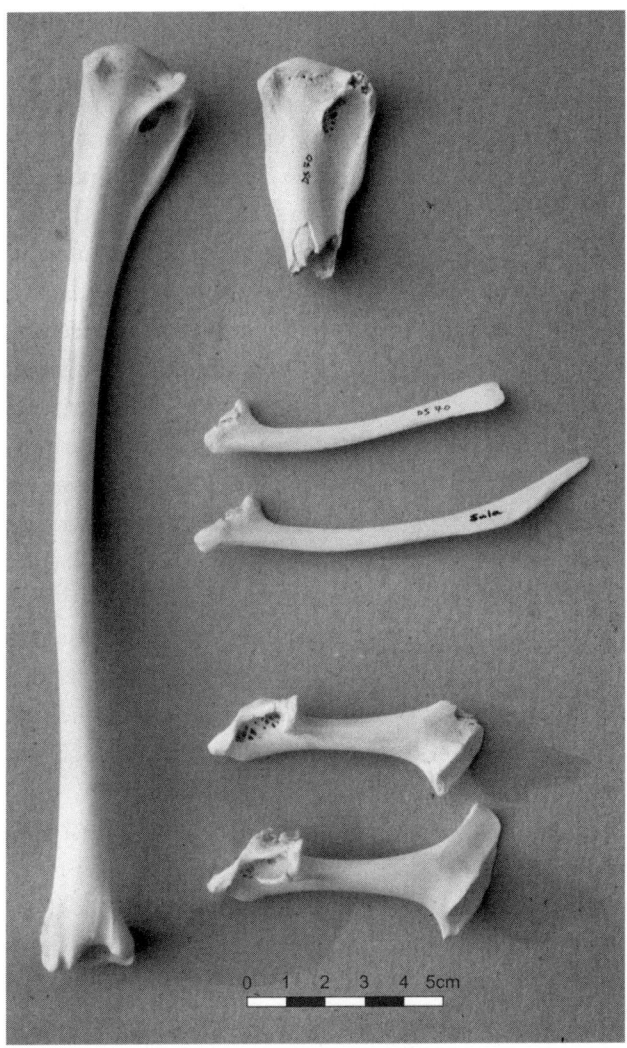

FIGURE 3.1. Elements of an adult gannet, *Morus bassanus*, and a newly fledged bird, a guga, compared. Humerus: left, adult and right top, guga; scapula (centre): above, guga and below, adult; coracoid (bottom): above, guga and below, adult. The guga bones are as large as those of adults but show slight porosity and have less well developed articulations. The breaks on the guga bones are from butchery and consumption (photograph by D. Serjeantson).

growth period of the large ground-living birds is also greatly extended – in some species of moa it lasted up to a decade (Turvey et al. 2005), and in these too the bones show changes with age. Most of what has been written on skeletal changes associated with age has been on domestic birds (e.g., Habermehl 1975; Whitehead 2004).

In hatchlings the skeleton is partly ossified, though the limb bones still comprise more cartilage than bone. A study which compared a precocial species (see

Chapter 2), the barred buttonquail, with an altricial one, the budgerigar, found differences in the degree of ossification. In the buttonquail, the bone which was ossified to the greatest degree in the hatchling was the femur (34 per cent ossified) and the least was the humerus (15 per cent). In the budgerigar, which was generally less ossified at hatching, the radius at 15 per cent was most ossified but the humerus at 6 per cent was least (Starck 1994).

It is very easy for the researcher to make a practical study of the immature bird skeleton, as the materials are to hand in most kitchens in the form of a chicken bought from a commercial source. Chickens raised today for roasting or broiling are killed before the skeleton has fully ossified, so they retain the immature form. If the bones are simmered gently in water for a short time and then cleaned, it is apparent that the limb bone articulations have the shape of those of a mature fowl, but the ends are present only as cartilage. Many of the elements which are fused in the mature fowl, such as the separate bones of the carpometacarpus, will be found as individual bones.

Fusion

Studies have shown that the growth rate differs between altricial and precocial birds: the more precocial the development of the young, the slower their growth. Growth rate is related to mature body weight within those groups. In general, the larger a species, the slower its rate of growth, but there are differences between closely related species such as the ducks which do not support the general hypothesis (Ricklefs 1968, 1973). It seems that altricial chicks, which remain for a long time in the nest, are effectively skeletally mature by the time they leave the breeding site. On the other hand, the chicks of precocial species such as the domestic chicken leave the breeding site young and are able to walk or swim very early, before the skeleton is mature. In these, fusion of the late-fusing bones is delayed compared to other birds.

The elements which fuse after hatching are summarised in Table 3.1. The elements of the carpometacarpus fuse early, before the tibiotarsus and tarsometatarsus. Fusion of the ilium, ischium, and pubis precedes fusion of the pelvis to the sacrum. In some species the ligaments of the thoracic vertebrae ossify to form the notarium. The spur in the Galliformes develops from a bony core within a keratinous sheath to a fully ossified spur fused to the tarsometatarsus shaft. Its development is described in more detail later. In chickens (Table 3.2) the first limb bone to fuse is the carpometacarpus: 'the fetal *Ossa carpi centralia* and *Ossa carpi distalia* fuse with the proximal ends of the metacarpals – i.e. metacarpals II and III – in early post-natal

Table 3.1. *Bones which fuse after hatching*

Bone	Fusing elements
Carpometacarpus	Fusion of central and distal carpals with metacarpals II and III
Tibiotarsus	Fusion of caput tibiae to corpus tibiotarsi
Tarsometatarsus	1. Fusion of hypotarsus to metatarsi II, III, and IV
	2. Fusion of spur core to shaft of tarsometatarsus (Galliformes)
Notarium	Fusion of thoracic vertebrae 2–5
Pelvis (os coxae)	Fusion of ilium, ischium, and pubis
Synsacrum	1. Fusion of synsacral thoracic, lumbar, sacral, and synsacral caudal vertebrae
	2. Fusion of os coxae to synsacrum

Note: Some species within the Galliformes have a spur which fuses to the tarsometatarsus.
Source: Information is based on Serjeantson (1998, tab. 1); data are from Baumel et al. (1993).

life to produce the compound bone, the Carpometacarpus' (Baumel 1979, 100). This takes place at about 14 weeks in the domestic chicken, though the timing varies between breeds (Habermehl 1975, 181). The last limb bone to fuse is the tarsometatarsus when the hypotarsus at the proximal end fuses to metatarsi II, III, and IV from 16 weeks onwards. In geese (Table 3.3) all elements are porous and unfused at 4 weeks, including the bones of the pelvis, but by 16 weeks the limb bones are fused. The tibiotarsus is fully fused before the tarsometatarsus, which, with the synsacrum and sternum, retains evidence of immaturity at 16 weeks. The unfused articulations of the tibiotarsus and tarsometatarsus of a crane from the Iron Age site of Haddenham, discussed in Chapter 5, are illustrated in Figure 3.2. Certain elements remain poorly ossified for a longer time (Hangay & Dingley 1985, 123). The sternum remains porous for up to three months in the domestic chicken, up to four months in geese, and up to six months in pigeons (Habermehl 1975, 181, 190). I have seen excavated examples of geese sterna in which the keel was distorted or bent; this could be ascribed to

Table 3.2. *Age of fusion in bones of domestic chicken*

Bone	Age
Carpometacarpus	14 weeks
Tarsometatarsus, proximal	16 weeks (modern breeds)
	19–27 weeks (older breeds)
Spur core to tarsometatarsus	34 weeks onwards

Source: Data are from Habermehl (1975), West (1985a), and Sadler (1991).

Table 3.3. *Evidence of age in skeletons of four immature domestic geese*

Element	4 weeks	Immature; age unknown	16 weeks	16 weeks approx.
Tibiotarsus	Porous, fused proximal and distal; distal fusion line visible	Fused proximal and distal	Fused proximal and distal	Fused proximal and distal
Tarsometatarsus	Unfused proximal; porous	Fused; proximal fusion line visible	–	Fused proximal, fusion line visible, slightly porous
Proximal phalanx	Unfused proximal; porous	Fused; fusion line visible	–	Fused proximal, slightly porous
Synsacrum	Not united; ilium unfused to pubis	Not united; ilium unfused to pubis	Partly united; ilium fused to pubis	Partly united, illium fused to pubis
Sternum	Porous	Porous	Mature; crest porous	Mature, crest porous
Femur	Porous	Porous	Mature	Mature
Scapula	Porous	Porous	Mature	Mature
Humerus	Porous	Porous	Mature	Mature
Radius	Porous	Porous	Mature	–
Ulna	Porous	Porous	Mature	–
Coracoid	Porous	Porous	Mature	Mature
Carpometacarpus	Porous; metacarpal II and III not united	Porous; elements not united	–	–

Source: Information is from Serjeantson (2002, tab. I).

disease, as discussed later in the chapter, but it may be no more than an indication that the bird was not fully mature and that the soft bone became distorted in the ground.

Ageing from Incremental Layers

Many animal classes show cyclical growth lines in the bone or other tissue (Reitz & Wing 1999, 79–83); when these are laid down annually, the age of the organism can be inferred. The research on ageing bird bones using this technique has had mixed success. Lines of arrested growth (LAGs) are laid down in the cortical zone of long bones; both endosteal and periosteal layers (see Figures 2.4 and 3.9) have been

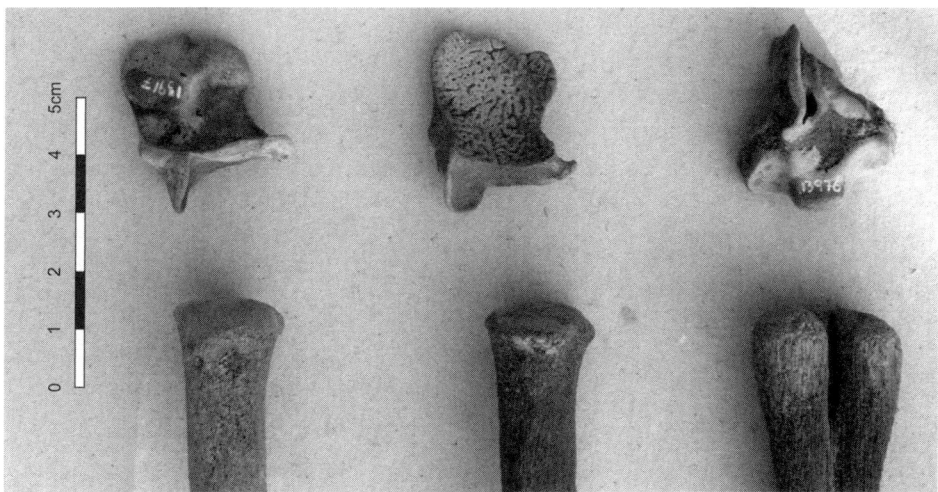

FIGURE 3.2. Unfused bones of a crane, *Grus grus*, from the Fenland Iron Age settlement of Haddenham, Cambridgeshire. Left and centre: proximal tibiotarsus; right: left proximal tarsometatarsus (photograph by D. Serjeantson).

shown to exhibit circumferential lamellae. For studies of LAGs in birds, limb bones are sectioned with a fine saw, embedded in resin, ground down, mounted on slides, and examined at 100× magnification or greater (Klomp & Furness 1992; Broughton et al. 2002; Van Neer et al. 2002). One study of the tibiotarsi of twelve wild birds of known age was partially successful in identifying age. Observers were able to count the endosteal layers correctly in four of the five species studied, that is, fulmar, shag, common redshank, and great skua, though they did not get consistent results with the Brunnich's guillemot (Klomp & Furness 1992). The LAGs in the mandibles of the house martin showed lines correlating with age only up to the age of two years (Figure 3.3), after which resorption blurred the results (Lapena et al. 1993). The LAGs in the femora, humeri, and tibiotarsi of five double-crested cormorants of known age gave consistent readings between observers, but the rings did *not* correlate with age (Broughton et al. 2002). An experiment with domestic chickens of known age also gave ambiguous results: in a sample of 53 elements, the endosteal line sometimes ran into the cortical bone, and sometimes into the medullary bone (see below), so there was no straightforward relationship between the number of layers and the age of the birds (Van Neer et al. 2002). It does appear that both wild and domestic birds have LAGs related to seasonal growth cycles but that they do not separate clearly, presumably because of local resorption. Van Neer and colleagues pointed out there was greater potential in studying the endosteal layers in archaeological material, since the periosteal layer is more likely to have suffered damage in the ground.

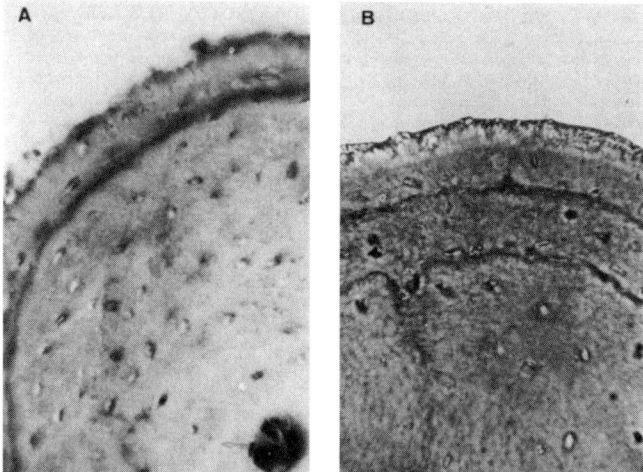

FIGURE 3.3. Transverse sections (40×) of the ascendant branch of the mandibles of house martin, *Delichon urbica* (Lapena et al. 1993, fig. 3). A, younger than two years, one line of arrested growth (LAG) visible; B, five years, only two LAGs visible, showing that the mandible has undergone remodelling.

Unlike flying birds, the large flightless birds do show cyclical growth lines. A study of the cortical growth lines in 21 specimens demonstrated that moa have annual growth rings, though they are sometimes paired (Figure 3.4). The 'growth marks follow the pattern of decreasing outward separation expected for true annual

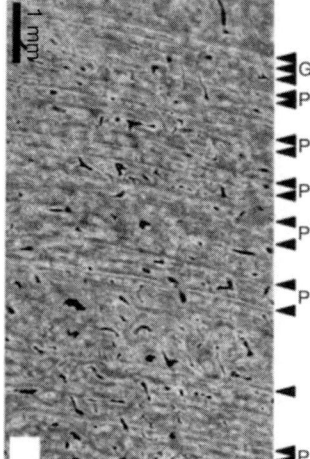

FIGURE 3.4. Cortical cross section of a femur of one of the moa, *Euryapteryx geranoides* (Turvey et al. 2005, fig. 2), showing eight single, paired (P), or grouped (G) lines of arrested growth (LAGs) (scale bar is 1 mm).

signals' (Turvey et al. 2005). This in turn demonstrated that moa had an extended developmental period, with some species taking up to ten years to reach maturity.

The method of ageing from incremental lines has been problematic with mammals and is equally insecure with birds. However, it is a technique which may yet prove useful in the future, and, if so, the greatest potential for future research is probably with wild birds in seasonal environments, and with endosteal rather than periosteal layers.

Ageing from Bone Length

Since bird limb bones grow by apposition, the length of immature long bones can in theory be used to establish age. This was attempted by Don Brothwell with the immature chicken bones from Uley, a Romano-British temple of the second to fourth century AD in southern Britain. Almost one third of the domestic chickens which were sacrificed at the temple were immature. Brothwell posed two questions: Were the immature bones from subadult birds only, or did they spread randomly from very young birds to mature ones? Furthermore, can age at death be estimated from the dimensions of the young bones? The breadth of the proximal humerus of the smallest specimens was comparable with modern chicks of two weeks of age, and the presence of very young birds was confirmed by the size distribution of the femora (Figure 3.5). It appeared that there were chicks of all ages at the site. When compared with modern birds, however, the archaeological specimens showed depressed growth (Brothwell 1997), so the implication is that it would be unreliable to estimate the age of an immature domestic chicken limb bone by comparison with modern immature birds of known age. This does not, however, rule out the use of long bone length as a measure of relative maturity. The attempt to age immature bones from their length and breadth may also be unreliable if the species is sexually dimorphic, as subsequently discussed, or, in the case of domestic birds, if breeds of different sizes are involved which mature at different rates, which seems to have been the case in the Roman period in Europe (Chapter 11).

We saw earlier how the spur developed with age. The increase in the length of the spur of male domestic chickens and turkeys is a potential source of information on the age at death. In chickens, according to Habermehl (1975, 182), spur length increases by approximately 10 mm per year until the age of five years. It continues to grow in capons but not in cocks. Habermehl also quoted lengths of the spur in different breeds which vary from his main data. A study by other researchers of twenty-five turkeys between one and nine years of age (Gilbert et al. 1981, 8) showed that the turkey spur continues to grow until the age of six years (Table 3.4).

Table 3.4. *Spur lengths in domestic chicken and turkey at different ages*

Age (years)	Length (mm)	
	Chicken, *Gallus gallus*	Turkey, *Meleagris gallopavo*
1	15	6.7
2	25	22
3	35	30
4	50	–
5	60	–

Note: Turkeys over three years of age were not examined.

Source: Information is from Habermehl (1975, 182) and Gilbert et al. (1981, 8).

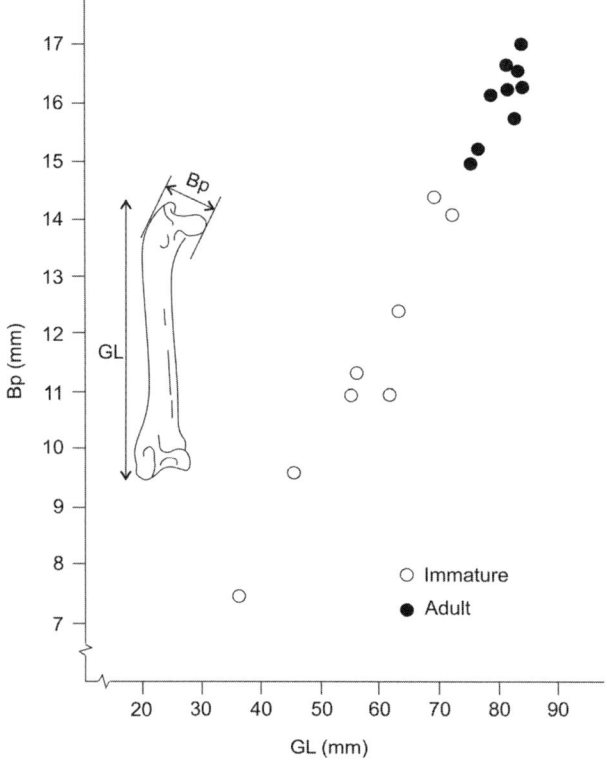

FIGURE 3.5. Scatter diagram showing the size of adult and immature chicken femora from the Romano-British temple at Uley, Gloucestershire: greatest length (GL) × proximal breadth (Bp). The immature specimens are from birds of all ages, the youngest little more than two weeks of age (drawing by P. Copeland).

FIGURE 3.6. Humeri of immature gulls from the Inuit site of Nipisat I, Greenland (Gotfredsen 1997, fig. 2). The light-coloured bones are recent specimens of a glaucous gull, *Larus hyperboreus* (centre), killed at the beginning of July and a kittiwake, *Rissa tridactyla* (right), killed at the end of July (photograph by G. Brovad).

Recording Age Stages

Most zooarchaeologists have distinguished mature from immature or porous bird bones, and some have added further categories. Avery and Underhill defined three age categories for the cormorants, albatrosses, gannets, and petrels from the South African shell middens: 'n' for nestling, 'j' for just fledged, and 'a' for adult. However, they were only able to separate the penguins into two age classes (Avery & Underhill 1986). The chicken bones from the Basilica area in the Romano-British town of Silchester were classified as 'mature', 'porous', or 'very juvenile', and immature tibiotarsi and tarsometatarsi were recorded as 'unfused' or 'fusing' in those instances in which the fusion line was still visible. The main species in a group of assemblages from the Skyring Sea in Patagonia were steamer ducks and various cormorants. Lefèvre divided the bones of the ducks into immature and mature classes only but was able to separate the immature cormorant bones into four age classes, that is, 'adults', 'subadults', 'young', and 'chicks', using skeletons of known age for comparison (Lefèvre 1997). Gotfredsen (1997) found remains of gulls in various stages of immaturity at the Inuit site of Nipisat in Greenland (Figure 3.6); she classified them in four age stages: '*adultus*', '*subadultus*', '*juvenilus*', and '*pullus*'.

The immense number of sacred ibises, both mummies and skeletons, excavated at Tuna el-Gebel (Hermopolis Magna) were grouped into five or six age classes: 'neonate', 'infantile', 'infantile-juvenile', 'juvenile', 'subadult', and 'adult' (Table 3.5). 'Subadults' were identified as those specimens in which the proximal articular end

Table 3.5. *Age classes and bone length of the sacred ibis,* Threskiornis aethiopicus, *from Tuna el-Gebel, Egypt*

Class	Approximate age (days)	Humerus (mm)	Femur (mm)	Tibia (mm)	Metatarsus II–IV (mm)
Neonate	1–2	27–30	27–30	32–50	21–25
Infantile	2–14	30–50	30–35	50–75	25–35
Infantile-juvenile	15–35	50–70	35–50	75–90	35–60
Juvenile	36–50	70–100	50–60	90–120	60–85
Subadult	50–70 (90)	>100	>60	>120	>85
Adult	>90	>113	>63	>133	>90

Note: Bone length is given as the greatest length of the diaphysis. Subadult specimens are those in which the proximal articular end of the tarsometatarsus was fusing or fused but all three metatarsi were still not fused proximally. Adult specimens are those in which the proximal articular end of the tarsometatarsus was completely fused.
Source: Information is from von den Driesch et al. (2005).

of the tarsometatarsus was fusing or fused but the three metatarsi were still not fused proximally, and 'adults' were identified as those specimens in which the proximal articular end of the tarsometatarsus was completely fused (von den Driesch et al. 2005).

Table 3.6 defines four age stages for bird bones, based on the examples just cited. The bones of very young chicks (hatchlings) are small and porous and comprise less than half of the length of the shaft. Those of immature birds (nestlings) are porous and, where relevant, unfused, but are more than half-ossified. Bones defined as subadult (just fledged) are of adult length but still have some evidence of porosity and, where relevant, a visible fusion line. The boundaries between the age stages are not clear, even with chicken bones, especially when just a few specimens are involved. In practice, with chickens if only one element is used to estimate the age structure of

Table 3.6. *Four age categories for recording excavated bird bones*

Age stage	Bone condition
Very young (hatchling/neonate)	Bone half-ossified or less
Immature (nestling/young/ juvenile/infantile)	Bone more than half-ossified, porous, and unfused
Subadult (fledgling)	Bone full size and fused, with fusion line visible, slightly porous
Adult	Bone fused, not porous

a population, it should be the tarsometatarsus. This element gives the most refined ageing data in chickens, as it is the last bone in the skeleton to fuse. For other species, a comparative collection with juveniles of all ages is needed and, in practice, fewer age stage distinctions are appropriate. The best source of evidence for age at death – despite its limitations – is the fusion stage of those elements which fuse. Porosity, especially in its early stages, is easily recognised, if less easy to record consistently. A record of the length of juvenile bones is repeatable, but hard to interpret. A record of the fused or unfused state of those bones which fuse is most reliably compared between assemblages.

SEXING

Spurs on Galliformes

The presence of a spur on the tarsometatarsus is not a fully reliable guide to the sex ratio, because hens occasionally have spurs. In natural conditions, cocks use the spur in fights in which they compete for females, behaviour which has intrigued people for millennia and which has been exploited in cockfighting, as discussed in Chapter 13.

For a long time it was not clear how the spur developed. In 1982 Barbara West published a paper on the significance of spurs in domestic fowl. At that time she had been unable to find publications which described the development of the spur, and proposed an explanation which in the event had to be revised (West 1982, 1985a, 1985b). Further research showed that the spur starts its development as a small oval thickening of the ectoderm and develops as a bony core within a keratinous projection. The spur core increases in length within the keratinous sheath in the direction of the tarsometatarsus shaft. As ossification approaches the shaft, a roughened area, the spur scar or socket primordium, develops on the tarsometatarsus (Figure 3.7). In an experimental study of domestic chickens the spur scar started to develop when the spur core reached 17–19 mm, at about four months. Actual fusion of the spur core to the bone takes place from six months onwards in chickens but is very variable (Table 3.2). Later, as we have seen, the spur increases in length (West 1985a; Sadler 1991; Baumel et al. 1993, 113, n. 300; Peters 1997a). Occasionally a spur core not yet attached to the bone has been recovered; these sometimes show a curved thin plate of bone (a 'shield') where it is about to attach to the tarsometatarsus. An example from Hellenistic levels at the sanctuary of Poseidon, on Kalaureia, Greece, is illustrated in Figure 3.8 (Serjeantson in press-a).

48 BIRDS

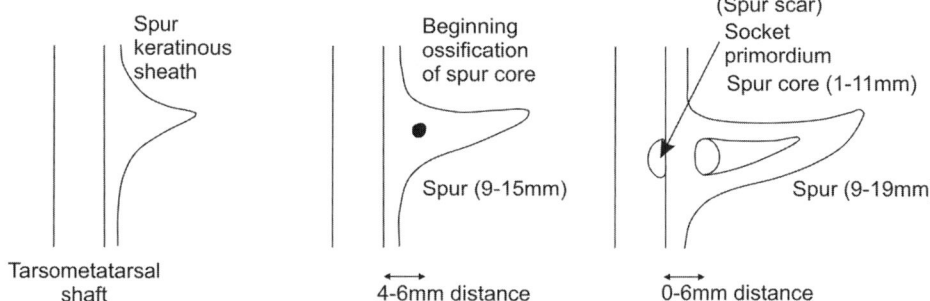

FIGURE 3.7. Stages in the development of the spur in the Galliformes (redrawn from West 1985a, fig. 1). Left shows a keratinous projection only; centre shows the initial ossification of spur core; right shows the development of the spur core and the spur scar (socket primordium) on the tarsometatarsus shaft.

The spur is by no means always absent in females; a percentage of female turkeys are spurred (Gilbert et al. 1981, 8), as are hens of some modern breeds. The spur may develop in hens with defective ovaries, but it is also found in normal hens. It is more common in the females of the Leghorn and other light Mediterranean breeds (Baker & Brothwell 1980; Sadler 1991). Spurs on hens often remain unfused or in the keratinous condition: in a pair of spurred tarsometatarsi on a female of the Light Sussex breed, one was still unfused to the shaft at 18 months (Figure 3.8). The incidence of hens with spurs may therefore have been lower in the past than the figures quoted in the recent veterinary literature suggest, since these may include unossified spurs. I have yet to find or read of an archaeological spurred tarsometatarsus which also contained medullary bone.

The presence or absence of a spur or the spur scar is the best guide to the ratio of adult male to female Galliformes in an archaeological bird bone assemblage. 'The presence of the metatarsal spur is acceptable proof of a male Turkey, recognizing the very small percentage of spurred females' (Gilbert et al. 1981, 8). Any count of the ratio has to exclude immature tarsometatarsi, since evidence for a spur would not be expected in these. It must also, of course, exclude any fragment of the tarsometatarsus where the relevant area of the bone shaft is not present. To make this count, it is essential to use a recording system that shows which areas of the bone are present, such as the 'bone-zone' recording system described in the next chapter. The results are usually shown as 'spur present', 'spur scar present', or 'spur absent'. The picture is complicated by the possibility that some males were caponised, a process which affects the development of the spur, as discussed in Chapter 11.

In those ducks which have an ossified syrinx, this structure is more developed in the males. According to Leif Jonsson, the syrinx of the red-breasted merganser

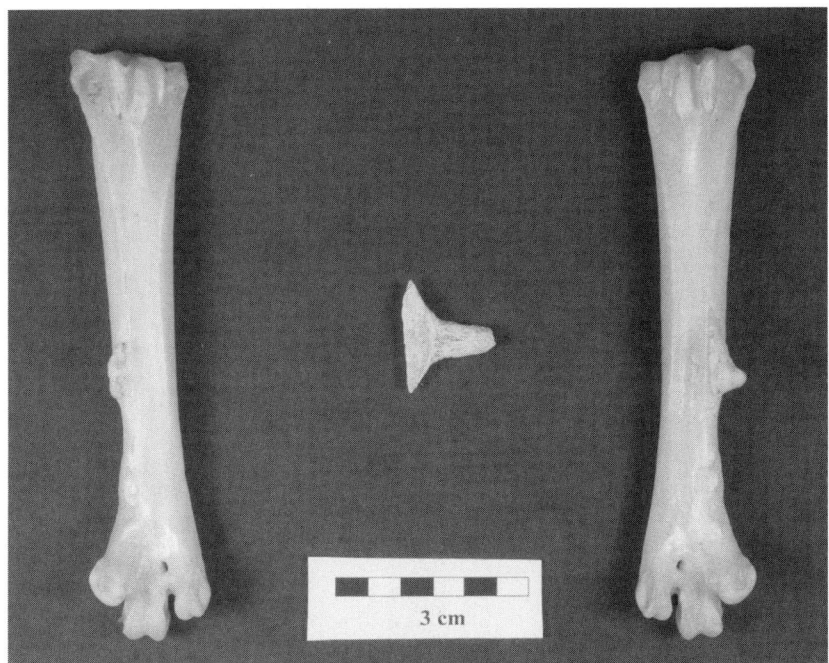

FIGURE 3.8. Pair of tarsometatarsi of a hen of the Light Sussex breed with spurs, aged approximately 18 months. The bone on the left has a spur scar; that on the right has a small fused spur. In the centre is an unfused spur and 'shield', presumably from a cock, from Hellenistic levels at the sanctuary of Poseidon, Kalaureia, Greece. (See Figure 14.6 in Chapter 14 for further examples of spurs with a shield; photograph by D. Serjeantson.)

is dimorphic. Relative humbers showed that there was an even ratio of males and female mergansers in the bird remains recovered from the Viking town of Sigtuna in Sweden (ZOOARCH archives 6 May 2003 – see Appendix 3).

Medullary Bone

Medullary bone is found just before and during the time of lay. Though it is most often seen in domestic chickens, it has also been found in other domestic birds and in wild birds. It consists of a granular deposit of calcium within the bone which provides a buffer supply of calcium for the development of the egg. In the domestic hen, the calcium is withdrawn from the blood into the gut at a rate of up to 140 mg per hour, drawing on the reserves which have been laid down within the skeletal elements. The eggshell calcifies over a period of 16 hours, during which time the bird has to provide more than 2 g of calcium, depending on the size of the egg and the thickness of the shell.

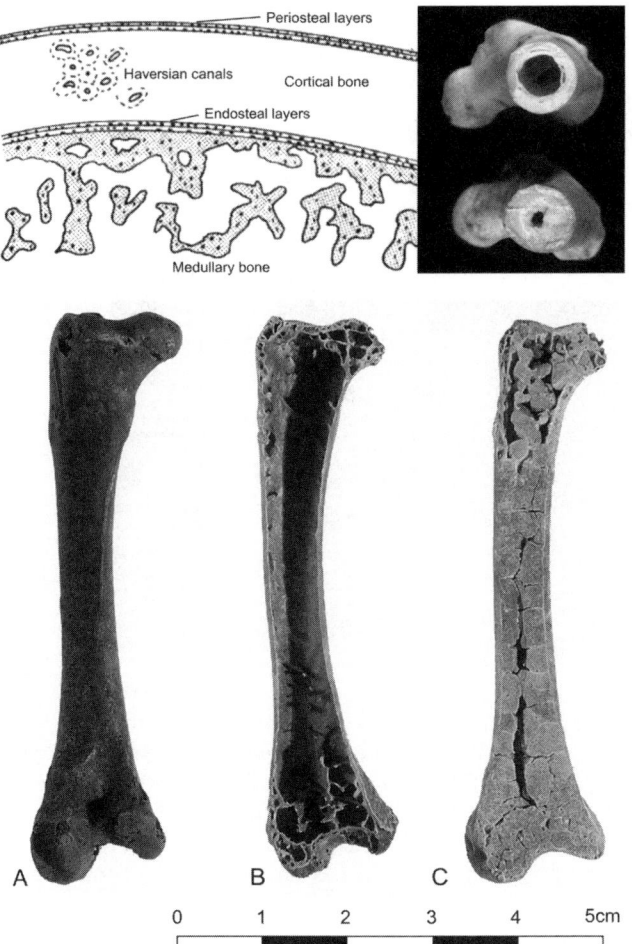

FIGURE 3.9. Medullary bone. Top left is a schematic cross section of a long bone of a female bird, showing cortical bone, periosteal and endosteal layers, and medullary bone (Van Neer et al. 2002, fig. 2); top right is cross sections through two chicken femora showing (above) medullary bone surrounding the bone wall and (below) medullary bone almost filling the marrow cavity. Bottom row shows femora of geese, *Branta* sp., from Nipisat I (Gotfredsen 1997, fig. 7): A, intact bone for comparison; B, longitudinally sectioned femur with no medullary bone; C, longitudinally sectioned femur filled with medullary bone (photographs by U. Albarella and G. Brovad).

Medullary bone is laid down first around the endosteal lining of the bone wall and then advances into the red marrow tissue in the bone cavity (Figure 3.9). The quantity varies from bird to bird and fluctuates during the period of lay. It is present to some degree in the buildup to the laying period and during the laying period and disappears at some point after egg-laying has ceased. In an experimental study of laying hens, Taylor and others found it to disappear slowly during the moult

(Taylor 1962; Taylor et al. 1971), though Van Neer et al. (2002) found that it had already disappeared from the skeletons of the moulting hens that they studied. Wildlife biologists and zooarchaeologists have found it in the domestic and wild turkey, sage grouse, passenger pigeon, short-eared owl, and Canada goose (Driver 1982; Munzel 1987; Gotfredsen 2002; Lentacker & Van Neer 1996; Van Neer et al. 2002). However, it was absent in arctic sandpipers, so there may be other species in whom it is not found. Little is known about how long it persists in the domestic chicken or in other species.

In archaeological material medullary bone has been observed in all states, from lining the bone wall to entirely filling the marrow cavity. It is more usual in archaeological assemblages of wild birds from later prehistoric sites for just a few elements to contain medullary bone. For instance, a handful of bones from the site of Ajvide on Gotland in the Baltic contained medullary bone: four of eider duck and one each of guillemot and razorbill. At this Neolithic settlement, crops and animals were the main resource, supplemented by some wild birds, of which only a few were females in lay (Mannermaa & Stora 2006). The implications are discussed in Chapter 10.

The experimental study of incremental growth lines referred to earlier was accompanied by an examination of medullary bone in modern hens. Van Neer and colleagues set out to test hypotheses about the husbandry of domestic chickens at two early sites – Berenike on the Red Sea Coast and Sagalassos in Turkey (Van Neer et al. 2002). At both sites an unexpectedly high percentage of the bones contained medullary tissue. In a sample of modern chicken bones it was most common in the femur and tibiotarsus and least common in the tarsometatarsus and humerus. At Sagalassos it was present in all the elements examined, though it was least common in the humerus. The researchers calculated a sex ratio for both assemblages from the spurred and unspurred tarsometatarsi. After they adjusted the numbers for the calculated number of hens, they found the ratio with medullary bone to be very high in the femur and tibiotarsus but lower in the humerus and tarsometatarsus (Figure 3.10). The percentage of femora and tibiotarsi with medullary bone was excessive, and this, together with the degree to which medullary bone filled the bone (see later), may have had more than one cause. It may indicate that the hens were invariably killed just when they ceased to lay, but it surely also indicates that hens were in lay for most of the year. The numbers of elements with medullary bone from five sites in England confirm that medullary bone is most often present in the femur and tibiotarsus (Table 3.7).

The degree to which medullary bone filled the marrow cavity in modern hens and in the archaeological specimens was also calculated (Van Neer et al. 2002, fig. 7). It was quantified as the percentage of the surface that filled the lumen of the bone section.

Table 3.7. *Presence of medullary bone in the different elements of chicken from sites in England*

Site	Date	Coracoid	Humerus	Radius	Ulna	Femur	Tibiotarsus	Tarsometatarsus
Silchester	Roman				1	3	4	
Carisbrooke Castle	Medieval			1	1	4	3	
St Gregory's Priory	Medieval		1			5	7	1
Eynsham Abbey	Medieval		1			24	12	
Winchester	Medieval	1			2	2	9	18
Total		1	2	3	4	45	44	1

Source: Information for Silchester Roman forum is from Serjeantson (2000b); for Carisbrooke Castle, Serjeantson (2000a); for St Gregory's Priory, Canterbury, Powell et al. (2001); for Eynsham Abbey, Oxfordshire, Ayres et al. (2003); and for the suburbs of medieval Winchester, Serjeantson and Smith (in press).

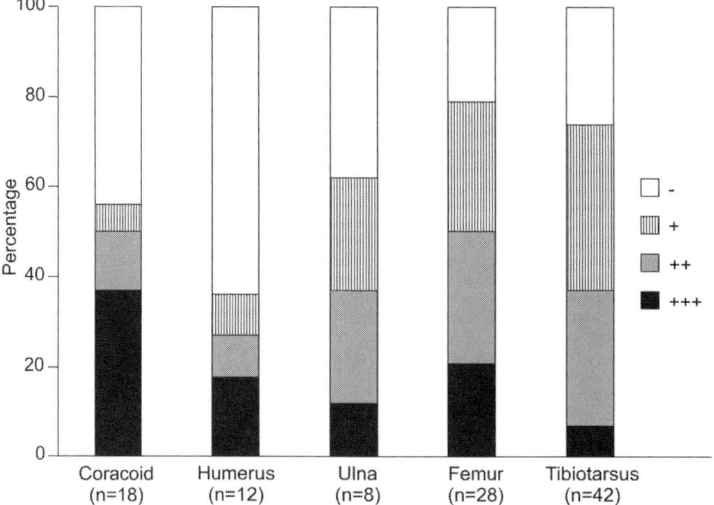

FIGURE 3.10. Percentage of chicken elements with medullary bone at the Roman port of Berenike (after Lentacker & Van Neer 1996, fig. 3). The legend shows: −, absent; +, visible only as a thin layer near the cortex; ++, intermediate; and +++, inner cavity of the bone almost completely filled.

As might be expected, the archaeological bones (humerus, femur, tibiotarsus, and tarsometatarsus) showed much variation. In some specimens it actually filled the medullary cavity to a greater degree than in recent hens. This result could not be fully explained but it was thought that an abundance of lime-rich soils at both sites played a role.

For a systematic analysis of the percentage of hens slaughtered when in lay, it is obviously more useful to select the elements most likely to show medullary bone and examine every specimen. Coy (1983) recommended that the femur should be selected, both because it often contains medullary bone and because it survives well in chickens. The research at Berenike and Sagalassos and the data from English sites confirm the importance of the femur but indicate that the tibiotarsus is also worth including in any analysis. A practical advantage of making a systematic study of the tibiotarsus is that this element is more often found broken than is the femur, which obviates the need to damage the bone. Medullary bone can be recognised in broken bones, provided they are clean, but unbroken bones also have to be checked. In this case, the most reliable method is to snap the bone in half, but, as this is a destructive technique, other methods have been tried. Coy (1983) drilled a small hole in the unbroken femora from the Saxon town of Hamwic, which allowed her to inspect the interior of the bone. Some of the chicken femora from the medieval abbey of St Albans have been x-rayed: medullary bone was visible in those elements in which it filled the medullary cavity, but could not be clearly distinguished in those instances in which it survived only as a lining to the bone wall.

Size Differences Between the Sexes

Some species are highly dimorphic, others less so, and some not at all. In the turkey and the great bustard, for instance (see Figure 6.16 in Chapter 6), males are so much larger than females that most elements can be sexed. In hawks the females are larger, which allowed the hawks from the Migration-period castle at Oldenburg to be sexed (Chapter 13). The length of the long bones in both domestic turkeys (Gilbert et al. 1981, tab. 2) and wild turkeys (Bochenski & Campbell 2006, 29), including the extinct *Meleagris californica* from Rancho La Brea, is highly dimorphic (Figure 3.11). None of the lengths in domestic turkeys showed any overlap between males and females, even of the shortest elements measured. The dimorphism of the greater sage grouse from the Connley Caves in Oregon led the original analyst to identify the larger group as wild turkey and the smaller as sage grouse. This implied an unexpected increase in

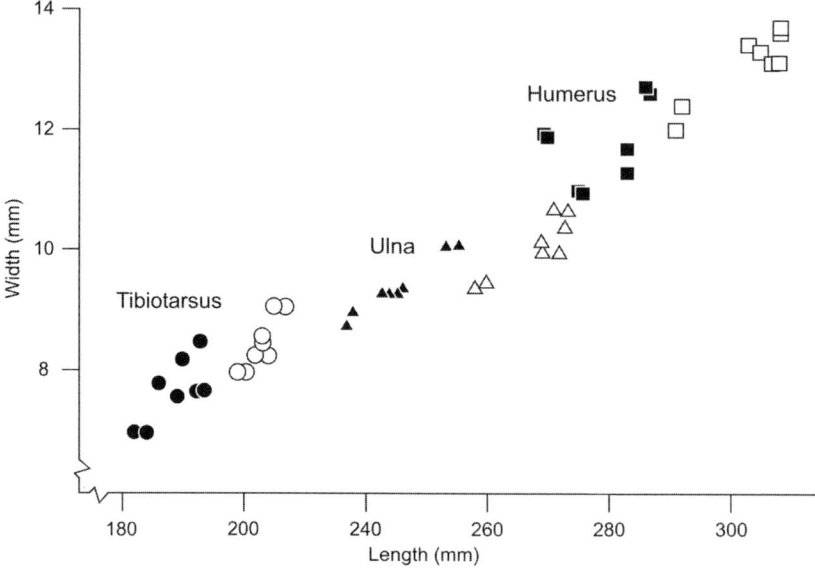

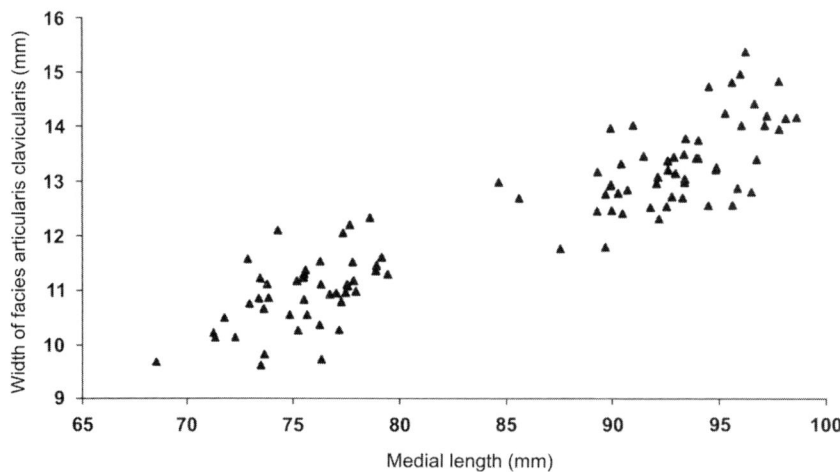

FIGURE 3.11. Size of long bones, showing examples of sexual dimorphism. The top graph shows limb bones (length × shaft width) of whooper swan, *Cygnus cygnus* (redrawn from Northcote 1980). The humerus, ulna, and tibiotarsus of males (white) and females (black) overlap in the middle of the range. The bottom graph shows the coracoid of the extinct California turkey, *Meleagris californica* (medial length measured between the processus acrocoradoideus and the cotyla scapularis × width of the sternal facet, or facies articularis clavicularis). Measurements fall into two discrete groups, interpreted as females and males (Bochenski & Campbell 2006, fig. 30).

the range of the wild turkey, which was disproved when it was shown that the two sizes present were in fact males and females of the sage grouse (Grayson 1977, fig. 3).

With the snowy owls from the Late Palaeolithic cave site of Bois-Ragot, Vienne, a species in which the female is 20 per cent larger than the male, about half of the identified remains could be sexed, including even second, third, and fourth phalanges (Laroulandie 2000, tab. 2). Both sexes had been targeted, but rather more females than males. Many of the economically important species such as the ducks (Woelfle 1967) are only weakly sexually dimorphic. The long bones of the whooper swan are also weakly dimorphic and cannot be separated at the middle of the range (Figure 3.11). In the corvids, too, the mean length of the long bones of the males was greater than that of the females, but there was 'a considerable overlap between the sexes' in the species studied (Tomek & Bochenski 2000, 67).

In many assemblages of prehistoric and early historic chickens, the bones fall into two size classes, reflecting the two sexes, but this simple picture is greatly complicated by the possible presence of capons and of more than one type or breed. The chicken is sexually dimorphic, but the sexes overlap; under domestication, sizes vary between and within the sexes, as discussed in Chapter 12.

PATHOLOGY *BY TONY WALDRON*

It is unusual to find much evidence of pathology in any assemblage of bird bones. Among domestic birds, those which are kept for egg production or as breeding stock generally survive longer than those kept for meat, and thus they are more prone to disease; breeding birds are liable to be affected by arthritis, while laying hens are prone to osteoporosis, especially during the laying season when the demand for calcium is high (Thorp 1994). Another factor that mitigates against finding evidence of disease in bird bones is that most assemblages are composed of disarticulated material frequently in the form of kitchen waste; as a general rule, the more complete the skeleton, the greater the likelihood of finding any pathology that might have been present. In archaeological contexts, the majority of pathology is found in chicken bones. The exception is birds kept as pets, or for purposes such as falconry.

Skeletal Malformations and Trauma

There are a number of malformations, congenital and acquired, that may affect the bird skeleton. None is very common, although in waterfowl at least, the rate of malformation is considerably increased by the presence of toxins in their habitats (Rockwell et al. 2003). In domestic birds, there is a relationship between the development of skeletal deformities and the size and weight of the bird, so that they occur more often in hens fattened for the table (compared with pullets and layers) and in turkeys (Cook 2000). The legs of broiler birds may show both torsional and rotational deformities (Duff & Thorp 1985), thought to result from mechanical forces acting on a rapidly remodelling skeleton that is not sufficiently strong to support the body weight of the bird (Reiland et al. 1978). Skeletal abnormalities in poultry may be brought about by nutritional deficiencies, especially of the precursors of vitamin D, giving rise to rickets (Reiland et al. 1978; Edwards 2000); this may be recognised by bowing of the leg bones. Kinky back is a form of spondylolisthesis in which there is displacement of the fourth thoracic vertebra resulting in curvature (kyphosis) of the spine, sometimes accompanied by paralysis of the legs if the spinal cord is compressed by the displaced vertebral body (Thorp 1994).

Crooked Keel

One form of deformity found in chickens and some other domestic birds is the so-called crooked keel in which the sternum is deviated to one side. The lesion tends to occur in heavier birds and was formerly thought to be the result of early perching, the weight of the bird forcing the sternum down onto the perch so that it was forced out of normal alignment. Male birds are slightly more often affected than female and in chickens the condition usually develops by 20 weeks. The more modern view is that a deviated sternum results from nutritional deficiencies during the period of rapid growth (Warren 1937; Blount 1964; Poulos et al. 1978). As discussed, an immature and porous sternum could become distorted in the ground, and this would have to be distinguished from skeletal malformation.

Fractures

Fractures are probably the most common type of pathology seen in assemblages of bird bones, most often affecting the legs, wings, or skull. Survival following fractures of bones other than the skull is possible, providing the bird does not starve or become predated during the period when healing is taking place. Fractures of the coracoid – usually resulting from an injury to the thorax – will prevent the bird from flying, and even if they heal, the bird may not be able to fly again if the mechanics of the wing are too greatly disturbed (Holz 2003); death is then inevitable. Among domestic

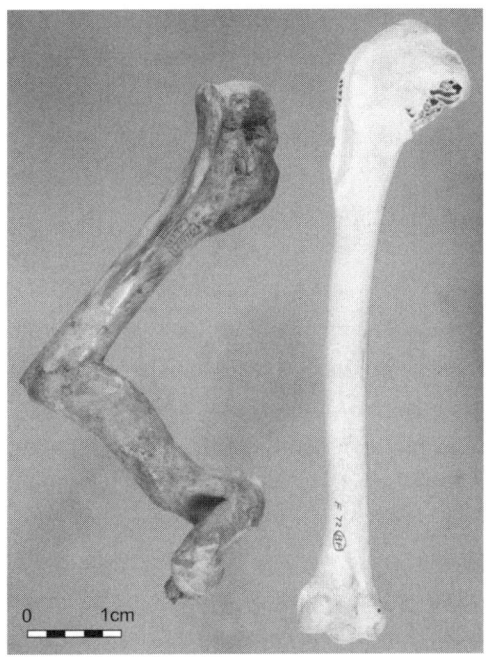

FIGURE 3.12. Fractured humerus of a goose, *Anser* sp., from medieval York which has healed with angulation (left), compared with normal specimen (right) (photograph by T. P. O'Connor).

birds, fractures of the legs are most common, sometimes resulting from overweight. Laying birds, which are prone to osteoporosis, are at particular risk, and up to a third of osteoporotic hens in lay may develop a fracture in modern flocks (Whitehead & Fleming 2000).

Bird bones heal much more quickly than those of mammals – the record seems to have been six days for a bantam hen which broke a tibia and was confined to a small box to restrict its movements (Wood 1941) – but they invariably do so with considerable displacement or angulation of the distal fragment, and often with the production of a large amount of callus. This can be seen in goose humeri from medieval Lincoln (O'Connor 1982, fig. 56) and York (Bond & O'Connor 1999, pl. XIX). It is obvious that rapid healing has considerable survival value since a crippled bird is not likely to survive for long in the wild, while a domestic bird would be likely to find its way into a cooking pot if healing were long delayed. In the case of domestic, and particularly pet, birds, it is likely that attempts would have been made to promote healing by splinting the affected limb; I am not aware that any archaeological examples of bone setting in birds have come to light, however.

The diagnosis of a fracture in a bird is perhaps the easiest of all to make because of the displacement, the angulation (Figure 3.12), and the presence of callus (e.g., Gilbert et al. 1981, fig. 12). Fractures which occurred shortly after or at the time of death may be difficult to differentiate from post-mortem injury; any evidence of remodelling, as shown by smoothing of the sharp edges of the fracture, or the production of callus, however, will indicate that the injury was sustained before the bird died.

Arthritis

There are many forms of arthritis, but the only one that is at all likely to be found in bird skeletons is osteoarthritis, which is fundamentally a disease of cartilage. It is more common in laying hens than in broiler birds (Anderson-Mackenzie et al. 1997). It is usually diagnosed by the presence of osteophytes around the margin of the joint; when this criterion is used, the disease seems to be relatively common, in wild birds at least. For example, Rothschild and Panza (2006) found that 3 per cent of hawk and 9.8 per cent of pigeon skeletons in museum collections in the United States had osteoarthritis on this basis. This is somewhat at odds with previous reports which suggest that the disease is rare in birds (Sokoloff 1963) and certainly it does not occur with anything like this frequency in archaeological assemblages. It is not mentioned at all, for example, in the review of Baker and Brothwell (1980), and it would be more reliable to confine the diagnosis to those cases in which eburnation (polishing) is seen on the joint surface since this indicates complete loss of articular cartilage, the polishing resulting from the movement of bone against bone, an unequivocal sign of osteoarthritis.

Osteoarthritis is more likely to occur in older birds; hence it tends to be more common in layers than in broilers, but it may also be a complication of other conditions in birds. It may, for example, occur when damage to ligaments results in the instability of joints (Duff 1990). It develops secondary to other forms of hip disease in male turkeys (Duff 1984). Although the diagnosis of osteoarthritis should present no difficulties if reliance is placed on demonstrating eburnation, it would not be possible to tell whether the condition was primary or secondary, except in those instances in which osteoarthritis may have been secondary to a fracture, when displacement or angulation of the distal fragment causes changes in the mechanics of the joint above or below the fracture. Even in such a case, the bird would have had to survive a long period following the fracture for osteoarthritis to supervene.

Other forms of arthritis do occur in birds but extremely rarely, and there is very little prospect of coming across them in an archaeological assemblage. Gout occurs in both wild birds (Murnane & Garner 1987) and domestic birds (Mert 1991) but rarely affects the joints, except in domestic strains specially selected to have high blood uric acid levels (Cole & Austic 1980). Where articular gout does occur, it may be recognised by the presence of punched out para-articular lesions (Rothschild & Ruhli 2007).

Infectious Diseases

Osteomyelitis

Infections with *Staphylococcus aureus* are common in breeding chickens and may give rise to infections of the knee (femuro-tibiotarsal) or ankle (tibiotarsal-hypotarsal) joints, or the vertebrae (Jensen & Miller 2001). Affected joints become swollen, painful, and inflamed, causing the birds to become lame, while vertebral infections may result in paralysis. Osteomyelitis supervenes when the bone marrow becomes infected, usually as the result of spread through the blood stream, so-called haematogenous spread. The bones most likely to be affected by osteomyelitis include (in order of frequency) the proximal tibia, proximal humerus, proximal femur, rib cage, and distal femur (Mutalib et al. 1996). The affected bones become enlarged and periosteal new bone develops around the shaft, forming what is referred to as an involucrum. As the disease progresses, pus is formed within the marrow cavity, raising the intramedullary pressure. Eventually the pus escapes to the outside through holes in the bone known as cloacae. This characteristic set of signs – swelling, involucrum, and cloacae – is pathognomonic of osteomyelitis and ought to make the diagnosis in a full-blown case relatively straightforward.

Tuberculosis

Tuberculosis is a disease that may occur in domestic, wild, captive, and pet birds and is usually caused by one of two species of mycobacteria, *Mycobacterium avium* and *M. genavense* (Tell et al. 2001). The disease may sometimes reach endemic proportions in wild bird populations with considerable loss of life (Kock et al. 1999). Humans, especially those who are immunosuppressed, may occasionally contract tuberculosis from birds, but pet birds may also become unwell by contracting the disease from their owners (Washko et al. 1998). By contrast with mammals, in which the skeleton is relatively infrequently involved, tuberculosis in birds seems always to affect the bones, being confined generally to the marrow cavity of the long bones of the leg (Lignereux & Peters 1999). Affected bones are swollen and there may be a considerable formation of periosteal new bone, again by contrast with the mammalian form of the disease. Tuberculosis may also affect the joints, especially the tarsus, knee, and shoulder joints, which will eventually become fused. The combination of a swollen long bone and the presence of periosteal new bone should raise the possibility of the diagnosis, although it may be difficult to differentiate from non-tubercular osteomyelitis.

Periosteal new bone as an isolated phenomenon is a relatively common finding on the shafts of long bones, sometimes very considerable in extent, as, for example, in some of the chicken bones from the medieval priory at St Mary of Ospringe (Wall 1980, pls. 1A and B). Although this is frequently attributed to an infection, usually unspecified, it is unusual to be able to determine the true cause, and in most cases there is nothing to be gained from making the attempt.

Osteopetrosis

Osteopetrosis (Figure 3.13) is an interesting condition which has been known for many years to be caused by the avian leucosis virus, an RNA retrovirus (Smith 1982). The virus interferes with normal osteoblast function with the resultant formation of dense layers of periosteal new bone and spread into the marrow cavity. (Osteopetrosis in birds must be distinguished from the disease of the same name in humans, in which the defect resides in the osteoclasts, not the osteoblasts.) The long bones are principally affected and they become enlarged and heavy; an illustration of the condition in live and plucked birds and the skeleton can be found in Biltz and Pellegrino (1965, fig. 1). There are many archaeological examples of avian osteopetrosis, mostly in chickens from southern and eastern Britain (Brothwell 2002), and it is one of the easiest of avian diseases to recognise and diagnose.

Recognising and Diagnosing Pathology in Bird Bones

There is generally little difficulty in recognising that a bone is abnormal but it is a much more difficult task to make the correct diagnosis. In many cases all that one will be able to do is to describe (and preferably photograph) the abnormality. Some conditions have pathognomonic signs – eburnation in osteoarthritis and the combination of swelling, periosteal new bone, and cloacae in osteomyelitis – but these are few. Fractures are probably the easiest lesions to recognise, but in the event that the bone is not greatly displaced or angulated, it might take an X-ray to reveal the

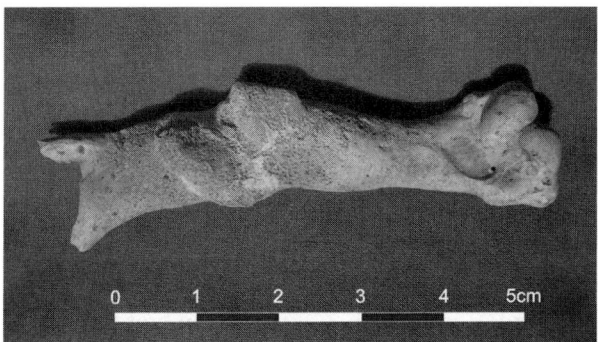

FIGURE 3.13. Humerus of a chicken from medieval Flaxengate, Lincoln, with avian osteopetrosis (photograph by S. O'Connor).

fracture line. Radiography is often disappointingly unhelpful in making a diagnosis, and, wherever possible, the help of a veterinary radiologist should be sought – if one can be found.

CONCLUSION

Though establishing the age at death in birds is less informative than in mammals, it is possible to do so from those elements which fuse after hatching and from porosity and bone length in immature bones. The sequence in which elements fuse seems to be similar between species, but the extent to which it follows the same pattern between families has yet to be confirmed. The porosity of juvenile bones is easy to recognise, though species identification can be difficult: for instance, it was not even possible to separate all the youngest chickens and pigeons in the food remains from the Post-Medieval manor of Hextalls in southern England (Bourdillon 1998). The synsacrum and sternum are late in reaching their fully mature form so are potentially useful for ageing. Unfortunately they can be very fragmented, so they are not always recorded. Certainly, if there is a real possibility that young as well as adult birds were being exploited, it is worth recording age data on these late-fusing bones if they can be identified. It is also important to separate hatchlings from older immature birds, since very young birds are likely to be casualties rather than food remains. In domestic birds, their presence suggests that the settlement was one where the birds were raised, as discussed in Chapter 12 in the context of the domestic geese from medieval Winchester.

So far as sexing is concerned, tarsometatarsi can be distinguished in chickens and turkeys, but in other domestic and wild species, size is the only guide. Distinctions are clear in those large birds which are strongly dimorphic but more difficult in species in which the sexes overlap in size. In this case it is possible to obtain a sex ratio where a large sample is available, but some specimens are always going to be ambiguous. Medullary bone is currently the subject of medical as well as zooarchaeological research because of its value for the study of osteoporosis in humans. Research into the length of time medullary bone persists in different avian species would have great potential for archaeological interpretation. Where large birds such as swans and bustards were caught for food, it is possible to infer from size differences in the bones whether either sex was preferred. It is likely that hunters deliberately selected males for feathers where these have more colourful plumage than females; in this case, establishing the sex ratio could be important.

Domestic birds kept for the table are short-lived, as are most wild birds, which reduces the likelihood that they will develop skeletal pathology. Pathology is seen more often in domestic birds kept for breeding. Avian osteopetrosis is a condition that is specifically linked to stocking densities, so it can therefore reveal interesting information regarding fowl husbandry in the past. The fact that it is not found until the Roman period is telling. Though occasionally seen in long-lived wild birds such as ravens, it in fact is rarely observed in archaeological material.

The biological data discussed here and in the previous chapter all contribute to the interpretation of a bird bone assemblage or a single element. In the next chapter we shall be concerned with how to set about identifying bones and recording biological data in a consistent form.

4

Identification, Recording, and Quantification

In this chapter we shall look at the practical steps needed to identify bird bones, the stages to be followed, and the comparative material available for use. The identification of bird bones often poses greater problems than that of mammals (though not more than fish). Some of the problems of identifying the more common species encountered in archaeological assemblages are summarised here. Having made the identification, the analyst has to make a record of the species and elements, and some of the protocols which have been used by avian zooarchaeologists and palaeontologists are described. Finally, we shall examine how bird bones have been quantified and compared between sites and assemblages.

IDENTIFICATION

The archaeologist reading an account of the birds from a site is probably happily unaware of the problems faced – and the decisions made – by the specialist who has identified the remains. Identification problems arise because some bird families include species whose skeletal elements are almost indistinguishable, a challenge similar to that encountered with, for instance, deer in North America and marsupials in Australia. One veterinarian has commented, 'When birds are compared with some other classes of vertebrates, such as the reptiles, it must be admitted that, despite their extensive adaptive radiation, the range of osteological differences found among them seems fairly small' (Bellairs & Jenkin 1960, 245). An experienced avian palaeontologist wrote, 'It should be remembered that bird bones present such slight differences amongst members of the same genus that specific identification is given with some reserve'. According to Bramwell (1959–1960) the confusion is particularly marked in such families as the ducks, crows, thrushes, and smaller passerines. Experience with bird bone identification led Morales (1993b) to be more, rather than less, cautious over time in identifying the elements of certain families. The same conclusion was reached by Ericson and Tyrberg (2004, 18): 'Perhaps the most important knowledge gained in recent years is a better recognition of when an accurate identification is possible, and – probably even more important – when it is not'.

One reason for errors and overconfident identification can be that, as Driver (1992) pointed out, the analyst makes the assumption that the likely species in the range is the one which is present. This is relevant for the identification of Galliformes in assemblages from medieval Europe, where an occasional pheasant bone may be present among the ubiquitous chickens, but in general it is probably a less serious source of error in bird bone identification than specific identifications made by reliance on a single reference specimen. What Driver's point does highlight is the importance of being familiar with distributions.

Past Changes in Distribution

Knowledge of the expected distribution of birds in the past in any particular area is crucial background information for bone identification. This includes both the current and the past distribution. There is a vast modern ornithological literature concerned with recent expansions and contractions in ranges, but there is also abundant evidence for past changes in archaeological and palaeontological assemblages. A few surveys have been published of distribution changes in the Holocene era based on archaeological finds. Harrison assembled records of the early avifauna of Britain, which he published in both scholarly and popular form (Harrison 1980; Harrison & Reid-Henry 1988). A recent survey of Swedish avifauna includes both Pleistocene and Holocene records, and domestic as well as wild birds (Ericson & Tyrberg 2004). Other countries which have been well served by synoptic works are New Zealand (Worthy & Holdaway 2002), Mexico (Corona-M. 2002), the Netherlands (Clason 1967; Clason & Prummel 1979), Bulgaria (Boev 1996), Hungary (Gál 2007), England (Yalden & Albarella 2008), and Scotland (Kitchener 2007).

Bird Bone Identification in Practice

In a recent text-book on zooarchaeology the author wrote of how 'the *process* of identification has received less attention [than other aspects of bone analysis], despite its obvious importance' (O'Connor 2003, 113). Here we shall review some stages of the process, as some aspects are not self-evident for the beginner.

Ideally, a researcher will learn to identify bird remains in the environment of a museum or laboratory with a comprehensive reference collection and with tutoring from others with wide experience. However, in reality, zooarchaeologists often have to work in less than ideal conditions. A reference collection is the first requirement; where this is limited, the researcher needs to negotiate access to a more comprehensive collection to check any unusual specimens.

A good recommendation for the student is to 'place before him at the outset skeletons of birds in five different size classes, in order to accustom him or herself to the relative sizes of the birds' (Olsen 1979, 56). This is good advice because novices often find that bones are smaller than expected in relation to the size of the bird because feathers make a bird appear larger. Since identification relies first on shape, and after that on size, correct identification depends on familiarity with the range of sizes within families and within species. We saw in Chapter 3 that some species exhibit sexual dimorphism, and in this case reference specimens of both sexes are needed. Size changes have occurred over time; the example of the common crane is discussed in Chapter 15. Domestic birds present challenges because of the great variety in size and shape which has developed under domestication (see Chapters 11 and 12). With chickens it is useful to have skeletons of breeds closest to the original wild species, as modern birds are larger and more robust than their prehistoric and early historic ancestors.

Use of Reference Collections

The major national collections such as the Natural History Museum in England, the Muséum national d'Histoire naturelle in Paris, and the Florida Museum of Natural History, the Vertebrate Zoology collection of the University of California and the museums of the Universities of Michigan and Kansas, aim to collect skeletons from all over the world (Olson 2003). Though formerly museums gave priority to collecting skins, the skeleton collections became increasingly prominent from the 1950s onwards (Hangay & Dingley 1985; Olson 2003).

Most working zooarchaeology laboratories cannot attempt to collect everything; they instead confine themselves to collecting comparative skeletons from the region in which research is being carried out. Even a small collection, however, needs to have depth as well as breadth (Stewart & Hernandez Carrasquilla 1997). As Ericson and Tyrberg (2004, 18), note, 'A high-quality comparative collection should not only be taxonomically broad ... but also reflect intra-specific variation in the size and morphology of most species'. Several specimens have to be consulted to accommodate the full size range. Bochenski and Tomek concluded that a single specimen is enough to identify 'species of the same body size but belonging to different genera' but set out to examine how many specimens were necessary to identify a bone in those families where species overlap in body size. They examined the morphology in three elements from two species of grebe (great crested and the red-necked), two corvids (carrion crow and rook), and two elements from two thrush species (song thrush and blackbird). Each articular end had up to five morphological characters. The researchers found that in a few cases one unequivocal feature served to separate the species successfully, but that two comparative specimens or even three were sometimes needed (Bochenski & Tomek 1995). An unstated implication is that any bone, or at least any complete bone, can be identified to species, but the fact is that there are families, especially the ducks, where even the most experienced workers have not been able to separate similar-sized species.

Creating a Reference Collection

The creation of a reference collection has become more difficult in the past 20 years. The days are gone when, as one long-retired museum curator wrote, 'if we needed a series of 200 birds we just went out and shot them' (Erritzoe 2005). Today it is illegal in many parts of the world to collect and handle the carcasses of certain wild birds; raptors are especially heavily protected. To collect today, one needs a licence or good contacts with wildlife authorities who have their own licences to handle dead birds. Museums today have an ethics policy for collections (see, e.g., the policy of the Florida Museum of Natural History, cited in Appendix 3). Wageningen University, a Dutch institution with a large reference collection (see Appendix 3), carries this disclaimer: 'No bird has been killed to get its skull or skeleton for this collection. All wild birds died of natural causes or accidental, and in a few cases due to legal hunting by others, or died in captivity'.

The first step in adding a bird to the collection is to confirm the identification, as this will be very much more difficult when the feathers and flesh have been removed. The minimum additional information needed is provenance, with date of death, cause of death, age, sex, and weight when known (Davis & Payne 1992). It is also good practice to record the measurements of the wing-length, bill, and tail.

Some of the methods used to clean mammal skeletons are suitable for birds, but only the more gentle ones. Bleaching with chemicals such as H_2O_2 has proved to damage the bone so that the reference skeleton is unsuitable for DNA analysis

(Barnes et al. 1998). Though bird bones have less marrow than mammal bones (Chapter 2), they do nevertheless have to be de-greased. Gentle maceration in water at about 35° C will remove some of the grease, and better results are obtained if this is combined with the use of enzymes such as neutrase or trypsin (Hangay & Dingley 1985; Davis & Payne 1992). Large museums maintain colonies of dermestid beetles (Dirrigl 2004). These are very effective at leaving a clean skeleton, but have to be very carefully curated to ensure that the beetles do not get into the collections. Beetles do not destroy all the ligaments and tendons, so they are not ideal when a completely disarticulated skeleton is required. Less hazardous is the use of other small animals such as woodlice, mealworms (Erritzoe 2005), or tadpoles (Legge 1993), though the latter are active only in spring. If the cleaning method leaves the bones bleached white, a good tip is to add a teabag to the final cleaning water, as this lightly stains the bones and highlights subtle variations in the areas of muscle attachment (Davis & Payne 1992). Burial in the ground is least labour intensive. Specimens need to be buried with an indelible label in a gauze bag. A carcass buried in the spring may be clean by the end of the summer, as fungi and soil fauna are more active in warm weather; specimens buried later in the year may take longer. Once dug up, the bones can be cleaned with warm water only. If the collection later develops any infestation, freezing is the best technique for killing insects and eggs (Erritzoe 2005).

A collection of any size is usually kept in boxes or drawers in taxonomic order, but some laboratories also find it useful to have index collections in which elements are arranged together. Index collections are quicker to use, but there are advantages in using complete skeletons, as the researcher learns the relative sizes of the skeletal elements. The Archaeological Science Department of English Heritage (formerly the Ancient Monuments Laboratory) uses an index collection arranged in taxonomic position in five size classes. The nine main limb and girdle bones, left side only, were selected, one of each sex. The rest of the skeleton and those skeletons not used for the index collection were stored in boxes (Corke et al. 1998).

Using the Literature

Bird identification guides for use in the field can help identification of the mandible and maxilla, but otherwise they are mostly useful for information on relative size. Specialist books and papers with illustrations of disarticulated post-cranial bones are needed.

Manuals

Bones of North American birds are illustrated in *Avian Osteoarchaeology*; this manual includes some fine detailed pencil drawing by Gilbert, but it has the disadvantage that illustrations are shown at different scales on the same page (Gilbert et al. 1981). It includes keys and, what are most valuable, ranges of bone lengths. Skulls of North American birds are illustrated by Olsen (1979). Post-cranial bones of some species commonly found in the British Isles have been illustrated by Cohen and Serjeantson (1996). The extinct moa and other New Zealand species are figured by Worthy and Holdaway (2002, 576, app. 2), who have also published a key to their identification. If used circumspectly, manuals are useful for the beginner, as they allow certain families and species to be quickly ruled out, and can suggest the family to which a bone belongs (Cohen & Serjeantson 1996, 3); however, for identification to species, reference specimens should be used, together with papers on individual families.

Papers on Individual Families

Even when a good reference collection is available, papers on individual families and species ought to be consulted, as they give a guide to minor morphological differences and also size ranges. This is especially important when a specimen is from a family in which there are many species which overlap in size, such as the ducks. If a collection contains only one skeleton of each species, it is tempting to make a positive identification when in fact the element in question fits within the size range for more than one species.

Internet Resources

Several internet sites have photographs of skulls and skeletons (see Appendix 3), but few have images of individual elements. The *Centro Austral de Investigaciones Cientificas*, Tierra del Fuego, Argentina, has a digital photographic file for species from the south of South America. An Expert System is being developed there for use in the field in which the user enters measurements of the element to be identified, and the programme lists species ranked in order of probability. Elements can be viewed from various perspectives in order of probability, or two species can be compared (Estevez et al. 2002).

Identification from Micromorphology and DNA

In mammals, measurements of both Haversian canals and secondary osteons have been used to identify species, but, as we saw in Chapter 2, only the former are present in bird bones (see Figure 2.3). In some cases an examination of the tibiotarsus wall in thin section separated domestic fowls, pigeons, geese, and ducks, but it did not separate wild and domestic birds except in pigeons (Strott 2005).

There are now many studies of the relationships between species based on mitochondrial DNA, but there are still few examples of its use for identifying ancient bird bones from archaeological contexts. DNA analysis has been used in connection with the origins of domestic geese (Barnes & Dobney 2000), turkeys (Speller In preparation), and chickens (Storey et al. 2008). The results are discussed in Chapters 11 and 12. It has also been used to identify the albatross species from excavated sites in Japan and elsewhere in the eastern Pacific. Measurements suggested that three species might be involved, the short-tailed albatross, the laysan albatross, and the black-footed albatross, but the elements sampled for DNA all proved to be from the short-tailed albatross (Eda et al. 2006). The research on domestic geese and albatrosses has highlighted the fact that size has varied so greatly over time that using the size ranges of modern specimens for comparison is not necessarily reliable.

As well as being used to examine the origin of domestic birds, microscopic techniques have potential for identification of material from archaeological sites, even if they are not likely to become routine because of the expense of the equipment required. They could be particularly useful for identifying the species where a bone has been used for a tool or decorative object and has lost its morphological features.

Measurements

The use of metrical analysis for identification, sexing, separating wild and domestic birds, and size change over time is referred to at many points in this book. Zooarchaeologists in Europe usually follow the protocols set out for bird bones in *A Guide to the Measurement of Animal Bones from Archaeological Sites* (von den Driesch 1976, 103–129); in North America the measurement points illustrated by Howard (1929) are also referred to. Research papers using metrical analysis normally illustrate the measurement points used, for instance on the humerus and femur, where the proximal articulations do not present obvious opposing surfaces

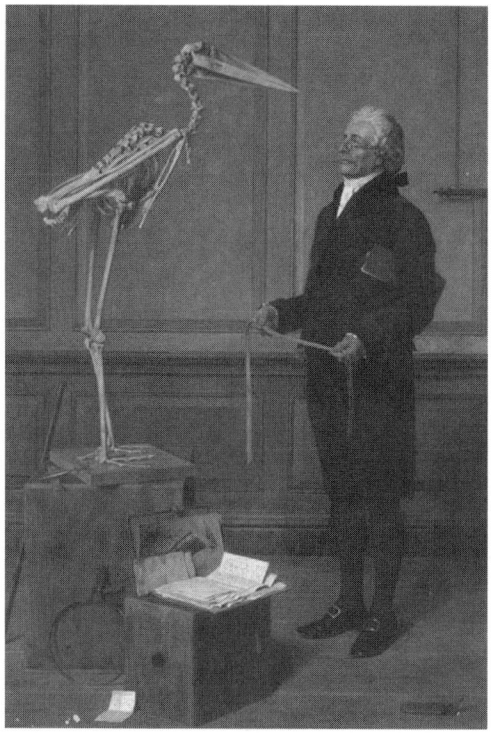

FIGURE 4.1. 'Science is Measurement', 1878, by Henry Stacy Marks. A scientist holds a tape measure with which he is about to measure a skeleton, probably a marabou, *Leptoptilus crumeniferus* (from Serjeantson 2005b).

(see, e.g., Figure 3.5). In those species in which the cnemial crest projects above the proximal articular surface of the tibiotarsus, it is useful to take the measurement of the greatest length excluding, as well as including, the cnemial crest, as this is often broken off in archaeological material. Measurements of bird bones can usually be taken with Vernier or digital callipers, but a measuring box is needed for complete wing bones of the largest flying birds and to measure the lengths of bones of the large ground-dwelling birds. Victorian naturalists seem to have relied on a tape measure (Figure 4.1). Results are usually displayed as univariate graphs (see, e.g., Figure 4.5 later) or bivariate graphs (see, e.g., Figure 3.11 in Chapter 3 and Figures 4.3 and 4.8 later).

In the past it was regarded as good practice to publish the raw measurements, but today this is less necessary, as it is becoming possible to make measurements available via the Internet (Appendix 3). Members of the International Council for Archaeozoology can post measurements on the *Bonecommons* internet site. The

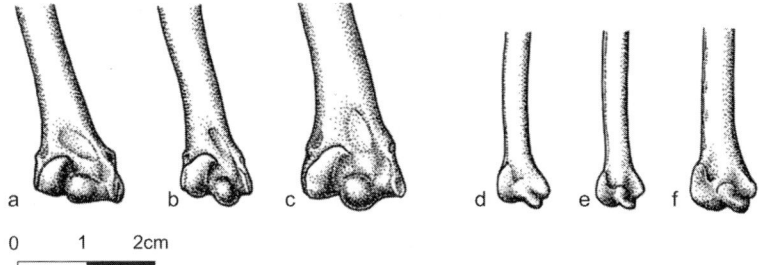

FIGURE 4.2. Morphological distinctions in the distal humerus and distal ulna of chicken and grouse: a and d, domestic chicken; b and e, willow grouse, *Lagopus lagopus*; c and f, black grouse, *Lyrurus (Tetrao) tetrix* (Boessneck & von den Driesch 1973, fig. I).

Animal Bone Metrical Archive Project is a source of measurements of domestic chickens and geese from English sites (Serjeantson 2005b).

Identification of Some Common Species

Domestic Chicken and Other Galliformes

The skeletal elements of domestic chicken can be confused with those of the pheasants and also in certain contexts with the Eurasian black grouse, willow (red) grouse, and guineafowl. The domestic chicken was introduced to Europe in the first millennium BC (Chapter 11) and the pheasant, in very small numbers, in the Roman period, so both have potentially been present since that time. The skeletal elements of the chickens of early historic times are unhelpfully similar to those of pheasants, and both are sexually dimorphic and quite variable in size. Most illustrations of chicken and pheasant suggest that they are different sizes (e.g., Erbersdorbler 1968; Cohen & Serjeantson 1996), but in fact they overlap. The most reliable distinctions are the presence of a hypotarsal (calcaneal) ridge running down the posterior internal border of the tarsometatarsus and a pneumatised area below the trochanter of the femur. Both are present in the pheasant (see Figure 2.7 in Chapter 2) but absent in the chicken (Eastham 1971; Cohen & Serjeantson 1996, 63).

The black grouse and even the smaller willow grouse can be confused with a small domestic chicken (Boessneck & von den Driesch 1973; Ericson & Tyrberg 2004, 18). Morphological distinctions in the humerus and ulna are shown in Figure 4.2. Willow grouse and ptarmigan, which has shorter legs, are hard to separate and the distinction between the two species was not attempted in the assemblage from

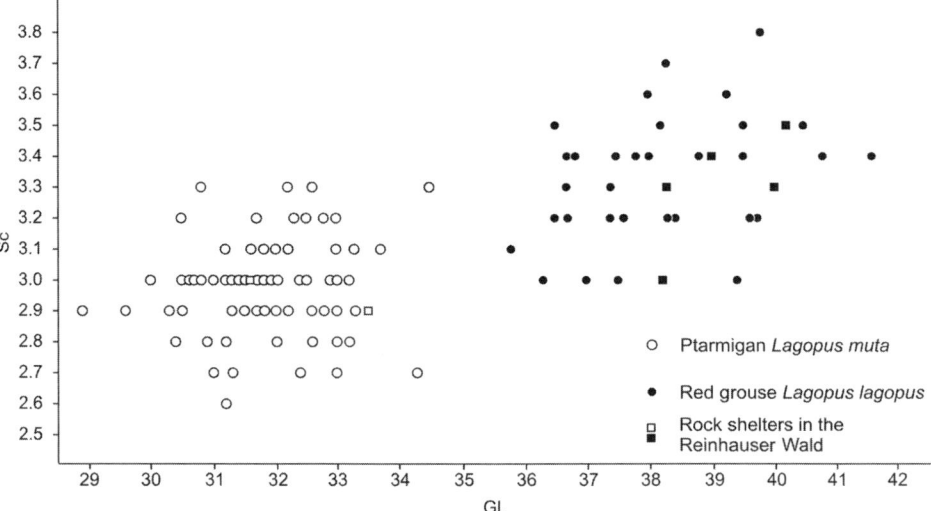

FIGURE 4.3. Size of tarsometatarsi of willow grouse, *Lagopus lagopus*, and ptarmigan, *L. muta*, from the Pleistocene cave site of Brillenhöhle (circles) and rock shelters in the Reinhauser Wald (squares; see Boessneck & von den Driesch 1973, diag. IV): greatest length (GL) × shaft breadth (Sc) in millimetres.

La Vache (discussed in Chapter 6), where most of the elements were fragmented (Laroulandie 2005a). At the Pleistocene cave site of Brillenhöhle (Boessneck & von den Driesch 1973), tarsometatarsus dimensions showed that both species were present (Figure 4.3).

Guineafowl and chickens may be present together on sites in Africa. Guineafowl were introduced to Europe, the West Indies, and Central America from the sixteenth century onwards, if not earlier (see Chapter 12). Though similar in size, some elements can be distinguished morphologically: the skull of the guineafowl has a 'cephalic bump' or bony casque, which is particularly pronounced in males (see Figure 12.8 in Chapter 12). Other features which distinguish the two species have also been observed (MacDonald 1992).

Turkey and Other North American Galliformes

Recent domestic turkeys can be distinguished from their wild counterparts by their shorter and more robust leg bones and broader sternum (Figure 4.4). However, remains from earlier than about the seventeenth century AD are difficult to separate, as discussed in Chapter 12. The size ranges and morphological distinctions between extinct and surviving wild turkeys have been the subject of research by

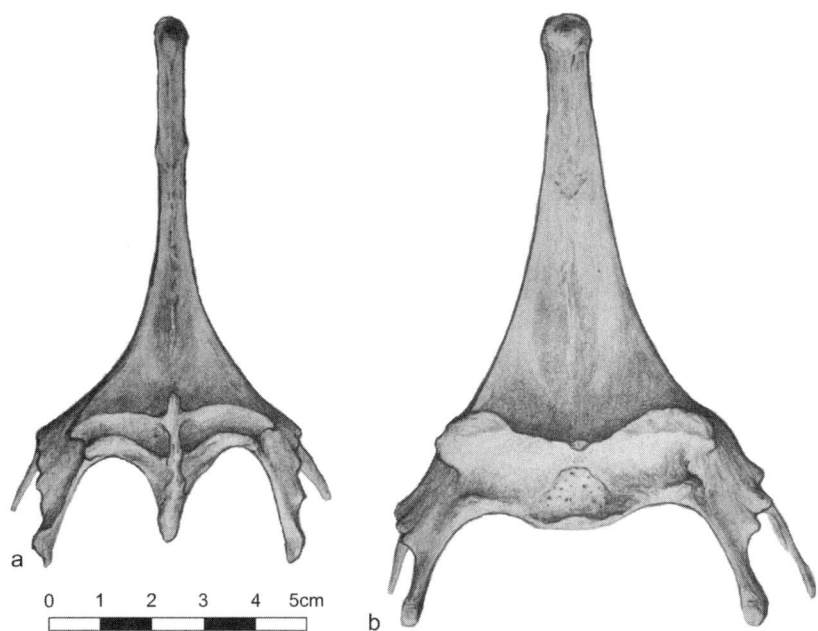

FIGURE 4.4. Sternum of a, wild and b, domestic turkey, *Meleagris gallopavo* (after Gilbert et al. 1981, fig. 5).

Steadman (1980), Gilbert et al. (1981), and Bochenski and Campbell (2006). The length of the limb bone in wild turkeys is quite variable (Table 4.1), compounded by the fact that turkeys are sexually dimorphic. Dirrigl (2002) found that among the North American gallinaceous birds, turkey, ruffed grouse, prairie hen, and bobwhite, morphological criteria alone distinguished only the proximal humerus and proximal coracoid between each of the species while other features were distinctive only between the Galliformes and the Phasianidae.

Geese

The *Anser* and *Branta* species overall have some morphological distinctions, but within and between families there is an overlap in size and shape (Bacher 1967; Barnes & Dobney 2000). In wild geese the presence of a pneumatic foramen in the furcula is characteristic of *Anser* but unusual in *Branta* (see Figure 2.12 in Chapter 2), which allowed Gotfredsen to identify the geese at the Greenland site of Nipisat as a small subspecies of Canada goose rather than a species of grey goose (Gotfredsen 2002). The leg bones of domestic geese become more robust than those of wild geese from the medieval period onwards in Europe, as discussed in Chapter 12.

Table 4.1. *Bone length range of male and female wild turkeys,* Meleagris gallopavo

Bone	Male		Female	
	Range	Specimen no.	Range	Specimen no.
Humerus	147–163	28	120–128	11
Coracoid	101–117	33	84–95	18
Ulna	144–159	23	119–126	16
Radius	129–142	23	106–119	17
Carpometacarpus	76–89	64	61–71	64
Phalanx second digit	28–32	25	23–26	11
Femur	138–146	24	112–124	23
Tibiotarsus	145–160	28	120–139	13
Tarsometatarsus	144–169	24	131–138	12

Note: Bone length range is the greatest length (in millimetres). The tibiotarsus was measured from the nutrient foramen to the distal end.

Source: Information is from Gilbert et al. (1981, tab. 2).

Ducks

The various dabbling and diving ducks are notoriously difficult to separate (Woelfle 1967; Pieper 1982). The elements overlap in size except at the smallest end of the size range. Most elements of the two smallest dabbling ducks, the common teal and the garganey, are absolutely shorter than those of middle-sized and large ducks, and most elements in the mallard are larger. A comparison of the humerus length of eight duck species found in Syria today with the archaeological specimens from the Pre-Pottery Neolithic site of Tell Mureybet (Figure 4.5) showed that most at that site were teal (or garganey or both), a few were clearly mallards, and that several unidentified middle-sized ducks were also present. Modern domestic ducks are larger and more robust than wild mallards (Chapter 12), but this size increase took place only in historical times.

Pigeons

The turtle doves are distinguishable from the larger doves or pigeons of Europe by size, but morphologically the skeletons of the pigeons are very similar (O'Connor 1993; LaBianca & von den Driesch 1995, 147–149). The woodpigeon is larger than

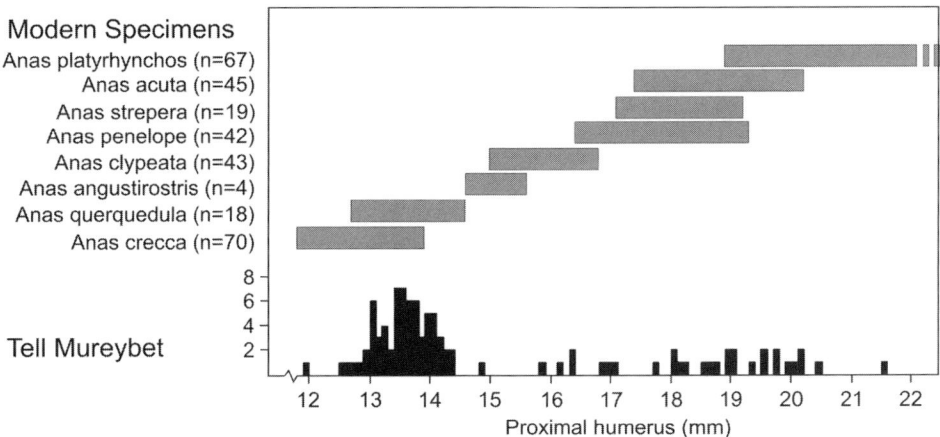

FIGURE 4.5. Size of humerus of ducks, Anatidae, from Tell Mureybet, Syria, compared with ranges for recent ducks. The *x* axis shows proximal breadth and the *y* axis shows the number of specimens (Gourichon 2004, fig. 3.13).

both the wild rock dove and the stock dove, but the latter two are very similar to each other. Research found some possible distinctions only in the sternum, ulna, and tibiotarsus (Fick 1974; also see Figure 4.6). Once domesticated, as discussed in Chapter 12, rock doves can grow as large as woodpigeons, in which case separation of the femur, tibiotarsus, and tarsometatarsus is difficult. Feral town pigeons today have reverted to the size of rock doves (LaBianca & von den Driesch 1995), so archaeological specimens attributed to rock dove could conceivably be any of truly wild birds, closely managed domestic birds, feral individuals from a formerly domestic population, or synanthropic individuals from a formerly wild population (O'Connor 1993).

Mute and Whooper Swans

The two large swans of Eurasia, the mute and the whooper swans, overlap in size and are also sexually dimorphic (Northcote 1981). The elements which are clearly distinct are the sternum and the furcula (Bacher 1967): the sternum of the whooper swan has a cavity which produces the whooping call and the furcula is more curved than in the mute swan (Figure 4.7). The wing bones of modern mute swans from the south of England are slightly shorter than those of prehistoric swans, and they show rather more variation, perhaps because they derive from a population which was closely managed in the Middle Ages (Northcote 1983).

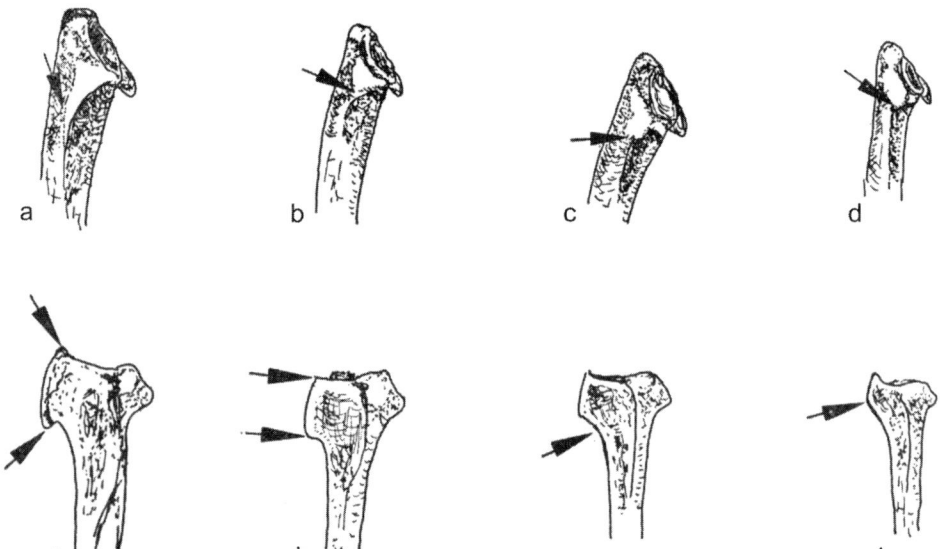

FIGURE 4.6. Identification of pigeons, Columbidae, showing distinctions in the proximal ulna (top) and proximal tarsometatarsus (bottom): a, woodpigeon *Columba palumbus*; b, stock dove, *C. oenas*; c, domestic pigeon, *C. livia domestica*; d, collared dove *Streptopelia decaocto*. Below: proximal tarsometatarsus, a, woodpigeon, b, domestic pigeon, c, stock dove, d, collared dove. Morphological distinctions are marked with arrows (Fick 1974, figs. 18 and 21).

Corvids

Among the corvids, the raven stands out as larger than the other species, but the carrion crow and the rook are difficult to distinguish except from the skull and mandible (Tomek & Bochenski 2000). Male carrion crows are on average larger than rooks, but there is an overlap between the two species, which makes distinctions in the long bones unreliable except at the extreme ends of the size range (Figure 4.8). There is also an overlap in the size of the smaller corvids (Hernandez et al. 1993; Tomek & Bochenski 2000).

Discussion of Identification

There is a hierarchy of confidence with which elements can be identified to species, from most to least reliable: (1) an element from a skeleton or part skeleton; (2) a single complete diagnostic bone; and (3) an incomplete but diagnostic bone. This leaves many fragments which can only be identified as 'probable' rather than certain.

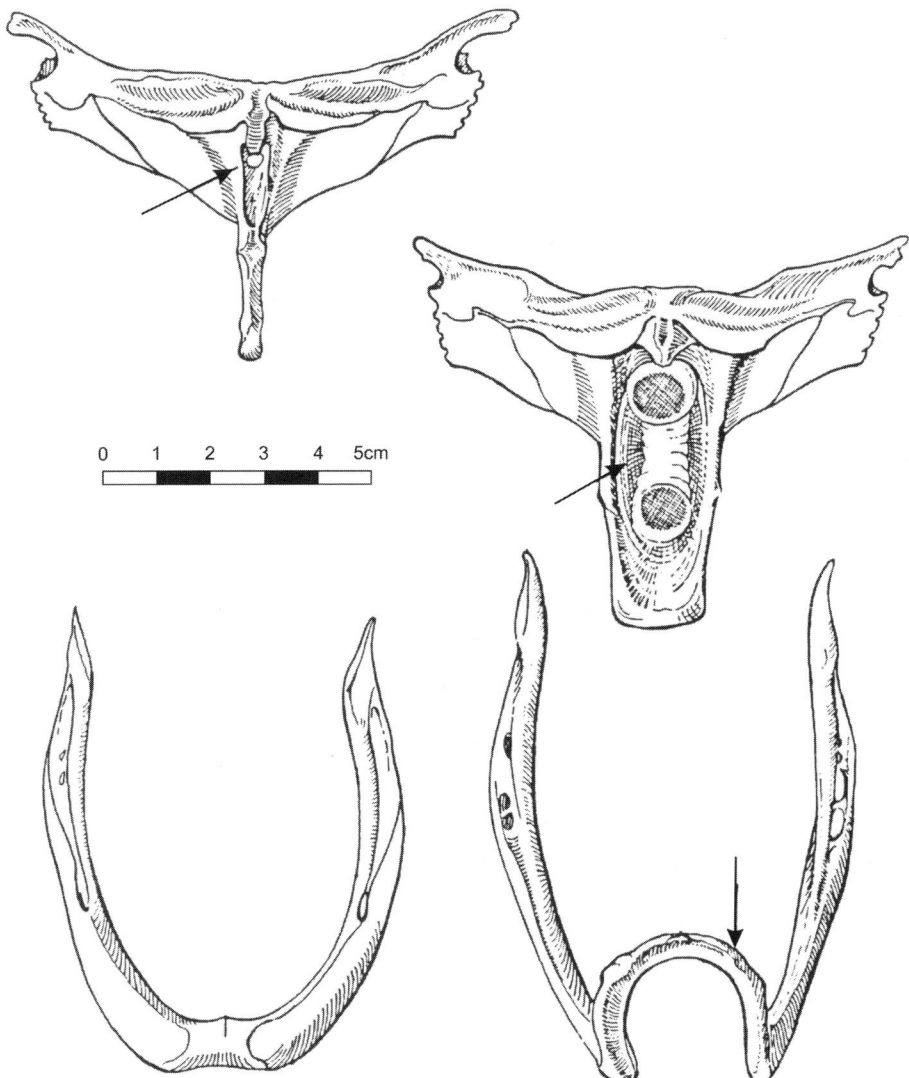

FIGURE 4.7. Furcula and sternum of swans. The left shows *Cygnus olor* and the right shows *C. cygnus* (after Bacher 1967).

My own practice has been to record elements as 'certain' (C) or 'probable' (P). I use 'probable' for fragments which are not complete enough for positive identification or where other species are possible, if unlikely, on zoogeographical grounds (see the previous discussion). In any discussion of past distributions, I rely only on those specimens identified as 'certain', but for discussion of butchery and other aspects of economic behaviour, the 'probable' specimens are included.

78 BIRDS

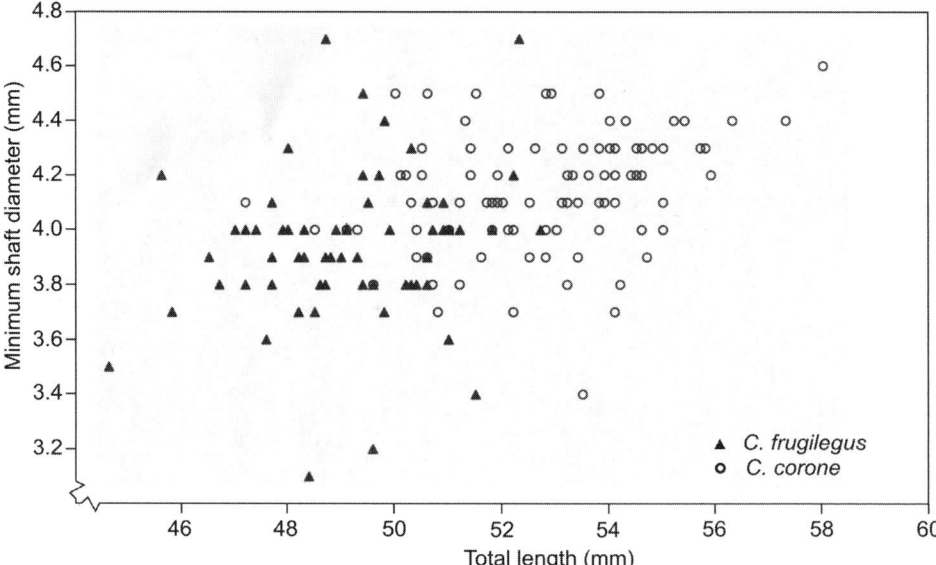

FIGURE 4.8. Scatter diagram of femur measurements (total length × minimum shaft diameter) of carrion crow, *Corvus corone,* and rook, *C. frugilegus* (Tomek & Bochenski 2000, fig. 145). There is an overlap in size except at the lower and upper ends of the size range.

No amount of comparative material and research will solve all problems of identification, but this is not necessarily a barrier to archaeological interpretation, as discussed. For instance, though Lefèvre was unable to identify the cormorants, steamer ducks, and members of the sheldgeese family to species, she was nevertheless able to give important insights into the changes in seabird fowling in Patagonia, as discussed in Chapter 10.

RECORDING

Actual identification is only the first step. Decisions then have to be made about which elements to identify, about how to record elements not identifiable to species, and about how to record the parts of a bone present.

Which Elements?

As with mammals, a researcher sometimes has to make the choice of restricting identification and recording to a selection of elements, based on their potential for identification, survival, and recovery. The degree to which survival is affected by density and shape is less clear-cut than in mammal bone, as discussed in Chapter 6, but relative survival will certainly affect any selection of elements to identify. Recovery methods, discussed in the next chapter, affect whether or not the smaller bones are present; elements such as the pygostyle, quadrate, wing digits, and phalanges are less often recovered than the main limb bones and are rarely identified, even though they are sometimes morphologically distinguishable.

The question of identifiability is rarely discussed explicitly, but the fact that some elements and some species are more identifiable than others can be significant in interpreting relative numbers in an assemblage. Morales (1993b) proposed a three-category scale of usefulness for different bone portions from the avian skeleton (Figure 4.9A): (1) diagnostic and very frequent element or portion; (2) diagnostic element or portion; and (3) neither diagnostic nor frequent. Figure 4.9C illustrates those elements and portions most frequent in Spanish archaeological assemblages, and Figure 4.9B is a qualitative estimation of the most diagnostic element. All skeletal elements were included except vertebrae, ribs, and some other minor elements.

Which Parts of the Bone?

When bones are fragmented, as they often are, the problem arises of how to record which parts of the bone are present. This has been overcome by some analysts by the use of abbreviations (P for proximal, M for medial, D for distal, etc.). I devised a method for recording mammal bone on a computer database using diagnostic zones which was later modified for bird bones (Cohen & Serjeantson 1996). Each of the major bones is notionally divided into eight regions or diagnostic 'bone zones' (Table 4.2). These are illustrated and defined for individual bones in Appendix 2. For each identified specimen, the bone zone is scored as present or absent (1/0). The zone is recordable if a definable characteristic in the zone is present or, in the absence of this, more than half of the zone is present. The advantage of using eight zones for each element, rather than a variable number, as anatomy might suggest (see, e.g., Figure 6.1 in Chapter 6), is that the bone zones present are recorded in a standard number of database fields. Eight zones might seem to be too many for species where the limb bones are too small to fragment into more than two identifiable pieces, but even with small birds there is merit in using zone recording, as it allows patterns of damage to be recognised. For instance, the olecranon process of some of the ulnae of thrushes from St Gregory's Priory, a medieval religious house in the south of England, had been snapped off in a consistent fashion when the birds were prepared

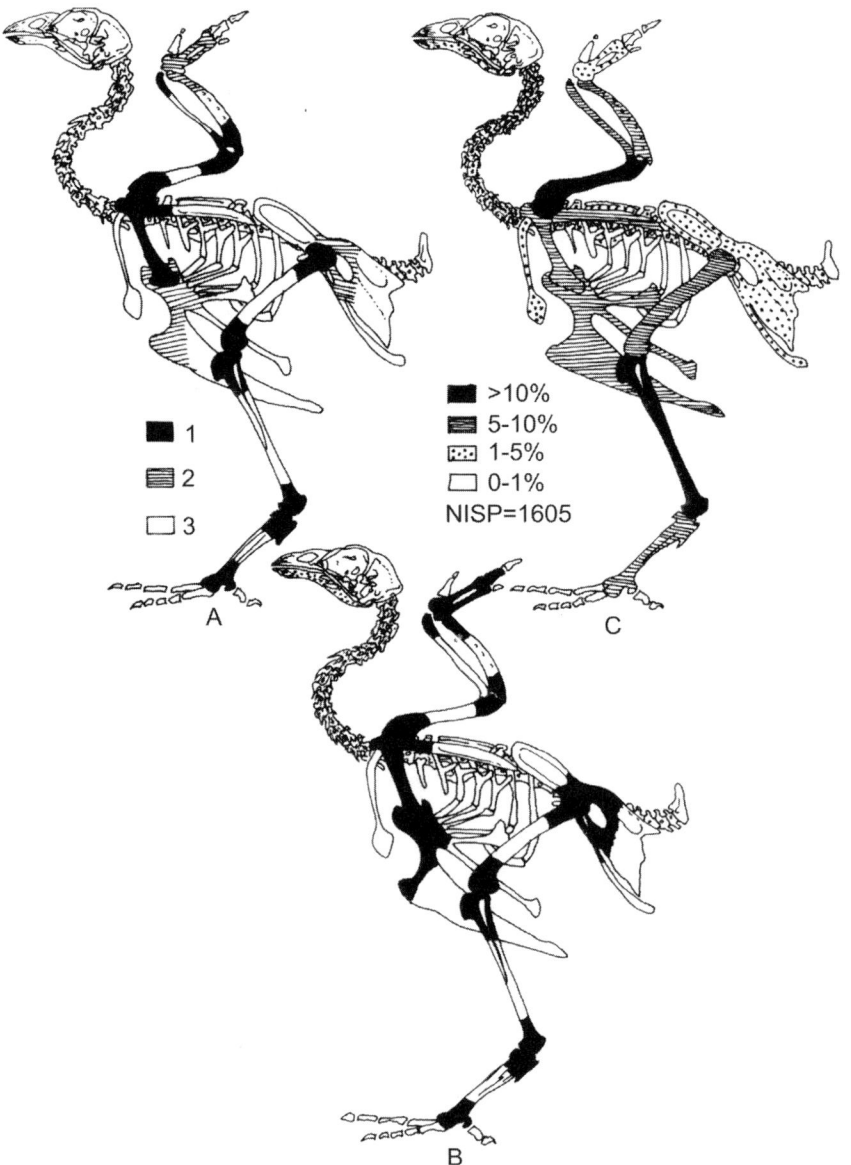

FIGURE 4.9. Identification of the elements of the avian skeleton: A, three-category scale of usefulness for identification (1 = diagnostic and very frequent element or portion, 2 = diagnostic element or portion, 3 = neither diagnostic nor frequent); B, qualitative estimation of the most diagnostic elements; C, elements and portions most frequent in Spanish archaeological assemblages (NISP = number of identified specimens; Morales 1993b, fig. 2).

Table 4.2. *Definitions of zones on avian limb bones*

Zone	Definition
1	Medial half of proximal end
2	Lateral half of proximal end
3	Medial half of proximal shaft
4	Lateral half of proximal shaft
5	Medial half of distal shaft
6	Lateral half of distal shaft
7	Medial half of distal end
8	Lateral half of distal end

Note: Zone definitions are modified for other elements (see Appendix 1).
Source: Information is from Cohen and Serjeantson (1996, figs. 8 and 9).

for cooking, as discussed in Chapter 6 (Powell et al. 2001). Proximally damaged ulnae were recorded thus:

0   1   1   1   1   1   1   1

The location of cut marks, superficial burning, and other damage can also be assigned to the appropriate zone, as discussed in Chapter 6.

Size Classes

It can be useful to assign fragments not identified to species to size classes. This allows fragments such as vertebrae and ribs to be included in the record. Size classes can also be used with identified or potentially identifiable elements. At the Neolithic site at the Links of Noltland, Orkney, Armour-Chelu found remains of an unexpectedly large number of small birds which could not be identified to species. She quantified the elements in eight size categories based on body length (Armour-Chelu 1988; see Table 4.3, Column A). The quantity of material in the three smallest size classes strongly suggested that this part of the assemblage was not from human food but from owl pellets, research to which we return in the next chapter. John Stewart classified the unidentifiable fragments from the Lower Palaeolithic site of Boxgrove into size classes (Table 4.3, Column B), and from this he was able to

Table 4.3. *Size categories used for recording bird bones, approximately correlated between authors*

A	B	C
Very short (VS)		
Short (S)	22–32 g (sparrow size)	Tiny (finch size)
Medium short (MS)	80–110 g (thrush size)	Small (thrush size)
Medium (M)	140–190 g (jay size)	Medium (pigeon size)
Medium long (ML)	250–440 g (teal size)	
Long (L)		Large (chicken size)
Very long (VL)		Very large (goose size)
Huge (H) (swan size)		

Note: Columns A and C show body length; Column B shows weight. Size classes in Columns A and B were designed for use with wild birds and those in Column C for assemblages with mainly domestic birds. The size classes were used for unidentified as well as identified remains.
Source: Column A is from Armour-Chelu (1988); Column B is from Harrison and Stewart (1999); Column C is from Ayres et al. (2003).

demonstrate that small birds, which could not be identified, as well as large birds were present (Harrison & Stewart 1999). Ayres et al. (2003) assigned identified as well as unidentified bones from medieval Eynsham Abbey, Oxfordshire, England, to five size classes appropriate for assemblages with mainly domestic birds (Table 4.3, Column C). The two larger size classes are 'goose-size' and 'chicken-size'; the 'medium-size' class includes pigeons and plovers; small birds are defined as 'thrush size', and 'tiny' birds such as passerines smaller than thrushes are finch size.

Unidentifiable Fragments

All assemblages contain unidentifiable fragments – if they do not, they have been poorly collected, or the bones have been incompletely sorted from the other vertebrate classes. Sieved assemblages normally contain large quantities. This fraction of the assemblage falls into two groups: bones which are potentially identifiable, and those which are too small and fragmentary to be identified even to family.

As we have seen, even when vertebrae, ribs, phalanges, and perhaps limb bone splinters are not identified to species or family, it can be informative to record them in a size class. In the assemblage from Eynsham Abbey the percentages of identified and unidentified bones in each size class were compared, as shown in Table 4.4. The

Table 4.4. *Identified and unidentified bird remains from Eynsham Abbey, Oxfordshire, England, by size class*

Recovery method	Identified		Unidentified	
	n	%	n	%
Hand				
Goose size	247	24.3	25	11.5
Chicken size	682	67.1	157	72.4
Medium	80	7.9	23	10.6
Small	7	0.7	6	2.8
Tiny	0	0.0	6	2.8
Total	1016	100.0	217	100.0
Sieved				
Goose size	9	5.0	69	26.6
Chicken size	149	82.8	147	56.8
Medium	19	10.6	34	13.1
Small	3	1.7	8	3.1
Tiny	0	0.0	1	0.4
Total	180	100.0	259	100.0

Note: The unidentified fraction includes a relatively higher number of medium, small, and tiny birds, probably a more accurate reflection of actual consumption.

Source: Data are from Ayres et al. (2003, tab. 10.20).

table, which includes all data from the eleventh to the fifteenth centuries, shows a reasonable correspondence between the identified and unidentified fraction in each size class. When the unidentified fraction, identified only to size class, is taken into account, the relative quantity of medium, small, and tiny birds is increased, which is probably a more accurate reflection of actual consumption at the abbey.

Discussion of Recording

Whether it is worthwhile to record all elements or only a subset is a decision which has to be taken at the outset of the research. The decision of what to record can be helped by including an assessment stage in archaeological projects. In an assessment all the excavated material is given a preliminary scan and crudely quantified to identify its main features (English Heritage 1991). The detailed recording which takes place later can then be tailored to highlight the research potential of the material. The finds should help to answer questions posed by the excavation as a whole, but they may also suggest a research interest of their own. A preliminary assessment also has the advantage that it can reveal when remains may be potentially difficult to identify, so that the archaeological project manager has advance warning that analysis will require special expertise or access to a specialist reference collection.

When time and funds are limited, some questions can be answered by identifying a subset only of the material; the aims and available resources will dictate how much attention is given to the fraction which can be identified only to size class. The recording protocols will also be modified to answer specific questions posed by the assemblage.

Classification

As we see in later chapters, the range of avian species excavated from archaeological sites is very often more diverse than that for mammals. Bird remains may also have more diverse origins, and there is greater likelihood that the origin is non-anthropogenic (see Chapter 5). This raises the question of the most appropriate categories to be used when listing and discussing remains from archaeological sites (Serjeantson 2000b). Taxonomic order is used when the purpose of the research is palaeontological, but this is not always the most appropriate order for zooarchaeological purposes. It can be inappropriate where the assemblage is mainly domestic. Wild and domestic animals are often shown separately, though this presents problems with geese, ducks, and pigeons where wild and domestic cannot always be separated (see Chapter 12). There are also categories of birds such as the mute swan which have been wild, semi-domestic, and feral in the past. It is desirable to separate anthropogenic and non-anthropogenic species, but, as we see in the next chapters, this distinction can be ambiguous where birds are concerned. The Humboldt Cave site, for instance, discussed in the next chapter, contained large numbers of bones of teal, some of which were from raptor pellets and some of which may have been from human meals (Livingston 1989). In this case, the author could not realistically have separated the anthropogenic from the non-anthropogenic. The non-anthropogenic or intrusive component of an assemblage can be further subdivided (Gautier 1987). The groups suggested are as follows:

- 'contemporaneous intrusives', that is, animals which ended up in the context during their life or shortly afterwards;
- 'late intrusives', that is, animals of which the remains are younger than the deposit in which they ended up, often the burrowing species; and

- 'reworked intrusives', that is, older material which ended up in a younger context.

These distinctions might seem excessively pernickety, but are in fact very important as far as birds are concerned, because of the significance of birds for reconstructing the season of occupation (Chapter 10) and past environments (Chapter 15).

Some researchers, such as Leach (1979), list species in decreasing order of abundance, which carries the implication that the birds were perceived in terms of their economic and food value, which may indeed have been the case. Some authors have resorted to listing birds in alphabetical order. Vigne and colleagues (1997) listed the species alphabetically in their study of faunal change on Corsica as a response to the changes which were taking place in avian taxonomy, discussed in Chapter 1.

So far as birds are concerned, regardless of how the discussion is set out, most authors do list the birds in taxonomic order. While this has the advantage of being a convention used by all scientists, the revisions to the Linnean taxonomy going on at the present time mean that researchers have to face the problem of when to change to using the revised taxonomy.

The record or list is only the beginning of the process of interpretation: for all but the smallest assemblage, the next decision is how to quantify the relative abundance of species and elements.

QUANTIFICATION

Many of the methods used to quantify animal bones of all classes are appropriate for bird bones (Lyman 2008). In avian palaeontology it is not always necessary to count every fragment, since establishing the presence alone of a species may be the aim of the research (Tyrberg 1998). In zooarchaeology, including the zooarchaeology of bird bones, fragment numbers are important basic data.

The debate about whether minimum number of individuals (MNI) as well as number of identified specimens (NISP) is a valid measure in zooarchaeology has taken on the status of opposed ideological positions (Lyman 1994, 97–112; O'Connor 2000). Germans and other European scholars influenced by them tend to use only NISP, while Americans, French, and most British scholars use MNI. NISP is more appropriate for small assemblages, often the case with bird remains. In Mesoamerican zooarchaeology, for instance, where assemblages are small and have high species diversity, the disadvantage of using a derived measure is believed to outweigh the advantage (Emery 2004, 28).

86 BIRDS

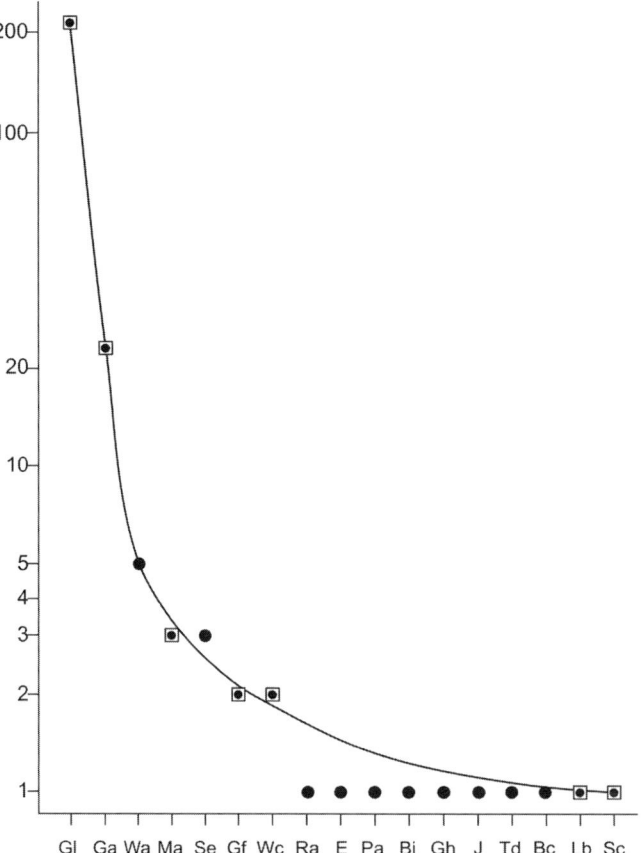

FIGURE 4.10. Birds from the Mesolithic site of Ølby Ling, Denmark. The *x* axis shows rank order and the *y* axis shows log abundance of species. Squares signify winter visitors; dots signify residents. Capture was specialised on guillemots, *Uria aalge* (Gl), and gannets, *Morus bassanus* (Ga); other species were of minor importance (redrawn from Grigson 1986, fig. 4).

Transformations of NISP

A refinement on the use of raw numbers is to convert NISP into log ratios when one is graphing the results. This technique is used by ecologists (Elston et al. 1996): it has the advantage that the data tend to be normally distributed on log transformation and it also reduces the scale on the *y* axis when plotting, since the log scale is generally contracted relative to the untransformed data. When the birds from Mesolithic sites in Denmark were compared by using log ratios, Grigson (1986) was able to contrast sites such as Ølby Ling (Figure 4.10) where bird hunting was specialised on a few

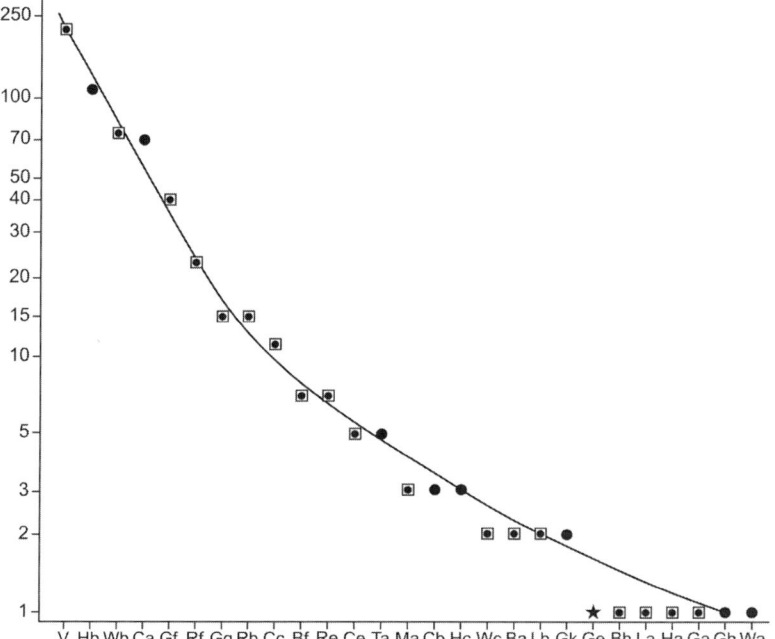

FIGURE 4.11. Birds from the Mesolithic site of Ertebølle, Denmark (axis and symbol information shown in Figure 4.10). Wildfowling was generalised rather than specialised (redrawn from Grigson 1986, fig. 5).

species, here guillemots and gannets, with others such as Ertebølle where fowling was generalised on a wider range of species (Figure 4.11). Fowling in the Danish Mesolithic is discussed in Chapter 10.

Derived Measures: MNE and MNI

Wildlife biologists quantify raptor prey by using minimum numbers. In a study of the prey of British owls, Glue (1972) used the cranium of rodents for the count but found that the avian cranium was unsuitable 'as decapitation of bird prey may occur before eating'. Instead he used the synsacrum and sternum, chosen because these elements survived well in the prey of owls and raptors (see Chapter 5). In this case Glue was selecting one or two elements on which to base MNI, rather than calculating it from all elements. The first avian palaeontologist to calculate MNI was Howard, who used to make the quantification of the fossil birds from Rancho La Brea comparable with the mammals (Lyman 2008, 38). MNI was not taken up at the time, and subsequently Foss Leach, one of the first zooarchaeologists to use MNI for bird remains, based his method on that described by Chaplin in 1971 for calculating MNI in mammals (Leach 1979).

The calculation of minimum number of elements (MNE) and MNI is useful in assemblages which contain a large number of bones from only a few species. Leach calculated minimum numbers of the most frequent species, the yellow- and red-crowned parakeets and the tui, at the Washpool site at Palliser Bay in the New Zealand (Leach 1979). He made his records on paper sheets by using letter codes and made the calculation manually, a technique now fortunately superseded by the use of computer databases.

I calculated the MNE for the chicken remains from Carisbrooke Castle, using the bone zone method described earlier, for two assemblages which dated from shortly after the castle was first constructed in the late eleventh century AD, one from a ditch and one from a midden (Serjeantson 2000a). In the raw records for the tibiotarsus from the midden, zones 3–6 are most frequent in the left elements and zones 5 and 6 in the right elements, giving an MNE of eight left and five right bones (Table 4.5). I calculated the MNE for other elements in the same way (Figure 4.12). Calculation of NISP only would have overestimated numbers of the tarsometatarsus, tibiotarsus, synsacrum, furcula, humerus, and even the femur, all of which had significantly higher numbers by NISP calculation. In this example, calculation of MNE gave a better idea of the relative frequency of the different parts of the carcass.

One of the arguments against the use of MNI is that it assumes that the whole carcass was present, which, with large mammals, was often not the case. With birds, on the other hand, except with the large ratites, the entire carcass was usually brought back to the camp site, though we look at some interesting exceptions in later chapters. The question of whether to use MNI as well as NISP is less acute for birds than for mammals, but even bird bones are sometimes chopped or break into more than one recognisable piece.

Bone Weight

Comparison of MNI provides information on the relative numbers of birds, but it is unhelpful about the relative amount of meat provided by each species. For this, other calculations are preferable. One which is sometimes used is the relative weight of bone, which can stand as a proxy measure for meat weight, as there is a reasonably constant relationship between the two. Bone was weighed as well as counted for the avifauna from the site of Schipluiden in the Netherlands (Zeiler 2006). The results showed that, at this Neolithic wetland site, 92 per cent of the remains in the hand-collected material were from ducks by NISP, but only 65 per cent by weight.

Table 4.5. *Database for chicken tibiotarsi from the Carisbrooke Castle midden, showing recording of bone zones 1–8 (Z1–Z8)*

Spec. No.	Side	Z1	Z2	Z3	Z4	Z5	Z6	Z7	Z8
5059	L	0	0	1	1	1	1	0	0
5060	L	0	0	1	1	0	0	0	0
5061	L	1	1	1	1	1	1	0	0
5062	L	1	1	1	1	0	0	0	0
5063	L	1	1	1	1	0	0	0	0
5063	L	1	0	1	1	1	1	0	0
5064	L	1	1	1	1	0	0	0	0
5064	L	1	1	0	0	0	0	0	0
5065	L	0	0	0	0	1	1	1	1
5066	L	0	0	0	0	1	1	1	1
5067	L	0	0	1	1	1	1	1	1
5073	L	0	0	0	0	1	1	0	0
5119	L	0	0	0	0	1	1	0	0
Total L		6	5	8	8	8	8	3	3
5068	R	0	0	0	0	1	1	1	1
5069	R	0	0	0	0	1	1	1	1
5070	R	0	0	0	0	1	1	0	0
5071	R	0	0	0	0	1	1	0	0
5072	R	0	0	1	1	1	1	0	0
Total R		0	0	1	1	5	5	2	2

Note: MNI = 8, based on the most frequent zones (zones 3–6, left side; L = left and R = right).
Source: The data are from the author.

Though ducks were more frequent than swans, geese, waders, and other species, especially in the final two phases, the comparison of bone weight showed that swans and geese must have contributed almost as much to the food supply, at least in phases 1 and 2a (Figure 4.13). However, intra-assemblage and inter-assemblage differences in bone weight can reflect the nature of the substrate and the mineral inclusions within the shafts of the bones as much as actual differences in meat weight.

Meat Weight

As well as extrapolating meat weight from bone weight, some authors extrapolate meat weight from MNI, both within and between animal classes. The biomass, that

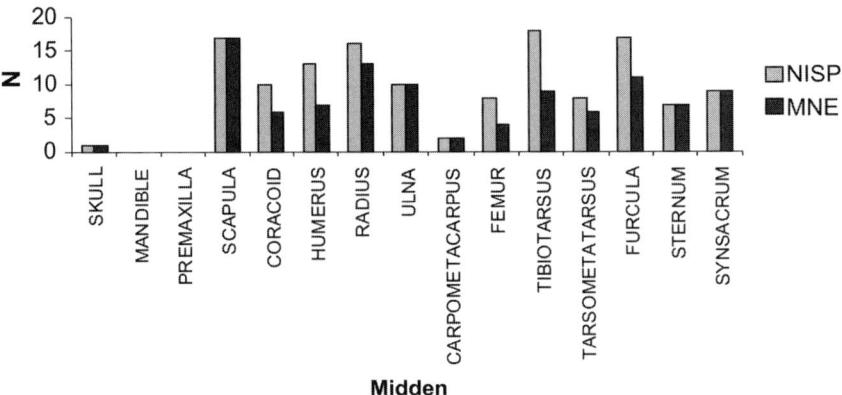

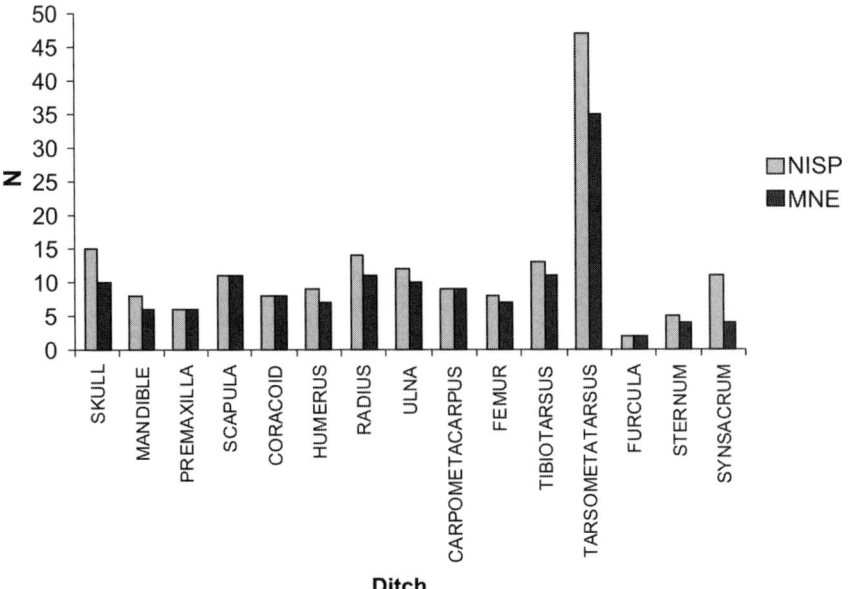

FIGURE 4.12. Comparison of NISP and MNE of chickens from Carisbrooke Castle, Isle of Wight, eleventh to twelfth century AD (author's data). The top section shows remains from the midden; the bottom section shows those from the ditch.

is, meat weight, was calculated for the seabirds from the successive layers at the Patagonian site of Túnel VII, a temporary camp of the nomadic Indians of Tierra del Fuego on the Beagle Channel which was occupied in the nineteenth century AD. Eight layers were identified, thought to represent short-term, perhaps annual, episodes of occupation. The biomass from large and small seabirds, penguins, cormorants, and

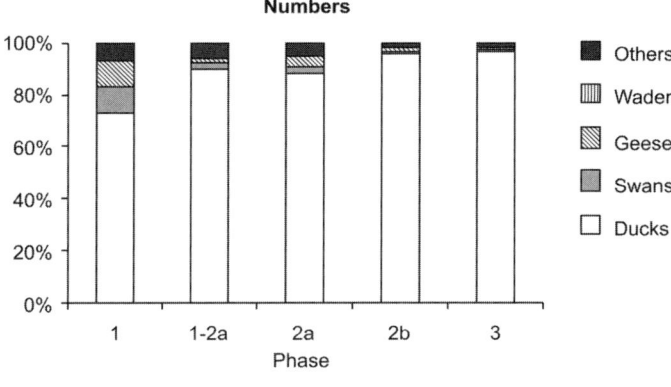

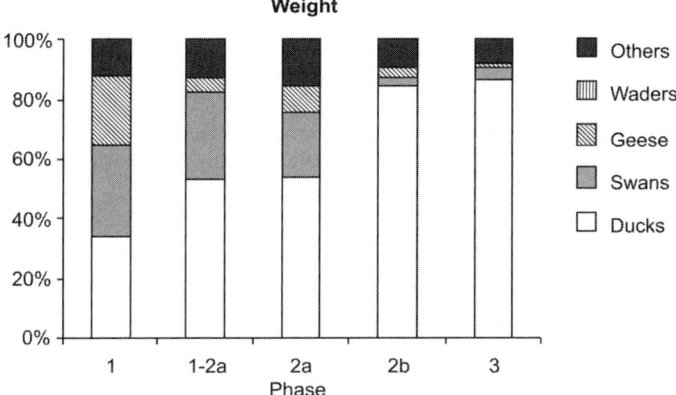

FIGURE 4.13. Comparison of numbers (NISP) and bone weight of the bird remains from the Neolithic site of Schipluiden, the Netherlands, phases 1–3 (after Zeiler 2006).

ducks over time was estimated (Figure 4.14). The absolute quantity of birds increased from the lower to the higher levels, but relative consumption of the different species and groups remained broadly similar, with the big seabirds, which were mainly albatrosses, penguins, and cormorants, providing the greatest quantity (Mameli 2002).

Comparing the Abundance of Birds with Other Vertebrate Classes

The different methods used to compare relative quantities of food or calories provided by mammals, fish, birds, and other vertebrate classes has been discussed many times (Reitz & Wing 1999, 191–205; O'Connor 2003, 156). Though there are

92 BIRDS

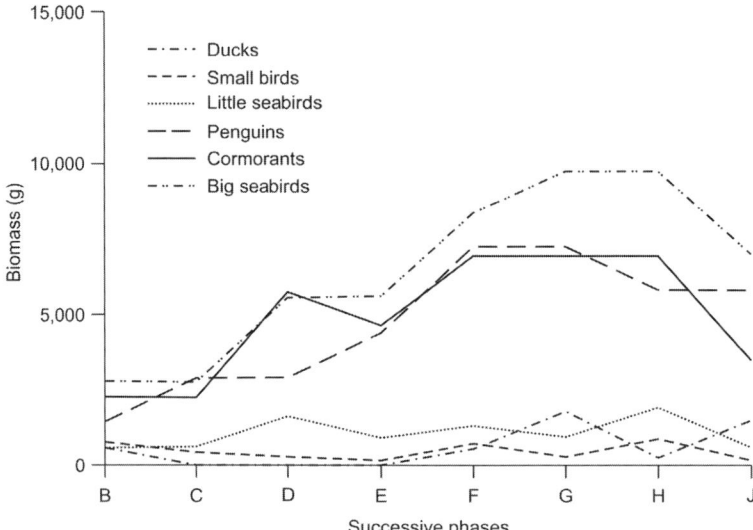

FIGURE 4.14. Biomass of birds extrapolated from MNI at Túnel VII on the Beagle Channel, Argentina, phases B to J. The absolute quantity of birds increased from the lowest level (phase B) to the higher levels, but the relative contribution of the different families and groups remained broadly similar (after Mameli 2002, fig. 4).

ways of modifying the imbalance in animal size, NISP and MNI become less helpful for estimating the relative contribution of different animals in the diet, as the mammals are normally larger than the birds while fish and molluscs are usually smaller. Methods such as bone weight and meat weight produce less biased comparisons.

NISP can be used as a basic comparison (see, e.g., Figure 10.10 in Chapter 10), so long as it is recognised that it will show a relatively low value for birds because there are fewer elements in the skeletons of birds than of mammals. Typical figures for mammals, birds, and fish were calculated by Jennie Coy, who counted the elements in skeletons in the reference collection at the Faunal Remains Unit at Southampton University. She quoted a figure of 100 bones in a domestic chicken, 250 in a sheep when individual teeth are included, and 300 in a cod, *Gadus morhua* (Coy 1982). More relevant is the number of bones which is identified to species: this again is fewer in birds than in mammals.

Mark Maltby used an innovative means of estimating the quantity of chicken eaten on different types of settlement in Britain in the Roman period. He restricted the comparison of chickens to mammals to the smaller species, sheep, and pigs. A problem with surveys such as this, acknowledged by Maltby, is that different workers selected different sets of elements to identify, not just of chickens but also of the mammals. The results were presented as percentages of the three species together, and of fowl as a percentage of sheep and goat (Table 4.6). The results showed

Table 4.6. *Percentage NISP of domestic fowl compared with sheep or goat on Romano-British urban and military sites, villas, and nucleated and rural settlements*

% fowl	Urban	Military	Villa	Nucleated	Rural
<1	3	8	20	6	71
1–2	0	8	0	41	18
3–5	18	23	13	29	9
6–10	15	23	53	24	3
11–15	10	15	7	0	0
16–20	23	0	0	0	0
21–25	21	0	7	0	0
>26	10	23	0	0	0
Samples (*n*)	39	13	15	17	34

Source: Information is from Maltby (1997).

that chickens were popular on Romanised sites such as towns but were less readily accepted as a food on native rural settlements (Maltby 1997).

Bone Weight Between Animal Classes

As well as being used to compare quantities within classes, bone weight is sometimes used for comparisons between different animal classes. The weight of the bones of bird, mammal, and fish better reflects the quantity of meat produced by each class.

Coy (1982) also calculated the relationship between the weight of the bones and the weight of the carcass for ten birds and seven mammals. The percentage of weight of bone in birds varied between 4.2 per cent in a common snipe and 9 per cent in a mute swan. In the mammals it varied from 5.3 per cent in a zoo wild boar to 10.5 per cent in a zoo wolf which had died in winter (Table 4.7). The percentage of bone by weight is slightly less in the birds than in mammals, but in general the range is not dissimilar. Column 3 in Table 4.7 shows the condition of the animal at death, and Coy points out that the animals with the highest percentage of bone to muscle had died possibly after having lost much of their body fat following poor feeding. Those with the lower percentages of bone weight may reflect more accurately the ratio in healthy animals.

In the small assemblage (25 bones) from the Post-Classic Mayan site of Laguna de On birds were 5 per cent by NISP but only 3 per cent by weight (21 g). As referred to earlier, it is typical of small Mayan sites for the fauna to comprise a variety of marine

Table 4.7. *Percentage bone in the carcass weight of seven mammals and ten birds*

Mammal or bird	% bone	Status and condition
Mammals		
Wild boar, *Sus scrofa*	5.3	Culled zoo animal
Brown bear, *Ursus arctos*	5.7	Culled zoo animal
Badger, *Meles meles*	5.7	Found dead
Domestic dog	5.8	Euthanised
Domestic pig	7.0	Immature, found dead
Fallow deer, *Dama dama*	8.7	Immature zoo animal, found dead
Wolf, *Canis lupus*	10.5	Zoo, winter death
Birds		
Common snipe, *Gallinago gallinago*	4.2	Shot
Pochard, *Aythya ferina*	4.3	Shot
Domestic hen	4.9	Killed
Teal, *Anas crecca*	5.6	Shot
Woodcock, *Scolopax rusticola*	6.2	Shot
Coot, *Fulica atra*	6.7	Killed by car
Partridge, *Perdix perdix*	7.8	Killed by car
Rook, *Corvus frugilegus*	8.2	Found dead
Common gull, *Larus canus*	8.6	Found dead
Mute swan, *Cygnus olor*	9.0	Died of injuries

Source: Data are from Coy (1983).

and land mammals, reptiles, amphibians, and fish as well as birds, with birds never a major dietary component (Masson 2004). By contrast, chickens were a major part of the food eaten at the temple of Mithras at Künzing in Germany (see Chapter 13). To compensate for the discrepancy in the size of the main species, chickens and pigs, the weight of bone as well as the NISP was calculated (von den Driesch & Pöllath 2000). Chickens were 39 per cent of bones by NISP and 18 per cent by weight (Table 4.8). Pigs made up half of the material by NISP and weight; their remains weighed relatively little, as most were very young.

Meat Weight

Both meat weight and kilocalories were calculated for the guanaco, sea mammals, birds, fish, and molluscs from the shell midden assemblages from Túnel, based on MNI (Estevez et al. 2001). In the first calculation, cetaceans made up 95 per cent of the food and swamped the results from the other species, so a second calculation

Table 4.8. *Weight and number of bones of food animals, horses, and dogs from the Mithraic temple at Deggendorf, Germany*

Animal	n	%	Weight (g)	%
Horse	11	0.1	421.8	1.2
Cattle	208	1.1	3,605.4	10.1
Sheep	130	–	–	–
Sheep or goat	1,513	8.4	6,613.2	18.6
Goat	4	–	–	–
Pig	10,078	51.6	18,284.0	51.4
Dog	4	–	12.9	–
Chicken	7,591	38.8	6,558.3	18.4
Red deer	6	–	58.1	0.2
Hare	3	–	9.0	–
Total	19,548	100	35,562.7	100

Note: Because the pigs were very young, the relative importance of chickens is high even when calculated by weight.
Source: Data are from von den Driesch and Pöllath (2000, tab. 1).

was carried out with whales omitted (Figure 4.15). Of the species other than whale, birds provided less than 6 per cent by weight but nearly 7 per cent by kilocalories. Pinnipeds, mainly sea lions, made the greatest contribution to diet, while molluscs provided greater weight of meat than birds but a smaller quantity of calories, no doubt, as discussed in Chapter 10, because birds are fattier.

One of the disadvantages of calculating meat weight from MNI in mammals is that many assemblages include immature as well as mature animals. It is potentially misleading if the weight of an adult animal is used in the calculation for extrapolating meat weight when immature as well as mature animals are present. This is not a problem with wild birds, which, as we saw in Chapter 2, reach adult weight at the time of fledging and are only rarely caught for food when smaller. However, weight at slaughter in domestic chickens varies greatly depending on whether the birds were killed as pullets (young birds), capons (male birds fattened for eating), or hens (Chapter 11).

Discussion of Quantification

Bird bones do not fragment into as many identifiable fragments as do mammal bones, so the use of MNE and MNI as well as fragment numbers has less utility,

96　BIRDS

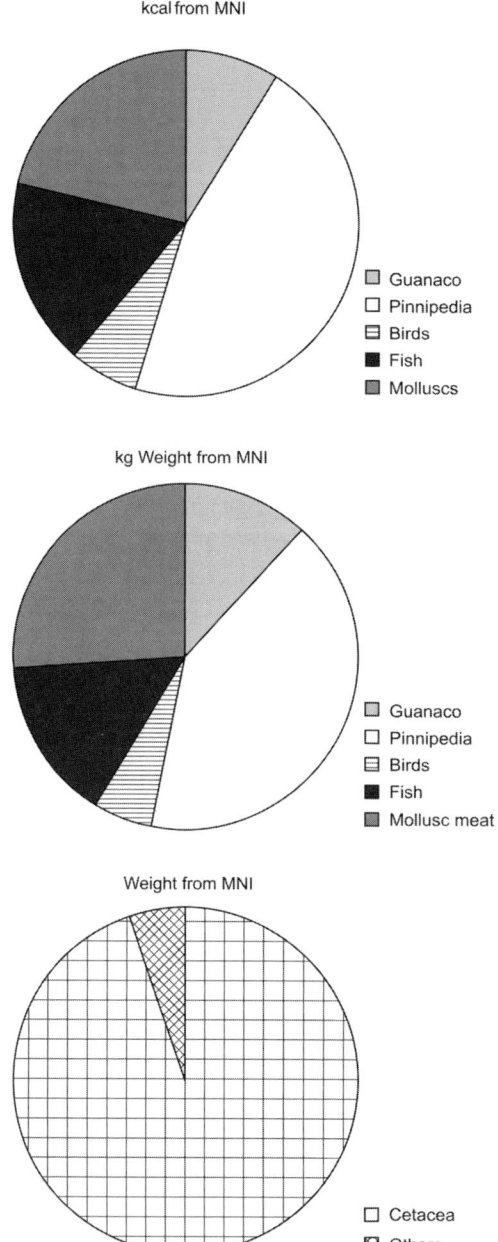

FIGURE 4.15. Comparison of kilocalories (top section) and meat weight (middle section) based on the MNI of mammals (excluding cetaceans), birds, fish, and molluscs at Túnel VII. When the weight of cetaceans is included in the calculation (bottom section), their contribution may have been more than 90 per cent of kilocalories (Estevez et al. 2001, fig. 3).

but it can refine the results. The calculation of bone weight as a proxy for meat weight is a useful method for comparisons between classes when the total food yield at a site is the goal. However, it is less relevant where secondary products such as eggs or feathers are the products for which the animals were exploited or kept. In this case, the calculation of minimum numbers is appropriate. These examples of quantification cited here are not going to resolve the arguments between those who prefer to use the unmodified raw data (NISP) and those who prefer to use modified measures, but they have shown the potential of different methods of comparison.

CONCLUSION

The identification and recording of bird bones can have more than one aim. To understand the past environment, accurate identification to species is necessary and material which cannot be identified at this level can be ignored, but for archaeological analysis, compromises are necessary. Two tiers of identification can be used; and it can also be worthwhile to identify elements to family and size class when they cannot be identified to species. The identification of bird bones carries more problems than that of with mammal bones, at least in Europe, so these compromises are often necessary.

The avian zooarchaeologist needs to use a reference collection and also to consult specialist publications where available. One implication of the research of Bochenski and Tomek (1995) is that a reference collection does not have to contain dozens of specimens of related birds *where separation is possible on a single criterion*, but that several species are needed where this is not possible. In addition, it is crucial to become familiar with the past as well as the present avifauna of the region. Even with all these aids available, work on ancient DNA is beginning to suggest that modern size ranges may not be adequate as a guide to the identification of early material. Problems have often been encountered with the reliability of past records (Morales 1993b), and these have often been the subject of re-identification (Harrison 1980). As Holdaway (2002, 631) observes, 'Published lists and museum collection data suggest high levels of uncertain or misidentification of birds from archaeological sites'. A conservative approach to identification is best, together with publication of the criteria for the identification of any contentious species.

Minimum lists of the data to be recorded have been proposed for mammal remains (Grigson 1978; Klein & Cruz-Uribe 1984; Davis 1992). If there is selection in the elements recorded, as Morales acknowledged, it will take into account the potential for survival as well as identifiability. In Table 4.9 a ranking is proposed for

Table 4.9. *Ranking of elements to be recorded*

Ranking	Reliable	Fairly reliable	Least reliable
Robust	Coracoid	Femur	Synsacrum
	Humerus	Ulna	
	Tibiotarsus		
	Tarsometatarsus		
Medium		Radius	Pelvis
		Carpometacarpus	Foot phalanges
		Sternum (articulation)	Cervical vertebrae
		Major wing digit	Pygostyle
		Scapula	Quadrate
Fragile	Cranium		Atlas
	Mandible		Axis
			Ribs
			Tracheal rings
			Patella

Note: The ranking has been modified to take into account the reliability of identification as well as survival.

identifiability which is further subdivided by likely survival (discussed in Chapter 6). Fragile elements such as the cranium and mandible are worth recording when they survive because they are among the most reliably identified elements. Many of those elements classed as 'least reliable' can be identified in certain species.

So far as quantification is concerned, NISP alone is appropriate where there are just a few specimens, but the use of MNE and MNI has revealed how birds were utilised and viewed in the past (see, e.g., parts of the body of the main species at Jerf el Ahmar, discussed in Chapter 8). The next step, calculation of meat weights and kilocalories, has also been used, but utility indices, widely used for understanding prey selection by hunter-gatherers (Lyman 1994, 225–234), to my knowledge have been established only for rheas (Giardina 2006). Each research project will have different demands and no single recording system will be suitable for every site.

The reasons why some bones are present and some are absent in an assemblage are complex. Explanations include selection and deposition by humans and other animals, the effects of natural processes of destruction, and the strategies employed in excavation. All these are discussed in the next two chapters.

5

Natural Taphonomy and Recovery

The term 'taphonomy', coined 60 years ago to define the process of the 'transition...of animal remains from the biosphere into the lithosphere' (O'Connor 2005), has been used by zooarchaeologists to encompass all the changes which take place between the death of an organism and its appearance on the laboratory bench (Lyman 1994). Probably none of the material discussed in this book has reached the stage of complete fossilisation, but, as we shall see in this and the following chapter, remains from archaeological sites have undergone much alteration. The taphonomy of bird bones is more intriguing and arguably more important than that of mammal bones, because the origin of the bird bones in archaeological deposits is often more ambiguous than that of the mammal remains.

Understanding both the natural and cultural modifications which have taken place is an essential prerequisite for interpreting how an assemblage accumulated. Only then is it possible to understand whether people were responsible for collecting the bones, whether they were accumulated by other predators, or whether they were the remains of natural deaths. In this chapter the natural modifications which affect bones between the death of a bird and the delivery of bones and bone fragments to the desk of the zooarchaeologist are discussed; the next chapter will be concerned with traces of butchery, cooking, and other human modifications.

The importance of recognising damage by non-human predators was acknowledged from the very early days of the study of ancient bird remains. Milne-Edwards, after examining the ptarmigan and grouse remains from a Palaeolithic cave in France, wrote, 'Their abundance can only be accounted for by admitting that Man used those birds as food, and brought thither the produce of his chase; for if the Grouse had been carried in by Birds of prey or carnivorous Mammals, the bones would generally be broken, gnawed, and the articular heads would have disappeared' (Milne-Edwards

1875, 238). He was well aware that bird remains, especially those from caves, may derive from more than one source. For instance, he thought that the many bones of the crag martin in caves at Lourdes and Bruniquel in southern France could be explained by the fact that the crag martin 'ordinarily nests in caves or in the crevices of rocks'. However, at Lacomb-Tayac, he was 'disposed to believe that it was principally streams of water that carried in the remains of a great variety of Passeres' (Milne-Edwards 1875, 247).

Nevertheless, there are many assemblages where researchers have found it difficult to work out whether bones were assembled and discarded by humans or whether they had other origins. Even excavated assemblages from sites of historic times can pose problems of interpretation. For instance, Becker was confronted with the problem of deciding whether or not the bird remains from the environs of a mosque in Syria were anthropogenic. The most frequent species were the house or rock sparrow, the starling, and the common swift; but domestic chicken was also present (Becker 2005a).

In this chapter we shall consider some of the environments where there can be uncertainty as to whether bones derive from human activities or from other sources. We shall also look at the criteria for distinguishing natural assemblages: traces on the bones themselves, element fragmentation, and the presence or absence of certain elements. The presence or absence of certain elements, as well as being related to bone density, is also directly related to the methods used to recover bones, so, as a preliminary, the implications of sieving and sampling or its absence have to be taken into account.

RECOVERY

The methods used to recover material impose a bias on a bird bone assemblage, as they do on other animals and on other classes of archaeological material such as coins. If birds are present, long bones of the larger species will be recovered even when deposits are not sieved (screened), especially when excavators are sharp eyed, but it is unrealistic to expect smaller elements which have taken on the colour of the soil to be seen and retrieved. Most birds are quite small; to recover these, sieving is necessary. Today, bulk sieving is carried out on many excavations, but in Europe it is usual for a subsample of the deposits to be sieved and certainly in the past there were many excavations on which no sieving took place: any conclusions about the role of birds on such sites must be suspect.

Mesh Sizes

Where sieving does take place, typical mesh sizes used in North America have been ½ in. (12.7 mm) and ¼ in. (6.4 mm). These meshes were used, for instance, in the 1969 excavations at Lovelock Cave, Nevada, where a large assemblage of bird bones was recovered (Livingston 1989). A 4-mm mesh sieve is commonly used in European sites. At the Neolithic site of Schipluiden, approximately 8 per cent of the deposits were sieved using 4-mm mesh. The number of bird bones was greatly enhanced by this, with one third of the total being recovered in the sieves (Zeiler 2006, 421). Excavations on Polynesian island sites regularly use a smaller mesh (⅛ in. or 3.2 mm; see Weisler 1995; Steadman & Rolett 1996; Steadman et al. 2002). This mesh was used for excavations of the dune site of Tahuata in the Marquesas Islands. There, one of the aims of the research was to examine the role of humans in the extinction of the endemic avifauna of the islands. As the sediments contained some very small birds, use of the small mesh was justified as several extinct species were found. The authors argued that the record from the earlier excavations in the Marquesas 'is unlikely to be complete, being biased against small species such as swifts, kingfishers, passerines, and certain shorebirds' as 'no finer mesh than ¼" was used to sieve the sediments' (Steadman & Rolett 1996, 92).

When the recovery of small bones is a priority, the mesh may be even smaller. At Lavezzi in Corsica the deposits were sieved through meshes of 2 mm and also 1 mm, so the excavators could be confident that nothing of importance was lost (Vigne et al. 1991). In this excavation too, one of the main aims was a study of the bird remains as a means of revealing changes in avian distribution, as discussed in Chapter 15, so here too the labour of sieving with a small mesh was justified.

Bulk Sieving

Bulk sieving is normal procedure on most excavations in North America, but it is less common in Europe, at least on sites of the historic period. The decision on whether to carry out bulk sieving depends not only on the priorities of the excavation but also on the properties of the soil matrix and the likelihood that small bones will be present. Light, sandy soils are more easily sieved than heavy clay soils, as light soils can be dry-sieved. Sieving is less time consuming and consequently cheaper than is the wet-sieving needed on heavy soils.

Sampling

The alternative to bulk sieving is the sampling of deposits, which may be either random, or the opportunistic sampling of selected contexts which appear to be exceptionally rich in bones. Some case studies described here emphasise the value of opportunistic sampling on sites which were not bulk sieved.

This was shown clearly at the site of Hextalls, a manor house in Surrey occupied by a wealthy family, perhaps one with royal connections. At some time in the early sixteenth century the occupants appear to have paid a visit during which they feasted on a large quantity of meat from wild and domestic animals, including small birds. The rubbish was disposed of in a large pit, probably dug for the purpose. The excavators sieved a sample of 65 litres of the pit fill using a 6-mm mesh sieve. In the material retrieved by hand, 9 per cent of bones were from thrushes, and none from the smaller songbirds, but in the sieved sample, small songbirds and thrushes made up 38 per cent of the bones (Bourdillon 1998; Serjeantson 2001a), a percentage which must be a closer reflection to the original quantities eaten.

A second example is an Iron Age site in southern Britain. Bones of small animals are in general rather rare on settlement sites at this time, as wild animals were not regularly part of the diet. However, during the excavation of Haddenham, an Iron Age settlement in the Fenlands of eastern England (see Chapter 3), it became obvious to the excavators that the floor of one of the houses contained an unusually dense layer of well-preserved small bones. They sampled a 1-m-wide transect across the house floor using 2-mm sieves. The site as a whole resulted in an assemblage of bird bones which was quite exceptional for the period. The settlement was close to the Cambridgeshire Fenland, an area with large expanses of shallow water in the Late Iron Age; as well as the birds, which were mainly waterfowl, remains of domestic mammals and beavers were recovered, though, interestingly, almost no fish bones, despite what must have been an abundance of fish in the fenland waterways (Evans & Serjeantson 1988; Serjeantson 2006a). As might be anticipated, there were relatively fewer ducks (31 versus 26 per cent) in the hand-picked sediments and more bones of swans (40 per cent of identified bones versus 27 per cent; see Figure 5.1).

A third example is the site of St Gregory's Priory in Canterbury in south-east England. Dense accumulations of tiny bones were noted in two separate areas. These were sieved through 1-mm mesh: as well as much fish, remains of small songbirds were recovered. One deposit from an oven floor proved to contain over 200 bones of passerines, of which even the wing digits and phalanges were recovered. It became clear that the deposit contained almost exclusively elements from the head, distal wings, and distal legs (see Figure 6.17 in Chapter 6). In this case the small

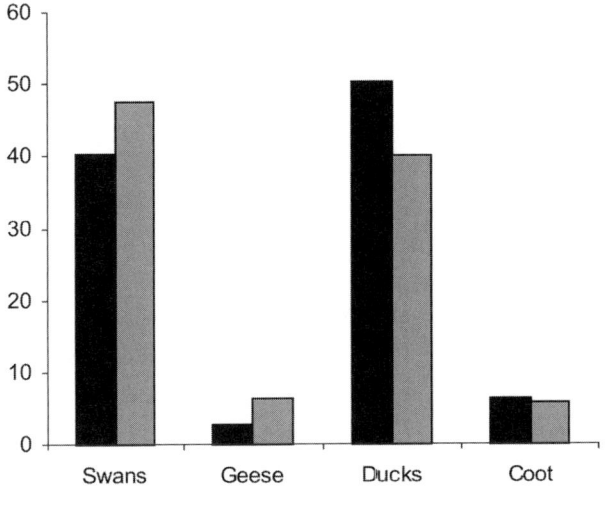

FIGURE 5.1. Percentage of bird bones from sieved and unsieved deposits at Haddenham site V, Cambridgeshire: ducks were relatively more frequent in the sieved samples and swans and geese in the hand-retrieved material (Serjeantson 2006a, fig. 5.102).

mesh size was justified, but it would not have been realistic for large quantities of sediment.

Careful excavation by hand will recover the larger bones of chickens and birds larger than chickens, so the absence of sieving gives undue emphasis to larger species such as geese and swans. Immature bones even of large species are liable to be lost or seriously underrepresented when material is retrieved by hand. Small elements such as wing digits and phalanges may not add to the list of species present, but they can inform on butchery, consumption, and feather use (see, e.g., Figure 6.19). For the recovery of birds of the size of pigeons and smaller, sieving is essential. Finally, as Steadman and Rolett pointed out, no credence can be given to the *absence* of small species where sediments are not sieved.

In Europe it has not been usual to sieve sediments from excavations of the later prehistoric and historic period. This may have been justified for some later prehistoric farming settlements where neither birds nor fish were significant in the diet and economy, but – as later chapters will reveal – important information can be lost when Roman and medieval sites are not sieved.

An equally important contribution to good recovery is made by the individual who undertakes the task of sorting and picking the contents of the sieves, as this is not always the same person as the one who identifies the bones.

However carefully recovered, no assemblage can be interpreted in the absence of an understanding of the effects of natural as well as human modifications to the skeleton which took place prior to burial and in the ground, and it is to these that we turn next.

NATURAL ACCUMULATIONS

There are several environments in which bird remains are found where natural deposits can be confused with those associated with human activity. They include places where birds have died a natural death from disease, starvation, or another cause and also places where remains have been discarded by predators. Raptors discard pellets which contain bones and also drop bones and part carcasses at the nest or feeding spot. The taphonomy of these natural accumulations has been a major concern of avian palaeontologists, and their findings are relevant for those who study bird remains associated with human activity. There is a very large palaeontological literature on natural collections of bird bones, but here we will consider mainly those publications which focus on how to distinguish natural from anthropogenic assemblages.

Natural accumulations of bird bones are found in caves and rock fissures, sand dunes fringing the sea, lakes, and rivers, and swamps. These do not exhaust the list of possible locations where remains are preserved following death (Weigelt 1989, ch. 2; Lyman 1994, 115), but they are the main places where bones survive. In New Zealand, where ground predators were absent, some caves preserve large numbers of bones of the extinct moa (Worthy & Holdaway 2002; also see Figure 5.2).

Of all these environments, caves pose the greatest problem as they are used by humans, birds, and indeed many other animals (Mourer-Chauviré 1983; Andrews 1990, 93; Bochenski 2005). Several species use caves or cave mouths to nest or roost, including rock doves, swifts, starlings, jackdaws, choughs and other corvids, swallows, and martins. These birds, both adult and young, die naturally in the cave. People, raptorial birds, and mammalian predators also bring killed or scavenged prey back to the cave or cave mouth for consumption. The bones survive in caves partly because they are protected from the weathering to which they would be exposed in the open air. Many of the remains found in the rock shelter of Vaufrey in south-west France were from the chough. Out of the 600 elements found, one third was from juveniles; and this, together with the fact that none showed cuts marks, indicated that they were from birds which had died in the cave (Laroulandie 2000, 175). Jackdaw remains were found in at least two of the Cheddar Caves in

FIGURE 5.2. Bones on the floor of Moa Cave, Honeycomb Hill Cave system, South Island, New Zealand (Worthy & Holdaway 2002, fig. 2.15; photograph by T. H. Worthy).

Gloucestershire, and they were also thought to be natural occupants (Harrison 1988, 1989). A cold environment makes survival in a cave more likely than a warm one (Bochenski & Tomek 1997). Some man-made environments such as chimneys and dovecots imitate the conditions in a cave, and skeletons are indeed found in such contexts. Remains of immature domestic pigeons are very often found in the base of medieval dovecots (Chapter 12).

The origin of bird bones from sand dunes can also be ambiguous (Ericson 1987; Weisler & Gargett 1993). Birds which are wrecked at sea by starvation or winter storms are washed up on the shore, and become incorporated into coastal dunes by currents and tides, and by winds blowing desiccated skeletons off the shoreline and on to the dunes at the back of the beach. The same phenomenon takes place around large lakes. Several species, especially members of the gull and tern families, breed on sand dunes and die at the nest site. Where birds use burrows to lay the egg and rear the chicks, the young may die in the burrow. A skeleton of a chick recovered in excavations on Moloka'i in Hawaii was so well preserved that it was judged that it could never have been exposed to the elements and must have been protected by a collapsed burrow (Weisler & Gargett 1993).

Swamps and fens trap and preserve birds as well as mammals. The most dramatic example of creatures preserved in swamp pits is in the liquid asphalt pits, commonly known as 'tar pits', at Rancho La Brea where huge numbers of animals became entombed (Weigelt 1989, 44–47; Bochenski & Campbell 2006). The skeletons of Dalmatian pelicans and swans have been found entombed in the peat in the Fenlands north of Cambridge. In the past the remains were often dug up by farmers while

Table 5.1. *Disarticulation sequence in ice-trapped American coots, birds of various species in a field, and manx shearwaters*

Ice-trapped coots	Birds in a field	Manx shearwaters
	Ribs from sternum	Ribs from sternum
Cervical from thoracic vertebrae	Hind limb (femur from pelvis)	Hind limb (femur from pelvis)
Skull from atlas		Skull from vertebral column
Trunk from pectoral girdle + wing	Synsacrum from vertebrae	
Sternum from coracoid + wing	Sternum from coracoid	
Synsacrum + hind limb from thoracic unit		Synsacrum from thoracic unit
Humerus from coracoid	Humerus from scapula + coracoid	
Femur from synsacrum	Radius and ulna from humerus	
Humerus from scapula + coracoid	Scapula from coracoid	
Tibiotarsus from femur	Wing digits from wing	

Note: The first elements lost from the skeleton are the ribs, followed by the cervical vertebrae and skull. Hind limbs disarticulated from the pelvis at an early stage in the birds exposed in a field and in the shearwaters, but later in the coots.

Source: Information for American coots, *Fulica americana*, is from Oliver and Graham (1994); for birds of various species in a field, from Bickhart (1984); and for manx shearwaters, *Puffinus puffinus*, preyed on by great black-backed gulls, *Larus marinus*, at the breeding colony, from Serjeantson et al. (1993).

draining the fens for agriculture: thanks to the peat diggers, we know that pelicans formerly lived and bred in Britain.

One obvious indication that bones have a natural origin, and have not been the prey of humans or other animals, is when a skeleton is complete. It is quite rare for a skeleton to remain complete and in articulation because of the many post-mortem changes which take place (Nicholson 1996). In natural conditions a bird skeleton will remain in articulation only when it is quickly covered by sediment after death; only locations such as a collapsed burrow, a swamp, or a lakebed fall into this category. The carcass must also avoid later predation and more than a minimum of biological degradation. One skeleton which appears to meet these criteria is an immature crane

FIGURE 5.3. Carcass of a manx shearwater, *Puffinus puffinus*, killed by a great black-backed gull, *Larus marinus*, on Skomer Island, Wales. The gull has removed the ribs, vertebrae, and synsacrum and has turned the head inside out (photograph by D. Serjeantson).

found at Haddenham (see Figure 3.2 in Chapter 3). The settlement was abandoned in the first century BC, when the water level of the nearby fen rose and the ground became waterlogged. The crane was found in the silted up fill of a ditch and, of the whole skeleton, only the skull was missing; none of the elements has suffered any damage and even distal phalanges, carpals, and caudal vertebrae survived. The conditions for preservation, silts which were almost anaerobic, were so perfect that as well as the skeleton, impressions of the feathers survived (Serjeantson 1998), which indicated that the fledgling had died a natural death.

Survival as complete as this is rare. It is more usual for different parts of the carcass to become separated, and for the bones to decay, with the more fragile bones decaying more quickly than the more robust ones. These are issues which will be examined next.

Natural Disarticulation Sequence

An appreciation of the sequence in which bird skeletons disarticulate under natural conditions is helpful for distinguishing human agency from other effects. Several studies have been carried out on this process on birds exposed to different conditions (Table 5.1). Schäfer (1972) looked at the disarticulation of birds which had been floating in the sea for some time; the birds had been exposed not just to the water but also to aquatic predators and to scavenging birds. Serjeantson and colleagues (1993) examined survival of skeletal elements in carcasses of manx shearwater collected from their breeding colony on the island of Skomer off the coast of Wales (Figure 5.3). They had been killed by great black-backed gulls but had not been exposed to mammalian

108   BIRDS

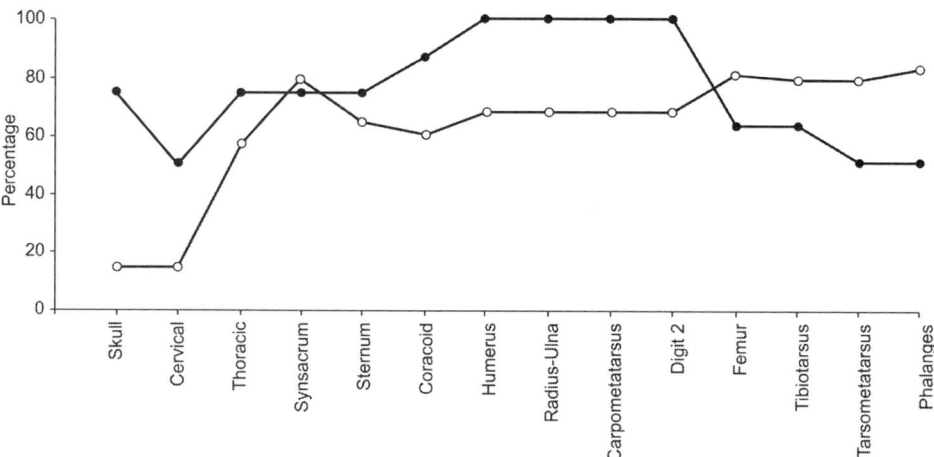

FIGURE 5.4. Element survival in American coots, *Fulica americana*, in bird-scavenged (solid circles) and mammal-scavenged (open circles) carcasses. Surviving elements are divided by MNI (redrawn from Oliver & Graham 1994, fig. 8).

predators, of which there are none on the island. Oliver and Graham (1994) recorded surviving body parts in 48 American coots out of 300 or more which had died when they became trapped in the ice at Spring Lake in Illinois on one December day when the temperature dropped from +9° C to –13° C in one day. The coots were then scavenged by both herring gulls and mammalian predators. Both Oliver and Graham (Figure 5.4) and Serjeantson and colleagues (Figure 5.5) calculated dispersal from the frequency of elements: the lower the survivorship, the earlier the element in question became disarticulated. Bickhart studied the natural disarticulation of 28 birds left in a damp field, some unprotected and others protected from scavengers in cages (Bickhart 1984; Lyman 1994, 447). The order in which elements became

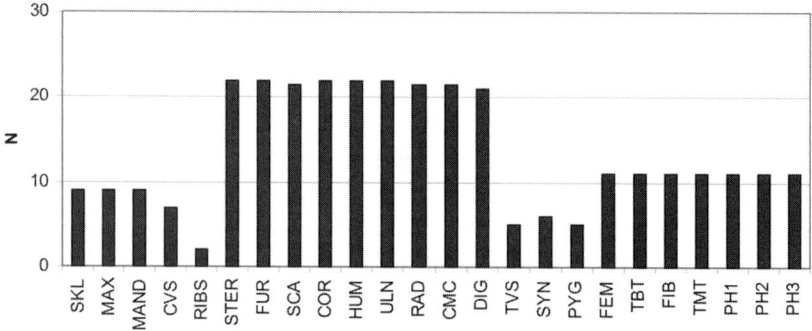

FIGURE 5.5. Element survival in manx shearwaters, *Puffinus puffinus*, killed by gulls on Skomer Island (author's data).

detached from the carcass was very similar to the order for the coots and the manx shearwaters, with ribs lost first, followed by the hind limb and vertebrae.

All these studies, summarised in Table 5.1, show a reassuring degree of agreement, despite the varied conditions to which the birds were exposed. Most show that the first elements to be lost are the ribs, which separate from the sternum. Another early event is that the head, sometimes attached to the cervical vertebrae, is detached from the rest of the vertebral column. In most studies the hind limbs disarticulate from the pelvis at a fairly early stage. This may be connected with the degree of scavenging, as carnivores preferentially removed the hind limbs of the coots, but these elements also disappeared early in the birds from Skomer, where no carnivores are present. The hind limbs remained articulated to the pelvis for a relatively longer time in some carcasses observed in a desiccated condition in the deserts of Peru (deFrance 2005). The next stage is the separation of the synsacrum from the thoracic unit. Carcasses then tend to continue to hold together as a unit for a long time as a pair of wings joined to the sternum (Schäfer 1972; Serjeantson et al. 1993; deFrance 2005; Bochenski 2005).

These final stages in the disarticulation sequence reflect the fact that the strongest ligament connections are between the humerus, scapula, and coracoid, and also between the bones of the wing. Consequently, in natural conditions, it is likely that the bones of the wing will survive in articulation for longer than the bones of the leg.

NATURAL DAMAGE AND DECAY

Out of the myriad processes of damage to which bone is exposed, I shall concentrate here on water sorting, weathering, and bioerosion on and in the ground. Many other processes have been discussed for mammal bones (Lyman 1994, ch. 9), but these topics have been the subject of specific research relating to bird bones. As with all vertebrate remains, survival of bird bone depends on the pH of the surrounding soil and the degree of water percolation, but microbial action also plays a major part in the early stages of bone disintegration. Experiments comparing survival of mammal, bird, and fish bone found that the bird bones, which belonged to feral pigeons, survived better in almost all conditions than those of a mammal (*Rattus norvegicus*) and fish (various species). The more compact periosteal surface of bird bones makes them more resistant to the invasion of micro-organisms (Nicholson 1996). This was evident in the relative lack of channelling on the surface of the bird bones compared with those of mammals. However, at later stages in the decay process, mammal bone appears to survive better than bird bone (Cruz 2008), which is what might intuitively be expected.

Hydrodynamic Sorting

The effects of water transport and sorting which have been observed on remains of mammals and other animals have been summarised elsewhere (Lyman 1994, 171–176), and here I shall discuss some of the studies and observations which have been made of bird bone dispersal by water. The frequency of different elements in fluviatile environments was established by Rich, who analysed 10,000 bones from natural sites of Tertiary date from Langebaaweg, in South Africa. They were in a variety of environments including floodplains, marshes, and tidal flats. She found that survivorship correlated with the hydrodynamic characteristics of the bones: the very small, very elongated, and very slender bones such as the radius and ulna were underrepresented, as were those with large surface-to-volume ratio such as scapulae, ribs, and skulls (Rich 1980).

An experimental project by Trapani (1998) which set out to examine the hydrodynamic sorting of bird bones examined their behaviour in different currents of water. Pigeon bones were cleaned, disarticulated, and introduced into flumes by use of a flat bed and a ripple bed. They were introduced into still water and water flowing at constant velocity. The degree to which the different disarticulated elements moved is shown in Table 5.2. The results were broadly similar, but elements were affected by whether the substrate was flat or ridged. The cranium, innominate (pelvis), vertebrae, ribs, and coracoid had the greatest potential for movement, apparently because of their irregular shape. The scapula and furcula travelled least, probably because they are flatter. The long bones, which are higher and rounder, were intermediate in their tendency to move in a current of water. They quickly settled in a trough on the bed with their long axis parallel to the flow, as do the long bones of mammals, and only when they were exposed again did they again travel in the flow. The conclusion was that dispersal potential did not correlate only with density but that shape also had to be taken into account.

Trapani (1998, 479) also studied partly articulated carcasses and found that these 'generally have a higher potential for dispersal than single, disarticulated bones'. Although these have a greater total weight, their increased surface area and height in the flow makes them more susceptible to being carried along in the current. A complete disarticulated leg was an exception: it behaved more like a single long bone.

Weathering

Weathering on bird bones takes the same basic form as weathering on all classes of bones. In open-air environments it takes the form of bioerosion, damage from

Table 5.2. *Dispersal sequences for bones of rock dove,* Columba livia, *in a flume*

Flat-bed trials		Ripple-bed trials	
Element	Rank	Element	Rank
Cranium	1	Cranium	1
Incomplete cranium	1	Innominate	2
Vertebral segment	1	Inc. cranium	3
Vertebrae (3)	1	Vertebral segment	4
Ribs (2)	2	Coracoid	5
Innominate	3	Ribs (2)	6
First phalanx	4	Vertebrae (3)	7
Coracoid	5	Tarsometatarsus	8
Caudal vertebra	6	Humerus	9
Sternum	7	Sternum	10
Tarsometatarsus	8	Sacrum	11
Femur	9	Tibiotarsus	12
Sacrum	10	Caudal vertebra	13
Mandible	11	Ulna	14
Ulna	12	First phalanx	15
Humerus	13	Femur	16
Phalanges (2)	14	Carpometacarpus	17
Radius	15	Phalanges (2)	18
Tibiotarsus	16	Mandible	19
Carpometacarpus	17	Radius	20
Furculum	18	Furculum	20
Scapula	19	Scapula	20

Note: Flumes included both flat and ripple beds.
Source: Data are from Trapani (1998, tab.2).

sunlight, or both; once bones are buried, damage results from acid etching by roots and organic acid in soils (Andrews 1990, 13, 19).

In an experimental study of the effects of weathering on bird bones, Bochenski and Tomek placed carcasses in three different types of locations in and near a cave in southern Poland: within the cave, outside it, and buried nearby. The carcasses, most of which were passerines and pigeons, had been accidentally killed on roads. They were left for periods of between 10 and 52 months (Bochenski & Tomek 1997). At the end of that time all femora, both experimental and those collected earlier, were examined for breakage and other damage. The researchers found that small corroded holes with irregular sponge-like edges appeared near the trochanter major

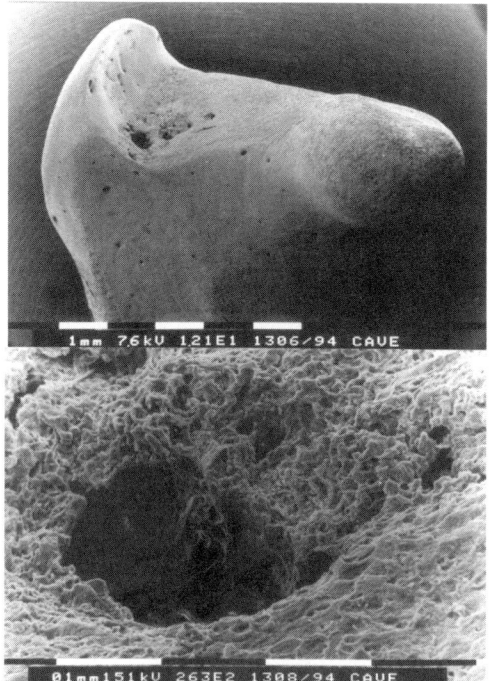

FIGURE 5.6. Weathering on the proximal femur of a pigeon, *Columba* sp., after ten months on a cave floor: small corroded holes are visible near the trochanter major (Bochenski & Tomek 1997, fig. 15). The bottom figure is an enlargement of one of the holes, showing irregular, sponge-like (but not rounded) edges. Scale bars show 1 mm on the top portion and 0.1 mm on the bottom.

(Figure 5.6), broken edges had become rounded, and some weathering had taken place over the whole surface of the bone. Table 5.3 summarises the weathering stages observed, which were scored by using the categories defined for large and small mammals (Behrensmeyer 1978; Andrews 1990). The stages of damage were similar to those which had been observed on mammal bones, though none reached the final stages of heavy weathering with splitting and splintering (Behrensmeyer's stages 3–5). This may be a function of the conditions of the trial, which took place in fairly cold conditions, but it may also be because, as we have seen, the surface of bird bones is more resistant initially than that of mammal bones to attack from micro-organisms.

Bioerosion

Even where preservation is apparently good, a certain amount of bioerosion does take place. It is caused by cyanobacteria, algae, and fungi, which colonise the bone

Table 5.3. *Weathering categories for bird bones, correlated with stages for large mammals and microfauna*

	Large mammal		Small mammal		Bird bones	
Stage 0	No modification	Range 0–3	No modification	Range 0–2	No modification	Range 0–4+
1	Cracking parallel to fibre structure; articular surfaces may show mosaic cracking; fat, skin, and other tissue may or may not be present	0–3	Slight splitting parallel to fibre structure	0–2	Articular ends: one or more small holes with rough edges; shaft: no modification or single small holes with rough edges, or merely depressions with rough bases; breakage may be sharp and rounded or semi-rounded; tendons and feathers may or may not be present	1–4+
2	Concentric flaking usually associated with cracks; crack edges usually angular in cross section; remnants of ligaments, cartilage, and skin may be present	2–6	More extensive splitting but little flaking	3–5+	Articular ends: sieve-like surface due to extensive pitting; holes with sharp and rough edges; shaft: many large and small holes with rough edges and depressions with rough bases. Concentric flaking. Breakage: sharp and rough, very fragile. Neither tendons nor feathers present	? (at least 1 year but probably many years)
3	Patches of rough homogeneously weathered compact bone, resulting in fibrous texture; weathering penetrates 1–1.5 mm	4–15+	Deep splitting and some loss of deep segments or 'flakes' between splits	4–5+		
4	Bone surface coarsely fibrous and rough; splinters of bone loose on surface; weathering penetrates inner cavities	6–15+				
5	Bone falling apart in situ, with large splinters lying around	6–15+				

Note: The weathering categories correlated with stages for large mammals are from Behrensmeyer (1978) and those for microfauna are from Andrews (1990). Range is given in years.

Source: Data are from Bochenski and Tomek (1997, tab. 4).

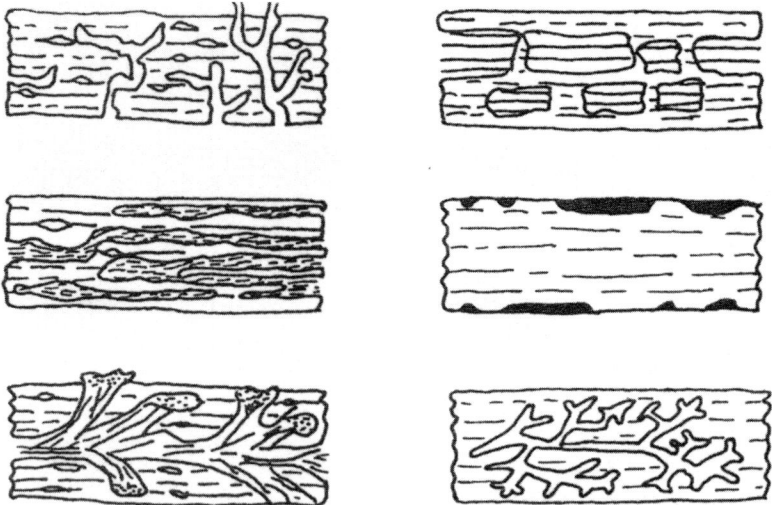

FIGURE 5.7. Schematic drawings of six types of tunnel made by bioeroding organisms such as cyanobacteria, algal filaments, and fungi on the bone surface (redrawn from Davis 1997, fig. 4).

surface both in the ground and in the presence of light (Lyman 1994, 395–397; Nicholson 1996; Davis 1997). When exposed to air and moderate soil moisture, colonisation takes place by fungal hyphae. This is the most usual cause of bioerosion in caves, while in shallow water the main agent is algae. *Mucor*, *Cladosporium*, and *Candida* are some of the known fungal agents. Erosion takes the form of shallow erosive tunnels in the bone surface, with a diameter from approximately 2 μm to 90 μm. These tunnels show various morphologies: branching ('Wedl') tunnels, linear, budded, lamellate, and a more extensive branching pattern parallel to the bone surface defined by Davis as 'Hackett' tunnels (Figure 5.7). The experiment did not succeed in associating tunnel morphology with individual organisms. Davis studied the rate and appearance of bioerosion by submerging carcasses of 56 birds of various sizes in shallow marine and freshwater bodies in southern Florida, an environment where decay and bioerosion is rapid. He found that, after 70 days, all bones which were neither removed by scavengers nor deeply buried had suffered bioerosion in the form of staining and tunnelling. Some fine bone in skulls and sterna had totally disappeared in that time: Davis suggested that the absence of marrow within these elements may have made them less resistant to erosion. The most important implication of Davis' study is that bioerosion can be responsible for a relatively rapid disappearance of bone, as well as for marking the surface in a characteristic way.

The studies of disarticulation, especially the study of the ice-trapped coots (Figure 5.4), showed that the condition of the skeleton varied according to whether the predator or scavenger was a mammal or another bird. Bochenski and Tomek (1997) also pointed out that erosion in natural conditions was potentially capable of being confused with erosion from digestive juices. For direct evidence of damage from predators, we have to turn to the actual traces on the bones themselves.

Traces of Natural Predators

Much of the literature on bird bones accumulated by predators other than humans has been published by naturalists and zoologists with the aim of identifying the prey species, either as a tool for understanding the status of the predator in question or as a means of revealing past environments (Andrews 1990). Their research is also relevant to the interpretation of remains from archaeological sites.

Avian Predators

Of the raptorial birds, a few prey mainly on other birds, and birds are one part of the diet for many more. The features of an assemblage which identify the predator are the prey species, avian and otherwise; damage to bones, including erosion; the breakage patterns; and the elements which predominate.

Prey Selection

Hawks and owls concentrate on prey of a certain size range, so the size of prey can be diagnostic of the predator, though prey varies according to environment and season (Yalden & Morris 1990). In times of food stress, raptors change their habits and take smaller creatures if their normal prey is scarce. They may also attempt to catch prey larger than usual (Bochenski 2005). The eagle owl, which takes both mammals and birds, takes birds as large as the capercaillie and mammals as large as roe deer, *Capreolus capreolus*. In an environment of low diversity some raptors are narrowly specialised: snowy owls, for instance, concentrate on grouse and ptarmigan. The prey size of these large owls overlaps with human food choices. The two grouse species were also common prey of the gyrfalcon (Bochenski et al. 1998). A species such as the rock dove is especially liable to have an ambiguous origin. It inhabits caves, is preyed on by several raptor species, and in addition is also caught by people. Grouse and ptarmigan do not naturally enter caves, but they may be brought there by natural as well as human predators. Smaller owls concentrate on smaller prey such as rodents, which are less likely to be confused with human prey. In the case where prey species potentially overlap, the absence of the cut marks and breakage patterns typical of human consumption, together with the presence of raptor damage (subsequently discussed), will indicate that the remains were not generated by humans.

The presence of a suite of prey species uncharacteristic of other deposits from Scottish coastal middens suggested that the assemblage from the Late Bronze Age at Tofts Ness was not anthropogenic. This prehistoric settlement on the island of Sanday on Orkney was occupied by farmers more or less continuously from the third millennium BC to the first millennium AD. In most periods the birds were mainly medium- and large-sized seabirds and waterfowl, but in the Late Bronze Age the bird bone assemblage comprised nearly 80 bones of small waders, Charadriiformes, and more than 20 of passerines, with just a handful of ducks and seabirds. The abrupt change in species and animal size suggested that, at that time, the area had been used temporarily as a raptor roost, and this was confirmed by the hundreds of bones of the Orkney vole, *Microtus arvalis orcadensis*, also present. Taking into account the raptors found in Orkney today and in the past and their preferred prey, I concluded that the most likely predator was the short-eared owl (Serjeantson 2007b), which hunts Orkney vole in summer and switches to small shore birds in winter (Glue 1977).

Dealing with the Prey

The diurnal birds of prey, the falcons and eagles, and also vultures actually derive nourishment from bone itself, and from the lipids within the bone. They digest bone itself, just as do mammalian carnivores. The most extreme example is the bearded vulture or lammergeier, which scavenges bones from mammalian carcasses, drops them on to rocks to break them, and eats the fragments. Interestingly, 'the kind of bones they take is not dictated by what other scavengers have left but by the best choice in terms of fat content'(Robert & Vigne 2002, 325). The bone-breaking sites, their ossuaries, are liable to be confused with human consumption sites.

Raptors which catch other birds consume their prey by two different methods. Owls typically catch the prey and eat it whole or in large pieces, and eject the fur, feathers, and bone in pellets. Others, mainly the diurnal raptors, retire to a roost with the prey, where they pluck it, tear off the flesh, and eat it. They consume some bones with the flesh and drop others below the feeding site. As with pellets, for these

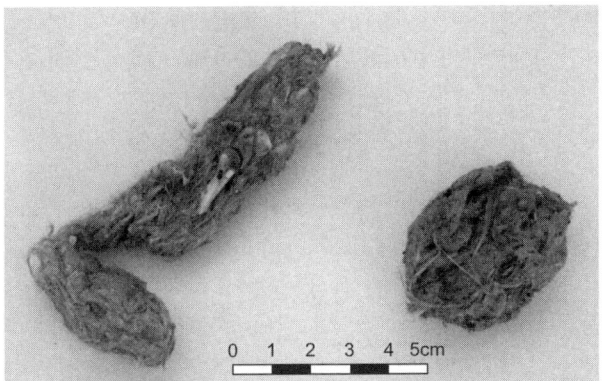

FIGURE 5.8. Pellets of a bald eagle, *Haliaeetus leucocephalus*: small fragments of bone are visible in the feather matrix (photograph by D. Serjeantson).

elements to survive, they have to find their way into a protected environment such as a cave or rock fissure.

Most people are familiar with the fact that owls eject pellets, but in fact many species of birds and also some mammals eject pellets. They are cast by species as diverse as gulls, corvids, waterfowl, and even some passerines (Brown et al. 1999, 82–89). The typical raptor pellet (Figure 5.8) consists of a mass of small bones, surrounded by fur or feathers (Glue 1977), but pellets of those species which eat fish or insects also contain fish scales or the remains of insect exoskeletons. Over time, in most contexts the pellet disaggregates. The fur, feathers, and insect remains quickly decay, leaving – in suitable environments – only the bones.

Beak and Claw Marks

Avian predators use their beaks and claws to hold and disarticulate the carcass, and sometimes they leave traces of beak and claw damage. The perforations made with the beak have an irregular square or triangular form, or a zigzag outline, as in Figure 5.9, which shows humeri of pigeons from pellets of the eagle owl. The pigeon bones in the owl pellets were compared with those discarded by a peregrine falcon. The humerus was the element on which beak marks were most often seen; the owl made the holes near the articular ends, sometimes opposing. A few were present at both ends of the humerus, but on the other long bones there was usually a single hole (Laroulandie 2002). The beak impact of the falcon was lighter and smaller (Figure 5.10).

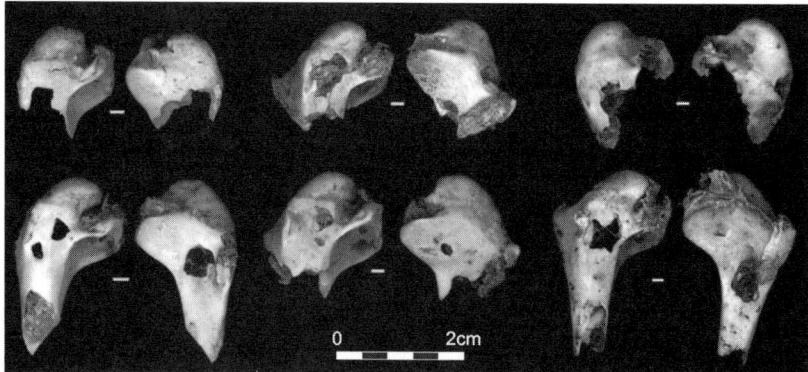

FIGURE 5.9. Beak impact of an eagle owl, *Bubo bubo*, on the proximal end of the humeri of pigeons, *Columba* sp. The bones have been snapped in half and show irregular squarish holes (photograph by V. Laroulandie; see Laroulandie 2002, fig. 2).

Raptors also attack the sternum and other flat bones when extracting meat and fat from their prey. Figure 5.11 shows the sternum of one of the manx shearwaters from Skomer referred to earlier; it has been pecked by a great black-backed gull (Serjeantson et al. 1993). Damage to the sternum seen on a moa bone from New Zealand was also thought to be caused by an avian predator, Haast's eagle (Figure 5.12). The pelvis has been broken by the beak of a bird which is thought to have attacked the carcass at that point to reach the kidneys and kidney fat (Worthy & Holdaway 2002, 274).

Digestion

The natural erosion of bird bones described earlier has been compared with digestion of bone by owls. The bones which were ingested and then rejected in pellets showed

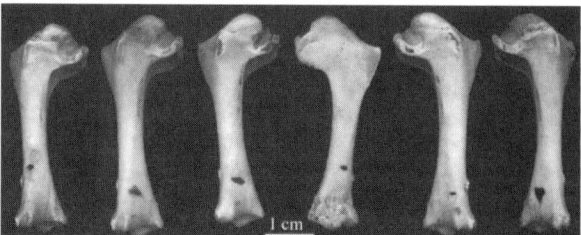

FIGURE 5.10. Humeri of pigeons, *Columba* sp., with holes from the beak impact of a peregrine falcon, *Falco peregrinus* (photograph by V. Laroulandie; see Laroulandie 2002, fig. 3). Note that the holes are smaller and lighter than those made by the eagle owl.

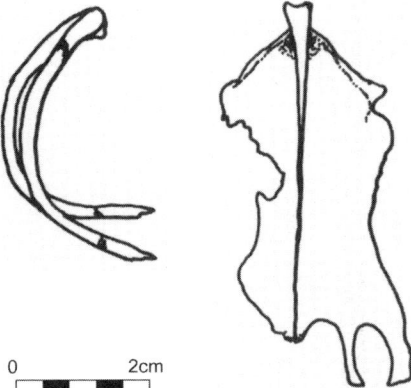

FIGURE 5.11. Furcula and sternum of a manx shearwater, *Puffinus puffinus*, from Skomer Island, showing beak damage from great black-backed gull, *Larus marinus* (Serjeantson et al. 1993, fig. 3).

some signs of digestion, mainly a rounding and thinning of the breakage edges. Fractured shafts and holes had rounded edges which had the appearance of 'plastic which has begun to melt in the heat' (Bochenski & Tomek 1997, 384). Digestion affected the articular and broken ends rather than the whole bone. Breaks on the control bones were sharp and at right angles to the shaft, while those from the owl pellets were rounded and partly thinned in a manner similar to those which had been exposed to weathering.

Diurnal raptors also eject pellets, but a study which compared the pellets of gyrfalcons with those of owls showed that the pellets of falcons contained only a

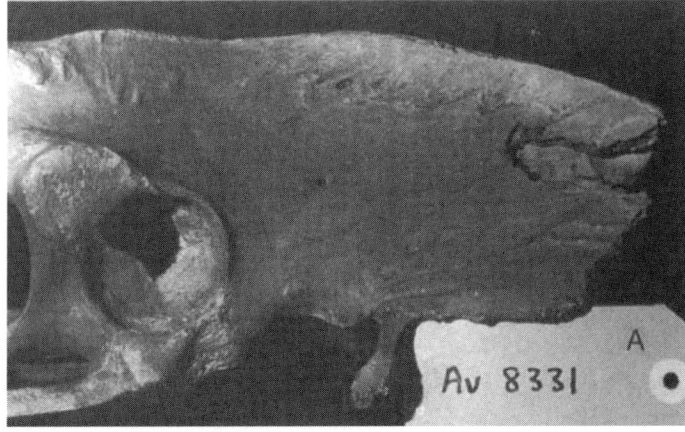

FIGURE 5.12. Pelvis of a moa, *Emeus crassus*, showing a notch in the anterior iliac plate made by the beak of a large bird, probably Haast's eagle, *Harpagornis moorei*. The perforations were made with the claws (Worthy & Holdaway 2002, fig. 8.18; photograph by R. Morris).

120 BIRDS

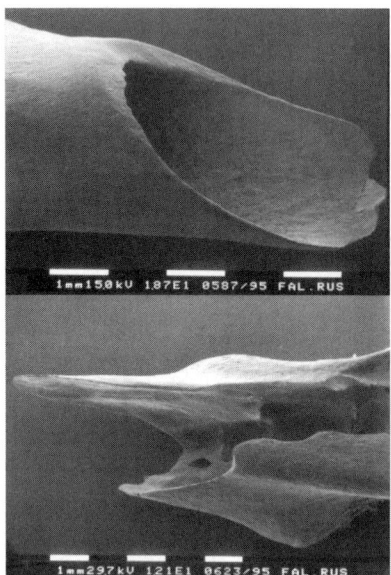

FIGURE 5.13. Bones of grouse, *Lagopus* sp., from the pellets of a gyrfalcon, *Falco rusticolus*, showing evidence of digestion. The top section shows an ulna shaft with green fracture rounded and thinned through digestion; the bottom shows the shaft of a coracoid with a long digested gap along its axis. All edges are thinned and rounded (Bochenski et al. 1998, figs. 2 and 3).

small quantity of bone as they 'digest significantly more bones of their bird victims than any of the owl species examined'. In the gyrfalcon pellets 'shafts of long bones showed traces of digestion significantly more often...than in snowy owls' and contained many shaft fragments 'heavily modified through digestion' (Bochenski et al. 1998, 432). Figure 5.13 shows an ulna and a coracoid from gyrfalcon pellets in which the breaks have digested edges; in both, the edges are thinned and rounded; in the coracoid, the strong digestive acids have completely eroded away part of the bone surface.

Bones from regurgitated owl pellets tend not to be much eroded (Andrews 1990, 19). As they are mostly undigested and are wrapped in a matrix of fur and feathers, they are protected from the effects of weathering and bioerosion. They consequently have a greater chance of surviving than bones of the same species which were captured and eaten by people. The bird bones from the Links of Noltland, referred to in Chapter 4, were scored as 'fresh' or 'weathered'. The 'weathered' material was abraded, and occasionally there was some loss of compact bone and exposure of cancellous tissue, while the 'fresh' group was almost 'greasy' and anatomical features were sharply defined and unabraded. Armour-Chelu found that the bones of the larger birds, those in categories 'huge' to 'medium long', were more broken and more weathered than those from birds in the categories 'medium' to 'very short'. For the bones of the larger birds, 35 per cent were weathered and only 9 per cent fresh, compared with only 13 per cent weathered in the smaller size classes and as many as 30 per cent fresh. The conclusion was that the 'medium' to 'very short' species had been the prey of owls (probably, as at Tofts Ness, the short-eared owl), and the larger remains had been human food (Armour-Chelu 1988).

Dispersal and Fragmentation

The degree of damage can be a criterion for distinguishing traces of birds of prey. Avian predators can be divided into three groups according to the degree of damage they do to their victims' bones (Bochenski & Tomek 1997). Elements reduced to the smallest sized fragments are those from the pellets of the large diurnal birds of prey: typically well below 30 per cent of the element is present. Bones from the pellets of owls are intermediate: the surviving share of the whole bone is between 30 and 60 per cent. Least damaged are bones discarded uneaten by diurnal raptors. However, elements from the pellets of certain owls, the barn owl, the long-eared owl, and the short-eared owl, are also relatively undamaged, as we have seen. In a comparison of the damage which occurred on individual elements, Bochenski (2005) showed that in all cases the scapular end of the coracoid survived better than the sternal end, but the proximal and distal ends of the long bones survive in different proportions according to the bird of prey involved. The relative density of the two ends of the coracoid could account for the regular pattern, but the reasons for the differences in the limb bones could not be explained.

Some of the criteria for distinguishing assemblages which derive from a bird of prey are open to ambiguous interpretations. The erosion from digestive juices of the birds of prey could potentially be confused with post-depositional erosion in the ground, and the predominant elements rejected by some of the raptors are disconcertingly similar to anthropogenic assemblages, as we see in the next chapter.

Mammalian Predators

There are few mammalian predators which rely exclusively on birds, though some may do so locally; for instance the arctic fox, *Alopex lagopus*, is a major predator on ground-nesting birds in the Arctic in the breeding season. Those carnivorous and omnivorous mammals such as rats, cats, pigs, and possums which were introduced to uninhabited islands turned to the adults, chicks, and eggs of ground-nesting birds as their main source of food, as they were freely available (Chapter 15). Herbivores have been known to scavenge the carcasses of birds from time to time. Their hoofprints in the snow revealed that deer had scavenged the coots killed in the ice in Illinois (Oliver & Graham 1994). The Shetland sheep on the island of Foula developed the habit of not only scavenging but actually killing and eating the chicks of the terns which breed there. In one year 200 chicks were found with heads, wings, or legs missing (Hall 1992). Manx shearwaters suffer in the same way from the red deer on the Hebridean island of Rhum. 'After biting off and swallowing their victim's head, the deer chew wings and legs to extract the bone. They then discard the remainder of the carcase. By selectively eating bone, the deer are presumably making good [the] mineral deficiencies in the montane vegetation they graze' (Brooke 1990, 49).

Prey Selection

Bird bones are less attractive to carnivores than those of mammals because the quantity of cancellous tissue and the bone marrow content is less. However, some carnivores do catch and eat birds and also scavenge carcasses. In the domestic context they scavenge bones discarded from human meals. In one instance, the carnivores, which were mainly foxes and coyotes, removed entire carcasses and broke limb bones when consuming the coots frozen into the lake ice while the scavenging herring gulls picked the carcasses clean in situ (Oliver & Graham 1994). The gulls preferred to attack the skull and breast, while the foxes consumed the legs, giving the contrasting pattern seen in Figure 5.4.

Gnawing Traces

Carnivore gnawing can be recognised by puncture marks and by ragged edges, defined by Binford (1981, 61) as 'crenulated' ends. Both are visible in the chicken bones (Figure 5.14) which were recovered outside dens used by foxes and badgers (Mallye et al. 2008).

The incidence of gnawing by dogs and small carnivores on bird bones from archaeological sites is usually low (Cruz 2008). Where it has been observed, not

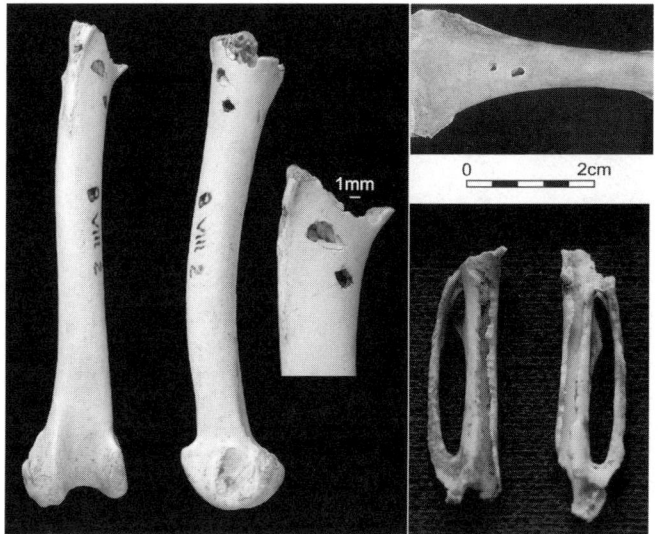

FIGURE 5.14. Marks of gnawing of bird bones by mammals. The left side shows a chicken femur gnawed by a fox, *Vulpes vulpes*, or a badger, *Meles meles*. The top right shows the coracoid of duck, *Anas* sp. from Pompeii, gnawed by a very small carnivore, probably a weasel, *Mustela nivalis*. The bottom right shows gnawing by a rodent, probably the house mouse, *Mus musculus*, on the carpometacarpi of chukar partridge, *Alectoris chukar*, from Neolithic Ganj Dareh, Iran (photographs by J.-B. Mallye, A. Powell, and N. Munro).

surprisingly, it has most often been on larger birds. In the remains from Haddenham, carnivore gnawing was recognised on a surprisingly high percentage (17 and 12 per cent) of the bones of the big birds, pelican and swan, but on three elements only of mallard, all humeri (Serjeantson 2006a). Dog gnawing was noted on 50 bones of Anatidae at the Pre-Pottery Neolithic site of Tell Mureybet in Syria, that is, between 1 and 2 per cent, a percentage comparable to that at Haddenham, and much lower than the incidence of gnawing on mammal bone at the site (Gourichon 2002). Gnawing was identified on approximately 9 per cent of the bones of domestic geese from Wood Quay in medieval Dublin, the traces consisting of punctures and shredding of epiphyses (MacDonald et al. 1993). The sequence of destruction on a series of tarsometatarsi can be seen in Figure 5.15. The bones were attacked on the proximal end, and then on the distal end, and caused damage from slight to major. The authors considered that dogs were responsible, but they also raised the possibility that the chewing marks were the work of humans or even pigs.

Cats are better known for eating birds, catching the birds themselves and also scrounging remains discarded by people. The damage and puncture marks made by cats are similar to those made by dogs, but the punctures made by their smaller canine teeth are finer. Whereas dogs completely demolish bones of smaller birds,

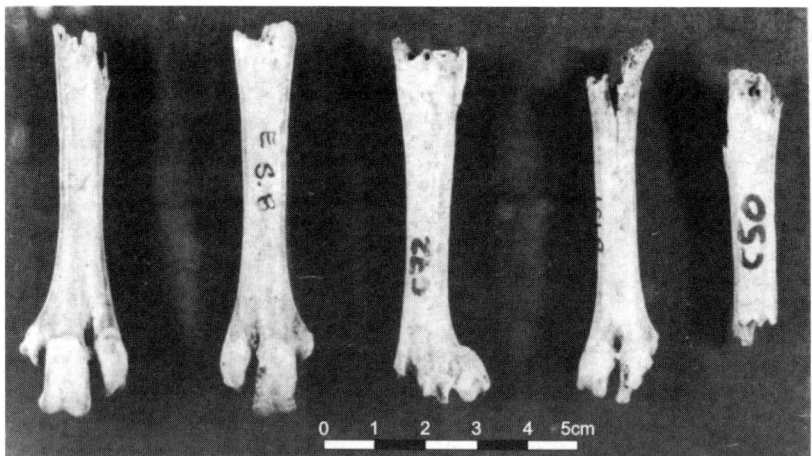

FIGURE 5.15. Gnawing, probably by dogs, on the tarsometatarsi of domestic geese, *Anser anser*, from medieval Dublin, showing a sequence from minor to major destruction (MacDonald et al. 1993, pl. V; photograph by R. Hutton MacDonald).

cats may damage them but not destroy them completely. The smallest carnivores will also bite bones if given the opportunity. Powell (1995–1996) found very small circular holes on one of the duck bones from Pompeii (Figure 5.14). Remains of weasels, *Mustela nivalis*, were also found nearby, and the holes are a perfect fit with their tiny canine teeth. Rodent gnawing is distinctive: the molar teeth produce flat parallel marks. Several of the bones of the chukar partridge from the Early Neolithic site of Ganj Dareh in Iran show substantial rodent damage. The culprit was probably the house mouse, *Mus musculus*, the most common rodent at the site (Figure 5.14). In the two carpometacarpi illustrated the rodent has gnawed through the shaft of the major metacarpal, exposing the marrow cavity, and has also chewed both ends. The presence of the house mouse, together with the gnawing evidence, supports the claim of Ganj Dareh to be one of the earliest sedentary settlements in the Near East.

The species present and the marks on the bones made by predators are the most reliable clue to the origin of an element or an assemblage, but the presence or absence of certain elements also gives a pointer to the predator involved.

ELEMENT SURVIVAL

The presence and absence of certain elements relies on two factors: the damage done when the carcass is eaten and digested, already discussed, and whether or not the

Table 5.4. *Survival of pigeon long bones in pellets of eagle owl,* Bubo bubo, *and in food remains of peregrine falcon,* Falco peregrinus

Bones	Bubo bubo pellets			Falco peregrinus food remains		
	NISP	MNE	% survival	NISP	MNE	% survival
Coracoid	32	22	50.0	16	15	37.5
Scapula	21	19	43.2	12	12	30.0
Humerus	46	32	72.7	37	34	85.0
Ulna	34	25	56.8	20	19	47.5
Radius	18	17	38.6	5	5	12.5
Carpometacarpus	35	34	77.3	14	14	35.0
Femur	41	27	61.4	6	6	15.0
Tibiotarsus	48	33	75.0	3	3	7.5
Tarsometatarsus	46	44	100.0	1	1	2.5
Total	321			114		

Source: Data are from Laroulandie (2002).

whole carcass was carried back from the kill site to the roost or nest. Some species dismember their prey at the kill site; the sparrowhawk, for instance, leaves the wings and legs at the kill site (Brown et al. 1999, 77). Whether or not birds are selective about what they carry to the nest also depends on whether or not they are feeding young. Owls ingest the whole animal and then eject the bones in pellets, while diurnal raptors, as we have seen, discard some and ingest the remainder. Their stronger digestive juices destroy some elements completely, though some are also ejected in pellets. Another criterion for identifying raptor prey is therefore the relative number of elements from different parts of the body.

In a pioneering study of bird bone taphonomy, Ericson (1987) argued that the relative numbers of wing and leg bones were a guide to whether or not an assemblage was anthropogenic, a subject discussed in the next chapter. Differential survival also distinguishes different types of assemblage of the prey of avian predators. In the pellets of the eagle owl, the elements of the wing and leg survived in almost equal numbers (Table 5.4). Laroulandie (2002) and a survey by Bochenski (2005) confirmed that the ratio of wing to leg elements was approximately equal in remains from pellets of several types of owl and diurnal raptors. It was more variable with uneaten remains recovered from below roosts (Figure 5.16). Here wing bones strongly predominated over those from the leg, except in the golden eagle. The elements which were most

126 BIRDS

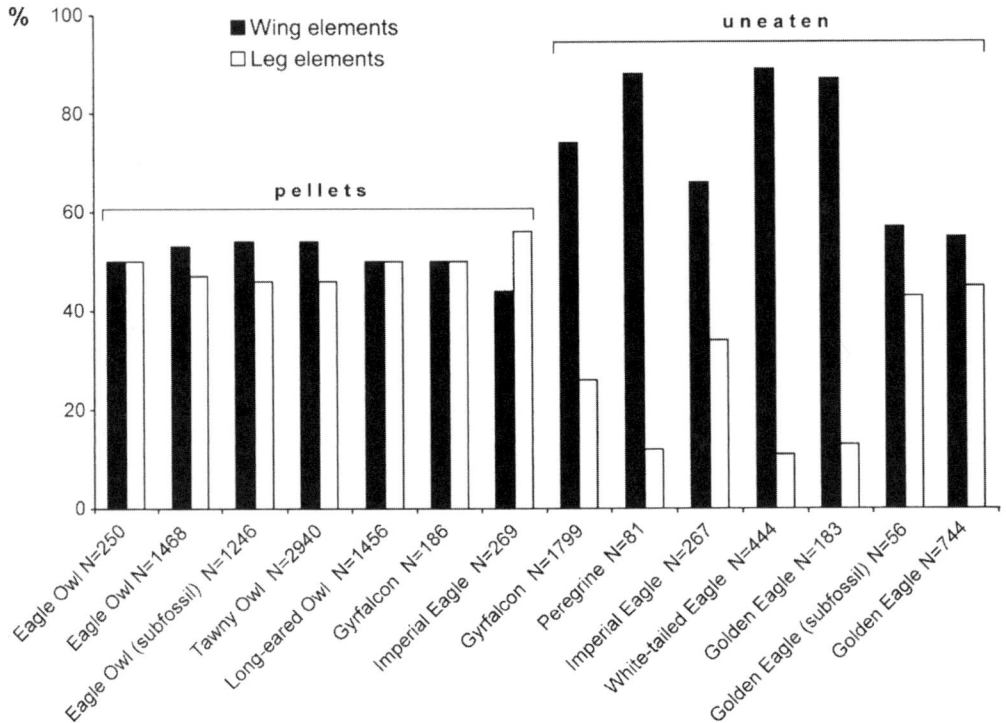

FIGURE 5.16. Proportion of the total number of wing (humerus, ulna, and carpometacarpus) to leg (femur, tibiotarsus, and tarsometatarsus) bones in bird pellets and in uneaten food remains of owls and diurnal birds of prey (Bochenski 2005, fig. 4.2).

abundant in the remains discarded by peregrine falcons were also those of the wing; the femur, tibiotarsus, and tarsometatarsus were fewest (Table 5.4). The absence of hind limbs was also a characteristic of the scavenging by mammals of the frozen coots, as we have seen.

In pellets and also in most collections of uneaten bones, elements from wing and leg predominate over those from the core of the body, sternum, pelvis, scapula, and coracoid (Figure 5.17). However, elements from the body, especially the sternum, were relatively more common in the discarded food remains of the golden eagle (Bochenski 2005, fig. 4.3). The remains of black grouse from a cave in Staffordshire, England, appeared to be prey of a golden eagle, as there were adults and also young among the discarded remains. The bone which survived best was also the sternum: the most robust area of the bone, the articulation, was the part that survived, as the rest had been broken away. The authors rejected the hypothesis that the eagles had dismembered their prey elsewhere, but considered that the limb bones had

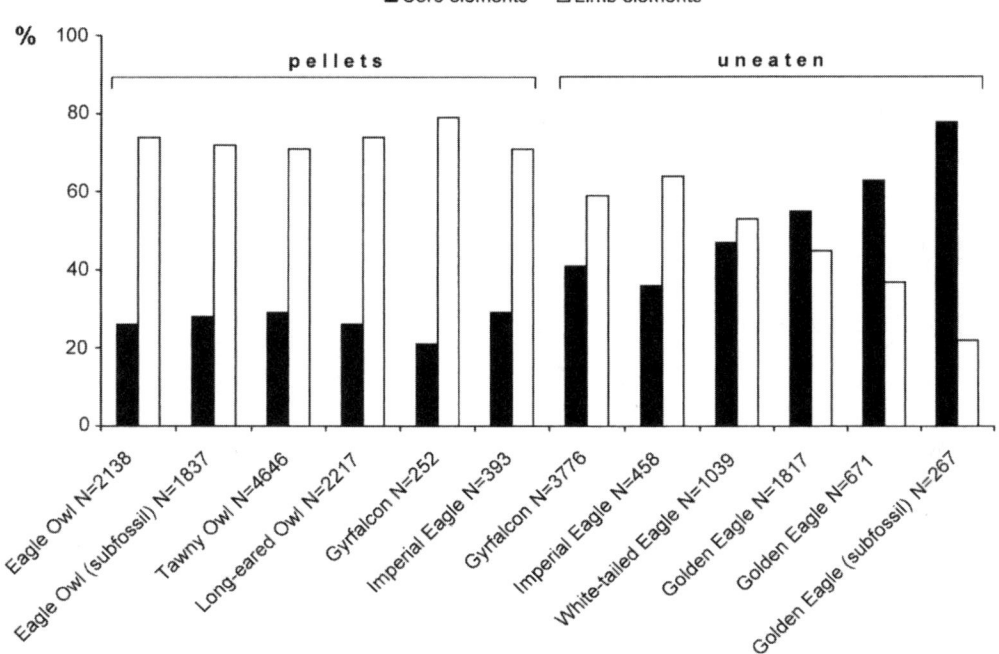

FIGURE 5.17. Proportion of the total number of core (sternum, pelvis, scapula, coracoid) to limb (humerus, ulna, radius, carpometacarpus, femur, tibiotarsus, tarsometatarsus) bones in pellets and in uneaten food remains of owls and diurnal birds of prey (Bochenski 2005, fig. 4.3).

been either digested completely or rejected elsewhere in pellets (Bramwell et al. 1987).

The clearest distinctions between groups and species can be seen when a single element predominates. For instance, the tarsometatarsus predominated in owl pellets and the carpometacarpus was the most frequent element dropped from a roost or nest by those raptors which snap off the wings before consuming their avian prey; this includes gyrfalcons, some eagles, and some of the owls (Bochenski 2005). The coracoid and humerus predominated in uneaten remains from eagles and falcon. Mourer-Chauviré (1983) distinguished remains from owl pellets from human refuse by the numbers of tarsometatarsi and carpometacarpi in the deposits. At the Middle Palaeolithic cave site of Sesselfelsgrotte, where none of the bird remains showed any trace of human intervention, there were almost twice as many tarsometatarsi as other elements (von den Driesch 2005). A predominance of other parts of the skeleton may derive from other raptor prey *or* from human prey, as discussed in the next chapter.

As a generalisation, owls digest very little of a bone, whereas in the hawks and eagles the digestive process has a strong effect on the bones ingested, to the extent that some are totally destroyed. Bones discarded uneaten do not suffer erosive damage from digestion, though they may suffer weathering before burial. These factors all affect bone condition, fragmentation, and the relative number of elements. They can suggest whether the predator is an owl or a hawk, but to work out which predator was involved also depends on prey species and size, for mammals as well as birds.

CONCLUSIONS

The main limb bones of chickens and birds larger than chickens are likely to be recovered in the trench except in the most adverse excavation conditions, but smaller birds will be overlooked and the smaller or more fragmentary skeletal elements of large birds will not be recovered. Where bird remains are present in the deposits, sieving enhances the material collected. Since, as we see in Chapter 10, humans have usually exploited birds of medium and large size, a 4-mm mesh is adequate for most anthropogenic material. It is only necessary to use sieves with the smaller mesh if there is a likelihood that small birds are also present.

Except for those rare occasions when a skeleton is found, it is usual for bones to be disarticulated and damaged. The question then arises as to whether the damage results from human cooking and eating, or whether it has some other origin. The most diagnostic marks of non-human predators are those made by bird beaks and carnivore teeth. Breakage patterns can also indicate the predator, but these criteria are ambiguous on their own. The erosion of the bone surface is greater in bones rejected by diurnal raptors, which digest more of the bones, than it is in owl pellets. Bones dropped uneaten below a roost are less damaged as they have not been ingested. Digestion causes the breakage surfaces of limb bones to become corroded, but the weathering which takes place in the ground or even on the ground surface after deposition has a similar effect. As few of these traces will be diagnostic on their own, survival of different parts of the anatomy can also be a valuable criterion for identifying the agent of damage.

The predominance of certain elements is certainly diagnostic in some contexts, but of all the factors discussed in this chapter, element survival gives the most ambiguous results. Above all, it is important to take into account species composition, context, and associated finds when interpreting the origin of deposits. For instance, bones distributed around a cave wall are more likely to be from pellets while those from the middle of the cave are more likely to be from people or carnivores. It is only when a natural origin for the bones has been ruled out that we can begin to understand how humans were catching, cooking, and eating birds and disposing of their remains, as we shall see in the next chapter.

6

Taphonomy: Human Modifications and Element Survival

Modifications such as cut marks and burning not only demonstrate whether remains were anthropogenic in origin but also reveal the purposes for which the birds were caught, whether for food, feathers, tools, or yet other purposes. The chewing of bones by humans also leaves traces, as does burning, which is almost invariably the result of human actions, whether related to cremation, cooking, or merely the disposal of remains on a fire.

There are several criteria which are helpful for recognising anthropogenic material; they include some related to behaviour and context as well as some which rely on the condition of the bones themselves (Laroulandie 2000), as shown in Table 6.1. In Chapter 5 we considered circumstances in which both natural and anthropogenic assemblages may be found together and looked at natural agents of destruction, including burial conditions and predators other than people. Here, I shall examine those features of assemblages and individual bones which are characteristic of human activity.

Four sources of evidence were invoked in a study of the remains of *Lagopus*, mainly ptarmigan, from the Upper Palaeolithic (Magdalenian) site of La Grotte des Eglises in France. The bones must have been introduced into the cave by humans or large raptors, several of which, as we saw in Chapter 5, preyed on grouse in the Late Pleistocene. Firstly, natural death could be excluded because grouse do not naturally use caves. Secondly, mammalian carnivores could be ruled out because the bones showed no marks of carnivore gnawing. Thirdly, the remains were associated with bones of ibex, *Capra pyrenaica*, and salmon, which certainly derived from human meals. Finally, and conclusively, cut marks were found on some of the bones (Laroulandie 1998).

There has also been a great deal of discussion on whether the presence or absence of certain elements can indicate whether or not an assemblage is anthropogenic. This question is related to the density or robustness of individual elements, and the

Table 6.1. *Criteria to consider when identifying whether an assemblage is natural or anthropogenic*

Criteria	Description
1 Behaviour	Species in or out of natural range or natural habitat
2 Age and sex	Presence or absence of juveniles; proportion of juveniles
3 Context	Natural site or site associated with human activity, or potentially either
4 Natural traces on bones	Presence or absence of digestion traces, gnaw marks, beak marks, etc.
5 Anthropogenic traces on bones	Presence or absence of cuts, chops, disarticulation and peeling marks, burning, or chewing
6 Degree of disarticulation	Bones partly in articulation or disarticulated
7 Fragmentation	Where fragmented; how much; survival of different areas of the bone
8 Frequency of skeletal parts	Expected or skewed anatomical distribution
9 Associated material	Absence or presence of artefacts and human food remains

relationship between bone density and element survival is considered in the second part of the chapter.

CUT MARKS

We have already noted how Milne-Edwards (1875, 238) rejected a natural origin for the *Lagopus* bones in some French caves, because he noted that 'on many of them we observe the *striae*, or notches similar to those produced by the flint implements made use of by the men of that period to detach the flesh of animals'. Subsequent research has greatly refined our understanding of the cut marks on bird bones (Laroulandie 2007). Cut marks may be confused with marks with a non-anthropogenic origin such as scratches from sandy soil or fine gnawing marks (Lyman 1994, 297), but they are usually recognisable. The presence of cuts confirms the anthropogenic nature of an assemblage, so they are usually mentioned in reports on finds of bird bones, even if sometimes in frustratingly little detail. The use of a scanning electron microscope to highlight the profile of the cuts (Figure 6.1) can give useful insights in assemblages where the cut marks reveal a consistent activity, as in some Palaeolithic assemblages, but cut marks are often visible to the naked eye. A lens with between 3× and 10× magnification is needed, together with a good source of light, something all too often

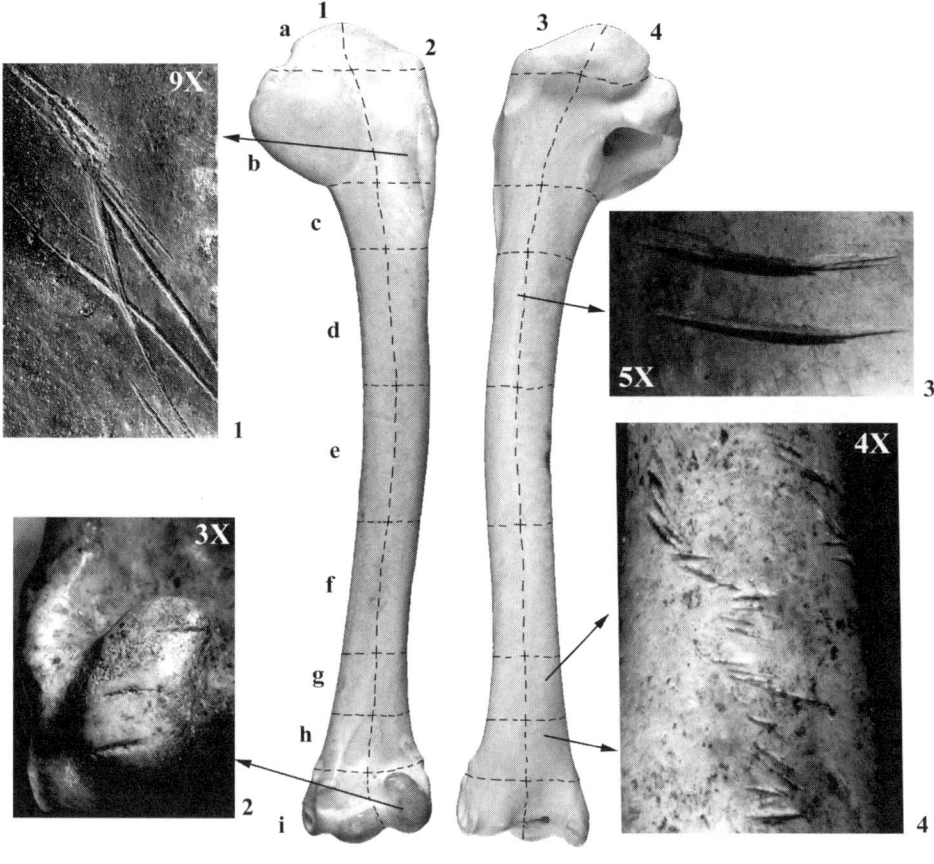

FIGURE 6.1. Cut marks on humeri from Grotta Romanelli, Italy. The centre view gives caudal and cranial views of the humerus, showing zones where cut marks were recorded. 1, wigeon, *Anas penelope*, at 9× magnification; 2, white-fronted goose, *Anser albifrons*, 3× magnification; 3, greylag goose, *A. anser*, 5× magnification; 4, wigeon, 4× magnification (Tagliacozzo & Gala 2002, fig. 2).

lacking in the dark museum basements and archaeological study rooms to which the study of bones is often consigned.

Cuts have three main functions: dismembering, filleting, and skinning. Short, sometimes quite deep, cuts at the area of muscle, tendon, and ligament insertions result from dismembering the carcass, including the removal of wings. Striated cuts or scraping marks result from filleting meat from the bone or from cleaning the bone in preparation for tool-making. Skinning cuts are rarely seen, probably because birds are usually plucked for cooking rather than skinned. The types of cuts made in disarticulating and filleting birds have been demonstrated experimentally.

Table 6.2. *Location of disarticulation and filleting cuts produced in experimental butchering of grey partridge,* Perdix perdix

Anatomical element	Disarticulation	Filleting
Coracoid		x
Furcula		x
Scapula (proximal articular end)	x	
Scapula (body)		x
Humerus (articular extremities)	x	x
Humerus (posterior proximal part of body)	x	x
Humerus (medial and distal part of body)		x
Ulna (articular extremities)	x	x
Ulna (body)		x
Radius (proximal articular end)	x	
Carpometacarpus (proximal articular end)	x	
Pelvis	x	x
Femur (proximal end)	x	x
Femur (medial and distal part of body)		x
Femur (distal articular end)	x	
Tibiotarsus (proximal articular end)	x	x
Tibiotarsus (body)		x
Sternum		x

Source: Data are from Laroulandie (2001).

Laroulandie (2001) butchered a batch of grey partridges and recorded the results (Table 6.2). She recorded the marks made on the proximal or distal ends (or both) of the long bones and the scapula when cutting through the ligaments to disarticulate the bird. Those on the scapula, coracoid, furcula, and sternum resulted from filleting, as did those on the body of the limb bones. Just a few regions on some elements showed marks from both processes: articular extremities of the humerus, posterior shaft of the humerus at the proximal end, distal ulna, pelvis, proximal femur, and proximal articular end of the tibiotarsus. Cuts on other elements and on other parts of elements related to only one process.

On the *Lagopus* bones from the Late Magdalenian cave site of La Vache in the Ariège, Laroulandie (2005a) observed dismembering cuts on articulations, and filleting cuts on the body of the elements, including on the scapula and sternum (Figure 6.2). Examples of the different types of cut marks are illustrated on humeri of various species from the Late Palaeolithic (Epigravettian) site of Grotta Romanelli in southern Italy (Figure 6.1): striated filleting cuts on the proximal shaft of the humerus

134 BIRDS

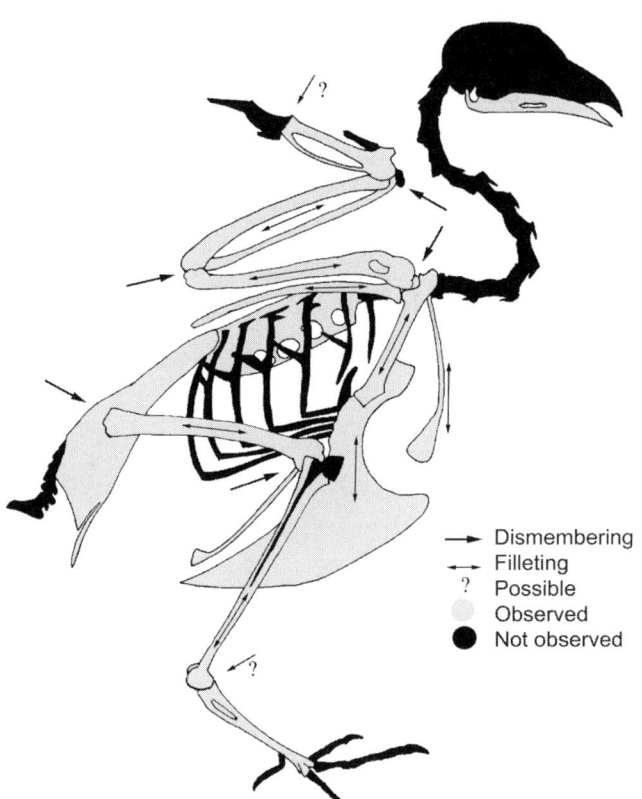

FIGURE 6.2. Outline of skeleton showing location of cut marks on the bones of grouse, *Lagopus* sp., from the Magdalenian site of La Vache, France. Arrows indicate disarticulation; double arrows indicate filleting cuts (Laroulandie 2005a, fig. 4; drawing by V. Laroulandie).

of a wigeon, very short repeated cuts at the distal articulation of a humerus of a white-fronted goose, and short, relatively deep, repeated cuts at muscle attachments on the humerus shaft of a greylag goose and a wigeon (Tagliacozzo & Gala 2002).

Incidence of Cut Marks

A comparison of the percentage of bones with cut marks at French and Italian Upper Palaeolithic sites shows that the incidence of cut marks is surprisingly varied. It is high at La Vache and Taï 2 (Figure 6.3), but it is much lower at the contemporary Grotte des Eglises (Table 6.3). The differences between the assemblages do not correlate with species. Ptarmigan was the main species at six sites; at Grotta Romanelli the little bustard and geese were the main species; and at the nearby Grotta della Madonna

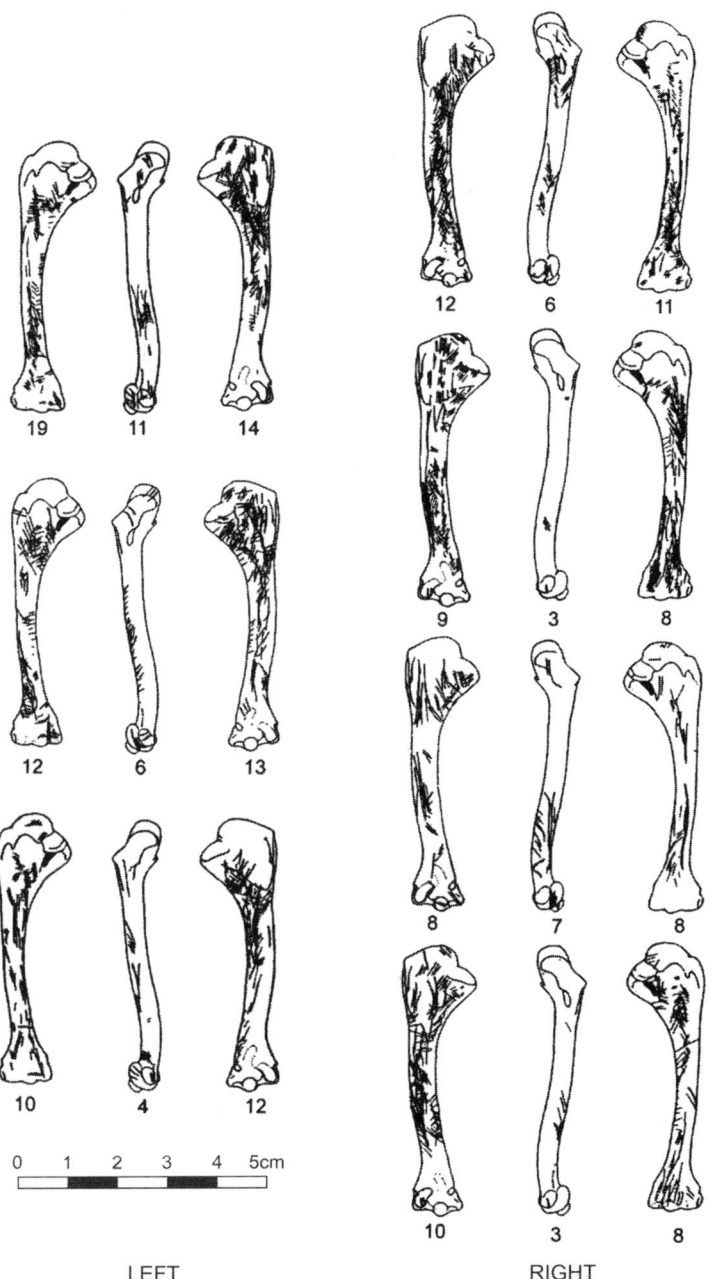

FIGURE 6.3. Location of cut marks on humeri at Taï 2, France. The number of specimens showing the cut marks in question is also shown (Louchart & Soave 2002).

Table 6.3. *Percentage of major elements with cut marks from eight Late Upper Palaeolithic sites*

Site	LAV	BER	GAZ	TOU	TAI	EGL	ROM 1	ROM 2	MAD
Sternum	5	x	x	x	x	x	x	0.6	0.0
Furcula	7	x	x	x	x	x	x	0.4	2
Coracoid	22	27	30	14	58	3	9	12	**26**
Scapula	11	x	x	x	48	x	0.9	1	5
Humerus	**73**	**100**	**40**	**23**	**100**	5	**18**	**60**	20
Ulna	14	x	9	10	84	8	0.1	2	0
Radius	12	x	x	0	90	**14**	x	3	2
Carpometacarpus	0.4	0	0	0	45	0	x	0.7	3
Pelvis	5	x	x	x	x	x	x	21	6
Femur	47	50	15	19	40	0	0.3	1	7
Tibiotarsus	8	x	18	11	66	6	0.6	2	7
Tarsometatarsus	0	9	0	0	6	0	x	0	0

Note: LAV = La Vache, *Lagopus*; BER = Berroberia, *Lagopus*; GAZ = Gazel, *Lagopus*; TOU = Tournal, *Lagopus*; TAI = Taï 2, *Lagopus*; EGL = Grotte des Eglises, *Lagopus*; ROM 1 = Grotta Romanelli, *Otis tetrax*; ROM 2 = Grotta Romanelli, Anseriformes, mainly geese; MAD = Grotta della Madonna di Praia, Anseriformes, mainly ducks. An x denotes an element excluded from the analysis. Percentages greater than 1 are rounded to the nearest whole figure. The element with the highest percentage of cut marks is shown in boldface type.
Source: LAV is from Laroulandie (2005a); BER is from Diez Fernandez-Lomana et al. (1995); GAZ and TOU are from Vilette (1983); TAI is from Louchart and Soave (2002); EGL is from Laroulandie (1998); ROM 1 is from Cassoli and Tagliacozzo (1997); ROM 2 and MAD are from Tagliacozzo and Gala (2002).

they were ducks, mostly mallard (Tagliacozzo & Gala 2002). The greatest consistency is that the element with the most cut marks at seven of the nine assemblages is the humerus. The carpometacarpus and tarsometatarsus of ptarmigan showed consistently fewer cuts than the other limb bones. There is an enigmatic contrast between Les Eglises with very few cut marks on the one hand and the remainder of the sites with ptarmigan where the percentage is high. Les Eglises was also unusual in that the bone with most cuts was the radius. For some of the sites at least, the contrast does not relate to observation method, as the same individual and method was involved. Furthermore, the contrast does not relate to date or environment (Laroulandie 1998), so it must relate to some cultural distinction in butchery and consumption which has yet to be explained.

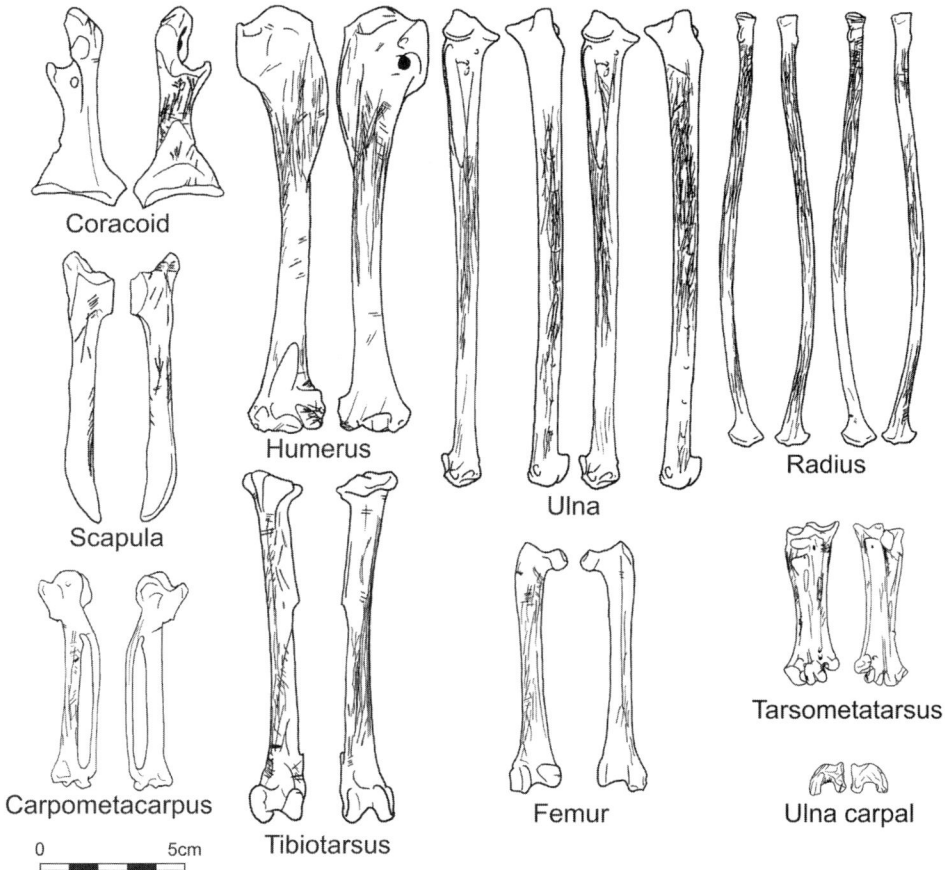

FIGURE 6.4. Location of cut marks on bones of snowy owl, *Nyctea (Bubo) scandiaca*, from the Magdalenian site of Bois-Ragot, Vienne, France. Cuts on the scapula and coracoid as well as the limbs show that the birds were eaten (Laroulandie 2000, figs. 84, 85).

Interpreting Cut Marks

Striated or scrape marks such as those illustrated on the humerus, ulna, and radius in Figure 6.4 were more difficult to interpret than the short cut marks. Though many were long and sinuous, some were quite short. Striated cut marks have been reported much more often on Palaeolithic sites than on sites of later periods, so they may be related to the conditions of the period, perhaps cold weather, which meant that birds were frozen at the time they were butchered. Diez Fernandez-Lomana and colleagues (1995) pointed out that removing meat from the bone, after it has been stored after being dried or smoked, leaves scraping marks. The large number of bones with visible cut marks is also probably related to the fact that, in the Palaeolithic era, birds were cooked over an open fire.

Striations also sometimes result from scraping the bone free of skin to remove the feathers. The remains of snowy owls from Bois-Ragot were covered with cut marks (Table 6.4), including both repeated short cuts and striations. The fact that cuts are frequent on the coracoid and scapula and on the body of the femur and tibiotarsus (Figure 6.4) does suggest that the meat was being recovered, but many of the cuts on the wing bones can only be explained as coming from feather removal. The cutting and scraping marks on the snowy owl bones extended, unexpectedly, over the phalanges (Figure 6.5). These striations too may have been made when feathers were removed – the snowy owl has feathers on the feet – but may have been made to clean the bones for ornament; some phalanges from the sites were engraved, as discussed in Chapter 9 (Laroulandie 2000, 2004). Detaching sinew should perhaps also be considered (see Chapter 8).

In some assemblages the elements from the body have more frequent cut marks than those of the limbs. At the Grotta della Madonna the coracoids had more cut marks than the humeri (Table 6.3). At Quebrada Tacahuay, a Late Pleistocene coastal site in southern Peru, cuts were also rare on the wing and leg bones of the seabirds from the site but more frequent on the furcula and scapula (Mameli 2002). This is very unlike the pattern of cut marks on contemporary sites in Europe.

Birds, unlike mammals, are rarely skinned because most have a layer of fat below the skin, which is desirable for its flavour and nutritional value (Chapter 11). Skins were removed only when they were to be used for clothing or for decoration, as discussed in Chapter 8. In those cases, skinning might leave cut marks on the skull (see Figure 14.10 in Chapter 14), but these have rarely been observed.

Once pottery vessels began to be used for cooking, it was necessary to butcher only the largest birds before cooking. With small- and medium-sized birds, the carcass is small enough to fit into a cooking pot. Stewing rather than roasting over an open fire also leaves the flesh tender, so it may be unnecessary to use a knife to remove meat from the carcass. Certainly, cut marks are much less frequent in later periods than in the Palaeolithic.

By the Bronze Age the question arises whether cuts were made with metal or stone knives. The cut marks discussed here were on assemblages from prehistoric sites where metal tools were absent, so there was no ambiguity about the implements used, but after metal knives came into use in about the fourth millennium BC, either material may have been used. It is generally accepted that cuts made with flint knives have a blunt V-shaped profile, and those made with metal knives have

Table 6.4. *Number and per cent of cut marks on remains of snowy owl,* Nyctea (Bubo) scandiaca, *from the Upper Palaeolithic site of Bois-Ragot, France*

Element	NISP	NO	NO with cuts	% with cuts
Cranium	4	4	0	0.0
Mandible	5	5	0	0.0
Vertebrae (total)	55	55	0	0.0
Synsacrum	6	6	0	0.0
Rib	0	–	–	–
Sternum	2	2	0	0.0
Coracoid	23	23	8	34.8
Scapula	14	14	8	57.1
Furcula	0	–	–	–
Pelvis	8	8	0	0.0
Humerus	80	79	37	46.8
Ulna	48	46	35	76.1
Radius	78	76	37	48.7
Ulnar carpal	13	13	4	30.8
Radial carpal	0	–	–	–
Carpometacarpus	33	33	8	24.2
Wing digit 2	0	–	–	–
Wing digit 3,1	3	3	0	0.0
Wing digit 3,2	2	2	0	0.0
Wing digit 4	0	–	–	–
Femur	41	41	12	29.3
Patella	0	–	–	–
Tibiotarsus	63	58	14	24.1
Fibula	8	8	1	12.5
Tarsometatarsus	25	25	6	24.0
Metatarsus 1	1	1	0	0.0
Phalanx I, 1	13	13	7	53.8
Phalanx I, 2	22	19	4	21.1
Phalanx Ii, 1	12	10	2	20.0
Phalanx Ii, 2	21	20	12	60.0
Phalanx Ii, 3	14	14	2	14.3
Phalanx Iii, 1	9	9	2	22.2
Phalanx Iii, 2	5	4	1	25.0
Phalanx Iii, 3	21	18	9	50.0
Phalanx Iii, 4	26	26	5	19.2
Phalanx Iv, 1	0	–	–	–
Phalanx Iv, 2	1	1	0	0.0
Phalanx Iv, 3	3	3	0	0.0
Phalanx Iv, 4	20	19	14	73.7
Phalanx Iv, 5	19	18	5	27.8
Penultimate phalanx	10	4	1	25.0
Ungual phalanx	2	1	0	0.0

Note: NO = NISP observed; an em dash indicates that the element was not analysed.
Source: Data are from Laroulandie (2000, tab. 73).

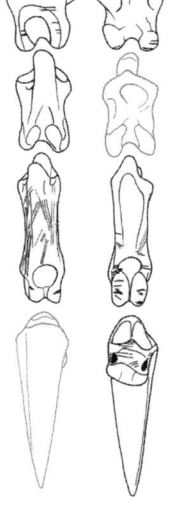
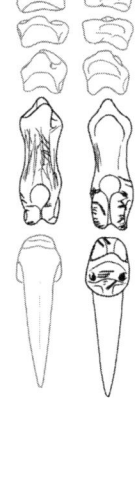

FIGURE 6.5. Location of cut marks on phalanges of snowy owl, *Nyctea (Bubo) scandiaca*, from Bois-Ragot, France. Unmarked phalanges and surfaces are outlined in grey (Laroulandie 2004).

a sharper profile. This distinction can be helpful, though it is now seen to be an oversimplification (Greenfield 1999).

Even after chopping tools came into use, cutting as well as chopping was used to prepare birds for cooking. In domestic chickens and in wild birds of a comparable size, cut marks are most often seen on the condyles of the distal tibia, presumably made when the muscle was cut from the bone (Figure 6.6). A peacock butchered at Carisbrooke, the medieval castle referred to in Chapter 4, had cut marks around the distal articulations of the tarsometatarsus, showing that the feet were removed from this large bird (Figure 6.7). Where the wing and feathers were saved for use, the wing was detached either at the elbow or wrist (carpometacarpal) joint, as discussed in Chapter 8. Removing meat from the bone during consumption also leaves cut marks: this is believed to explain the series of nicks or short cut marks below the head of several chicken femora from the Mid-Saxon town of Hamwic, present-day Southampton (Coy 1989).

CHOP MARKS

Once heavy metal knives and cleavers came into use, birds, like mammals, were sometimes butchered by use of crude chops as well as with knives. The area of the

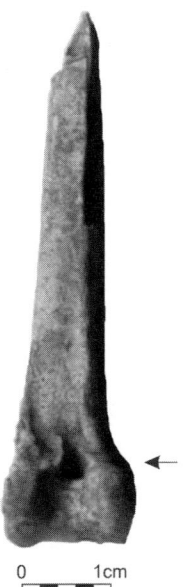

FIGURE 6.6. Distal tibiotarsus of a great auk, *Pinguinus impennis*, from Norse levels at Pool, Sanday, Orkney, with a cut mark (arrowed) on the condyle (photograph by D. Serjeantson).

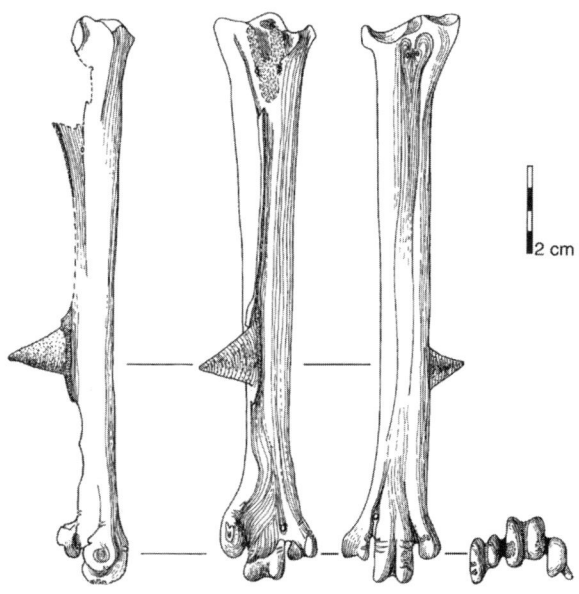

FIGURE 6.7. Tarsometatarsus of a peacock, *Pavo cristatus*, from Carisbrooke Castle with cut marks round the distal condyles (drawing by D. Webb).

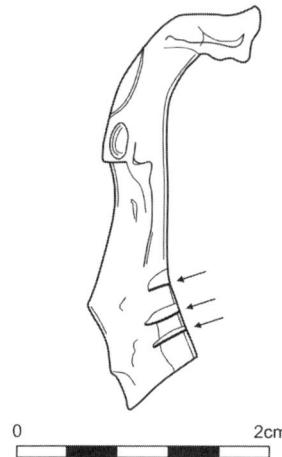

FIGURE 6.8. Butchered coracoid of a great auk, *Pinguinus impennis*, from the Iron Age site of Hornish, Outer Hebrides, Scotland. The bone shows three initial surface marks followed by a final chop (drawing by P. Copeland).

chop sometimes shows preliminary surface marks close to the final clean chop (Figure 6.8). The placing and number of chopping marks seen on the bird bones from Late Medieval deposits at St Gregory's Priory, Canterbury, are listed in Table 6.5. Those interpreted as resulting from preparing the bird for cooking (primary butchery) are distinguished from those deriving from consumption (secondary butchery). The chops most often seen were through the shaft of the tibiotarsus and the tarsometatarsus, which is typical of chicken butchery in all periods (Powell et al. 2001). If the wing was removed with a chop, the chop itself sometimes went through the humerus (see Figures 3.1 in Chapter 3 and 8.9 in Chapter 8). Chops used to divide a carcass for cooking or eating are seen mainly on large birds, such as the longitudinal chopping through the synsacrum seen on domestic geese from medieval Dublin (Figure 6.9; also see MacDonald et al. 1993).

Unlike with mammal bones, midshaft chops usually result from chopping the carcass into pieces rather than from exposing the marrow cavity. The large flightless landbirds are an exception; in this respect, as in many others, their treatment was more like that of mammals. At Hawksburn, an early Moa hunter site in the South Island of New Zealand, nearly half of the unburned tibiotarsi from the butchery area of the site had long spiral fractures; as this element in moa held the greatest quantity of marrow, these were presumably the result of marrow-fracturing chops (Anderson 1989b, 146).

The experimental butchery has clarified the origin of many cut marks, especially those made on small- and medium-sized birds in the Palaeolithic. However, as we

Table 6.5. *Number and location of chop marks observed on the bird bones from St Gregory's Priory, Canterbury, Kent*

Element	Location	P/S	GAL	ANS	ANA	LIM	PER	Total
Scapula	Through articulation	S	2	1	1		1	5
Humerus	Through distal articulation	P?		1		1		2
Radius	Midshaft	P?		2				2
Ulna	Through distal articulation	P	1					1
Coracoid	Midshaft	S	2	1				3
Furcula	Shaft	S		2				2
Synsacrum	Transverse	S	1					1
Femur	Through femoral head	S	1		1			2
Femur	Midshaft	S	2					2
Tibiotarsus	Midshaft	P	6	1	1			8
Carpometacarpus	Through proximal articulation	P	1	1				2
Tarsometatarsus	Through proximal articulation	P		1				1
Tarsometatarsus	Midshaft	P	3	1				4
Total			19	11	3	1	1	35

Note: P = primary butchery (chops presumed to result from preparing the bird for cooking); S = secondary butchery (chops deriving from consumption); GAL = chicken; ANS = domestic goose; ANA = ducks, *Anas* spp.; LIM = Godwit species, *Limosa* sp.; PER = grey partridge, *Perdix perdix*.
Source: Powell et al. (2001, tab. 53).

have seen, many cut marks remain unexplained. As Laroulandie has pointed out, cuts, breaks, and peeling are epiphenomenal; that is, the aim was not to leave marks on the bones but to get consumable products. Consequently, 'for a single processing pattern, modifications will not appear on all the bones' (Laroulandie 2005b, 28). This can be because different individuals approached the task in a different way or were more or less skilful in technique. People may have been dealing with fresh or preserved birds, and they may or may not have also wanted to recover wings and feathers.

The absence of cuts does not mean birds were not eaten, though it is rare to find an anthropogenic assemblage in which cut marks are totally absent. The absence of burning traces certainly does not mean that birds were not cooked, since even cooking

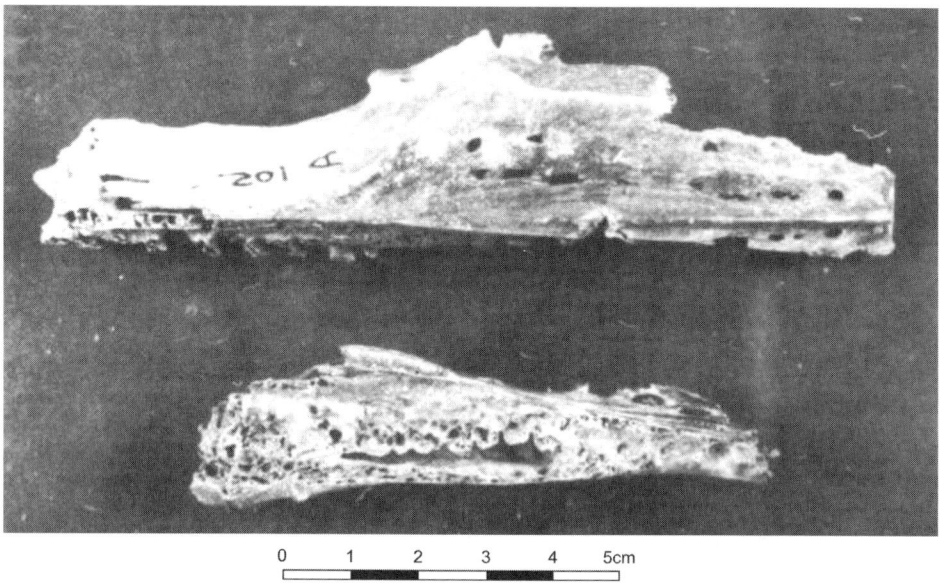

FIGURE 6.9. Butchered synsacra of domestic geese from medieval Dublin, chopped transversely (MacDonald et al. 1993; photograph by R. Hutton MacDonald).

over an open fire can be done without leaving traces on the bones. The contrasts between the incidence and location of cut and burn marks certainly suggests that butchery and consumption were influenced by cultural as well as directly economic influences.

BUTCHERY WITHOUT TOOLS

Birds can be dismembered without the use of knives or chopping tools. According to Thomas McGovern, fishermen in Iceland used to dismember puffins by pulling them apart (ZOOARCH archives 13 Oct 2004 – see Appendix 3). Laroulandie (2005a, 2005b) demonstrated the effect on the different bone elements of disarticulating the main joints, especially the wing joints, by bending and overextending the joint. Overextension of the elbow joint of partridges left a depression, perforation, or notch in the olecranon fossa of the distal humerus, caused by pressure from the olecranon process of the ulna. Perforations of this type were present on humeri of ptarmigan from La Vache (Figure 6.10), and similar notches were seen on the radius and ulna. Neither avian nor other mammalian predators dismember their prey by using this technique, so it is evidence of human activity.

'Peeling' of the bone surface at the articulation is further evidence of the disarticulation of bird carcasses by pulling them apart (Laroulandie 2005b). Some

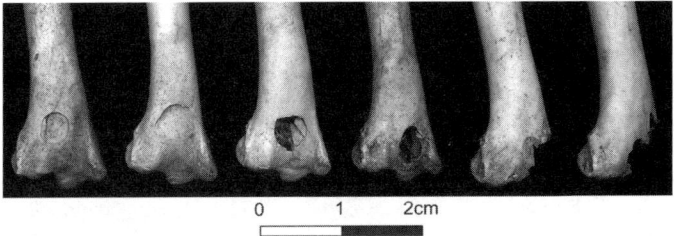

FIGURE 6.10. Notches and perforations in the olecranon fossa of humeri of grouse, *Lagopus* sp., from the Palaeolithic site of La Vache, France, made by overextending the joint to disarticulate the wing (Laroulandie 2005a, fig. 3.4; photograph by V. Laroulandie).

ligaments adhere so firmly to the bone that when they are put under strain as the joint is disarticulated, some of the bone surface is peeled off. Personal experience with the preparation of skeletons for a comparative collection has shown that this is most likely between the bones of the scapular girdle (scapula, coracoid, proximal humerus), and also between the bones of the wing (distal humerus, proximal ulna). Bone peeling is always adjacent to the zone of fragmentation of the articular end, and the articulation itself may be damaged or partially or totally removed (Figure 6.11). Laroulandie (2000) found examples of peeled bones at Combe Saunière and Bois-Ragot, and the same damage was reported on bones of the geese at Grotta Romanelli. As with notches, the presence of peeling on the wing bones confirms human intervention, even if it does not tell us whether the birds were dismembered for consumption or for obtaining feathers.

Damage to the olecranon process has been observed on the ulna of small birds, probably from where the wings were snapped off as the birds were prepared for cooking. There were a few examples on the ulnae of thrushes from St Gregory's

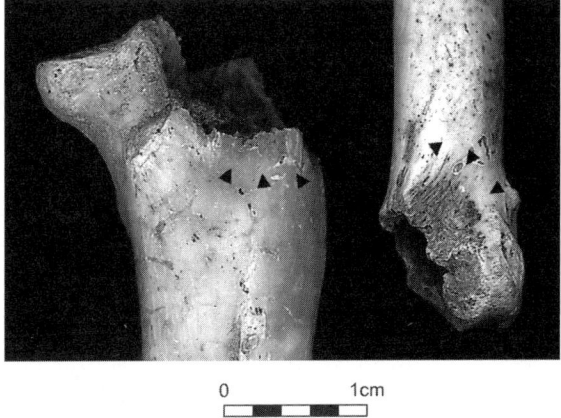

FIGURE 6.11. 'Peeling' marks (indicated by small arrows) on the proximal (left) and distal (right) articulations of a left ulna of snowy owl, *Nyctea (Bubo) scandiaca*, from Combe Saunière, France (Laroulandie 2000, fig. 112; photograph by V. Laroulandie).

146 BIRDS

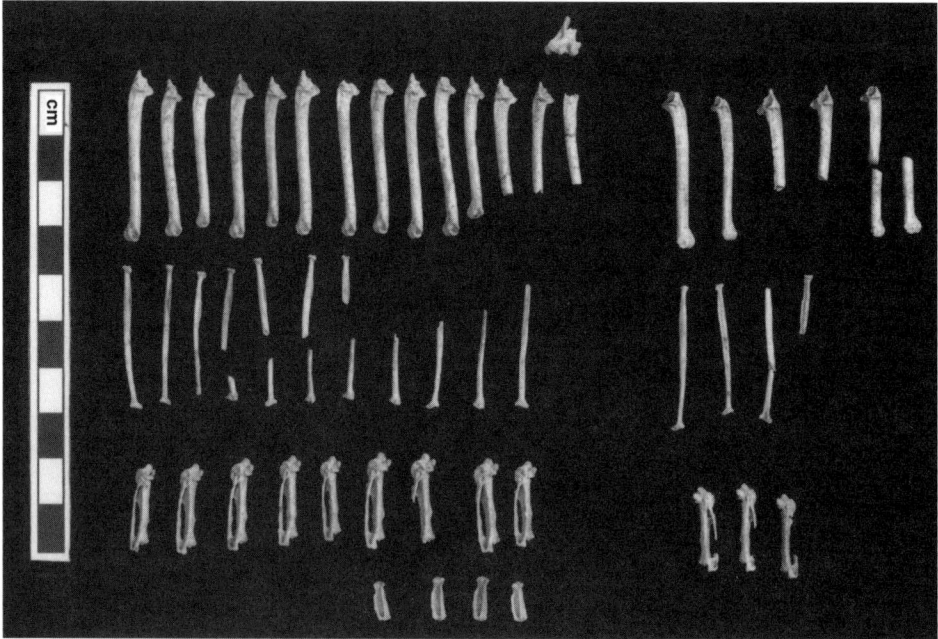

FIGURE 6.12. Wing bones of thrushes, Turdidae, from the garden of the house of Amarantus in Pompeii. The wings (MNI = 14) were snapped off, leaving a single fragment only of distal humerus and damage to the olecranon process of several ulnae (photograph by N. Bradford).

Priory, and similar damage was seen also on ulnae of thrushes (Figure 6.12) in the assemblage from the garden of the House of Amarantus in Pompeii (Powell 1995–1996). The intriguing assemblage from Pompeii is discussed later and in Chapter 14.

Most bird bones are small enough to be broken midshaft without the benefit of tools. Mammal bones, when broken fresh, show a spiral or helical fracture (Lyman 1994, 319). Weisler and Gargett (1993, fig. 3), after experimentally fracturing bird bones, found that the breaks were approximately spiral though the spiral fracturing was less marked than in mammal bones. The spiral fractures caused by fresh breaks can be distinguished from later breaks in dry bone, which have a straighter fracture angle, a combination of oblique and irregular offsets, as in dry mammal bones (Mannermaa & Stora 2006).

HUMAN CHEWING

In the days when people in Europe ate small songbirds, they consumed the body minus wings and head whole, bones and all (Serjeantson 2001). Evidence for the

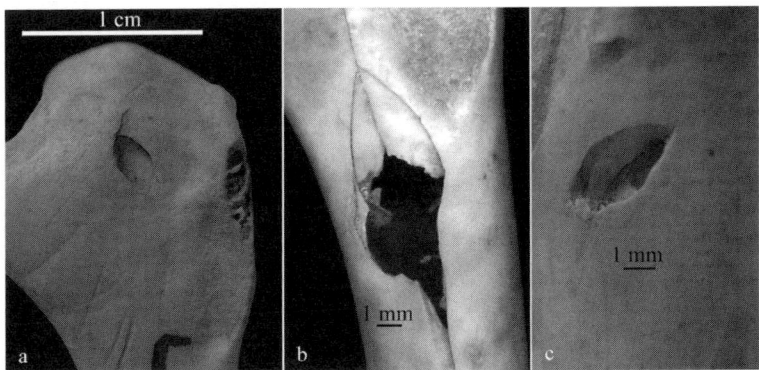

FIGURE 6.13. Holes in the humeri of grouse, *Lagopus* sp., from La Vache, interpreted as human bite marks. They are distinguished from carnivore gnawing and beak marks by the oval shape and associated crushing (Laroulandie 2005b, fig. 3.7; photograph by V. Laroulandie).

eating of bones is sometimes found in coprolites, which sometimes survive in arid environments. Some in Lovelock Cave, discussed later, contained fragments of bones of American coot.

With larger birds, people damage bones accidentally when eating the birds and also chew bird bones for the same reason as do carnivores and some of the raptors: so that they can eat the marrow and the fat within them. Some intrepid researchers have experimented with chewing bird bones and recording the marks. The puncture marks made by human incisor teeth when a person is eating wings and legs with meat on (Figure 6.13) should be distinguishable from carnivore gnawing and beak marks by their oval shape and by associated crushing (Laroulandie 2005b).

Chewing bird bones for marrow has been reported among communities in the Pacific Northwest and from Polynesia (Wigen & Stucki 1988; Weisler & Gargett 1993); archaeological evidence shows that it was once more widespread. As Weisler and Gargett (1993, 88) noted, a quarter of the bones from nine sites on the island of Moloka'i in Hawaii were broken at one or both ends: 'The breaks have a ragged, irregular edge often associated with one or more longitudinal cracks. Sometimes the cross-section of the bone appears compressed'. These authors suspected that this damage might have resulted from consumption by humans, so they experimented with consuming various birds and chewing the bone articulations and reported that they were able to replicate attributes of the archaeological sample.

Long bones with the articular ends broken in the manner described have been observed in other assemblages. Many of the humeri and ulnae of gulls from sites in Greenland have broken articular ends which appeared to have been bitten off (Figure 6.14). Examples were found on sites of all periods from 1900 BC to AD 1600

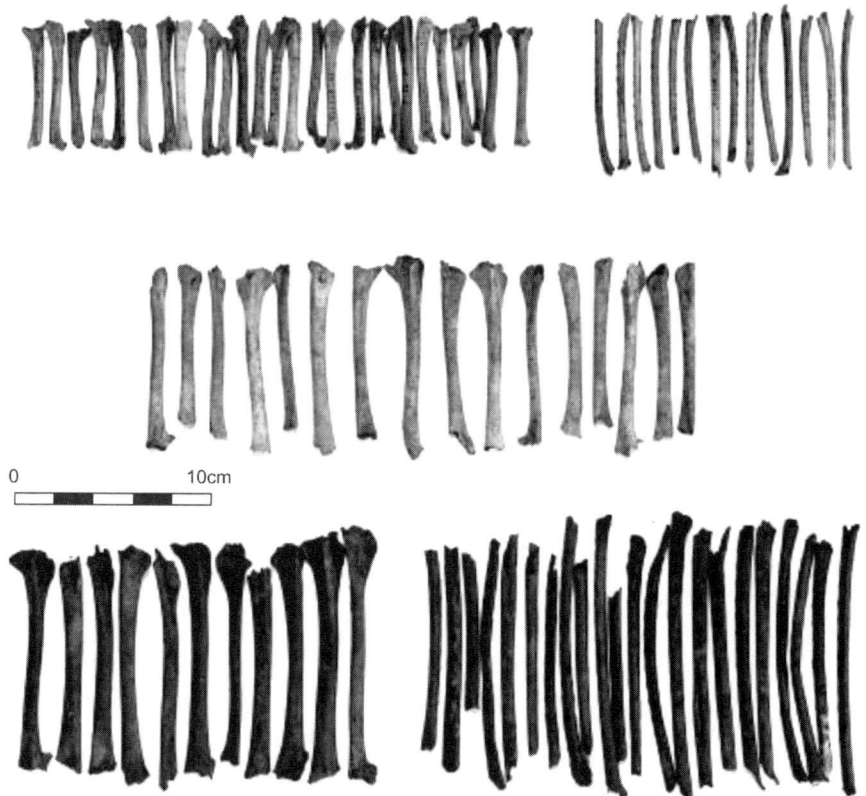

FIGURE 6.14. Gull remains from Greenland sites with articulations broken or bitten off, apparently chewed by humans (Gotfredsen, 1997). The top section shows humeri and ulnae of kittiwake, *Rissa tridactyla*, from Orkrusset; the middle shows humeri of Iceland gull, *Larus glaucoides*, from Qoormoq; the bottom shows humeri and ulnae of glaucous gull, *L. hyperboreus*, from Qajaa (photograph by G. Brovad).

(Gotfredsen 1997). Many of the radii and ulnae from sites in Patagonia were also chewed or crunched 'to consume the cartilaginous epiphysis and marrow content' (Lefèvre & Pasquet 1994). Over 80 per cent of the articular ends of the wing bones of the gulls from the Neolithic settlement of Tofts Ness in Orkney had damaged ends (Table 6.6) which were also thought to result from chewing (Serjeantson 2007b). Though some elements also had midshaft breaks, these by contrast were straight, 'dry', rather spiral fractures, so they were thought to be post-depositional. Chewed bone extremities have also been recorded on Palaeolithic sites in France, including Grotte de Bourouilla in the Pyrenees and Morin in the Gironde (Gourichon 2002).

Higgins (1999) questioned whether the Greenland bones were deliberately damaged for marrow extraction, basing her view on the analysis of a skeleton of a double-crested cormorant in which she found little marrow in the radius and ulna.

Table 6.6. *Incidence of damaged articular ends of radii and ulnae of gulls, from Tofts Ness, Sanday, Orkney*

Condition	n	%
Complete, both ends intact	2	3.7
Broken midshaft, end intact	18	18.9
Subtotal undamaged	20	13.4
Complete, one end damaged	7	13.0
Complete, both ends damaged	45	83.3
Broken midshaft, end damaged	77	81.1
Subtotal damaged	129	86.6

Note: The gulls included great black-backed gull, *Larus marinus*, together with herring gull, *L. argentatus*, or lesser black-backed gull, *L. fuscus*, or both. The damage was interpreted as human chewing. The midshaft breaks were mostly post-depositional.

Source: Data are from Serjeantson (2007b).

What marrow was present was 'thin in consistency and low in fat content', so she thought that the damage on the Greenland material must be natural. However, the fact is that this is not typical of natural damage. In most assemblages the articular ends are *not* broken open in this way. The damage has no obvious function in removing feathers or muscle. As we have seen, overextension of the joint to disarticulate the bones of the wing also produces some crushing and loss of the bone ends, but the damage pattern is different and does not destroy the ends of the bones (see, e.g., Figures 6.10 and 6.11). The damage does have similarities with the chewing illustrated in Chapter 5 in Figure 5.15, which is thought to be by dogs, but the bone ends were less 'crenulated' as defined by Binford (1981, 61). The bones were clearly chewed purposefully at the Greenland sites and also at Tofts Ness and elsewhere. It may be that in these communities every source of food, however small, was exploited. It is probably not a coincidence that the damage has most often been observed in marginal environments where food was limited.

BURNING

The burning of bones, including bird bones, is almost invariably the result of human actions. Occasionally, in a dry environment, bones are burnt by spontaneous fires (Lyman 1994), but this is extremely rare. Bones are also sometimes attacked by a black fungus (see Chapter 5), which can be confused with charring, but where a fungus is involved, the black areas are located in arbitrary positions on the bones and do not show the gradations in colour found in charring associated with cooking and other fires. 'Burning' can describe charring, calcining of bone until it is white in colour, or any stage in between (Lyman 1994, 384–392). The activities which produce the different degrees of burning tend to have quite different aims or origins, so it is important to distinguish the different types.

Calcination

Bones become fully calcined at about 600° C (about 1,100° F), but they show signs of partial calcining if they are exposed to lower temperatures for any length of time. When burnt, bones lose organic matter and shrink in size and change colour. The colour changes are not fully consistent with changes in temperature, but in general calcined bone is white, blueish-white, or grey in appearance, while bones charred from a briefer contact with fire are partially burned, with charred areas varying from brown to dense black.

In one experiment, chicken bones exposed to a fire in a pit and added to fuel in an earth oven which reached at least 500° C became white or grey. In addition, joints were disarticulated and the bones became very fragile. The only element which remained in one piece was a femur (Spenneman & Colley 1989). This experiment confirmed that bird bones may become calcined and not just charred if discarded into a very hot domestic fire. It also confirmed, as might be expected, that heavily burnt bone is very prone to fragmenting.

Moa bones were sometimes deliberately used as fuel. A collection of bone from Hawksburn, found near a group of ovens, had been very heavily burnt. At this butchery site, the meat was cooked in ovens and the bones used as fuel. They were fragmented into what was described as 'bone gravel' (Anderson 1989b, 144–147).

Bones placed on a sacrificial fire become calcined, as do those placed on a pyre as an accompaniment to human cremation. Head and foot bones of cockerels from the garden in Pompeii referred to earlier were calcined. They are thought to have been part of a sacrificial deposit. Cremated animal bones from cemeteries also become calcined. At the Late Iron Age cemetery at King Harry Lane, St Albans, north of London, the remains of chickens and also pigs were calcined to a grey colour, fragmented, and reduced in size just as was the human bone (Davis 1989). Two wing bones of small shorebirds from an Early Medieval funeral pyre in the Netherlands were calcined to a grey colour (Prummel 1993).

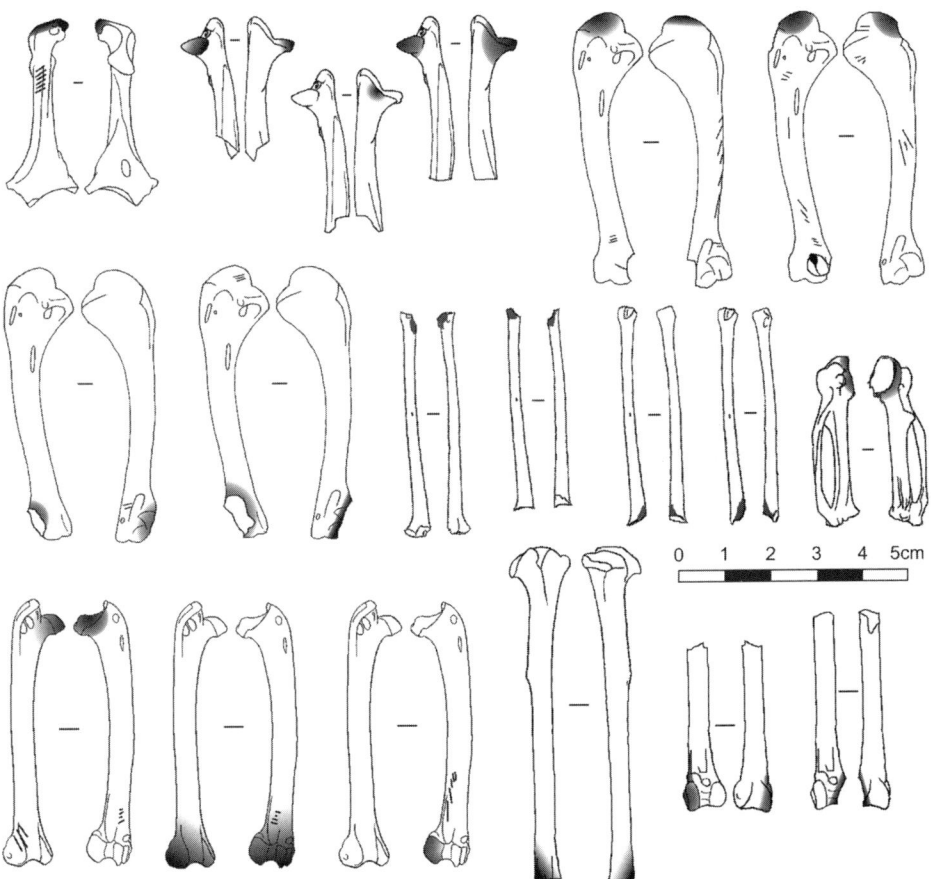

FIGURE 6.15. Location of traces of charring on bones from La Vache. The presence of burning traces on many elements suggests that portions of the carcass were cooked on hot stones or over the embers of an open fire (Laroulandie 2005a, fig. 16).

Charring

Contact with the heat of the fire caused the meat to shrink away from the bone, exposing the end to burning. Dawson (1969, 360) pointed out that Hildegarde Howard had recognised that 'Many of the broken limb bones [from Emeryville shellmound] are charred at the broken end'. At La Vache traces of charring were observed on the extremities of several elements of ptarmigan. To replicate this, Laroulandie cooked disarticulated portions on stones heated by the embers of a fire and found that this did cause burning localised on the articular extremities if the portions accidentally came into direct contact with the embers (Figure 6.15). In the experimental bones, the burnt ends were chestnut-brown or orange to black in colour (Laroulandie

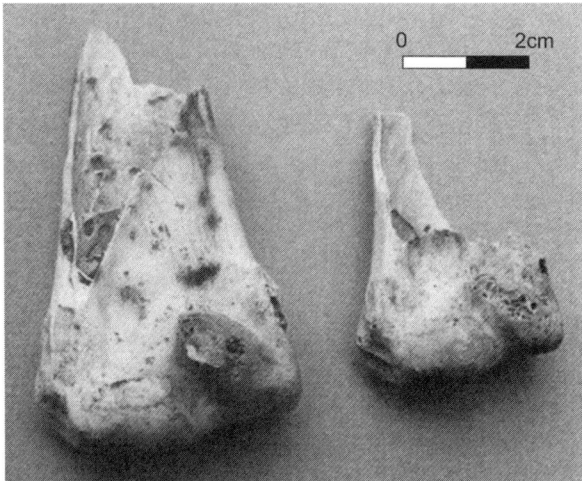

FIGURE 6.16. Charring on distal humeri of male and female great bustards, *Otis tarda*, from the Upper Palaeolithic levels in Klisoura Cave, Greece (Tomek & Bochenski 2002, fig. 2).

2001). The location of the marks of burning on the bones from La Vache indicated that portioned carcasses were cooked at the site after the wings had been removed. The areas which were burnt showed that some wings were cooked with the humerus attached and others without it (Laroulandie 2005a). Charring on the humeri of the great bustards from the Palaeolithic cave at Klisoura in Greece shows that these large birds were also disarticulated and cooked by contact with an open fire (Figure 6.16).

Several other Palaeolithic cave sites show systematic traces of charring in the bird bones. At Grotta Romanelli, out of 5,821 humeri studied, one third showed traces of burning at the proximal end. The damage ranged from slight charring in some to others where fire had destroyed the articulation. The pattern was reasonably consistent between the main food species: 38 per cent of the humeri of the little bustard are burnt in this fashion, 22 per cent of the great bustard, 36 per cent of anserine geese, and 37 per cent of *Branta* species (Cassoli & Tagliacozzo 1997, tab. 1). It was clear that both large and small birds had been cooked in the same way. This contrasted with the raptor bones from the site, which were less affected: fewer than 5 per cent of the humeri of eagles, falcons, and owls were burned (Cassoli & Tagliacozzo 1997). A swan from a Mesolithic site in the Netherlands also appears to have been cooked on an open fire. At the temporary camp site of Bergschenhoek, the remains of a small fire were found behind a windbreak, and associated with it were bird and mammal bones including part of a skeleton of a Bewick's (tundra) swan which was partly burnt. As the burning was on the trunk, it suggested that the bird had been roasted whole on the fire (Clason & Brinkhuisen 1993).

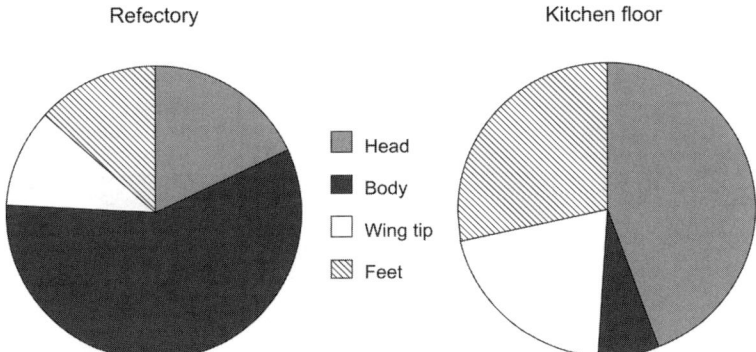

FIGURE 6.17. Relative numbers of elements of thrushes, Turdidae, and other passerines from two deposits at St Gregory's Priory, Canterbury. Elements from the body predominate in the refectory, where meals were taken, and elements from the head, wing tips, and feet predominate in the kitchen, where the food was prepared (Powell et al. 2001, fig. 240).

Traces of charring on the bone extremities are the best evidence for cooking. They have been seen mainly on sites of hunter-gatherers, as they are diagnostic of cooking done over an open fire. However, at some Upper Palaeolithic sites with otherwise similar environments, evidence for burning is absent, so even in the Palaeolithic era it was possible to cook birds – and other animals – without leaving traces on the bone (Laroulandie 2005a). Most later cooking methods are undetectable: cooking in earth ovens leaves few or no traces (Steadman et al. 2002), and neither does boiling, stewing, or roasting in enclosed ovens.

Probably the most usual reason for finds of burnt bones is that they were thrown on to a fire to clean up the living space. This was the explanation for the burnt bones of seabirds from Quebrada Tacahuay (deFrance 2005). A surprisingly large number, more than half, of the elements of rock dove from Qumran Cave 24 were reported as burnt. They were certainly associated with human activity, as some elements had cut marks (Recchi & Gopher 2002). No consistent pattern was reported, so these presumably were bones thrown on to a fire.

DIFFERENTIAL DISPOSAL

Butchery methods are also revealed when parts of the body are disposed of in different areas of a settlement. One of the deposits in which thrush remains were found at St Gregory's Priory was an area of the kitchen floor. It comprised almost exclusively elements from the head, wings, and feet, which must be waste from food preparation (Figure 6.17). This suite of elements contrasts with the remains

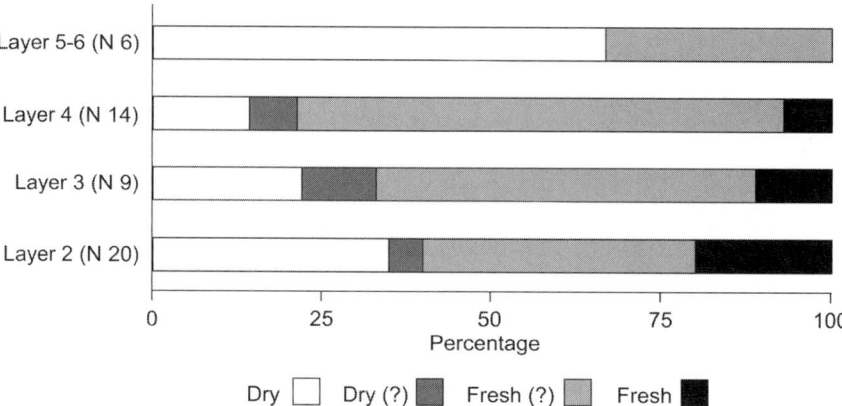

FIGURE 6.18. Percentages of dry and fresh fractures on the bird bones from the lowest layer (2) to the uppermost layers (5–6) at Ajvide, a Neolithic site on the island of Gotland in the Baltic Sea (Mannermaa & Storå 2006, fig. 8).

from the refectory, where food was eaten, which were mostly from the body. It also contrasts with the elements of thrush inside a pot recovered from Roman Nijmegen (Chapter 10), where the only elements present were from the body and proximal wing. Two deposits at Carisbrooke Castle showed a similar contrast (see Figure 4.12 in Chapter 4). Tarsometatarsi were the most frequent element in a ditch deposit, presumably waste from preparing the birds for cooking, while the rest of the carcass was present in more equal numbers in a midden deposit, presumably dumped there after consumption.

FRAGMENTATION

The types of breakage discussed up to now were deliberately inflicted to disarticulate the bird and to cook and eat it. These only involve midshaft breaks when the wing or foot was removed. Many, perhaps most, of the breaks observed in bird bones are probably post-depositional, the result of trampling, sediment movement, and sediment compaction. This was demonstrated in the midden material at the Neolithic site of Ajvide on Gotland. The percentage of breaks identified as fresh declined from the lowest to the highest levels, with the percentage of 'dry' breaks highest in the uppermost level (Figure 6.18; also see Mannermaa & Storå 2006). Because so much fragmentation is post-depositional, fragmentation patterns in bird bones do not show clear distinctions between natural and anthropogenic assemblages. The degree of fragmentation, together with surface damage, is probably informative only of the absolute amount of damage which the assemblage has suffered from all sources.

RECORDING MODIFICATIONS

The research discussed in this chapter has relied on the fact that bone modifications were recorded consistently. The analyst has two possibilities. Modification can be sketched on the outline of a bone (as in Figure 6.4), something which is now feasible with computer recording as well as manuscript. One can elaborate on this by depicting a single cut mark, for example, and recording the number or percentage observed next to each cut mark, as was done to illustrate the pattern of cut marks at the site of Taï 2 (Figure 6.3). Alternatively, one can record the nature and location of modifications by using codes and then quantifying them, but for this bone zones have to be identified. We saw in Chapter 4 how bone zones are used to record which parts of an element are present. If the Cohen and Serjeantson zones are used (see Appendix 2), a further code is needed to indicate whether it is the cranial or caudal side of the bone which has been modified. Figure 6.1 shows the codes which were used for recording cut marks on the humeri from Grotta Romanelli and Grotta della Madonna. They distinguish the caudal and cranial aspects of the bone and allow for cuts in nine zones along the length of the bone, 'a' to 'i'. This allowed great precision in identifying the location of cuts on the longer elements.

Discussion

Traces on the bones themselves are the least equivocal evidence for the origin of an assemblage or an individual bone, but as these are rare on many sites, researchers in the 1980s turned to relative numbers of wing and leg bones to investigate whether the presence of certain elements and the absence of others indicates whether or not an assemblage was anthropogenic (Mourer-Chauviré 1983; Ericson 1987).

ELEMENT PRESENCE OR ABSENCE AND BONE DENSITY

Ericson (1987) made the assumption that different parts of the carcass were given differential treatment in cooking, and that this would be reflected in the elements discarded. He was concerned specifically with the wild birds from the well-known Mesolithic and Neolithic 'kitchen middens' or shellmounds on the shores of the Baltic: coastal shellmounds, as we saw in Chapter 5, potentially contained material of mixed origin. The ratio was calculated of the bones from the anterior extremity, humerus, ulna, and carpometacarpus, to those from the posterior extremity, the femur, tibiotarsus, and tarsometatarsus. The radius was excluded to make the number of bones from the extremities equal. Ericson assumed that, in a natural assemblage, the elements would be present in the ratio 1:1. The shellmound assemblages were compared with natural dune deposits and human midden material, with chickens and geese analysed separately. In the natural deposits the bones of the wing predominated over those of the leg, ranging from more than twice as frequent to four times as frequent, whereas leg bones dominated in the domestic fowl and geese. In the kitchen middens the wing bones predominated, as in the natural material, which raised the serious possibility that many of the remains were unrelated to human activities. This conclusion contradicted the generally accepted interpretation of the remains in the shell middens as mainly anthropogenic. Ericson did suggest some other explanations, including the possibility that a ratio of 1:1 between wing and leg bones might not be expected if density and potential for survival was not equal.

The method was taken up by Livingston, who compared numbers of wing and leg elements from two sites in western Nevada, Lovelock Cave and Humboldt Lakebed. Lovelock Cave was used by people as a 'storage facility for caching food, raw materials and personal effects; [it was] a place of burial, and may have been the locus of short-term residential occupation' (Livingston 1989, 538). However, raptors, coyotes, packrats, bats, and pigeons also lived in and used the cave, so these had contributed to or disrupted the faunal materials that accumulated there. The remains of the small animals, including the teal, were thought to have come from raptor pellets, as they, like the many rodent and small mammal remains in the cave, exhibited characteristic raptor damage. The other birds, which were mainly coots, medium-sized ducks, mallards, and grebes, were thought to be human prey. This was confirmed from the fragments of bird bone in the coprolites which survived in the cave, and by finds of decoy ducks and nets which confirmed that wildfowl had been deliberately hunted. The percentage of anterior elements for Lovelock Cave and Humboldt Lakebed was 48.4 and 48.8 per cent across all avian taxa, not significantly different from the expected 50 per cent. However, when the species were calculated separately, the percentage of wing bones of the grebes and the coots was significantly lower than the expected 50 per cent and the percentage for medium-sized dabbling ducks was significantly higher (Table 6.7). The survival pattern for diving ducks was more like that of the coots. According to Livingston (1989, 543) 'The pattern can more readily be interpreted in terms of the morphology of taxa as expressed in the relative robusticity of the two sets of extremities'. Furthermore, the teal from the Humboldt lake sites, which were anthropogenic in origin, had a preponderance of wing elements (74 per cent) just as did those from the cave (81 per cent), which were from raptor pellets. Livingston believed that survival could best be explained by the feeding and escape

Table 6.7. *Ratio of anterior to posterior elements from Lovelock Cave and Humboldt Lakebed Site, Nevada*

Bird	Lovelock Cave		Humboldt Lakebed	
	NISP	Ratio	NISP	Ratio
Podicipedidae				
Podilymbus podiceps	89	24.0	22	59.1
Podiceps nigricollis	36	47.2	14	64.5
Aechmophorus occidentalis	28	25.2	50	28.0
Anatidae				
Geese	15	66.7	25	62.7
Anas spp. (teal size)	362	81.2	46	73.9
Anas spp. (medium size)	167	62.3	75	72.0
Anas platyrhynchos	161	86.5	22	86.4
Aythya valisineria	6	83.3	23	65.2
Aythya (medium size)	31	48.4	79	46.8
Bucephala albeola	16	37.5	5	40.0
Oxyura jamaicensis	23	43.5	63	65.1
Rallidae				
Large rails	750	42.1	786	39.2

Note: Anterior elements are the humerus, ulna, and carpometacarpus; posterior elements are the femur, tibiotarsus, and tarsometatarsus. The percentage of wing bones of the grebes and the large rails (mainly coots) was lower than the expected 50 per cent and the percentage for medium-sized dabbling ducks was significantly higher.

Source: Data are from Livingston (1989).

behaviour of the birds. Dabbling ducks and geese escape by flying up directly from the water, so they should have stronger wing bones. Diving ducks and coots, which feed in deeper water, escape by 'spattering' with the legs before flying or by diving, so they should have relatively stronger leg bones. The element ratios at the two sites did fit the predicted model.

Bovy (2002), like Livingston, set out to investigate the relationship between survivorship and functional anatomy. She analysed wing-to-leg ratios in assemblages from the Pacific Northwest Coast, comparing element survival between albatrosses, dabbling ducks, gulls, auks, and diving ducks. These were also discussed in relation to whether they predominantly used flying or diving as their main means of escape. Four of the assemblages discussed were clearly strongly affected by human selection: the main wing bones (humerus, ulna, and radius) were scant or absent at British Camp (Figure 6.19), Watmough Bay, and Whalen Farm in the Gulf of Georgia and

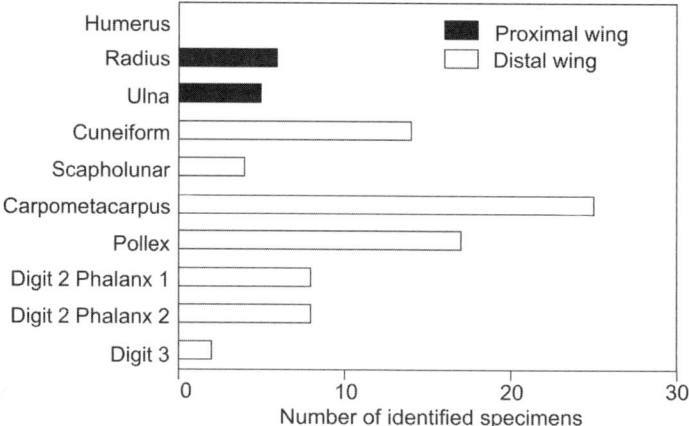

FIGURE 6.19. Frequency of wing elements of aquatic birds from British Camp, San Juan Islands, Washington State (redrawn from Bovy 2002, fig. 3).

Maple Bank on the southern tip of Vancouver Island. (As discussed in Chapter 9, the absence was probably because these elements were curated or traded for tool use.) This cultural bias invalidates the results from these sites, but the findings from the remaining assemblages with less biased element distributions showed that survival did *not*, as Livingston had concluded, reflect the preferred means of locomotion. Wing bones predominated in all the assemblages, especially in gulls, but also in all the other species studied. There was no contrast in the relative number of leg bones between diving birds and dabblers.

The hypothesis that the bones of the wing survive best in flying birds and those of the leg in ground-living birds has been tested more effectively in bird bone assemblages from Patagonia, because these include species which use flight for locomotion, the rheas (Rheidae) which use walking exclusively, and the penguins, which use swimming exclusively. The bones of the wing predominated in the flying birds and the bones of the leg were less frequent even than those from the scapular girdle and axial skeleton at some sites. In the flightless ground birds the elements from the leg predominated, as might be anticipated. The relative numbers of wing and leg bones were approximately equal in the swimming birds (Cruz 2005).

Structural Density

For more than 30 years, zooarchaeologists have recognised the extent to which the density of different elements in mammals had an important effect on their survival in the archaeological record (Brain 1976; Binford 1981). The original density studies

Table 6.8. *Average bulk density for five skeletal elements of weak and strong flyers*

Element	Average bulk density (g/ml)
Aythya and Podicipedidae	
Humerus	0.93
Coracoid	0.84
Femur	0.82
Tibiotarsus	1.0
Tarsometatarsus	0.78
Anas	
Humerus	0.68
Coracoid	0.75
Femur	0.48
Tibiotarsus	0.72
Tarsometatarsus	0.43

Note: Weak flyers are *Aythya* spp. and Podicipedidae; and strong flyers are *Anas* spp.
Source: Data are from Higgins (1999, tab. 5).

on mammals were concerned with how gnawing by domestic dogs affected bones, but later work, which has confirmed and refined the original hypothesis, showed that similar patterns of bone survival can be produced by different mechanisms (Laroulandie 2005b). Recently, several authors have worked on the hypothesis that the density of the different elements in birds must also have had an influence on survival. Density can refer either to structural density or to the density of bones per unit area (Lyman 1994, 189–192, 235–258); here, it is the structural density with which we are concerned. Structural density denotes the ratio of the mass of a substance to its volume; it is defined as grams per cubic centimetre. As the porosity varies within a single bone, the 'true density' cannot be measured, so it is the 'bulk density' that is measured (Lyman 1994, 237).

Higgins (1999) analysed the bulk density of five elements (coracoid, humerus, femur, tibiotarsus, and tarsometatarsus) of 13 species of ducks and grebes. The bulk density was calculated by measuring the volume by water displacement and the mass. Species were grouped, following Livingston, as strong or weak flyers. The results suggested that the bones with the lowest density were the tarsometatarsi and femora in both weak and strong flyers and also that the density of the wing elements of the gracile-winged birds was actually higher than the density of the wing elements of the strong flyers (Table 6.8). This seemed to contradict Livingston's

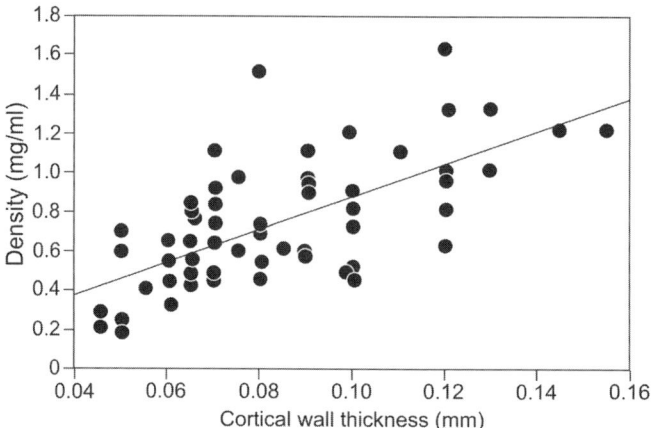

FIGURE 6.20. Regression of bulk density to cortical wall thickness for 65 duck and grebe species, *Aythya*, *Anas*, and Podicipidae (density = 0.06 + 8.02 × thickness; R^2 = 0.468; redrawn from Higgins 1999, fig. 4).

conclusion, and suggested that other factors had to be taken into account. Higgins also measured cortical wall thickness. The results, shown as a regression against bone density (Figure 6.20), suggest that the variation in bulk density can be explained – at least in part – by cortical wall thickness. The survival of the five elements in a series of assemblages from Túnel, the Patagonian shellmounds referred to in Chapter 4, fitted the predicted pattern insofar as the femur and tarsometatarsus, the least dense of the bones, were the least well represented. Otherwise findings were inconclusive.

Subsequently, densitometry has been used to derive bone mineral densities. The density of eleven elements of North American Galliformes was measured with a densitometer which had been developed for use with small animals, that is, a dual-energy X-ray bone densitometer (DEXA; see Dirrigl 2001, Dirrigl 2004). Densitometry studies of mammal bones in the past have measured scan sites; with birds it proved necessary to use a larger area of the bone to take into account pneumatisation and changes between trabecular and cortical bone, so 28 rectangular 'regions of interest' were defined on the articulations and shaft of the elements to be measured. The regions of interest were modified at the proximal or distal end of a bone to take into account irregular shape. The DEXA measures density in two ways, that is, areal bone mineral density (or BMDa g/cm^2) and density per unit volume (or BMDv g/cm^3), and there has been some debate about which is more relevant for archaeological comparisons. When applied to bird bones, the two methods gave very different results, both on absolute and relative measures (Dirrigl 2001). The bone shaft was found in general to be denser than the articular ends, but otherwise the rank order yielded by the two methods show little agreement.

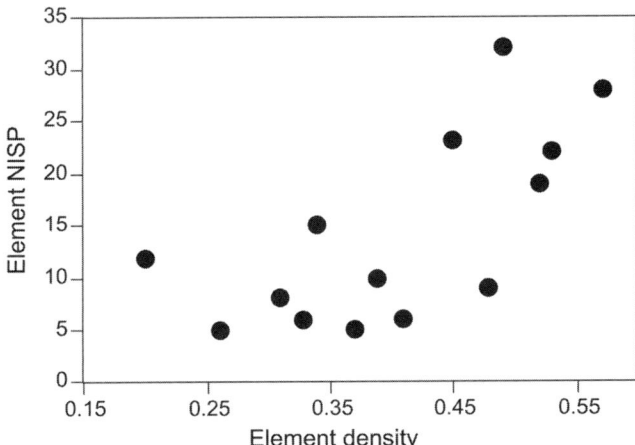

FIGURE 6.21. Relationship between number of elements and density (bone mineral content/volume) of duck remains from the Yerba Buena shellmound, San Francisco Bay (after Broughton et al. 2007, fig. 8).

A second analysis of bone density using a dual-energy X-ray machine which employed a dual-photon absorptiometric system presented values for cormorant, goose, and ducks. It provided density for whole elements rather than scan sites (Broughton et al. 2007). The bone mineral content was measured and bone volume calculated by the use of a water hydrostatic weighing method. Elements and portions of elements were then divided by bone volume to produce volume density (g/cm). The research was carried out to evaluate whether the taxonomic abundance in Emeryville and other San Francisco Bay shellmounds, and in particular the decline in geese and cormorants, could be explained by density-mediated attrition, so the focus was on the density of species as a whole as well as individual elements. The research showed that the elements of double-crested cormorant and the merganser, a diving duck, had significantly higher densities overall than those of the Canada goose and the dabbling ducks, whose skeletons had the lowest overall density. In ducks the relative number of elements present correlated with element density (Figure 6.21), but this was not consistent for other families.

Discussion

It is not at all clear whether bulk density, volume density, cortical thickness, size, or shape is the main influence governing resistance to decay in bird bones, since the experimental studies up to now have given unexpectedly inconsistent results. As a generalisation, the thin plate-like bones such as the sternum and skull are more vulnerable to crushing than the limb bones. Of the elements of the body, the coracoid, which is compact, also survives well. Most experimental and actualistic studies have confirmed that wing bones survive better than leg bones in flying birds and that in ratites and in the Galliformes, and other families which spend much of their life on the ground, the legs survive better – compare, for example, the skeletal parts of geese and cranes with those of francolin and chukar in Figure 8.8 in Chapter 8. This certainly suggests that functional anatomy plays a part at a simple level.

We might expect the survival of bird bones to be subject to the same processes of relative destruction as mammal bones, but, as we have seen, there are significant differences. Firstly, the smaller size of bird bones makes them more vulnerable to destruction, even if, as we saw in Chapter 5, the bone surface is initially more resistant to decay in the soil than that of mammal bones. The effect of dogs gnawing is reasonably well understood so far as mammal bones are concerned, but, as discussed in Chapter 5, it is observed mainly on the bones of large birds. With mammal bones, the degree to which bones are consumed is related to the presence of marrow combined with relative density, but in birds there are no strong differences in the quantity of marrow between elements and no element in the bird skeleton is dense enough to cause a dog to lose interest. The survival pattern of the scavenged coots trapped in the ice, discussed in the previous chapter, suggested that carnivores go first for the legs and leave the wings in whole birds, but this is doubtless because, unlike humans and raptors, they are unable to deal with the feathers.

CONCLUSIONS

Modifications

The many circumstances in which the origin of an assemblage of bird bones is ambiguous led Weisler and Gargett (1993) to claim that it is more important to confirm the anthropogenic origin of bird bones than of mammals and fish by seeking positive evidence for traces of human modifications. This was explicitly contested by Steadman and colleagues (2002), who demonstrated that the percentage of wild birds with cut marks and burning, though low, was similar to the percentage of modified chicken bones, the latter undoubtedly anthropogenic. Steadman was certainly correct in pointing out that it is unusual for a high percentage of bird bones to have visible anthropogenic modifications, but the point that Weisler and Gargett make is important as a reminder that there are many sites where the origin of the bird remains is uncertain, and in this case visible modifications can be an important clue. As Steadman and colleagues argued, the absence of butchery marks does not necessarily rule out human exploitation, since, as we have seen, it is not necessary to use knives or choppers to butcher and eat birds. The use of scanning electron microscopy has the potential not only to illuminate whether or not there are cut marks on bones but also to show whether these were made with flint or metal tools. Cooking, too, may leave no evidence. In the absence of these positive signs, inferring human exploitation may rely on the absence of evidence for other predators or a natural origin for the bones. Other criteria listed in Table 6.1 such as species, age, and associated material all contribute to the interpretation. The presence or absence of elements can only be used with caution, as we have seen.

Thanks in a large degree to the experimental research of Laroulandie, we can now often identify the function of a particular cut mark, but it is still an enigma why some assemblages have a high percentage of visible cut marks and others have few. One reason may be differences between observers and, crucially, may depend on whether or not elements are examined with a lens, but this certainly does not account for the great variation which has been noted. Future research might profitably explore the effect of carcass freshness on the quantity and type of cuts. The fact that cuts seem to be most frequent on Palaeolithic assemblages and on those from sites in high latitudes may be because birds were disarticulated before they were cooked, and perhaps were even dried or frozen at the time that they were butchered. Since the feathers have to be removed before cooking, the wing was often removed, so it is worth looking for evidence of where it was disarticulated and whether this was done using cuts or was pulled off, leaving perforations or peeling. Bones with random marks of burning and calcining, when they are not from a cremation, are probably from a domestic fire, so tell us little, but charred bone ends can suggest the cooking method. The consumption of marrow from bird bones is evidenced not from a pattern of chop marks, as with mammals, but by chewing of the bone ends.

Element Survival

In a temporary or permanent settlement where dogs have gnawed the mammal bones, we should expect them to have eaten bird bones as well, but the effect of this on anatomical distribution is unclear. While they may ignore wings with feathers attached, dogs are as likely to eat the wing bones as other parts of the carcass if the feathers have been plucked.

So far as the relative survival of the different elements is concerned, it does seem clear that it is quite usual for the humerus to be the most frequent element in an assemblage of wild birds, so this alone is not diagnostic of the activity which led to the formation of the deposit. A predominance of wing elements may result from density mediated survival, but it may also represent wings collected for use. It is also characteristic of the remains left by certain raptors, as discussed in Chapter 5. Equally, the absence of carpometacarpi, skulls, and feet may be a function of natural attrition of these small and fragile elements, but in a well-preserved assemblage their absence may indicate that the birds were dressed elsewhere. In both cases, the interpretation depends on other factors such as the species, the other elements present, and on whether the assemblage has suffered post-depositional damage (Table 6.1).

Where the anatomical distribution is highly skewed other than towards the main wing bones, it is always worth seeking an explanation. This pattern can be produced by humans, as with the tarsometatarsi in the Carisbrooke Castle ditch, or the carpometacarpi in the Pacific West Coast sites, but it can also be produced by other predators, as for example the predominance of sterna of black grouse below the roost of a golden eagle discussed in the previous chapter.

As we saw in the previous chapter, assemblages tend towards equifinality, whether generated by people or by other predators, especially when later destructive processes are severe (Pike-Tay et al. 2004). Many processes result in the same end pattern of element survival, even if the reason is uncertain. For the time being we have to rely on empirical studies of element survival to suggest what is and what is not the expected survival pattern when the whole carcass was originally present. Even in those cases where the breaks are mainly a consequence of natural damage (N-transformations), it does not mean that the birds were not exploited. And even when consumption by people has been established, the question still remains as to whether the birds were primarily killed for their feathers or tools, with meat the secondary aim. These questions will be explored in the chapters which follow.

7

Eggs and Eggshell

Today eggs are an important source of food all over the world, thanks to the prolific laying of domestic chickens. Collecting and eating the eggs of wild birds, on the other hand, which was once common among hunter-gatherers and some farming communities, has ceased in all but a very few parts of the world. A few communities avoid eating eggs altogether, probably because of their powerful associations with fertility (Simoons 1994, 163–167), but even these may use eggs in ritual contexts. In this chapter we shall investigate the circumstances which favoured collecting the eggs of wild birds as well as the contribution of the eggs of domestic birds to the food economy. The structure of eggshell and the methods which have been used to identify and quantify it are summarised. The shells of the large eggs of the ground-dwelling ratites such as the ostrich are large and robust, and we shall look at some of their uses as a raw material.

At least four aspects of the egg-laying and brooding behaviour of birds govern whether eggs may provide a regular source of food or just a casual snack: the size of the egg, the number per clutch, whether nests are colonial or solitary, and the accessibility of nests.

One egg of an ostrich, a cassowary, or a South American rhea provides a meal for a group of people. Darwin found that people were eating rhea eggs at the time of his visit to South America (Darwin 1897, 85), and ostrich eggs continue to be eaten in Africa, providing the equivalent of between 24 and 28 hens' eggs. The egg of the extinct elephant bird, the largest known, had a capacity of as much as 11 litres (Dewar 1984). Smaller eggs provided enough food for a group of people if the clutch contained a large number of eggs; species such as the wild red junglefowl, ancestor of the domestic chicken, and some of the partridges lay more than a dozen eggs in a single clutch. Where species breed in colonies a large number of eggs can be collected at once, even if the species in question laid only one egg. Breeding colonies have been the most significant source of wild birds' eggs in the past. It was clearly easier

166 BIRDS

FIGURE 7.1. Gathering eggs from the sea cliffs in Orkney, during the nineteenth century (photograph courtesy of the Orkney Library and Archive).

to gather eggs when the nests were in accessible places such as moorland or sand dunes, and no doubt it is for this reason that the eggs of terns, gulls, and plovers have always been sought after. It was much more difficult to collect the eggs when nests were in trees or on rock faces, though this inaccessibility was overcome by those who collected eggs from sea cliffs. Nests in marshy areas were easier to rob than those on sea cliffs, if harder than those on moors and dunes.

ETHNOGRAPHY AND HISTORY OF EGG-COLLECTING AND PRODUCTION

In a few parts of the world, including Iceland and the Faeroe Islands, the collection of wild birds' eggs is still an important economic activity; it was still widespread as recently as 100 years ago in other parts of Europe (Figure 7.1). Even at its peak, however, the consumption of the eggs of wild birds may never have matched that of the eggs of chickens and other domestic birds. Since chickens have been bred to have an extended laying season, their eggs have been an important part of the diet all over the world.

Egg Collection from the Wild

Seabirds have provided the most abundant source of eggs in the wild. On the Pacific Northwest Coast, the Tlingit used to travel to offshore islets in June to eat birds' eggs (Oberg 1980, 70). The eggs of the arctic tern were eaten by the Nunamiut, though the birds themselves were not eaten as they were too hard to catch (Nelson 1969, 166). The Maori took the eggs of the white-fronted tern (Crowe 2001, 74) and those of the sooty tern were eaten on the Seychelles (Love 2005). In the Faroe Islands the eggs of the arctic tern were a delicacy (Williamson 1948, 148). In the nineteenth century the eggs of a wide range of seabirds were eaten in the British Isles, especially in Orkney and Shetland, including those of the eider, razorbill, herring, and great black-backed gulls (Mudie 1835; Baldwin 1974; Fenton 1978; Hull 2001, 183–186). In the past, until it became extinct, the eggs of the great auk were gathered from the coastal skerries off Iceland where it bred (Grieve 1885); their eggs were collected and eaten or sold in May and June. In the Orkney Islands, eggs were collected in bags of sealskin or baskets. The best known community in the North Atlantic to exploit seabirds' eggs was on St Kilda, an isolated island group which lies 66 km off the west coast of Scotland. Here, eggs were collected from high cliffs around the islands which held huge colonies of gannets, fulmars, and puffins. These are some of the largest seabird colonies in the world. As few crops could be grown on the islands, one mainstay of the economic life was the barter and sale of seabird eggs as well as the birds themselves for grain.

There were several areas of northern Norway where seabirds and their eggs were taken for sale until the last century. Seabird areas there were divided into 'egg-og-dunvaer' (egg and down areas) and 'fuglefjell' (bird rocks or nesting cliffs). The egg-and-down areas were islands, islets, and skerries on which gulls, eiders, and other birds nested: most important for eggs were the three large gulls, great black-backed, lesser black-backed, and herring. Others whose eggs were taken included terns, geese, ducks, shags, cormorants, black guillemots, and oystercatchers (Bratrein 2005).

Inland, the nests of ducks and swans provided eggs in the greatest quantity. In Iceland even today, up to 10,000 duck eggs are collected each spring from around Lake Mývatn (McGovern et al. 2006). Many communities used to eat swans' eggs: they were eaten in Ancient Greece (Pollard 1977, 107) and are known to have been eaten in Kamchatka, Iceland, and the Hebrides in the nineteenth century: 'those of the tame swan being esteemed in all countries where they can be procured' (Sibley 1794, 5, 135; Sinclair 1978). Historically, eggs of swans and other waterfowl were collected in the marshy Fenlands of England by men known as Fenland slodgers who used boats and sometimes stilts to reach the nests.

The collection of eggs from nests on the ground was often the job of women. The film *Atanarjuat*, which is based on Inuit life in the Canadian Arctic, shows the women with babies and small children collecting eggs in summer and bringing them back for the rest of the group to eat. However, taking the eggs of seabirds such as the auks and the kittiwake, which were laid on steep cliffs, was a very dangerous activity and was a task for men. A seventeenth-century account describes how the men of St Kilda, terrifyingly expert cliff climbers, used ropes of horsehair to scramble down the cliffs and collect the eggs as well as the birds themselves (Baldwin 2005).

In temperate regions, even with prolific wild birds, the breeding period is seasonal and short so the presence of eggshell on a hunter-forager site indicates that the site was occupied during that brief time of year. Even on St Kilda, where the egg-collecting season was prolonged, it lasted only from mid-March to July, covering the period when the gannets, puffins, and fulmars were brooding. However, eggs can be stored. In Scotland and the Faroe Islands they were preserved for winter in peat ash or 'waterglass', which is peat ash and salt water (Williamson 1948, 146), just as hens' eggs were on the mainland. On St Kilda, those eggs which were not eaten immediately or exported were stored for the winter in 'cleits', which are circular stone structures with apertures open to the constantly blowing cold wind.

Sustainable Harvesting

Whether or not the collection of wild birds' eggs was sustainable depended partly on clutch size but mostly on how egg collecting was carried out. In some areas the practice was to leave one egg on the nest (Bratrein 2005). In Norway, eggs were gathered every third day, up to a certain date, after which the bird was left alone. In Orkney in the nineteenth century, when the farmers who owned the rights to the breeding grounds first found a nest they discarded all the eggs. The next day they returned and collected all the eggs laid that night, thus ensuring that the eggs were fresh. They then left the colony alone so that any further eggs were left to hatch (Fenton 1978). The species involved at this stage laid a further egg if the first was taken, but one reason for the decline of the great auk in the eastern Atlantic is that the expanding population of prehistoric farmers around the coast of the British Isles took the single egg which was laid each year. Eventually, there were no more birds to return and lay.

Domestic Birds' Eggs

With domestication, eggs were more readily available, and in Chapters 11 and 12 we shall examine the extent to which the domestic birds were kept for their eggs. As the eating of eggs became more common it brought great benefit to the diet, especially of the poorer sections of society. 'Next to milk production, egg protein is the most efficiently produced animal protein. An estimated 27 per cent of the plant protein fed to the chickens is converted into egg protein; that is about 180 kg of egg protein is produced from about 670 kg of feed protein' (Pimentel & Pimentel 1979, 55). These figures refer to egg production under modern conditions, but even in the past eggs were a source of protein available on a small scale which carried less cost than the eating of meat. In medieval Europe, hens' eggs were eaten in large quantities, especially in those households which followed the religious dietary rules for the avoidance of flesh meat on certain days (Harvey 1993). They were avoided only in Lent (see Figure 11.6 in Chapter 11), which conveniently coincides with the time of year when hens naturally lay few eggs. In the Middle Ages egg production reached almost modern levels: an anonymous English farming treatise of the thirteenth century says that hens should produce 122 eggs, and the fourteenth-century writer Walter of Henley gives a figure of 180 eggs per year (Stone 2006).

The presence of eggshell in archaeological deposits is a guide to whether eggs were eaten. Its presence on a settlement may also indicate that birds were being raised there. To establish whether chickens and other domestic birds were being raised for eggs, we are not restricted to finds of eggshell but can also examine the incidence of medullary bone, as discussed in Chapter 11. However, if we are to use the eggshell from archaeological sites to provide time depth to our understanding of egg collecting and of rearing birds for eggs, favourable conditions of survival are needed, together with careful recovery.

SURVIVAL AND RECOVERY OF EGGSHELL

Like bone, eggshell survives better in alkaline than acidic soils; it also survives in anaerobic and desiccated conditions. Being composed mainly of calcite, it is more liable to dissolution in the soil than bone and it is also more vulnerable to damage from trampling. Most archaeological finds have come from protected environments such as tombs, wells, pits, and ditches, though eggshell has also been found in the organic build-up of material on house and kitchen floors. Where eggshell survives, it is occasionally present in quantities large enough to be visible to the naked eye, as in the layers of kitchen floor at Eynsham Abbey in Oxfordshire (Woolgar et al. 2006, pl. 1.1), but usually pieces are so fragmentary that they are scarcely visible. Eggshell is normally recovered in samples retrieved by wet sieving. The mesh necessary for the recovery of eggshell is 2 mm or less, except where it has survived in very large pieces (Keepax 1981).

EGGSHELL STRUCTURE

The basic ovoid shape of an eggshell varies, with some eggs more spherical, some conical, and some biconical. The variations in size and shape are helpful to identification if a significant proportion of the shell survives, which it may do if the egg was originally intact. The colours and markings, so important in modern eggshell identification, occasionally survive in archaeological material and can be diagnostic. More useful for identification are the thickness and microscopic structure.

Eggshell is mainly composed of calcium carbonate in its stable crystallographic form, calcite, with an organic component. Other minerals such as phosphate and vaterite may also be present. In addition to the calcite, eggshell has an organic outer coating of protein, fat, and polysaccharides and a proteinaceous inner membrane. The inner membrane has a characteristic pattern at the time the egg is laid which is lost when shell resorption by the embryo begins to take place. Being organic, the inner and outer membranes do not survive in archaeological material, but membrane impressions have been observed (Keepax 1981; Sidell 1993; Mikhailov 1997).

The range of variation in the microstructure of eggshell can be seen in the reference atlas of micrographs (Mikhailov 1997) which was compiled originally with the aim of identifying relationships between avian families. Variations between the main bird families are shown as scanning electron micrographs and schematic diagrams. The interior or mammillary layer of the shell is a zone of columnar organic cones with basal caps. Crystals of calcite form from these cones, producing rounded tips. The mammillae form tightly packed columns. They grade into a continuous layer with a squamatic structure on an organic matrix of large membranes, fine fibrils, and vesicles. Outside this is the external zone, sometimes referred to as the palisade layer. Some shell shows a distinct boundary between these layers and some a more diffuse junction (Figure 7.2). The external zone has an outer compact crystalline layer, the cuticle, which is overlaid with a chalky cover or a covering of another

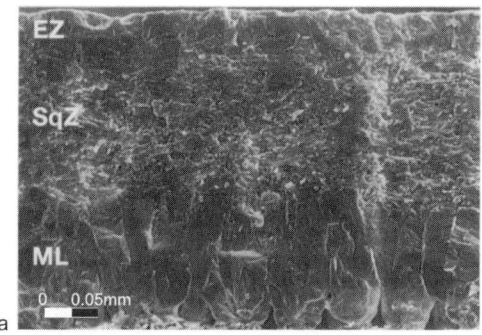
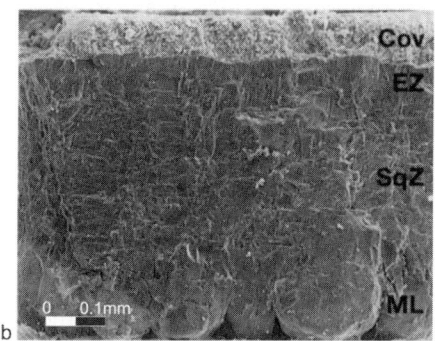

FIGURE 7.2. Scanning electron micrographs of a cross section through eggshell of a, turkey, *Meleagris gallopavo*, and b, greater flamingo, *Phoenicopterus ruber*, showing the mammillary layer (ML), the squamous zone (SqZ), the external zone (EZ), and the cover (Cov). The relative thickness of the layers differs between families (Mikhailov 1997, pls. 9A and 4F).

accessory material such as vaterite. This is microglobular in form. The layers are of variable thickness (Figure 7.3). The outer layers have usually been lost in archaeological material (Sidell 1993). Openings or pores between the mammillae allow the transfer of gases and water vapour. The pores continue through the shell (Figure 7.4) and are present as pore mouths at the outer surface of the eggshell. They can be simple or bifurcating. In fresh eggs they are plugged, but they usually exist as open pores in archaeological finds. Some of the variations in the relative thickness of the mammillary layer and the squamous zone are set out in Table 7.1, and those in the Cygninae, the Anserinae, and the Anatinae are shown schematically in Figure 7.3.

IDENTIFICATION AND QUANTIFICATION OF EGGSHELL

Eggshell from archaeological sites has been identified by a combination of methods. In recent eggs, size, shape, and colour are the best guides to identification. In archaeological finds of whole eggs, where colour survives poorly if at all, the size and

Table 7.1. *Thickness range and other characteristics of eggshell of some common families*

Family	Thickness range (μm)	CL:ML	EZ/SqZ	Traces of cover
Cygninae	350–700	2.5–4	0.1–0.2	present
Anserinae	200–520	1–2	0.1–0.2	present
Anatinae	180–310	2–3	0.2–0.5	not found
Tetraonidae	140–310	1–1.5	0.1–0.2	not found
Phasianidae	90–290	1–1.5	0.1–0.3	not found
Meleagrididae	320	1.5	0.1	?not found
Numididae	380	2.5	0.1	present

Note: CL:ML = ratio of continuous (squamatic) layer to mammillary layer; EZ/SqZ = ratio of external zone to squamous zone.
Source: Data are from Mikhailov (1997, 41).

shape can be compared to eggs of known species. In a series of whole eggs found on medieval sites in England, Keepax (1981) plotted the maximum length against the maximum diameter and compared these with domestic and some common wild birds to suggest possible identifications. One egg, from a castle in Otford in Kent, was within the size range for domestic goose, and the rest fell within the size range for chicken or small duck. Curvature as well as thickness has been used with large pieces of shell. In a study of the eggshell of extinct moa from New Zealand, curvature was measured with a surface gauge modified by the addition of two fixed probes. The result was converted to diameter width and length by use of a formula based on cylinder measurements (Gill 2000).

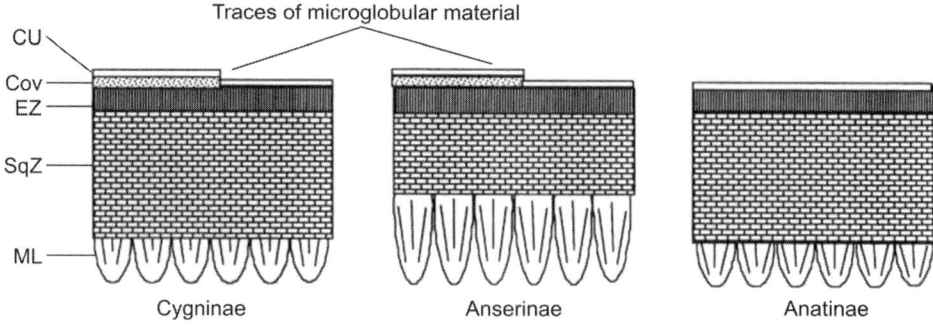

FIGURE 7.3. Diagrammatic radial cross section through eggshell of Cygninae, Anserinae, and Anatinae, showing relative thickness of the cuticle (Cu), external zone (EZ), squamous zone (SqZ), and mammillary layer (ML). Some species have traces of a microglobular chalky cover on the external surface of the shell (Mikhailov 1997, fig. 12).

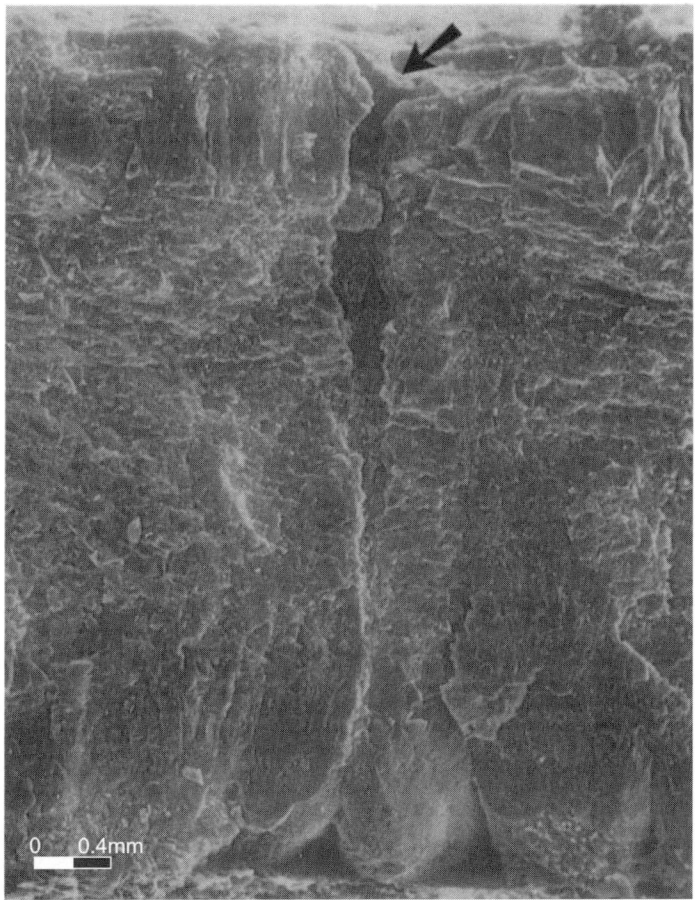

FIGURE 7.4. Scanning electron micrograph of a cross section through eggshell of a guillemot, *Uria aalge*, which is penetrated by a pore canal. The arrow indicates where the cuticle covers and partly infills the canal (Mikhailov 1997, pl. 12C).

Thickness

For the identification of small fragments, establishing thickness by use of a micrometre is the first step (Keepax 1981; Sidell 1993; Eastham & Gwynn 1997; Boyer 1999). Shell thickness has been measured for certain recent domestic and wild species by various authors (Table 7.2). Their results are not fully consistent. In domestic birds, thickness varies according to breed or to diet. Thickness measurements alone cannot distinguish eggs of closely similar size, but they are used as an initial guide. Eggshell thickness in Roman and medieval deposits in Leicester (Figure 7.5) showed a single peak in each period, suggesting that most egghell fragments

Table 7.2. *Eggshell thickness of selected domestic and wild species*

Species	Thickness (μm)			
	Keepax	Murphy	Boyer	Sidell
Domestic				
Chicken – various breeds	220–480			325–350
Bantam		260		
Leghorn		310		
Cochin china		360		
Guineafowl	400–710			
Turkey	280–450			
Domestic duck	250–550			350–400
Domestic goose	400–700			525–650
Quail			180–200	175–200
Wild				
Struthio camelus				2100–2000
Phalacrocorax carbo				300–325
Anser anser				525–550
Cygnus olor				500–600
Columba palumbus			140–160	150–200
Columba livia				150–200
Catharacta skua				300–325
Larus argentatus			250–260	300–350
Rissa tridactyla				200
Alca torda			330–350	
Perdix perdix			180–210	200–250
Vanellus vanellus			120–140	
Phasianus colchicus	200–400			200–250
Gallinula chloropus			210–220	
Corvus frugilegus			160–190	

Source: Data are from Keepax (1981), Murphy (1985), Boyer (1999), and J. Sidell (personal communication, June 2006).

are from a single species, probably chicken, as they are within the thickness range for chicken. The Roman was fractionally thinner than the medieval eggshell. Thickness is also informative if eggs fall into one or two clear size groups. The most likely interpretation of eggshell fragments from a medieval household which separates into two groups, one thinner and one thicker, is that the thinner shell is from domestic chickens and the thicker from goose.

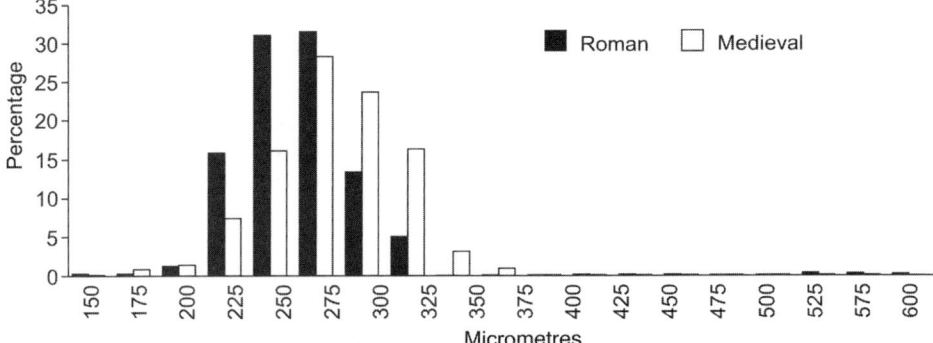

FIGURE 7.5. Thickness of eggshell fragments from Roman and medieval deposits at Causeway Lane, Leicester. The size distribution (see Table 7.2) is compatible with the eggshell being mostly from domestic chicken (redrawn from Boyer 1999).

Microscopic Features

For identification to species, scanning electron microscopy is needed. Preparation of the samples includes cleaning and drying. In one study, each subsample was first scanned under a stereo microscope and sorted into superficial types and then representative fragments of different thicknesses were selected for study. Subsampling was necessary, since resources, equipment, and time did not allow all fragments to be analysed. The selected fragments were mounted on aluminium stubs and gold coated under vacuum (Sidell 1993, 1997). Species identification was made by comparing the internal structure, the sculpturing, and the measurements of the different layers in radial cross section with modern reference material.

A new approach to eggshell identification has recently been attempted using neural network software (Eastham & Gwynn 1997). For the analysis of eggshell from Skara Brae in Orkney, rather than relying on visual distinctions, the researchers experimented with the use of artificial neural network software of a type used to classify multivariate biological data. Skara Brae, a well-known Late Neolithic village which was first excavated by Gordon Childe, was re-excavated in the 1970s, when the deposits were sieved. Remains of many more bird and fish species were recovered, as well as eggshell fragments, with the major midden level producing about 600 pieces. For the neural network analysis, micrographs were taken of the patterns of mammillary cones and pores on the inner surface of the shell of 25 recent species which breed in Orkney today or whose bones were present in the deposits. The software identified the modern samples with an accuracy rate of 70 per cent. The analysis was then run three times on the archaeological samples. The results were not fully consistent internally, but they did suggest that most of the eggshell fragments were from the pintail and the larger gulls. These were not the most frequent species among the bone remains, which were very diverse, but, as discussed earlier, all are species whose eggs might be expected as the eggs are fairly easily collected.

Quantification

In the studies described, fragments were counted, but counting is probably uninformative as well as being unrealistic in many cases. Other methods are available which can suggest quantity: the percentage of samples in which eggshell fragments were found, and the volume of eggshell per sample. At the site of Mons Claudianus, a Roman quarry site in Egypt where the living quarters of the workers was excavated, eggshell, preserved in the arid desert sediments, was found in 64 per cent of the soil samples (Hamilton-Dyer 1997; Maxfield & Peacock 2001). The fragments were not positively identified, but chickens were by far the most frequent species at the site so it is most unlikely that the eggshell is from another species. Some of the samples from the kitchen floor at Eynsham Abbey contained more eggshell than bone (Ayres et al. 2003, 385). The percentage by volume was estimated by eye and assigned to bands of 1 to 10 per cent, 10 to 20 per cent, and so on. Every layer of the kitchen floor of the Early Norman abbey contained some eggshell; in three layers eggshell made up between 30 and 50 per cent, and in two it was between 50 and 70 per cent by volume. The weight of moa eggshell from a sample column at the site of Wairau Bar in South Island was extrapolated for the whole site. The calculation suggested that the huge quantity of 2,380 eggs had been eaten there over the lifetime of the site (Anderson 1979, 124).

EGGSHELL FROM ARCHAEOLOGICAL SITES

The techniques of analysis described have been used in combination for the study of eggshell from excavations. Some are more appropriate for eggs of wild birds, some for domestic, and some for what are potentially ritual deposits.

Wild Birds

Thickness and curvature were used in the study of moa eggshell from Tokerau, a natural deposit of eggshell and bones in a coastal sand dune in the North Island (Gill 2000). Curvature measurements showed that all eggs were within the known range for moa eggs, which had been established from the dimensions of the 18 whole moa eggs known from New Zealand.

Eggshell, both burnt and unburned, was excavated at Nunamira Cave, Tasmania, from an occupation layer dated to 16,000 BP. The curvature, surface sculpting, and colour of the 333 fragments matched the eggshell of the Tasmanian emu. As Cosgrove (1995, 76) noted, 'The crenelated surface is easily distinguishable while the inner surfaces are smooth and pale yellow or cream in colour'. The fragments also retained their external colour, which was dark green to olive. The likely identification was confirmed by some bone fragments of emu from the same deposits. The fact that the eggshell was found on a living site and that some was burned certainly suggests that the eggs had been eaten at this early date.

The finding of shell fragments within the floor of a house at the Iron Age settlement of Haddenham was unexpected, as both birds and eggshell are rare on Iron Age settlements in Britain. Two types of eggshell were present. One was thick shelled with grey-green external pigment; the second was thinner walled with dark brown speckling. Preservation of the pigment on eggshell at this site was probably due to the waterlogged conditions. The thickness, pore, and mammilla count, and surface sculpturing of the thicker shell were a good match with the mute swan. The thinner shell could not be identified from the limited reference collection available (Sidell 2006).

Eggshell was found throughout the midden at the Viking site of Mývatn in northern Iceland. It was identified from the thickness and relative size of mammillae. Most fragments were from waterfowl, ptarmigan, guillemot (*Uria aalge* or *U. lomvia* or both), and other members of the auk family. Though the site is inland, where ducks and ptarmigan would be expected, seabird eggs as well as the seabirds themselves were present. As the nearest breeding colonies of the guillemot are 60 to 70 km distant, it was clear that the site must have retained close connections with the coast, which was confirmed by the remains of marine fish among the food remains (McGovern et al. 2006).

Domestic Birds

Eggshell from sites in the arid American Southwest contributes to our understanding of the early stages of domestication of the turkey. Bones as well as eggshell were found at Tularosa Cave, a Mogollon site dating from the early first millennium AD in an area interpreted as a corral or pen for turkeys (Rea 1980). Even if the turkeys were still wild at this time, the finds suggest that they were kept in captivity. Turkey eggshell has also been found at several other Pueblo sites, including Black Mesa, Arizona, and Chaco Canyon. The Pueblo people were concerned with raising turkeys (see Chapter 12), and the eggshell is evidence that turkeys were breeding at the sites in question.

From the middle of the first millennium BC hens' eggs have been found on sites in Europe and North Africa. The ubiquity of eggshell at Mons Claudianus is an early example of what must have been highly efficient poultry raising for eggs. The site was the camp quarters of quarry workers in the Eastern Desert of Egypt and in a very isolated location, so chickens must have been transported to the camp to provide eggs for the workers (Hamilton-Dyer 1997, 1998). We have seen how eggshell fragments have been found in medieval sites in England, retrieved in soil samples (Murphy 1985, 1990; Boyer 1999; Ayres et al. 2003).

Whole Eggs and Ritual Deposits

Eggs have been assigned symbolic and cosmological value in some cultures and were sometimes placed as offerings in temples and graves. These eggs were deposited whole, and in some cases they even survived intact.

A group of 26 complete hens' eggs was placed within the Maussolleion at Halikarnassos (Bodrum), Turkey among the other sacrificial deposits. All were found within a metre square, which was thought to 'indicate that . . . they were carried down the steps in a basket after which the eggs were removed and placed nearby' (Hojlund 1983). This appears to be part of a tradition of placing eggs in graves, which is found throughout the Greek world in the Hellenistic period. Both real eggs and clay copies were used (Kurtz & Boardman 1971). Eggshell fragments, which have not been identified to species, were found in a well or cistern at the Sanctuary of Poseidon, Kalaureia, on the island of Poros in Greece. Much of the fauna in the cistern, which included a snake and several puppies, was sacrificial in nature; the shell may therefore be from eggs deposited in the cistern, perhaps as a chthonic or fertility ritual (Serjeantson in press-a).

In the Roman world the tradition of placing eggs with the dead was also widespread. A child's grave in the Roman-period cemetery in Solymár in Pannonia in present-day Hungary contained eggshell, originally complete eggs, on a tray. These were thought to be hens' eggs as several cemeteries in Pannonia contained chickens as grave offerings (see Chapter 14). The find was interpreted as having cosmological significance, rather than a food offering (Gál 2005b). In a Regensburg cemetery of the third century AD, one grave included a complete cow skeleton and two clay vessels as well as numerous eggs (Luff 1982, 193). Eggshell was also found with a Late Iron Age (early first century AD) cremation at Baldock, a Romano-British site to the north of London. The thickness was compatible with domestic fowl (Murphy 1990). In these examples the eggshell was not positively identified, but Roman tradition suggests that most or all was from hens' eggs.

The tradition of placing eggs with burials seems to have a widespread human resonance. Whole moa eggs have been found in association with burials in New Zealand. Perforated eggs were found with burials at Wairau Bar in the South Island and two whole eggs were found at the more southerly site of Awamoa, Shag Mouth (Figure 7.6), also apparently associated with a nearby human burial (Anderson 1979, 125, 135).

Some finds of whole eggs are more enigmatic. At Castle Acre Priory in Norfolk two intact eggs were found in a crack in a sixteenth-century wall. One, identified on the basis of size, shape, and thickness, was considered to be from one of the Galliformes. It was thought to be a better match with guineafowl than with domestic chicken (Keepax 1981). The identification is not unreasonable, as guineafowl had already been introduced to England by this time (see Chapter 12), but how it came to be within a wall is a mystery.

OSTRICH EGGSHELL

Complete ostrich eggshells were used as flasks. In South Africa a single hole was drilled in the top of a shell through which the egg was removed. The flasks were used to carry water, with a plug or stopper inserted to prevent spills. Fragments with evidence for a circular hole have usually been interpreted as pieces of flasks, but it has recently been shown that some of the carnivores which scavenge ostrich eggs leave a pair of holes which can scarcely be distinguished from holes made by humans (Kandel 2004). Ostrich eggshell was recovered from two Middle Stone Age sites in the Geelbek Dunes in the Western Cape. The eggshell from one had features which suggested the eggshell modifications were anthropogenic even at this very early date, but the only modifications to the eggshell at the other site were circular holes. The authors considered that these were most likely caused by a large carnivore so the eggshell at that site was natural rather than anthropogenic. They

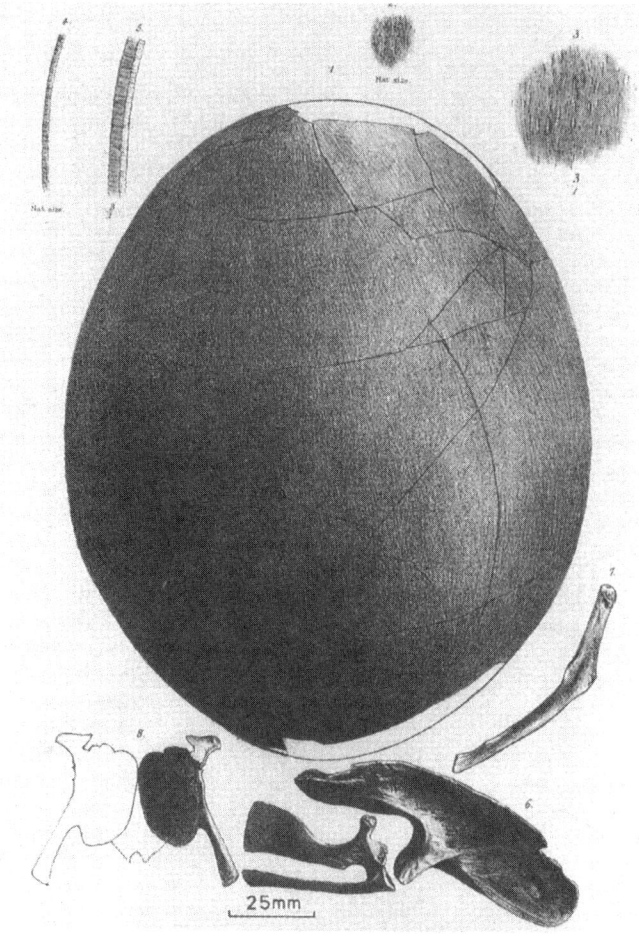

FIGURE 7.6. Reconstructed moa egg from Awamoa, Shag Mouth, South Island, New Zealand, and fetal bones (Anderson 1989b, fig. 5.17). The bones were probably not associated with the egg.

proposed that other criteria should be used for the positive identification of flasks (Table 7.3).

Ostrich eggshell has also been used for beads and other artefacts in Africa and the eastern Mediterranean (Poplin 2000; Kandel 2004, 2005). Beads and the residue from bead manufacture were found at several sites in the Western Cape dating from the first millennium AD. All the stages of bead-making were present (Kandel 2005). First, the fragments were cut into angular blanks. They were then further cut or ground to a circular shape and a hole was drilled for suspension (Figure 7.7). Finally, some were deliberately burned black and others were polished. The identification of ostrich

Table 7.3. *Criteria to be taken into account in identifying flasks of ostrich eggshell at archaeological sites*

Criterion number	Criteria to identify whether modified fragments of ostrich eggshell at archaeological sites represent rim pieces of flasks
1.	Well-stratified site with no evidence of carnivore activity
2.	Complete or refitted, single-holed ostrich eggshell
3.	Subsequent modification to opening (e.g., resin spout, stopper)
4.	Engraving (e.g., geometric patterns, lines)
5.	Decoration (e.g., charcoal, ochre)
6.	Use-wear on the outer surface (e.g., polish, staining, or discoloration from organic materials)
7.	Trace of contents (e.g., specularite, ochre, ant larvae, eggshell fragments)
8.	Openings consistently made at one location on several eggs (e.g., cache)
	Criteria which may indicate flasks, but which should not be used independently:
1.	Undecorated opening with conchoidal fracturing on the inner surface
2.	Opening with a chipped, bevelled, or ground outer surface

Source: Data are from Kandel (2004).

eggshell, whether used for artefacts or as remains of meals, is less problematical than the identification of eggshell of smaller birds, but the problems posed about whether or not it is anthropogenic, and whether or not the eggs were collected and eaten, are mirrored in smaller birds.

DISCUSSION AND CONCLUSIONS

The eggshell finds discussed here show that there are four, perhaps more, reasons for the presence of eggshell on an ancient settlement.

1. The shell is from eggs which were eaten. They will be associated with other food remains in a midden or in an area where food was prepared and eaten, as in the kitchen floor at Eynsham Abbey. The eggshell will be broken and usually present in a large quantity and the eggs will have been recently laid. Where eggs were food, the further questions are whether eggs are eaten in large or small quantities and which species they are from. However, the question of the importance put on the eating of eggs of domestic poultry is probably best answered *not* by collecting and studying eggshell but by examining the incidence of medullary bone.

182 BIRDS

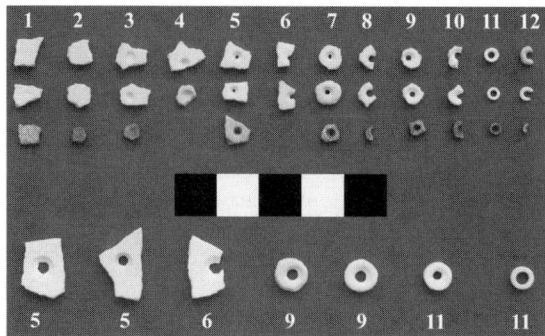

FIGURE 7.7. Manufacture of small and large beads of eggshell of ostrich, *Struthio camelus*, from archaeological sites of the first millennium AD in the Western Cape, South Africa. All stages are shown, from blanks (1) to completed (11) and broken (12) beads. The scale bar is 5 cm (photograph by A. W. Kandel, courtesy of the Iziko–South African Museum and the Department of Early Prehistory and Archaeology of the Middle Ages, University of Tübingen).

2. The second possibility is that the eggs are from birds raised at the site. The remains may be in a pen, as in the Pueblo sites, but they may also be in more diffuse areas of the site. The shell will be from eggs which have hatched so it will be broken into small fragments. Eggshell is also found on sites where people were keeping tamed wild birds, such as the sacred ibises in Egypt discussed in Chapter 14. In this case, there may be no doubt about the species involved, but the question of whether the shell is always from hatched birds would be worth exploring.
3. The eggshell is from an offering or other ritual deposit. Remains from a grave or site where ritual offerings were made will not be hatched and will have been whole at the time they were deposited, as in the Maussolleion at Halikarnassos. Such deposits can help to interpret ritual behaviour even if the species cannot be identified. Eggs in this condition have the greatest likelihood of being identified, as they will be more complete.
4. The eggshell is intrusive. Non-anthropogenic eggshell from the nests of birds which nested at the site will be hatched and fragmentary. The context and associated material – or lack of it – may be suggestive. Identification of the species helps the interpretation of the deposit as cultural or non-anthropogenic. If, for instance, the shell was from jackdaw rather than a domestic bird (see Chapter 5), it is likely to be intrusive.

As we see, though species identification is a desirable goal, there are some questions which can be answered without identification of every fragment. Where scanning electron micrographic analysis is unavailable, species identification may sometimes be inferred from the associated bone remains. Quantifying the presence or absence in soil samples can be informative for pinpointing where cooking or consumption took place, or where birds were penned. The condition of the eggshell, whether in large or tiny fragments, can distinguish whole eggs from eggs that have been eaten or hatched. This is potentially possible from the appearance of the inner surface of the eggshell and it is probably the most useful direction for future experimental work.

Identification to species is possible with large birds where the range of possible species is few, as with emu in Australia and with ostrich. In those contexts where it is likely that the eggshell is mainly from chickens and geese, measurement of fragment thickness can suggest the ratio of eggs consumed between the two species. This technique might, of course, be applied in any environment where it was suspected that only one or two species were involved. The positive identification of avian eggshell from archaeological sites cannot yet be done routinely. It requires expensive equipment and materials, a reference collection larger than is usually available, a high level of expertise, and a great deal of time. At present, it is ruled out as a routine procedure.

Nevertheless, there are two areas where it would be highly desirable to carry research into eggshell identification further. The first is in the exploitation of wild birds. Do those who exploit wild birds target different species for the collection of eggs from those targeted for meat? Expectations based on biology and ethnography and historical records suggest that we might expect the eggs of any of the colonial nesting birds to have been exploited, where available, and that on coastal sites we might expect a preponderance of gulls' eggs and on inland sites those of ducks and other waterfowl. A detailed study of suitable assemblages would help to answer these questions. The second area where research is desirable is in the early stages of the domestication and keeping of domestic chickens. At some time the production of hens' eggs overtook that of every other domestic species. As we have seen here and in Chapter 3, some of the Roman sites in Egypt seem to suggest that the process had already taken place by the first centuries AD, but it may well have taken place earlier, in Italy, further east in the Roman Empire, or quite possibly elsewhere in Western Asia. Recovery and identification of the eggshell as well as the bones themselves will help to pin down this important breakthrough for human economic life.

8

Feathers, Skins, and Other Products

There is hardly a community in the world which has not used feathers and bird skins for decoration. For many they have also had a symbolic value. Feathers have been a focal element in the culture of the peoples of New Guinea, Polynesia, New Zealand, and North and South America (Leach 1979; Sillitoe 1988; McGovern-Wilson 2005; Pressman 1991; Reina 1991); though used for decoration in Eurasia, they seem to have been less important in ritual there. Feathers also have practical uses. In high latitudes they are useful for warmth and insulation. Flight feathers are needed for fletching arrows, and in the past the primary flight feathers provided the quill pen, the main writing implement in Europe and the western world until the nineteenth century. Feathers can be a secondary as well as a primary product.

In this chapter I shall consider the significance of feathers for past societies before I describe their composition, the different types of feathers and their uses, and their identification. Some of the feather and skin finds from archaeological contexts are discussed to show the range of environments in which they may survive. The carcass of a bird provides other raw materials of lesser importance: sinew and oil, which are also briefly discussed.

FEATHERS: INTRODUCTORY COMMENTS

It is likely that feathers were first used both for decoration and warmth from at least the Upper Palaeolithic era onwards. The immense advances in human social development at that time, probably associated with speech (Lieberman 2007), were accompanied by symbolism in other areas such as art and decoration.

Unfortunately in view of their importance, the feathers themselves survive only rarely in archaeological situations. As they consist of keratin, they survive only in exceptional circumstances. We therefore often have to rely on depictions of people and feathers, and on the proxy evidence from bone assemblages to find out whether birds were hunted or kept for their feathers. The earliest European evidence for the use of feathers for fletching arrows is the depiction on pebble engravings at La Colombière, an Upper Palaeolithic site in France (Clark 1948). Indirect evidence for the exploitation of feathers and other products relies on the presence of certain elements and the butchery marks, and for archaeological interpretation these are likely to be of more value than feathers themselves.

ANTHROPOLOGICAL FEATHER USE

The very wide range of values that have been assigned to feathers has been summarised by Sillitoe (1988, 301): 'Throughout the world people use birds' plumes to decorate themselves, particularly to create headdresses.... The plumes used, and the manner in which they are worn, may, for instance, mark the wearer's achievements, as in the coup complex of the Plains Indians. Or they may indicate initiatory status and knowledge, as among the Baktaman of New Guinea. In other societies they may indicate social standing and wealth... plumed headdresses may serve as regimental insignia to distinguish warriors clearly in battle, as among, for example, the Zulu last century.... Other peoples include the plumes of certain birds in their headwear in the belief that this will effect some sympathetic transfer of the birds' qualities to them, that an owl's plumes, for instance, might improve their sight in the dark'. It is clear that the colour, shape, texture, and flexibility of feathers are important, but equally significant are the associations of a particular species for the wearer.

The symbolic value placed on feathers is exemplified by the ceremonies of the Cashinahua peoples of Peru, where the initiates wear their most beautiful headdresses 'to attract the attention of the people and the spirits' (Reina 1991, xv). Headdresses, more than other garments, identified the wearer and his status within the group. Among the WaiWai of Guyana, these took the form of hair tubes decorated with feathers; one example exhibited in the Horniman Museum, London, in 2006 used complete wings as decoration (Horniman Museum 2006). They were also used on belts, necklaces, pendants, and cloaks. War gear, battleaxes, shields, and even warships were decorated with feathers, often with eagle feathers, and feathers of all types have been used to decorate masks. They were often woven into flax garments and into basketry to add decoration. On their own, or tied to dream-catchers, feathers had magical importance and acted as good luck charms. The feathers and skins of the northern flicker brought good luck in North America, as did the wing feathers of swans (Stewart 1977, 173; Nelson 1983, 91, 112). Feathers were used in traditional medicine in Mexico, where feathers of the laughing falcon, the king vulture, and the turkey vulture were burnt and applied in the form of ashes to alleviate wounds, to prevent hair growth, and as a cure for syphilis and ulcers (Corona-M. 2005).

Selection by Association

In many cultures, eagle feathers were more highly desired than those of other birds. 'Their efficacy was not merely mechanical; it was also magical'. The user was 'appropriating some of the eagle's power and keenness of vision.... The potency of the eagle is identified not only with the pinions on which it soars in the heaven, but also with the beak and claws by which it secures its prey' (Clark 1948, 128). Over and over again we find that it is eagle feathers which are sought for their association with the qualities needed in hunting and warfare. Hesiod in the eighth century BC refers to the use of eagle feathers in Greece (Clark 1952, 39). Mozino, the first European to spend a long period among the First Nations of the Pacific Northwest, described his life with the Mowachat. He wrote that 'eagles were hunted for their feathers, but I have not been able to learn whether they use eagles for food' (Mozino 1991, 20). The use of feathers of the bald eagle to decorate cloaks continues in the Pacific Northwest among the Nuchanulth of Haida Gwaii (Figure 8.1).

Among the Plains Indians, headdresses and bonnets made with eagle feathers could only be worn by proven warriors (Penney & Longfish 1994, 100). Feather use was also often specific to gender. In some groups men retain for themselves the privilege of wearing feathers: in Hawaii men wore cloaks and helmets of feathers, while the only feathers worn by women were in the lei which they wore around the neck.

Colour

In nature, colour is rare. It is found in plants, especially in flowers and fruits, but these are transitory; feathers survive longer. They provide a wider range of colours than the pigments which were available to paint the body. The colour which has been prized most highly is red (Pressman 1991; McGovern-Wilson 2005), with yellow, black, white, and iridescent feathers also sought after. In Polynesia, red was associated with chiefs and used in gifts (McGovern-Wilson 2005). The most famous feather garment in the world, the cloak given to Captain Cook by the king of Hawaii, is decorated with red and yellow feathers. This cloak, now in Te Papa Tongarewa, the Museum of New

FIGURE 8.1. Nuchanulth cloak decorated with appliquéd feathers of the bald eagle, *Haliaeetus leucocephalus*, Haida Gwaii, British Columbia, shown with a hat of woven bark (photograph by A. Yeoman).

Zealand in Wellington, was made with feathers from the I'iwi, the Hawai'i mamo, and the flanks of the o'o (see http://www.tepapa.govt.nz/TePapa; July 4, 2006). In the myths of traditional South Amerindian peoples, the colour red was regarded as the most intense colour, and feathers of other colours were explained as having derived their colours from the lesser quantity of blood in which the feathers were dipped or from other, less desirable body fluids such as bile. In fire myths, feathers of other colours had failed to reach the intense red heart of the fire, so they were duller (Pressman 1991). It was the red feathers on the scalp and nape of the flicker which were also associated with blood (Penney & Longfish 1994, 185). In Mexico at the time of contact the red feathers from the head of the golden-fronted woodpecker were used to cure headaches (Corona-M. 2005). Though the resplendent quetzal was traditionally the most important source of feathers, the iridescent black tail feathers of the great-tailed grackle have also been prized in Mexico since the fifteenth century (Christensen 2000). The iridescent quality of hummingbird feathers made them prized for feather artwork in Mexico (Corona-M. 2005). White feathers, important in New Zealand as well as North America, were obtained from seabirds such as gannets and albatrosses (McGovern-Wilson 2005).

Fletching Arrows

Feathers attached to an arrow stabilise its flight. It does not appear that those of any one species are better than others from the technical point of view. Archers today use turkey and goose feathers, as these are easy to obtain. In the past, however, the selection of feathers for fletching arrows was based more on the qualities of the bird. The Sioux used the feathers of hawk, eagle, or other bird of prey in the hopes that the qualities of these raptors were imparted to the arrow. The Omaha preferred owl feathers because they were light and durable and because they 'helped the arrow find its mark silently, as the owl flies, and accurately, as the owl catches its prey at night' (Laubin & Laubin 1980, 12). Throughout the Americas, the tribe and even the individual archer could be recognised from the feathers used and the method of hafting. Two or three feathers are used and the individuality comes in the way in which they are combined, trimmed, possibly twisted, and attached to the shaft. Fletched arrows and feathers for fletching arrows have been found on North American sites, though rarely in the Old World. Though the bow and arrow has been in use since the Upper Palaeolithic in Eurasia, the evidence for this relies almost exclusively on arrowheads. Some wooden arrows recovered from bogs at Vimose in Denmark and Thorsbjerg in Schleswig-Holstein had impressions of the thread binding on the shaft, but the thread itself and feather used for fletching did not survive (Clark 1948).

Quills

Quill pens made from primary feathers (see later) have been in use as writing implements since at least the sixth century AD. Those of geese and swans are among the sturdiest, though feathers of other species can be used. The second and third primaries are best, with those from the left wing being the ideal fit for right-handed writers, and those from the right wing for left-handers. The feathers of older birds are of better quality than those of juveniles, and plucked feathers are better than those from slaughtered birds (Serjeantson 2002).

Trade and Exchange

Feathers have been used for gifts and exchange throughout the world. In northern Europe they were a source of income for the inhabitants of St Kilda and the Northern and Western isles of Scotland until a century ago. They were initially paid to clan chief or landlord as rent in kind, and later sold in the market (Fenton 1978; Shaw 1980, 128, 168, 173). The feathers of the scarlet macaw and other parrots were probably the most significant trade item in the American Southwest in pre-contact times, and in New Zealand feathers were used in gift exchange (Anderson 1988). In South America, feathers were a source of wealth which could be used for trading and in marriage alliances, and in Polynesia they acted as currency (McGovern-Wilson 2005).

FEATHER TYPES AND STRUCTURE

Many of the practical as well as symbolic uses of feathers made use of the flight feathers, while the other feathers provided insulation and warmth. There are three basic feather types: contour feathers, down, and filoplumes. The contour feathers cover the body; of these the most evolved are those of the wing, which are also known as flight or quill feathers, and those of the tail. Each individual contour feather on the Poitou goose, a domestic breed which was kept mainly for feather production, had a different name (Figure 8.2); one expert in the last century distinguished 250 different feather types. Each wing feather had a different specialised use, including for brushes, toothpicks, shuttlecocks for badminton, and pens (Lecuyer & Pujol 1975).

Contour feathers comprise a central hollow shaft or rachis with branches on each side, the vanes (Figure 8.3). The base of the shaft, the calamus, is oval or circular in cross section while at the distal end the rachis is circular or square in most feathers. The vane is made up of pennaceous and plumulaceous barbs. The pennaceous barbs link together with hooks known as hamuli; when a bird preens it is restoring these links. The pennaceous barbs are stiff and the plumulaceous barbs at the base of the vane are silky or fluffy. The plumulaceous barbs themselves consist of a rachilla or ramus with vanules on either side which are made up of barbules. The contour feathers on the body have a larger area of fluffy plumulaceous barbs than the feathers of the wing and tail and so are used for insulation and warmth. True down grows in between feather tracks and is covered by the contour feathers. This type of down has a small shaft or calamus and may lack a rachis.

Filoplumes are hair-like underfeathers (Voitkevich 1966; Dove 1997). Down has many qualities: it is soft, light, elastic, and does not become matted. Today feathers are used for warmth mainly in padded anoraks and waistcoats, pillows, sleeping bags, duvets (the French word for down) and eiderdowns, a term which reminds us that originally down from the eider duck was one of the main sources of feathers for

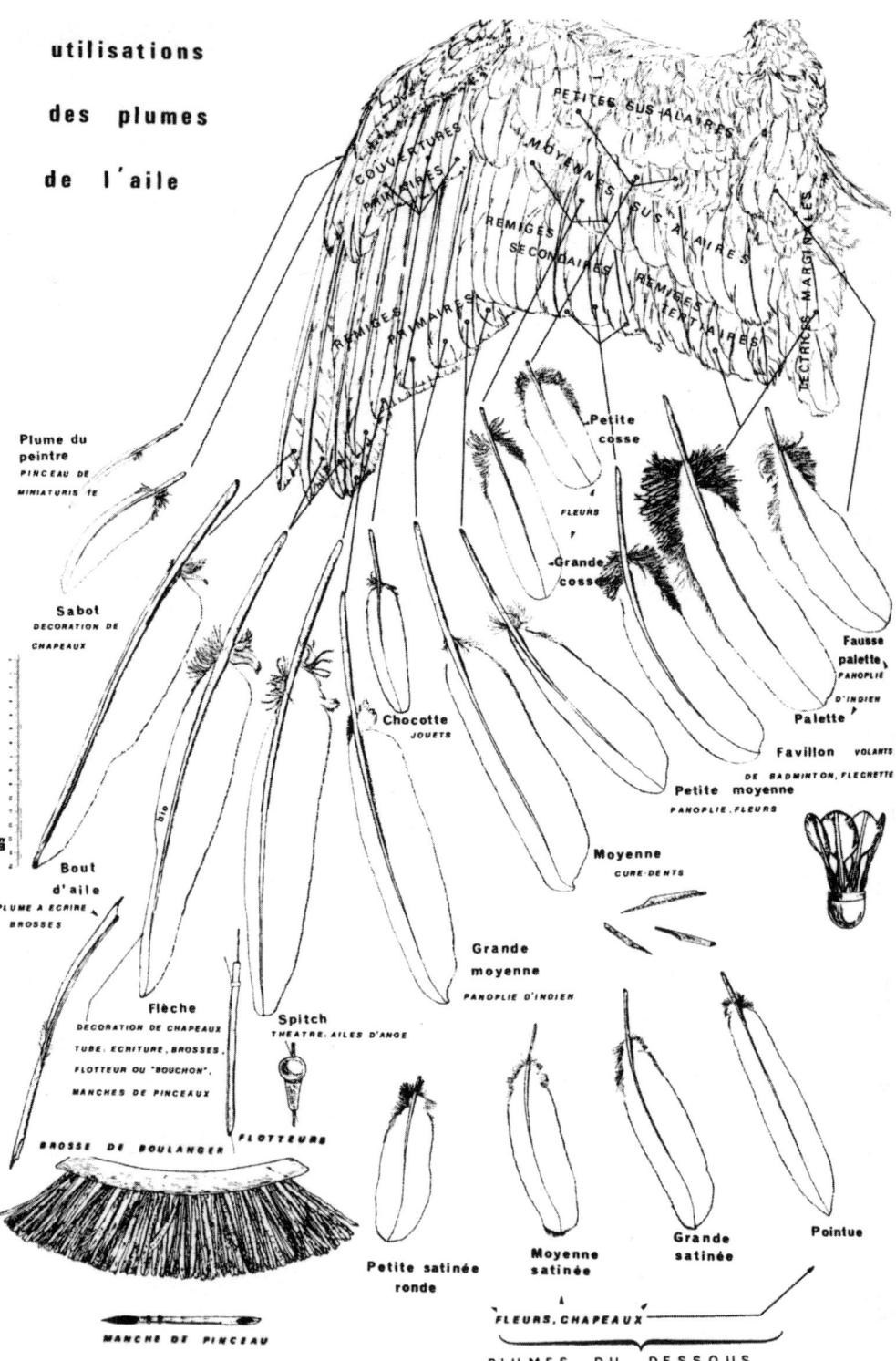

FIGURE 8.2. Wing feathers of the domestic Poitou goose, showing the different names given to the feathers and their specialised uses in the early twentieth century (after Lecuyer & Pujol 1975, 210).

FEATHERS, SKINS, AND OTHER PRODUCTS   191

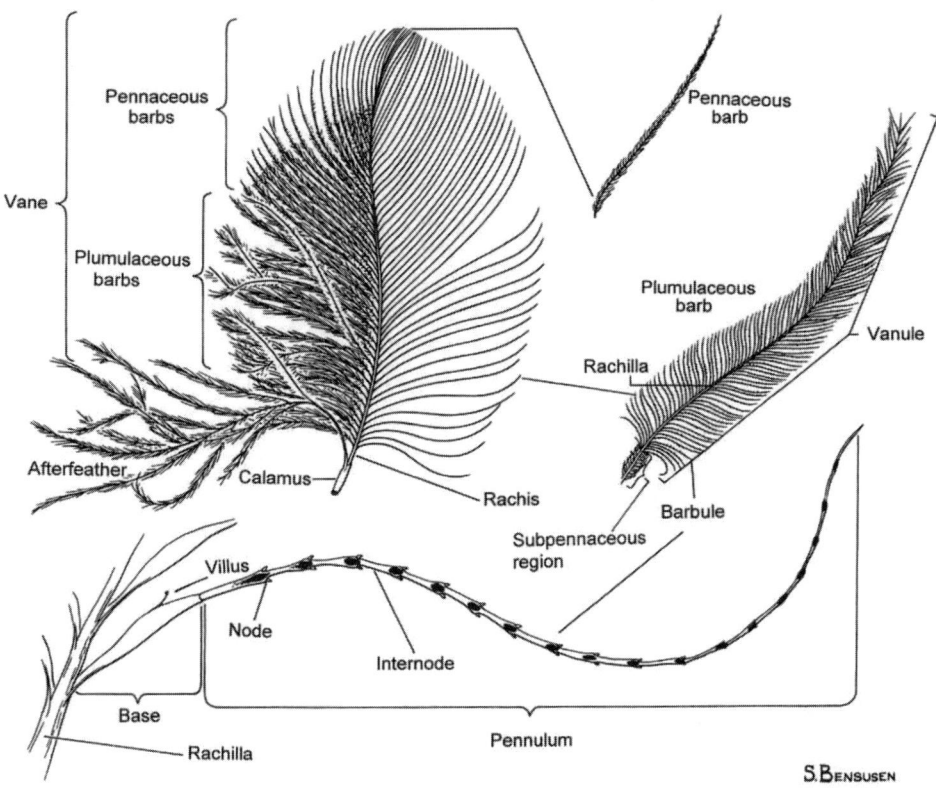

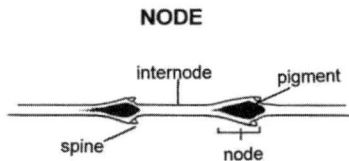

FIGURE 8.3. Topography of a contour feather, showing calamus, rachis, and vane with pennaceous and plumulaceous barbs and barbules. The enlarged diagrams on the right show pennaceous and plumulaceous barbs (Dove 1998). The enlarged bottom section shows detail of a barbule, and below that the diagram shows the arrangement of nodes and internodes (drawing by S. Bensusen).

bedding. The down feathers of geese and other waterfowl have the smallest relative density and are reputed to be the fluffiest of all (Serjeantson 2002). All feathers on the ratites are soft, and, unlike on other birds, lack barbules (Worthy & Holdaway 2002, 219).

The primary wing feathers are carried on the carpometacarpus and the digits (Figure 8.4). The secondaries, which number from fewer than 10 to more than 40,

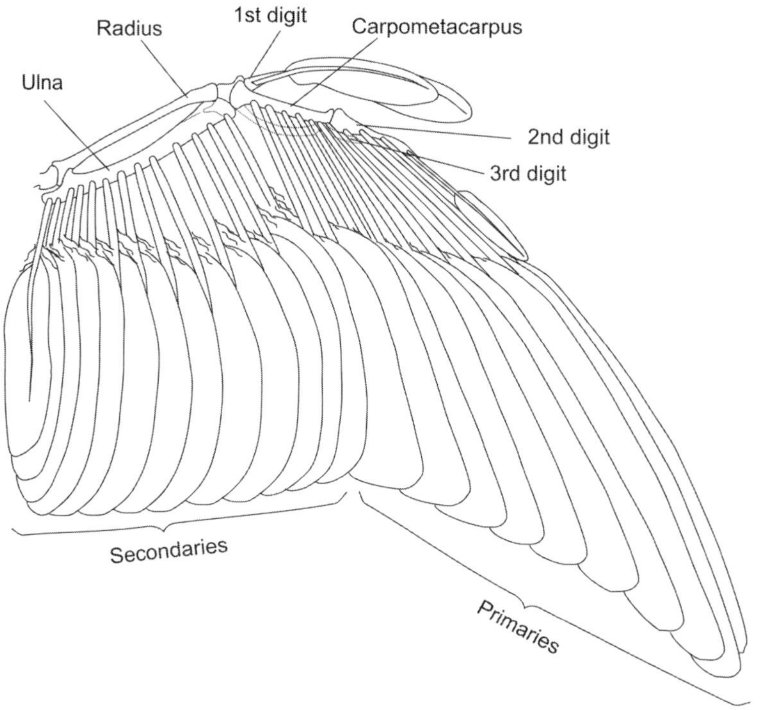

FIGURE 8.4. Wing showing the primary and secondary flight feathers and the skeletal elements to which they are attached (drawing by P. Copeland).

depending on species, are carried on the ulna and radius, and the tertiaries are carried on the humerus. The number of tail feathers, which are carried on the pygostyle, ranges from 10 to 24 (Lecuyer & Pujol 1975; Brown et al. 1999). They vary from insignificant small feathers to the magnificent plumes of peacocks, pheasants, quetzals, and birds of paradise.

Birds grow several sets of feathers between hatching and maturity. Gulls grow and moult three or four sets of feathers of different colours before they become adult at the age of about four years. Birds grow a new set of feathers every year, and some grow two sets: the breeding and non-breeding or eclipse plumage. The very practical reason for this is that feathers readily become damaged, so migratory birds need to grow new flight feathers, often just before the migration. The down beneath the feathers provides insulation and waterproofing, and these feathers also need to be renewed. Most birds lose flight feathers one at a time over a protracted period and continue to fly while moulting, but some ducks, geese, and swans lose all flight feathers at the same time, and they are restricted to swimming or walking on land during the period when the flight feathers are regrowing.

FEATHER IDENTIFICATION

Size, shape, and colour are the best guides to identification in ancient as well as recent material (Dove 1998; Brown et al. 1999), but where feathers are damaged or fragmentary, or where the whole feather is not available for study, microscopic analysis can be used. This relies on the microscopic characters such as the nodal morphology, internodal length and width, basal cell length, and pigmentation pattern in the nodes of the barbs and barbules (Figure 8.3; also see Dove 1997). Microslides are prepared of individual barbs or barbules and examined under magnification up to 400× (Messinger 1965; Dove & Peurach 2002; Dove 1999; Dove et al. 2005). Some field guides illustrate individual feathers at the macroscopic level (Brown et al. 1999), but, as with skeletal elements, a reference collection of feathered skins is needed to check any identification at the macroscopic level and a collection of slides showing morphology in recent feathers is needed for comparisons at the microscopic level. The preliminary washing needed before excavated finds can be studied, the conservation and the storage of feathers are also skilled procedures because of the vulnerability of feathers to mechanical damage, light, heat, mould, and insects (Dove 1999; Schaeuffelhut et al. 2002).

ARCHAEOLOGICAL FINDS

Feathers from archaeological excavations have survived in arid, cold, and anaerobic conditions.

Finds from Arid Environments

Feathers are quite common on archaeological sites in the American Southwest, where they survive in the arid deserts of Utah, Colorado, and Arizona. As well as mummified birds complete with feathers, bundles of feathers were sometimes found and individual feathers used as decoration of basketry and clothing. They were usually of turkey or scarlet macaw (Messinger 1965; Rea 1980; McKusick 1980; Parmalee 1980; Jolie & Hattori 2005). There are some very early finds – feathers in Hogup Cave in Utah dated from 6440 ± 50 BP – but most date from the first millennium AD. A quantity of feathers survived in the West Ruin at Aztec Ruins National Monument in New Mexico, mostly from turkey. A turkey feather there was used as fletching on an arrowshaft, one of the first microscopic identifications

FIGURE 8.5. Bunch of feathers, probably of chicken, from the Roman quarry camp at Mons Claudianus in the Egyptian desert (photograph by S. Hamilton-Dyer).

of an archaeological feather fragment (Messinger 1965). Feathers were woven with fibres for clothing and decoration. A feather-string robe from Canyon Del Muerto, Arizona, was wrapped round a flexed burial (Olsen 1968, pl. I) and a squirrel pelt sash from a Pueblo context in Lavender Canyon, Utah, was decorated with feathers of the scarlet macaw. The small feathers used were lashed to fine fibre (Borson et al. 1998).

The arid Egyptian desert also provides an environment where feathers have survived. One of the few early finds of fletched arrows was a quiverful found in the tomb of Tutankhamen (Clark 1948); the tomb also held fans of ostrich feathers. Several feathers were recovered in the fibrous and dusty matrix of the site of Mons Claudianus in the Eastern Desert, referred to in the previous chapter. Most were either white or brown and compared well with domestic chicken, the only bird found at the site in quantity. As well as the isolated feathers, six were found tied in two bundles of three (Figure 8.5). These must have been intended for decoration or ritual use (Hamilton-Dyer 1997).

In New Zealand feathers, fragments of feathers, and skins from cloaks were found during the excavation of rock shelters on Lee Island in Lake Te Anau. The sites date from the sixteenth to seventeenth centuries AD and the feathers were preserved by the dry conditions; they too still had some colour. They were primarily of kakapo and kaka large parrots endemic to New Zealand. Two bundles of kakapo feathers seem to have been deliberate caches while others were scattered about the site. Most were tail feathers (Holdaway 1991; McGovern-Wilson 2005).

Finds from Cold Environments

Feathers have also survived in circumpolar regions from Greenland to Alaska, where they have been preserved in ice or by freeze-drying, the latter a combination of low ground temperature and dry air. In the Yukon, feather fragments were recovered from ice patches, some associated with artefacts, some attached to sticks and others wrapped with sinew. They dated from between 4500 and 190 BP. Out of the twelve fragments examined, six were identified to species or family (Table 8.1); three were from raptors, one from a flicker, one from a duck, and one from ptarmigan (Dove et al. 2005). Mummified remains of 34 adults and children from Kagamil Island in Alaska were found wearing garments of feathers, and bird and mammal skins. As the mummies could not be examined using invasive methods, fragments only of feather were available for study so microscopic identification was required. The feathers proved mainly to come from the Charadriiformes, Anseriformes, and Pelecaniformes; the mammal fur was from Phocidae, Otariidae, Mustelidae, Ursidae, Canidae, and Cervidae (Dove & Peurach 2002).

Finds from Anaerobic Environments

Most fossilised palaeontological feathers originally came from what were originally anaerobic sediments (Davis & Briggs 1995), and these conditions sometimes preserve more recent feathers. When the Gokstad Viking ship was excavated from a burial mound of about AD 870 in Norway, the 'exotic and unexpected discovery' was made of bones and also feathers of a peacock next to the steering oar (Dawson 1969). This was not the wealthiest of the burial mounds of the Viking chiefs, but it did also contain garments with gold thread and chess pieces. Feather fragments survived in a pocket of organic material in a medieval stone-lined pit at Pluscarden Priory, Scotland. They were identified as coming from pheasant (Ceron-Carrasco 1994). At the Fenland site of Haddenham (see Chapter 5), the conditions for preservation in the anaerobic silts of a waterlogged ditch were so perfect that impressions of the feathers were visible with the skeleton of a crane, though the feathers themselves did not survive. An unusual form of preservation was encountered in Finland, where feather fragments have been used as temper in pottery (Mannermaa 2003).

Table 8.1. *Identification, description, and date of ancient feathers associated with artefacts recovered from ice patches in the Yukon*

Artefact no.	Identification	Artefact description	Washed	Radiocarbon date	Location
JbVa-1:1a	Eagle (*Aquila* or *Haliaeetus*)	split flight feather	Yes	440 ± y50 BP	Texas Gulch IP
JcUu-1:8	Unidentified	pennaceous flight feathers	No	n/a	Friday IP
JcUu-1:9	Unidentified	two pennaceous feather shafts attached to stick	No	1250 ± y40 BP	Friday IP
JcUu-2:1	Unidentified	fragmented feathers*	Yes	4580 ± y70 BP	Alligator IP
JcUu-2:1c	Northern flicker (*Colaptes auratus luteus*)	birch shaft with large feather rachis and small yellow feather wrapped with sinew	No	4580 ± y70 BP	Alligator IP
JcUu-2:2h	Duck (Anatidae)	single primary feather*	Yes	3900 ± y70 BP	Alligator IP
JcUu-2:16	Unidentified	split feathers on spruce stick	No	190 ± y40 BP	Alligator IP
JcUu-2:22	White-tailed ptarmigan (*Lagopus leucurus*)	one white feather* and various other dark flight feathers	Yes	n/a	Alligator IP
JcUu-2:24	Gyrfalcon (*Falco rusticolus*)	a clump of approximately eight flight feathers	Yes	n/a	Alligator IP
JdUt-17:3e	Unidentified	large pennaceous feather attached to tip of artefact	No	1840 ± y40 BP	Granger IP
JdVb-2:1	Unidentified	small feather shafts wrapped in sinew on artefact	No	4360 ± y50 BP	Thandlat IP
JgVe-1:11	Short-eared owl (*Asio flammeus*)	single flight feather	Yes	n/a	Thulsoo IP

Note: n/a = not applicable; the asterisk denotes a notched feather.
Source: Data are from Dove et al. (2005, tab. 1).

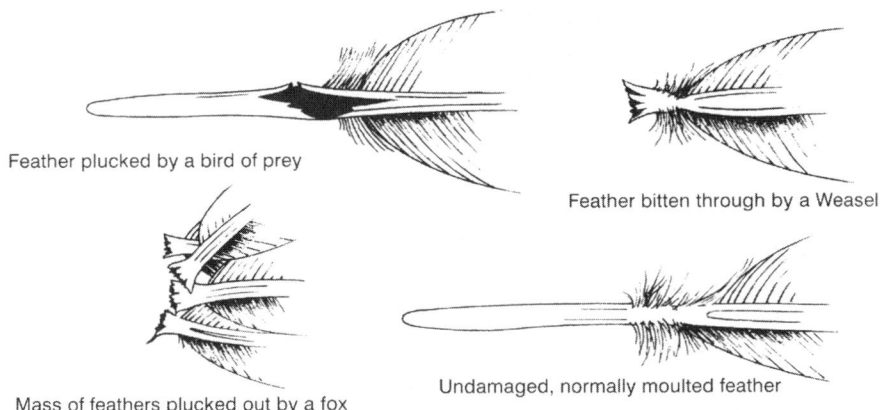

FIGURE 8.6. Types of damage to feathers by avian and mammalian predators (Brown et al., 1999, 75; drawing by M. Lawrence).

TAPHONOMY

Avian and mammalian predators damage feathers when they kill or pluck a bird. Birds of prey pluck feathers, leaving a hole or broken section in the base of the shaft; foxes, weasels, and other small mammals bite through the shaft just below the vane (Figure 8.6). Some feathers also show a type of natural damage known as 'hunger marks'. These are horizontal grooves across the vane which are caused by poor development of the barbules, a result of stress.

People cut or notch feathers; those used for fletching are invariably cut and the shaft is trimmed (Laubin & Laubin 1980, 113; Lyon 1991). Several of the feathers found in the ice patches in the Yukon were notched (Table 8.1 and Figure 8.7), and they are believed to have been intended for fletching arrows (Dove et al. 2005). The shaft was usually trimmed in the feathers used for feather-string objects in the Southwest (Borson et al. 1998). The kaka feathers from Lee Island referred to earlier were obliquely trimmed, probably for decoration. Because the Pluscarden feathers appeared to have been chopped into pieces, they were thought to have come from padded clothing or a cushion.

FEATHERS AS A SECONDARY PRODUCT

Feathers can be plucked from the live bird so, like wool, they can be a secondary product. The feathers regrow naturally after the bird has been plucked as part of the annual cycle of feather moult and regrowth. Geese of the Poitou breed were plucked

FIGURE 8.7. Feather of a white-tailed ptarmigan, *Lagopus leucurus*, cut or notched with a sawtooth pattern, preserved in a melting ice patch, Alligator site, Yukon, Canada (Dove et al. 2005, fig. 5; photograph by M. Heacker).

three times a year (Lecuyer & Pujol 1975), and it is said that in the heyday of intensive goose rearing in the eighteenth and nineteenth centuries, geese were plucked up to five times a year. Geese can first be plucked cleanly at about 12 to 15 weeks, the age at which goslings come into 'full feather' (Serjeantson 2002). Feathers and also down plucked from live birds are of higher quality than those from birds which have been killed, especially if the geese have lived where winters are cold. The most expensive duvets in an English department store are filled with 'hand plucked Siberian goose down'. Goose feathers used to be so valuable that geese were kept as much for their feathers as for their meat in the past (see also Chapter 12), something which is hinted at by the predominance of adult birds in early medieval assemblages. The tail feathers of the peacock are of higher quality, with better colour and less damage, if they are plucked before they moult, and one of the original impulses for the domestication of the peacock was for the feathers, as it was for the turkey (Chapter 12).

Tamed birds have also been kept in many societies so that the feathers can be plucked. Recent ethnographic examples include some Amerindian tribes of South America who tamed members of the parrot family, so that they could pluck the feathers, though they also kept the birds around the settlement to enjoy their ability to imitate human speech (see Chapter 13). The scarlet macaw was kept for its feathers, which were a 'necessary ritual item' in the Medio and Pueblo cultures (Minnis et al. 1993). The intriguing relationship between the pre-Columbian peoples of the Americas and the scarlet macaw is discussed again in Chapters 12 and 14. The Maori used to keep great white egrets in a cage for the white wing feathers which they plucked and wore in their ears (Crowe 2001, 81). In Central Asia in the eighteenth century, eagles were kept tethered by the yurts of the Kuriles to provide feathers for trade (Clark 1948). Just as with domestic birds, a captive bird provided its owner with a reliable source of feathers, and with feathers of higher quality.

The down of eider ducks is also a secondary product. The female birds pluck the down from the breast to line the nest and cover the eggs. The Inuit of Northern Canada gather eider down from the nests and use it to make clothing padded with down (Oakes & Stone 1990, 17). In areas where eiders breed in northern Europe, farmers collected the down for use and for sale. In northern Norway the farmers did not kill eiders, but protected them carefully from predators so that they would produce down and also eggs each year. To encourage nesting, the farmers built artificial nest sites. They kept human visitors away from the nests and even kept their cats tied up during the breeding season. The birds would allow themselves to be lifted off and replaced on the nest when feathers were removed (Bratrein 2005).

PROXY EVIDENCE FOR FEATHER USE

In the absence of feathers themselves, three lines of evidence can suggest that the feathers were used: the species, the elements, and the butchery marks.

Species

At the rock shelters of Lee Island, discussed earlier, where feathers as well as bones were found, the species – parrots, parakeets, and New Zealand pigeons – were those whose feathers had traditionally been sought after for decorating capes and other objects. The kaka bone remains lacked the distal wing bones, which had been detached at the proximal ulnar joint, and one interpretation of this absence is that the wings with the feathers had been taken away for use or exchange. Here, the birds had also been eaten and carcasses carried away from the site, which made interpretation of the relative numbers of the different elements rather complex (Anderson 1988; Anderson & McGovern-Wilson 1991; McGovern-Wilson 2005).

At the Palliser Bay site in New Zealand referred to in Chapter 4, the species present and also the predominant elements indicated that the parts of the birds brought to the site were those with particularly bright feathers. The main species were parakeets, both red- and yellow-crowned, and the tui. One of the most frequent elements of the tui was the mandible, an element which was scarce in the parakeet remains. The tui has a very distinctive tuft of long curled white feathers below the beak, which would most easily be removed by cutting the mandible. The parakeets have red and yellow feathers on the top of their heads: by contrast, there were relatively more crania of parakeets (Leach 1979). The Mesolithic site of Aggersund in Denmark was thought to be a special-purpose hunting camp where the white feathers of swans were obtained, since the bird bones at the site were exclusively of whooper swan (Grigson 1986).

Elements

In Chapter 6 I drew attention to the excess of distal wing bones at sites in the Pacific Northwest (see Figure 6.19). One possible explanation for the imbalance is that the distal wings had been collected for the feathers. Other sites have similar element patterns. At the Pre-Pottery Neolithic site of Jerf el Ahmar in northern Syria, the greatest number of elements of the griffon vulture were from the distal wing and feet (Figure 8.8), a contrast with the food species, geese, cranes, and partridges, where the pectoral girdle, femur, and tibiotarsus were common. The contrast led the author to the conclusion that the vulture was valued for features other than food, not only feathers but also tools and amulets, as we see in the next chapter. At other Syrian Pre-Pottery Neolithic sites vultures, both the griffon and black vulture, are thought to have been captured for their black feathers (Gourichon 2002).

At the Inca site of Potrero-Chaquiago in Argentina, the evidence for feather use is even clearer. In a storage area within the administrative centre of the city the bird bones recovered were almost exclusively carpometacarpi and associated carpals and phalanges from two raptors, the black-chested buzzard-eagle and a buzzard. They were found close together, some still in articulation; a minimum of 62 birds were represented (Rodriguez Loredo de March 1993). The author drew attention to the fact that the weaving of feather textiles was an activity in this Inca city; here the wings appeared to represent a store of feathers for use or for exchange. The choice of black, brown, and white feathers was enigmatic in a region where brightly coloured feathers were available, and usually seen as more desirable.

There is evidence for the collection of goose wing feathers in three medieval towns in England where there was an excess of carpometacarpi and wing digits of geese in certain deposits. In Beverley the wings are thought to have been used as dusters in weaving, but at Norwich and Winchester the predominance of left hand bones and

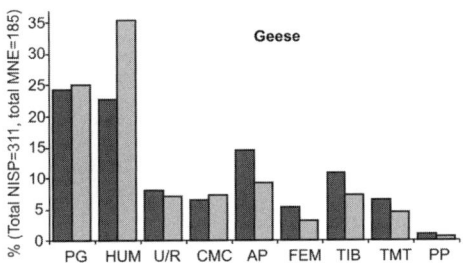
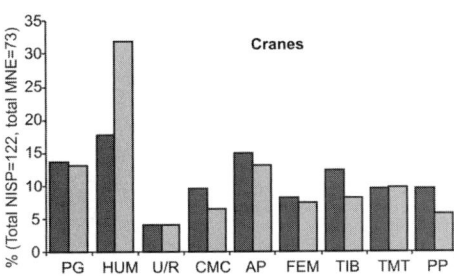
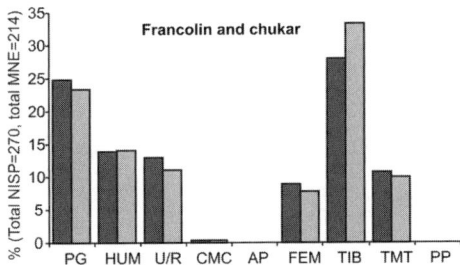
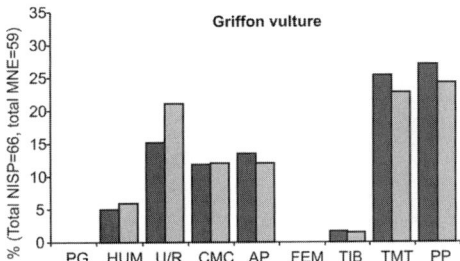

FIGURE 8.8. Elements present of geese, crane, *Grus grus*, partridges (francolin and chukar), and griffon vulture, *Gyps fulvus*, at the Pre-Pottery Neolithic site of Jerf el Ahmar, northern Syria. The most frequent elements of the griffon vulture are from the distal wing and the feet, suggesting a concern with the feathers and also with the claws for amulets. PG = pectoral girdle, HUM = humerus, U/R = ulna/radius, CMC = carpometacarpus, AP = anterior phalanx, FEM = femur, TIB = tibiotarsus, TMT = tarsometatarsus, PP = posterior phalanges (from Gourichon 2002, fig. 2.5).

the find of a stylus, another writing implement, suggested the bones were from wings with primary feathers attached which were collected for use as quill pens (Serjeantson 2002).

The *absence* of the elements of the left wing of scarlet macaws was a consistent pattern in Mimbres sites where macaw remains have been found. The birds were killed and given ceremonial burial, and the assumption is that the feathers and the left wing were retained whole for ritual use or decoration. Wings seem to have been used as part of the temple furniture in the fourth to sixth centuries AD Nubian temple at Qasr Ibrim in Lower Egypt (Rowley-Conwy 1989), and the wing of a swan placed beneath a child buried in a Mesolithic cemetery also surely had ceremonial use. Ceremonial and ritual uses of birds are discussed again in Chapter 14.

At the site of The Farm Beneath the Sand (GUS) in Greenland, the excavators found in one house the articulated wing bones broken off through the humerus, but no other elements, of a white-tailed sea eagle (Figure 8.9) and in another house four

FIGURE 8.9. Bones from the left wing of a white-tailed sea eagle, *Haliaeetus albicilla*, from the Viking site of The Farm Beneath the Sand (GUS), Greenland, probably collected for the feathers or for use as a brush (Enghoff 2003, fig. 8; photograph by G. Brovad).

articulated goose wings. Enghoff considers that the wings were probably collected for the feathers, but she also raised the possibility that they might have been intended for use as brushes (Enghoff 2003). Feathers pick up dust very effectively (Oakes & Stone 1990, 14), which is the reason why they are still used in feather dusters today.

Cut Marks

Albatrosses were hunted for meat and raw material for bone tools as well as for feathers at Hamanaka 2 in Northern Japan, a site of the Okhotsk Culture period (1500–600 BP). Cut marks on almost 20 per cent of the carpometacarpi indicated the removal of wing feathers; the cuts were either on the metacarpal process to detach the extensor ligament, or on the bone shaft (Eda et al. 2005). Though the predominance of bones of the feet and wings of snowy owl was not highly pronounced at the Late Magdalenian site of Le Bois-Ragot in France, the cut marks suggested that the owl feathers were used. As discussed in Chapter 6, wings had been detached at the distal humerus or at the wrist. Careful cut marks on the proximal carpometacarpus indicated where the distal wing was detached. Similar cuts were noted on carpometacarpi of geese from medieval Winchester (Serjeantson 2002).

Many owl radii and ulnae at Le Bois-Ragot also had longitudinal cuts or scrapes along the length of the bone, and even the carpometacarpus and tarsometatarsus had been treated in the same way (see Figure 6.4 in Chapter 6). These elements have little muscle, suggesting that the cuts were not to recover the meat, so they must therefore have been for removing feathers (Laroulandie 2004). The fact that there were cuts on the tarsometatarsus is a reminder of the fact that the snowy owl is one of the very few species which has feathers on the legs.

Age

Most remains of domestic geese from archaeological sites are of adult birds, but in the Late Medieval period in several towns in England the relative number of immature birds increased (see Figure 11.7 in Chapter 11). Immature geese, as we have seen, have produced at most one crop of useable feathers. This change in the age profile reflects the decrease in importance of feathers relative to meat in later Middle Ages (Albarella 1997b; Serjeantson 2002).

FEATHERED SKINS

Feathered bird skins, like feathers, were used for both decoration and warmth (Oakes & Stone 1990; Rae & Wills 2002). In Northern Canada, for instance, the common loon and other species were caught for skins and feathers, chosen both for their beauty and their practical uses (Nelson 1983, 87). In headdresses, feathered skins were usually for ritual use, as in the cap made from the white-feathered skin of a kelp goose which was worn by the shamans among the Ona of Patagonia until the early twentieth century (Lothrop 1928, 55). As discussed in Chapter 14, Californian Indians used buzzard skins to make ceremonial garments (Fraser 1963, 654–655), while other groups used those of turkeys. As well as the feathers, fragments of feathered skin of a kaka were recovered from Lee Island. Both had been part of a cape which was found partially burned. Medicine bundles were also wrapped in bird skins (Ubelekar & Wedel 1975).

Bird skins were worn outside for decoration, but inside other clothing for warmth. At least one of the human infant mummies found in caves on Kagamil Island in the Aleutians was wearing an undergarment of bird skin (Dove & Peurach 2002). Bird skins are thinner and less pliable than those of mammals, and have deeper follicles, so they are not as strong as mammal skins though they can be as warm or warmer. They were used in the Arctic for clothing, boots, slippers, and shoes. The best quality skins come from birds killed in October and November, because the moult is finished, the down is thick, and the skin is at its strongest (Oakes & Stone 1990). A skin with feathers can indicate the season of the year when the bird was killed, from the state of feather development. Among the Arctic communities, the skins of eider, puffin, cormorants, and sometimes raptors were used.

The method by which eider skin clothes were sewn has been recalled by Silatik Meeko and other women from the village of Sanikiluaq in Belcher Island, Northern Canada, where the skill is not quite lost (Oakes & Stone 1990). Using an *ulu*, a woman's curved knife, the seamstress cut away the duck's feet and wings. She then sliced through the skin at the neck area and away from the beak. She forced her hand between the skin and the body, and, holding the beak in her mouth, pulled the skin from the body. The fat was sucked from the skin to clean it (Figure 8.10a). Skins were sewn using bird bone needles and sinew, and large stitches were used so as not to weaken the skins. In parkas the wrist and face edge were strengthened with the skin of a dog or other mammal. Men's and women's parkas were made from up to 30 bird skins (Figures 8.10b and 8.10c), and those of children from as few as eight.

The skin covering of the foot of web-footed birds was used as a waterproof pouch. The naturalist Joseph Banks wrote that the 'webbed feet of albatrosses make capital tobacco pouches by drawing out all the bones and using the claws as ornament' (O'Brian 1987, 85). The Yámana in South America also removed the membrane over the feet for use (Mameli 2002). In the early nineteenth century, according to the entomologist Fabricius, the skin from the feet of the great auk was sometimes sewn together with pieces of seal skin to make small bags in which items could be stored (Meldgaard 1988). There is a bag made from the skin of a swan's foot in the Royal Ontario Museum (Gilbert et al. 1981).

Skinning Traces

As we saw in Chapter 6, cut marks made by skinning have rarely been recognised on bird remains, as birds are usually plucked rather than skinned before they are cooked. Cuts around the skull and the mandible may be diagnostic of skinning. At

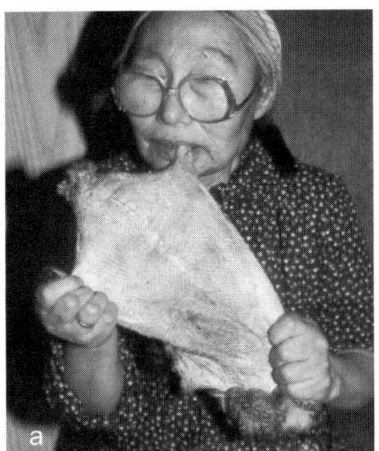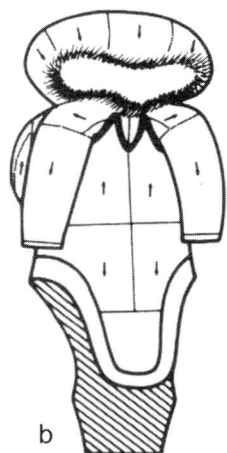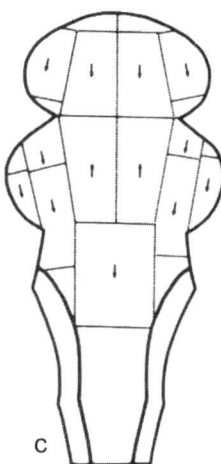

FIGURE 8.10. Preparation and sewing of clothes from the feathered skins of eider ducks, *Somateria mollissima*: a, seamstress Silatik Meeko from Belcher Island, Nunavut, Canada, removes the fat prior to using the skin to make a child's parka; b and c, diagrams showing how eider skins were used by the Ingava Inuit to make up a parka (photograph by J. Oakes; drawing by Z. Chun).

Jerf el Ahmar, fine cut marks on the parietal region of a griffon vulture cranium (see Figure 14.10 in Chapter 14) suggest that the bird had been 'scalped', that is, the skin cut from the skull, at this point (Gourichon 2002).

SINEW AND OIL

Sinew

Tendons or sinew have been an important raw material for those people living close to the glacial margins, where few plant fibres were or are available. During the Upper Palaeolithic era, sinew was used for sewing clothes, tents, and bags, and for binding objects such as bows, just as it has been among Arctic communities until recently. It has the great advantage over vegetable fibres of providing a waterproof seam. Bird as well as mammal sinew was used; the eider clothing described earlier was sewn with sinew from gulls, caribou, and bearded seal. Cuts needed to detach sinew are short repeated cuts. In mammals, such cut marks on the toe bones have been interpreted as evidence of sinew removal (Parkin et al. 1986). Cut marks have sometimes been noted on bird phalanges (see, e.g., Figure 6.5 in Chapter 6). When cut marks are found on the toes as well as other elements, especially from Palaeolithic assemblages, sinew removal is worth considering.

Oil

Bird fat was consumed, as discussed in Chapter 10, and the fat and oil was also used for heat and light. Seabirds and waterfowl are particularly oily. Their oil has been used for lamps and for lubrication among the Ainu (Eda et al. 2005), the Inuit (Oakes & Stone 1990), and also in northern Europe. The Procellaridae project oil at intruders, a reflex which was exploited by the fowlers on St Kilda who collected oil from fulmars before they killed the birds. The fowler, after catching the bird, 'dips the bird's beak into a small leather bag suspended to his waist, and there the oil is vomited' (Gray 1871, 500). Bird fat or oil has a low melting point, and it was formerly a commercial source of light oils until superseded by mineral oils; in the nineteenth century, fulmar oil was exported to the city of Glasgow and sold as a rust preventative. Bird grease has been used as the basis of ointments and liniments, and today it is still possible to buy ostrich oil, which is said to be good for the skin. The most dramatic use of bird oil was in the Faroe Islands where, according to a nineteenth-century naturalist, storm petrels were used as lamps: 'the Faroese convert them into lamps or candles, by drawing a wick through them, and setting fire to it' (Mudie 1835, 391). This surely would leave the bones burnt or charred, but has this ever been seen in archaeological material?

DISCUSSION

Oil from birds as a fuel was relied on most heavily by those who lived in high latitudes, though its use for liniments and ointments was worldwide. The best hope of identifying the use of oil from birds is probably from the chemical analysis of ceramics, as has been done for fish oils (Brown & Heron 2005). Most societies have had access to thread made from plant fibres, so sinew, including bird sinew, was important for sewing only where these were not available. With the sinew itself unlikely to survive, needles with very small eyes (see Figure 9.4 in the next chapter) are a potential guide to its use in the past.

Feathers and skins, on the other hand, were immensely important, whether used for symbolic, decorative, or practical purposes. Some ornithologists can identify feathers at the macroscopic level, but expertise in using microscopic techniques is limited. The techniques were originally devised as an aid to understanding evolutionary relationships, as with eggshell identification, but they have since been applied to forensics and the identification of birds killed in aircraft strikes as well as to anthropological research. Individuals skilled in identification of feathers work mainly in the larger national natural history museums. In view of the expertise needed to identify and curate feathers, it is advisable to contact an expert if they are encountered on excavations. Microscopic as well as macroscopic analysis has been used in North America, where feathers are quite often recovered.

Elsewhere they survive so rarely in archaeological contexts that we have to rely on the proxy evidence of species, elements, and cut marks. The presence of powerful birds such as raptors or colourful birds such as turkeys, parrots, and parakeets are a strong indication that they were caught for their feathers, even if they were also eaten. A disproportionate number of wing bones may suggest the wings were collected for the feathers while the rest of the carcass was discarded. We saw in Chapter 6 that the humerus, radius, and ulna may predominate in an assemblage because they are among the largest and most robust bones in the skeleton, but if smaller wing elements such as the carpometacarpus and wing digits are present in unexpectedly high numbers *and* the other elements which are discarded during primary butchery such as feet and heads are absent, it indicates that feathers were collected and used. Cut marks detaching parts of the wing, particularly the carpometacarpus on which the primary feathers are found, are also indirect evidence for the use of feathers. Repeated longitudinal cuts or scrapes on the wing bones may also indicate that feathers were removed from the bones. These longitudinal cuts on the ulna and radius have been observed in Palaeolithic assemblages, but not in those of later periods, and it would be worth investigating if the marks were so prominent on the bones from that period because the feathers were removed when the wing was desiccated or frozen. If cuts are present which are apparently from skinning, they would be unequivocal evidence that the community had been using the skins, something for which there is up to now little archaeological evidence.

The use of feathers for fletching arrows was widespread, and the need for feathers for arrows has always been considered one of the possible reasons for catching birds in North America. In the Old World this connection has not always been made, but feathers for fletching arrows may well have been the main reason for the occasional presence of bird remains on settlements where otherwise birds were a very minor element in the fauna.

The most widespread use of feathers has always been for decoration, for ceremonial purposes, and for marking special status or wealth. This is self-evident in those parts of the world where the tradition has persisted, such as Polynesia and the Americas, but it is less obvious in Europe. Especially in later prehistoric Europe, early farmers in general had little interest in hunting and eating birds, as we see in Chapter 10, but from time to time a few bones, often from large birds, are found on prehistoric sites. It is likely, as Albarella (1997a) suggests, that the cranes and vultures whose remains were found at the Bronze Age site of La Starza in Italy were prized for their huge feathers, which, as we have seen, may well have had symbolic or ceremonial value. Where the quantity of bird remains is large, it is a challenge to distinguish the relative importance of meat and feathers, but in those societies which avoid eating birds or eat very few, there is a very real possibility that any remains that are present are from birds caught for their feathers.

9

Tools and Ornaments

Bird bones are uniquely functional as tools because the bone wall is both dense and thin. The bird bone objects which have attracted most attention are the flutes, pipes, and whistles made from the long, tubular wing bones of large birds, but these elements and others were also made into delicate tools such as awls, points, small chisels, arrowheads, fishhooks, pins, and needles. Tubular bones were also used as drinking straws. With the ends blocked, they were used as containers and, cut into segments, they were used as beads (Crockford et al. 1997; Wijngaarden-Bakker 1997; Walker & Parmalee 2004; Gál 2005a).

MANUFACTURE OF TOOLS

In most collections of bone tools, the percentage made on bird bones is low, but sites in the Arctic and the far south of South America can be exceptions: at Túnel I, two thirds of the tools were made from bird bones (Scheinson 1990–1992). The analysis of the sequence of actions which contributed to the selection, modification, and use of tools and other objects, sometimes referred to as the *chaîne operatoire*, reveals why some species and some elements were preferred.

Selection of Species and Elements

Unlike feathers which, as we saw in the previous chapter, were often selected for symbolic reasons, function as much as association dictated the choice of bird bones for tools. At the Upper Palaeolithic cave site of Les Eyzies in France, the bones of crane 'by reason of their length and solidity, supplied material for the fabrication

Table 9.1. *Bird species represented in artefacts and food remains at Dutch Neolithic sites*

Site	Species	Element	Function	Also food remains
Aartswoud	White-tailed eagle, *Haliaeetus albicilla*	Carpometacarpus	Sharp awl	–
Aartswoud	Crane, *Grus* sp.	Tarsometatarsus	Sharp awl	–
Vlaardingen	Bewick's swan, *Cygnus bewickii*	Radius	Tube	–
Vlaardingen	Greylag goose? cf. *Anser anser*	Radius	Tube	+
Hazendonk	Bewick's swan/Greylag goose	Humerus	Bead?	–
Hekelingen III	Whooper swan, *Cygnus cygnus*	Ulna	Tube	+
Hazendonk	Swan ?mute *Cygnus* cf. *olor*?	Tibiotarsus	Tube	(+)
Bergschenhoek	Swan ?mute	Tibiotarsus	Awl	+
Swifterbant	Crane, *Grus* sp.	Ulna	Awl	–

Note: All species whose bones were used for tools were large; some were absent from the food remains. Symbols are as follows; +, present; (+), probably present; –, absent, ?, uncertain identification.
Source: Data are from Wijngaarden-Bakker (1997).

of needles, arrow-points and other similar implements' (Milne-Edwards 1875, 247). In high latitudes, bones were used from small as well as larger birds, but in general there was a preference for elements from large birds (Table 9.1; also see Wijngaarden-Bakker 1997; Godula et al. 2002; Gál 2005a). The species selected for bone tools on Neolithic sites in the Netherlands were white-tailed sea eagle, crane (Figures 9.1a and 9.1b), the three species of swans found in Western Europe, and greylag goose. These are six out of the ten largest birds, by weight, found in the Netherlands in the past. Out of the nine implements discussed, five, possibly six, were made on bones of species which were not represented among the food remains (Table 9.1; Wijngaarden-Bakker 1997). The only bird bone from the Neolithic site at Barrow Hills, Radley, Oxfordshire, was an awl which had been made from the ulna of a white-tailed sea eagle (Barclay et al. 1999, fig. 4.34). The use of elements from species not eaten may suggest that birds were sought specifically as raw material for tools. Elements from birds as small as the horned and tufted puffins were used to make needles in Alaska and the Pacific Northwest (Stewart 1996).

At coastal sites where seabirds were available, the bones of gulls and albatrosses were preferred because the bones of the wing are long and straight. Baskets containing both finished tools and manufacturing materials were found at Ozette, a waterlogged Late Prehistoric village site on the Pacific coast of Washington State. They contained

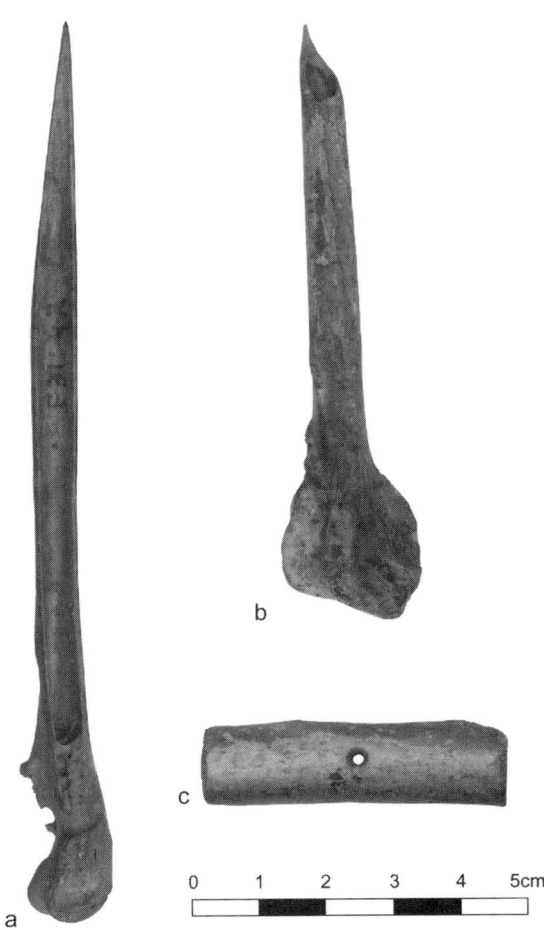

FIGURE 9.1. Neolithic bone tools from Aartswoud, the Netherlands: a, an awl made on the tarsometatarsus of a crane, *Grus grus*; b, an awl made on the tarsometatarsus of a white-tailed sea eagle, *Haliaeetus albicilla*; c, a tubular object with opposing holes made on the humerus of a crane (Wijngaarden-Bakker 1997, figs. 2, 3, and 6).

collections of wing bones of gulls and of short-tailed albatross, a species now confined to islets off Japan, but formerly more widespread in the North Pacific (DePuydt 1994, 223; Crockford et al. 1997; Lefèvre et al. 1997). Most caches of tools or elements destined for tools have come from cemeteries. At the Modoc Rock Shelter site in Illinois, approximately 160 radii of goose, including both Canada and snow goose, and six tarsometatarsi of sandhill crane were found with a human burial of the Archaic period. Most of the bones were unaltered but one or two had been made into awls. The earliest recorded cache of bird bones for tools is of Paleoindian date, from the basal levels in Dust Cave, Northwestern Alabama. It comprised 23 humeri of

Canada goose, of which 19 had cut or scrape marks from disarticulation or defleshing (Walker & Parmalee 2004).

At Túnel, the bones of large birds were concentrated in the central area of the settlement 'inside the hut', apparently because that is where tool-making took place. The tools included burins (chisels or awls) made on the humerus, radius, and tibiotarsus of large seabirds (Mameli 2002; Mameli & Estevez 2004).

Sources of Raw Materials

The elements used for tools and other objects must usually have come from birds which were caught and killed, though not necessarily for food. The bones may have been scavenged from carcasses (see Chapter 5). As Weisler and Gargett (1993, 85) point out, 'At present there is no way to determine whether bird bone artefacts such as awls and tattooing needles were produced using bones from human kills, as opposed to bone scavenged from natural death locales'. This comment referred to the Hawaiian island of Moloka'i, where dead birds could readily be found washed up on the beaches, but it is relevant for any site on the coast. Marta Moreno (personal communication, 26 July 2004) has described how shepherds in Spain used to collect wing bones to make into flutes from the carcasses of the griffon and the black vulture which they encountered in the mountains. At sites in the South Island of New Zealand, bones of moa, Dinornithidae, were used for making fish hooks long after the moa themselves were extinct, and at North Island sites bones for tools were thought to have been imported from elsewhere as raw material (Anderson 1989b, 112).

Wings and individual wing bones appear to have been traded in the Pacific Northwest. Though it is possible that the albatross bones at Ozette (DePuydt 1994) were from carcasses washed up to the beach, a more probable explanation is that they were imported from neighbouring bands through trade or exchange. There are relatively few humeri, radii, and ulnae of albatross at the Maple Bank site in Victoria, and more carpometacarpi and phalanges. By contrast, at the contemporary site of Yuquot, further north, all parts of the albatross skeleton were found. We saw in Chapter 8 how a high percentage of carpometacarpi can indicate that the distal wing was collected for the feathers. Here, in addition, the hypothesis is that the principle wing bones were traded away for use as tools elsewhere (Crockford et al. 1997). As discussed in Chapter 6, other sites in the Gulf of Georgia have the same suggestive predominance of the carpometacarpus (see Figure 6.19), either because feathers were collected, or because proximal wing bones were exported, or both.

Curation and Survival

There are hints that bone tools survive better than waste bone. One reason for the better preservation of bone tools compared with bones from food remains at archaeological sites may be that the bones were not cooked by boiling. Rex Garniewicz suggested that another reason might be that bone tools were intentionally greased to keep them from cracking or splitting, something supported by a number of ethnographic references in North America (ZOOARCH archive 20 February 2003 – see Appendix 3). Awls used to pierce skin develop polish from contact with the fats in the skin, which gives some protection from erosion in the soil. Other tools too may have been protected inside a bag or with clothing. All these factors may go some way to explaining why bird bone tools are sometimes found even when other bird remains are absent or rare.

TYPES OF TOOLS, FLUTES, AND BEADS

Awls and Points

Awls made from bird bones take the same basic form as those made from mammal bones: one epiphysis was left on the bone to provide a strong handle, the unwanted epiphysis was cut off, and the bone was split all or part of the way up the shaft and ground or cut to a point (Figures 9.1a, 9.1b, and 9.2). The humerus was often used as it is a robust bone (see Chapter 6), but the other straight hollow elements were also used. Two longitudinal sections of crane humerus from Neolithic Aartswoud were presumably points or awls even though they lack handles; one was decorated and perforated for suspension at one end (Figure 9.3).

Needles and Pins

Needles and pins were also made from elements with a strong, straight bone wall. Needles were used for tattooing as well as for sewing and weaving. Milne-Edwards describes an early find from Les Eyzies, the 'lower portion of a tibia, which had been separated from the body of the bone, not by an accidental fracture, but evidently by the hand of Man and by means of a sharp instrument which played the part of a saw. The fragment bears also numerous longitudinal grooves made by an analogous instrument, probably for the purpose of detaching needles or arrow-points'

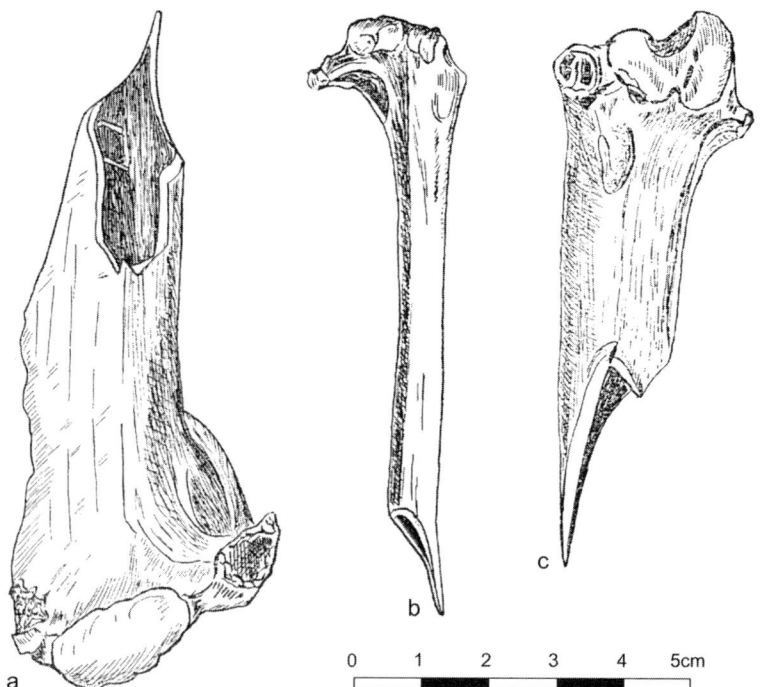

FIGURE 9.2. Bird bone awls from New Zealand: a, the right proximal humerus of a mollymawk, *Thalassarche cauta*, from Pounawea; b, the proximal humerus of a sooty shearwater, *Puffinus griseus*, from Papatowai; c, the right distal humerus of a mollymawk from Pounawea (after Lockerby 1959).

(Milne-Edwards 1875, 247). Several more examples of needle manufacture have subsequently been discovered on Palaeolithic sites in Europe (Laroulandie 2000, fig. 18), and an albatross humerus from the site of Amaknak in the Aleutian Islands has been worked in almost exactly the same way (Figure 9.4a). Needles from Whale Cove, Oregon, and from New Zealand were made on bird bones, but the element and species could not be identified. In the Pacific Northwest, the eyes of some needles were incised and others were drilled; some have the eye near the point which interlocks two threads, as in the needle of a modern sewing machine (Stewart 1996, 98). Those from Amaknak have very tiny holes, some too small for most types of thread (Figure 9.4b), so they must have been used with fine sinew (see Chapter 8). An alternative explanation for the very small eyelet holes, suggested for some of the bone needles from New Zealand, is that human hair was used for sewing (Lockerby 1959). Eight needles, some of bird and some of mammal bone, were found together in a needle case made from a caribou metapodial at the coastal Archaic site (*c.* 2000 BC) of Port au Choix in Newfoundland. Some of these too had extremely fine eyelet holes (Tuck 1971). Pins, similar in morphology to needles but without an eye,

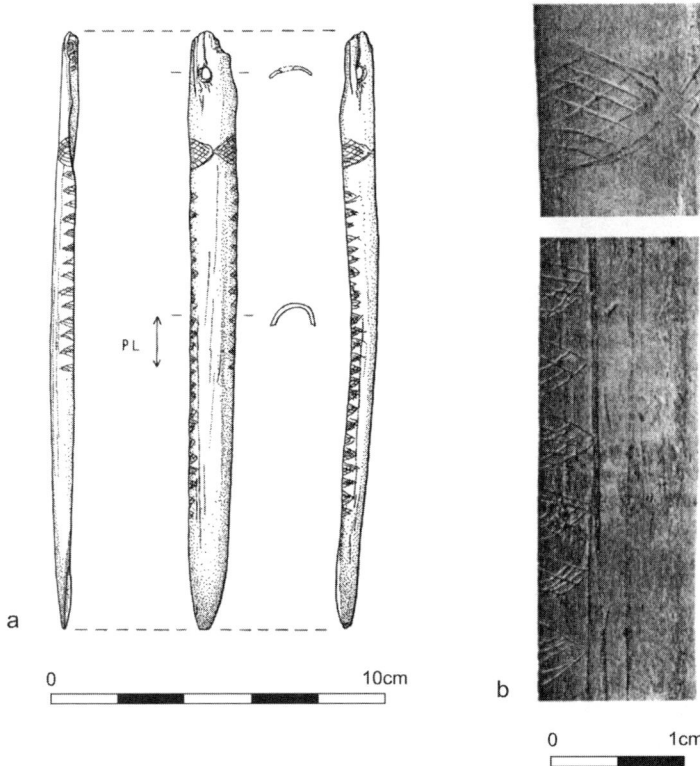

FIGURE 9.3. Neolithic bird bone point from Hardinxfeld-Giessendam De Bruin, the Netherlands: a, perforation, rounded ends, and traces of use-wear on the distal end; b, details showing cross-hatch decoration and scrape marks on the shaft where the bone was cleaned before manufacture (from Louwe Kooijmans 2001, fig. 10.15; photograph by C. H. Maliepaard).

were used for composite fish hooks and larger examples were used as blanket pins (Bennet & Lyman 1991, 31).

The use of the beaks as pins has occasionally been referred to in the ethnographic literature. The long beak of a curlew was used as pin on the island of St Kilda, an environment where, as we have seen in earlier chapters, birds, eggs, and feathers were a mainstay of the subsistence economy. In Finland the sharp, pointed beaks of divers were used as arrowheads (Mannermaa 2003, 18).

Tubes and Tubular Objects

Ethnographic literature from all over the world describes how bird bone tubes were used as straws for drinking, sniffing, and blowing, including blowing paint. They have

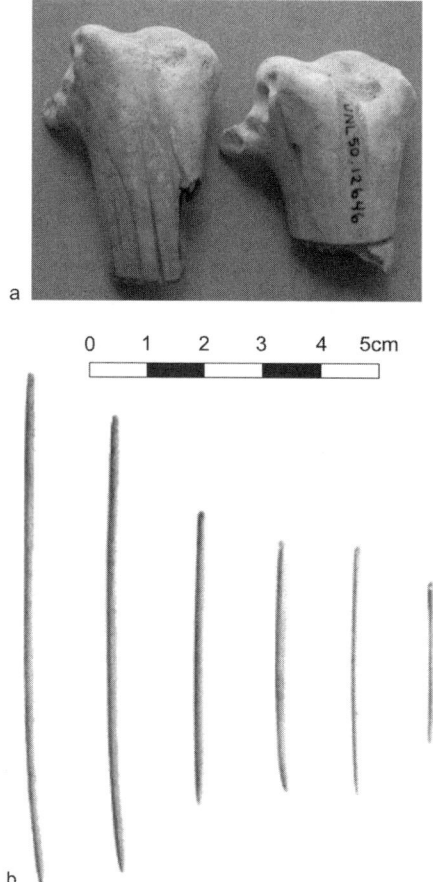

FIGURE 9.4. Needle manufacture at Amaknak, Aleutian Islands: a, humeri of albatross, *Phoebastria* sp., with grooves from needle manufacture; b, bird bone needles, some with fine holes suggesting the use of bird sinew as thread (photographs by R. Wigen).

been used as ritual drinking straws for menstruating women in some communities of the Pacific Northwest, and as ritual milking straws in the Old World. Tubes of bird bone have also been used for the storage of ochre and other precious materials and as needle cases. Two tubular pieces from Pool, Sanday, Orkney, made on ulnae of goose were interpreted as needle cases by analogy with similar objects elsewhere in Europe in the Viking period (MacGregor 1985, 193). The inhabitants of Pool had a choice of bones of gannet and cormorants as well as goose. The ulnae of the former are as large and robust but those of geese may have been selected because the diameter is greater and more circular (Serjeantson 2007a).

To make bone tubes, the long bone was carefully cut round the proximal and distal shaft to detach one or both epiphyses, usually leaving a distinctive clean straight cut. Cleaning prior to use often left scrape marks along the length of the bone (Wijngaarden-Bakker 1997; Recchi & Gopher 2002, fig. 10) which remain visible even when the implement was decorated. Three complete Neolithic bone tubes in the Archaeological Museum in Krakow have a fairly consistent length of approximately 70 mm, which suggests a common use (Godula et al. 2002). One day perhaps use-wear analysis or chemical analysis will identify traces of milk, food, pigment, or some other substance which helps to reveal the use. The perforation in one of the tubes from Aartswoud (Figure 9.1c) might suggest its use as a bead or toggle but the function of most tubes is unknown. Some Neolithic pottery in Europe is decorated with impressed rings which are thought to have been made with bird bones, but research in progress has shown no elements which might have had this function. A systematic examination of wear on the cut ends of bird bone tubes may one day identify this use.

The offcuts from making bone tubes consist of the proximal or distal end of the long bone, removed above or below the epiphysis. The distal ulna of griffon vulture from the site of Tell Hesban in Jordan was severed approximately 20 mm above the distal articulation (LaBianca & Driesch 1995, 135–137), perhaps so that the rest of the bone could be used for beads or some other tool. In the worked distal humeri of cormorants from Amaknak, the cut was angled (R. Wigen personal communication July 2007).

Flutes, Pipes, and Whistles

Flutes or pipes – which are distinguished from whistles by having more than one finger or tone hole – represent the most elaborate use of long tubular bird bones. In the past the bone used for a flute was sometimes described as made on a 'tibia' when in fact it was another element. Roman flutes were referred to as 'tibiae', which may have led the inexperienced to assume the instrument was always made on a tibia or tibiotarsus, but recent research has shown that this identification was incorrect so far as bird bone flutes are concerned (Moreno-Garcia et al. 2005). The ulna or radius of a vulture was most often chosen in southern Europe (Milne-Edwards 1875, 230; Moreno-Garcia et al. 2005). In medieval England the ulna and occasionally other elements of goose, swan, and crane were used (Leaf 2007). In China most flutes are made on bones of red-crowned crane (Zhang et al. 2004). Flutes made on albatross bones were displayed in the Te Papa Tongarewa Museum in New Zealand in 2006 and wing bones of stork were used for flutes in the Netherlands in the Middle Ages (Esser & Verhagen 2001).

It has been suggested that bird bone whistles and flutes were originally made as bird decoys, but it now appears that the earliest flutes known are already more sophisticated than is needed for a decoy whistle (D'Errico et al. 2003). The earliest examples date from the early Upper Palaeolithic (Aurignacian) levels in Germany and France. Fragments of several flutes were identified among the bones excavated from the cave of Aurignac in the nineteenth century: 'From the condition of these bones it seems that the inhabitants of the Caves carefully sought after them, their dimensions being considerable, and their remarkable pneumatic state permitting them to be easily converted into pipes. Indeed the ulnae are generally broken so as to separate the articular extremities; and on several of them we observe outlines or regular lines' (Milne-Edwards 1875, 230). Parts of two flutes were found at Geissenklosterle in southwest Germany, also from an Aurignacian level, with a date of $36,800 \pm 1000$ BP. The most complete example was made on the radius of a whooper swan; the shaft survives to 130 mm in length. It has three holes on the dorsal side, circular to oval in shape, which were cut with a flint and bevelled (Hahn & Munzel 1995). Several flutes have been recovered in excavations at the Pyrenean site of Isturitz from Upper Palaeolithic levels. One, with at least three holes, came from Aurignacian levels; no less than nine were associated with Gravettian tools, six with Perigordian, and two with Solutrean or Magdalenian industries. All were made on the wing bones of vultures (Laroulandie 2000; D'Errico et al. 2003; Moreno-Garcia et al. 2005). At least two from Gravettian levels show wear around the finger holes; they also show regular incisions (Figure 9.5).

The tradition of making flutes from bird bone ulnae or radii has continued from Later Prehistoric times until the present day. Bird bone flutes or whistles were excavated from Late Neolithic barrows at Normanton and Avebury in Wiltshire; the Normanton flute was made on a tibiotarsus of a large bird which has not been identified. There are many examples from the Roman world and from the early historic times in Europe and the Near East (Figure 9.6). Some Islamic examples from the Iberian Peninsula and Syria are decorated (Figure 9.7; also see Megaw 1960; MacGregor 1985; Becker 2005b; Gál 2005a; Moreno-Garcia et al. 2005). Though several flutes are now known from medieval England made from both bird and mammal bones, none is illustrated in contemporary manuscripts, suggesting that at this time bone flutes were used only in informal contexts (Leaf 2007). Double pipes or flutes are known from the Carpathian Basin in the Avar period, sometimes made on a pair of tarsometatarsi of the same bird (Gál 2006a). There is an internet site devoted to the playing of reproductions of early prehistoric bone flutes (see Appendix 3).

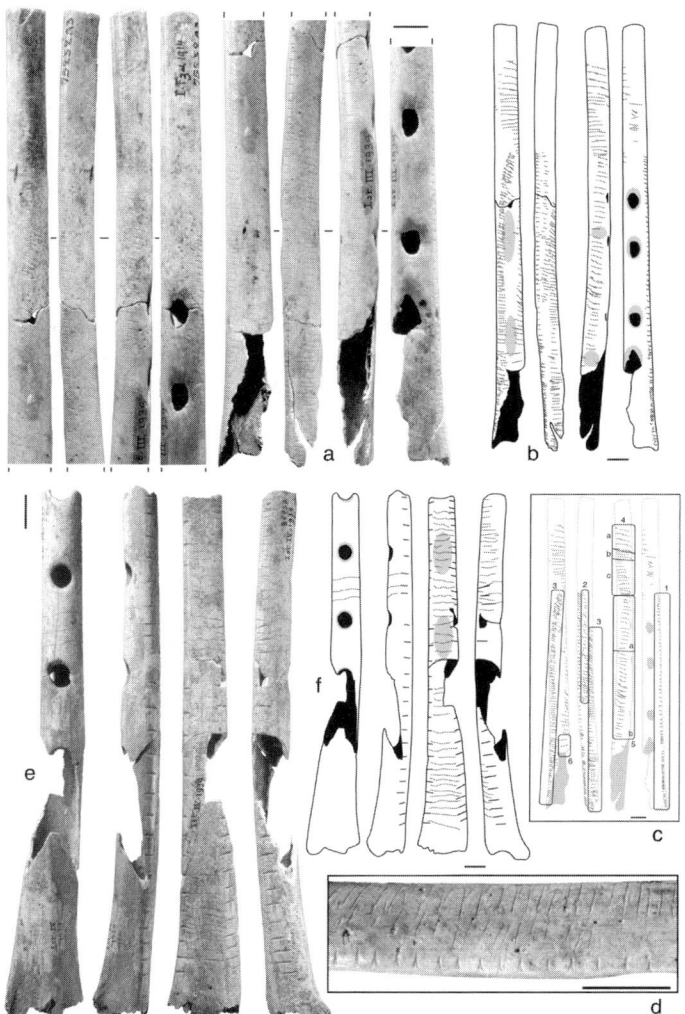

FIGURE 9.5. Pipes (flutes) with four holes from the Gravettian levels of Isturitz Cave, made on the ulnae of black vultures, *Aegypius monachus*: a and e, photographs, and b and f, tracings, of the two most complete examples (grey areas around the finger holes and at the rear of the pipe indicate polish interpreted as use-wear); c, sketch identifying marks and incisions made by different tools; d, close-up views of sets 1–3, scale 1 cm (D'Errico et al. 2003, fig. 10; photographs by F. D'Errico).

A series of flutes from Roman, Visigothic, Islamic, and recent periods in Spain and Portugal was all made on ulnae. Even when the bone lacked both ends, the element used could be identified from the curvature, the triangular cross section at the distal end, and surviving traces of the quill knobs (*papillae ulnare*). The Iberian

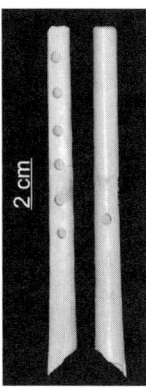

FIGURE 9.6. Flute from medieval Visegrad, Hungary, with at least six holes, made on the ulna of an eagle, possibly *Aquila chrysaetos* (Gál 2005a, fig. 7). The finger holes are worn. The left side shows the cranial view; the right shows the caudal view (photograph by E. Gál).

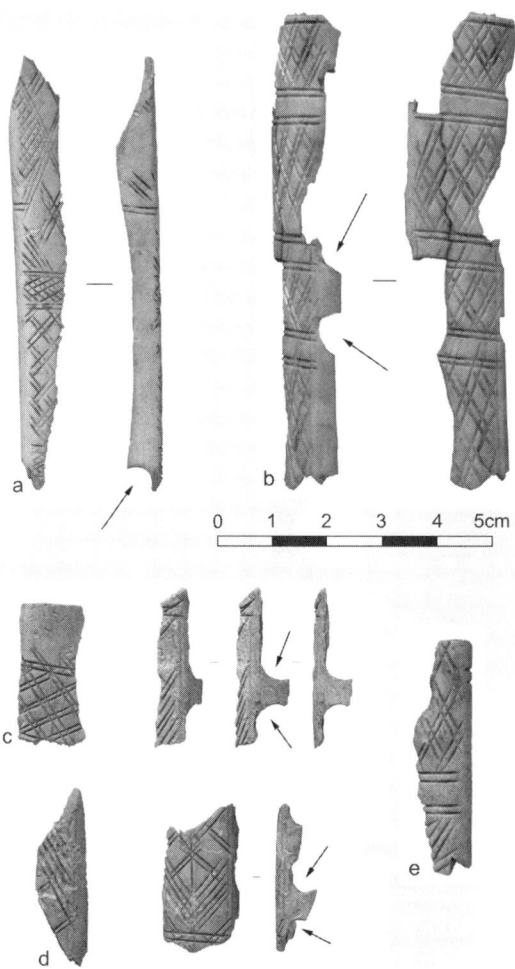

FIGURE 9.7. Five pieces of Islamic bird bone musical instruments from Mértola, Portugal. Arrows show the position of the holes (Moreno-Garcia et al. 2005; photograph by J. P. Ruas).

bones were all from either the black or griffon vulture. In some cases the authors were able to distinguish the species, using the criterion of the distance between the nutrient foramen and the actual or estimated beginning of the *cotyla ventralis* of the proximal epiphysis (Moreno-Garcia et al. 2005). The re-examination of bone flutes by Moreno-Garcia and colleagues and by D'Errico and colleagues has exposed how casual archaeologists have been in the past about attempting to identify the element and species from which these instruments were made.

The Iberian flutes have up to five holes, which are not necessarily positioned in a straight line or at regular intervals. Polish has been detected around the holes on the two Gravettian flutes from Isturitz, which has been interpreted as use-wear (D'Errico et al. 2003, fig. 10). Polish has been observed on many later examples, including on a flute made on the ulna of a griffon vulture from early Islamic Raqqa (Becker 2005b, fig. 2) and on an example from medieval Hungary (Figure 9.6).

In a fragmentary find, the presence of a hole or holes may be diagnostic of a whistle or flute, but some prehistoric perforated bones originally claimed as flutes have since been rejected because the hole was subsequently found to have been made by a carnivore tooth or by natural erosion. The presence of wear round the hole (see Figures 9.5 and 9.6) is stronger evidence that the piece was originally a flute. Decoration may confirm this, but, as we have seen, other objects made with bird bone tubes were also decorated.

Beads

The earliest necklaces of tubular beads made from bird bones also date from the Palaeolithic era. A perforated tibiotarsus of a Eurasian stone curlew was found with perforated mammal teeth in a Late Glacial rock shelter in the Pyrenees, the Abri Dufaure (Altuna et al. 1991), and finished beads and bones worked for the production of beads have been found on several Natufian and Pre-Pottery Neolithic sites. At Hayonim a young man was buried with a bracelet of at least 14 beads made from the distal tibiotarsus of the chukar, cut off at the supratendinal bridge (Pichon 1988). These and other similar beads, sometimes referred to as 'pearls', from elsewhere on the site were polished from wear. The distal epiphyses of tarsometatarsi of eider, cormorant, and crane excavated at the Middle Neolithic site of Ajvide on Gotland were cut and also polished, leading the researchers to think that they may also have been used as beads or ornaments (Mannermaa & Lougas 2005). The polish will have come from contact with skin or clothing. Bird bone tubular beads were sometimes used as spacer beads in necklaces made up of more than one material. Another type

222 BIRDS

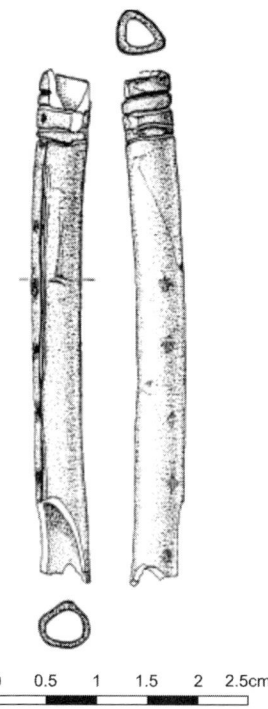

FIGURE 9.8. Method of manufacture of annular beads at the Pre-Pottery Neolithic site of Qumran Cave using the ulna of a corvid, *Corvus* sp. (Recchi & Gopher 2002, fig. 12). The shaft has been grooved with a sharp implement preparatory to removing bone rings.

of Natufian beads comprised thin rings cut from the shaft of a long bone. Figure 9.8 illustrates how these were made: a corvid ulna from Qumran Cave has the distal epiphysis cut off, and a series of deep grooves around the shaft made to remove rings of bone a few millimetres wide. Just as with the flutes and other tubular objects, there are longitudinal striae or scrape marks on the bone from cleaning (Recchi & Gopher 2002, fig. 12). Beads can be readily recognised if they are found as part of a group, and especially if found with human burials. Isolated short tubes are more difficult to identify as beads unless they show some wear on the cut edges or traces of polish.

Other Utensils

An unusual object of bird bone was found at the Late Hallstatt settlement of Balatonboglár–Berekre-dűlő in Hungary: the lower mandible of a spoonbill (Figure 9.9) had been detached from the skull perhaps for use as a spoon or spatula (Gál 2005a).

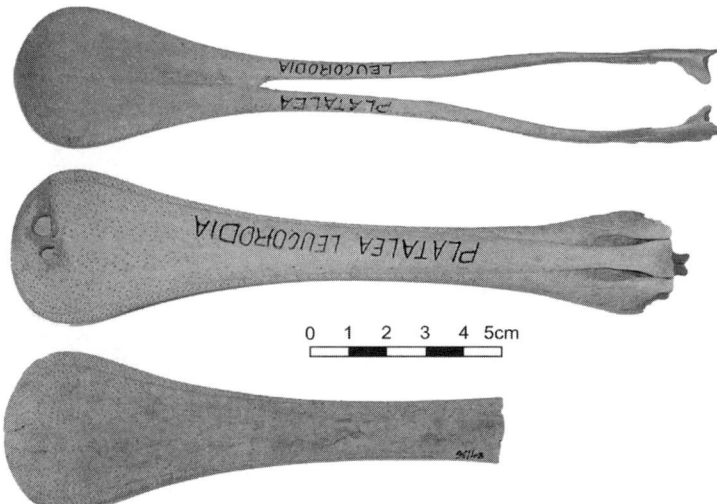

FIGURE 9.9. Maxilla of spoonbill, *Platalea leucorodia*, cut from the skull, perhaps for use as a spoon (Gál 2005a): the bottom shows the maxilla from the Iron Age site of Balatonboglár–Berekre-dűlő, Hungary; the top and middle show a maxilla and mandible of a recent spoonbill for comparison (photograph by E. Gál).

Tools Made from Bones of Flightless Birds

The leg bones of heavy ground-living birds have similar qualities to those of mammalian herbivores, so they were selected for tool-making for rather different reasons than the finer bones of flying birds. Limb bone splinters of moa were carved into points and chisels (see Figure 2.5 in Chapter 2) and also into gorges and fishhooks (Figure 9.10) at sites from the Archaic period in New Zealand (Lockerby 1959; Anderson 1989, 119, 134, 156).

Discussion

A tool or an offcut from tool-making can be recognised where a bone has been carefully cut or sawn, since day-to-day butchery of birds, as discussed in Chapter 6, used simpler techniques. Traces of grinding, polish, or wear on a point or awl is also evidence that the bone was used. The longitudinal striations or scrapes seen on the radius, ulna, and carpometacarpus may indicate that the bone was cleaned for use, but they are not on their own diagnostic of bones used as tools, as these marks were also made when the feathers and meat were removed.

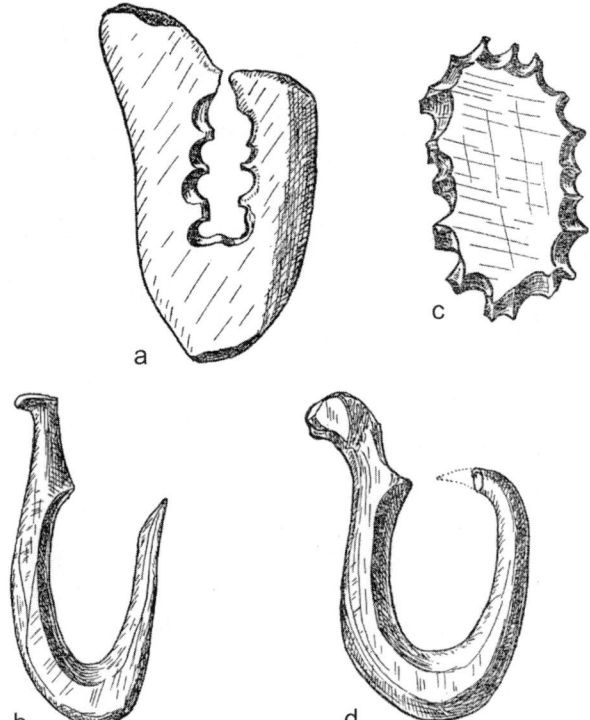

FIGURE 9.10. Fishhooks of moa bone from Archaic sites in New Zealand, showing the method of manufacture: a, partly worked; b, offcut; c and d, completed hooks. Note that a and d are from Papatowai, b is from Pounawea, and c is from King's Rock (from Lockerby 1959, figs. 24–27).

Functional tools of bird bone were most important in the Late Palaeolithic and Mesolithic, and they continued to be so in high latitudes in the Americas but are relatively sparse elsewhere. In later prehistoric Europe, from the Neolithic period onwards, 'artefacts made from bird bones do not seem to be a very usual occurrence in prehistoric contexts' (Wijngaarden-Bakker 1997). They fell out of use partly, no doubt, as the exploitation of birds declined, and, later, because bronze took over as the material of choice for delicate tools such as awls and needles.

DECORATIVE OBJECTS

As well as the beads made from bone tubes, other parts of the skeleton have been used for decoration and – as discussed in Chapter 14 – as amulets or talismans.

FIGURE 9.11. Perforated claw of an eagle owl, *Bubo bubo*, from the Tibocoaia Cave, a Palaeolithic site in Romania (Gál 2005a, fig. 12; photograph by E. Gál).

Complete wings and heads were sometimes used (see, e.g., Gilbert et al. 1981, fig. 2), as well as skulls, beaks, and the phalanges.

The use of claws or talons (distal or ungual phalanges) for decoration and as talismans was widespread. Invariably they were from raptors. Not only are raptor claws larger and more distinctive than those of other birds – raptors are capable of using their claws to carry off prey which is almost as heavy as they are – but the association with power and with hunting skill must have been a strong inducement for hunters to wear or carry the claws of eagles and vultures. Distal phalanges have been found as parts of a necklace or as isolated finds in contexts where they appear to have been collected or perhaps worn. At the Abri Dufaure, as well as bone beads, 65 distal phalanges of the eagle and the snowy owl were found, more than any other element (Altuna et al. 1991). At Qumran Cave almost half of identified elements of the Falconiformes were phalanges, compared with a maximum of 16 per cent for other families (Recchi & Gopher 2002). In the assemblage of 53 bird bones from Brzesc Kujawski, a Polish Neolithic site, the avian fauna comprised mostly ducks and geese, but of the three raptor bones, one is a distal phalanx of a greater spotted eagle (Bogucki 1979).

Though often unmodified, in some the articular end of the phalanx is drilled through for suspension (Figure 9.11). Perforated claws of raptors have been found in Iron Age Scandinavian graves (Clark 1948) and with a burial in the Anglo-Saxon cemetery of Spong Hill in eastern England (Bond & Worley 2006). A very complex example was found in Eralla Cave in the Pyrenees, in Late Upper Palaeolithic (Magdalenian) levels. The claw of a falcon or accipiter was pierced with three holes, 'one bored vertically through the end, just below the epiphysis and two others horizontally and at right angles into the centre below the epiphysis.... Microscopic examination of the holes shows no marks of cutting, but the edges are extremely smooth, even polished' (Eastham 1985, 68). The claw was found, appropriately, in a context interpreted as a ritual deposit. At Tell Hesban a distal phalanx was found with an unfinished perforation. The bone had been drilled on one side, but the perforation had not been completed (LaBianca & Driesch 1995, 135).

The presence of a perforation is conclusive evidence that the bone was worn around the neck or on clothing, but otherwise we have to rely on the context and the associated finds to suggest if the claw had cultural significance. Certainly, any group of claws found together or an articulated foot suggests deliberate collection.

Other Phalanges

The proximal and medial as well as the distal phalanges of birds of prey also seem to have been worn or used as amulets. A large number of proximal phalanges of vulture were recovered at the site of Jerf el Ahmar (Table 9.2), suggesting that phalanges may have been collected (Gourichon 2002). Phalanges of snowy owls from Upper Palaeolithic Bois-Ragot in France were engraved with a series of parallel lines (Figure 9.12), showing a decorative or talismanic use. These, like some of the worked bone, have scrape marks from cleaning (Laroulandie 2004, fig. 5).

Beaks and Skulls

The mandibles and skulls of some birds were worn for the same reasons as claws: they brought luck from their favourable associations with certain birds, and they were also decorative. In one of the graves in the cemetery of the Archaic period at Port au Choix in Newfoundland, one individual was buried with 150 maxillae of the extinct great auk (Tuck 1971). The great auk, which formerly bred on offshore islands within reach of the site, had a large prominent beak. A hair pin carved in the likeness of a great auk was also found with the burial. The peoples of the Kamchatka and the Kuriles wore puffin beaks round the neck as talismans (Clark 1948), and one such collection was found on a human mummy from Kagamil in Alaska (see Chapter 8). It consisted of 13 maxillae of the tufted puffin (Dove & Peurach 2002). The mandible of a grebe was found in a Mesolithic cemetery at Vedbaek in Jutland; it too had been worn around the neck, perhaps as an amulet or talisman (Mannermaa 2003, 18). Grebes are skilled at fishing, which may be at least part of the reason why the beak was chosen. In the Aleutian Islands the beaks of ravens were worn, perhaps because there the raven was a totem bird (see Chapter 14). Inuit garments on display in the Bow River Museum in Calgary are decorated with bird skulls, and at Túnel 'the presence of wear traces on the frontal bone of a penguin – probably *Eudyptes*

Table 9.2. *Element distribution of griffon vulture,* Gyps fulvus, *from Jerf el Ahmar, Syria*

Anatomical elements	Left	Right	NISP
Cranium			3
Premaxillary			1
Mandible			5
Quadrate	5	3	8
Cervical vertebrae			8
Furcula			1
Humerus	1	3	4
Ulna	10	4	14
Radius	5	7	12
Cuneiform	1	3	4
Carpometacarpus	3	5	8
Anterior phalanges			
1 of digit II		4	4
2 of digit II	5	3	8
1 of digit III		1	1
Tibiotarsus		1	1
Tarsometatarsus	9	6	15
Metatarsal I	1		1
Posterior phalanges			
1 of digit I	5	2	7
2 of digit I	5	1	6
1 of digit II	2	3	5
2 of digit II	5	6	11
3 of digit II	7	9	16
1 of digit III	4	4	8
2 of digit III	2	5	7
3 of digit III	6	4	10
4 of digit III	3	6	9
1 of digit IV	2	4	6
4 of digit IV	3	1	4
5 of digit IV	1	2	3
2 of digit I or 3 of digit II			3
Total NISP			193

Note: The unusually large number of phalanges suggests that they were curated for use as amulets or for decoration.
Source: Data are from Gourichon (2002, tab. 2).

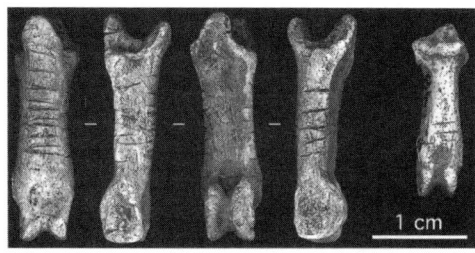
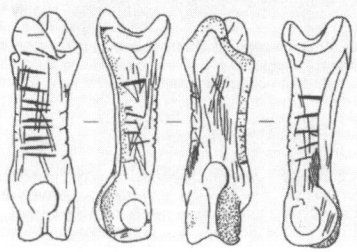

FIGURE 9.12. Engraved proximal phalanges of snowy owl, *Nyctea (Bubo) scandiaca*, from the Magdalenian site of Bois-Ragot, France (Laroulandie 2004, fig. 5). The bottom section is a drawing of four views of the phalanx shown on the left in the photograph (photograph and illustration by V. Laroulandie).

sp. – and a cormorant was probably related with the Yámana use of the crests of those birds for decoration' (Mameli 2002, 159).

Just as with phalanges, the significance of a skull or mandible will be clear if it is found in a grave or with clothing or as part of a necklace, or with other ritual objects. Alternatively, as at Túnel, wear or polish may suggest its former use.

CONCLUSIONS

Not so long ago, Wijngaarden-Bakker (1997) wrote, 'A systematic review of artefacts made from bird bones has not yet been undertaken'. This remains true. In this chapter we have looked at examples of some of the main types of implements and bone objects, and a few surviving pieces have indicated how bone tools were made. But it has not been possible to say much about decoration, use-wear, and wear damage, all important for understanding the function and life history of a bone tool.

Bones used for tools can be recognised by the fact that they have been cut or sawn in a careful and regular fashion. Just as with mammal bones, straight, regular cuts distinguish bones intended for tools from butchered bones, which more often have spiral fractures. The presence of polish or wear, which comes from use or from contact with the skin or clothing, can provide confirmation that a bone was more than a discard from a meal.

In some assemblages, bird bone tools have been found in numbers which were out of all proportion to the relative number of bird bones in the assemblage. Differential survival might explain this, but it may also indicate that some bones were sought after, even if flesh and feathers were ignored. Tools and objects have even been found in a place or time where the species would not be expected because out of its geographical range or even extinct, thus providing evidence for trade.

As we have seen, certain elements and certain species have been chosen over and over again. For tools, choice of elements was mostly functional, with straight, strong elements more useful than smaller and weaker ones. However, just as with claws as amulets, bones for flutes and even for tools were sometimes chosen because they carried the associations of a particular species – a crane with song, or an eagle with power – as for functional reasons.

Flutes and whistles are evidence for an aesthetic consciousness in humans. 'Music has ever accompanied the sacred rites of past recorded time no less than the present' (Megaw 1960, 13). The appearance of bone flutes in Europe very shortly after the arrival of fully modern humans is surely not a coincidence, but must be a sign that humans who by now had speech also appreciated music and rhythm. The earliest decorative objects of bird bone also appear to be no earlier than the Upper Palaeolithic. The fact that bird bones were selected for tools even when mammal bones were more readily available shows how the physical properties of the bones as well as the associations were also appreciated. It also demonstrates how, by the Upper Palaeolithic era, humans had developed the skills needed to catch or trap large elusive birds such as eagles, something discussed in the next chapter.

10

Wild Birds as Food

Birds have rarely been as important for food as mammals and fish, but locally, and in certain seasons, they have been crucial to existence for some hunter-gathers and for some farmers in areas marginal for agriculture. There is a large body of ethnographic literature on hunting wild birds for food (MacPherson 1897; Stora 1968; Nelson 1969; Randall 2005), as well as many zooarchaeological studies. In this chapter I will discuss aspects of bird biology and behaviour which led to some species being more frequent prey than others, with ethnographic as well as archaeological examples. The means by which people caught birds were a subject of great fascination to nineteenth-century sportsmen who have left us accounts of the methods, sometimes highly skilled, which were used, and we shall touch here on those which are detectable in archaeological remains. We shall also examine the environments in which birds have been a major or a significant minor resource. Because so many species have strongly seasonal behaviour, wildfowling was often a seasonal occupation, and the birds from a site can indicate the season at which it was occupied. The chapter concludes with a brief overview of the capture of wild birds for food from the Palaeolithic era onwards, and the role of birds as food in the transition from hunting and gathering to farming.

THE ECONOMICS OF BIRD CAPTURE

The factors which influenced the decisions of hunters and farmers to catch birds for food approximate to the criteria proposed for optimal foraging in general but with subtle differences. Optimal foraging among hunter-gatherers depended on the weight of the prey, the aggregation size of the herd, its mobility, and the 'non-food benefits' (Jochim 1976). Weight of prey alone is useful as a crude measure, but the nutritional value of birds is very variable, so this too has to be taken into account.

'Aggregation', so far as birds are concerned, refers to whether birds are solitary or flocking, which, as discussed in Chapter 2, varies between species and between seasons. The greater mobility of birds – most can fly away – has an important effect on whether species were targeted for food. The 'non-food benefits' of birds are mainly feathers, but they can also include the prestige which accrues with the capture of large birds. Jochim subsequently acknowledged that there were many features which were omitted from his initial calculations; from the point of view of wildfowling, the most significant of these is technology: many birds could be captured only when quite complex technologies had been devised.

Weight

Size has been an important criterion in the selection of birds for food. In Table 10.1 some examples are given of bird weights; they are shown grouped from the largest to the smallest. The large flightless birds, the ostrich, the emu, and the various extinct moa of New Zealand yield or yielded as much food as a medium or large mammal and provided food for a large number of people. The largest flying birds such as turkeys, geese, and cranes also provide enough meat for a group larger than a nuclear family. Birds below 1 kg in weight, however, provided only enough meat for a small family, and a bird below about 200 g such as a snipe or a thrush is insufficient even for a single individual. To provide a significant quantity of food, birds smaller than about 200 g have to be caught in large numbers (hence the importance of birds which can be caught in a flock). Stiner and colleagues, however, made the interesting suggestion that small game, in which they included birds, provided meat in 'small packets' in the late Upper Palaeolithic era. The smaller animals, which could have been trapped by women, may have provided women and children with a more regular source of protein than they would otherwise have had if they relied for meat only on large herbivores which were available only occasionally. A regular supply of protein would have been beneficial to their health and to the children's growth, so it may have contributed to the increase in the population which took place at the end of the Pleistocene era (Stiner et al. 2000).

The selection of larger rather than smaller species is exemplified in the assemblage from Buldir Island in the Aleutians. The larger auks and auklets were the most frequent avian species in the middens of the fifteenth to sixteenth century AD. The least auklet, today the most common auk in the area, is rare, and storm petrels (fork-tailed and Leach's petrels), the most common breeding birds on Buldir Island today, are absent. The authors concluded that the selection of the larger species

Table 10.1. *Weights of selected birds in approximate size classes*

Size class	Weight range
>10 kg	
Ostrich, *Struthio camelus*	90–135 kg
Emu, *Dromaius novaehollandiae*	31.5–36.9 kg
Dodo, *Raphus cucullatus*	10.6–17.5 kg
Mute swan, *Cygnus olor*	7.0–14.0 kg
>2 kg	
Great bustard, *Otis tarda*	3.8–8.5 kg
Wild turkey, *Meleagris gallopavo*	4.1–8.2 kg
Crane, *Grus grus*	4.5–7.0 kg
Greylag goose, *Anser anser*	2.1–4.3 kg
Gannet, *Morus bassanus*	2.4–3.6 kg
Shag, *Phalacrocorax aristotelis*	1.76–2.15 kg
>1 kg	
Brent goose, *Branta bernicla*	1.3–1.6 kg
Mallard, *Anas platyrhynchos*	0.75–1.5 kg
Herring gull, *Larus argentatus*	0.79–1.4 kg
>200 g	
Little bustard, *Tetrax tetrax*	700–950 g
Grouse, *Lagopus lagopus*	450–750 g
Chukar, *Alectoris chukar*	365–595 g
Woodpigeon, *Columba palumbus*	284–587 g
Francolin, *Francolinus francolinus*	400–500 g
Puffin, *Fratercula arctica*	320–480 g
Teal, *Anas crecca*	200–450 g
<200 g	
Snipe, *Gallinago gallinago*	80–140 g
Song thrush, *Turdus philomelos*	65–100 g
Greenfinch, *Carduelis chloris*	81–96 g
Linnet, *Carduelis cannabina*	15–22 g

Note: Weight range is from the smallest female to largest male (see also Table 10.2 and Table 13.1). Emu range is for females.

Source: For the emu, means are from Worthy and Holdaway (2002, tab. 5.4); for the dodo, *Raphus cucullatus*, the reconstructed weight is from Kitchener (1993); other species are from Snow and Perrins (1998).

indicated that food rather than feathers was the main focus of the hunt (Lefèvre & Siegel-Causey 1993).

One reason for preferring large birds is because the feathers have to be removed whether the bird is large or small. Less time is spent processing a single large bird than a large number of small birds. One study showed that that mass capture of birds and also mammals was less efficient in terms of return of food for the energy expended than the capture of a single large animal. With mass capture, only 9 to 33 per cent of time and effort was spent on the actual pursuit and the remaining 66 to 91 per cent of effort was spent on processing (Ugan 2005). With ducks, for instance, the processing involved the preparatory tasks of net making and travelling to the hunt and also plucking, preparing, and cooking the birds. Though small passerines were and are caught for food, this practice may have developed only later in Europe. The only anthropogenic assemblages I know of with remains of the small songbirds in quantity are from complex societies, the Roman Empire, and the Late Middle Ages (see Chapters 4 and 14). The recipes of the period suggest that small birds were eaten as much for show as for their food value (Serjeantson 2001a; Serjeantson 2006b).

Nutritional Value

Nutritional value is as important as absolute size. The maximum percentage of daily food intake which can be derived from protein is 50 per cent. More is lethal; fat and carbohydrate is also necessary (Noli & Avery 1988), so the nutritional value of a bird carcass is related to the ratio of fat to protein. In mammals, a substantial proportion of the available fat derives from the marrow and from within the bone itself; these sources of fat, though present (Chapter 2), are limited in birds. The percentages of fat and protein in bird carcasses vary more widely than might be expected: this can be seen in Table 10.2, where data are set out for some wild and domestic birds (Paul & Southgate 1978). Values for chicken depend on whether the chicken was boiled or roasted. The lower percentage of fat recorded for a boiled chicken must presuppose that the fat in the cooking broth was discarded, but in the past this fat would have been consumed. Ducks and geese are fatty birds and consequently have a higher calorific value than chickens and pheasants. The latter may have relatively more muscle but less body fat.

Seabirds are also notoriously fatty; waterfowl, for example, need body fat to survive in cold water. An informant from Stornaway in the Outer Hebrides, where gannets are still eaten (see Figure 3.1 in Chapter 3), described how they have a thick layer of fat underneath the skin (M. MacLeod personal communication, 1985). The same is true

Table 10.2. *Nutritional value (kilocalories, protein, and fat) of some domestic and wild birds*

Bird	kcal	Protein	Fat
Duck	339	19.6	29.0
Goose	319	29.3	22.4
Pigeon	230	27.8	13.2
Chicken (roasted)	216	22.6	14.0
Pheasant	213	32.2	9.3
Partridge	212	36.7	7.2
Chicken (boiled)	183	29.2	7.3
Grouse	173	31.3	5.3
Turkey	171	28.0	6.5

Note: Nutritional value is shown as constituents per 110 g: figures are for roast meat including skin, except where shown otherwise.

Source: Data are from Paul and Southgate (1978, 107, 111).

for the chicks of the shearwaters (Chapter 2). The high fat content helps to explain why the hunting of seabirds has been carried on worldwide. After moa became extinct, the Maori on the South Island of New Zealand turned to the muttonbird (the sooty shearwater), one of the fattiest species available (Anderson 1996). The preference for fatty seabirds may be in evidence in the assemblages from the sites in Patagonia (Chapter 4), where penguins, cormorants, and albatrosses outnumbered ducks and geese, though all were available (Table 10.3; see also Figure 4.15 in Chapter 4 as well as Lefèvre 1993, 1997; Mameli 2002).

On inland sites, we might expect waterfowl to be caught in preference to Galliformes, and this does indeed seem to have been the case in many parts of the world. Ducks were the main species at two Neolithic sites in the Netherlands. At Swifterbant, an encampment on a levée beside fresh water, the hunt concentrated on mallard (102) and other ducks (513) out of a total of 642 identified birds, and at Hazendonk on a river dune, out of 71 specimens, 32 were from mallard and 22 from goose (Zeiler & Clason 1993). At Brzesc Kujawski, referred to in Chapter 9, ducks and geese were also the main avian prey (Bogucki 1979). The preference for waterfowl is not confined to Europe. In prehistoric sites in Utah, Parmalee (1980) found that geese and ducks were the main species in all periods. Out of more than 5,000 bird bones, they were more than 50 per cent of the avifauna in the Archaic period and rose to more than 70 per cent in the succeeding Fremont period from about AD 750 onwards.

Table 10.3. *Number of identified specimens of birds and mammals from Skyring Sea sites in Patagonia*

Site	Birds	Small mammals	Artiodactyls	Marine mammals	% birds
Central zone					
SK 33	17	1			93.8
SK 26	58	1			98.2
SK 25	73				100.0
SK 29	48	8		3	81.4
SK 49	33			103	24.3
SK 24	82			35	70.1
SK 3	2443	29			98.8
SK 6	44				100.0
Western zone					
SK 16	66				100.0
SK 11	32				100.0
SK 12	27		1		96.4
SK 14	471	39	1		92.1

Note: Birds were a major resource, greatly outnumbering mammals at all sites except SK 49.
Source: Data are from Lefèvre (1997, tab. 3).

Flocking

Medium and small birds which are uneconomical and inefficient to catch in isolation can provide enough food when taken in large numbers. When prey is taken through the use of mass capture techniques such as nets, the return is higher than would be predicted by size alone (Nagaoka 2001). Gourichon demonstrated how most of the birds from Tell Mureybet were those which aggregate in large flocks. Though birds were not a significant element in the total fauna of this large Pre-Pottery Neolithic tell by the Euphrates, the species which occur in large flocks outnumbered those which are normally solitary or occur in pairs or small flocks (Figure 10.1). The number of taxa was also relatively smaller among the flocking birds, which confirms that it was the latter which were deliberately targeted (Gourichon 2004). Birds congregate in flocks in winter to take advantage of the fewer sources of food, when on migration, and when they come together to nest colonially.

Winter was the season in which corn buntings and twites, known collectively as 'snaa fowl', visited the corn yards in flocks and were caught for food by Orkney farmers (Fenton 1978, 522). Wildfowl which breed in the Arctic and migrate south in winter follow routes along the east and west coast of North America, which makes the

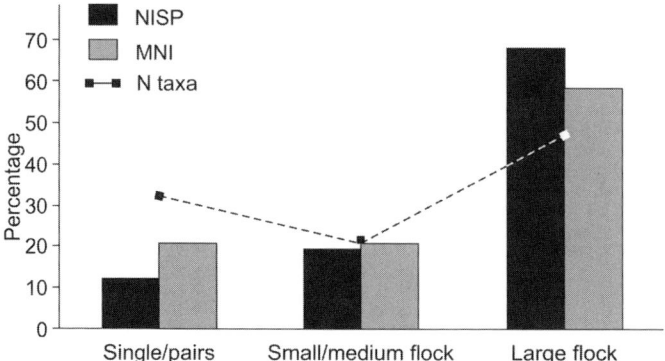

FIGURE 10.1. Birds (NISP, MNI, and number of taxa) from Pre-Pottery Neolithic Tell Mureybet in Syria shown in aggregation classes: single or pairs, small or medium flocks, and large flocks (Gourichon 2004, fig. 4.38); most are species which form large flocks.

flock movements very predictable. Nelson described how the Inuit hunted waterfowl on migration in May and June, and rarely at other times of year. The geese and ducks were shot from the ice as they flew along the open leads, and the dead birds were picked up in the water (Nelson 1969, 154). Birds on spring migration were a particularly important resource as they were returning at the time of year when people were most likely to starve (Nelson 1983, 78). Flocks of honey buzzards were caught on their southerly autumn migration until the nineteenth century. They were taken at Falsterbö on the southern tip of Sweden as they roosted in the sparse trees on the peninsula. The honey buzzard is one of the few raptors which was killed for food rather than for feathers. It was 'killed in the darkness and stored in salt barrels for the winter food supply' (Schmitz 1971, 300).

Most seabirds come to land only in the breeding season. Many of the seabird families referred to here and in earlier chapters breed in colonies, including penguins, albatrosses, petrels and shearwaters, gannets, cormorants, and gulls. Around the north and west coast of Scotland and on the islands, prehistoric settlements have a consistent percentage of about 2 to 5 per cent of birds in the bone assemblages, and invariably most are seabirds (Serjeantson 1988). In the earliest occupation of Tofts Ness on the island of Sanday in Orkney, the three large gulls, that is, great black-backed, herring, and lesser black-backed gulls, were the main avian species. It is probable that they were killed on their breeding colony on sand dunes near the settlement. Over time, gulls became less abundant, suggesting that the breeding colonies became depleted after livestock and cereal cultivation were introduced to the island (Serjeantson 2007b). In New Zealand the muttonbird was harvested from breeding colonies on offshore islands in the Foveaux Straights south of the South Island, and the geese and seabirds from sites in Greenland also appear to have been taken at the time when they were present in breeding flocks, as discussed in Chapter 3.

Ease of Capture

In general, birds are difficult to catch but there are some circumstances when they are more easily taken. Those which did not perceive humans as predators were easiest to capture because they did not attempt to escape. This applied to most birds which nested on uninhabited islands and 'obtaining these birds... may have resembled our concept of gathering more than hunting' (Steadman & Kirch 1990). The early historic descriptions of the unconcerned behaviour of the dodo and the great auk in the presence of sailors in search of a meal are painful to read. Authors have concluded that the moa in New Zealand, too, must have behaved in the same confiding way in the presence of the Polynesian colonists (Anderson 1989b; Worthy & Holdaway 2002).

Some nesting and roosting sites act as traps, which also makes capture easy. In caves, birds could be taken with the minimum of technology. There are accounts of how cormorants and shags were captured in sea caves in Scotland with the aid of smoke and sticks (Ritchie 1920; Baldwin 1974). Wild rock doves were also caught in caves where they roost and nest, behaviour which, as discussed in Chapter 12, led to their domestication. Species which lay their eggs in burrows are also easily trapped. The adults are vulnerable while incubating the eggs, and the fledglings are at risk until they can fly (see Chapter 2). Fowlers took puffins and manx shearwaters from their burrows on offshore islands around Scotland and the Faroe Islands (Baldwin 1974; Williamson 1948). In Patagonia the Magellanic penguin was harvested from its burrow at the breeding site by the Canoe Indians (Lefèvre 1988; also see Figure 10.2) and the muttonbird was caught in the same way in the Foveaux Straits (Anderson 1996).

Some birds are vulnerable during the moult. As we saw in Chapter 2, some waterfowl moult all their flight feathers together. At this time they congregate and are more easily killed than when they can fly away (Clark 1948). 'In August they lose their feathers, and are not able to fly, when the natives of Iceland and Kamchatka hunt them with dogs, which catch them by the neck, and easily secure them in their defenceless state' (Sibley 1794, 135). Swans were caught at this time in Kamchatka in what were known as 'battues'; they were driven by boats into small gulfs, where 'the boatmen killed them with clubs and the governor with firearms' (Stora 1968, 317–320). It is thought likely that the velvet scoters, one of the main species at the Danish Mesolithic site of Havnø, were caught when flocking together during the moult which takes place in the area between late July and early October (Grigson 1986).

FIGURE 10.2. Magellanic penguins, *Spheniscus magellanicus*, at the breeding site by the Skyring Sea, Patagonia. Penguins were one of the main species caught from sites in southern Patagonia (photograph by D. Serjeantson).

Another period of the life cycle when birds can be taken relatively easily is when they are on the nest, as they are less likely to fly off when incubating eggs. Geese were taken at this time at the site of Nipisat in Greenland. Chicks at the nest site are also vulnerable until they fledge. In historical times in Scotland and elsewhere in northern Europe, the young of certain species were caught just before they left the nest sites: this was the case with the fat young gannets (Beatty 1992).

TECHNOLOGY AND FOWLING METHODS

The technologies required for catching birds are an important key to understanding how and when birds have been exploited. They range from simple clubs to complex nets, snares, lures, and decoys (MacPherson 1897; Baldwin 1974; Reina & Pressman 1991). The killing of birds which could not escape with clubs or stones was within the capability of early hominids, but it is likely that only fully modern humans had the ability to make tools such as snares, nets, bows, and arrows and blowguns, the devices which have been used to catch birds until the recent past (Diamond 2002). The use of boats has also been significant, as this permitted the exploitation of breeding sites on small offshore islands as well as the colonisation of previously uninhabited islands, which invariably held seabird colonies.

The most elaborate method of catching birds was hawking. It required an immense investment of time on the part of the falconer, so although trained hawks might catch a lot of birds, hawking can scarcely ever have been economically efficient. It is more appropriate to regard hawking as a sport (Chapter 13).

Scavenging

Only scavenging requires no skill. In Chapter 9 we saw how bird bones used for tools were sometimes scavenged from dead birds; it is more difficult to establish whether carcasses were scavenged for food. Seabirds are often found dead or moribund along a strandline, especially after bad weather, having suffered exposure or a failed food supply (Chapter 5) and the carcasses may retain enough flesh to be edible. Avery and Underhill (1986), who set out to identify the season of occupation of three Late Holocene shellmounds in South Africa, proposed that the hunter-gatherers of the Western Cape had obtained the birds by scavenging. They found that the relative numbers of the different species and the relative numbers of mature and immature birds correlated with the birds washed up on the beaches today. The species in the middens included many which were normally inaccessible, such as the jackass penguin, the Cape gannet, and various albatrosses, petrels, and shearwaters (Table 10.4). All breed on offshore islands, but the hunter-gatherers of the Western Cape did not have the use of boats to reach the islands. Today, none of these species normally approaches the shore unless sick, dying, or washed up dead (Avery & Underhill 1986). The authors did not discuss the possibility that some species may have bred on the mainland in the early Holocene.

DeFrance considered the possibility that scavenging was the origin of the birds in the Late Pleistocene coastal midden at Quebrada Tacahuay in southern Peru. The site is in an area where fluctuations in El Niño or the Southern Oscillation can bring about catastrophic natural mortalities. The main species, cormorants and gannets, are sometimes washed up on the shore today, but the natural casualties included immature birds which were absent from the excavated remains, so deFrance rejected scavenging as the means by which the birds were obtained (deFrance 2005). Eda and colleagues also considered scavenging as the origin of the albatross remains from shell midden sites in Northern Japan referred to in Chapter 4 (Eda et al. 2005). They rejected scavenging as an explanation of how the birds had been obtained because

Table 10.4. *Species and age classes of birds from the Paternoster site, a Late Holocene shell midden on the Western Cape, South Africa*

Species	Adult	Juvenile	Nestling	Total
Jackass penguin, *Spheniscus demersus*	17	10	0	27
Cape gannet, *Morus capensis*	1	0	0	1
Great (White-breasted) cormorant, *Phalacrocorax carbo*	5	0	4	9
Cape cormorant, *P. capensis*	14	0	18	32
Crowned cormorant, *P. coronatus*	1	0	2	3
African black oystercatcher, *Haematopus moquini*	3	0	0	3
Kelp gull, *Larus dominicanus*	1	0	1	2
Swift tern, *Sterna bergii*	2	0	1	3
Common tern, *S. hirundo*	1	0	0	1
Spotted eagle owl, *Bubo africanus*	1	0	0	1
Total	46	10	26	82

Note: Age classes correspond with the age classes defined for natural casualties washed up on the beaches. The high percentage of immature birds shows that the site was occupied in summer.

Source: Data are from Avery and Underhill (1986).

there was no deficit of leg bones, even though, as we saw in Chapter 5, the legs become detached from a carcass rapidly in the natural disarticulation sequence.

As discussed in Chapters 5 and 6, the survival pattern of the different skeletal elements is affected by so many different processes that *on its own* it is an unreliable guide to the origin of a deposit. It is notable that very few ethnographic accounts make any reference to scavenging and in view of the range of simple as well as complex methods used to catch birds, scavenging may have been a rare strategy of last resort.

Sticks and Stones

Birds which could not escape could be killed with the bare hands, a stick, or a stone. No devices were needed to take those species which could be caught when roosting at night, but it did require a great deal of skill to approach the birds without disturbing the flock. The Canoe Indians of Patagonia caught king cormorants on offshore islets as they slept. The Indians immediately wrung the birds' necks so that no sound was made to disturb other birds in the flock (Lefèvre 1988). The same technique was used for cormorants and gannets around the coast of Scotland (Baldwin 1974). Birds which nest in burrows were pulled out by hand or with a hooked stick (see Figure 10.6b later) or dug out with spades or trowels (see Figure 10.6c), sometimes with the aid of dogs.

The moulting swans in Kamchatka referred to earlier were clubbed. Unlike wringing the necks, this disturbed the flock, so it was only possible when the rest of the flock could not immediately fly away. Cormorants and gannets were killed on the nest with sticks as they are reluctant to abandon the eggs when brooding (Baldwin 1974, 2005). There are also many accounts of how great auks were killed on shore with sticks and stones, unable to escape even as some in the colony were being killed (Birkhead 1993).

Spears

Bird spears, which have been used in Australia, New Zealand, and elsewhere in the recent past, are more elaborate than ordinary sticks as they are finely balanced and have specially crafted heads. Long, slender bird spears with barbed harpoon points were used by the Nuchanulth and other peoples of the Pacific Northwest (Stewart 1996, 106). In Patagonia, long spears were used to kill the Magellanic penguins as they were swimming (Lefèvre 1988). Objects interpreted as bird spears have been found in archaeological contexts. Clark refers to rock shelter sites in the Lower Murray River region of Australia where large birds as well as kangaroo and wallaby were caught with the use of barbed spears (Clark 1961, 256). Some prehistoric bone arrowheads from Mesolithic sites in Russia are thought to have had the same function (Figure 10.3).

Bolas and Sling-Stones

The bolas, three stones attached to a line, is mostly found in South America. Darwin (1897, 84) described how rheas were 'caught without much difficulty by the Indian or Gaucho armed with the bolas'. The Nunamiut around the Arctic used a killamittaun, a type of bolas which had seven or eight weights and as many strings (Nelson 1969, 158). Sling-stones are more universally known. Slings with walnut-sized sling-stones were used by the Ona of Southern Patagonia to catch birds (Lothrop 1928). In Iron Age Europe, sling-stones found on prehistoric sites are usually presumed to have been used to kill human enemies rather than wild animals, though there is an Irish legend which was recounted to emphasise the magical prowess of the hero

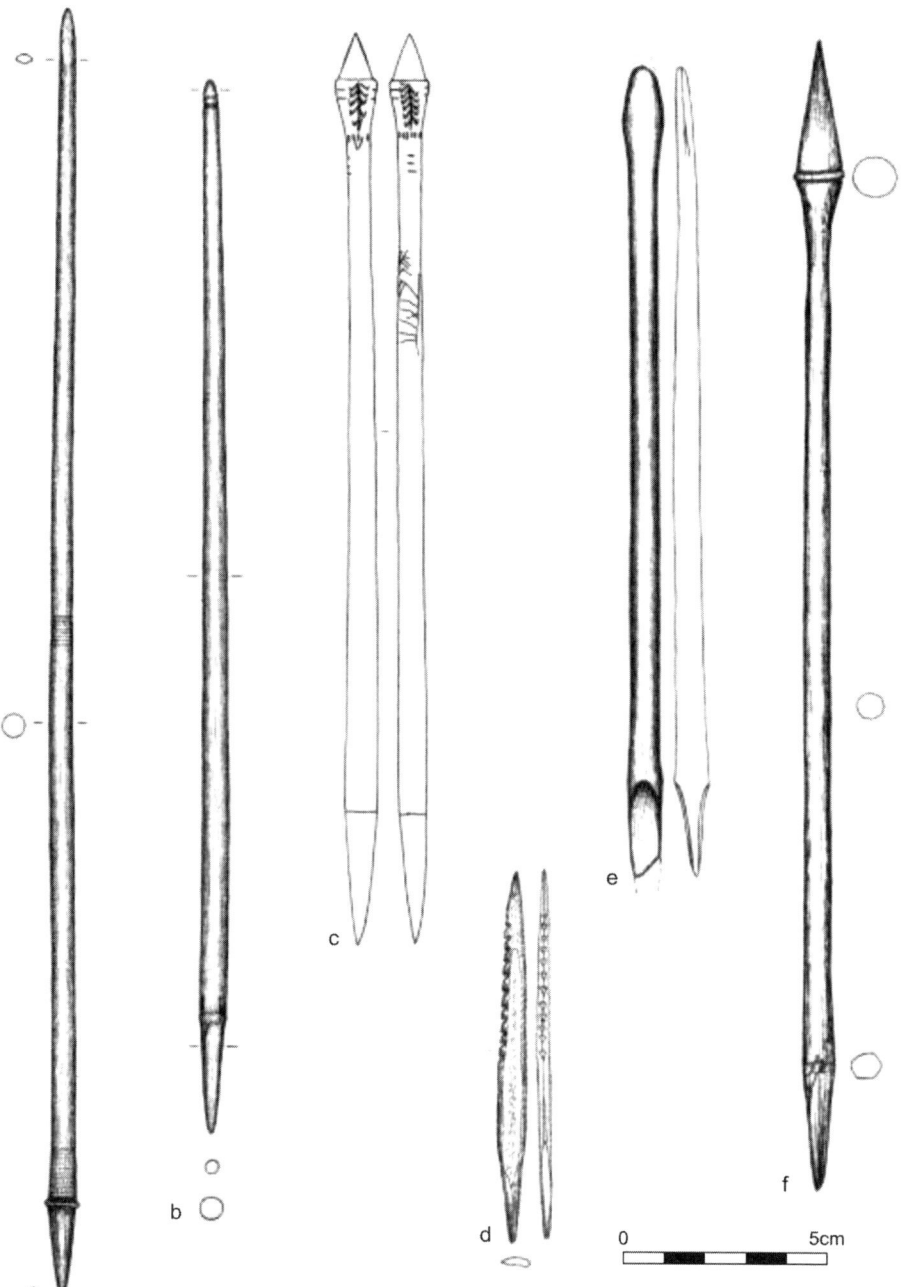

FIGURE 10.3. Mesolithic bone arrowheads from the Upper Volga region of Russia, thought to have been used for hunting birds: a–d are from the Ivanovskoye area, and e and f are from the Stanovoye area (after Zhilin & Karhu 2002, fig. 2).

Cu-Chulain which tells how he stunned 'eight swans with a single sling-stone' (Baldwin 1974, 68). Groups of excavated stones at sites in South America are thought to have had this purpose, including some at the very early site of Monte Verde, where round rocks of the size of an egg were recovered. These are thought to have been collected for use as bird missiles in view of the later tradition of the use of bolas and slings in Chile (see http://whc.unesco.org/en/tentativelists/1873; 22 April 2007).

Snares

Snares and nets are more elaborate (MacPherson 1897, xxxiii–xxxvii). In the Late Upper Palaeolithic in Europe, both were made with sinew and hair; later, plant fibres were also used. Snares, sometimes referred to as springes or gins, may originally have been developed to catch small mammals such as foxes and hares, but they were then found to be effective in capturing birds which forage on the ground for food, especially those which follow regular trails as do grouse, ptarmigan, and woodcock. The Buglé people of Panama set snares for the great curassow and the great tinamou, the two large ground birds which raid their garden crops (Smith 2005). The Canoe Indians of southern Patagonia caught steamer ducks by enticing them into snares on shore (Lefèvre 1988). In Orkney, the 'snaa fowl' were caught with horse hair nooses fixed to a board (Fenton 1978, 522).

The method used to catch woodcock in the eighteenth century probably differs little from that used in northwest Europe at the end of the last glaciation (Clark 1948). 'The woodcock comes abroad at night, keeping always to the little paths' [and] . . . 'springes or nooses were set along the paths regularly traced by the birds as they forage in search of worms' (Sibley 1794). The 'springe' referred to would entrap the bird when the hunter was absent, but in some snares the hunter had to be present to pull the string. A snare for kaka, which was on display in the Invercargill Museum in the South Island of New Zealand in 2005, consisted of a loop attached to a tree branch; when the string was pulled the bird's feet were trapped on the branch.

A series of snares or loops on a single line was used to catch seabirds in southern Patagonia (Lothrop 1928, 83; also see Figure 10.4) and similar snares were used to catch puffins on St Kilda (see below), which has a large puffin colony as well as colonies of other seabirds (Baldwin 1974). A row of loop snares across a pond was used for catching ducks as they flew in to land (MacPherson 1897, xxxv). Snares with multiple loops may have been developed especially for birds which flock.

As they are made of organic materials, snares rarely survive, though one was found in a Late Bronze Age context in Sweden (Clark 1948). Snaring leaves no physical trace

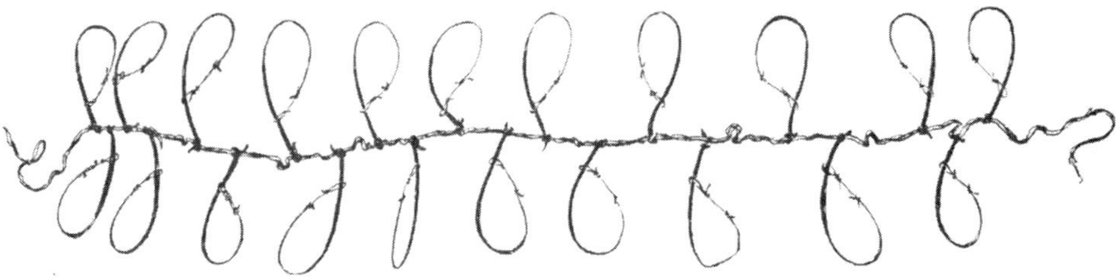

FIGURE 10.4. Snare with 21 loops, used by the Ona of Patagonia in the early twentieth century for catching ducks (after Lothrop 1928, 83).

on the carcass, but the use of snares can be inferred for catching those species which spend most of their time on the ground, as it was the most effective way of trapping those species such as the ptarmigan, grouse, and bustards whose remains are so common in caves of Late Glacial Europe, where the faunal assemblages also contained hare, fox, and other smaller mammals presumed to have been snared (Diamond 2002, 40).

Nets

The aboriginal Australians made nets of sinew, bulrush, flax, grass, reed, rush, and spinifex, sometimes using smoke as a preservative. The nets used to funnel birds could be hundreds of metres long, while some were small enough merely to cover a burrow or water hole (Satterthwait 1986).

Mist nets (also known as air nets) were hung across flyways, suspended from trees or poles. In Australia mist nets were used to catch parrots, pigeons, and budgerigars, and in Europe they were used to catch waders and small flocking birds. In the Netherlands the process was highly complex: 'The fowler uses a single 20 m long net, that initially lies flat on the ground. Decoy golden plovers and lapwings...are placed before and behind the net. A living golden plover is placed on a little seesaw. With a flute the fowler attracts the plovers from the air. When the plovers landed, the fowler pulled the net up and let it fall across them' (Prummel 1993, 103). Vertical nets ('stake nets') were set out along the shore to catch gulls and waders. Both vertical and horizontal nets were used in the water to catch birds which swim, rather like fishing nets (MacPherson 1897, xxxvii–xl; Stora 1968, 328). In the lagoons near Perpignan in the South of France, nets fixed horizontally in the water with floats and sinkers (Figure 10.5) were used to catch tufted ducks, pochards, and coots. The vertical arrangement prevented the ducks from rising to the surface (Boissier 1984). Horizontal nets (clap nets) trap birds on the ground and were used to throw over

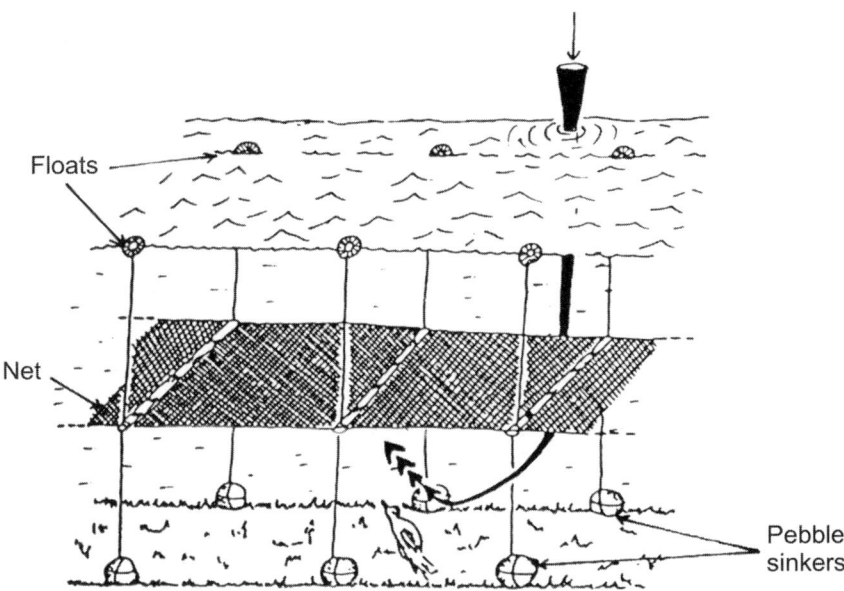

FIGURE 10.5. Underwater net for catching ducks and coots, recently in use in Perpignan, France; the duck takes the route marked by the arrow and comes up under the net, which is fixed horizontally in the water with floats and pebble sinkers (redrawn from Boissier 1984, fig. 3).

sleeping birds. In Australia, nets were set at the end of a funnel-shaped brush or grass enclosure on land where birds were plentiful and they were driven into it (Satterthwait 1986). Unlike snares, which are suitable for solitary birds, the main value of nets is to catch flocks in places where they can be predicted to fly or land (Satterthwait 1986).

Nets on poles rather like landing nets for fish or large butterfly nets were used all over the world (MacPherson 1897). In the Faroe Islands the nets (Figure 10.6a) were used to catch puffins (Williamson 1948); in Orkney they were known as 'swap' nets and used to 'swap' puffins, razorbills, and guillemots (Figure 10.7). Tasmanian aboriginals used traps of woven basketry to catch birds (Satterthwait 1986). Nets were sometimes used with pitfalls, which are appropriate for large birds which could not escape. Both are thought to have been used in hunting moa (Anderson 1989).

The netting of birds is depicted on a stone slab at Abydos in Upper Egypt. The slab shows a clap net in which wildfowl have become entangled (MacPherson 1897, 272). The Greek and Roman authors refer to catching birds with nets, but, as we have seen, the practice undoubtedly began much earlier. Netting, together with notched pebbles which could have been used as netsinkers, was found at the Neolithic site of Twann in Switzerland. Studer concluded that, as the main avian species (the

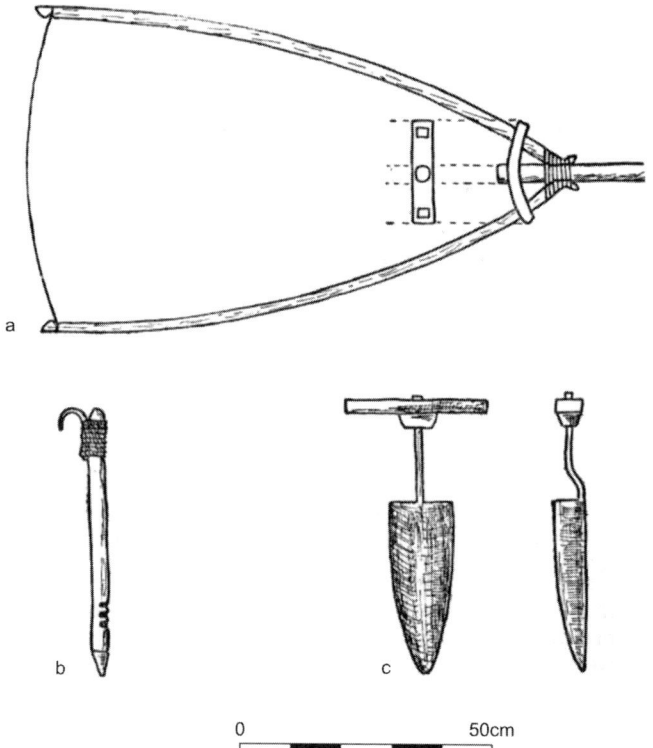

FIGURE 10.6. Implements for catching puffins, *Fratercula arctica*, Faroe Islands, in the early twentieth century (after Williamson 1948, 150): a, frame for the net (see Figure 10.7); b, hooked stick; c, trowel for digging puffins out of the burrows.

goosander) was a diving duck, it had been caught in nets. Fish as well as bird remains were found at the site, so the birds may have been an incidental by-catch of fishing (Studer 1992).

Bow and Arrow

In the Old World the bow and arrow was an invention of the Upper Palaeolithic period; as with snares and nets, either sinew or fibre can be used in its construction (Bergman 1993). In central Alaska a blunt bone arrowhead was used to shoot birds (Rainey 1939, 371) and the use of a similar arrow in South America stunned the bird but kept it alive so that the feathers could be plucked (Reina & Pressman 1991). Arrows of this type are known from at least the Mesolithic period (Clark 1948; Clark 1952, fig. 14). Arrow damage was recognised in the pelvis of an Arctic grouse (ptarmigan) at the Late Glacial site of Meiendorf in North Germany. The bird was apparently

FIGURE 10.7. Late nineteenth-century wildfowlers on Orkney with puffins, *Fratercula arctica*, and guillemots, *Uria aalge*. They hold the large 'swap' net with which the birds were caught as they flew close to the cliff (photograph courtesy of the Orkney Library and Archive).

perforated by an arrow discharged from below. The sternum of a crane from the same site had no less than four arrow wounds (Clark 1948, 116). A transverse arrowhead was actually lodged in a swan humerus at the Late Mesolithic site of Vedbaek in Jutland (Mohl 1978). As discussed in Chapter 8, arrows require feathers for fletching, and arrows with traces of the binding have been recovered from Scandinavian bog sites.

Blowguns

The blowgun is typically a weapon of Central and South America. It is used mainly for birds which would otherwise be inaccessible in the high canopy of the tropical rainforest. It has the great advantage of being silent. The blowgun was known to the Maya, as it is depicted on Maya vases (Ventura 2003). Small clay pellets were used instead of a dart in some parts of the world: small pellets found at Casas Grandes in Mexico are thought to have been for use with blowguns (Jett 1991). The weapon is thought to have originated in Southeast Asia but it is so widely distributed that independent invention cannot be ruled out (Jett 1991; Krim 1992).

Guns

Guns, originally known as 'birding pieces' or 'fowling pieces', were first used for wildfowling in England in 1533 but had been used earlier in Continental Europe (Fisher 1947). Though no more difficult to use than a spear or a bow and arrow, they were much more difficult to make and so were available initially only to the wealthy. At the end of the sixteenth century, however, the mechanism was simplified so that it did not need an expert to make and maintain it, and the gun went into more widespread use, though shooting did not supersede nets for obtaining birds on a commercial scale (Fisher 1947, 15). The invention of the shotgun allowed whole flocks to be slaughtered at a time and, as discussed, there was a significant increase in the consumption of birds, especially small birds, in the Late Middle Ages and the early Post-Medieval period (Albarella & Thomas 2002; Serjeantson 2006b) which may be attributable to the use of the fowling piece.

Other Hunting Aids

The implements and devices described do not exhaust the variety of means of catching birds. 'Guns, lime twigs, nets, glades, gins, strings, baits, pit falls, pipe calls, stalking horses, setting dogs, and decoy ducks' were all listed as means by which birds were caught in eighteenth-century England (Strutt 1810, 34). 'Bird lime' is any glutinous substance spread on a twig or perch, by which birds are caught and held fast. Bird pipes or whistles, as we saw in Chapter 9, are known from Palaeolithic times, though a skilful hunter can imitate bird calls without an artificial whistle. A 'stalking horse' was a small mobile hide or blind, which the hunter moved gradually towards

FIGURE 10.8. Fixed decoy for capturing ducks in Borough Fen, Lincolnshire. The view is of the main pond and a curving pipe, temporarily closed off with a log; the screens and the arches over the pipe are also visible (photograph by D. Serjeantson).

the unsuspecting bird. 'Decoy ducks' are birds or model birds put down to entice wild birds to land, often used in conjunction with nets and devices. Some were found in excavations in Lovelock Cave, Nevada, discussed in Chapter 5. It was suggested that the Bewick's swan found at Bergschenhoek in the Netherlands, referred to in Chapter 6, may have been used to make a decoy, as the skeleton lacked head, legs, and the majority of the wing bones, all of which would have been removed to make a decoy bird (Bakels & Zeiler 2005).

Elaborate structures, combining ponds and nets, also known as decoys, were created to catch ducks. They consist of a central pond with channels or 'pipes' leading off it. The tapering pipes are lined with screens and overtopped with an arching structure covered with netting (Figure 10.8). Decoys of this type devised in the Netherlands and used there and in England in early modern times consisted of a pond with several pipes. Ducks were enticed into the pipes by a dog running behind the screens, which the ducks followed out of curiosity. The decoyman chose which pipe to use according to the direction of the wind and blocked off the others with a log (Cook & Pilcher 1982).

The simple technologies described here could have been used by an individual or a small band foraging for a diverse range of resources, but, as Satterthwait (1986) points out, a complex technique such as net hunting comes into its own only when prey selection shifted from targeting large-game (k-resources) to small-bodied animals (r-resources). Though the original discussion referred to Australia, his conclusion also applies to Europe at the end of the last glaciation. Net hunting implies a greater degree of social organisation as well as technical competence in the group. The elaborate structures such as constructed decoys only came into use when fowling became a commercial activity. However, there seems to be no strong correlation between the complexity of the technology and the importance of birds as a food resource.

BIRDS: A MAJOR OR MINOR FOOD RESOURCE?

The food resources of hunter-gatherers have been assigned to a hierarchy of importance. Those identified for the Kung! Bushmen were primary, major, minor, supplementary, and rare (Lee 1968, tab. 3). A primary resource provided over half of the food and was eaten daily; a major resource was eaten daily when it was in season; and a minor resource was eaten several times per week in season. Supplementary and rare resources were those eaten when other resources were unavailable, perhaps several times a year but irregularly. For archaeological material, quantification of food resources into these categories has proved difficult because of the problem of quantifying plant foods, and the quantifications which have been done (see, e.g., Chapter 4) have usually been confined to animals or to vertebrate remains only.

In a survey of the role of wildfowling in the Mesolithic and Neolithic periods in northern Europe and around the Baltic, the consumption of wild birds was graded in four degrees of intensification on the basis of the percentage of bird bones relative to mammals, or, where these data were not available, the absolute number of bird bones. The categories were intensive (>20 per cent), subintensive (10–20 per cent), subsidiary (3–10 per cent), and occasional (<3 per cent). Out of the approximately 180 assemblages for which data were available, intensive fowling by this definition took place on only 7 per cent and subintensive fowling on a further 8 per cent of sites (Guminski 2005). This range is probably typical for mainland Europe in general at this period, but there are environments in which birds have greater importance. In view of the discrepancy in size between birds and most mammals, where birds were 20 per cent or more of the assemblage it does not of course imply that they were 20 per cent of the food.

As we saw in Chapter 4, intensive fowling was defined differently in a study of wildfowling at Danish Mesolithic sites. With these assemblages, the degree to which a single species or a few species were targeted was the criteria for intensive fowling rather than the absolute percentage of bird bones (Grigson 1986). Where an assemblage was dominated by one or two species (see Figure 4.10), fowling was

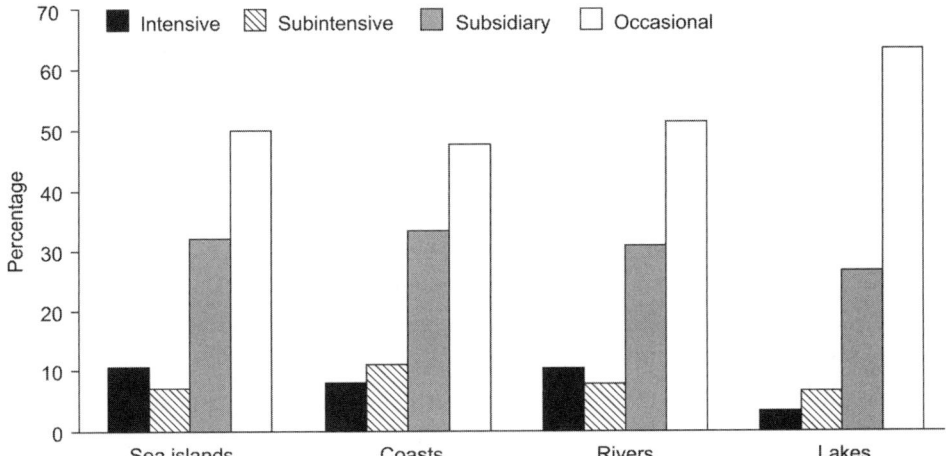

FIGURE 10.9. Mesolithic and Neolithic wildfowling in northern Europe and the Baltic region on settlements in four types of location: sea islands (28 sites), coasts (63 sites), rivers (39 sites), and lakes (60 sites). Percentage of sites where wildfowling was intensive, subintensive, subsidiary, or occasional is based on relative numbers of bird and mammal bones (redrawn from Guminski 2005, fig. 8).

regarded as specialised and where an assemblage was very diverse (see Figure 4.11), it was regarded as unspecialised. It is likely that the birds provided by an intensive hunting strategy were a significant minor resource, probably seasonal, but the status of birds as a resource in the 'diverse' assemblages is less clear.

MAJOR RESOURCE

Birds may never have been a primary food resource, but they have been a major resource in at least three environments: on islands, in high latitudes or at the glacial margins, and on the coast. In the Mesolithic and Neolithic settlements in northern Europe already referred to, the most intensive fowling took place in settlements on islands and on the coast, but it was also interpreted as intensive on some riverine sites (Figure 10.9).

Islands

Islands without ground predators hold large populations of birds, both landbirds and seabirds. The birds are naïve in the presence of humans when first encountered, so, as discussed, they are easily killed. In the first years after colonisation, birds provided a major food resource on many islands. Indeed, the readily available supply of birds probably encouraged exploration among the Polynesian islands (Milberg & Tyrberg 1993). Birds were a source of meat for island peoples of the Pacific whose crops provide mostly carbohydrates and whose domestic animals were few (Reis & Steadman 1999). The importance of birds to initial colonists is exemplified by the first occupation of the Auckland Islands in the Antarctic. In the thirteenth to fourteenth centuries AD explorers from New Zealand visited the islands, leaving a midden with occupation debris. In the midden were remains of marine shells, 124 large birds, and 14 seals, and deriving perhaps from a single summer's occupation. The main avian species was the muttonbird, with which the Polynesian explorers were already familiar, and albatrosses and penguins, the other large taxa available. Though the island also had a population of landbirds, few were found in the midden (Anderson 2005).

When the first voyagers from Polynesia landed in New Zealand between the eleventh and thirteenth centuries AD, they encountered a country without land mammals. Instead, the herbivorous fauna consisted of the flightless moa, other ratites, and rails whose only predator was Haast's eagle. The moa ranged in size from *Dinornis giganteus*, which weighed up to 200 kg, to small *Euryapterix* and *Pachyornis*, which weighed between 20 and 30 kg (Worthy & Holdaway 2002, tab. 5.3). In the North Island the colonisers continued to live by garden agriculture as they had done in Polynesia, but the kumara (sweet potato) could not be cultivated in the south of the South Island, so there people relied on moa together with seals. The birds were killed away from the site and floated down the river to the settlements, where they were butchered and cooked in ovens. The minimum number of moa killed and eaten at one large site, Shag Mouth, has been estimated at more than 6,000, and at some other sites the density of bone suggests that tens of thousands of birds may have been killed. At Shag Mouth and elsewhere a lower layer with charcoal and moa bones was succeeded by layers with shellfish, fish bones, and a few moa bones only (Anderson 1989, 131–148). In other words, moa were a major resource only in the initial period of occupation.

On the Marquesas, Tonga, and Tikopia islands in Polynesia, the lowest occupation levels on each island also have abundant remains of endemic birds (Steadman & Rolett 1996; Steadman et al. 2002). On the Marquesas, both local seabirds and indigenous landbirds were exploited in the initial occupation of the Hanamiai site (*c.* AD 1025–1300), but numbers of domestic animals increased in the later layers. On each of the islands the pattern was for the landbirds and the seabirds which bred on the main island to be exploited until they were extirpated or greatly reduced and for subsequent exploitation to be of less accessible breeding colonies of seabirds, usually from small offshore islets (Weisler 2001).

Seabirds were a major element in the diet in the Aleutian Islands, which have seen millennia of occupation. On Buldir Island, Steller's sea lion, *Eumetopias jubatus*, was the main food but fish and birds were also an important part of the diet. The abundance of the main avian species varied over time, probably in relation to climate fluctuations, but their exploitation continued (Lefèvre & Siegel-Causey 1993; Lefèvre et al. 1997).

The best known historic example of an island where people relied on seabirds as a major resource is St Kilda (Kearton 1902; Baldwin 1974, 2005). The islands in this group are surrounded with cliffs which hold vast colonies of nesting seabirds, mainly fulmars and gannets. The birds were caught over the summer and, like the eggs, preserved for winter in stone cleits. The islanders also kept sheep and imported cereals from the more fertile Scottish islands, but they probably ate birds every day, even in winter when preserved birds were available. Wildfowling here was sustainable, as the quantity of birds breeding on the cliffs was immense. The capture of seabirds continued into the nineteenth century on islands all over the world. On the island of Lewis in the Outer Hebrides, the Faroe Islands, and Iceland, it continues today (Beatty 1992; Randall 2005; McGovern et al. 2006).

High Latitudes

On the glacial margins, birds were an important resource on large land masses as well as on islands. In southern France in the Late Pleistocene period, birds were a major food source; at La Vache food procurement concentrated on ibex and ptarmigan, with MNIs of thousands of each in the Magdalenian levels (Laroulandie 2005a). In the High Arctic the percentage NISP of birds in a series of Palaeoeskimo sites ranged from 11 to 14 per cent, except in the later pre-Dorset phase, when it was only 6 per cent (Figure 10.10). The pre-Dorset phase was during a particularly cold period, when marine mammals supplied most of the food and no fishing took place (Darwent 2004). In Greenland, birds continued to be a major resource from the Palaeoeskimo (Saqqaq) period until the later Thule culture, which overlapped with Norse occupation. Palaeoeskimo sites tended to concentrate on two or three main families: gulls, auks, geese, and eider duck, but in the Thule period capture was often concentrated on a single species: Brunnich's guillemot at eight sites, eider at one site, and Iceland gull at another (Gotfredsen 1997).

Coasts

A high biomass of birds as well as mammals and fish is characteristic of coastal regions in the temperate zone (Anderson 2001). Even in low latitudes, seabirds are

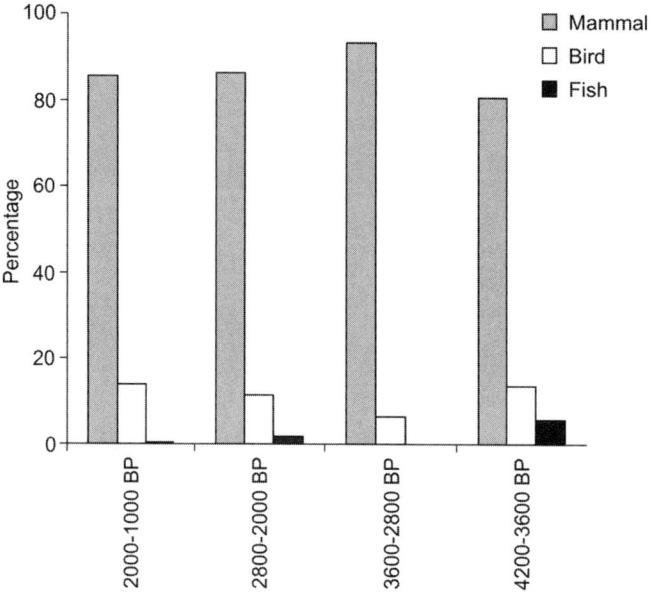

FIGURE 10.10. Numbers (NISP) of mammal, bird, and fish remains from High Arctic sites: mammals were the major and birds a minor food resource (data from Darwent 2004).

abundant on coasts if food is available. Along the South American coast the cold Humboldt Current brings nutrients which enhance fish numbers, and the fish in turn provide food for gulls, penguins, and other seabirds.

Seabirds are plentifully available in spring and summer around the coast when they come ashore to breed, while in winter ducks and waders are abundant on the seashore and in estuaries. Cormorants are resident so they are available all year round. At Quebrada Tacahuay, seabirds, together with fish, were the main subsistence base. This rather specialised adaptation occurred during a Late Pleistocene cold episode when plants and other food resources were scant. There was an 'overwhelming predominance of birds over mammals' (Lefèvre 1997) at all sites but one in the shell middens around the coast of the Skyring Sea, an inland sea in Chilean Patagonia. Marine mammals and some artiodactyls were also exploited, and the principal avian species were cormorants and the steamer duck (Figure 10.11). The primary resource at Ponsonby, a coastal site on Isla Riesco in southern Patagonia, was the guanaco, *Lama guanacoe*. At this site, occupied between the sixth and third millennia BC, birds were a major resource, second in importance to the guanaco. The presence of immature cormorants and ducks (see Chapter 3) made it plain that the sites were visited in summer, but as the main species were resident in the area, visits at other times of year are not ruled out. At Ponsonby, the importance of birds and other marine resources increased over time at the expense of the guanaco. The capture of

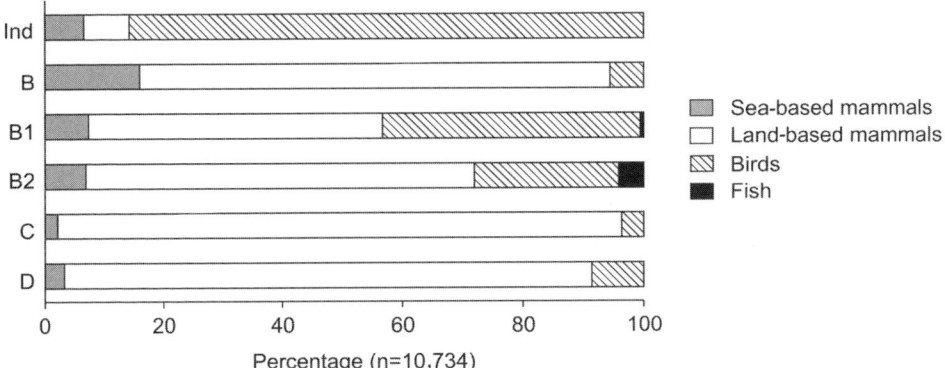

FIGURE 10.11. Numbers (NISP) of marine mammals, terrestrial mammals, birds, and fish from the site at Ponsonby, Isla Riesco, Patagonia, from the sixth to the third millennium BC (Lefèvre et al., 2003). The bar labelled 'Ind' refers to material thought to be from the upper layers (B2, B1, and B). Over time the relative number of terrestrial mammals, mainly guanaco, declined and marine mammals and birds increased.

birds was specialised on a single species or a few species at most sites in Tierra del Fuego and southern Patagonia: in many sites the main species were the cormorants, but at some it was steamer ducks, and on Herschel Island it was the sooty shearwater (Lefèvre 1997; Lefèvre et al. 2003).

MINOR RESOURCE

Where birds have been an important minor food resource, it has usually been at certain seasons, either when other foodstuffs were hard to obtain or when birds were particularly abundant locally. Several examples have been referred to earlier. According to the Spanish naturalist Mozino, who spent a year in Nootka Sound on Vancouver Island in 1792, fish and whale blubber were the main foods of the local Mowachat (or Muchalacht) band. They ate birds in one month of the year in spring before the start of the whaling season. 'The month of Orcu-mi-gl', which translates as 'geese moon', 'is known for its abundance of ducks and seagulls' (Mozino 1991, 62).

As elsewhere in Patagonia, in the Beagle Channel sites referred to in Chapter 4, sea lions were the main prey, but birds were also an important minor food resource (see Figure 4.15). For farmers living near the coast, too, birds often provided a minor but essential resource; this was especially true for farmers in northern latitudes who were raising livestock and growing a few crops at the margins of cultivation (Fenton 1978, 510–523; McGovern et al. 2006).

As discussed, birds were a minor or subintensive resource at fewer than 10 per cent of sites around the Baltic (Figure 10.9). In later prehistoric times in the British Isles, sites where birds were caught in quantity were restricted to a very few settlements adjacent to wetlands. The fenlands of East Anglia and the Somerset Levels held vast populations of waterfowl before they were drained for agriculture, but only a handful of early settlements are known where these were exploited. At Haddenham in Cambridgeshire, discussed in Chapter 7, the Iron Age farmers caught mute swans, mallards, and coots. The swans must have been a significant minor item in the diet – remains were more numerous than those of pigs – though feathers rather than food may have been the main reason for taking the birds (Evans & Serjeantson 1988; Serjeantson 2006a). As the main avian species are resident, fowling was not necessarily a seasonal activity at this site.

SUPPLEMENTARY AND RARE RESOURCES

In many societies, birds are no more than a supplementary or rare resource, if an important one. Among the Nunamiut of Wainwright and Point Hope 'a good catch of waterfowl could provide the margin between adequate food supply and hunger' in a lean year (Nelson 1969, 157). Birds have been an incidental resource in strongly seasonal regions and also where seasonality is less marked. The killing of birds by the Buglé people served the dual purpose of protecting the crops and providing an incidental supply of meat (Smith 2005).

Birds were a supplementary ('subsidiary' or 'occasional') resource in more than 80 per cent of the sites surveyed by Guminski. The goosanders netted at Twann, referred to earlier, were no more than an occasional addition to the food supply. This also seems to have been the case at the Late Bronze Age (1000 BC) site of Hauterive-Champréveyres on the shores of Lake Neuchâtel in Switzerland. In that small assemblage of 156 bird bones, 75 per cent were mallards. They were certainly anthropogenic, as the majority have cut marks, but contributed little to the food supply, which relied on crops and domestic animals (Studer 1992).

BIRDS AS INDICATORS OF SEASONAL OCCUPATION

Since hunter-gatherer sites were normally occupied at one time of year only, one of the first research questions asked of an excavated site is the season in which it was occupied. Bird remains are particularly valuable for identifying season of occupation (Clark 1948). They indicate the season of occupation, regardless of whether they were a major, minor, or incidental resource. The season of capture can be inferred from migratory species present for only part of the year, from bones of immature birds, from eggshell (see Chapter 7), and from the presence of medullary bone (Serjeantson 1998).

Seasonal Migrants

In his pioneering studies of the bird remains from the Danish Mesolithic kitchen middens, Winge demonstrated how some of the sites must have been occupied at certain seasons as some species were seasonal visitors only (Clark 1948). Many authors have since applied the same test to avifauna assemblages.

Seasonal occupation of the Abri Dufaure, an Upper Palaeolithic (Magdalenian) cave site in the Pyrenees, was indicated by the presence of winter visitors and residents and the absence of summer visitors. The winter visitors included the great northern diver and at least two species of goose, the greylag and the bean goose. The anthropogenic origin of the assemblage was confirmed by butchery on some of the goose remains. The age at death of elements in the mammalian fauna confirmed the season of occupation (Altuna et al. 1991). At the Late Upper Palaeolithic site of Wadi Kubbaniya on the River Nile near Aswan, the birds, though a minor item of diet, were also all winter visitors, confirming winter occupation. This was also inferred from the bird remains from the fourth millennium BC site of Aggersund in northern Denmark. The birds present were all swans; those which could be identified to species were whooper swan (see Chapter 4). Flocks of whooper swans spend the winter in the inlets of northern Jutland, but they are absent in summer when breeding on the northern tundra (Grigson 1986; Mohl 1978). Winter occupation was also confirmed at the Mesolithic site of Polderweg in the Netherlands (Wijngaarden-Bakker 2002) from the presence of red-breasted merganser and a suite of other winter visitors.

Occupation in summer was demonstrated by the presence of crane and stork – both of which winter in southern Europe and North Africa – on a number of Mesolithic sites in the British Isles and northern Europe. These two species are among the few bird bones from the well-known site of Star Carr in northern England, where the mammal remains confirm that the site was occupied in summer (Legge & Rowley-Conwy 1988, 38–39).

At the site of Dudka, an island in the lakelands of northeast Poland, most of the birds are thought to have been caught on migration in spring and autumn. Very few of the main species winter in the area, and not many more breed there today (Guminski 2005). The area is a stopping-off point for migratory waterfowl.

Immature Birds

The presence of immature bones is reliable evidence for summer occupation (Clark 1948, 1952). The classic research in which immature birds demonstrated seasonal occupation was Howard's study of the avifauna from Emeryville shellmound (Chapter 1). Nearly half of the cormorants were immature nestlings, and the author deduced that they had been captured between mid-June and the end of July (Howard 1929).

Other sites tell the same story. We have already seen how immature seabirds were present in the middens of the Western Cape hunter-gatherers, showing that these coastal sites were occupied in summer. More than half of the cormorants were nestlings and more than one third of the jackass penguins were juveniles at the Paternoster site (Table 10.4; also see Avery & Underhill 1986). The presence of one-month-old spectacled eider and one-month-old snow goose demonstrated occupation in summer at the site of Umingmak on Banks Island in the Arctic (Munzel 1987). We saw in Chapter 3 how almost half of all bird bones were of immature birds, mostly gulls, kittiwake, and cormorants, at the Nipisat site in Greenland (Gotfredsen 1997) and that at the Skyring Sea sites many of the steamer ducks and cormorants were immature. The percentage of immature cormorants at these sites ranged from approximately 30 per cent to almost 90 per cent. These sites too must have been occupied in the summer months, between November and March in the southern hemisphere (Lefèvre 1997). Summer occupation was inferred at the site of Mullerup from the Danish Boreal period, where the assemblage also included remains of immature cormorants. At the contemporary coastal site of Klintsø, some of the remains of great auk were immature, so this site must have been occupied in summer (Grigson 1986).

Medullary Bone

Medullary bone, described in Chapter 3, is found in the bones of females in lay. Its presence in the bones of wild birds demonstrates that the site was occupied in the breeding season, normally early summer. Nearly two thirds of the femora of the Canada geese at Nipisat I contained medullary bone. Medullary bone forms in the subspecies *Branta canadensis minima* during the last six to seven days of rapid ovarian development, which is presumed to take place after the birds have arrived at the breeding grounds (Gotfredsen 1997). It confirms that the site was occupied in early summer (Figure 10.12). Similarly, at Umingmak on Banks Island, medullary bone in snow geese confirmed that the site was occupied in June (Munzel 1987).

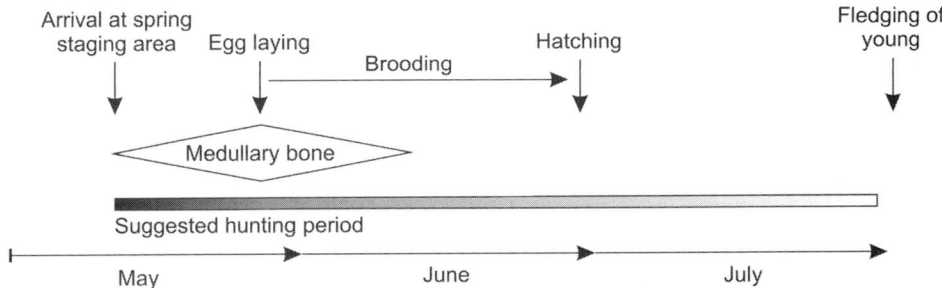

FIGURE 10.12. Season of occupation at Nipisat I, based on the presence of medullary bone and immature birds (Gotfredsen 2002, fig. 8).

In view of the fact that many species, especially seabirds, must have been captured in the breeding season, it is surprising how rarely medullary bone is observed in wild birds. No medullary bone was present in the remains of ptarmigan in six Magdalenian sites in France, despite the fact that both species of grouse must have been resident in the area (Laroulandie 2003). At Ajvide, for instance, the Neolithic Baltic site referred to in Chapter 3, it was seen in only six out of nearly 680 identified bones, less than 1 per cent (Mannermaa & Stora 2006). This is probably a typical figure for bird remains from farming settlements.

It may be unsafe to infer that people were absent from a site in early summer from the absence of medullary bone. It may persist for only a very short time in some species, especially those which lay only one or two eggs. It is even possible that fowlers deliberately avoided female birds in lay as a conservation strategy, or targeted birds which were apparently not paired off. It is also possible that farmers mostly caught seabirds as soon as they returned to the colony to breed, rather than later in the year, because food is scarcest in farming communities, as it is for hunter-gatherers, in early spring.

For the archaeologist, the bird remains, even if scant, can be one of the most important weapons in the arsenal of evidence available for determining seasonal use of a site, since for each of the criteria the evidence is unambiguous. Seasonal indicators are more reliable for sites in high than in middle and low latitudes, but in sites from low latitudes human activities are governed less by the seasons and the question of the season of occupation is less pressing.

PRESERVATION OF WILD BIRDS FOR FOOD

Wild birds were caught for exchange and sale widely until the nineteenth century (Serjeantson 1988). In the days before rapid transport of goods, a precondition was

FIGURE 10.13. Preservation of birds: a pottery vessel from a latrine in a Roman military settlement at Nijmegen, the Netherlands, containing the remains of bodies of song thrushes, *Turdus philomelos*, minus heads, distal wings, and legs (Lauwerier 1993b). The vessel with contents had been imported from the Ardennes or the Eifel region.

that foodstuffs could be preserved. The ability to preserve food was not confined to farming societies but is also found among hunter-gatherers (Ingold 1986). Muttonbirds caught in the Foveaux Straits were traded with neighbouring groups for foodstuffs not available in the South Island (Anderson 1996). They were stored in fat within kelp or bark containers. As we saw, seabirds were preserved by wind-drying on St Kilda and the honey buzzards in Sweden were salted down in barrels like fish. In circumpolar regions, the Inuit preserved birds killed in the autumn by freezing (Nelson 1983, 90). An early example of preserved birds are the 28 song thrushes which were found in a pottery vessel excavated from a latrine in a Roman military settlement at Nijmegen in the Netherlands (Figure 10.13). Petrological analysis of the vessel showed that it had not been made locally but several hundred miles to the south, revealing that the preserved birds had been imported from the Ardennes or Eifel region (Lauwerier 1993b). These examples remind us that we may be able to pin down the season of slaughter, but not necessarily the season of consumption.

PREHISTORY OF BIRD CAPTURE

Up to now this chapter has been concerned with the factors which influenced where and when fowling took place in the past, and it has drawn on archaeological case studies from all periods and all continents with little chronological perspective. Here, I shall close with a brief overview of the origins, prehistory, and history of fowling.

Bird remains have been found on a few Lower Palaeolithic archaeological sites in Africa and Eurasia, but positive evidence that these early samples were anthropogenic is hard to find (Gala et al. 2005). The likelihood that that they were human food was rejected at most sites, though this has been claimed for one or two. Mourer-Chauviré pointed out that most Lower and Middle Palaeolithic assemblages are raptor prey: at Lazaret, for instance, the birds date from a time when humans were absent from the site. However, the Acheulian site at Aridos in Spain, a terrace of Middle Pleistocene date where humans butchered an elephant and deer, was an open air site, and the author thought that it was difficult to explain the presence of ducks, partridges, pigeons, crakes, and Passeriformes except by acknowledging that they had been killed and eaten by the Lower Palaeolithic hunters (Mourer-Chauviré 1979, 1205). Some seabirds, including a great auk and a cormorant, were found at Boxgrove, a Lower Palaeolithic site in the south of England. The site was a short distance from the coast, so the bird must have been carried to the site, most likely by the early hominids (Harrison & Stewart 1999). At Klasies River Mouth in South Africa (100,000–70,000 BP) some penguin remains were found among the fauna; they would have made up less than 0.5 per cent of meat consumed but were thought to be food remains (Avery 1983). It is unsurprising that some of the avian species from the most ancient sites were flightless, as it is these which can most easily be approached and killed.

In the Near East and Europe there was a distinct increase in the consumption of birds from the Upper Palaeolithic period onwards. The concentration on a few large mammals characteristic of the earlier Pleistocene gave way to the hunting of a much wider range of animals, the 'broad spectrum' revolution, in which birds and small mammals such as hare, rabbit, and fox played a part (Tchernov 1993; Stiner et al. 2000). Birds were included in the broad spectrum of resources at the lakeside camp at Ohalo II, though they were only a small element in the diet. The assemblage was diverse: among the nearly 500 identified bird bones from the site, at least 40 species were identified, from 16 families (Simmons & Nadel 1998). As we have seen, the diversity may suggest that fowling was an occasional or casual activity. At many Upper Palaeolithic sites in the Levant and Europe, a narrower range of bird species was targeted. In Klisoura Cave in the Peloponnese region in Greece, fowling was concentrated on just two species: in one layer, out of 285 identified bones, nearly 70 per cent were rock partridge and 30 per cent great bustard (Tomek & Bochenski 2002). At Grotta Romanelli, now near the coast but further inland in the Pleistocene era, bustard was also the main prey (Table 10.5). While the main species in Near Eastern and Italian sites were also grey and rock partridge and quail, further north, as at some of the French sites and at the Late Glacial site of Petersfels in Germany,

Table 10.5. *Species with more than 500 identified bones from Upper Palaeolithic levels at Grotta Romanelli, Italy*

Species	NISP
Little bustard, *Tetrax (Otis) tetrax*	21,829
White-fronted goose, *Anser albifrons*	3,433
Brent goose, *Branta bernicla*	1,829
Bean goose, *Anser fabalis*	1,388
Great bustard, *Otis tarda*	561

Source: Data are from Cassoli and Tagliacozzo (1997).

hunting was so specialised that ptarmigan and willow grouse made up over 90 per cent of all birds (Clark 1948; Laroulandie 2003).

Though some fowling occurred in the Early Upper Palaeolithic (Aurignacian) period at Hayonim Cave, in the main wildfowling both there and in Italy took place later (Figure 10.14). Sites in these two areas show how there was a shift in the Late Pleistocene from harvesting animals which were easy to collect such as molluscs

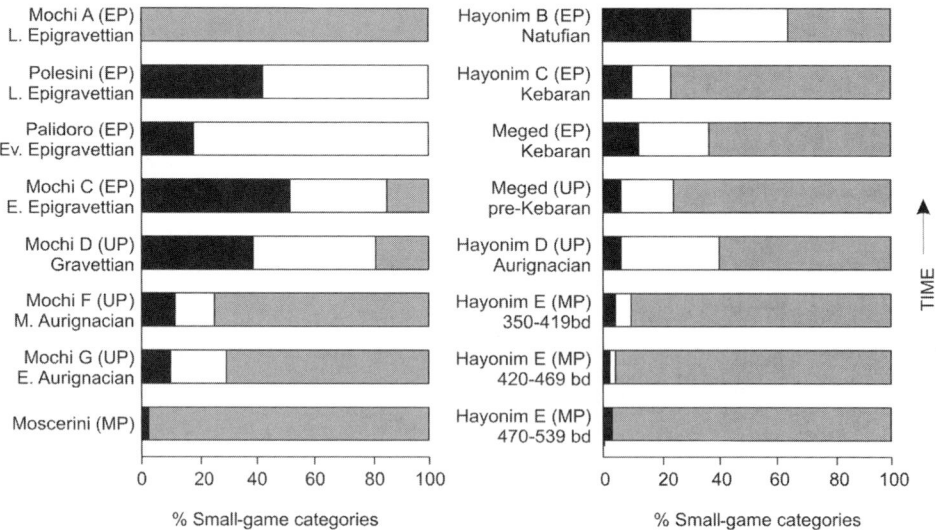

FIGURE 10.14. Relative frequencies of slow or sessile prey (marine molluscs or tortoises; grey bars), versus birds (white bars) and lagomorphs (black bars) in the small-game fractions of Palaeolithic assemblages from (on the left) Italy, 110,000–9000 BP and (on the right) Israel, 200,000–11,000 BP, ordered from oldest at the bottom to youngest at the top: EP, Epipalaeolithic; UP, Upper Palaeolithic; MP, Middle Palaeolithic; Ev, Evolved (from Stiner et al. 2000, fig. 2).

and tortoises to hunting fast, elusive animals such as birds and hares. It was made possible, as we have seen, by the use of snares and nets. It correlated with an increase in the human population which, as Stiner proposed, was encouraged by the increase in the resource base or was a response to technological changes (Stiner et al. 2000). In southwest France, Laroulandie concluded that before the Upper Palaeolithic period birds were killed (or scavenged?) mainly for tools and feathers and that it was only from the Magdalenian period onwards that there is unequivocal evidence of the use of birds as food. As discussed in Chapter 6, the cut marks on the bones, as well as the overwhelming numbers of birds, confirmed that by that time birds were caught primarily for food (Laroulandie 2003, 2005a). In South America we have seen how seabirds were one of the main prey items at Quebrada Tacahuay, one of the few Late Glacial sites in the region with faunal remains.

The abrupt fluctuations in climate and the associated changes in bird distribution at the end of the Pleistocene era (Chapter 15) brought about disruptive changes in the exploitation of birds as well as mammals. Specialised hunting of grouse and other game birds ceased. This was exemplified at the site of Taï 2 (Drome). Grouse were a major prey item in the Magdalenian levels with remains more numerous even than those of ibex and reindeer (Table 10.6), but in the succeeding Epipalaeolithic (Azilian) phase birds played little part (Louchart & Soave 2002).

As sea levels rose at the start of the Holocene, marshy areas were created all over Europe and North America in which waterfowl flourished. Fowling for waterfowl developed in two areas of northern Europe (Guminski 2005, fig. 1). One was northern Denmark together with parts of southern Sweden and north Germany. As we have seen, there were different strategies at different sites, but most have large numbers of ducks, swans, and other waterfowl, attracted to the estuaries and bays which remained free of ice in winter (Grigson 1986). The second area where fowling was significant in the Mesolithic was northeast Europe, especially in the Kunda culture of the eastern Baltic. The same range of species was exploited as in northwest Europe, mainly waterfowl, but also grouse and raptors in drier environments (Guminski 2005). It is likely that seabirds, especially great auks, were eaten on coastal sites (Tuck 1971; Grigson 1981), but as few early Holocene coastal sites have survived the Holocene rises in sea level, this is difficult to prove.

Once farming became established in Europe and Western Asia, communities narrowed their resource base to the cultivated crops and domestic animals (Bogucki 1979). Foods from the wild became no more than a supplementary resource and the exploitation of birds was restricted to areas where agriculture was marginal (Schulting et al. 2004). Fowling, often combined with fishing, became restricted to 'dwellers by marsh, lake and seashore' (Clark 1952, 55). Coastal farmers in Scotland

Table 10.6. *Birds and mammals from Magdalenian and Azilian levels at Taï 2, southern France, showing the change in the consumption of grouse*

Taxon	Magdalenian	Azilian
Swan, *Cygnus* cf. *olor*	1	
Anatinae indet.		1
Eagle, *Aquila* cf. *chrysaetos*		1
Willow grouse, *Lagopus lagopus*	66	1
Ptarmigan, *Lagopus muta*	21	
Lagopus sp.	350	3
Black grouse, *Tetrao tetrix*	4	
Great bustard, *Otis tarda*	1	
Short-eared owl, *Asio flammeus*		2
Chough, *Pyrrhocorax graculus*	18	1
Aves indet.	7	2
Total birds	468	11
Ibex, *Capra ibex*	187	203
Reindeer, *Rangifer tarandus*	91	53
Chamois, *Rupicapra rupicapra*	19	17
Red deer, *Cervus elaphus*	22	9
Horse, *Equus* cf. *gallicus*	2	3
Aurochs, *Bos primigenius*	1	1
Wolf, *Canis lupus*	3	
Badger, *Meles meles*	1	2
Total large mammals	326	288

Note: Magdalenian refers to the Upper Palaeolithic period, or 14,450–13,110 cal BC; Azilian refers to the Epipalaeolithic period, or 13,620–12,800 cal BC.
Source: Data are from Louchart and Soave (2002).

(Serjeantson 1988), Iceland (McGovern et al. 2006), and Greenland (Enghoff 2003) exploited seabirds to supplement farmed produce. Farmers living near wetlands caught predominantly waterfowl (Zeiler & Clason 1993; Gál 2007), as at Schipluiden in the Netherlands (see Figure 4.13 in Chapter 4). Those few Neolithic communities in northern Europe which continued to hunt birds focused on a narrower range of species (Guminski 2005).

In the Americas exploitation followed a different pattern. The scarcity of domestic animals meant that wild animals, including birds, continued to be exploited by farmers as well as by hunter-gatherers. So far as the turkey was concerned, exploitation led eventually to its domestication, as we see in Chapter 12.

Far from ignoring wild birds, in the complex societies of Western Asia and in the classical world, wild as well as domestic birds were kept in captivity for sacrifice at ritual and ceremonial occasions (Chapter 14). In Inca societies scarlet macaws and other birds were kept for ritual purposes. All sorts of birds were kept for sport and pleasure, as discussed in Chapter 13. In medieval Europe, dietary rules required abstinence from the flesh of quadrupeds on certain days of the year, which encouraged the consumption of fish and birds (Woolgar et al. 2006a). Domestic chickens met the need of providing meat on days when meat from four-footed animals was forbidden in most of continental Europe and mainland Britain, but at Illaunloughan, a coastal monastery in Ireland, the manx shearwater filled the role (Murray et al. 2004).

The consumption of wild birds was also a means by which the elite in hierarchic societies marked itself off from the rest of the population. In medieval England, eating large birds such as crane, heron, and bittern was a sign of households of high status (Albarella & Thomas 2002; Dobney & Jaques 2002). The lists of animals provided for banquets include an astonishingly wide range of wild birds as well as mammals and fish (Bourne 1981; Sykes 2004; Serjeantson 2006b). The sale of wild birds to townsfolk began at this time, and has continued to the present day, supplementing agricultural produce and the much more widely traded fish. It survives on a small scale only, and, in Europe at least, has more to do with sport than economics. Even the harvesting of seabirds and their eggs from high sea cliffs (see Figure 7.1 in Chapter 7) was such a hazardous activity that it was an important initiation and test of manhood in places as diverse as St Kilda and Easter Island (Routledge 1917; Bratrein 2005; Love 2005).

DISCUSSION

The consumption of wild birds in the past depended on two interacting factors: availability and how birds were caught. People ate large birds where these were available, but in their absence ate smaller birds which flocked together. It was rare for people to catch birds below 200 g in weight, though it was certainly not unknown. The physical evidence for the means of capture has only rarely survived, but it is often possible to deduce how the birds were caught from the methods documented ethnographically. Nothing in this survey of methods of catching birds in the past has contradicted Clark's conclusion that 'One of the first points to emphasise is that the early fowlers relied only to a very limited extent upon taking birds on the wing' (Clark 1948). However, Clark probably underestimated the antiquity of techniques such netting and the use of bird lime. These are now known to be so widespread that there is no reason to suppose their use did not go back to Late Palaeolithic times.

The importance of birds as a nutritional resource varied according to the environment. They were a major resource on islands, especially newly colonised islands, around the coast where seasonal seabirds came ashore for a short period in the year to breed, and in high latitudes where food resources were limited. The exploitation of birds in high and medium latitudes was probably always a seasonal activity. Immature birds and females in lay were exploited in summer at sites on the Arctic and Antarctic margins, but both are rarely found on sites in more temperate environments. Where the birds are exclusively adults, it suggests that birds were a food exploited in winter and early spring rather than in late spring and summer. Though birds have rarely been a major resource, they were an important minor resource in a wide range of places in the past, not only to hunter-gatherers but also to farmers in certain environments. As well as the examples cited in this chapter, there are many more in other chapters. However, if birds were relatively insignificant in terms of nutrition, it does not mean that they were unimportant in other ways. As discussed, in some complex societies the consumption of birds carried a social significance out of all proportion to their value as food.

On many settlements, remains are so few that birds can never have been more than a very rare supplementary or fallback food resource, and they may even have been avoided as food. In these settlements, as discussed in Chapter 8, feathers may have been more important than meat, even if the birds were also eaten. Though the focus of this chapter and indeed much of the book is on those communities which *do* eat birds, we cannot avoid the fact that there were many hunter-gatherers who caught birds only occasionally. There were also many farming communities where birds were scarcely eaten until the domestic chicken found its way into every farmyard, the subject of the next chapter.

The Domestic Chicken

The chicken, *Gallus gallus*, is the most widespread domestic animal in the world; chickens are kept in every continent and eaten by a wider range of peoples and societies than any other animal. They provide protein for the poor who otherwise rarely eat meat as well as a reliable source of meat for the rich, and they can be kept by townspeople as well as villagers. The other domestic birds, discussed in the next chapter, are all less significant on a world scale, even if locally important. Despite their ubiquity, theories of domestication proposed by different authors have scarcely mentioned the chicken (let alone other birds) or have ignored it (Clutton-Brock 1981a; O'Connor 1997). The chicken is not even included with the 'domestic animals of major world-wide importance' in a recent zooarchaeology textbook, but with the 'small domestic animals kept for various purposes' (Reitz & Wing 1999, 291).

The three basic stages of domestication are taming, breeding in the presence of people, and full human control of breeding. Once the last stage is reached, morphological changes take place and we find diversification into varieties under artificial selection by humans (Darwin 1868; Peterson & Brisbin 1999). Identifying where one stage grades into the next from archaeological finds of chickens presents serious challenges in the initial stages, but the full domestic status of chickens becomes very clear as they became widespread beyond the area of their natural distribution.

Gallus gallus has traditionally and formally been referred to as 'domestic fowl', though the common usage in English today is 'chicken'. 'Domestic fowl' can be confusing in the plural. Are 'domestic fowls' a flock of chickens? Or are they a collection of domestic birds of many different kinds? Although 'chicken' is also ambiguous as it is sometimes used to refer to the young of any bird, I shall use 'chicken' here. Some authors use the scientific binomial *Gallus gallus* or its modification, *G. gallus* f. domesticus, while others, following the principle set out by Clutton-Brock (1981b), use *Gallus domesticus*. Some of the names given to the different age classes are listed in Table 11.1.

Table 11.1. *Some of the names given to chickens of different ages and sexes*

Name	Age and sex
Hatchling or chick	Newborn
Cockerel	Immature male
Pullet	Immature female
Cock or rooster	Mature male
Hen	Mature female
Capon	Castrated male or male fattened for eating

Note: The term is 'cock' in England and 'rooster' in the United States.

The chicken has filled many roles in the past. At first its symbolic qualities were more important than food – it was associated with the dawn and rebirth, with valour, and with victory in combat. As discussed in later chapters, chickens were kept for sacrifices and for cockfighting; only later did meat and eggs take over. Once they were kept as a food animal, their success as a domesticate lay in their small size. Compared with cows and sheep, chickens need little food. Their natural diet is seeds, other vegetable matter, and invertebrates, and it is one which they can seek out for themselves around the house and garden, so it is easy for a small household to keep a flock provided it can protect them from predators.

WILD ANCESTOR

In the nineteenth century, Darwin and others identified the wild ancestor of the domestic chicken as the red junglefowl (Darwin 1868). There are four species of wild *Gallus* and five subspecies of the red junglefowl, all of which are found in Southeast Asia, southern China, and the Indian subcontinent (Crawford 1984a, 299). The skeletal anatomy, the plumage, and the wide distribution of the red junglefowl initially suggested that it was the sole ancestral species. Later work on behavioural differences between the junglefowl species confirmed this (Crawford 1984). DNA analysis is now also making a contribution. One study of chicken DNA concluded that Thailand and neighbouring regions were the maternal home of the chicken (Akishinonomiya et al. 1994) while others, after analysis of wild and domestic chickens from many parts of the world, proposed that domestic chickens had multiple origins, including in southern China and neighbouring countries, southeastern China, and the Indian subcontinent (Liu et al. 2006). In each of these studies, questions can be raised about the origin of the species used: modern breeds may not be descended from local wild populations because new breeds have been introduced everywhere in the past 200 years. There is also a real possibility that few or no fully wild red junglefowl still exist in the wild today which have not been exposed to genetic mixing with domestic chickens, since domestic chickens are kept in all those areas where the junglefowl survives and they interbreed freely with the wild population. There is a danger that the wild genes will become, or have already become, swamped by hybridisation (Brisbin 1995; Peterson & Brisbin 1999). The hypotheses for chicken origins have still to be tested with ancient material.

HISTORY

The early history of the domestic chicken has until recently relied on iconography and written sources (Crawford 1984a; Peters 1997b; Limet, 1994, n. 2150). The earliest depictions known are a figurine and an engraving on a clay seal from Mohenjo-Daro, the third to second millennium BC site in Pakistan excavated in the 1930s by Mortimer Wheeler (Zeuner 1963; Benecke 1994). As this site is in the plains, it is some distance from the natural environments of the junglefowl, so it was inferred that chickens had already been introduced to the site and so were under human control. There are pottery figurines of chickens and also ducks at earlier sites in China, from the Late Neolithic (second to third millennium BC) site of Lung Shan (Watson 1969) and the third millennium sites of Qujialing and Shijiahe (West & Zhou 1988).

The earliest written references date from the middle of the second millennium BC. The cuneiform texts from Mesopotamia are rather ambiguous. Limet (1994) concluded that either 'dar.Me.luh.ha' (bird from Meluha) or 'dar.lugal' must refer to the chicken; these two terms are found from the fifteenth century BC onwards but not earlier. The first mention in Egypt of a bird which may refer to a chicken is found in a text of the mid-fifteenth century BC which states that Tuthmoses III 'received from Syria four birds which lay every day' (Limet 1994). However, chickens were not depicted on monuments in Egypt until the time of the Ptolemies in the late first millennium BC, and no chicken mummies have been found (Houlihan & Goodman 1986, 79–81), so the chicken cannot have been at all widespread until Egypt was exposed to the external influence of the classical world towards the end of the first millennium BC.

These sparse illustrations and references together suggest that the chicken was carried beyond its natural range in the second millennium BC, and that some birds were taken to Western Asia by the middle of the first millennium BC. The number must have been very few, as the Greeks were still unfamiliar with the chicken in the ninth century BC: the Minoans do not depict the cock in any of the frescoes found up to now and the birds are not mentioned by Homer or Hesiod. It is only from the seventh century BC that cocks were depicted on coins and vases and are referred to by the Archaic and Classical Greek writers (Wood-Gush 1958; Zeuner 1963; Boev 1995; Serjeantson In press-a). By the first century BC, the Roman farming writers, Varro and Columella, were already familiar with chickens of different breeds and knew of some very sophisticated means of raising them for meat and eggs, especially in the cities (Hooper & Ash 1935; Columella 1941; Peters 1997a). The historic evidence suggests that the main spread of domestic chickens westwards took place in the last 500 years of the first millennium BC.

EARLY ARCHAEOLOGICAL RECORDS

The archaeological record, however, raises the possibility that the domestication and spread took place earlier. There have been a few claims of chicken bones in Pleistocene sites in Europe. According to Milne-Edwards (1875, 241), 'Bones of this bird... are found associated with those of *Ursus spelaeus*, *Rhinoceros*, and the large *Felis*' in the French caves. These and other finds claimed from Pleistocene Europe are now viewed with grave suspicion and believed to be intrusive (Garcia Petit 2005, 156–157). The earliest archaeological records were assembled by West and Zhou (1988), who listed nearly 30 published and unpublished records of chicken bones which predate 2000 BC; they are from sites in China, Iran, Turkey, Syria, Greece, Romania, and the Ukraine (West & Zhou 1988, tab. 2). In China, chicken remains have now been recorded from a total of eleven Neolithic sites (Underhill 1997). Some from the sixth millennium sites in China are now known to be from pheasants (Benecke 1994, 364; Peters 1997a, 1997b) and some may be from wild birds, since the range of the wild red junglefowl may originally have extended further north in China than it does today. However, the presence of chicken remains on a number of sites (Bellwood 2005, 111–127) makes it likely that China was an early centre of domestication, if not the earliest. In the Indian subcontinent there are some early Neolithic finds in the north, including quite a few bones on two settlements of late hunter-gatherers, which might indicate emerging chicken husbandry there amongst semi-sedentary hunter-gatherers or hunter-cultivators (Fuller 2006). Chickens have been reported from quite a few third and second millennium sites in the Indian subcontinent, both from sites within the known range of the red junglefowl but also from outside it. Those from peninsular India are from sites of the mid-second to late second millennium BC and are from outside the range of wild junglefowl, suggesting that they are introduced domestic birds (Badam 1984, tab. 1; Pawankar & Thomas 1997; Thomas et al. 1997; Fuller 2006). In Thailand, where we might expect early records, remains of chicken are surprisingly scant. The scarcity of records from the cemetery and settlement at Phum Snay in Cambodia suggests that domestic chickens were still rare there even as late as the Iron Age (500 BC to AD 500; see O'Reilly et al. 2006).

West and Zhou hypothesised that chickens reached Europe by way of China and Central Asia rather than by way of Western Asia, as early records for chicken have been claimed in the countries of the former USSR. It has also been claimed that there was a native wild Caucasian/Ukrainian-Moldovan and Crimean *Gallus* species (Boev 1995). Certainly a transmission route north of the Caspian and the Black Sea is perfectly plausible geographically, though whether social conditions there in the second millennium BC would have favoured the importation of the chicken is a different matter.

The earliest finds from Western Asia include some from Tell Sweyhat in Syria (*c.* 2400 BC) and from Korucutepe in Anatolia (Benecke 1994, 365). There is a possible mid-second millennium find from Egypt, but there, as the historical records suggest, the main spread was a millennium later (Peters 1997b). The initial spread of the chicken around the Mediterranean may have been in the boats of the Phoenician traders and colonists, since the earliest chicken bones in Spain come from one of the Phoenician colonies dating from the eighth century BC onwards (Hernandez Carrasquilla 1992; Peters 1997b; Garcia Petit 2002). The earliest in Italy are also from Phoenician settlements in the south (MacDonald 1992), including the site of Lattera where as many as 10 per cent of the bird bones ($n = 2,080$) were of chickens (Garcia Petit 2005).

The archaeological evidence certainly includes some suggestive early finds, but, together with the historical record, it supports the hypothesis of some early writers that Alexander the Great was inadvertently a key figure in making the domestic chicken more widely known. Between 331 BC and 323 BC Alexander campaigned as far as India with his huge army; this must have provided regular contact between Persia, India, and the Greek world. Perhaps the soldiers brought back a taste for eating chicken as well as for cockfighting, as well as bringing back new, more prolific, breeds. It is only from about this time that remains are found in any quantity: in the town of Nea Halos in Greece (third century BC), chicken was the second most common species after the rock dove. In Spain the earliest site where chickens have been found in quantity is also from the third century BC, at the site of Barchin del Hoyo (Hernandez Carrasquilla 1992). Only a few records of chicken in Egypt predate the Roman sites of Berenike and Mons Claudianus (see Chapter 8), where chickens were abundant (MacDonald 1993; Hamilton-Dyer 1997; Van Neer & Ervynck 1999).

The earliest finds of chicken remains from central Europe date from the mid-first millennium BC (Early Iron Age; see Benecke 1993), and the earliest find from the British Isles may not be until much later (Poole in press). In Sweden the earliest record is from the first century BC. It is of a bird which was sacrificed in the Skedemose fen near Malmö in southern Sweden (Ericson & Tyrberg 2004, 15). In southern Britain, chickens only became common from the beginning of the first millennium AD onwards. During the 400 years of Roman occupation, chickens were eaten on military sites and in towns and to a lesser degree in villas, but they were not taken up by the native population in the countryside (see Table 4.6 in Chapter 4). From the mid-first millennium onwards in Europe, chickens are present on most sites. If remains are scarce, the small numbers are more likely to reflect poor survival and recovery than the absence of chickens from the farmyard and the pot (Serjeantson 2006b). In the later first millennium AD on coastal areas of Ireland, the monks ate seabirds instead of chickens (Murray et al. 2004), and around the coast of western and northern Scotland, where seabird fowling also continued, chickens were known but rare until the later Middle Ages (Serjeantson 1988).

The spread of the domestic chicken through Southeast Asia and on to the islands of the Pacific must have been as early as or earlier than the westward spread, as remains have been found on Polynesian islands associated with Lapita pottery which dates from the second millennium BC (Storey et al. 2008). These birds must have been semi-domestic if not fully domestic. For unknown reasons, the spread into Polynesia was patchy: chickens have been recorded on up to 20 per cent of the islands of Far Oceania, but on less than 3 per cent of the islands of Near Oceania, and they were never taken to New Zealand. At the site of Tahuata in the Marquesas Islands, which were referred to in Chapter 10, chickens were rare when the island was first occupied in the eleventh century AD but became more abundant in the thirteenth century as the local wild bird populations were extirpated (Steadman & Rolett 1996). This pattern of an increase in chickens in parallel with a decline in the consumption of native birds does not hold for all sites, and the reasons for the presence or absence of chickens on any one island are still enigmatic (Storey et al. 2008).

The spread into sub-Saharan Africa was rather late, even later than the spread into Egypt. East Africa had trading contacts with Egypt, the Near East, and also India from early in the first millennium AD, so chickens might be expected to have featured in these exchanges, but current research does not indicate that the chicken was adopted before about AD 800. When it was, it is thought to be as a result of contacts with Asia (Chami 2004). In West Africa, the earliest known finds are from the important site of Jenne-jeno in Mali, in cultural layers of *c.* AD 500–800 (MacDonald 1992; Blench & MacDonald 2000).

Tantalising evidence has emerged from time to time which suggests pre-Columbian contacts between Polynesia and South America. The chicken is one of the possible links. The Spanish found that when they first reached the Amazon Basin and the Andes, people already kept chickens. The word used for chicken in Chile is similar to an Asian name for the bird. Recent DNA analysis on directly dated bones has shown a close match between the DNA of chicken bones from a pre-Columbian site in Chile and those from the Polynesian island of Niue as well as with the Araucana, the breed of chicken native to South America, confirming that chickens were indeed taken to South America from the South Pacific (Storey et al. 2007). The sweet potato, native to South America, occurs early in Polynesia, and the blowgun is used in both parts of the world (Carter 1971; Jett 1991; Anderson et al. 2007), confirming the early date for contacts across the Pacific.

CHANGES FOLLOWING DOMESTICATION

If chickens were domesticated for ritual purposes (Chapter 14) and for cockfighting (Chapter 13), there is no reason to expect rapid size change in the first centuries following domestication. The modern breeds known as the Aseel in Southeast Asia and the English Game Fowl in Europe are closest to the original red junglefowl. Once the birds were taken beyond their natural range in the wild and reared for food, people intervened to caponise the males, encourage larger breeds, and select for birds with extended egg-laying capabilities. They also bred for different coloured plumage, including white and black.

Caponisation

The natural family group is a cock with four or five hens and young; in a domestic flock the number of hens can be increased. The cocks fight naturally for females, an instinct which has been encouraged in those breeds kept for cockfighting, so, when several male birds are kept for the cooking pot, castration in some form is advantageous. The evidence for this in the past is largely based on the condition of the tarsometatarsus. It is reviewed here in some detail, as it is one of the most contentious issues in the study of chicken bones from archaeological sites.

The word 'capon' is ambiguous, as it has been used to refer both to castrated males and to any young bird fattened for consumption. Today, males are castrated

Table 11.2. *Condition of tarsometatarsus in domestic chickens, showing likely and possible interpretations of the presence and absence of a spur or spur scar*

Bone condition	Interpretation
1 Tarsometatarsus fused, spur absent	HEN
	Cockerel approximately 7 months?
2 Tarsometatarsus fused, spur present	COCK
	Capon
	Hen of certain breeds
3 Tarsometatarsus fused, deformed spur present	CAPON
4 Tarsometatarsus fused, spur scar present	COCKEREL 7–18 months
	Hen up to any age
5 Tarsometatarsus unfused, spur scar present	COCKEREL approximately 7 months
	Capon

Note: Capital letters indicate the likely interpretation and lowercase letters indicate a possible but unlikely interpretation.

with a chemical implant, but before this method was developed castration was carried out by removal of the testicles. These organs are internal in birds, located next to the kidneys, so the task required great skill. Because a small incision was required, it was also hazardous to the bird. This operation may have been carried out in ancient China, and many researchers consider that it was done in classical times, but Joris Peters, after a close study of the descriptions of chicken husbandry by Varro, Martial, Columella, and other agricultural writers of antiquity, concluded that Roman poultry keepers did not practice castration in the true sense. The process which these authors describe is cauterisation of the spurs. Both have the effect of preventing cocks from fighting (Peters 1997a).

Physical castration on birds carried out before about three months of age has the same effects as it does in mammals: bones increase in length and fusion is delayed (Blount 1964). It also leads to an increase in the length of the spur, a phenomenon noted by Aldrovandi in the sixteenth century and confirmed by an experimental study (Peters 1997a). Cauterising the spur should not affect bone growth as it does not affect the gonads; this operation should be visible only as damage to the spur. The development of the spur on the tarsometatarsus was described in Chapter 3. Tarsometatarsi from archaeological assemblages are found in four conditions: fused but lacking a spur or spur scar; fused and with a spur; fused and with a spur scar; and unfused and with a spur scar (Table 11.2). Spurs are sometimes unusually small or malformed (West 1982, 1985a, 1985b; Sadler 1991; Peters 1997a; Peters 1997b). The

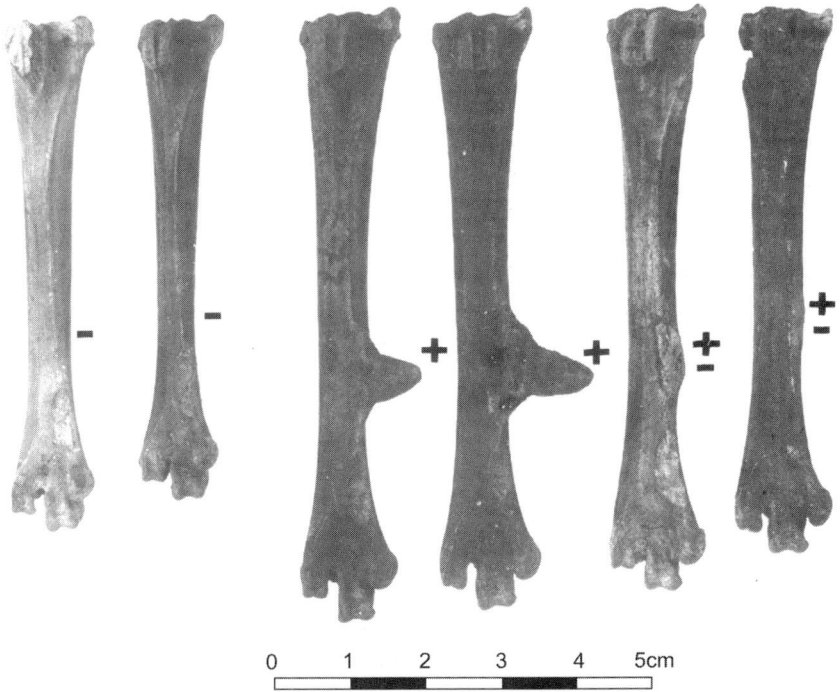

FIGURE 11.1. Examples of tarsometatarsi of chickens from the Roman castellum at Velsen, the Netherlands: –, hens with no spur; +, cocks with spur present; ±, immature cocks with spur scar (Prummel 1987; photograph by R. J. Kosters).

interpretation of these four conditions has been the subject of much confusion, not least because writers have not defined the type of caponisation to which they were referring.

1. Tarsometatarsus Fused, with Spur or Spur Scar Absent

These belong to hens (see the left side of Figure 11.1). The possibility that they are from young cocks in which the tarsometatarsus has not yet reached the stage at which the changes start to occur prior to fusion of the spur is very remote (see Table 3.2 in Chapter 3).

2. Tarsometatarsus Fused and Spur Present

These belong to adult cocks, including castrated birds (see the centre of Figure 11.1). Some normal hens of modern breed develop a spur, and a spur also develops occasionally in old hens as hormone levels drop (Sadler 1991; Cupere et al. 2005), so a few bones in this condition may be from hens. Spurs on hens are less well developed than those on cocks, and they often remain unfused to the tarsometatarsus. Figure 3.8 in Chapter 3 shows a pair of spurred tarsometatarsi from hens of the Leghorn breed; at the age of 18 months, one spur has fused and the other has not. Agricultural writers in the classical period and in the Middle Ages were unanimous in recommending that hens with spurs were contrary to nature and should be killed off, so in archaeological material from early periods it is a reasonable assumption that there were few or no spurred hens. When relatively short tarsometatarsi with spurs are present, they are usually interpreted as coming from cocks of a small breed.

2a. Tarsometatarsus Fused, Small or Deformed Spur Present

Many – probably most – of the assemblages of tarsometatarsi from the Roman period, and some from other periods, include among the spurred bones a small group with poorly formed spurs. Often these tarsometatarsi are longer than those with fully developed spurs. They have usually been identified as capons. For instance, among the tarsometatarsi from Roman-period sites in northern France (Figure 11.2), spurred and unspurred birds fall in two discrete size groups, the shorter females and the larger males, but seven out of 17 bones in the 'male' group have poorly formed spurs, and, of these, six are longer than the bones of those with well formed spurs. The same phenomenon was seen in two sites in Hungary from the Roman period (Bökönyi & Bartosiewicz 1983). Peters' conclusion (1997) that castration proper did not take place in the classical period raises an interesting dilemma for the interpretation of these bones. The fact that the spur is poorly formed should rule out the possibility that these larger birds were physically castrated, since, as already discussed, this operation leads to an increase rather than a decrease in spur length. The specimens are best explained as birds which suffered cauterised spurs, but it leaves open the question of why the bones are longer.

3. Tarsometatarsus Fused and Spur Scar Present

At one time it was believed that the presence of a spur scar denoted a caponised bird, and this interpretation can be found in reports written in the 1980s and earlier. This is now known to be incorrect (West 1982, 1985a, 1985b). Rather, these bones are

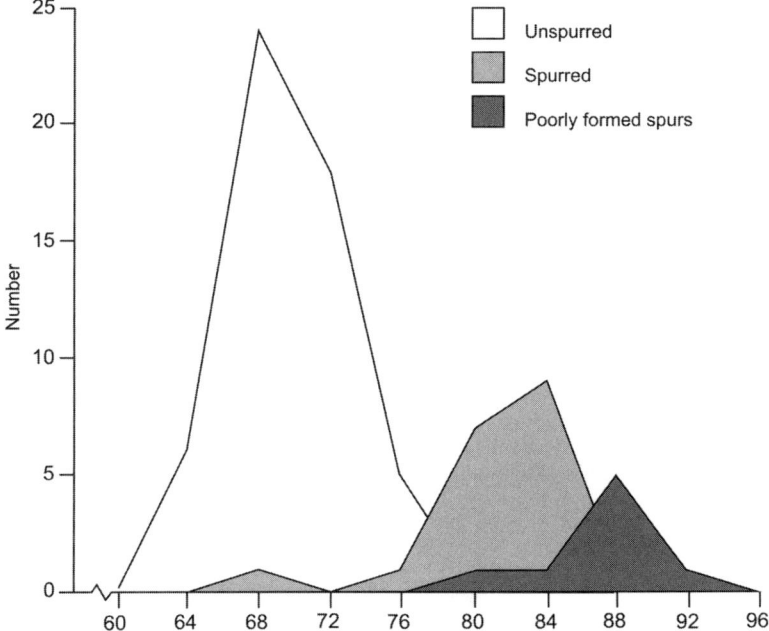

FIGURE 11.2. Distribution of length (in millimetres) of chicken tarsometatarsi from Roman-period sites in northern France, showing the spurred and unspurred separately (after Clavel et al. 1997). The spurred tarsometatarsi include a category with spurs which are poorly formed; most of these are longer than those with normal spurs, so are interpreted as being from caponised birds.

usually from males, still quite young, in which the spur has not yet fused to the bone shaft (see the right side of Figure 11.1). It is also possible that they are from hens which are developing spurs.

The tarsometatarsi with spur scars are sometimes longer than the spurred examples in an assemblage, which complicates the interpretation. The tarsometatarsi from the sixth- to seventh-century deposits at the Byzantine site of Sagalassos in southwest Turkey showed this phenomenon (Figure 11.3). Two out of the five longest tarsometatarsi have spur scars (Cupere et al. 2005, fig. 5). Other examples of assemblages in which this was evident are the Roman-period occupation in York where more than one type or breed is present (O'Connor 1988, fig. 15) and the castellum at Velsen in the Netherlands (Figure 11.4) where a single type or breed is present (Prummel 1987). The obvious deduction is that the long-legged birds are some which were castrated, which had the effect of delaying fusion of spur scar to the tarsometatarsus shaft. Alternatively, in the second type or breed, the cocks had longer legs and delayed fusion of the spur to the tarsometatarsus.

278　BIRDS

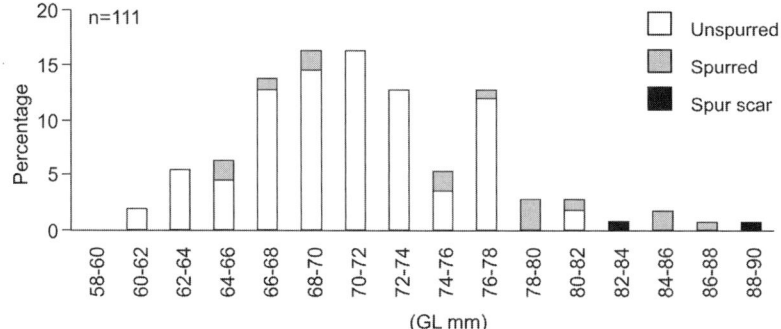

FIGURE 11.3. Distribution of the greatest length in millimetres (GL mm) of tarsometatarsi of chicken from the Byzantine site of Sagalassos, Turkey, from the seventh to eighth century AD (redrawn from Cupere et al. 2005, fig. 6). Two size groups are present within the unspurred and spurred specimens, which are interpreted as two different types or breeds. The two specimens with a spur scar are among the longest elements.

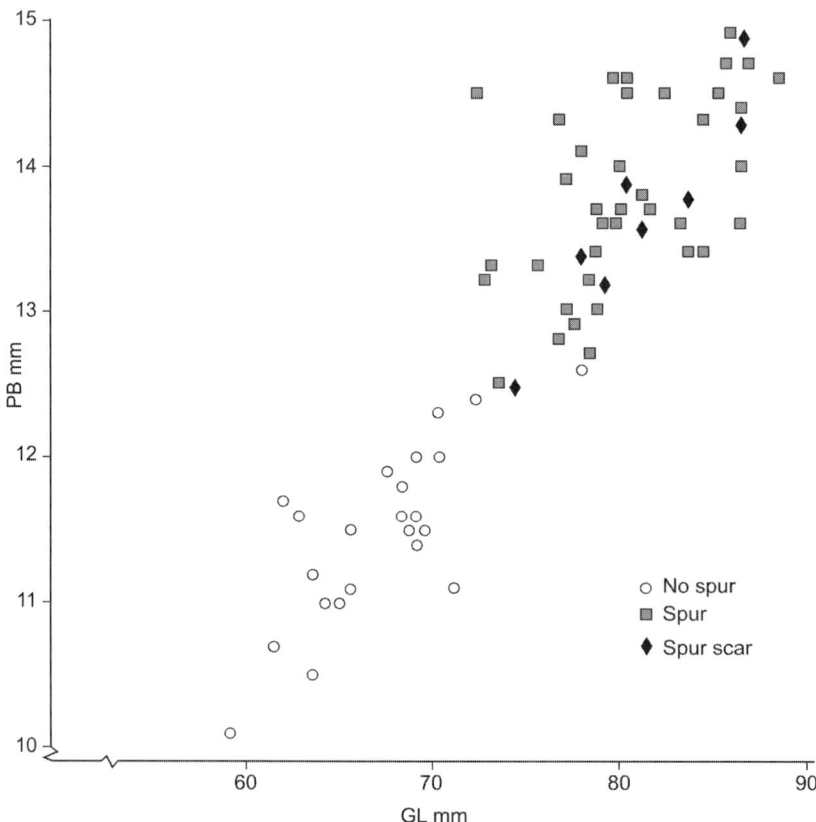

FIGURE 11.4. Size of tarsometatarsi of chickens from the Roman castellum at Velsen in the Netherlands, c. AD 15–30: greatest length in millimetres (GL mm) × proximal breadth in millimetres (PB mm). The small overlap between spurred and unspurred elements suggests that a single type or breed is present (Prummel 1987, fig. 3).

4. Tarsometatarsus Unfused and Spur Scar Present

There are occasional finds of bones in this condition with delayed fusion of the proximal tarsometatarsus. It is sometimes found in the birds with the longest legs, contrary to the case just discussed. It has been suggested that these are from birds which have undergone castration, as they combine delayed fusion of the tarsometatarsus with enhanced spur development (West 1985b). The alternative is that they are from cockerels of a slow-maturing breed in which fusion of the tarsometatarsus occurred at a relatively advanced age.

It is clear that the age of fusion of the proximal tarsometatarsus and of the spur to the shaft of the bone itself have been very variable in the past, as they are today. It seems to have been particularly true for the Roman period, a time when we know, from written accounts, that the breeding of different strains took place. The zooarchaeological evidence also seems to support the theory that caponisation in the past, whatever form it took, led to an increase in tarsometatarsus length.

Size Change and the Development of Breeds

Though plumage changed under domestication, this is only visible in the depictions and descriptions. For the zooarchaeologist the most significant change is in the size. As well as birds bred for large size, specialised small breeds were developed (Columella 1941; Darwin 1868).

Any analysis of size change in chickens has to take into account their sexual dimorphism (see Chapter 3) and so must be carried out on elements which can be sexed. A survey of size change in northern France from the Gallo-Roman to the Post-Medieval period was based on the femora of female birds only, identified from the presence of medullary bone, and on the tarsometatarsus. The authors used an index based on the skeletons of twelve modern hens. Multipliers were established for each of the main limb bones which were applied to the archaeological specimens. The results showed that chickens grew larger between the first and fifth centuries AD, and then plummeted in size from the fifth to the eleventh centuries. There was then a gradual increase between the twelfth and fourteenth centuries, and a substantial increase in size in the sixteenth century (Figure 11.5). This did not fit with an earlier survey (Erbersdorbler 1968) which suggested a different timing for the medieval size increase. The two datasets are hard to compare as the earlier survey used very broad time bands, but the increase in size which took place in the Middle Ages may have occurred at different times in different parts of Europe (Clavel et al. 1997).

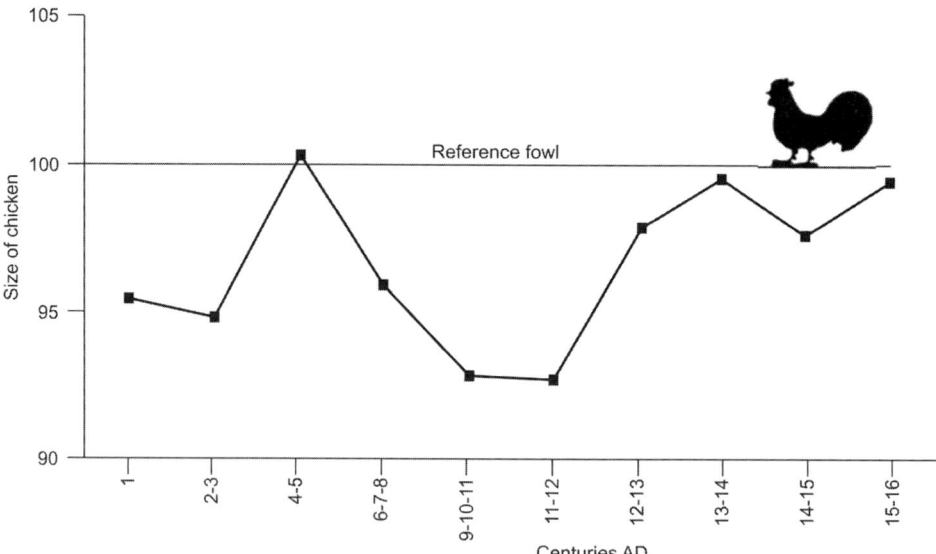

FIGURE 11.5. Size change in chickens from northern France over time, based on tarsometatarsus length; stature is shown in relation to reference chickens (redrawn from Clavel et al. 1997, fig. 9).

In those parts of south Asia where the wild red junglefowl is still found, people continued to capture wild birds for cockfighting, and wild and domestic birds have interbred. This would have inhibited size change in domestic birds locally. Where domestic chickens are left to forage for food rather than fed liberally, they also remain small, as was the case in sub-Saharan Africa in the first millennium AD, where the chickens were as small as junglefowl (MacDonald 1992).

The Development of Breeds

The presence of different breeds can also only be established when sexual dimorphism has been ruled out as an explanation for two different size classes. Despite the ambiguities over caponisation, the tarsometatarsus is especially suitable for identifying breeds because it varies more in length according to breed than other elements. There appeared to be more than one breed among the chickens from Sagalassos (Cupere et al. 2005). Compared with the remains from those assemblages from northern Europe such as Velsen, and Early Medieval Haithabu and Eketorp, which contained homogenous populations of chickens, at Sagalassos the size range was greater. This suggested that more than one breed was present and it was confirmed by the tarsometatarsus and also other elements. The tarsometatarsi from Sagalassos do not fall into two discrete groups of males and females according to bone length, but they do include a few small spurred examples in the short group and some unspurred examples towards the upper end of the distribution (Figure 11.3). The short-legged birds were interpreted as coming from cocks of a different, smaller, breed than from hens with spurs. The femora confirmed the conclusion that two distinct breeds were present, as the length showed a bimodal distribution *within* the specimens with medullary bone (Cupere et al. 2005). The size distribution elsewhere confirms the presence of more than one breed in the Roman period, including York and Exeter (Maltby 1979, fig. 20).

Eventually, the development of specialised breeds in the modern period led to some with skeletal abnormalities. The Polish breed, which has a feathery crown, has a protuberance on the skull, and 'rumpless' fowls have a distorted sternum and lack caudal vertebrae (Darwin 1868).

Age at Death

As chickens became important as a source of meat, more were slaughtered while still immature. This is exemplified in the city of Exeter: only 11 per cent of the bones from the Roman period were immature, while in the Middle Ages this rose to 20 per cent (Maltby 1979). For the medieval cook, 'chickens' and 'hens' were different commodities, and 'capons' few and reserved for feasts and special occasions (Figure 11.6; also see Harvey 1993, 53; Stone 2006). The percentage of immature chickens was similar to that in Exeter in other medieval towns, but it was higher in religious houses and in the households of the wealthy (Serjeantson 2006b, fig. 9.7). From as early as the twelfth century at Eynsham Abbey, no less than half of all birds eaten were immature. In the towns such as medieval Norwich (Figure 11.7), the percentage of immature birds increased from the sixteenth century onwards. Consumption of chickens and capons was a mark of wealth and social status and in the later Middle Ages it reflected the trend towards eating more meat (Albarella 1997c; Serjeantson 2006b).

Extended Laying Period

Like other Galliformes, the red junglefowl lays a large clutch of eggs, and will continue to lay if some are removed. This tendency has been very much enhanced under domestication. The statement about the 'bird which lays every day' in Egypt, if it does refer to chicken, suggests that this transformation in behaviour may already have begun by the middle of the second millennium BC. As early as the fourth century BC,

282　BIRDS

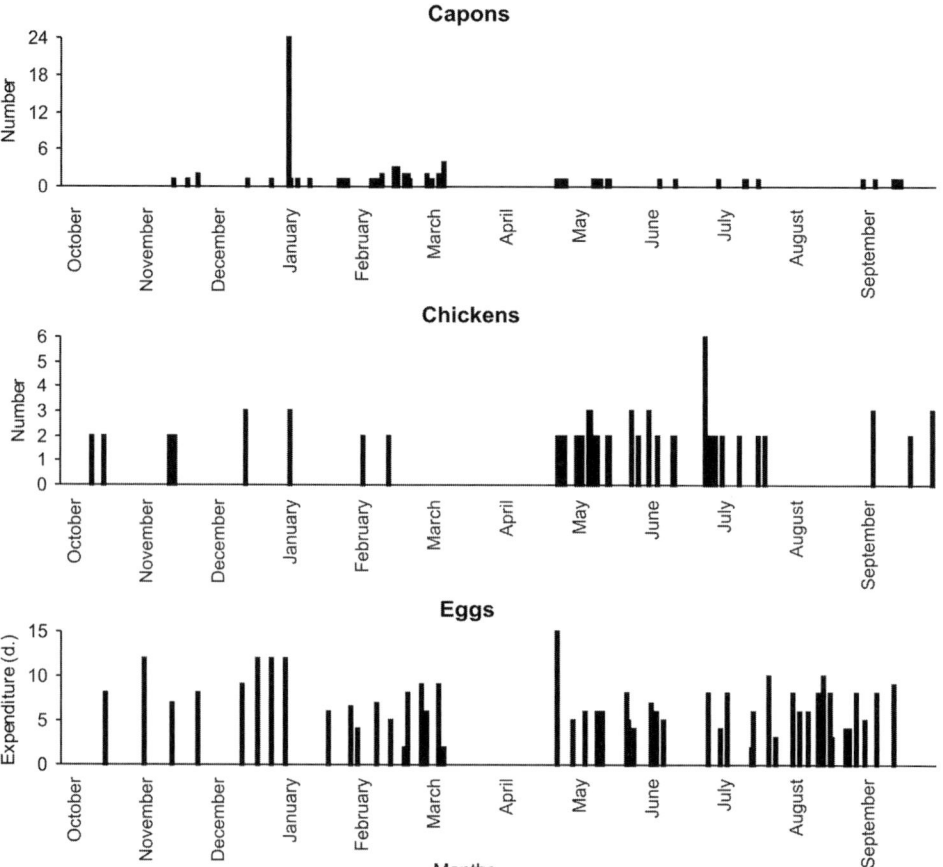

FIGURE 11.6. Seasonal consumption of capons, chickens, and eggs in the medieval Suffolk household of Alice de Bryene, 1412–13, shown as numbers of capons and chickens and expenditure in pence (d.) on eggs (Stone 2006, fig. 10.2). Capons were fattened for feasts, especially the Christmas and New Year feast. April was the Lenten fast, when birds and also eggs were avoided.

according to Aristotle, a hen would lay up to 60 eggs per year (Wood-Gush 1958). In the birds' natural environment, which is tropical and subtropical, laying is not markedly seasonal, but it becomes so in environments with greater seasonal contrasts. Columella, three centuries later, referred to a laying season from 13th January to 13th November, indicating that hens did cease to lay in winter. The dates are suspiciously exact, but they do already suggest a laying period comparable with that of birds today kept under natural conditions. Egg production and consumption in medieval Europe is discussed in Chapter 7.

To identify flocks kept mainly for egg production we need to look at the incidence of medullary bone. We saw in Chapter 3 how the chicken remains from the Roman

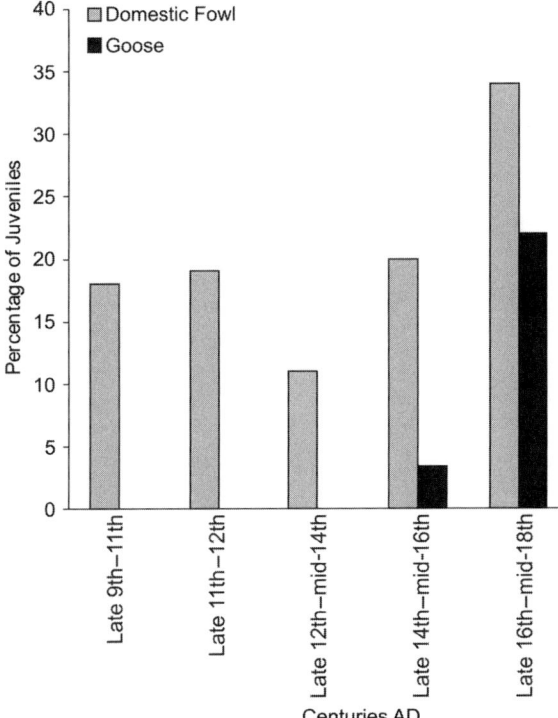

FIGURE 11.7. Comparison of the percentage of juvenile domestic chickens and geese from medieval Norwich (Albarella 1997c, fig. 7). Immature chickens are present throughout the Middle Ages, but immature geese only from the fifteenth century onwards.

port of Berenike on the Red Sea had a very high percentage of medullary bone, which indicated that egg production must have been important at the site. This was also the case in Gaul. Clavel and colleagues (1997) found that the femora in their Gallo-Roman sample fell into two size classes, and almost all of those in the smaller size class contained medullary bone, which suggests that the period during which hens were laying must have been much prolonged even in Europe at this time. In Britain, the incidence of medullary bone is lower in Roman-period assemblages but rises in the Middle Ages to more than half of all femora (Table 11.3), suggesting that laying was extended in the later period.

DISCUSSION

There is little good evidence at present for the earliest stage of the domestication of the chicken, though the group of early records from Neolithic China are worth

Table 11.3. *Incidence of medullary bone in chicken femora from Roman and medieval sites in southern Britain*

Site		Total	Number with medullary bone	%
Silchester (Forum)	Roman	15	3	20.0
Dorchester	Roman	5	1	20.0
Carisbrooke Castle	12th	9	4	44.4
Eynsham Abbey	12th	22	6	27.3
Eynsham Abbey	13th–14th	20	13	65.0
St Gregory's Priory	14th	10	5	50.0
Eynsham Abbey	15th–early 16th	12	8	66.7

Note: The incidence is calculated from the presence or absence of medullary bone in the femora of adult birds.

Source: Data for Dorchester are from Maltby (1993); data for other sites are from the author.

further investigation. The confirmed records which predate about 1500 BC may be of tamed, possibly even domesticated birds, carried beyond their natural range in small numbers. The picture will only become clear when the contribution of the various subspecies of the red junglefowl to the domestic chicken gene pool has been clarified. Our understanding of chicken domestication will also have to be reassessed if, in fact, the natural distribution of junglefowl extended south of the foothills of the Himalayas in the Indian subcontinent (Fuller 2006) and also if, contrary to West and Zhou (1988), the range extended further north in China in the Early Holocene.

Chickens were certainly carried to the Polynesian islands in the second millennium BC, and they also reached northern China, the Middle East, and as far west as Turkey, Greece, and the Balkan Peninsula. These first birds are likely to have been exchanged as exotic gifts between rulers, as were peacocks. Until the middle of the first millennium BC the chicken was probably no more than a rare curiosity. The scarcity of archaeological record would fit the theory that initially they were kept for sacrifice and for cockfighting. The third stage of domestication, when breeding was fully controlled and different types of bird were developed, did not occur in Europe until some time between the fifth and third century BC on present evidence. After that time chickens are found in substantial numbers at some sites, so they must have been kept more widely around the Mediterranean.

The spread into western and northern Europe coincided with the expansion of Roman influence (Peters 1997b). It was delayed in the villages compared with the towns and was also delayed around the Atlantic coast where seabirds were available as an alternative food. On present evidence, the spread of the chicken was also delayed in Africa. From the mid-first millennium AD onwards in Europe, chickens had lost their ritual connotations and were kept by people of all ranks. Large institutions such as the crown, the aristocracy, and religious houses kept their flocks, but they also relied heavily on peasant farmers to raise chickens for eggs and meat (Stone 2006). In early modern times, chickens were carried all over the world by European colonists, only for the explorers to find them already present throughout Asia and Polynesia.

The explosion in chicken numbers which occurred around the Mediterranean in the last centuries of the first millennium BC may well have been the result of a change in behaviour which made it more attractive for people to keep the birds in captivity. Did they become easier to manage? Or did the period of lay become much more extended? Or had the chicken's status as a bird with religious links and prophetic powers initially restricted it to temples and sanctuaries, so that only later was it allowed into the hands and farmyards of common folk? The chicken had an important role in the religious and ritual sphere, which is discussed in Chapter 14.

If the earliest spread of the domestic chicken in Eurasia and also in the Americas is to be pinned down more closely, it is essential that finds of possible early chickens are treated rigorously. There are three criteria which have to be satisfied before an early record of domestic chicken can be claimed. The first is that the bone really is from chicken and not from the pheasant or one of the other medium-sized Galliformes with which it can be confused (Chapter 4). The second is that the date of the bone is as old as is claimed and that it is not a contaminant from a later level (Benecke 1994, 367). The third is that the bird is domestic rather than wild. In the past it was difficult to satisfy these conditions, but today two, and perhaps all three, of these criteria can be met. Provided that DNA can be extracted, a specimen can be tested to confirm that the bone was in fact from chicken and not from some other galliform bird (Storey et al. 2008). If there is any uncertainty about the date or the integrity of the context, this can also be confirmed, as new radiocarbon dating techniques can be used which require only a few grams to be tested, so allowing a bone as small as that of a chicken to be dated (Storey et al. 2007). This is worthwhile for any pre-Columbian find in South America and any find which predates about the sixth century BC in Western Asia and Europe.

More than geese and the other domestic birds discussed below, for the last two millennia, chickens have been found in households in every country of the world, but they have been invisible in discussions of the transmission of culture and economy

(Storey et al. 2008), overlooked no doubt because of their very ordinariness. It is now clear that the significance of their presence in certain contexts should not be overlooked. When found on Iron Age sites in Europe, they are evidence – no less than coins – of contact with the Roman world. Their presence on Polynesian islands – and certainly on pre-Columbian sites in South America – demonstrates long-distance contacts at a period in prehistory when these are otherwise elusive.

12

Other Domestic Birds

Depending on how domestication is defined, about two dozen species of birds other than chicken have been domesticated (Table 12.1), and many more have been tamed and kept in captivity. Of the 24 species described in *Evolution of Domesticated Animals* (Mason 1984), some are recent domesticates and several are cage birds. Here I shall consider a smaller number: the turkey, geese, ducks, and the pigeon. I shall also briefly discuss other domestic and possibly domestic birds for which there is archaeological evidence: peafowl, guineafowl, and the scarlet macaw.

The main characteristic of mammals which have been domesticated is their capacity to tolerate the presence of humans and the absence of an instinct for instantaneous flight from humans. To breed under human control they should not be excessively territorial and should lack a complex courtship ritual. If they are domesticated for food, they should be at the bottom of the food pyramid and convert plant food to meat efficiently. Many domestic mammals have a well-organised social structure with a dominance hierarchy in which humans assume the dominant role (Reitz & Wing 1999). In the case of birds, some of these criteria are met, but others are modified: geese, for instance, are moderately territorial. In particular, species with a strong instinct to migrate are unsuitable for domestication, one of the reasons why the greylag goose, the swan goose, and the mallard were domesticated and other closely related species were not.

TURKEY

Wild Ancestor and Domestication Process

As well as several extinct Pleistocene forms of *Meleagris*, there are two surviving species of wild turkey in North America: the ocellated turkey, *Meleagris ocellata*, and

Table 12.1. *Domesticated and possible domesticated birds*

Species	Original distribution of wild ancestor
Major domesticates	
Domestic fowl, *Gallus gallus*	Southeast Asia
Turkey, *Meleagris gallopavo*	North America
Greylag goose, *Anser anser*	Eurasia
Swan goose, *Anser cygnoides*	Southeast Asia
Common duck, *Anas platyrhynchos*	Eurasia
Muscovy duck, *Cairina moschata*	South America
Pigeon, *Columba livia*	Western Asia, Southern Europe
Minor domesticates	
Peafowl, *Pavo cristatus*	Southeast Asia
Guineafowl, *Numida meleagris*	West Africa
Scarlet macaw, *Ara macao*	South and Central America
Ostrich, *Struthio camelus*	Africa and Near East
Pheasant, *Phasianus colchicus*	Far East, Middle East
Mute swan, *Cygnus olor*	Eurasia

Note: Recently domesticated species are not included.
Source: Data are from Mason (1984).

M. gallopavo, which is the ancestor of the domestic turkey (Bochenski & Campbell 2005). Up to seven subspecies of *M. gallopavo* have been recognised; their distribution and their contribution to modern domestic turkeys has been revisited many times over the years (Schorger 1966; Steadman 1980; McKusick 1980; Crawford 1984b; Olsen 2000). The modern domestic turkey is thought to be descended from the subspecies originally found in Northern Mexico, *M. g. gallopavo*. The ocellated turkey may briefly have been domesticated locally on Cozumel Island, in Mexico, where *M. gallopavo* is absent (Bochenski & Campbell 2006).

Two hypotheses, at least, have been proposed to account for their domestication. One is that turkeys were attracted to cultivated gardens and crops, where they were hunted and then domesticated (Pinkley 1965). They may have been tolerated or encouraged because they controlled garden pests. The alternative theory is that they were deliberately taken into captivity so that the feathers and feathered skins could be used. These were a very important item of trade in pre-Columbian America, as we saw in Chapter 8.

Archaeology and History

The earliest excavated remains of turkeys which are believed to be a domesticated form are from the site of Tlatilo, Mexico, dating from 1250–600 BC. Bones were found in both domestic rubbish and in funerary contexts here and on later sites in Mexico (Lefèvre & Marinval-Vigne 1992). Otherwise, some of the earliest finds are of feathers, objects decorated with feathers, and desiccated skeletons from the American Southwest on sites of the Basketmaker II culture. Individual elements, turkey pens or corrals with droppings and eggshell and also feathers and skeletons have been found dating from AD 500–700 onwards (Basketmaker III). In Tularosa Cave in New Mexico, referred to in Chapter 7, turkeys were kept in a corral within the cave: droppings, eggshell fragments, and desiccated birds, including chicks, were present (Rea 1980). Similar turkey corrals are also known at other sites in the Southwest (Olsen 2000). At the site of Canyon de Chelley, remains of 300 desiccated birds were found, but no disarticulated remains, suggesting that birds were raised at the site but were not eaten.

It is only from Pueblo III times (thirteenth century AD) that disarticulated and butchered remains are found in quantity as well as burials, feathers, and pens, suggesting that turkeys had become an important source of food (Muir & Driver 2004). At Mug House Ruin in the Mesa Verde National Park, 1,074 bones from a minimum of 183 turkeys were excavated, many of which were butchered and charred (Olsen 2000). In thirteenth-century Anasazi sites, turkeys, together with lagomorphs and deer, were the principal sources of meat (Muir & Driver 2004; also see Figure 12.1). There are also rock engravings and depictions on the walls of the kivas (ceremonial houses) of the Pueblo culture and on Mimbres pottery (Olsen 2000).

Some authors have regarded the turkeys in the American Southwest to be derived from a native wild population which was domesticated locally. The alternative is that turkeys were initially introduced as one element in the contact and exchange of foodstuffs and other products with took place between the Anasazi and the civilisations to the south. At various times in the first millennium AD, corn (maize), squash, the bottle gourd, various species of beans, and scarlet macaws (see below) were all introduced from Central America. The turkey was yet another of these items of trade (Rea 1980). Metrical analysis has failed up to now to fully clarify the domestication process in the American Southwest.

In Mexico, turkey became an important foodstuff for the elite. At the time of contact they were known in Guatemala, Honduras, Nicaragua, Costa Rica, and

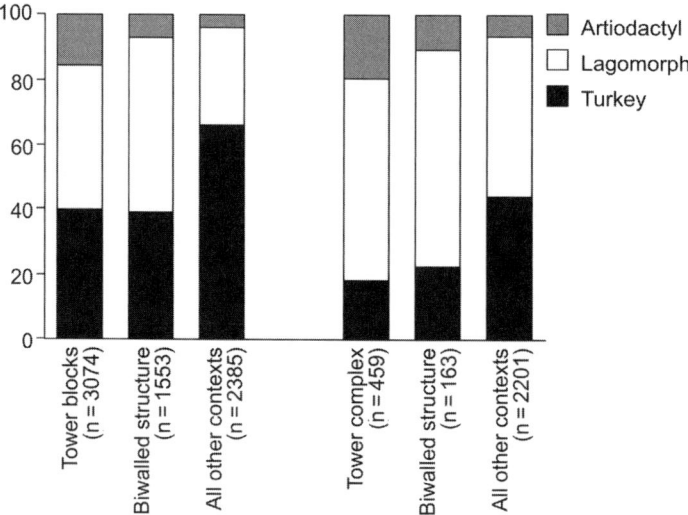

FIGURE 12.1. Relative numbers of artiodactyl, lagomorph, and turkey at two Colorado sites: Sand Canyon Pueblo (left) and Yellow Jacket Pueblo (right; redrawn from Muir & Driver 2004, fig. 5).

some of the Caribbean islands as well as Mexico (Crawford 1984b). Montezuma's household ate a large number daily. The first birds may have been exported as early as AD 1500, when Vicente Yáñez Pinzón was given turkeys to carry to Europe (Crawford 1984b), a visit which predated the fourth voyage of Columbus in 1502, when he too was given 'gallinas de la tierra' to eat (Olsen 2000).

The earliest historical mention of a turkey in France is in 1534 and the earliest archaeological records are from late-sixteenth-century deposits in the Jardins du Carrousel in Paris (Audoin-Rouzeau & Pichon 1992). The earliest finds from Germany are from Lübeck (Benecke 1994). Numbers increased gradually over time, though turkeys were never common (Audoin-Rouzeau & Pichon 1992). Numbers increased in Northern France between the fifteenth and the seventeenth centuries (Clavel 2001). The price declined from eight times that of a chicken in 1538 to four to five times in 1620 as turkey numbers increased in relation to chickens (Audoin-Rouzeau & Pichon 1992). One of the first turkeys sent to Italy had white feathers, indicating that a type had already developed with plumage which differed from that of wild turkeys. According to Jacopo De Grossi, it or one of its descendants, is depicted on the ceiling of a gallery in the Palazzo Altemps in Rome, originally painted in the 1580s (ZOOARCH archives 18 October 2001 – see Appendix 3). When colonists went to North America in the early seventeenth century, they took domestic turkeys *back* with them (Lefèvre & Marinval-Vigne 1992).

Table 12.2. *Plumage characteristics of some subspecies of turkey,* Meleagris gallopavo

Subspecies	Retrix tip	Tail covert	Rump
M. g. merriami	Buff/gray-white	Buff/white	Blue-black
M. g. gallopavo	White	Pinkish white	Coppery/green
M. g. mexicana	White	Pinkish white	Coppery/green
Eastern races	Cinnamon/chestnut	Dark chestnut	Glossy black

Source: Data are after Schorger (1966) and Rea (1980).

A recent analysis of the ancient DNA of turkey bones from Pueblo sites in the Southwest compared specimens from archaeological sites with reference sequences of mitochondrial haplotypes of wild turkey. The ancient specimens contained several different subspecies. The majority of the specimens were most closely related to a wild subspecies currently found outside the four-corners, though a few of the local Merriam's subspecies (*M. g. merriami*) were also identified. Most of the Merriam's birds were recovered from earlier time periods which could support the hypothesis that there was an initial attempt to raise local birds but that most excavated turkey remains are from a domestic subspecies originally introduced from elsewhere (Speller and Yang 2006).

Changes under Domestication

Thanks to the survival of feathers in sites in the Southwest, the plumage of the earliest domestic turkeys is known. The oldest were black but later the colouring became more variable (Table 12.2). Some developed a white tip, which, it has been argued, may have resulted from a diet which was restricted to corn (Olsen 2000).

The remains from Basketmaker II sites are of a small bird, but from the seventh century AD onwards larger as well as smaller birds are present. These two types have been interpreted as two distinct breeds, that is, the Small Indian Domestic and the Large Indian Domestic (McKusick 1980). The birds in the oldest sites were mostly small, but later sites included both small and large types. The turkey is strongly sexually dimorphic (Chapter 3), which can confuse results. In historic times, domestic birds were much larger than wild turkeys (Gilbert et al. 1981), but production of the extremely large birds farmed commercially today does not predate the twentieth century.

Discussion

Thanks to the exceptional preservation of material in the American Southwest, we are in the unusual position of being able to give a good account of why the turkey was domesticated and of some of the processes. It is clear that in the first centuries of their history as domestic birds, turkeys were kept for their feathers and for ritual purposes and were raised for meat only from Pueblo III times. It is only since they were carried round the world in the sixteenth century that meat has been the main product, and it is only from the twentieth century that they have been raised for consumption year-round, rather than restricted to Thanksgiving and Christmas. What has still to be clarified is whether the Mexican subspecies was the original progenitor of the Anasazi turkeys as well as of modern domestic turkeys. The answer to this question – as with many species discussed here – lies in DNA analysis, combined with studies of metrical variation in large, well-preserved and well-dated osteological samples.

GEESE

Two species of goose have been domesticated, the greylag, *Anser anser*, and the swan goose, *A. cygnoides*. In their domestic form, they are usually known as the common and the Chinese or African goose. The former is more successful in temperate conditions and the latter is better adapted to hotter parts of the world. The Egyptian goose, *Alopochen aegyptiacus*, was kept in captivity for millennia in Ancient Egypt and is frequently depicted, but it is a pugnacious bird which requires a lot of space, so it was not fully domesticated (Houlihan & Goodman 1986, 65).

The natural distribution of the swan goose is in Eastern Asia, where it breeds in Siberia and winters mostly in China (Dohner 2001). The original distribution of the greylag was throughout Eurasia, where it bred further south than the other grey geese. Today its breeding range is fragmented, but in the past it must have encompassed much of temperate Europe and Western Asia. There are two races, the Western form, *A. a. anser*, and the Eastern form, *A. a. rubirostris*. Zeuner (1963) considered the Western form the probable ancestor of modern domestic geese, but Kear argued for the Eastern form (Kear 1990; Albarella 2005).

Wild and domestic greylag geese have co-existed for millennia so it is likely that there has been some back-crossing of domestic with wild birds. Riddell thought that goose domestication probably took place in many places at different times (Riddell 1943). In Scotland it was common until the nineteenth century for farmers to take greylags from the wild to rear on the farm (Ritchie 1920, 105). Once in the farmyard, geese had to be prevented from indulging their – not very strong – instinct to migrate, so the primary feathers were pinioned or plucked; this was unnecessary if the birds grew too heavy to fly.

Historical Evidence

Written evidence indicates that the Chinese goose was domesticated by 1000 BC in the Far East (Albarella 2005). The earliest accounts of the domestication of the greylag goose are also based on depictions and written accounts (Riddell 1943; Zeuner 1963; Crawford 1984a; Kear 1990). There are depictions of geese in some Egyptian tomb paintings. One from Thebes and another on a wall in the Northern Palace of Akhenaten in El-Amarna (Houlihan & Goodman 1986, fig. 72) clearly show a greylag. Both date from the eighteenth Dynasty (mid-second millennium BC). The flock of geese in the Amarna painting have heterogeneous colours, and this, together with the presence of goslings, was taken as evidence that they were domestic (Boessneck 1991, fig. 1). There are references to flocks of tame, possibly domestic, geese in Mesopotamia at approximately the same time (Zeuner 1963). There, geese were sacrificed to important divinities (Limet 1994). The Odyssey, composed in about the ninth century BC, describes how Penelope, wife of Ulysses, kept a flock of white geese, which suggests that the feathers had already undergone a change from the natural grey colour. Columella in the first century AD recommended that large, white birds should be selected to breed from and described a regime of husbandry and feeding which is substantially the same as until recent times. The Roman writer Varro suggests that there were domestic geese in Rome but that they were uncommon (Hooper & Ash 1935, 483).

Archaeological Evidence

Domestic geese are not mentioned in a survey of the biological evidence for domestic plants and animals in prehistoric China (Pearson & Underhill 1987). Archaeological evidence is unhelpful at present for the domestication of the Chinese goose. There is more evidence for the greylag, but this too is problematic. As wild greylags are widespread in Eurasia, we cannot use the evidence of finds outside the natural range as evidence as we can with chicken. We have to rely on a marked increase in numbers, size change, or increased numbers of immature birds.

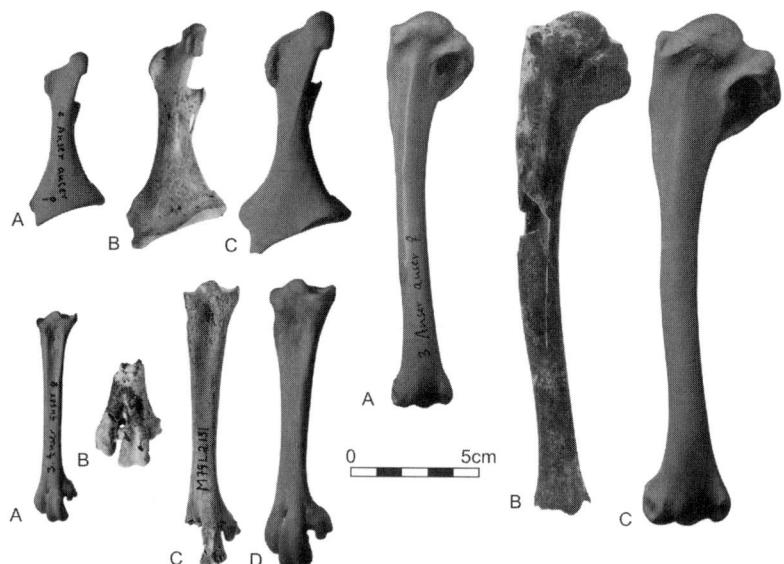

FIGURE 12.2. Large goose bones from Egypt: A, bones from a modern wild greylag; B, bones from Tell el-Maskhuta, Egypt; and C, bones from a very large modern domestic breed, the Toulouse (Boessneck 1991). The top left section shows the coracoid; the bottom left shows the tarsometatarsus; the right section shows the humerus.

The zooarchaeological evidence from Egypt is at odds with the wall paintings. The workers at El-Amarna ate few birds, and geese there were fewer than pigeons and even than cormorants. If the goose was domesticated for food, consumption was restricted to the upper classes (Luff 2001). Certainly the remains of possible domestic geese have been found in burial chambers (Boessneck & von den Driesch 1982). By the Late Dynastic period some of the remains of geese were so large that they can only be domestic: elements from Tell el-Maskhuta, a town in the Nile delta, are as big as those of the Toulouse goose (Figure 12.2), which is one of the largest modern breeds (Boessneck 1991).

Numbers

The scarcity of geese compared with chickens on sites of the Roman period confirms the implication in Varro that geese were not widely kept. Both geese and chickens were present at the early Roman castellum at Velsen (Chapter 11), but the geese were morphologically indistinguishable from wild birds, so are thought to have been wild rather than domestic. In Britain, goose remains are rarer than ducks in the Roman period and not thought to be domestic. It is only after about the sixth century AD that

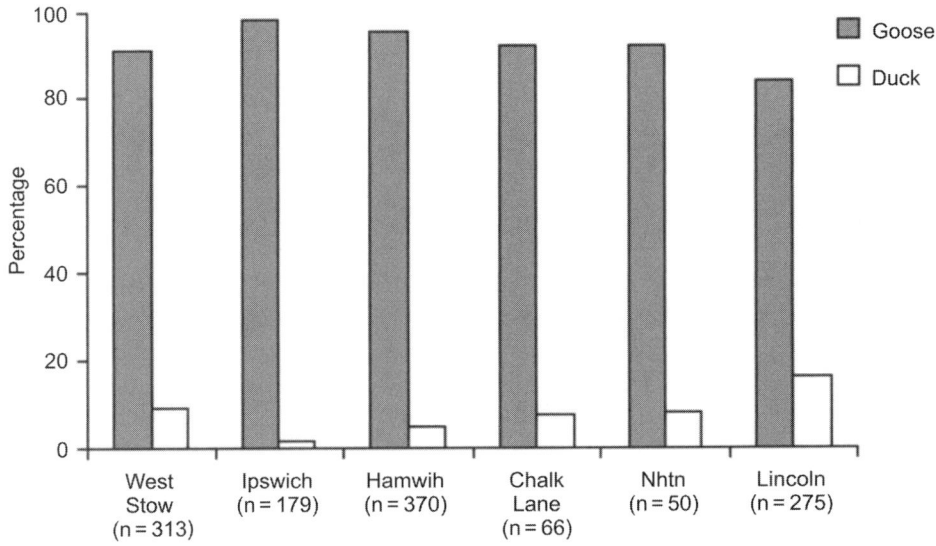

FIGURE 12.3. Relative percentages of goose and duck from Saxon sites (later first millennium AD) in southern England, showing the importance of geese (Albarella 2005); Nhtn = Northampton.

we find evidence that geese were widely kept and clearly domestic: in six Mid and Late Saxon towns and settlements in England, geese were ten times as frequent as ducks (Albarella 2005; also see Figure 12.3). In Saxon England, the Laws of Ine stipulated that the rental from a farm should include 10 geese and 20 hens. Charlemagne in France recommended flocks of 30 geese and 100 chickens on royal farms, and 12 geese and 50 chickens on smaller ones (Hagen 1995). In view of the larger quantity of meat on a goose, more goose meat may in fact have been eaten than chicken in the first millennium AD in Western Europe.

Size

The wild grey geese all overlap in size; wild and domestic greylags also overlap (Bacher 1967; Boessneck & von den Driesch 1979; MacDonald et al. 1993; Barnes & Dobney 2000; Barnes et al. 1998). However, by the later Middle Ages, most elements of the wing and leg were shorter than those of the wild greylag. Their length was compared between two sites on the Schlei Estuary in North Germany, Early Medieval Haithabu and medieval Schleswig. Over time, each of the main wing and leg bones other than the tibiotarsus became shorter (Reichstein & Pieper 1986). Skeletal proportions changed between the tenth and the thirteenth century. The tarsometatarsi

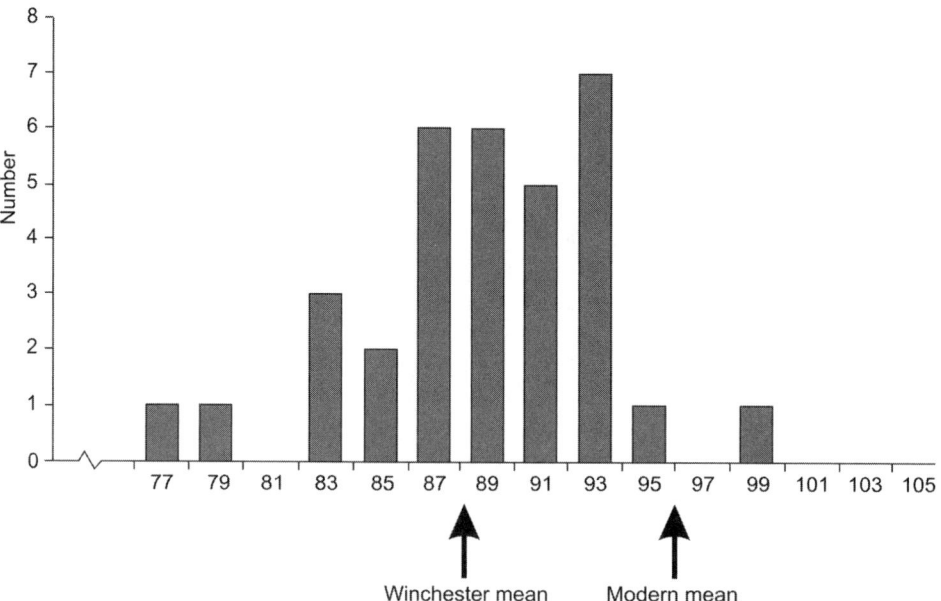

FIGURE 12.4. Distribution of the length (greatest length in millimetres) and mean of carpometacarpi of domestic geese from medieval Winchester; the modern mean (from Bacher 1967) is also shown (Serjeantson & Smith in press).

of domestic geese became more robust than those of wild geese from the eleventh century onwards, as, for example, at Eketorp (Boessneck & von den Driesch 1979, fig. 44) and Kings Lynn (Bramwell 1977). The wing bones also became shorter in England (Figure 12.4).

DNA

The ancient mitochondrial DNA of a sample of goose bones was studied with the aim of distinguishing wild and domestic geese from Post-Medieval Lincoln and from Flixborough, an ecclesiastical site in Yorkshire occupied from the seventh to the eleventh century AD. Metrical and morphological analysis did not distinguish wild from domestic (Barnes et al. 1998; Barnes & Dobney 2000). The authors analysed the mitochondrial cytochrome b gene sequence, which separated *Branta* from *Anser*, but they did not separate the different grey geese. They then analysed the first domain of the mitochondrial control region, and it showed distinctions which successfully separated the greylag and the pink-footed goose. Surprisingly, the results suggested that a significant number of the geese at Flixborough were pink-footed

Table 12.3. *Biometric and molecular identification of ancient goose bones from sites in England*

Site	Element	GL	SC	Bp	Bd	Biometric interpretation	DNA identification
VC93	Humerus	–	–	42.2	–	Large	*Anser anser* domestic
VC93	Humerus	–	–	–	24.8	Large	*A. anser* domestic
VC93	TMT	92.3	8.7	20.3	20.4	Large	*A. anser* domestic
FLX89	Humerus	156.0	11.1	32.8	23.0	Medium–small	*A. brachyrhynchus*
FLX89	Humerus	–	12.0	33.0	–	Large–medium	*A. brachyrhynchus*
FLX89	Humerus	178.0	12.1	35.3	25.7	Large	*A. anser* domestic
FLX89	Humerus	172.4	11.5	–	23.8	Medium	*A. anser* domestic

Note: VC = Vicar's Court, Lincoln, Post-Medieval; FLX = Flixborough, Anglo-Saxon; GL = greatest length; SC = shaft diameter; Bp = proximal breadth; Bd = distal breadth.
Source: Measurements (in millimetres) are after von den Driesch (1976). Tabular information is modified from Barnes and Dobney (2000).

geese. Disconcertingly, there are both large and small greylags and both large and small pink-footed geese at that site (Table 12.3). In all but one sample, the DNA matched that of the Western race of greylag, but a single divergence in one of the Post-Medieval samples from Lincoln suggested that there may be some genetic input from the Eastern race, as suggested by Kear (1990).

Changes under Domestication

The plumage changed from grey to white in some domestic breeds. White feathers have two advantages: they and the down are a more attractive colour and the birds fatten more readily (Kear 1990). In Chapter 8 we saw how both feathers and down of geese have superior qualities to those of most other birds.

Geese fatten readily for the table, as force-feeding is an extension of the natural instinct to cram with food in advance of migration. Most geese used to be eaten in the autumn, but some goslings were fattened in the early summer and killed at the age of about four months and eaten as 'green geese' (Chapter 3). In one year's consumption in the household of Alice de Bryene, seven geese were eaten in July, but otherwise geese were eaten between November and March, with twelve being eaten at the New Years day feast (Figure 12.5). According to Columella, geese were fattened

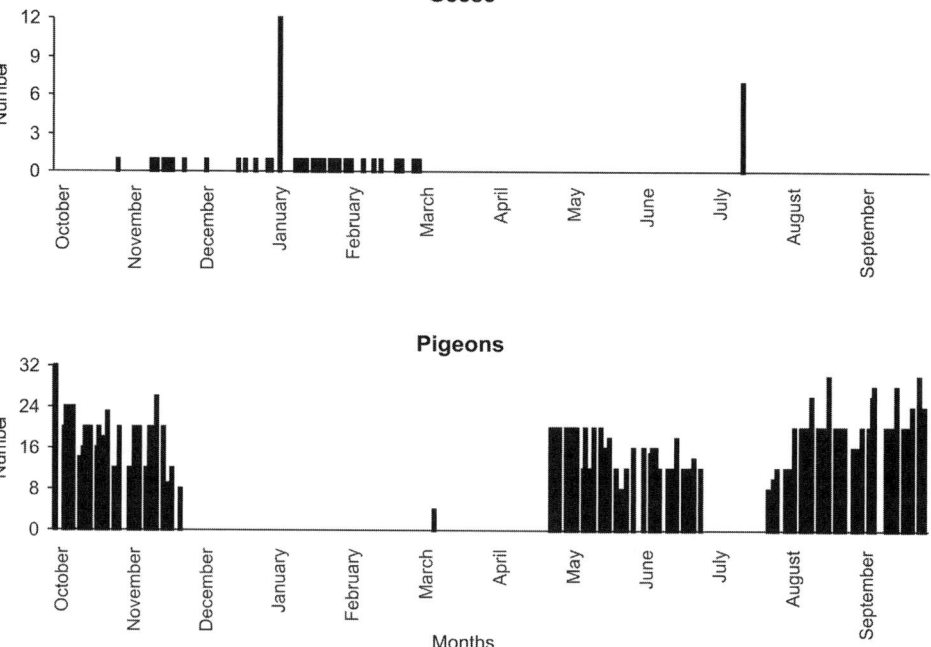

FIGURE 12.5. Seasonal consumption of domestic geese and pigeons in the medieval household of Alice de Bryene. Geese were eaten in autumn and winter, except for a few 'green geese' eaten in July. Pigeons were eaten from May to November but avoided in winter (Stone 2006, fig. 10.2).

over 40 days in Roman times. It is during the autumn that geese are crammed so that they develop the distended liver which is eaten as *pâté de foie gras* (Serjeantson 2002).

An increase in the percentage of immature goose bones was evident in the later Middle Ages at sites in England such as Winchester and Castle Mall, Norwich. This suggests that, though the feathers were more important in the Early Medieval period, in the later Middle Ages geese were raised for meat (Grant 1988; Albarella 1997c; Serjeantson 2002). This was associated with a general trend towards a higher consumption of meat in the later Middle Ages referred to in Chapter 11.

The number of eggs laid increased, as with all domestic birds. What is probably goose eggshell has been identified on at least one medieval site in England, as discussed in Chapter 7. As adult females were not normally eaten in the breeding season, it is rare to find medullary bone in domestic geese.

A flock of geese can be herded to market, hundreds of miles if necessary, so long as they can graze as they walk. This practice started in Roman times and was widespread in medieval Europe. Archaeological remains from a town need not be from animals reared in the town or even from the immediate hinterland, but may be from some distance (Serjeantson 2002; Albarella 2005).

Conclusions

The initial impulse for keeping geese in the Middle East and in Classical Greece may have been to have them available in the temple precinct for sacrifices. There is little archaeological evidence to suggest that domestic geese were kept in any number in prehistoric times. It is likely that the Anglo-Saxon colonists from north-west Europe brought geese to England with them, having become accustomed to using the feathers and eating the meat of the abundant local wild geese. At the Roman Iron Age site of Feddersen-Wierde several species of geese were present, but all apparently wild, but in Sweden the greylags from Pre-Roman Iron Age sites were regarded as domesticated (Tyrberg 2002). If the Swedish greylags were domestic, it could support Riddell's suggestion that geese were domesticated in more than one place. The first real sign of the presence of large numbers of domestic geese in England is in the Anglo-Saxon period, and there was then a further increase in domestic geese at the end of the first millennium AD with the spread of Norman influence. Until the later Middle Ages the feathers, used for warmth as well as for writing implements, were probably more important than the meat.

DUCKS

Two species of duck have been domesticated: the common duck, domesticated from the wild mallard, *Anas platyrhynchos*, in Eurasia; and the Muscovy duck, *Cairina moschata*, domesticated in South America. The two species are often crossed today by commercial duck breeders, but the offspring are infertile.

Common Duck

The history of the domestic duck has been admirably summarised by several authors (Clayton 1984a; Kear 1990, 54–60; Benecke 1994, 379–383; Luff 2000; Albarella 2005). The wild mallard is distributed throughout the northern hemisphere. Northern populations are migratory, but the mallard is the most sedentary of the temperate ducks. The initial domestication may have taken place in different places at different times. It has plausibly been argued that it took place in an area with high temperatures, as these can compensate for poor feeding in captive birds. The wide range of types or breeds of domestic duck in Southeast Asia suggested to Zeuner (1963) that the mallard was first domesticated there, and the importance of the duck in the Eastern Asian diet would certainly support this.

The mallard may have been commensal for a long time before becoming fully domestic (see Chapter 15). In China and elsewhere in Southeast Asia, ducks fit very well with rice agriculture, as they eat the nymphs of land crabs and locusts, which otherwise destroy the crop (Luff 2000). In the West, they are good to graze with sheep, as they eat the snail which is the secondary host to the liver fluke parasite in sheep. Wild mallards can readily be raised in captivity. Ducks, like geese, have to be pinioned to keep them in the farmyard, and also, like geese, lose the ability to fly when they grow too heavy to become airborne.

Changes under Domestication

Though the duck was a sacred bird in China and was sacred to Aphrodite in Greece, it is not thought to have been domesticated for ritual purposes. The main reason for keeping domestic ducks is for the meat. Ducklings fatten quickly and are eaten from the age of nine or ten weeks. Like all waterfowl, they have a carcass with a high percentage of fat (see Table 10.2). Today some people regard this as a disadvantage, but it was a virtue in Southeast Asia where the diet lacked dairy foods and so people needed fat from other sources.

As with other birds, there have also been changes in plumage and breeding behaviour. The first change which takes place when ducks are tamed is the appearance of white plumage (Bottema 1989), which – as in geese – is an advantage only if birds can be protected from hawks and other predators. The down is of almost as good quality as that of geese. The number of eggs laid per year has increased from seven to twelve in the wild to as many as 240, which is almost as many as a chicken. Under domestication, the normally monogamous wild mallard has learned to live under a polygamous regime with a ratio of one drake to four to six ducks.

History

Some of these changes are visible in the historical and zooarchaeological record. Figurines of ducks have been found in China and the Middle East. They suggest a ritual importance for ducks but are not necessarily of domestic birds. The first written references to ducks in China date from the Warring States period (475–221 BC; see Luff 2000). The ducks illustrated in ancient Egypt include other wild anatids as well as mallards. Like so many other birds in Egypt, mallards were probably kept in captivity but not fully domesticated. Roman farmers were encouraged to keep ducks and fatten them for the market and the table, but they do not appear to have bred them successfully in captivity. However, a mallard depicted on a mosaic in Cologne is shown with domestic rather than wild animals, which suggests that it was a farmyard bird. References to domestic ducks in the Early Middle Ages are scant. In the German *Capitularum de Villis* ducks are included with ornamental wildfowl. Wild and domestic ducks were distinguished in documents only from the twelfth century onwards, when domestic ducks were listed by St Hildegard of Bingen, though she regarded them as unclean because they fouled the ponds in which they lived. In England they were not referred to in accounts until the fourteenth century. In 1329–1330 the manor of Cuxham, which had a duck pond, provided Merton College, Oxford, with five ducks, as well as a goose, 18 capons, 63 cocks and hens, and 635 pigeons (Stone 2006).

Archaeology

Ducks were more common than geese on Roman sites in Central England (Albarella 2005). Duck remains from the villa at Fishbourne, in the south of England, were variable enough in size, with many larger than the wild mallard, that some were regarded as from captive, 'probably' domesticated, ducks (Eastham 1971), but other authors do not regard remains from Roman-period sites as domestic. Once domesticated, ducks grow larger than wild mallards. Remains of ducks from the Germanic provinces of the Roman Empire were indistinguishable from wild mallard, as were those from the fort at Velsen referred to earlier. The ducks from the Roman town of Dorchester in southern Britain were the same size as mallards, but some from the medieval deposits were larger, so thought to be domestic. In the Middle Ages in France ducks have been found mostly on rural sites (Clavel 2001) and the same is true in England (Albarella 2005). Ducks which were possibly domestic were noted from medieval Portchester Castle (Eastham 1977) and from the town of Exeter (Maltby 1979). In each case a few specimens were larger than wild mallards. At Eketorp in Sweden there were more immature ducks in the medieval period than in the fifth to sixth century AD, another plausible indication of their domestic status (Boessneck & von den Driesch 1979).

The history of the domestic duck in Europe is insignificant compared with its main history in Southeast Asia. The erect posture of the Indian Runner breed evolved in Asia, a feature thought to be associated with a history of droving there. The prolonged laying period, almost as long as that of the domestic chicken, also evolved in the East. It is there that we are likely to find the earliest evidence for the intensive rearing of young birds for consumption as well as for older birds carried or driven to market. We must hope that ancient settlements will be found on which bones are preserved, so that zooarchaeologists of the future are able to take up the challenge.

Muscovy Duck

The wild Muscovy duck has no connection with either Moscow or Cairo, as the common and scientific names imply; rather, it is a native of neotropical South America with a range from southern Mexico to Peru and northern Argentina. As with so many other domestic birds, it has been carried to other parts of America as well as elsewhere in the world and has gone feral in some environments. Its habitat preference is for swamps and river banks flanked with trees, in which it nests (Clayton 1984b; Kear 1990; Gade 2000; Stahl 2005). It is an omnivorous feeder, a virtue for a potential domesticate. It was encouraged to come inside houses to keep down insect infestation; it also keeps drainage ditches cleaned of vegetation. Both are possible forerunners of commensalism and full domestication.

History and Archaeology

The first Europeans in Central and South America and the southern Caribbean encountered people who already kept domestic ducks. The osteological evidence for Muscovy ducks comes from 'a few, widely scattered localities' according to Stahl (2005, 2006), who collated the finds from prehistoric South America and found that all were from the first millennium AD onwards. The largest assemblage is from the cemetery of Ayalán in Ecuador and settlements at Pailón (Bolivia) and in Panama. At some sites bones were found in association with domestic guinea pig and llama, supporting the hypothesis that the ducks were also domestic. The Pailón assemblage, in which some bones showed butchering marks, included birds in two size classes, interpreted as the two sexes. The equal numbers of males and females reflected either the hunting of pairs of birds or, more probably, the fact that they were domestic. The duck is beautifully represented in Peruvian Moche pottery. The spread of the Muscovy

FIGURE 12.6. Feral Muscovy ducks, *Cairina moschata*, with mixed plumage, from Guayaquil, Ecuador (photograph by D. Serjeantson).

duck is seen as 'associated with the movement of goods and exotics throughout the wider pre-Columbian world' (Stahl 2006, 662).

The Muscovy duck was taken to Europe in the sixteenth century. The first reference in England is in AD 1550. 'La grosse cane de la Guinée' – presumed to refer to the Muscovy duck which had not yet been given a local name – was first mentioned in France in 1555. Aldrovandi in Italy was familiar with the bird by 1603. Muscovies were also carried to Southeast Asia not long afterwards, as they were referred to in a document from Taiwan of 1693; they were also taken to West Africa (Clayton 1984b).

Changes under Domestication

The Muscovy duck has become much larger under domestication, the number of eggs laid per year has increased, and the colour of the feathers is now quite variable (Figure 12.6), but otherwise it is not much changed. In an attempt to establish from measurements whether birds from sites in Ecuador were wild or domestic, Stahl made a statistical study of 32 modern skeletons from known domestic and wild birds. Muscovy ducks are strongly dimorphic – males are more than twice as heavy as females – and domestic birds are larger than wild ones. The size of wild males and domestic females overlaps. Stahl's study used principal components analysis because multivariate statistics allow sexual dimorphism to be taken into account. The first component, size, accounted for almost 77 per cent of the total variance: it separated males and females. The second component, which accounted for 6.04 per cent of the variance, separated wild and domestic (Stahl 2005).

Discussion

Several important research questions remain to be answered in connection with the Muscovy duck. Stahl's analysis showed that even in the early second millennium AD, not all remains from settlements were from domestic birds, which raises the question of how early the duck was domesticated. Other features of an assemblage such as relative numbers, associations, and age may be as helpful as analysis of size. The Muscovy duck was carried to Europe before the end of the sixteenth century, and also to West Africa and Asia. No zooarchaeologist has recorded finds from the Post-Medieval period in Europe, Africa, or Asia. Have they been missed? Or were Muscovies always rather rare? Any archaeological find would make an intriguing addition to our knowledge of trading contacts in the modern period.

PIGEON

Some authors reserve the term 'pigeon' for the *Columba* species and 'dove' for the turtle doves, the *Streptopelia* species. This is tidy, but it is not strictly correct because 'pigeon' and 'dove' are synonymous in English (Snow & Perrins 1998). In this chapter I will use 'pigeon' to refer to the domestic bird and to the feral town pigeon.

Wild Ancestor

In *The Variation of Animals and Plants Under Domestication*, Darwin showed how the ancestor of the domestic pigeon was the rock dove, *Columba livia*; the 'aboriginal parent must have been a species which roosted and built its nest on rocks; and I may add that it must have been a social bird' (Darwin 1868, 180). Since this publication, Darwin's conclusion has 'not been contradicted by the evidence' (Johnston 2000). There is a second domestic pigeon, the barbary dove, *Streptopelia 'risoria'*, which was domesticated from the African collared dove, *S. roseogrisea*. It is kept in captivity and has gone feral in the Southern United States but does not have economic significance (Hawes 1984).

The original distribution of the wild rock dove is uncertain because feral populations have now colonised almost every country and city in the world (Simms 1979; Snow & Perrins 1998). The original range centred round the Mediterranean; it extended as far east as Western India, and as far south as the southern border of the Sahara. In Europe it extended as far north as the Alps, though on the west coast rock doves spread to Ireland, the Scottish islands, and the Norwegian seaboard (Ericson & Tyrberg 2004). The rock dove could, therefore, have been domesticated in many places (Johnston 2000), but in fact domestication probably took place in the Near East. It is likely that once communities there became sedentary, cultivating grain, processing it, and storing it within settlements, the rock dove became commensal and later fully domestic.

The wild rock dove is sedentary. It roosts and breeds in colonies on ledges on cliffs and in caves. It was the fact that, unlike the other pigeon species, it was naturally accustomed to breeding in dark, confined spaces that persuaded Darwin that the rock dove was the sole ancestor of the domestic pigeon. It forages on the ground for seeds, shoots, buds, and invertebrates (Snow & Perrins 1998), though feral birds eat almost any food scraps they can scrounge around human settlements. Except in the northern part of its range, even in the wild, rock doves may breed more than once a year, laying two eggs per clutch.

Both feral and domestic birds inter-breed readily with wild rock dove, so there are now few or no populations of pure-bred rock doves. As late as the thirteenth century AD, dovecots in England were sometimes restocked from wild roosts (Simms 1979); this presumably also occurred in other countries. DNA analysis has been undertaken to distinguish the degree of separation between different breeds (Traxler et al. 2000). It separated out some of the extreme fancy breeds, but the extent to which the domestic pigeons separate from wild ones has not yet been tested.

History

The brief history of the domestic pigeon by Zeuner (1963) has been augmented by more comprehensive recent surveys (Hawes 1984; Benecke 1994; Hansell 1998; Johnston 2000). As with the chicken and the goose, the earliest records and depictions of what may be domestic birds are from Mesopotamia and Egypt, and, just as with other domestic species, they suggest that pigeons were initially sacrificial birds. A Halafian clay figurine of a rock dove or other pigeon of *c.* 4500 BC (Benecke 1994, fig. 237) may be either wild or domestic, but a statue of the Babylonian goddess Ishtar shows pigeons perched on her arms, which does suggest that pigeons were domestic by the first millennium BC. In Egypt by 2000 BC, Rameses was able to sacrifice 58,810 pigeons to Ammon (Hawes 1984), a quantity so great that it is clear that the Egyptians must already have built structures to house colonies of pigeons. However, 500 years later, the plumage of the rock doves depicted in Minoan frescoes is indistinguishable from wild ones (Masseti 1997). By the second half of the first millennium BC domestic birds were known in Greece, and the references to pigeons in Roman literature make it clear that their breeding was under human control as different types were already known. In the Middle Ages, the Emperor Frederick II, whose treatise on falconry is referred to in the next chapter, built dovecots at each of his castles, and brought novel types of pigeon back from the Crusades, including a 'Syrian' bird (Haskins 1921). The first pigeons in North America are said to have been introduced by Europeans who settled in Canada in the early 1600s (Schorger 1962).

Archaeology

During the Pleistocene era, humans and rock doves often occupied the same caves and rock shelters, especially around the Mediterranean (Tchernov 1993; Cooper 2005). Tchernov did not consider that the pigeon was yet truly commensal in the Neolithic in the Levant because, though other birds were eaten in the Natufian and Pre-Pottery Neolithic (Chapter 10), remains of rock doves were rare. The rock dove was the most frequent species (498 bones) in the Neolithic occupation levels of Qumran Cave, but the other two common species in the cave were corvids (65 bones) and starlings (21 bones; see Recchi & Gopher 2002), all species which occur naturally in caves. There is support for Tchernov's view that pigeons were not yet commensal in the Neolithic period from the fact that they did *not* apparently spread with the earliest agriculture into northern and western Europe.

In much of Europe and Western Asia, it is not possible to identify a pigeon as domestic from its presence outside its natural range because pigeons are native to Western Eurasia and North Africa. One of the earliest assemblages with possible domestic pigeons is the mid-first millennium BC assemblage from Nea Halos in Greece, where there were more pigeons than chickens. They were identified as being from domestic pigeon because they were the best represented bird species and because five of the 76 elements were from juvenile birds (Prummel 2005). The eating

Table 12.4. *Archaeological finds of domestic pigeon from Central Europe and Scandinavia in the Late Iron Age and Roman period*

Site	Date	Number
Magdalensberg	1st BC–1st century AD	12
Ersigen-Murain	1st–2nd century AD	13
Berg	c. 2nd century	10
Wels	2nd century	Skeleton
Rainau-Buch	AD c. 150–260	3
Rottweil	1st–3rd century AD	1
Avenches (Aventicum)	1st–3rd century AD	12
Eining	2nd–3rd century AD	4
Augst	3rd century AD	3
Bad Kreuznach	2nd–4th century AD	110
Kővágószőlős	2nd–4th century AD	'Bones'
Epfach-Lorenzberg	'Roman'	1

Source: Data are from Benecke (1994, tab. 29).

of pigeons, presumably domestic, was attested at El-Amarna (Luff 2001). As the excavations were of the workmen's quarters, it suggests that pigeons were eaten by the workmen, even if, as discussed, the geese were not. The association of pigeons with intensive grain cultivation is exemplified well at Mas Castellar, where one third of the bird bones (of a sample of 768) were from pigeons. This Iron Age settlement was an agricultural site in the hinterland of Empuries, a trading port in Iberia founded by the Greeks in the sixth century BC (Garcia Petit 2005). Did the Greeks take domestic pigeons with them to their Iberian colony? Or did a population of commensal pigeons expand spontaneously round the Mediterranean and colonise Iberia?

The earliest domestic pigeons in Central Europe are from Late Iron Age and Roman-period sites (Table 12.4). Three partial skeletons were found in Roman deposits in Dorchester. They had been carefully disposed of, which suggested that they were domestic, but they were skeletally indistinguishable from the rock dove (Maltby 1993). There are surprisingly few records of pigeons in the Early Medieval period, but they become more common in domestic waste from the eleventh century onwards. From this time onwards pigeons are found all over Europe. They became a routine part of the upper- and middle-class diet. A dovecot at a Norfolk manor supplied up to 800 birds a year between 1298 and 1358 (Stone 2006). In monastic houses, pigeons were eaten as pittances (suppers) rather than at the main meal (Harvey 2006). There has been a persistent tradition that pigeons were valued as a source of protein in winter in medieval England, but this has been shown to be a myth. The accounts of Alice de Bryene showed that pigeons were in fact mostly eaten in the summer and autumn (Figure 12.5).

Changes under Domestication

Pigeons have been kept for sacrifices, for their meat, and for their dung. Their strong homing instinct is what made them suitable for carrying messages, as well as to take part in races. Wall paintings in Pompeii show that they have also been kept for pleasure from early times (Sparkes 1997).

There was little or no opportunity to select birds for size when they were kept in large dovecots, and consequently in the Middle Ages domestic birds were similar in size to the wild rock dove. Indeed, some were smaller: at both Faccombe Netherton (Sadler 1990) and Hextalls (Bourdillon 1998) in the south of England, some elements, morphologically identical to the rock dove, were even smaller than those of wild rock doves. When close control was exercised over breeding, as in Rome and in later historic times, larger strains were selected. As Darwin observed, modern domestic pigeons range from smaller than the wild rock dove to larger than the woodpigeon, and the changes include proportions of the limb bones and greatly modified beaks (Darwin 1868; Fick 1974, figs. 1–11). These changes are potentially recognisable in archaeological material, especially in a complete skeleton.

If size is problematic as a guide to whether birds are domestic, specimen numbers and immaturity may be a better indication, as at Nea Halos. Immature bones in household rubbish are probably birds reared in dovecots. In medieval households, squabs – immature birds eaten when 30 days old – were specified for the table. Remains of immature birds are found only occasionally among food remains from medieval sites; in England they have only been found in quantity only in the feasting deposit from the sixteenth-century manor of Hextalls referred to in Chapter 5 (Bourdillon 1998).

Pigeon Towers and Dovecots

Towers of clay were built as pigeon houses in Egypt and elsewhere in the Middle East while in Europe dovecots and pigeon lofts have more often been built in stone

FIGURE 12.7. Dovecot from the sixteenth century AD at the Château de Puyguilhem, France (photograph by D. Serjeantson).

(Stone 2006), first as part of the house or castle and later as free-standing structures (Figure 12.7). All have small apertures for the birds to get in and out, and some also have external perches. Internally, they have nest holes and ladders to allow people to climb up and harvest the birds. Dovecots were often constructed as tall narrow buildings, which suited the pigeons and also allowed the excrement to be collected from the base (Johnston 2000). Pigeon dung was recognised as valuable manure from Roman times (Columella 1941). Dovecots can be recognised even when little more than the foundations remain, not just from the circular shape but also from the bones of dead birds, especially squabs, which are often found in the floor deposits. At least five examples of dovecots have been excavated with skeletal remains in the base; juvenile pigeon bones from deceased fledgling birds are often found in large numbers in such contexts (Serjeantson 2006b).

Carrier pigeons were used in Assyria and the Greek writer Aelian reported that 'a certain Taurosthenes of Aegina dispatched a pigeon from Elis to carry to his home the news of his victory at the Olympic Games'. He used a brooding hen bird, and hens are still chosen today (Jennison 1937, 13). Carrier pigeons have been employed wherever people have kept pigeons, continuing even in the Second World War, but racing with pigeons started only in the nineteenth century (Zeuner 1963).

Discussion

In some respects pigeons are unsuitable domestic birds. They lay only two eggs per clutch, so are poorly adapted to intensive rearing (Hawes 1984), though they do make up for this by laying several times a year. They also compete with humans for food; in eighteenth-century France the pigeons belonging to the nobility were eating the grain cultivated by the peasants, which was one of the sources of discontent which led to the Revolution. Nevertheless, pigeons do well around human settlements and were encouraged as companion animals (see Chapter 13) as well as for food. Remains are generally much less common than those of chickens and geese on medieval sites, which is rather surprising in view of the large numbers listed in some household accounts.

MINOR DOMESTIC BIRDS

Peafowl

Two species of peafowl have been domesticated: the one usually kept is the Indian peafowl, *Pavo cristatus*, as it is easier to keep in captivity than the green peafowl, *P. muticus*. The natural range of the Indian peafowl is the Indian subcontinent and that of the green peafowl is Southeast Asia. Peafowl are well adapted to domestication: they are hardy, omnivorous, and polygamous, and even in the wild live around human settlements (Grahame 1984). The spectacular feathers of the peacock's train have always been very highly valued.

By the end of the second millennium BC peafowl were known in Babylon: some were kept by King Tiglathpileser I, probably having been obtained on his military campaigns in the East (Zeuner 1963, 456). The Persians also kept peacocks among other ornamental birds. One of the first early written references to a peacock is in the well-known list of the cargo brought to King Solomon from the East in the early first millennium BC: 'gold and silver, ivory and apes, and peacocks'. They are sacred birds in many religions of the East and became a symbol of resurrection and immortality quite early in the history of the Christian church, so they were often illustrated in devotional books of the Middle Ages. According to Varro a flock was kept in the temple of the goddess Hera on the Greek island of Samos, as the peacock was sacred to Hera (Hooper & Ash 1935; Jennison 1937). These were, or must have become, domestic. Though the feathers must have been the primary reason for domestication, the Romans also served peacocks at grand banquets. From the time of Charlemagne onwards, peafowl were recorded among the poultry kept on demesne farms (Stone 2006) and they also feature in lists of birds eaten at banquets and in recipes.

The criterion for recognising domestic peacock has always been finds outside the natural range of the bird. Very early remains were found at Harappa in the second millennium BC, but at this site in the Indian subcontinent they were thought to be wild (Zeuner 1963). There are few recorded finds of the birds from Greece and Rome. A peacock bone was found at Velsen, which was unexpected in view of the location of the castellum at the northeastern limit of the Empire (see above). Peafowl remains have been found on at least five Roman sites in Central Europe (Benecke 1994, 400) and on at least four villas in Britain (Poole in press) and in a rural sanctuary in France (Yvinec & Lepetz 2002). The trade in birds as well as feathers seems to have continued throughout the Early Medieval period: bone remains were present on two Saxon sites in East Anglia (Dobney & Jaques 2002) and in the tenth-century Gokstad ship burial in Norway (Dawson 1969).

In the Middle Ages, the keeping and eating of peacocks was confined to the upper classes. Remains have been found only in wealthy households, though these do include rural manors and wealthy town houses as well as abbeys and castles (see Figure 6.7 in Chapter 6). A few finds are also known from Post-Medieval sites in Europe (Makowiecki & Gotfredsen 2002; Gál 2006b).

Guineafowl

The guineafowl was domesticated from the helmeted guineafowl, *Numida meleagris*, a species native to Africa, and it is a common domestic bird there today. Where and when it was domesticated is uncertain. The guineafowl was known in Classical Greece, Egypt, and Rome; the distinctive chequered plumage was illustrated, and the bird was described by Varro and Columella (Hooper & Ash 1935; Columella 1941). The bird was also known to the Emperor Frederick II, but otherwise it was a rarity until the mid-sixteenth century when it was carried to southern Europe by Portuguese ships returning from West Africa. At that time birds were transported to Europe, and also to the West Indies, Central America, and Malaysia (Lamblard 1975; Mongin & Plouzeau 1984; Benecke 1994, 390–391).

Skeletal elements can be confused with the chicken and other Galliformes (see Chapter 4). Some of the earliest identified remains are from Senegal from sites of the fourth to tenth centuries AD, but their status as wild or domestic was inconclusive (Van Neer & Bocoum 1991); remains have also been found on later sites in West Africa

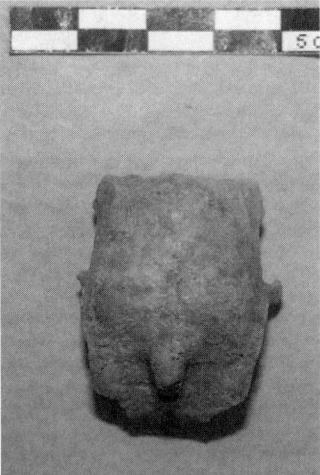

FIGURE 12.8. Skull of a guineafowl, *Numida meleagris*, from a wealthy household in medieval Genoa (twelfth to thirteenth century AD; photograph by A. Spinetti, by kind permission of Doctoressa P. Melli, Soprintendenza per i Beni Archeologici della Liguria).

(MacDonald 1992). The earliest recorded guineafowl claimed for Europe is from the Roman camp at Saarburg in Germany (Zeuner 1963, 457). Keepax (1981) identified some late medieval eggshell fragments as possibly from guineafowl (Chapter 7). The most convincing medieval find from Europe is a distinctive skull (Figure 12.8) recently excavated from a twelfth- to thirteenth-century deposit in Italy. This remarkable find was associated with rich pottery in the Torre della Curia, home of the wealthy Embriaci family in Genoa (Alessandra Spinetti, personal communication, 29 January 2007). The guineafowl has gone feral in several parts of the world, including in Madagascar and Haiti.

Domestication has had little effect on the guineafowl skeleton, which has 'retained all the characteristics of its wild counterpart' (Mongin & Plouzeau 1984), so its status even in Africa is difficult to ascertain. Guineafowl were rare exotics in Europe until the twentieth century, but the possibility that an occasional bone is present among the chickens is worth bearing in mind with archaeological assemblages.

Scarlet Macaw

As we saw in Chapter 8, the feathers of the scarlet macaw, *Ara macao*, were highly prized items of trade between the eleventh and fourteenth centuries AD in Mexico and the American Southwest. The macaws themselves were kept in captivity, but whether or not this amounted to full domestication is an interesting question. The feathers of other macaws and parrots, the military macaw, *A. militaris*, and the thick-billed parrot, *Rhynchopsitta pachyrhyncha*, were also used and traded, but these last two were not kept under such close control (Hargrave 1970; Rea 1980; Minnis et al. 1993; Creel & McKusick 1994).

The natural habitat of the scarlet macaw is Southern Mexico and Central America, but the fullest evidence for keeping macaws has been found further north. It was centred at the site of Casas Grandes (Paquimé) in the province of Chihuahua in Mexico, the city at the heart of the Medio culture. Altogether 322 skeletons of the scarlet macaw were found at the site, together with feathers and eggshell. Dozens of adobe structures, referred to as nesting cages, were found. These are rectangular boxes that are 1.2 m deep by 0.8 m wide with perches inside. The front wall had a hole which was blocked with a doughnut-shaped stone with a plug, which allowed access to the inside of the cage. Excrement was found in some of the cages. A field survey in Casas Grandes revealed more than 100 cage stones and also stones embedded in cages. Several dozen more cage stones were found in Chihuahua. Though the survey of Chihuahua covered many hundreds of square miles, all the cage stones were found within 30 km of Casas Grandes, which suggested that the rearing of scarlet macaws was controlled from the city (Minnis et al. 1993).

Macaws were also kept in Mimbres villages further north, where they are as early as those from Casas Grandes. Macaws and parrots were depicted on 24 pots or sherds out of more than 6,000 vessels of Mimbres pottery which have been located in museum collections. Feathers, some eggshell, and bones have been recovered from settlements, most of the latter in burials (see Chapter 14). The skeletal remains which have been tracked down – some were identified on site but not retained – included nine which were certainly scarlet macaw, one which was of military macaw, and five of a parrot species (see Table 14.1). The great majority were from new-fledged juvenile birds rather than adults, a characteristic of macaw bones also found on other Pueblo sites. Some of the pottery vessels also depict juveniles. This prevalence of young birds may have had ritual significance (Chapter 14). There are many Pueblo sites where feathers but only a few skeletal elements have been found, which raises the question of whether birds were kept at these sites or whether the feathers were carried there as gifts. Feathers and artefacts made using scarlet macaw feathers have been found in Utah, but bones are absent from these sites, so the birds themselves may never have been carried so far north (Rea 1980; Borson et al. 1998).

We have an unusually vivid picture of how scarlet macaws were kept in captivity in pre-contact times, but they did not undergo the changes in morphology or behaviour which have taken place with other domestic birds; the scarlet macaw remains a cage bird rather than a domesticate.

GENERAL DISCUSSION

Many other species have been kept in cages, aviaries, and parks in the past just as they are today, something documented historically from at least the second millennium BC (Zeuner 1963). We saw in Chapter 8 how people kept wild birds captive for their feathers in South America and New Zealand, an impulse which lay behind the domestication of some of the species discussed here. Other minor domesticates such as the ostrich and the pheasant were originally tamed and carried beyond their natural environment for display or sport. The pheasant may have been brought to England in Roman times; it was certainly reintroduced in the Middle Ages by the Norman kings just as they introduced peacocks and mammals which they had encountered elsewhere (Sykes 2007). The mute swan was brought under such close control in medieval England that its behaviour and morphology was changed (see Chapter 13). Several small species, including especially the finches, adapted to life as cage birds. The little egret has been tamed for its feathers and the great cormorant to catch fish for its owner.

As we have seen, domestication has been recognised from various lines of evidence. Most straightforward is the presence of a species outside its natural habitat. After that, an increase in numbers or a change in the age profile to include more juveniles (or both) may indicate that birds were domestic rather than wild. Changes in the plumage are conclusive, but this can only be reconstructed from illustrations except in those exceptional environments where feathers survive. Size change is the most reliable criterion for the zooarchaeologist, though this takes place only after domestication is fully established. As the study of ancient DNA becomes easier and cheaper to carry out, this too is going to reveal relationships which traditional zooarchaeological methods cannot discern.

Most if not all of the major domestic birds as well as some of the minor ones were originally kept in captivity so that they would be available for sacrifice. However, there were many species in which this did not lead to domestication. As well as the Egyptian goose, the ancient Egyptians kept thousands of sacred ibis in captivity (Houlihan & Goodman 1986) but did not domesticate them (Chapter 14). The species which did become domesticated acquired the ability to flourish around human settlements. Indeed, to some extent they may all have domesticated themselves, as Pinkley (1965) suggested for the turkey. This may well have been the case with the rock dove; it may also have been the case with junglefowl, guineafowl, mallards, Muscovy ducks, and even peacocks. Even geese must have been attracted to cleared agricultural land in the vicinity of settlements where they could graze in winter. Domestication modified the behaviour as well as the body shape to provide products of economic as well as ritual benefit. As with mammals, the unintended consequence of domestication of some species was that meat and the secondary products, eggs and feathers, became the main reason for keeping the birds.

13

Sport and Pleasure

This chapter is mainly about two sports in which people have taken a keen – indeed obsessive – interest for millennia: hawking and cockfighting. I shall also briefly discuss other sports in which birds have been involved. Birds have also been kept purely for pleasure: they are kept for their beauty, their voice or song, and for companionship. Even domestic birds, especially pigeons and peacocks and chickens, have been bred to be ornamental rather than practical. There is good archaeological evidence for hawking and some for cockfighting, but the archaeozoological evidence for birds kept purely for pleasure is less tangible, despite the fact that people must always have kept wild and domestic birds for this reason.

HAWKING

Hawking or falconry is the capture of wild mammals and birds using birds of prey. Today it takes place all over the world but it is most common in the East, especially in Arab countries. Some authors use 'hawking' to refer to the short-winged hawks (Accipitridae) and 'falconry' for the use of long-winged birds (Falconidae), but strictly the two words are interchangeable. In the past, hawking had the dual purpose of sport and to supply food for the table (Prummel 1997). However, as we saw in Chapter 10, the most effective way to catch birds for food was to use nets and traps, so it does seem that hawking has always been primarily a sport or carried out as a symbol of status.

In the earliest treatises on hawking in medieval Europe, most of the text was devoted to cures for the diseases to which captive hawks were very prone. These accounts were based on texts and information from the eastern Mediterranean which were disseminated to Europe and also to eastern Asia (Lagae 2005; Haskins 1921; Chun 2005). Dozens of books have been written on the history of hawking from at least the eighteenth century onwards (Strutt 1810; Harting 1978; Reeves 1995; Oggins 2004). Recently, several authors have discussed how hawking might be identified in the archaeological record (Prummel 1997; Cherryson 2002; Dobney & Jaques 2002).

Hawks and Prey

Fisher and Peterson (1964) estimated that 28 species of raptors had been used for hawking worldwide. The habits of the raptor species separate them into those which were most suitable for sport and those which were less suitable (Mulkeen & O'Connor 1997). Table 13.1 lists some of those used for falconry. Eagles were, and are, used for hawking in Central Asia but rarely in Europe. The buzzards are easy to train but do not provide such good sport as the Falconidae. There is even some evidence that the eagle owl was used, but Tyrberg (2002) suggests that it was probably used to lure birds rather than as a hunting bird in its own right. The prospective falconer looks for sport which provides an exciting spectacle, so chooses species such as the gyrfalcon and peregrine which 'stoop' on other birds in flight, rather than the slower hawks which take animals on the ground. A bird which is more difficult to train may be used so long as it provides better sport. Female raptors are larger than males (Chapter 2) and hunt larger prey, so they are the preferred of the two. The two sexes were known by different names and the subspecies of peregrine falcon were also known by different vernacular names (Table 13.1), at a time when there was no concept of a fixed species as there is today (Chapter 1): for instance, the male of more than one species was referred to as a 'tercel' (Reeves 1995).

Certain species were regarded as appropriate for different social ranks and for men and women. The personages listed in Table 13.1 are based on the list in the well-known *Book of St Albans* and are thought to apply mainly to the fifteenth century and may even be more applicable to Sicily than to northern Europe (Yapp 1981, 33). Once trained, birds will fly at different and larger species than they would normally take in the wild (Prummel 1997). Prey includes birds and mammals which were eaten and also other species such as corvids and kites which were hunted for sport but not eaten.

Catching and Training Hawks

'The hawk never becomes domestic or even tame' (Prummel 1997, 333). Each bird must be captured in the wild as hawks will not breed in captivity. In the Middle Ages

Table 13.1. *Raptors used for hawking in Europe and main prey species*

English name	Scientific name and sex	Appropriate for	Examples of main wild prey species	Examples of main prey when trained
Eagle	*Aquila* spp.	'emperor'	Mammals to 4 kg (fox, hare, rabbit), birds to 1200 g (grouse, ptarmigan), carrion	wolf, small deer
Merlin	*Falco columbarius*	'lady'	Birds to 100 g (lark, pipit, finches, wheatear, stonechat, dunlin, redshank, snipe)	lark
Gerfalcon or Gyrfalcon	*Falco rusticolus*; F	'king'	ptarmigan, grouse, seabirds, ducks	crane, heron, bittern
Jerkin or tercel	*Falco rusticolus*; M		ptarmigan, grouse, seabirds, ducks	
Goshawk	*Accipiter gentilis*; F	'yeoman'	Birds to 1200 g (pigeons, thrushes, pheasant, grouse, partridge, corvids), mammals to 1500 g (rabbit)	heron, goose, bustard, crane, hare, rabbit, pheasant, partridge pigeon
Tercel gentle	*Accipiter gentilis*; M	'poor man'	Birds to 1200 g (pigeons, thrushes, pheasant, grouse, partridge, corvids), rabbit	
Sparrowhawk	*Accipiter nisus*; F	'priest'	Birds to 500 g (woodpigeon, thrushes, lark, grouse)	moorhen, partridge
Musket	*Accipiter nisus*; M	'holywater clerk'	Birds to 500 g (woodpigeon, thrushes, lark)	
Peregrine or falcon gentle	*Falco peregrinus*; F	'prince'	Birds to 600 g (pigeons, grouse, thrushes)	pheasant, partridge, rook
Tercel	*Falco peregrinus*; M		Birds to 600 g (pigeons, grouse, thrushes, waders, seabirds)	partridge, rook
Kestrel	*Falco tinnunculus*	'knave'	Mammals to 100 g (voles), small birds, insects	
Buzzard	*Buteo buteo*	–	Mammals to 500 g (rabbit), birds to 600 g, carrion	rabbit, moorhen, squirrel
Hobby	*Falco subbuteo*	'young man'	Birds to 100 g (lark, pipits, finches, sparrow, warblers), insects	

Note: Medieval English name, Latin name and sex, personage for whom the bird was appropriate. Information is from *The Book of St Albans*; M = male and F = female.

Source: Data on weight and main prey species are from Brown (1976, tab. 15), Thom (1986), and Prummel (1997).

FIGURE 13.1. Method of capturing hawks in the Netherlands in the nineteenth century AD, using poles with long lines and a bow-net disguised with heather. The tethered peregrine falcon, *Falco peregrinus*, the two pigeons, and the great grey shrike, *Lanius excubitor*, are decoys (MacPherson 1897, 199).

professional hawk catchers took young birds ('eyases') from the nest or caught adult wild birds ('haggards') in nets and traps (MacPherson 1897, 189–202). The manner of catching peregrines in Valkenswaard in the nineteenth century was astonishingly complex. This province of the Netherlands is on the migration route for peregrines (hence its name of 'falcon wood'), and many birds were caught there to be supplied to falconers all over Europe. The method involved a tethered peregrine, a wild *and* a tame pigeon, and a great grey shrike, all of which acted as decoys for different stages in the procedure. It also required the use of a hide or blind, four long lines, and a bow-net. The fowler tied a decoy hawk and a decoy pigeon to a line, which was tied to a pole close to a hide. The wild hawk was attracted by the decoy hawk as it tried to catch the pigeon, and stooped on the pigeon itself. The fowler then dragged the pigeon towards him with the wild hawk still gripping the decoy bird and dropped a bow-net over the hawk (Figure 13.1). A trained hawk in the past, as today, was worth a great deal of money, and the value of land was enhanced if it held an eyrie of a wild hawk (Gurney 1921, 40; Tyrberg 2002).

Once delivered to the new owner, birds had to be trained, a highly skilled task which was often carried out by specialist falconers. Kings and nobles in the Middle Ages had professional falconers, who were highly paid and highly regarded. Hawks are trained to fly at artificial lures, with morsels of food as the incentive. The food is usually scraps of meats such as beef and mutton, but birds are sometimes fed

320 BIRDS

FIGURE 13.2. Hittite engravings of the first millennium BC: falconer with a hawk and a dead hare on the left (the curved stick similar to a short shepherd's crook on the other arm is a *lituus*); frieze showing a goddess with a hawk apparently wearing jesses on the right (after Canby 2002).

morsels from species such as pigeons and moorhens, their prospective prey (Gurney 1921, 40). Birds have a 'flying weight' which cannot be exceeded, so they are fed sparingly, and are not fed at all in advance of a day's hunting. The bird is carried on the falconer's arm and is attached by a leather thong, and some birds wear a hood. A lightweight bell is attached to the leg, so that the bird can be recovered if it strays. In the Far East, ownership is marked with a tail tag (Chun 2005).

History

The remote origins of falconry may lie in the Asiatic steppes as early as the second millennium BC (Benecke 1994, 453–457; Dobney & Jaques 2002). Whether or not it took place as early as this, the Hittites certainly seem to have been familiar with hawking, as it is illustrated on reliefs and seals of the second and first millennia BC from Anatolia. In one a god carries a raptor and a dead hare on one arm. Another shows people wearing jesses, the leather thongs that attach a bell to the hawk, and what appears to be a falconer's gauntlet (Figure 13.2; also see Canby 2002). There are also hints that hawking was practiced in Thrace and in Persia, though it is not mentioned in the literature of Classical Greece and Rome (Pollard 1977, 108). It was depicted in Japan from the fourth century AD and in Korea (at the time, part of China) from the fifth to sixth century.

Clemens Lunczer has found that the earliest references to the sport in Roman Europe are in the works of Julius Firmicius, a fourth-century astrologer, and Paulinus of Pella, a fifth-century poet (ZOOARCH archives 5 March 2006 – see Appendix 3). Paulinus had spent some time in North Africa as a child, so he may have seen hawking there. A mosaic in Sicily of the fourth century AD appears to show a small raptor used for hawking. The sport may even have taken place as far away as the British Isles: remains of a sparrowhawk were found together with thrushes in a Late Roman villa belonging to a wealthy family in southeast England (Murphy et al. 2000). From the first millennium AD onwards, hawking became popular in the Near East, the Middle East, North Africa, and all over Europe. In Sweden the earliest evidence, summarised by Tyrberg (2002), is skeletons of raptors in graves which date from the sixth century AD. In the second half of the first millennium AD, hawking was brought to a high art in Arab countries. The Emperor Frederick II, a native of Sicily, had the treatise on falconry, *De Arte Venandi*, translated from the Arabic in the eleventh century. He claimed that falconry was nobler than other forms of hunting because of the difficulty in acquiring the necessary skill (Haskins 1921). It was an activity which every nobleman learned to master as part of his education in courtly life. In the Middle Ages, hawking was regarded as 'so honourable an occupation that people carried a hawk on their fist when there was no intention whatever of hunting' (Gurney 1921, 40).

Archaeological Evidence

Prummel summarised five types of archaeological and zooarchaeological evidence which might indicate that hawking was practiced at a given site: the presence of falconers' equipment, a skeleton of a bird of prey, disarticulated remains of raptors, a preponderance of female hawks among the remains, and the presence of typical game from hawking (Prummel 1997).

Equipment

The most unequivocal evidence is falconer's equipment. This comprises the *jesses* (the short leash which the falconer holds), the *long leash* (which attaches the hawk to its perch), the *swivel* (the metal rings which connect the jesses to the long leash), the *bell*, and the *bewit* (the strap which attaches the bell to the leg of the bird). The falconer wore a heavy leather *glove*, and from the thirteenth century onwards in Europe, the hawk wore a leather *hood* (Prummel 1997). The *lure* consisted of a leather cushion, sometimes with articulated wings of a bird attached; it was used

FIGURE 13.3. Tail feather of Korean hawk with identity tag and bell (Chun 2005, fig. 4).

for training and to tempt the bird back at the end of an unsuccessful flight. A pair of articulated wings of a prey species might be from a lure, especially if found in a suggestive context. Korean hawks sometimes had identity tags attached to the tail feathers (Chun 2005), another object which might survive (Figure 13.3). Hittite falconers used a curved stick referred to as a *lituus*, similar to a short shepherd's crook (Figure 13.2). Leather and wooden equipment is likely to survive only in exceptional deposits, but those items made of metal, the swivel and the bell, have sometimes been found. Hawk rings, for instance, were found at Castle Hedingham and in excavations in the town of Biggleswade (Prummel 1997). Hawk bells have been found in excavations at the Valkhuis in The Hague, Netherlands (Pavlović & Nieweg 2007), and also in an early-sixteenth-century house in Puerto Real in Haiti (Reitz 1986).

Skeletons of Raptors

The presence of a skeleton of a falcon is unambiguous in certain contexts. The skeletons in graves of the Migration period onwards (sixth to tenth centuries AD) were in graves of high-status warriors (see Figure 14.6 in the next chapter). In Sweden most species were goshawks, but there were also peregrines, sparrowhawks, and gyrfalcons (Ericson & Tyrberg 2004, 47). A similar range of species and burials have been found in North Germany and England (Cherryson 2002). Even where the warrior was cremated, hawk remains have occasionally been found cremated with their owners (Prummel 1997; Cherryson 2002; Tyrberg 2002). The tradition of accompanied burial died out in Christian Europe, and in the Middle Ages hawks were disposed of with general refuse. Even in these contexts we can be fairly sure that the raptor in question was kept for sport if it was a species used in hawking, it was out of its natural habitat, and if it was not one of those raptorial species such as a kite which scavenge around human settlements (Chapter 15; also see Mulkeen & O'Connor 1997). Several raptor skeletons were found at the Slavonic stronghold of Oldenburg in Ostholstein, a castle with much other evidence for hawking (Prummel 1997). The skeletons of a goshawk, a sparrowhawk, and a peregrine falcon were recovered together from a pit at the Bishop of Winchester's rural manor at Faccombe in Hampshire (Sadler 1990, 505). The presence of these three different raptors, which normally occupy different ecological niches, within a single deposit provides strong evidence for the practice of falconry (Cherryson 2002).

Disarticulated Remains

Even single elements of raptors are also likely to be from trained birds if they are found outside the usual range, are immature, or show pathological changes. Disarticulated remains as well as partial skeletons were found at Oldenburg. Remains of at least two gyrfalcons were excavated in eleventh- to twelfth-century deposits close to the royal mews in Winchester. Though the gyrfalcon is frequently mentioned in descriptions of hawking in England (Dobney & Jaques 2002), it is not a native species so must have been imported from Norway or Iceland for falconry (Serjeantson 2006b). The evidence for hawking at Faccombe is strengthened by the fact that two elements showed pathological changes. A female goshawk had slight exostoses on the left tarsometatarsus, thought possibly to be the result of the use of jesses, and another had what was described as a possible false joint on the dorsal end of the left coracoid (Cherryson 2002). At least two hawks from medieval Scandinavia also exhibited pathological changes (Tyrberg 2002). An immature bird may also be significant: at Tell Hesban, a site of the first millennium AD in Jordan, a proximal humerus of a peregrine or lanner falcon was from a bird of about four weeks of age and was possibly a chick which had been caught to be trained for falconry (LaBianca & von den Driesch 1995).

324 BIRDS

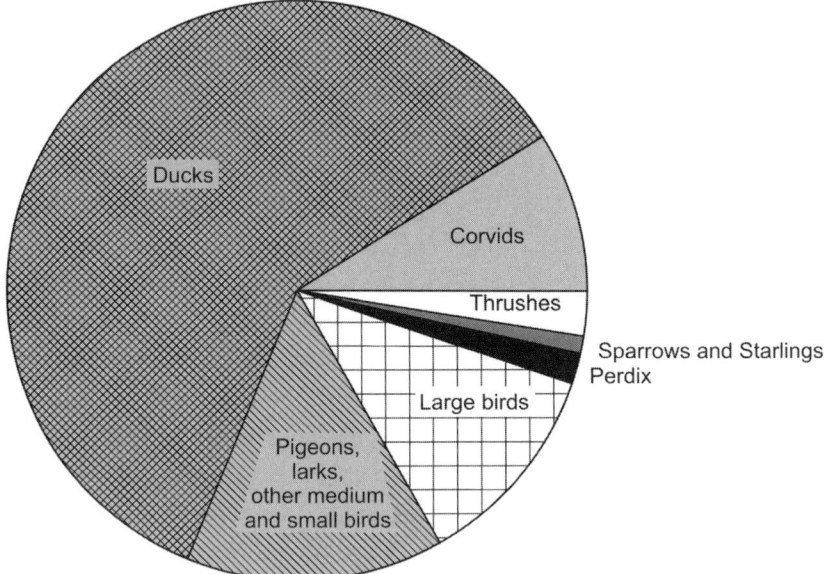

FIGURE 13.4. Relative numbers of wild birds excluding Accipitridae and Falconidae from the Slavonic stronghold at Oldenburg, Ostholstein, AD 750–1100, presumed to be the prey of the goshawks, *Accipiter gentilis*, sparrowhawks, *Accipiter nisus*, and other raptors which were also found at the site (redrawn from Prummel 1997, fig. 3).

More Females Than Males

At Oldenburg there were twice as many female as male goshawks and three times as many female sparrowhawks as males. This was interpreted by Prummel (1997), surely correctly, as a further argument that at Oldenburg these hawks had been deliberately selected for sport.

Prey Species

Prummel argued that the wild birds and mammals at Oldenburg were those which most often featured in falconers' prey. Ducks were most frequent (60 per cent of all wild birds), followed by grey partridge, pigeons, larks, and other medium-sized birds (Figure 13.4). The hare was the most frequent wild mammal. Corvids were a significant percentage of the remains. Elsewhere, however, the presence of the species caught by falconry does not necessarily prove that hawking took place, as the prey of hawks is much the same as the species usually taken in nets and traps. Ducks, as we saw in Chapter 10, were one of the most frequent wild birds caught for the table.

Discussion

Finally, as hawking was the province of the upper ranks of society, most finds of raptors have been in castles, palaces, hunting lodges, and in other households of high status (Cherryson 2002; Dobney & Jaques 2002). Hawking was an enormously popular activity in Europe and Asia among those of high rank for a thousand years, from the middle of the first until the middle of the second millennium, but 'The practice ... declined from the moment the musket was brought to perfection' (Strutt 1810, 27). It did not die out and was carried to the New World by early colonists, who found new hawk species to use. Today hawking still has tremendous social importance in some Arab countries, but in Europe and the English-speaking world it is a sport kept up by a devoted few. The relationship of a falconer with his hawk is unique among the relationships of humans and animals because people have never succeeded in domesticating or even taming hawks. Nevertheless, people have persisted in using the birds because of the thrilling sport they provide.

COCKFIGHTING

As argued in Chapter 11, cockfighting was one of the earliest reasons for keeping chickens. Most other spurred Galliformes, quails, partridges, and francolins, have also been set to fight; indeed quail fighting may initially have been as important as cockfighting in the classical world. Cockfighting is illegal today in most countries of the world, but it survives legally in the Philippines and elsewhere in Asia, in several Central American countries, and in one or two states of the United States. Every now and then a prosecution testifies to the fact that elsewhere, too, people still set cocks to fight. The fascination with cockfighting in Britain is clear from the histories of the sport written over the past 250 years (Pegge 1775; Strutt 1810; Scott 1957; Humber 1966). Some details of how fights were conducted in Asia differ from Europe, but the intense interest is the same (Lansang 1973; Geertz 1993).

Cocks which are strangers to each other have a natural tendency to fight, and if encouraged, will fight to the death. The procedure in a formal fight is for a pair of cocks of approximately equal weight and with spurs of equal length to be set to fight each other in an enclosed space. The fight, known in England as a 'main', consists of a series of bouts which last for a fixed length of time or until one of the birds kills the other. The birds leap into the air against each other, slashing the opposing bird with the spur (Scott 1957; Lansang 1973). They are encouraged to attack the head and breast rather than the wing, so as to draw blood, as it is usually loss of blood that kills the opposing bird. In nature, birds do not necessarily fight to the death, as the weaker one is able to fly away (Brisbin 1993), and it is to prevent this that cockfights are held in confined spaces.

Cockfighting birds are chosen for their agility and temperament – they must have a belligerent nature and be nimble footed. The best breeds for fighting are of small to medium size, though in the Philippines large birds are used. The traditional European breed, the English Game Fowl, had a small head, a short beak, a stout breast, and 'small and sturdy legs'. A 'sharp heel', that is, sharp spurs, is essential (Lansang 1973). The descendent of the English Game Fowl in North America is the 'Cornish' Game Fowl, but it is now kept for food rather than sport. Young male birds are segregated from others from about three months until two years of age, when they are old enough to fight. In the past birds were often fed an idiosyncratic diet which included things like chilli peppers and brandy. When artificial spurs were used, the natural spurs were cut off some time in advance of the fight so that the wounds would heal. Birds which did not live to fight another day were usually eaten (Scott 1957; Lansang 1973).

History

Texts and illustrations show that cockfighting took place from the first millennium BC in the Indian subcontinent, China, Sumeria, and Persia. A cockfight was held annually in classical Athens which had the purpose of reminding the citizens of the victory of the city over the Persians in 480 BC (Pollard 1977, 104–109), but cockfighting was known earlier in Greece: a krater from Corinth of *c.* 600 BC depicts a battle between two warriors, one of whom carries a circular shield with a depiction of a cock with comb erect, tail spread, and two prominent spurs, suggesting an existing association between gamecocks and human combat. A black-figure Attic vase shows men holding fighting cocks and squaring up for a fight. Cockfighting became very popular in Rome, especially with young men and soldiers: fighting cocks were depicted in a painting in the House of the Vettii at Pompeii and in a relief in Smyrna (Toynbee 1973, 256). Domestic chickens were known in southern Britain in the Iron Age (Chapter 11) but, according to Caesar, the British did not eat them but kept them 'animi voluptatisque causa', that is, for both spiritual and secular pleasures. The secular pleasure referred to is thought by some to refer to cockfighting (Scott 1957, 92). During the Middle Ages, cockfighting took place all over Europe. It was referred to in London in the twelfth century (Humber 1966, 73; Reeves 1995, 100). Annual cockfights were even held in boys' schools until the nineteenth century

(Humber 1966, 73). The sport was carried to the American colonies and round the world with the domestic chicken in the age of exploration, but when the Spanish reached the Philippines, 'they found our ancestors already addicted to it' (Lansang 1973).

Archaeology and Zooarchaeology

The presence of dedicated cockpits and certain items of equipment are evidence for cockfighting. There are also zooarchaeological correlates, though these are more ambiguous.

Cockpits

In Athens, birds fought on a platform. The traditional cockpit in England was a circular area surrounded with a wall or fence outside which were tiers of seating. Enclosed cockpits were circular with wooden or brick walls and at Whitehall in the seventeenth century there was a Royal cockpit which was octagonal. The recommended diameter was approximately 6 m (Humber 1966). Cockpits in the open air were set in artificial or natural circular hollows. In more elaborate cockpits, the sides of the depression were cut into terraces to form an amphitheatre, or the rim of the depression was artificially raised to allow more people to watch. A large circular open air cockpit at Gwennap with tiers of seating cut into the banks was chosen for the Methodist Charles Wesley when he preached in Cornwall in 1743. He had to wait until the 'main' was finished before he could begin (Humber 1966, 72). A Welsh cockpit reconstructed in the National History Museum at St Fagans (Figure 13.5) is covered to protect the birds and the spectators from the rain, rather more necessary in Wales than in countries with a dryer climate.

Artificial Spurs and Other Equipment

The natural spur on the tarsometatarsus was sometimes enhanced or replaced with an artificial spur. These were usually made of metal but sometimes of bone. A spur of Roman date from Cornwall was made of silver (Scott 1957, 53). Fighting cocks displayed in the Somerset Rural Life Museum in the 1980s had the natural spur removed and particularly vicious metal spurs attached (Figure 13.6). Other

FIGURE 13.5. Circular brick cockpit with a thatched roof in the Welsh National History Museum, St Fagans (photograph by D. Serjeantson).

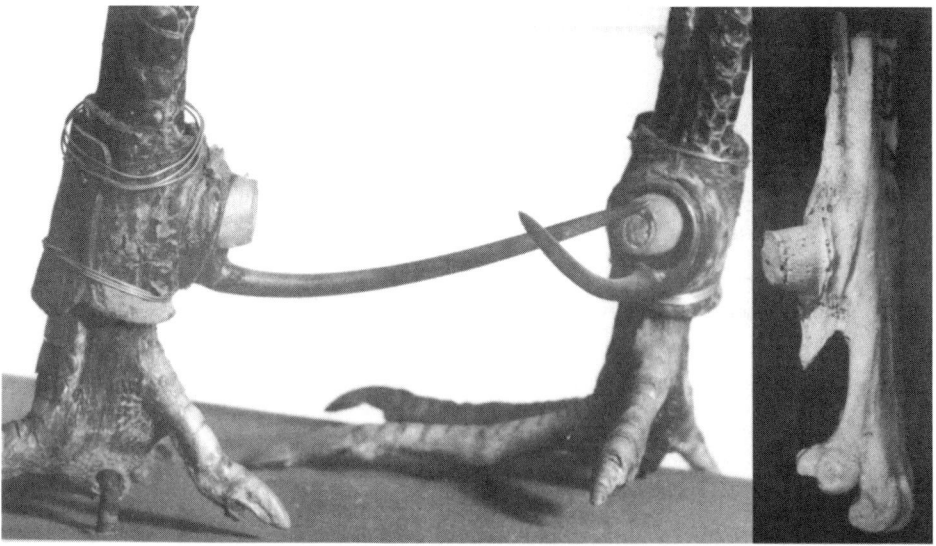

FIGURE 13.6. Modified spurs: artificial metal spurs attached to the leg of a cock in the Rural Life Museum, Somerset on the left; tarsometatarsus with the spur sawn off, Oxford, eighteenth century AD, on the right (West 1982, pl. 2).

cockfighting equipment included spur tags, identification tags, and wooden mufflers for the spur tip. One box of equipment confiscated from the owner by the police after cockfighting had been made illegal in Britain held scissors, pencil, safety pin, chalk, folding foot rule, iodine tube, ointment, and a sponge (Scott 1957). None of these items in isolation would indicate cockfighting but would be suggestive if found together. In an assemblage of chicken bones, a tarsometatarsus with a sawn-off spur is clear evidence for cockfighting: two such tarsometatarsi were found among material from eighteenth-century deposits in Oxford (Figure 13.6; also see West 1982). Tarsometatarsi damaged in this way have not been reported often, but this is not unexpected, as 'naked heel' fighting as well as fighting with artificial spurs has continued to be part of the cockfighting tradition from classical times to the present day.

Excess of Cocks

A sex ratio in which males equalled or exceeded females may also suggest that the birds had been kept for cockfighting, as a barnyard flock calls for a lower ratio (Chapter 11). A high proportion of cocks – based on the ratio of spurred and unspurred tarsometatarsi – were present in deposits from the Forum at the Roman town of Silchester in southern Britain. Cockfighting was a possible reason for their presence (Serjeantson 2000b); cockfighting certainly took place in the town as artificial cockspurs had been excavated there. In Roman Dorchester, too, there were more males than females in most periods (Maltby 1993, microfiche tab. 53) and in Roman deposits at the Coppergate site in York, about 75 per cent of tarsometatarsi were spurred. At Velsen, the Roman castellum referred to in earlier chapters, the sex ratio was two cocks to each hen (Prummel 1987). However, we have to bear in mind that there can be an alternative explanation for the imbalance, as cock birds were sometimes specially selected for sacrifice, as discussed in the next chapter.

Skeletons of Cocks

A complete skeleton suggests that the bird was buried with some special purpose, perhaps because it was highly regarded in life. A quail skeleton found in a pit of the Late Mamluk period (c. AD 1200–1456) at Tell Hesban in Jordan is thought possibly to be a victim of quail-fighting (LaBianca & von den Driesch 1995).

Conformation

As mentioned, birds specialised for cockfighting have a different conformation from those raised for meat, being smaller and leaner. The Roman writer Columella describes how the Greeks 'esteemed most highly the Tanagran and Rhodian breeds and likewise the Chalcidian and Medean' . . . 'since they desired height of body and determined courage in the fray' (Columella 1941, VIII, 2, 6). We saw how more than one breed or type of bird was present on some Roman sites, and in this case the smaller birds may be a cockfighting breed.

The spurs preferred were those of normal size and shape, not excessively long, which, as we saw in Chapter 11, were characteristic of caponised birds.

Symbolism of the Cockfight

Cockfighting has always carried a heavy load of symbolism. In the Roman world it was a pastime of soldiers and other young men, the fights providing a model of how combat should be fierce and if necessary carried to the death. In England it was positively encouraged among soldiers and schoolboys to teach them valour (Scott 1957). As well as encouraging bravery, cockfights in Rome were staged to foretell the results of a battle (Simoons 1994, 147). Cockfighting conflates sex and violence. The cockfight was seen not just as a fight between birds, but as a demonstration of masculinity, a fight between men. According to Csapo, writing about the cockfight in ancient Greece, 'the chicken was chosen to symbolise androcentric and phallocentric values in Athenian society' (Csapo 1993b, 124). In Greece several of the vases which depict cocks show them being presented by men to their prospective young male lovers, but this was interpreted as much a token of domination as of desire (Csapo 1993a). In Athens, cockfights were also seen as a battle between ranks in society, though in the United States, by contrast, cockfighting used to be regarded as democratic – George Washington and Andrew Jackson both went to cockfights. In England it was a sport of royalty and the aristocracy as well as of the poor but was not indulged in by the middle classes. In most countries it was an activity for men; women take no part (Lansang 1973; Geertz 1993).

Cockfighting has always attracted moral disapproval, even in those cultures where it was part of everyday life. Columella condemned it as a pastime in which young men wasted their own time and their fathers' money. He also expressed disapproval of farmers who bred birds for fighting instead of for meat. In Enlightenment times it came to be regarded as both cruel to the birds and brutalising to the spectators (Pegge

1775). The nineteenth century, a time when all forms of cruelty to animals began to be outlawed, also saw the first prohibition set on cockfighting. Massachusetts, one of the first places to make it illegal, banned it in 1836 and England in the 1840s (Humber 1966, 72).

Discussion

With chickens now one of the most common forms of meat it is difficult to appreciate that it may well have been the natural inclination of cocks to fight which provided the original impulse for domestication. Paradoxically, the very scarcity of chicken remains at early sites (Chapter 11) might support this, especially when remains are of male birds. In the absence of material remains, the only indisputable evidence for cockfighting is a modified tarsometatarsus; other indications such as a predominance of adult male birds or a complete skeleton of a cock may indicate cockfighting but may also signify birds kept for sacrificial purposes, as discussed in the next chapter.

HUNTING AND OTHER SPORTS

Though hawking was the chief means of hunting birds for sport, some large birds were hunted by other methods, using horses, spears, bow and arrow, and dogs. The hunting of ostriches is attested in Mesopotamia from the sixth century BC and also seems to have taken place in North Africa in Roman and Vandal times (von den Driesch & Baumgartner 1997, 163). Remains of cranes on Roman-period sites suggest that these large birds were also hunted for sport. Large numbers were found at Caerleon (Hamilton-Dyer 1993), a fort on the Welsh border which had a permanent garrison throughout the Roman occupation of Britain; at the castellum at Velsen, cranes were the third most frequent species (Prummel 1987). The soldiers no doubted hunted cranes as a pastime with feathers and meat the prize.

Ostriches were ridden from at least the first millennium BC. The earliest depiction is on a Babylonian limestone plaque from Kish. Ostriches were tamed by the Egyptians and the Romans, but, according to Zeuner (1963), not domesticated. As well as being ridden they were fattened for food – butchered bones have been found in Roman and early medieval sites in North Africa – and the Romans also used them in their Games where they were both ridden and used to pull chariots (Burke 2001). Racing with pigeons started only in the nineteenth century. Postcards on sale in France in 2002 show that there even geese were once used for racing and in Russia goose fights used to be held. The use of birds for sports such as these is unlikely to recognisable from skeletal remains.

BIRDS FOR PLEASURE

Some domestic birds have been kept for the pleasure offered by their appearance and behaviour. Peacocks (Chapter 12) are certainly kept mainly for their elegant appearance. Specialised breeds of chickens and pigeons have been selected for their plumage, and roller and tumbler breeds of pigeon have been selected for their acrobatics and aerobatics. It is even said that when they first encountered domestic chickens the Yanomamo in the Amazon Basin kept them as pets rather than for food. In simple and complex societies alike, wild birds have also been kept for ornament and as companion animals. People have always been fascinated by the degree to which birds and other animals can communicate and, especially, can imitate human speech (R. W. Serjeantson 2001).

Aviary, Cage, and Ornamental Birds

Corvids and parrots have been popular as pets because they communicate, but the range of species kept is surprisingly wide. In New Zealand the Maori kept tui and kaka as pets because they can speak long phrases and imitate tunes (Crowe 2001). In the early civilisations of the Near East, many species were kept for pleasure as well as for sacrifice (Houlihan & Goodman 1986). In Rome, the keeping of flocks of wild birds in aviaries may have originated in sacred practice but it spread to the secular domain. Wealthy citizens kept aviaries and caged birds and painted scenes of aviaries on the walls of their houses. The paintings were highly naturalistic, even if they combined elements which would not occur together in nature (Sparkes 1997). Among the birds kept in Rome were flamingos, purple gallinules, cranes, nightingales, blackbirds and other thrushes, starlings, goldfinches, ravens, crows, magpies, and parrots, as well as francolins and quail (Jennison 1937; Toynbee 1973). The last two species, as discussed, may have been kept for fighting but others were kept for their song, their appearance, or as curiosities. Ravens, the most intelligent of birds, were taught to talk. In the eleventh century AD, the Emperor Frederick II, as well as keeping hawks, had a zoo of exotic animals, including exotic birds, which travelled Europe with him (Haskins 1921).

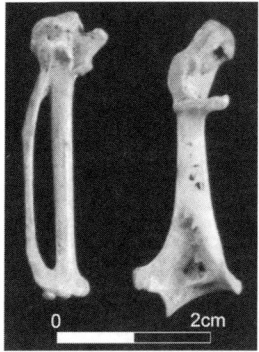

FIGURE 13.7. Carpometacarpus and coracoid of a parrot, Psittacidae, from Norwich, England, seventeenth century AD (photograph by G. Norrie).

Zooarchaeological evidence for cage and aviary birds has only occasionally been recognised. The only unequivocal evidence is a specimen found outside the bird's natural distribution, exemplified by a carpometacarpus and coracoid from a member of the parrot family from an eighteenth-century deposit in Norwich (Figure 13.7). This bird must have been imported – probably by a sailor – from Africa or the Americas (Albarella & Thomas 2002). A duck buried in its own coffin in Egypt is thought to be a pet bird buried with its owner (Ikram 2005). The scarlet macaws included in human burials in the American Southwest discussed in the next chapter had ritual importance, and they were probably more than pets. It is possible that the remains of jackdaws which have been found in deposits in the city of York and other towns were tame birds, but as jackdaws are found naturally in towns, this could not be proved (O'Connor 1993).

Mute Swan

The mute swan was kept in the parks of palaces and castles in England for ornament. As the largest British bird, the swan was associated in the medieval mind with power, as well as with elegance and grace. The control of swans was such that from the twelfth century onwards every mute swan in England was recognised as the property of an individual or an institution. They were marked by pinioning or were branded on the beak or leg; lists of these markings, known as 'swan rolls', are known from the sixteenth century onwards. At this time swans became sedentary in England (Ticehurst 1957; Northcote 1983; Ogilvie 1984; MacGregor 1995). The limb bones of modern mute swans are shorter and more variable in length than those of their antecedents in the Bronze Age, both changes thought to be a consequence of their domestication in the Middle Ages. Northcote even considered that the current population in England was feral rather than truly wild; certainly their behaviour today reflects centuries of breeding in proximity to human settlements. Like the peacock, the fact that the swan had symbolic value did not prevent it from being eaten, and it was an ornament on the dining table as well as on the lake. This is celebrated in the thirteenth-century poem set to music by Orff in the *Carmina Burana* in which a swan lamented 'once I swam on a lake but now am black and well-roasted'. From late medieval times onwards cygnets were removed for fattening in a yearly occasion known as 'swan-upping'. Deliberately fattened birds are probably the source of many of the swan remains found in Late and Post-Medieval bone assemblages.

CONCLUSION

Of all the sports and pastimes in which birds are involved, hawking leaves the clearest archaeological signature. Some raptors, as we saw in Chapter 8, were caught for their feathers, especially in North America in pre-contact times, but in Asia, North Africa, and Europe from medieval times onwards, it is reasonable to interpret skeletons, partial skeletons, and even single elements as coming from birds used for sport. Certain features, including spurs cut short, are evidence for cockfighting, but in the absence of this, the occasional bird used for fighting will be hard to identify among the mass of birds eaten. It is worth considering cockfighting where certain features are found together such as a predominance of adult male birds in a location such as a garrison fort. Remains are most reliably identified as pet birds if they are an exotic species, but this possibility should also be considered if remains are found with other pets or given special burial. However, special burial was also a feature of birds kept for ritual and symbolic reasons, as discussed in the next chapter.

14

Birds in Symbol and Ritual

Birds have played a powerful role in symbolic ideas since modern humans became capable of abstract thought. This is now believed to have happened quite suddenly between about 60,000 and 40,000 BP and it took place in tandem with the development of speech, music (see Chapter 9), and dancing. Indeed, it is only after this time that there is good detailed evidence for the capture of birds, as discussed in Chapter 10. Symbolism is more difficult to detect in the prehistoric archaeological record than are the material aspects of human behaviour which have been considered in earlier chapters. It is best inferred from art: iconography, engravings, sculpture, and paintings show birds most clearly in their symbolic roles, but physical remains – the focus of this chapter – can also do so. 'Self-consciousness and reason, symbolism and language, can at best only be inferred by the most tenuous extrapolations from the available prehistoric data' (Higgs 1973, 1) was the prevailing view in the 1970s, but since that time archaeologists have reacted against this pessimistic view and have placed greater emphasis on understanding the symbolic basis of human actions and detecting the evidence for symbolic and ritual behaviour in the archaeological record. This has brought with it an obligation to analyse material culture more critically, in order to separate non-economic from economic behaviour. We saw in Chapter 8 how the choice of the feathers of eagles and other birds of prey derived from the symbolic value of these birds rather than the intrinsic quality of the feathers, and in this chapter we shall survey some of the other symbolic roles of birds. Birds and parts of birds which formed an element in rituals, especially rituals involving food and food consumption, can be detected more readily, as the physical remains may leave traces in the context of the activity.

DIVINE AND TOTEM ANIMALS

In some religions and spiritual beliefs birds were actually regarded as divine, and in others a bird stood for the deity or was seen to have some of the deity's attributes. According to Ingold (1986a), the animals, including birds, which were worshipped were not sacrificed and eaten. In those societies where the gods or the creator spirit took the form of a bird, it was not killed, but was treated with respect. This was the case with eagles and crows over much of North America. In Celtic myth it was the swan whose power was so great that swans were never killed (Ross 1974); indeed, the killing of a swan remained taboo in Scotland into historical times (Kear 1990, 240). Though in most cultures the divine animal was protected, in others it was slaughtered in a special ceremony and consumed, perhaps once a year, to ensure its reproduction (Ingold 1986a). Fraser in *The Golden Bough* recounts several examples where birds are involved. The Ainu of Northern Japan revered eagles, hawks, and bears: these powerful animals were respected because they were good hunters. Some were kept in cages and later killed, at that time being invited to return again 'for the special benefit of Ainu hunters' (Fraser 1963, 676). According to Fraser's nineteenth-century sources, the Acagchemem of Southern California 'adored the great buzzard, and once a year they celebrated a great festival called Panes or bird-feast in its honour... the bird was carried into the temple in solemn procession and laid on an altar erected for the purpose.... The ceremonies being concluded, they seized upon the bird and carried it to the principal temple [where] they killed the bird without losing a drop of its blood. The skin was removed entire and preserved with the feathers as a relic for the purpose of making the festal garment or pelt. The carcase was buried in a hole in the temple'. Their belief too was that 'as often as the bird was killed, it became multiplied' (Fraser 1963, 654). The Hopi had a very similar ritual with eagles: they kept the young until fully fledged, at which time they were sacrificed. The bodies of the birds were buried carefully in a special cemetery outside the villages (Muir & Driver 2004). Even if Fraser distorted the function of the ritual, the activity is clear enough. The archaeological correlates are the buried body of the bird, possibly lacking some elements which had been incorporated in the 'festal garment'.

Totem Animals

When the members of a clan or social group appropriated a bird or other animal as their totem, the creature itself was not hunted or eaten; indeed it was avoided as food (Oberg 1980, 45). In this case, though it might very well be depicted, the remains would be absent. A series of megalithic limestone pillars at the Pre-Pottery

FIGURE 14.1. Bas relief on a Pre-Pottery Neolithic pillar at Göbekli Tepe in Anatolia, showing two cranes, *Grus grus*, lines depicting snakes, and pictograms (Peters et al. 2005, fig. 9; photograph courtesy of Deutsches Archäologisches Institut, Berlin).

Neolithic site of Göbekli Tepe were engraved with bas reliefs of cranes (Figure 14.1), snakes, wild boar, foxes, and bucrania of aurochs. The pillars at this site in southwest Anatolia are thought to have enclosed a series of ritual spaces. The faunal remains from the site did not correspond with the animals depicted, which could indicate that the pillars depicted the totem animals of the group. However, the variety in the species depicted would indicate that several different groups must have been involved (Peters et al. 2005).

BELIEFS ABOUT BIRDS

Divination

Certain forms of divination or ornithomancy rely on birds. For the Greeks and Romans, the cries of certain birds, including those of ravens, crows, and owls, signified the divine will. For other species such vultures, hawks, and eagles, the flight pattern was significant: the flight of an eagle from left or right foretold the outcome of a battle or another life event (Ross 1974, 295). The behaviour of a chicken *as it dies* in the course of the sacrifice foretold the future in Rome and beyond. A similar ritual takes place in West Africa. The 'answers to deep human concerns lay in the direction to which the dead body of the bird pointed as it came to rest, like the last breathless click of the roulette wheel' (MacDonald 1995). The small chickens originally introduced to West Africa performed this ritual more effectively than did the larger breeds which have been imported more recently. Cockfighting, discussed in the previous chapter, was also 'a sophisticated offshoot of divination', used to foretell the outcome of battles (Simoons 1994, 147). Divination by flight would be invisible in the archaeological record. A chicken killed for prophecy would leave a trace only if it was not then eaten.

Harbingers of the Seasons

The arrival of spring in the northern hemisphere is heralded by the arrival of migratory birds, one of the signs which triggered the ceremonies of spring. One possible explanation for the significance of cranes on Neolithic sites in the Near Eastern sites is that they were harbingers of spring. Smaller migratory birds such as swallows also herald spring, but when remains are found in any number, as in some cave sites, they are most likely the prey of raptorial birds (Chapter 5) and not connected with human actions. The arrival of these and other migratory birds may have been important in the annual round of the hunter and farmer alike, but there would have been no reason to kill the birds themselves. On Rapa Nui (Easter Island) a Bird-man cult flourished in the nineteenth century which was associated with the arrival of spring. Each clan chief appointed a servant to compete to collect the first egg laid by a sooty tern after the sooty terns returned to breed. The sooty terns nested on a small offshore island which could be reached only by a dangerous swim. Many Bird-men were commemorated on engraved stones (Figure 14.2). The first laid tern egg signified the start of the season for deep sea fishing, which was an important part of subsistence on Rapa Nui, more so than the birds and the eggs themselves (Routledge 1917; Martinsson-Wallin & Crockford 2001).

Messengers from the Gods

Because birds can fly, they have often been associated with the human spirit and its journey – in a trance or after death – towards the gods and the heavenly regions.

FIGURE 14.2. Rock engraving of a 'Bird-Man', a human figure with the head of a bird, from Rapa Nui or Easter Island (photograph by P. Copeland).

Their capacity for flight allows birds to fly to the spirit world, so it was thought that they carried messages to the gods or the ancestors. In return, the gods or the ancestors sent messages to the world of humans via the medium of birds. Bulmer described how in New Guinea the pied chat occasionally approached a person and gave its alarm call, which was interpreted as the ghost of a dead father or brother bringing a message to the living (Bulmer 1979, 69). Birds even carried food to the gods: during a ritual fast, a widow in Lucknow would offer a portion of food to the crow so that the bird would feed her husband's ancestors (Goody 1982, 118). Among the WaiWai in South America the shamans wore feathers so that they might transform themselves into birds and themselves carry messages to the sky (Horniman Museum 2006).

Fear of Birds

Ethnographic sources widely separated in time and space bear witness to how some birds are feared. The last great auk seen off the islands of St Kilda was killed because the local people believed that it was a witch (Fuller 1999). In New Guinea the friendly fantail was regarded as a witch because it gives a cry which warns bigger birds of human approach (Bulmer 1979, 70). In the Roman world owls were feared and reviled as witches and in medieval bestiaries the owl was described as a bird of evil and darkness and a harbinger of death (Klingender 1971, 256; Yapp 1981). In this case an owl or other feared bird might be killed, but it would not be eaten. This is a possible reason for the presence of a skeleton of a tawny owl which was recovered from a medieval ditch at Carisbrooke Castle. The skeleton showed no traces of disarticulation or butchery (Serjeantson 2000a). Other explanations for the presence of skeletons of owls are discussed later.

Inferences that excavated remains are from birds with one of these symbolic roles will be ambiguous at best. Much clearer and much easier to interpret are remains associated with rituals of death and worship.

BIRDS IN GRAVES

Animal remains, including birds, were placed with burials and cremations in many cultures. Remains from funeral feasts also find their way into grave fill, sometimes deliberately and sometimes no doubt accidentally. Individual birds with a function unrelated to food were also placed in graves.

Food and Offerings with Burials

One context in which bird remains were frequently placed in graves is in the territories of the Roman Empire and its periphery: chickens, eggs, and sometimes other birds were deposited with human burials and cremations (Parker 1988; Lauwerier 1993a; Benecke 1994; Gál 2005b). In Europe the custom of accompanying burials with parts of animals began in the first century BC on the fringes of the Empire and continued until the Christian burial tradition prevailed. A pig or a joint of pork was the most usual accompaniment of a burial; the chicken was the second most frequent, followed by joints of cattle, sheep, and goat (Figure 14.3; also see Lauwerier 2004).

Some animals and joints were placed on a dish. In a grave of the fourth century AD in a Roman cemetery at Nijmegen, a chicken was laid out on a Coarse Ware dish, together with the head of a suckling pig (Figure 14.4). The position of the articulated bones of the wing, the long bones, and ribs suggest that originally a complete bird was interred in an intact state. In a second grave a chicken lacking the head and right foot was laid on a Terra Sigillata dish. The absence of the left leg is not thought significant; it was probably cleaned away before contents of the dish were recognised (Lauwerier 1986). In Winchester, three burials in a Roman cemetery in the city had

BIRDS IN SYMBOL AND RITUAL 341

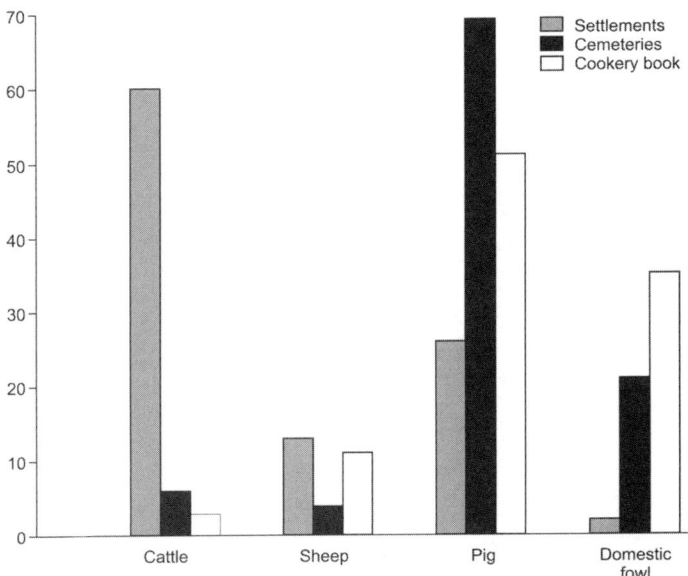

FIGURE 14.3. Frequency (NISP) of cattle, sheep and goat, pig, and domestic fowl in settlements and cemeteries within the Roman Empire, compared with the frequency of references to the animals in the cookery books of Apicius (Lauwerier 1993a, fig. 2).

FIGURE 14.4. Grave gifts from a cemetery of the fourth century AD in Nijmegen (Lauwerier 1993a). The left section shows a Coarse Ware dish containing the head of a suckling pig, and some remains of a chicken (grave 126). The position of the articulated bones of the wing, the long bones, and the fragments of rib suggest that a complete bird was interred intact. The right section shows a Terra Sigillata dish containing the articulated skeleton of a chicken, lacking the head and right foot (grave 190-1; photographs by R. Lauwerier).

FIGURE 14.5. Grave of a Roman soldier from Aquincum-Testverhegy in Roman Pannonia with a chicken (4) and parts of a young pig (5, 7, and 8) beside the left leg (Gál 2005b, fig. 4).

chickens placed between the legs and in a grave in another cemetery outside the North Gate a chicken was laid out with its head resting on the pot accompanying the burial (Maltby in press). At the other end of the Empire in Roman Pannonia, in the cemetery of Aquincum-Testverhegy in Hungary, a soldier was buried with a chicken and part of a young pig beside the right leg (Figure 14.5; also see Gál 2005b). A more elaborate rite was exposed in excavations in the island of Lipari off Sicily. A *bothros* or a sacred pit of the sixth century BC contained remains of animals consumed in ritual meals. They had been placed in votive containers and deposited in the pit. The sacrificed animals included at least one partridge, *Alectoris* sp., and six cocks, the latter a novelty around the Mediterranean at that time, as we saw in Chapter 11. A partridge ulna had a healed fracture, suggesting that the bird had been kept in captivity (Villari 1991). Chicken remains also accompanied a cremation on a grand scale which took place in a cemetery in Southwark, South London. A large pit, a *bustum*, had been dug beneath the cremation pyre, which was then used to hold the cremated remains and food offerings, including chicken (Mackinder & Reilly 2000).

Large mammals buried with the dead were usually represented by joints only, but chickens were typically found whole or with just the head and feet cut off.

More intriguingly, one of the cremation urns from a Late Iron Age necropolis at Lamadeleine in Luxemburg was accompanied by a chicken which had been butchered and partly reassembled in two heaps. One comprised the disarticulated humeri on top of the vertebral column and synsacrum and the second consisted of a chopped sternum with furcula, coracoids, and a scapula (Méniel 1995).

Cremated Remains

In the classical world, the food offerings which accompanied cremations were not necessarily themselves cremated, though in some rites the accompanying animals were cremated with the dead. Cremated remains can be distinguished from bones burned in cooking by the colour changes which take place at high temperatures (Chapter 6); they are also liable to be extremely fragmentary. As Bond has pointed out, only the most scrupulous archaeological project managers and human bone analysts pass on apparently unidentifiable scraps of calcined bone to a specialist so that any scraps of animal bone can also be identified. It is likely that there have been many unrecognised examples of cremated birds and other animals in graves (Bond 1996; Bond & Worley 2006).

Distinguishing Food from Offerings

There are two possible reasons for including the remains of chickens and other animals in graves: they were either intended as food for the deceased on his or her journey to the underworld or they were intended as an offering to the gods to ensure safe arrival in the afterlife (Lauwerier 2002). If the second, the species and numbers should be similar to the figurines found in graves, as these were thought to be representations of the animals associated with the different deities. Lauwerier showed that the figurines do not correlate with the remains: they often represent animals which were not eaten such as horses. The relative frequency of cattle, sheep, goat, pig, and chicken remains from graves does, however, correlate with the meats listed in the recipe book of the Roman writer Apicius (Figure 14.3). This does indicate that the grave contents were indeed intended to represent food rather than offerings. The recipes were for luxurious rather than everyday meals, which implied that the food accompanying the dead represented meals that were out of the ordinary. The analysis also explored the question of whether chickens were more usually placed in graves of women and pigs in those of men, as had been suggested in the past, and found that there was no correlation (Lauwerier 2002).

Selection of Species

In the Late Iron Age (La Tène) cemetery at Bucy-le-Long, the animals and also meat joints were cremated: these were young pigs, sheep, and cattle in the earlier phases, but they were exclusively pork and birds, presumably chicken, in the later phases (Auxiette 1995).

Parker suggested that the reason why chickens were found in graves in the Roman period was that 'the cock was an appropriate grave offering' (Parker 1988) because of what it symbolised. The cock was a symbol of the dawn and also of salvation, and it was the bird of Mercury, the messenger to the underworld. However, burials in Roman graves are more often than not of hens rather than cocks. For instance, three out of four chickens placed with burials in a cemetery of the Tylos period (200 BC–AD 200) in Bahrain were hens; the fourth was indeterminate (MacDonald 2003). One of the chickens in the *bustum* contained medullary bone, so it must also have been a hen. Also, as we have seen, the chickens mostly represented prepared food rather than whole birds. All this tends to give support to Lauwerier's conclusion that the chickens were deposited mainly because they were a luxury food. This is not to say that chickens did not also have ritual connotations; they clearly did, as discussed later.

Burials and cremations in cultures beyond the limits of the Roman Empire also occasionally included chickens as well as other animals. Some pagan Saxon and Scandinavian burials and cremations contained food remains as well as those of pets or companion animals (Chapter 13). A few of the Anglo-Saxon cremation graves at Spong Hill and Sancton in eastern England included chickens as well as the more usual larger mammals. All the accompanying animals were cremated, so the chicken remains were found in a calcined state (Bond 1996).

Roman funerary rites also included avian species other than chickens. Geese, eider ducks, quails, and woodcock have all been placed in Roman graves (Lauwerier 1986; Parker 1988; Gál 2005b). The Anglo-Saxons and Vikings kept geese in large numbers, and remains of these have also been found in graves and cremations (Bond 1996; Tyrberg 2002). The Egyptian goose was a traditional grave accompaniment in Egypt, again placed there as food for the dead (Houlihan & Goodman 1986; Boessneck & von den Driesch 1988).

Non-Food Remains in Graves and Cremations

Accompanying Animals

Some remains from graves and cremations have nothing to do with food. Individuals of high status were buried with their companion animals in the Scandinavian Late Iron Age. These included the falcons kept for hawking, discussed in Chapter 13, as well as horses and dogs (Tyrberg 2002; Bond & Worley 2006). Thirty-four graves are known in Sweden dating from AD 500 to 1000 in which hawks were buried with their owners (Figure 14.6), the majority in the province of Uppland.

Scarlet macaws (discussed in Chapter 12), parrots, and turkeys were interred in graves in the American Southwest (Ubelekar & Wedel 1975; Creel & McKusick 1994; Muir & Driver 2004). In the Mobridge cemetery in South Dakota, birds of prey (hawks, owls, and eagles) were generally buried with adult males, while crows and ravens were associated with children, and women were not usually buried with birds at all (Ubelekar & Wedel 1975). Turkeys were interred whole from Basketmaker III times (AD 700–600; see Rea 1980); at this early period, turkeys were prized for their use in rituals and their feathers but not for food (Chapter 12). At least six examples of birds interred with humans are known from sites in the Mimbres area of New Mexico (Table 14.1). Five were macaws and one was a thick-billed parrot. The macaws were buried whole, but only the head of the parrot was deposited (Creel & McKusick 1994). A child burial from the Grasshopper Ruin site in Arizona was also accompanied by a complete macaw, which was placed on the breast (Olsen 1979, 90).

Wings in Graves

There are some poignant examples in which only the wing was placed in a grave. A young child buried next to a female in the Late Mesolithic cemetery at Bøgebakken near Vedbaek in Denmark was laid on the wing of a swan, as deduced from the wing bones in the grave (Petersen & Meiklejohn 2003). In a Late Neolithic burial at Tamula, Estonia, a young child was buried holding part of the wings of a crane in each hand (Mannermaa 2003). The Vedbaek wing was thought possibly to be a cradle or shroud, but a more likely explanation is that the wings were intended so that child or its spirit would be carried to the afterlife on the wings of a bird.

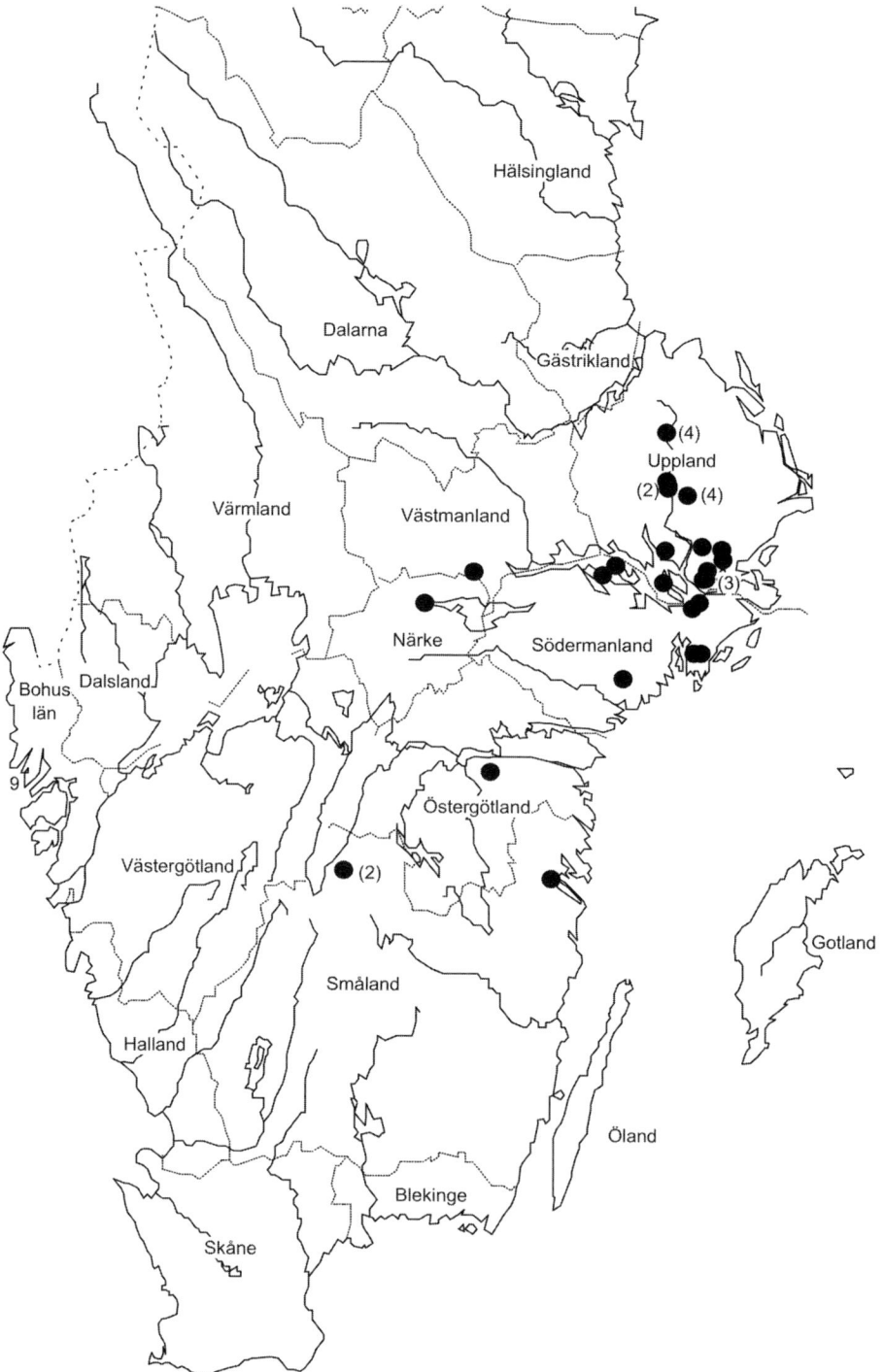

FIGURE 14.6. Map of Sweden, showing graves with raptor burials, sixth to eleventh century AD. There is a concentration in the province of Uppland (Tyrberg 2002, fig. 11; drawing by T. Tyrberg).

Table 14.1. *Burials of scarlet macaw, military macaw, and thick-billed parrot from Mimbres sites in New Mexico*

Site	Species	Age	Provenience	Temporal assignment
Cameron Creek	Parrot	?	Room 148, lower floor	Pit-house
	Scarlet macaw	?	Room 60, burial (male, adult)	Classic
	Macaw or parrot	?	West room block	? Classic
Galaz	Scarlet macaw	newly fledged	Burial 2–278, near Room 35 (child, 1 year)	Classic
	Scarlet macaw	newly fledged	Room 73	Classic
	Scarlet macaw	newly fledged	Room 73	Classic
	Military macaw	newly fledged	Room 73, in floor	Classic
	Parrot	?	Room 73	Classic
	Parrot	?	Room 73	Classic
	Macaw or parrot	?	Room 27A, below 3rd floor	Classic
	Macaw or parrot	?	Room 84, Burial 15–97 (child <1 year)	Classic
	Macaw or parrot	?	Room 15, below floor	Classic
	Macaw or parrot	?	Room 19, Burial 2–85 (female, 30–40 years)	Classic
	Macaw or parrot	?	Room 19, between floors 3 and 4	Classic
Old Town	Scarlet macaw	breeding age	Room A3, Feature A3–9	Classic
Osborn collection	Scarlet macaw	older than newly fledged	unknown	? Classic
Treasure Hill	Parrot	adult	Herrington Room 4, Burial 14 (male, adult)	Classic
Wind Mountain	Scarlet macaw	newly fledged	extramural, Block 20A	? Classic
Gila Cliff Dwellings	Scarlet macaw	newly fledged	Room 10A	Post-Classic
	Parrot	?	Room 30	Post-Classic
Freeman Ranch	Scarlet macaw	newly fledged	291 FR-6, burial (female, adult)	Post-Classic
	Macaw or parrot	?	below floor of Salado Room	Post-Classic

Note: The scarlet macaw is *Ara macao*; military macaw, *A. militaria*; and thick-billed parrot, *Rhynchopsitta pachyrhyncha*. Birds not identified to species are known from excavation records only and were not examined.

Source: Data are after Creel and McKusick (1994).

Ornaments and Talismans in Graves

Some bird bones from graves and cremations were probably ornaments or talismans (see below) rather than an accompanying deposit. The calcined carpometacarpi and other wing bone fragments of a small shorebird from Oosterbeintum, a cremation cemetery in the north of the Netherlands from the fifth to eighth century AD, may represent birds added to the funeral pyre with the horses and dogs, but they may alternatively have been from wings used to decorate clothing (Prummel 1993). Some of the objects discussed as possible ornaments in Chapter 9 may well be talismans or fetishes, as Clark (1948) suggested for the perforated raptor claws found with a human burial in a prehistoric stone cist in Scania.

Skeletons and partial skeletons of birds in a grave are likely to be either companion animals or intended as food for the dead. The origin of disarticulated bones in the grave fill is more doubtful. We have seen examples where they may be directly associated with the burial, but if in the fill, but not closely associated with the burial or cremation, they may be remains of a funerary meal partaken by the mourners. Alternatively the bones may be reworked, perhaps having come from an *earlier* funerary meal in the same cemetery. They may even be from some unrelated earlier activity at the site. Careful analysis of the species, the elements, the fragmentation, and other modifications and also of the associated finds is needed to establish the significance of the remains.

BIRD BURIALS

In some cultures birds themselves were given separate burial. Egypt provides the most prolific examples in the bird mummies recovered from temples and catacombs. Burials of whole birds have also been identified from the completeness of the skeleton taken together with the context of the find.

Pueblo Macaw Burials

Bird burial was a notable feature of the Pueblo peoples in the American Southwest (see Chapter 12). At the Mimbres sites referred to earlier, as well as birds with human burials, some birds were formally buried on their own (Creel & McKusick 1994, 519). Most were scarlet macaws, but some were military macaws, and some were the thick-billed parrots (Table 14.1). As well as macaws and parrots, bird burials also included eagles, hawks, and turkeys. The macaw and parrot burials were within the settlement, but those of raptors and turkeys were outside the walls, which is in accord with known Hopi practice. At the site of Galaz Ruin, skeletons and skulls were buried beneath the floor of certain rooms, all in the North cluster, an area which may have been devoted to the sacrifice of macaws. It may also be where they were kept, as it was the elite area of the settlement. This distribution of macaw remains was mirrored at other Mimbres sites where macaws and parrots were associated with areas used by the elite. The fact that no remains of macaws have been found at settlements of lesser status confirms this association. The macaw burials which have been studied recently all lacked the left wing. (Where bones were not retained on old excavations, the records are not complete enough to say whether or not this was the case.) The wing is thought to have been retained for use as a fan, as were wings of ravens and crows elsewhere. Out of ten of the macaw burials, seven were subadult, killed or died just at the age at which they had attained adult plumage. This suggests that they were ritually slaughtered in spring, when just fledged (Creel & McKusick 1994).

TEMPLE SACRIFICES, FEASTING, AND RITES

Sacrifice and feasting took place as part of funerary rites but are most often thought of in the context of temples and shrines. The animal was sacrificed to the gods – but it was then normally consumed by the human participants (Ingold 1986a). As in funeral feasts, it was usually food animals that were sacrificed. Any of the domestic animals might be sacrificed, though in Roman ritual the more choice food animals such as pigs were often chosen in preference to cattle, sheep, and goats. There was no requirement that animals should be of high quality or prime age (Lauwerier 2004). So far as chickens were concerned, there was rarely a concentration on one age cohort or sex.

There are descriptions of how, in Greece and Rome, selected parts of the animal were placed on the fire. The gods were content with the smell of the food as it rose from the sacrificial fire on which the animal was cooked. For cattle and other mammals, the femur and tail were removed and placed on the fire.

Archaeological Evidence for Chicken Sacrifice

Archaeological finds from Pompeii suggest that the heads and feet of chickens were placed in the sacrificial fire. An excavation in the garden of what appears to have

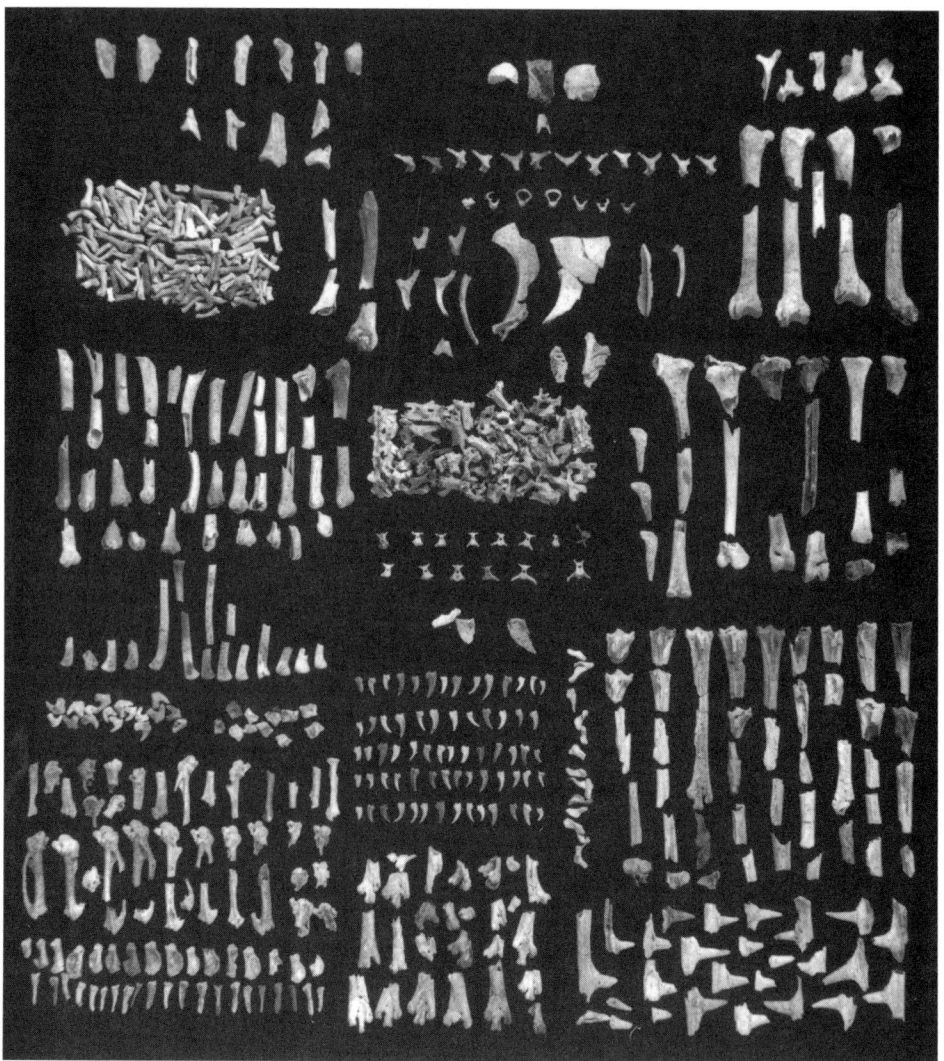

FIGURE 14.7. Burnt chicken bones, mainly foot bones, from cockerels, from domestic sacrifices in the garden of the house and bar of Amarantus at Pompeii (Powell 1995–1996; photograph by N. Bradford).

been a bar or wine shop in Pompeii exposed a rectangular cist containing remains of a minimum of 17 chickens. The extremities of the birds present, mostly bones of the foot, were burned (Figure 14.7). The ratio of spurred to unspurred tarsometatarsi was 38:3, showing that the great majority were cockerels. They were associated with figs and stone-pine nuts, plants traditionally included with household sacrifices, making it clear that the chicken remains too were from domestic sacrifices (Powell 1995–1996).

In Roman times, the temples in which chickens were sacrificed in the largest numbers were those dedicated to Mercury, and to the exotic deities Mithras and Isis. At the temple of Mercury on the hill at Uley in southwest England (Levitan 1993), among the large assemblage of sacrificed goats and chickens were birds of both sexes and all ages (Chapter 3). At the Temples of Isis in Egypt the bullock was the usual sacrificial animal in this cult, but when the cult was taken to the Western Mediterranean the chicken seems to have taken over as the sacrificial animal. In this way the cult was allying itself with other contemporary local cults (Lignereux et al. 1995). At the temple of Isis at Bélo, near modern Gibraltar, charred chicken remains were found in a blackened layer near the temple of the early first century. There were more hens than cocks, and both adult and immature birds were again present. In this case the heads and feet were lacking, presumably disposed of elsewhere. At the sanctuary of Isis and Magna Mater in Mainz, Germany, chickens were again overwhelmingly most frequent – in one phase more than 6,000 fragments were recovered. They were not butchered, but, like those at Bélo, they were burned. Unlike at Bélo, most were male.

In Mithraism, cocks were central to the rite. Mithraism, like the cult of Isis, was one of the mystery cults which originated in the Near East and spread throughout the Roman Empire in the first three centuries AD. The deity was identified with the invincible sun, and the crowing of the cock at dawn was seen as a welcome to the rising sun. In the temple of Mithras at Künzing in Germany, referred to in Chapter 4, 18 per cent (7,591 bones) of the faunal remains were of domestic chicken (see Table 4.8); this was in contrast to the local town, where chickens were only 1 per cent (von den Driesch & Pöllath 2000). The excavations at the Mithraeum at Tienen in Belgium revealed an even more focussed deposit: one pit was filled with remains of what the pottery suggested was a single feast which had taken place during the second half of the third century AD. Out of nearly 14,000 bone and shell remains from the pit, more than 7,500 were chicken bones, and a further 2,000 fragments, too small to be identified, were also probably from chicken. The estimated minimum is 238 chickens, more than two thirds of the animals present. The other remains from the pit were from a few fish, piglets, and young lambs (Lentacker et al. 2004). Chickens were also prominent in other Mithraic temples in Europe, from Aquincum in Hungary to London. There, in the temple of Mithras at Walbrook, chickens were the most frequent species in the first phase but were fewer in later phases, when the cult of Bacchus took over (King 2005).

In Künzing, the mammals were mainly immature but more than 70 per cent of the chickens were mature. Most elements were present, but again heads and feet were few. The tarsometatarsi were burnt, as at Pompeii. At Tienen, subadult chickens made up about one third of the total. No statistics were given for the ratio of spurred tarsometatarsi, but measurements of the humerus – unexpectedly – showed a unimodal distribution, in contrast to assemblages from contemporary sites where size was bimodal (Chapter 11). From this the authors proposed that all the sacrificed birds at Tienen were male. At both sites, head and foot bones were few, indicating that these had been removed before the chickens were cooked and eaten (Lentacker et al. 2004).

Sacrifice of Other Birds

At both Mainz and Pompeii, small songbirds as well as chickens were sacrificed. At Pompeii (see Chapter 6) they were members of the thrush family, but at Mainz most were finches (Hochmuth et al. 2005).

Bird Mummies

Nowhere was the symbolic role of birds given physical form more dramatically than in the temples and catacombs of Egypt, where mummified birds were deposited. Using the techniques with which they mummified the human dead, the ancient Egyptians mummified birds and the other animals. One bird was seen as the actual incarnation of the god with which the bird was associated. After death, this bird would be mummified. Most of the vast number of bird mummies were votive offerings, dedicated to the corresponding deity (Houlihan & Goodman 1986; Ikram 2005).

A few mummified birds were thought to be pets (see Chapter 13) and some were food mummies, so they had real rather than symbolic significance. One goose mummy in a burial had been prepared for eating: the head was removed, the wing was cut off at the distal humerus, and the feet were cut off at the distal tibiotarsus. The liver and gizzards were replaced in the body, just as in dressed poultry today. The carcass was wrapped in linen and interred in a wooden coffinet carved in the shape of the body. The fact that the bird was butchered and ready for consumption indicated that it was intended as food for the dead (Ikram 2005). There are examples of pigeons and ducks which have received the same treatment in Egypt, but none of chickens. Since the practice of mummifying animals continued into the Graeco-Roman period, by which time chickens were well known in some parts of Egypt, this is surprising. It may have something to do with the fact that the chicken was a recent and alien introduction (Chapter 11), whereas mummification was carried out to emphasise the national Egyptian character of the cult practice (Ikram 2005).

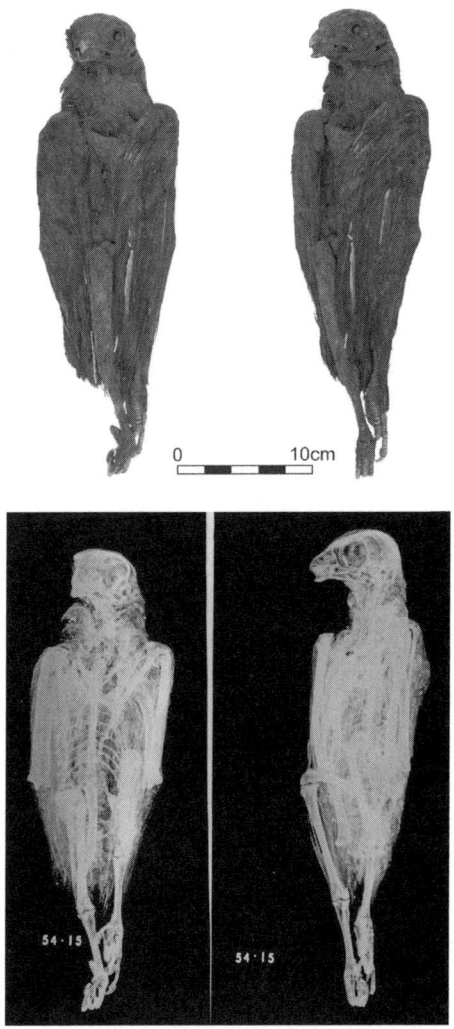

FIGURE 14.8. Mummified saker falcon, *Falco cherrug*, from Saqqara, Egypt; an extra femur has been included with the bird. The top section shows the external view; the bottom shows the X-ray view (photographs courtesy of The Natural History Museum, London).

At Saqqara, falcons and the sacred ibis were mummified. They were dedicated to the gods and placed in the catacombs. It has been calculated that up to 10,000 mummified ibises were produced each year at Saqqara; the sacred ibises must have been very carefully reared and husbanded to produce such large numbers. Most of the Saqqara mummies in the Natural History Museum are of falcons: examination and X-rays have shown that the birds were sometimes incomplete when mummified and many have broken bones, perhaps because they were deliberately killed (Cooper 2007). A saker falcon mummy included parts of other birds with the main mummy (Figure 14.8).

An astonishing series of up to four million sacred ibises were placed as votive deposits in the catacombs at Hermopolis Magna (Tuna el-Gebel), together with baboons, falcons, and other animals. After mummification, the birds were sealed within lidded pottery jars. The earliest consisted of macerated bones wrapped in linen. Later, bitumen and oil of turpentine was used to help with preservation. Eventually the entire bird was embalmed in a characteristic position with the beak pointing downwards. Some of these mummies did not contain the whole skeleton but just a few bones, or even just feathers or reeds. One explanation for this was that the priests and their assistants who produced the votive mummies in large numbers for pilgrims did the work carelessly, but a recent study suggests that the rite may actually have required the cult servants to collect up and mummify all dead birds, feathers, and even nesting material from the breeding site in the lake around the sacred enclosure. This could explain the single examples of mummies of other species such as flamingo; if another bird got into the sacred enclosure, it too became sacred and had to be preserved (von den Driesch et al. 2005). The fact that ibises of all ages were mummified (see Table 3.5 in Chapter 3) may suggest that it was birds which died naturally which were mummified, but if so, this calls in question why some of the falcon mummies had broken bones.

Temple Furniture and Rites

As well as being sacrificed, remains of birds were sometimes used as temple accoutrements. Raptor remains were found at Qasr Ibrim in Lower Egypt in a temple of the early first millennium AD. A large sandstone statue of a hawk as well as painted wooden plaques on which were depicted hawks, gazelles, and snakes were found inside the temple. In the outer room the excavators recovered avian wing bones. They comprised a pair of humeri and three carpometacarpi of spotted eagle, three humeri of peregrine falcon of which two seemed to be a pair, and a right humerus of the Cape or spotted eagle owl. The species, the intact state of the bones, the fact that all are from the wing, and that some were pairs from the same individual left little doubt that they were not food remains but that the wings formed part of the temple furniture (Rowley-Conwy 1989).

At Catal Höyük, and also at other early Neolithic sites in Anatolia and the Near East, there are hints that people performed a crane dance, wearing the wings of real cranes. The bones of a wing (Figure 14.9) were recovered from an area associated with Building 1 at Catal Höyük, where they had lain over a cattle horn, several goat horns, and a dog skull. The radius and ulna were modified: three sets of deep cut marks were visible on the proximal radius and on the ulna in the interosseus space between

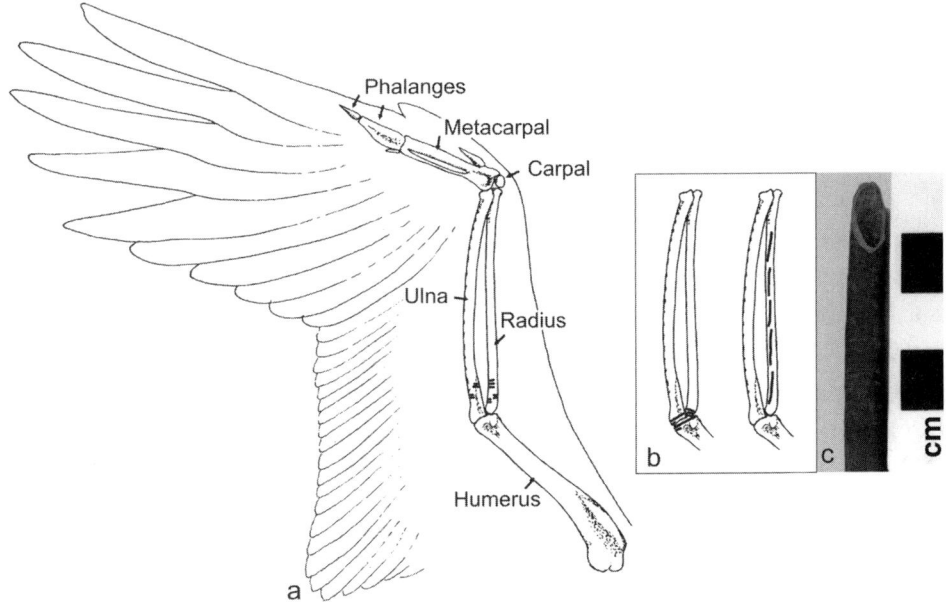

FIGURE 14.9. Cut marks on the radius and ulna of a crane, *Grus grus*, from Catal Höyük suggesting the wing had been worn or suspended: a, wing showing the location of the cut marks; b, hypothetical dismembering and filleting cuts for comparison; c, ulna showing cut marks (Russell & McGowan 2003; photograph by N. Russell).

these elements. As this is an area which would not be touched by disarticulation cuts and does not yield meat, and the authors suggested that a hole had been pierced through the skin at this point through which a fibre was run to attach the wing to a dancer's shoulder. This would allow the suspended wing to withstand stress from motion (Russell & McGowan 2003). Dancing cranes are featured on a painted wall of one of the shrines (F.V.1) at Catal Höyük; the crane carving at Göbekli Tepe has already been mentioned. All crane species perform a mating dance, and cultures all over the world have devised crane dances in imitation. In the classical world the crane dance was referred to by Homer and Plutarch: for them it was a winding dance first performed by Theseus to celebrate his escape from the Cretan Minotaur.

MEDICINE BUNDLES AND TALISMANS

Medicine Bundles

Medicine bundles were collections of bones and other objects wrapped in a skin which were owned and curated by an individual, a family, or a community. A bundle might protect an individual or a group from sickness or evil, or it might confer special power and rights on the holder. Individual bones had a similar significance as talismans, amulets, or fetishes. Medicine bundles were used in the Great Plains in the United States at the time of contact and have been used all over the Americas. The core of the bundle was the skeleton of a bird, often a raptor but sometimes a macaw or a turkey (Ubelekar & Wedel 1975). Hummingbird bundles are still sold in some markets in Mexico; they are considered to be love fetishes (Corona-M. 2005).

Two sets of bone remains found at the Mobridge Site in South Dakota, clearly not normal food refuse, were identified as medicine bundles by comparison with examples in museum collections. One set, from a grave (Burial 71c), consisted of a skull, wing bones minus the digits, the femora, tibiotarsi, and tarsometatarsi of a prairie falcon. The skull was cut. The second was a cut skull of a raven, also with the wing bones, including the major wing digit, the femora, and tibiotarsi and one tarsometatarsus. The X-ray of a complete medicine bundle in the Museum of Anthropology at the University of Michigan showed that it contained a set of elements similar to those described wrapped in a cured skin. The skull has the back cut away, and wing and leg bones are present, but none of the elements from the body. Another medicine bundle consisted of the 'skin of an owl filled out over a stuffing of dried grass with both wings folded in a natural attitude and both legs' (Ubelekar & Wedel 1975). A skull of a whooping crane collected from a burial site of the Assiniboine Indians at Ft Berthold, North Dakota, in the nineteenth century also has the occiput cut. It too is thought to be from a medicine bundle. Cutting away the back of the skull may have permitted the brain to be removed and allowed the skull to be attached to the bundle.

An assemblage from Phipps Mill Creek, Iowa, consisted of elements thought to be generated by the production of medicine bundles. Almost 90 per cent of the assemblage was foot bones of raptors: hawks, eagles, and turkey vulture. One feature contained more than 260 broken and splintered tarsometatarsi, approximately 100 phalanges, and more than 80 talons (ungual phalanges) together with shell beads, sherds, and other objects. The deposit was dated to about 900 BP (AD 1100). The tarsometatarsi were smashed and some of the ends were burned. The author rejected the possibility that the damage was caused by the method of capture or the removal of marrow, which is scant in the tarsometatarsi, and concluded that the feet were deliberately smashed to release the spirit of the birds as they were ritually killed. The fact that the rest of the body was missing suggested that the bodies were traded to other villages, perhaps as medicine bundles. The contemporary Mitchell site in South Dakota, for instance, had elements from legs and wings, but no feet (Fishel 1997).

Table 14.2. *Element distribution of red-tailed hawks from a pit in the settlement of La Playa, Sonora, Mexico*

Skeletal elements	NISP	Body regions
Vertebrae	57	Vertebral column
Coracoid	15	Pectoral girdle
Scapula	6	
Humerus	8	Wings
Radius	19	
Ulna	7	
Carpometacarpus	5	
Carpalia	22	
Pelvis	4	Pelvic girdle
Femur	17	Hind limbs
Tibiotarsus	14	
Tarsometatarsus	15	
Phalanges	124	

Note: The remains of red-tailed hawk, *Buteo jamaicensis*, in the pit are thought to represent medicine bundles.
Source: Data are from Martinez-Lira et al. (2005, tab. 1).

Remains of at least ten red-tailed hawks in a pit in the settlement of La Playa on the Gulf of California were also thought to represent medicine bundles. These were deliberately buried some time shortly before AD 150. Other pits at the site contained food refuse with cut marks and traces of burning, but the remains from this one pit lacked these. Skulls and sterna were absent and there was a paucity of bones from the pelvic area, but many normally fragile bones such as the carpal bones, vertebrae, and foot phalanges survived (Table 14.2), suggesting that the bones had been protected by skins (Martinez-Lira et al. 2005). Though the skeletal elements do not correspond with those from the medicine bundles found further north, they do at least show that hawks were given special treatment when buried at this early date in Mexico. As well as being curated in medicine bundles, in Mexico the body parts of birds were used in traditional medicine, but in most cases the references show that it was the soft tissue and 'grit' or gizzard stones which were ingested rather than the bones (Corona-M. 2005, fig. 1).

Medicine bundles and talismans owned by a community or lineage would be handed on from one generation to the next, so they would survive only incidentally, but a medicine bundle which belonged to an individual might be buried with the owner. Certain suites of bones can be recognised as medicine bundles, even if the wrapping has decayed and they are found outside contexts which were clearly of a ritual nature.

Talismans

Ethnographic references to talismans of bone do not suggest that one skeletal element rather than another was selected. Though the skull might seem to be an obvious choice – an illustration of the shield of Chief Rotten Belly has a crane skull attached (Gilbert et al. 1981, fig. 2) – it does not necessarily seem to have been chosen over other elements. In the Kalam country of Papua New Guinea the family life of the great woodswallow, conspicuous because it nested in the gardens, epitomised domestic virtues. Good housewives were likened to swallows. A ritual was performed over a newly married couple which involved the burning of wood swallow feathers in the fire, and the presentation to the bride of the beak and plumage of the bird for her to keep in a bag (Bulmer 1979, 70). This ethnographic account of the origin of a talisman makes it clear that the only circumstances in which such a bone might be recognised would be if it was protected by being in a bag, or was accompanied by other ritual objects, or, as already discussed, if it was found in a grave. The identification of a single bone as a talisman or fetish is much trickier. It would only be worth considering if the element was found in a position which suggested that it had been suspended around the neck or on a belt, or if found with other more durable objects in a bundle.

SKY BURIAL

Grave goods, votive offerings, and birds consumed at funerals and ritual feasts are easily recognised, but other birds which may have played a role in funerary rites are more elusive. Today in the so-called sky burial rites of the Parsees in India and the Tibetans, the dead are carried to a special place where they can be consumed by vultures. In Bombay the dead are ceremoniously carried to the dakhmas or towers of silence where white-rumped vultures and other birds such as kites and crows consume and disperse the corpse. In Tibet the bearded vulture is encouraged specifically for its role in dispersing bodies after death. The corpse is carried to a hilltop, where it is ritually dismembered by professional dissectors, and once that is complete, the waiting vultures are 'called' to the site (Peters & Schmidt 2004).

There is iconographic and archaeological evidence that vultures played this role in the Near East between the twelfth and seventh millennia BC (Solecki 1977; Gourichon

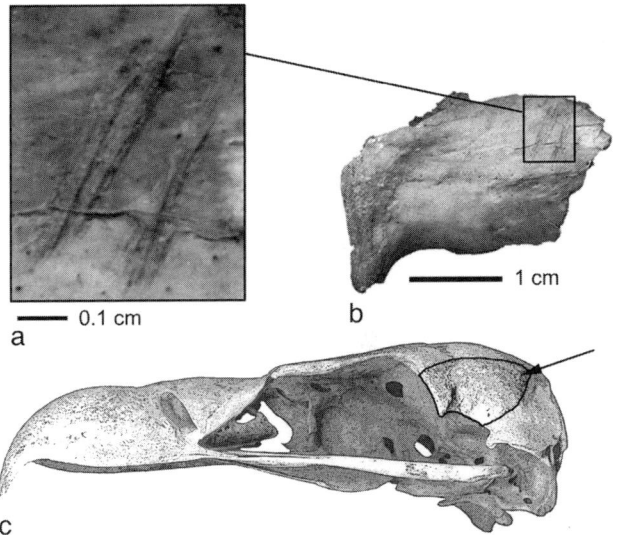

FIGURE 14.10. Temporal bone of the skull of a griffon vulture, *Gyps fulvus*, from Pre-Pottery Neolithic Jerf el Ahmar, Syria, with cut marks from scalping: a, cut marks enlarged; b, fragment showing location of cuts; c, outline of skull showing area of surviving fragment (Gourichon 2002; photographs by L. Gourichon).

2002; Helmer et al. 2004; Peters & Schmidt 2004; Peters et al. 2005). At Catal Höyük a wall painting shows griffon vultures pecking at headless corpses. The painting includes a human figure that Peters believes was intended as the professional 'caller'. Limestone sculptures of vultures were excavated at the sites of Nevali Cori in Anatolia and Jerf el Ahmar in Syria, and disarticulated remains were found at Jerf el Ahmar, Göbekli Tepe, and Gürcütepe, also in Anatolia. At Jerf el Ahmar, bones of the griffon vulture made up 12 per cent of the total assemblage (Gourichon 2002). Their phalanges were collected as amulets, as we saw in Chapter 9. On one skull, there were cut marks on the parietal bone, showing how the scalp had been removed (Figure 14.10). These sites were probably used for rituals associated with the deceased. Ethnographic analogy, together with the archaeological and zooarchaeological evidence, demonstrates the importance of vultures in the ritual life in the Pre-Pottery Neolithic and also its probable role.

Did raptors and ravens fill the same role in prehistoric Europe? We are ignorant of many aspects of the funerary ritual in much of Neolithic and Iron Age Europe. Where the dead were not buried in cemeteries, human remains survive as disarticulated elements, placed in chambered tombs in the Neolithic, but found as disarticulated elements incorporated into pits and occupation deposits in the Iron Age. The degree of disarticulation suggests that the dead were exposed, in which case avian scavengers such as the white-tailed sea eagle, the buzzard, and also the raven may well have had some role in dispersing the human remains (Baxter 1993). The skeletons of a minimum of five white-tailed sea eagles excavated from the Neolithic tomb of Isbister in Orkney – the 'Tomb of the Eagles' (Jones 1998) – have now been dated to a millennium later than the Neolithic use of the tomb (Pitts 2006), so they are now known not to be associated with the Neolithic funerary rituals there, but elsewhere the skeletons of these birds sometimes received special treatment (Serjeantson in press-c). As with the vultures in the Middle East in the Early Holocene, their role in death rites may have prompted the special treatment.

SPECIAL DEPOSITS AND RITUAL REFUSE

Several authors have attempted to find ways of separating out special deposits or 'ritual rubbish' from day-to-day domestic rubbish. Some of their approaches can be applied to birds. Grant and later Hill identified 'special animal deposits' from Iron Age sites in England from some of the subtle ways in which they stood out from domestic refuse. 'Special deposits' were placed in pits, apparently deliberately, sometimes in association with other distinctive material remains (Grant 1991; Hill 1996). Though bird remains are in general very rare from Iron Age sites in southern Britain, most of those present are corvids (ravens and crows) and buzzards, which were buried in pits. Crows are commensal around human settlements (see Chapter 15), so these could be natural deaths, but the fact that they were buried in pits often as whole or partial skeletons makes it likely that they had some ritual significance for the Iron Age population (Serjeantson 1991). As suggested, they may have been associated with the treatment of the dead.

Muir and Driver have shown that it is possible to identify what they term 'ritual refuse' at Pueblo sites. They divided the faunal remains from a group of Pueblo sites into three categories: common refuse, ritual internments, and ritual refuse. Identification of the first and second was fairly straightforward. The last category is the most difficult to identify, as it can be confused with common refuse. Their criteria are those used by Grant and Hill. Ritual rubbish was distinguished from common refuse when it contained species which were never or rarely eaten such as deer and raptors, when bones did not show traces of butchery and consumption, and when collections of these special bones were found together. From this they were able to show that at Sand Canyon Pueblo the ritual refuse, which consisted mainly of remains of wild birds (Table 14.3), was concentrated towards the centre of the site in a D-shaped, bi-walled structure. Both the contents of the room and also its unique shape marked it out as a room where ceremonies took place (Muir & Driver 2004).

Table 14.3. *Ritual refuse: wild birds from a D-shaped structure at Sand Canyon Pueblo*

Common name	Kiva Floor	Kiva Roof	Room Floor	Room Roof	Midden	Other	Total
Poor-will, *Phalaenoptilus nutalli*				1			1
Mourning dove, *Zenaida macroura*				1		2	3
Sandhill crane, *Grus canadensis*		2					2
Raven, *Corvus corax*					4	6	10
Jay, crow, or raven			3	3	8	16	30
Small passeriform		2		1	6		9
Small bird		4		1		10	15
Great horned owl, *Bubo virginianus*	1						1
Owl				1			1
Hawk					7		7
Falconid		1			1	2	4
Turkey vulture, *Cathartes aura*			8			1	9
Total	1	9	11	8	26	37	92

Note: The wild birds from within the D-shaped structure account for 64 per cent of all wild birds from Sand Canyon Pueblo excavations. The NISP is shown for wild birds from various contexts within the structure. 'Other' includes disturbed and indeterminate deposits.
Source: Data are from Muir and Driver (2004, fig. 4).

A much earlier example of the ritual treatment of raven skeletons has been identified. Driver argued that two ravens from Charlie Lake Cave, with dates of 10,500 – 9500 BC, comprised special deposits. The site is distinctive: it is a cave marked by a large isolated rock known as the Parapet. The birds were buried in front of the rock. The skeleton of the first was in good condition, with the only missing elements lost through natural decay. The second was less well preserved but it was found with a microblade and some ochre. None had cut marks or gnawing. In theory the ravens might have died as they roosted on the rock, but neither had been scavenged by other predators as would have been expected, so the most plausible explanation is that both were deliberately buried, perhaps as a means of memorializing the site (Driver 1999).

PRE-EMINENT SPECIES

It is clear from the foregoing discussion that certain birds stand out as having relationships with people which were not just those of prey and predator. As we have seen, the turkey and the scarlet macaw fall into this category in North America and the ibis and falcon in Egypt. The chicken, the raven, and several raptorial species have symbolic importance worldwide.

Chickens

It is paradoxical that the chicken, so important for providing food (Chapter 11), has also played a major role in sacrifice, funerary rites, and divination which was unconnected with their food value. The earliest references to chickens are to the crowing of cocks which greeted the dawn and to cockfighting as an emblem of warfare. It is likely that the chicken was first carried from the East into Western Asia and Europe because it carried ritual importance. The fact that when it first appeared in a region it was considered to be a sacred bird can be seen in the many places where the earliest records are from graves: chickens first appear in Slovakia and Germany from the first century BC in cemeteries (Benecke 1994, 368). MacDonald discussed the reason why the chicken rapidly became the primary sacrificial animal in West Africa, where even today it has many roles in addition to providing food. In the Yoruba regions the Giant Chicken created the Earth's terrestrial surface by its scratching, perhaps at some time after its introduction, having taken over that role from the native pigeon. At first its rarity in West Africa probably gave the chicken prestige, but as it became more familiar, the exaggerated differences in behaviour between the cock and the hen, the fecundity of the hen, and the crow of the cock in the morning made 'good pegs upon which to hang the regalia of symbolism' (MacDonald 1995).

Raptors, Vultures, and Owls

For quite different reasons, the diurnal raptors and owls were symbols of power (or dread). Their importance in human cosmology is affirmed by the many occasions on which they were given special burial and, as we saw in earlier chapters, how the feathers and bones were selected for tools and ornament. Though the scavenging behaviour of vultures must have been the feature which first drew them to human attention, they were valued in some parts of the world, as we saw in Chapter 9, for their wing bones which were used to make flutes.

Table 14.4. *Worldwide beliefs about the raven,* Corvus corax

General and specific actions by ravens	Society
1. Ravens find animals	
a. Locate game animals for human hunters	Blackfoot
b. Invoked in song to call bison	Cheyenne, Kokuyon, Dene, Apache
c. Drive caribou to hunters	Dene
d. Help elk find straying wife	Blackfoot
2. Ravens scavenge	
a. Steal bait from traps	Nunamiut, Koyukon
b. Scavenges coyote's bison kill	Mandan
c. Scavenges dead bison	Blackfoot
d. Hunters attract bears by imitating noises made by ravens while scavenging	Koyukon
e. Scavenge human dead on battlefields	Medieval Europe
f. Hunters leave part of their kill for ravens	Dene, Medieval Europe
3. Ravens communicate with people	
a. Human placenta fed to ravens allows child to understand them	Kwakiutl
b. Predict disasters and epidemics	Dene
c. Warn of storms at sea	Various, Alaska
d. Men wear raven skins to warn of enemies	Blackfoot, Cheyenne, Sioux
e. Calls over camp tell of approaching people	Blackfoot
f. Tells man where son is hidden	Mandan
g. Carried on ships, to be released and guide ship to shore	Europe
h. Brings message during vision quest	Blackfoot
i. The sun's messenger in cult of Mithras	Roman
j. Gather news for Odin	Norse

Note: The beliefs are connected with the raven's ability to find animals, its scavenging habits, and its call.

Source: Data are from Driver (1999, tab. 1).

The Raven

Worldwide, the raven, creator of the world and trickster, was the subject of a constellation of beliefs which had to do with its ability to find animals for the human hunter, its scavenging habits, and its calls, in which it communicates with people (Table 14.4). More sinisterly, ravens, like vultures and white-tailed sea eagles, were scavengers of human corpses: in the Anglo-Saxon poem *Judith* it was 'the corpse greedy bird, the black coated raven'. The crow, like the raven communicative and a scavenger, shares many of these characters; folk taxonomy may hardly have distinguished the two. In North America, and in Europe from the first millennium BC, ravens were sometimes given special burial in pits and wells. As well as occurring in Iron Age pits, their skeletons have been excavated in many towns and forts in Roman Britain. Two from a pit in Sheepen, the Roman town of Camulodum, were thought to have been foundation deposits, and one from a 9-m-deep shaft in Dunstable was thought to be a votive deposit (Parker 1988).

DISCUSSION AND CONCLUSION

A myriad of symbolic roles has been assigned to birds in cultures all over the world, and they have featured in many human rituals. Many more than those discussed here were appreciated – and possibly given ritual treatment – for those qualities for which people appreciate birds, that is, their song, their colourful plumage, their flight, and even, as in the case of the crane, their dance. In many of the examples discussed here, skeletons and other remains were found in a context such as a grave or shrine which was clearly a ritual environment. Outside such contexts, certain types of finds may suggest that remains had a symbolic character, especially when found in combination. The species, the condition of the skeletal elements, and the associated finds may suggest that there was significance beyond the material for the people who deposited the remains. As we have seen, contrary to the pessimistic conclusion of Higgs, many of the non-material roles of birds in symbol and ritual can indeed be detected. Archaeological finds confirm how long-lived some of these roles are.

15

Birds in the Environment

The ways in which birds have fulfilled material and spiritual needs of humans have been the subject of the preceding chapters but here the wider environment and the birds themselves take centre stage. Two different but related topics are examined: (1) the role of birds in understanding the environment in the past; and (2) changes in the distribution of birds in the past, including extinctions. The topics often interact. It is these areas of research which most interested the ornithologists and palaeontologists to whom bird remains from archaeological sites were submitted in the nineteenth and early twentieth century (Dawson 1969); since then, as the earlier chapters of this book have shown, the scope of archaeological bird studies has widened, but reconstruction of environments and past distributions remain important subjects of research.

The evolution and the early avian palaeontological record (Feduccia 1999) are outside the scope of this book. Here, we shall look at changes in the environment and in avian distributions during the last glaciation and in the transition to the early Holocene. The subsequent changes discussed here were often a consequence of clearance for agriculture, human colonisation of ever larger areas of the globe, and the growth of towns.

BIRDS AS ENVIRONMENTAL INDICATORS

For both research aims, it is essential to use the information from both natural and archaeological assemblages (Steadman & Kirch 1990). Each has its own biases. In the Pleistocene era, much of the data are from cave assemblages, which may be non-anthropogenic, anthropogenic, or a combination of both, as discussed in Chapters 5 and 6. In the Holocene era, archaeological assemblages are the main source of information. Whether the aim is palaeontological or archaeological reconstruction, understanding the origin of the assemblage is important, since no assemblage contains a complete sample of the local avifauna (Morales 1993b; Causey et al. 2005). This is even the case with natural collections; the Rancho La Brea tar pits contained mostly turkey and raptors, not because these were the most frequent species in the area but because the turkeys were attracted to the surface of the deposit to feed, and the raptors were then attracted to the turkeys and themselves became entrapped (Bochenski & Campbell 2006).

Each type of predator has a very different catchment area: that of a white-tailed sea eagle is between 30 and 70 km^2; human hunters range up to 20 km from a camp site (Vita-Finzi & Higgs 1970), while the territory of a barn owl is no more than about 3 km around the roost. Each predator selects prey of a different size: owls sample the small vertebrates in their territory (Pichon 1991) while carnivores and humans concentrate on larger prey, giving a bias towards larger avian species. There are, for instance, very few of the local passerines in human middens, since small birds were too much trouble to catch and prepare (see Chapter 10). Indeed, if more than one predator is involved, as in some of the Gibraltar caves (see later), the range of species present is increased, which is desirable for ecological reconstruction.

Because humans hunted selectively, the absence of a species from an archaeological assemblage does not equate to its absence from the environment. The little auk was absent from food remains of the seventeenth-century whalers on Spitsbergen not because it did not breed on Spitsbergen at the time but because fowling was done in autumn and winter when the little auk was at sea (Prummel & Zeiler 2002). Another potential bias in anthropogenic assemblages is the presence of birds which were traded or exchanged, something which even took place in hunting societies. Remains of manx shearwater and gannet have been found on inland sites in England in the Middle Ages. Finds such as these can be wrecks (Driver & Hobson 1992; Stewart 2002; Cooper 2005), but in this case it is much more likely that they were birds traded as food (Serjeantson et al. 1993; Albarella & Thomas 2002). People also transported and traded live birds, feathers, and individual elements as medicine bundles, talismans, ornaments, and tools, as discussed in earlier chapters. People may even have used bones from earlier deposits for tool-making; for instance, it has been suggested that later cultures in New Zealand used bones of moa for tools after the birds themselves were extinct, which influenced discussions of the date of their extinction before radiocarbon dating became available (Anderson 1989b, 112).

Correct identification to taxon (see Chapter 4) is extremely important for ecological reconstruction, but numbers are less so. Most significant information comes from the presence or absence of a species, as we see in studies from different places and dates (Bramwell 1960; Grayson 1981; Tyrberg 1995; Cooper 2005). Relative abundance can also be informative. The number of occurrences of a species in the archaeological record was compared between Ireland and mainland Britain to investigate whether species absent on Ireland had been extirpated or had never arrived. Ireland has more than one tenth as many records of open ground species and water-birds as Britain and a similar number of woodland birds but fewer than 4 per cent as many records of owls. The relative numbers suggest that the tawny owl and probably also the short- and long-eared owls never became established in Ireland, perhaps because the absence of so many small mammal species deprived them of adequate prey (Yalden & McCarthy 2004).

The presence of immature birds is informative. 'As far as palaeoecological interpretation of birds is concerned, positive identification of a breeding population is the ultimate achievement for two fundamental reasons. Firstly, it establishes the seasonal status of a given species and secondly, the breeding distributions of modern species can often be more clearly defined in terms of ecological parameters than their wintering regions' (Cooper 2005, 106). Identifying an area where birds once bred – and perhaps no longer do so – relies on finds of immature birds, whose presence suggests breeding nearby. Medullary bone (see Chapter 3) also confirms breeding females. Although medullary bone normally forms only after the female reaches the breeding ground, in geese, for example, build-up may begin while the birds are at the final staging areas en route to the breeding grounds (Gotfredsen 2002). Eighteen species from the Pleistocene deposits in the Gibraltar caves had evidence of breeding (Table 15.1), of which two no longer breed in southern Iberia. Two species of scoter, velvet and common, were represented by immature tarsometatarsi. The velvet scoter today breeds north of 55° longitude, so in 55,000 BP, the date of the deposit, its breeding range must have extended as far south as southern Spain (Cooper 2005).

The Study of Environmental Change

Environmental and climate change in the past, once the province of a few specialists, is now of vital interest to us all. The sources of information about past ecological conditions include lithology, pollen, invertebrates (ostracods and diatoms), as well as macrobotanical and vertebrate remains. For Pleistocene environments, mammals have traditionally given more information than other vertebrates and birds have had 'a reputation for being both scarce and uninformative' (Cooper 2005), but recently authors have made the point that birds have some important advantages over micromammals. They have distinct and sometimes very narrow environmental requirements, and their environmental tolerances are well known, thanks to two

Table 15.1. *Bird species from four Late Pleistocene cave deposits on Gibraltar with positive evidence of breeding*

Taxon	Status	Devil's Tower	Ibex Cave	Vanguard Cave	Gorham's Cave
Alectoris sp.	R	B/M	–	B	B
Melanitta fusca	W	–	–	–	B
Melanitta nigra	I	–	–	–	B
Gyps fulvus	I	–	–	B	–
Falco naumanni	S	B	–	B	B
Falco cf. *tinnunculus*	I	M	–	–	–
Columba cf. *livia*	R	–	–	–	B
Columba cf. *oenas*	I	–	–	B	–
Columba livia/oenas	I	B/M	–	B	B/M
Columba palumbus	I	–	–	B/M	–
Bubo bubo	R	–	–	–	B
cf. *Strix aluco*	R	B	–	–	–
Tachymarptis melba	S	–	–	B	–
Apus apus/pallidus	S	–	–	B	B/M
Hirundo sp.	I	–	–	B	B
Cyanopica cyanus	R	–	–	B	–
Pyrrhocorax pyrrhocorax	R	B	B	B	B
Corvus monedula	I	–	–	B	–
cf. *Corvus corone/frugilegus*	I	–	–	–	B

Note: R = resident, W = winter, I = indeterminate, S = summer breeder, B = breeding, and M = migratory.
Source: Data are from Cooper (2005, tab. 1).

centuries or more of ornithological observations (Cramp 1977, 1980; Hoyo et al. 1992).

In a study of the palaeoenvironment of South Australia, Baird used the bird remains from four caves because he regarded fossil bird assemblages as 'more precise indicators of Late Quaternary environments than microfloral and micromammalian assemblages' (Baird 1989, 241). His reasons were fourfold. First, the ecological niche of the target taxon could be defined with accuracy, compared, for instance, with nocturnal mammals where it is less well known. Secondly, avian assemblages are present throughout the Late Quaternary period of Australia. Third, bird remains can be identified to genus and often to species, unlike, for instance, pollen, which can often only be taken to family. Finally, the taphonomy of the deposits could be determined. In the caves studied, material derived from four sources: the barn owl, the Tasmanian devil (*Sarcophilus harrisii*), a natural trap, and a pitfall. As all catchments would have been circular territories close to the fossil deposits, the avifauna was a more reliable source of local information than the pollen, which could have travelled an unknown distance and from an unknown direction (Baird 1989). The same argument was used in a study of the Old Crow Basin in the Yukon in northern Canada. The various duck species suggested that there had been local episodes of warmer wetter conditions in the past than did the pollen, which consistently reflected cold steppic conditions (Fitzgerald 1991).

While biases in prey selection normally preclude using the absence of evidence as evidence of absence, it has been used in at least one case where very large samples were concerned. Tyrberg surveyed 84 assemblages ('faunas') from 40 sites from the Lower Pleistocene to the Holocene; he found that ptarmigan and willow grouse were the most abundant species in Europe in cold phases of the Pleistocene, present in 100 per cent of all sites with a fauna of more than 15 species. Tyrberg argued therefore that their absence from an assemblage of at least this size did indicate a real absence. As these two grouse species were the principle prey of both humans (see Chapter 10) and raptors (Chapter 5) in the Pleistocene, the origin of the assemblages was immaterial to the argument. The data showed that in the warmest stages of the last glaciation (Isotope Stages 5a–5d), grouse were absent from Southwest France and the fringes of the Mediterranean. As we saw in Chapter 10, their place was taken mainly by partridges. At that time the ptarmigan was restricted to Eastern Europe and the British Isles, while the willow grouse was present throughout northern Europe (Figure 15.1). In the subsequent cold stages, both species were again present as far south as the Mediterranean and the Pyrenees (Tyrberg 1995).

Analogue and Non-Analogue Faunas

Inferring past environments depends on the use of modern analogues or palaeoecological proxies. It is assumed that 'birds co-vary with the vegetation and that vegetation co-varies with climate' (Baird 1989, 241) in the past as today. However, many assemblages are in fact 'non-analogue', that is, they contain species in combinations unknown anywhere today. Some environments must have existed in the Pleistocene which have no parallel today. In particular there was a compression of biomes along the shores of the Mediterranean. Southern Spain was one of a chain of *refugia* for temperate species throughout Late Glacial times; Italy, the Balkans, and the Caucasus held others (Sanchez Marco 2004; Cooper 2005).

There are, however, other reasons why what appear to be non-analogue faunas are present. A deposit may cover a wide date range, at a time when climate and

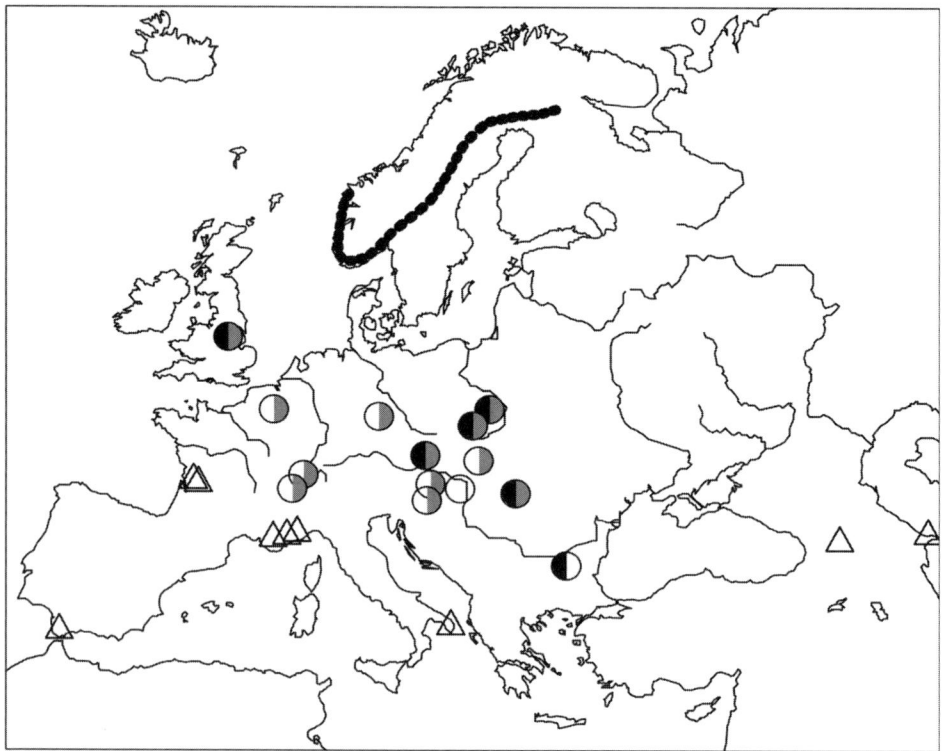

FIGURE 15.1. Map showing records of grouse, *Lagopus* spp., in Europe from Isotope Stages 5a–5d. Open circle indicates *Lagopus* sp. present; circle with left half shaded indicates ptarmigan, *L. muta*, present; circle with right half shaded, willow grouse, *L. lagopus*, present; circles with both halves shaded, both species present. Triangles signify faunas of more than ten species without *Lagopus*. The dotted curve marks the possible extent of the Scandinavian icecap during Isotope Stage 5d (Tyrberg 1995, fig. 6; drawing by T. Tyrberg).

environment were changing rapidly. Layers became mixed by bioturbation or burrowing animals. In the past, discrete layers were not always recognised in excavation. All these factors have been only too common in Pleistocene cave sites. Further, bird communities are usually taken to mean breeding communities, but a deposit may lie on a migration route, so species which migrate through the area may also be present. Birds on migration stop to feed or when under stress, and it is just at those times that they have a higher than usual chance of mortality (Steadman et al. 2002).

Four Late Pleistocene cave sites on Gibraltar had what might be regarded as non-analogue faunas, in that they contain northern species as well as those which breed in the area today (Table 15.1; also see Cooper 2005). Some bones may have been human prey, but most were from raptors, carnivores, and natural deaths. Cooper was largely able to rule out taphonomic reasons for the anomalous fauna, as control over the stratigraphy was meticulous and the layers from which the assemblages had come were closely dated. Rather than assume that Gibraltar had an environment for which there is no modern parallel, Cooper concluded that the fauna was explicable as deriving from a combination of breeding and migrating birds. Gibraltar is a bottleneck on two migration routes: a north-south route across the Straits of Gibraltar which is used by a very high proportion of Western European migratory birds and an east-west route used by seabirds entering and leaving the Mediterranean. Today, no less than 75 per cent of Western Palaearctic birds may occur on Gibraltar in the course of a year. Taking this into account, only about half a dozen of the species present have never been recorded in Gibraltar in recent times. The immature scoters referred to earlier indicated that at 55,000 BP there was an extension of Boreal water masses into the latitude of the Straits of Gibraltar (Cooper 2005). This is confirmed by another boreal species, the long-tailed duck, found in the Gibraltar caves and also in another contemporary site in Portugal.

PLEISTOCENE AND HOLOCENE CLIMATE CHANGE

The bird remains have been used to examine environmental change from the Late Pleistocene into the Early Holocene in several different parts of the world: North America, South Australia, North Africa, and the Near East.

Great Basin

The transition from the Late Pleistocene to Holocene conditions was the subject of the investigation of an alluvial channel in Nevada, which involved sedimentology, faunal study, and archaeology. A section was cut across the valley fill. The sediments at the base contained a substantial collection of Paleo-Indian tools, bifaces, points, and flakes, and a fauna with both anthropogenic and non-anthropogenic elements. The birds were thought to have been part of Paleo-Indian subsistence; certainly most were large species. All but two of the species present were waterfowl, indicative of wetlands in the vicinity of the site, but sharp-shinned hawk and black-billed magpie, today usually found in more mesic habitats, were also present. The avifauna together with the sediments indicated a moist period in the Younger Dryas between 9800 and 11,000 BP, a conclusion confirmed by other contemporary sites in the Great Basin. It has been succeeded by 8,000 years of a dry environment (Huckleberry et al. 2001).

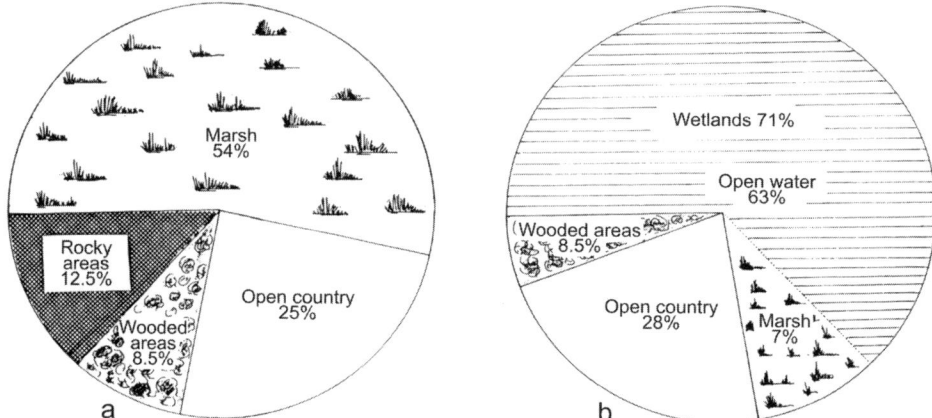

FIGURE 15.2. Environmental conditions at Ain Mallaha (Eynan) during the period of occupation from the eleventh to ninth millennia BC, as inferred from a, breeding and b, resident and migratory species (redrawn from Pichon 1991, figs. 6 and 7).

Southern Australia in the Late Pleistocene

The avifauna from the four Southern Australian cave sites referred to earlier indicated that there had been a lowering of precipitation around 30,000 years ago in South Australia which lasted until 10,000 BP, after which rainfall increased again to present-day levels (Baird 1989). This finding is very broadly in line with the conclusions about conditions in the Younger Dryas in the Great Basin.

The Near East in the Late Pleistocene

Most of the species from excavations at the Late Pleistocene (Natufian) sites of Hayonim and Ain Mallaha are still present in the area today as residents, winter visitors, or passage migrants. Of the 132 species from Hayonim and Ain Mallaha, only a dozen are no longer found in the area. As in Gibraltar, the species now absent are geese and ducks such as the mergansers which today are Palaearctic species. The little and great bustard which today, like the geese and ducks, winter north of the Levant, were also present. Their absence after the tenth millennium BP confirms the warming of the climate in the Holocene and also higher winter rains (Pichon 1991). At Ain Mallaha the wildfowl hunted by the inhabitants were from several different ecological zones: open water, marsh, woodland, open country, and marsh (Figure 15.2). The majority came from open water, and the site was indeed near a large inland lake at the beginning of the Holocene, the Lake of Huleh. Relative numbers of

Table 15.2. *Birds from an Early to Mid Holocene lakebed in the Erg of Murzuq*

Species	Ecological requirements
Ostrich, *Struthio camelus*	Savannah
Great crested grebe, *Podiceps cristatus*	Large water bodies, reed and water plant fringe
White stork, *Ciconia ciconia*	Marsh
Yellow-billed stork, *Mycteria ibis*	Slowly moving shallow water
Mallard, *Anas platyrhynchos*	Fresh or brackish water, wide environmental tolerance
Pintail, *Anas* cf. *acuta*	Small water bodies, reed and water plant fringe, fresh or brackish water
Ferruginous duck, *Aythya nyroca*	Slowly moving shallow water, reed and water plant fringe, fresh or brackish water
Quail, *Coturnix coturnix*	Marsh
Moorhen, *Gallinula chloropus*	Small water bodies, reed and water plant fringe
African fish eagle, *Haliaeetus vocifer*	Large water bodies, tree fringe

Note: The Erg of Murzuq is in the Eastern Sahara.
Source: Data are modified from Pachur and Peters (2001, tab. 1).

the different waterfowl show that wetlands diminished and open country increased over the centuries during which the site was occupied.

Holocene Environmental Change in the Eastern Sahara

Birds also contributed to understanding the palaeoclimate of the Eastern Sahara in the Early Holocene. Sediments in the bed of a former lake in the Erg of Murzuq in the Egyptian Eastern Desert which had held water between 8000 and 5000 BP preserved an invertebrate and vertebrate fauna. Some animals had died naturally in the lake and some remains were from campsites around the perimeter where pastoralists had used the lake for watering cattle and hunting. The birds were non-anthropogenic. 'Based on the ecological requirements of the different bird species (see Table 15.2), larger ... as well as smaller ... water bodies existed, with fresh to brackish, slowly moving, shallow waters, bordered by trees, reeds and other water plants and marshes' (Pachur & Peters 2001). The fish (cichlids and mochokids) confirmed the status of the lake as probably brackish at certain times of the year, while remains of mammals and ostrich which were also present indicated more varied ecological conditions of the wider hinterland.

The Early Holocene in Western Europe

The avifauna from Polderweg, a seasonal hunting camp on a dune in the Rhine delta in the Netherlands, consisted of the prey of the Late Mesolithic people who occupied the site in the eighth millennium BP. As well as demonstrating that the site was occupied in winter (Chapter 10), the bird remains revealed the former environment of the site. They came from two ecological groups. Nearly 90 per cent were wetland species, foremost among which were ducks, geese, and swans, but also red-throated diver, little grebe, herons, rails, and reed bunting. Their presence points to open, oxygen-rich water bordered by a lush vegetation of reeds. The remaining 10 per cent were characteristic of a wooded environment: sparrowhawk, buzzard, eagle owl, woodpecker, and woodcock. The botanical evidence from the site confirmed that both habitats had been present close to the site. Polderweg is just one example of the hundreds of Early Holocene sites in northern Europe where the predominance of waterfowl (Guminski 2005) confirms how the rising sea levels created wetland all over northern Europe.

The avifauna has assisted environmental reconstruction in a wide variety of sites, but – like all environmental evidence – it is best taken in conjunction with other evidence. Among the birds from the Near Eastern sites as well as the Gibraltar caves were some cold adapted species which disappeared at the end of the Pleistocene. The sites in each case confirmed the increasingly moist conditions at the end of the Pleistocene, with a site such as Polderweg in the Rhine delta having overwhelmingly wetland species. In areas which are arid today, such as the Sahara and the Great Basin, the wetlands present in the Late Pleistocene and Early Holocene had disappeared by about 8000 BP. There has since been little major change over the course of the Holocene, except where the environment has been altered by human activity, the subject of the second part of this chapter.

INTRODUCTIONS AND RANGE INCREASES

In the Holocene, many of the changes in avian distributions have been the result of human activity: species which are favoured by forest clearance, agriculture, and drainage have benefited at the expense of woodland and wetland birds. Some species flourished because of their association with human settlement. These include domesticates which became feral, commensal species, and some synanthropic species which have benefited from increasing numbers of humans.

Feral Domesticates

The most successful feral domesticate is the rock dove or town pigeon. These have established feral populations all over the world, thanks to their tolerance of towns and buildings which derives from their habit of nesting in caves (Chapter 12). Domesticated mallards have also reverted to a feral state all over their range, but, unlike pigeons, in many parts of the world they can rejoin their wild counterparts which are themselves highly tolerant of the presence of humans (O'Connor 1993). Few feral flocks of chickens and turkeys survive, since they need cover, a warm climate, and, above all, freedom from ground predators. In practice feral flocks occur mainly on islands. Feral chickens and turkeys have become established in Hawaii and other tropical islands. Some also survive in Florida and the states of the Southeastern United States, where temperature and environmental conditions resemble those in their native Southeast Asia (Brisbin 1993). The plumage of feral birds is variable (see Figure 12.7 in Chapter 12), but skeletally most revert to the size of the wild ancestor. The mute swan in England is a possible exception, as discussed in Chapter 13. Feral birds are difficult – perhaps impossible – to detect in the archaeological record since skeletal remains found outside the distribution range of the wild species would probably be interpreted as domestic.

Commensal and Synanthropic Species

A commensal species lives in a permanent close association with another and gains a benefit from the association without causing serious disadvantage, while synanthropes are adapted to living in association with humans and in habitats modified by human activity, but do not otherwise directly benefit. Even predators which become commensal increase in numbers to a much higher level than would be typical if they were living as predators in the wild, as is the case with kites living in cities (O'Connor 1998).

Birds Synanthropic with Hunters

Certain species may have been synanthropic with humans even before the beginnings of farming. The choughs and martins must have become tolerant of the hunters with whom they shared caves and rock shelters (Eastham 2001). It is likely that, as discussed in Chapter 14, the larger corvids have been synanthropic for millennia, bringing benefits to, and deriving benefits from, human hunters (Driver 1999). The bald eagle may have been synanthropic in the Pacific Northwest, its numbers encouraged by the waste generated seasonally when Bands living along the coast processed salmon for winter.

Species Encouraged by Agriculture and Stock Rearing

The most successful commensal species associated with farming is the house sparrow, its spread assisted by its habit of feeding on spilt cereal grains. The beginnings of this process can be seen in the rock shelter of Hayonim (Pichon 1991). There were few remains of sparrows in the Upper Palaeolithic (Aurignacian and Kebaran) levels in the cave but in the later Natufian levels more than one fourth of all avian remains are of the sparrow. The avifauna at Hayonim derives from owl pellets (Chapter 5) so should reflect relative numbers in the vicinity of the cave. The increase in sparrow numbers at this time fits well with the increase in the use of wild cereals and sedentism on contemporary Near Eastern sites. It also parallels the increase in the house mouse, *Mus musculus*, the presence of which is also an indication that the peoples of the Near East were becoming increasingly sedentary (Pichon 1991; Tchernov 1993). The spread of the sparrow into Europe is not easy to trace because remains survive only by accident in archaeological deposits. It is found on islands in the Mediterranean only after they were colonised by people: the earliest remains are from Early Neolithic Corsica (prior to the fifth millennium BC; see Vigne et al. 1997). In Northwest Europe, sparrow remains have not been found before the Bronze Age (Table 15.3). The earliest record in Sweden is from 1200 to 800 BC in Apalle Cave; there its presence coincided with that of the horse, and the two may have been connected (Ericson et al. 1997). In Britain the Late Bronze Age was a time of agricultural intensification, and records of domestic sparrow in Britain are also known from that time onwards on sites such as Danebury (Coy 1984). The sparrow has also been recorded on Roman sites in Britain (Parker 1988) and France (Ericson et al. 1997).

Some eagles, vultures, and corvids, if not already synanthropic with hunters, became so with agriculturalists, as the rearing of livestock provided carcasses for the birds to scavenge. The raptors which have benefited from pastoralism include the bearded vulture (Vigne et al. 1997) and the white-tailed sea eagle. In Sweden the latter is rare in the Pleistocene but became more numerous in the Holocene (Ericson & Tyrberg 2004, 102–104). White-tailed sea eagles are also common in Holocene sites in the British Isles (Serjeantson forthcoming). The presence of these as well as ravens

Table 15.3. *Some Holocene records of the house sparrow*, Passer domesticus, *in Europe*

Country	Site	Date	Species
Ukraine	Fatma Koba, Krim	Early Holocene (Azilian)	*Passer domesticus*
Ukraine	Alimovskii Caves, Krim	Early Holocene (Azilian)	*Passer domesticus*
Corsica	Monte Leone	5th millennium BC	*Passer domesticus*
Sweden	Apalle, Uppland	1200–800 BC	*Passer domesticus*
Bulgaria		1000 BC	*Passer domesticus*
Spain	Soto de Medinilla, Valladolid	800–400 BC	*Passer* cf. *domesticus*
Britain	Various sites	700 BC–AD 50	*Passer domesticus*
Corsica	Monte di Tuda	Iron Age and Roman	*Passer* cf. *domesticus*
Egypt	Tell Maskhuta	600 BC–AD 200	*Passer domesticus*

Source: Data are from Ericson et al. (1997) and Vigne et al. (1997).

and other corvids on prehistoric settlements was explained by their symbolic roles in Chapter 14, but it was their synanthropic habits which brought them in contact with humans.

The advent of agriculture and its consequent disturbance of the natural vegetation is one reason why species from a wide range of habitats are present on prehistoric settlements. Up to 70 avian species were identified out a sample of 4,000 bones from the Pottery Mound site in New Mexico. The number of species was high because many different habitats were available, including agricultural fields, the margins of the irrigation systems which provided water for the fields, and the vegetation on the river bank. The human settlement also attracted insects, as discussed later, which in turn attracted those species which depend on insect prey (Emslie 1981).

Clearance of the land for agriculture and the creation of *chinampas* in the Mexican basin following the Aztec invasion favoured the spread of *teozanatl*, the great-tailed grackle. It is absent in Pleistocene deposits (Corona-M. 2002). Its natural habitat is coastal wetlands, but it colonised the Mexican Basin from the Gulf Coast lowlands in the fifteenth century, having initially been introduced for its feathers (Chapter 8). The evidence for this comes not from skeletal remains but from the writings of Bernardino de Sahagun, who reported that the ruler Ahuitzotl 'commanded that they [the grackles] be brought here from Cuextlan and Totonacapan' together with other exotic mammals and birds. This description must refer to the great-tailed grackle, even though that species did not breed in the Basin of Mexico again until the twentieth century (Christensen 2000).

Agriculture was accompanied by clearance of the forest on many islands as well as on the mainland. On Corsica, 31 taxa out of a total of 119 recorded are present only in deposits of the Neolithic period and later. Some of the new species were birds of open fields, whose survival on Corsica was facilitated when the ecology was modified to include low to medium vegetation (Vigne et al. 1997). The creation of wet meadows as well as deforestation in mainland Europe encouraged some wetland species such as the stork, which is now synanthropic in parts of Europe (Esser & Verhagen 2001).

Synanthropes in Towns

Towns have a range of their own synanthropic species, which tolerate human presence while making use of the 'warmer climate, scarcity of predators, abundance of food, and the variety of environments' (Albarella 1997). It is the broad-spectrum omnivores which have been most successful together with those species which feed on the insects attracted by human refuse. The feral street pigeon and the starling have been most successful worldwide, but towns have also provided pickings for the sparrow and the jackdaw, with its habit of nesting – and dying – in chimneys. The hirundines benefit from the large numbers of insects in towns: their nesting was encouraged from the sixteenth century onwards by the provision of special pots, long-necked jars with a hole in the shoulder, which people attached to their houses. Some are illustrated in Dutch paintings. The earliest bird pots found in London were made in the Low Countries, but from the seventeenth century onwards, ceramic bird pots were locally made (Stephenson 1991). Some members of the thrush and finch families flourish in town gardens. If large numbers of bones are present in a refuse deposit, they probably derived from food remains (see Chapter 10), but the occasional starling or house sparrow is likely to be a natural death or a cat victim.

Avian scavengers were encouraged in towns in the past because they cleaned up the streets. One of these, the red kite, has been recorded on at least 18 urban sites in Europe. The corvids, ravens as well as crows, were also urban scavengers, the raven only disappearing from towns in Western Europe in the eighteenth century AD. The white-tailed sea eagle is thought to have become a scavenger in towns as well as in villages (Ritchie 1920; O'Connor 1993; Boev 1993; Mulkeen & O'Connor 1997).

DIMINISHED RANGES

The number of species which has done well alongside human settlement is greatly outnumbered by the number whose population has diminished.

The relative effect of human colonisation on herpetofauna, birds, and mammals has been studied on Corsica, in a comparison of faunas from seven sites which spanned the Late Pleistocene and Holocene periods. There were only small changes in the amphibians and reptiles but a 100 per cent turnover in the mammals, including the loss of all the endemic mammals. The birds were intermediate, with 6 per cent extinct or extirpated from the island since the Pleistocene. Of these, three were boreal species which were absent from all Holocene deposits and one was the endemic Corsican owl, *Bubo insularis*. The former disappeared with climate change, as we have seen elsewhere; the latter became extinct only in the Mid Holocene, the victim of humanly created environmental change rather than climate (Vigne et al. 1997). Birds became extinct over ten times as frequently as reptiles, but they were less vulnerable than the mammals.

One large bird whose range has greatly decreased in Europe over the course of the Holocene is the pelican, of which two species are still present in Europe but with very restricted distributions. It came as a surprise to early-twentieth-century palaeontologists to find remains of pelicans in two areas of southern England, the Somerset Levels in southwest England and the Fens near Cambridge, both formerly large areas of wetlands (Andrews 1917; Harrison 1987; Northcote 1980). Pelicans have also been identified in the Netherlands at the same period (Clason & Prummel 1979). The remains proved to be from the Dalmatian rather than the white pelican. They included immature as well as mature bones, demonstrating that the birds were breeding and not merely vagrants. In Europe today the Dalmatian pelican breeds only in the Danube delta, but the finds from Southern England and the Netherlands show that 2,000 years ago its breeding range extended to Western Europe. The crane, another large bird, has also declined in the western part of its range: there is abundant evidence of its presence from early Post-Glacial times to the Middle Ages, after which time there were probably several centuries during which it did not breed in the British Isles (Boisseau & Yalden 1998; Serjeantson in press-c).

One of the explicit aims of the excavation of deposits within the ruined chapel on the island of Lavezzi off the south coast of Corsica was to examine how the distribution of the local breeding seabirds had changed over time. The chapel contained midden material from human use, including bird remains. The main species were the yelkouan shearwater and the shag. Today the latter continues to breed on the island but there is no shearwater colony. There is also a large breeding colony of Audouin's gull today but this species is absent from the archaeological deposits. It is unlikely that those who visited the island in the sixteenth to eighteenth centuries to catch birds for food would have ignored the gulls, so the authors concluded that the shearwater colony has disappeared and the gull colony become established since the eighteenth century (Vigne et al. 1991).

These are only a few examples out of dozens which could have been cited to demonstrate changes in the former ranges of birds which took place before detailed written records were made. If the experience of the British Isles is typical, it is mainly the larger species whose ranges have contracted most in the Holocene era. Human predation contributed to the decline, but vegetation changes, especially drainage, probably had a greater effect (Serjeantson in press-c).

There is one example of a European species where palaeontological remains have demonstrated the absence of change. The origin of an endemic Iberian population of the azure-winged magpie was an enigma. It is otherwise known only in the Far East, China, Japan, and Korea, leading some to suppose it a recent introduction. Remains were recently identified in two of the Gibraltar caves referred to earlier, demonstrating that it has been present in Spain for millennia. A relict population must have survived in southern Iberia, which, as discussed, was a *refugium* for temperate species in the Pleistocene (Cooper 2005). Here, palaeontological evidence was able to show that the range of the azure-winged magpie must formerly have been widespread over Southern Europe and Asia, and this has been confirmed by genetic studies (Fok et al. 2002).

EXTINCTIONS

The most drastic distribution change of all is total extinction. Over the period of geological time in which birds have existed, the turnover of species has been of the order of every five to ten million years. The rate has been speeded up a hundredfold since the Pleistocene (Steadman & Martin 2003). The degree to which the extinctions of the large mammals at the end of the Holocene was caused by human action or climate change has been widely debated. The processes by which birds have become extinct in the Holocene are not necessarily the same, and they provide an important insight into mammalian extinctions (Anderson 1984).

Role of Climate

There is much concern at the present time about whether climate change will bring about the extinction of avian species. It certainly played a role in the extinction of the large mammals at the end of the Pleistocene. The populations of some became restricted to small areas or 'islands' of vegetation as environmental zones contracted until they reached the point where they could no longer support viable populations.

The changes in climate at around 12,000 BP did not directly cause avian extinctions. As we have seen, boreal species such as the grouse and snowy owl declined at the end of the Pleistocene, but they survived, if with contracted ranges and in smaller numbers. In New Zealand a comprehensive survey of the avifauna showed that climate was not a factor in the extinctions of either the large or small endemic birds. As in Eurasia, the distribution of some species changed at the end of the Pleistocene but none became extinct until the arrival of human colonists (Holdaway 2002).

Role of Humans

The hundreds of avian extinctions which have taken place in the Holocene can be shown almost without exception to be the direct or indirect result of the spread of human settlement. Nearly all have resulted from colonisation of new lands, the Americas, New Zealand, and smaller islands. The majority of the species which have become extinct in the Holocene were endemic to offshore islands. The reasons for this have been examined by several authors; they agree about the range of causes even if they sometimes disagree about the relative strength of each. Once humans reached offshore islands, a combination of factors contributed to the extinction of local species. They succumbed to overkill, habitat destruction, and to the introduction of predators, competitors, and avian diseases (Diamond 1984, 2002; Milberg & Tyrberg 1993; Steadman & Martin 2003). Populations endemic on islands were small, so by definition they were more vulnerable than those which lived on the large continents. More than 200 extinct island species were known by 1993. The families with the largest number of extinct species are the Rallidae and the Anatidae (Table 15.4), families found in both the Atlantic and Pacific Oceans. Many of these and other island endemics had become flightless (Figure 15.3) or almost flightless after they reached offshore islands with no ground predators (Milberg & Tyrberg 1993).

Breeding colonies of seabirds were wiped out or severely depleted by the first colonisers of offshore islands, who relied on seabirds and other marine resources such as turtles and reef fish to sustain them until agriculture was established. Colonies of procellariids and other seabirds on subtropical islands were extirpated, but those on islands in the temperate and circumpolar zone were more resilient. Firstly, colonies were larger on temperate islands and secondly, the depleted colonies could recruit constantly from breeding colonies on islands in the subpolar zone (Anderson 2001).

Overkill

Overkill is responsible for the extinction of 15 per cent of those species which have become extinct in the Holocene period, according to Diamond (2002). The large

Table 15.4. *Numbers of extinct Holocene birds by family*

Family	Mediterranean	Atlantic Ocean	Caribbean	Indian Ocean	Pacific Ocean	Total
Aepyornithidae				7		7
Dinornithidae					13	13
Procellariidae	1	2			2	5
Pelecanidae					1	1
Sulidae					2	2
Ciconiidae			1			1
Threskiornithidae			1		3	4
Anatidae	2		1	2	20	25
Cathartidae			1			1
Accipitridae	1		4		8	13
Falconidae			3			3
Megapodiidae					5	5
Phasianidae		1				1
Undescribed					1	1
Gruidae	1		1			2
Rallidae			4	1	29	34
Rhynochetidae					1	1
Aptornithidae					2	2
Burhinidae			1			1
Scolopacidae			2		3	5
Laridae					1	1
Alcidae					2	2
Columbidae	1		1		11	13
Psittacidae			2		3	5
Cuculidae				1		1
Tytonidae	2		5		1	8
Strigidae	3		6		5	14
Aegothelidae					1	1
Caprimulgidae			1			1
Apodidae			1			1
Xenicidae					3	3
Rhinocryptidae			1			1
Emberizidae			1			1
Muscicapidae					2	2
Meliphagidae					3	3
Drepanididae					23	23
Icteridae			2			2
Fringillidae	1	1				2
Estrildidae					1	1
Sturnidae					1	1
Corvidae	2		1		4	7
Total	14	4	40	11	151	220

Note: Between 6 and 12 species are now accepted for the elephant birds, Aepyornithidae, and 11 are accepted for moa, Dinornithidae.

Source: Data, in general, are modified from Milberg and Tyrberg (1993, tab. 2). Information for Aepyornithidae is from Dewar (1984) and that for Dinornithidae is from Worthy and Holdaway (2002).

FIGURE 15.3. Flightless cormorant, *Phalacrocorax harrisi*, on the Galapagos Islands. Many island endemics became flightless, so they were vulnerable to predation as soon as the island was colonised (photograph by D. Serjeantson).

ground-living birds which had evolved on the larger offshore islands were all wiped out by humans, the dozen or so species of moa in New Zealand, the elephant birds in Madagascar, and the dodo in Mauritius. As well as being large, these birds were slow to reproduce and were naïve in the presence of humans. The dodo became extinct exactly 174 years after it was first encountered by humans.

The mechanism and timing of the extinction of the moa in New Zealand has been examined by using a re-analysis of radiocarbon dates, and calculations of prey numbers and reproductive rates (Anderson 1989a; Holdaway & Jacomb 2000). Their breeding rate was low. In the South Island moa ranges were restricted, perhaps to a single valley. Overkill was certainly responsible for their extinction, but what form did it take? One theory is that the moa were wiped out by an expanding wave of people (a 'blitzkrieg') as the human population expanded from north to south, as has been argued for the large mammals in North America (Martin 1984). The radiocarbon dates do not support this; instead they show that sites in the south of the South Island were occupied as early as or earlier than any in the north. As we saw in Chapter 10, the South Island population rapidly came to rely heavily on moa hunting, because of the lack of alternative resources. Only after the first colonisation did settlement on the South Island spread inland. Moa were probably wiped out valley by valley. On North Island, where agriculture was possible and the moa habitat was forest, which made them harder to find and hunt, the peak of killing was later, but even casual hunting was enough to wipe out these slow-breeding birds (Anderson 1989a). Anderson concluded that moa hunting lasted from 900 BP to about 500 BP, but this length of time has been challenged by Holdaway and Jacomb (2000). These authors argued that given the low rate of reproduction, the moa could have withstood human pressure for fewer than 160 years. If these calculations do reflect reality, it would make the extinction of the moa one of the 'fastest recorded megafaunal extinctions', as fast as that of the dodo (Holdaway & Jacomb 2000).

Unlike the extinctions of large mammals at the end of the Pleistocene, there is no room for ambiguity in the extinction of the moa. 'In the extinction of the moas... we have a case which can be confidently removed beyond the first-order debate of Quaternary extinctions; that is beyond the question of cultural or non-cultural causation' (Anderson 1984, 729). Climate change can be ruled out as moa became extinct only in the past 1000 years, within 200 years of the arrival of the Polynesian colonists of New Zealand.

Overkill was also responsible for the extinction of many smaller species. It was the reason for the final demise of the great auk, since this species too suffered neither habitat loss nor climate change. Its flightlessness and naïveté combined with its practice of breeding on offshore islands ultimately made it vulnerable to human predation. In historic times the known breeding sites were on islands off Newfoundland and Iceland, but it was much more widespread in the Early Holocene. As discussed in Chapter 10, the great auk was killed for food by the first farmers to colonise Scotland. The first farmers to settle on the island of Sanday in the Orkneys were able to catch large numbers, but over the first hundred or so years of occupation numbers declined, and in later periods great auks were present only in ones and twos (Figure 15.4). The great auk may well have bred on the island, which was free of ground predators, until direct human predation put an end to the colony. This story of decline on a single island is repeated all round the coast of Scotland. It makes it highly likely that human predation brought about an absolute reduction in numbers in the eastern Atlantic as early as the first millennium BC (Serjeantson 2001b).

The most conspicuous recent example of human overkill is the passenger pigeon, which was wiped out by an urbanised human population who killed for sport rather than food. In the eighteenth and nineteenth centuries the passenger pigeon formed huge flocks in the hardwood forests of the eastern seaboard of North America, but archaeological finds show that its range formerly extended further west. Finds from Charlie Lake Cave show that it was present in the Boreal zone of northern British Columbia from about 9000 BP onwards. At least one specimen has been found in

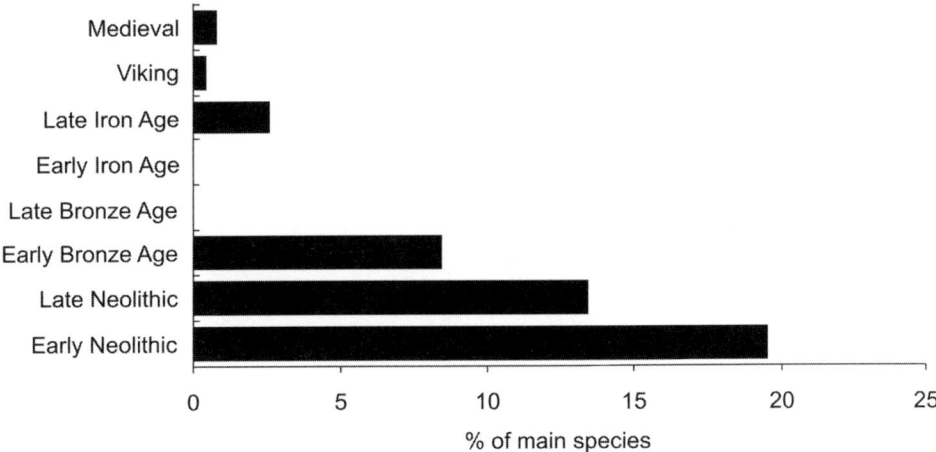

FIGURE 15.4. Decline in numbers of great auk, *Pinguinus impennis*, as a percentage of all birds at two sites on the island of Sanday, Orkney (Serjeantson 2001b). The great auk declined from nearly 20 per cent of all birds in the Neolithic period (third millennium BC) to 1 or 2 per cent only in medieval times (eleventh to thirteenth century AD).

Utah (Parmalee 1980), and a survey of archaeological records included some from west of the Rockies (Hargrave & Emslie 1980).

Overkill has also been responsible for some drastic reductions in range as a result of hunting. Ostriches, today only found south of the Sahara, were formerly also widespread in North Africa and Asia. Remains have been found in Syrian sites (Gourichon 2004, 134) and in Tell Hesban and Petra in Jordan (LaBianca & von den Driesch 1995; Studer 1996) as well as in Central Asia. In Roman times the large size of the ostrich made it a target for hunting for sport and food, as discussed in Chapter 13. It survived in Western Asia and North Africa into the first millennium AD (von den Driesch & Baumgartner 1997) and indeed into historical times, but much depleted in numbers.

Habitat Destruction

We have already seen how habitat destruction brought about the extinction of the endemic Corsican owl. In the form of clearance for agriculture and logging, it has brought many more endemic island species, especially woodland species, to extinction. In Mauritius twelve species have become extinct as a result of the logging of the tropical rainforest. Grazing and browsing by goats and rabbits destroyed the

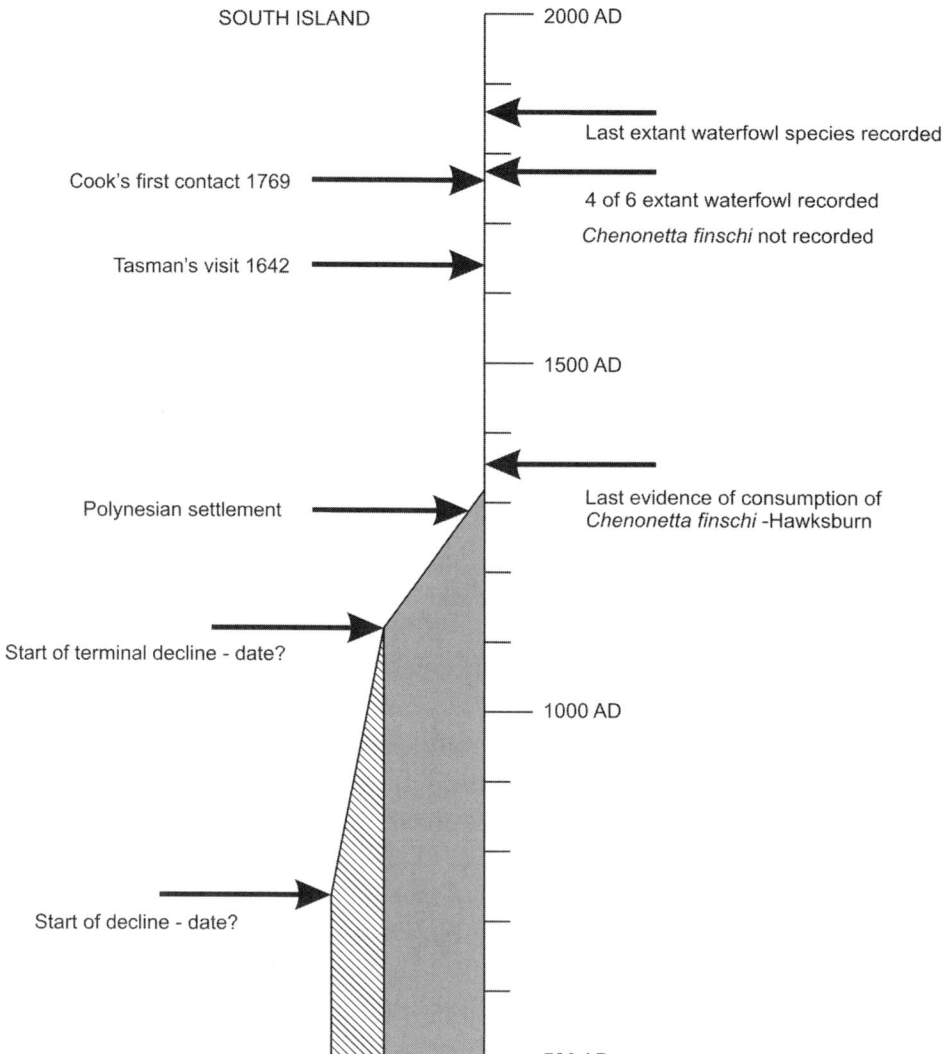

FIGURE 15.5. Hypothesised decline to extinction in New Zealand of Finsch's duck, *Chenonetta finschi*. 'Last extant waterfowl species recorded' indicates the date of the first published record of the last living species of waterfowl to be recognised in New Zealand, and 'last evidence of consumption' indicates the latest calibrated radiocarbon age for the most remote archaeological site from which Finsch's duck has been recorded. Hatching represents the proportion of total population of Finsch's duck lost during range contraction under predation pressure; shading represents the core population (after Holdaway 2002, fig. 5).

forests when they were introduced to offshore islands. On Mangaia in the Cook Islands, first colonised in about AD 1000, the extinction of the endemic fauna can be seen in successive levels in the Tangatatau Rockshelter. In the lowest zone (J) the inhabitants consumed almost as many local endemic landbirds as fish; in the middle part of the sequence, numbers of native landbirds plummeted and fish and domestic animals increased, and in the upper zones the relative number of birds increased, but they were seabirds rather than endemic landbirds (Steadman & Kirch 1990). Though direct predation contributed to the extinction of the endemic species on the island, the destruction of the *makatea* forest had a greater effect, as the pigeons, doves, and parrots depended on this undisturbed forest (Steadman & Kirch 1990).

Predators

The introduction of predators is thought to have caused half of all island extinctions (Diamond 1984). Rats were the worst culprit, having exterminated birds on at least 26 islands; cats have been second only to rats in their effect. Introduced pigs, dogs, foxes, weasels, mongoose, and monkeys have all affected the bird fauna and caused extinctions. Some of these predatory species were deliberately introduced as food; not only pigs, but dogs and even the Pacific rat, *Rattus exulans*, were eaten in Polynesia. The birds which suffered most were ground-dwelling species such as the rails and seabirds which came ashore to nest. The only islands where introduced predators did not cause extinctions were those with land-crabs, because the local species were adapted to ground predators. On other islands, endemic birds were naïve in the presence of ground predators. On some Polynesian islands the Pacific rat has been found in bird pellets in deposits with dates which precede the earliest cultural horizons, probably because rats travelled on visiting canoes (Anderson 2000) and so had an impact on some islands even before human occupation began. The range of the extinct New Zealand duck, Finsch's duck, had contracted even before Polynesian settlement became visible in the archaeological record (Figure 15.5). With environmental and other reasons rejected, the rat is seen as the most likely cause (Holdaway 2002). On the smaller Polynesian islands, where remains of rats have also been found in the earliest occupation layers, their effect on the bird fauna has been seen in succeeding layers (Table 15.5). Rat remains were almost absent from the lowest zone on Mangaia but then become much more common, and at the same time the local endemic avifauna declined, as witnessed both by numbers of bones and number of species (Figure 15.6; also see Steadman & Kirch 1990).

Table 15.5. *Summary of the vertebrate fauna from Tangatatau Rockshelter*

Fauna	A	B	C	D	E	F	G	H	I	J
Fish	51	667	973	937	2464	1206	875	735	1379	80
Reptiles										
Sea turtle	1			1						
Lizard		1					1		3	
Birds										
All native species	7	27	22	4	7	1	9	13	49	47
Gallus gallus (chicken)	1		2	3	13	3	6		3	
Mammals										
Pteropus tonganus (fruit bat)							1	2	15	13
Rattus exulans (Pacific rat)	19	125	83	50	39	14	61	34	40	1
Sus scrofa (pig)			3	10	13	2	1	1	1	
Delphinidae sp. (dolphin)							1			
Homo sapiens (human)	1	1								
Unidentifiable bird	5	27	20	10	23	4	11	13	36	52
Unidentifiable mammal		2		2	4	2	1			

Note: Tangatatau Rockshelter (MAN-44) is on Mangaia, Cook Islands: J, the lowest zone, may predate permanent occupation of the island.
Source: Data are from Steadman and Kirch (1990, tab. 2).

Competitors

The introduction of species which competed with the endemic birds for food has rarely led to total extinction, though the introduction of herbivores is thought to have had an effect on the population of the New Zealand takahe, a rare species which was once thought to be extinct but was rediscovered in 1948 (Diamond 1984). The endemic Rallidae on Polynesian islands may have suffered from competition with the domestic chickens introduced by Polynesian settlers (see Chapter 11) as well as from predators (Steadman & Rolett 1996).

Disease

In historical times, disease has made some contributions to the extinction or decline of some species, inadvertently introduced by domestic poultry. Pathogens are thought to have contributed to the decline of the heath hen in North America and

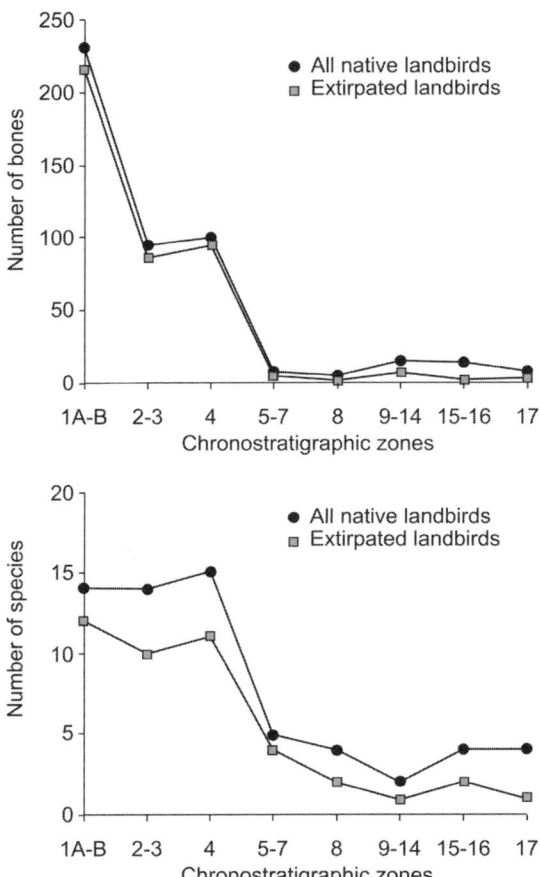

FIGURE 15.6. Decline in numbers of bones (top) and number of species (bottom) of native landbirds in Tangatatau Rockshelter, Mangaia, Cook Islands (redrawn from Steadman & Martin 2003, fig. 3).

the endangered Norfolk Island green parrot (parakeet; see Diamond 1984), perhaps carried there by domestic chickens. Introduced avian malaria may have contributed to the extinction of the many species of Hawaiian honeycreeper, Drepanididae (see Table 15.4); it is certainly thought to be holding back the increase in their numbers (Atkinson et al. 2000).

Multiple and Unknown Causes

On many oceanic islands it is not possible to point to a single cause for the extinction of the endemic bird faunas, though the process is often only too evident in sequential

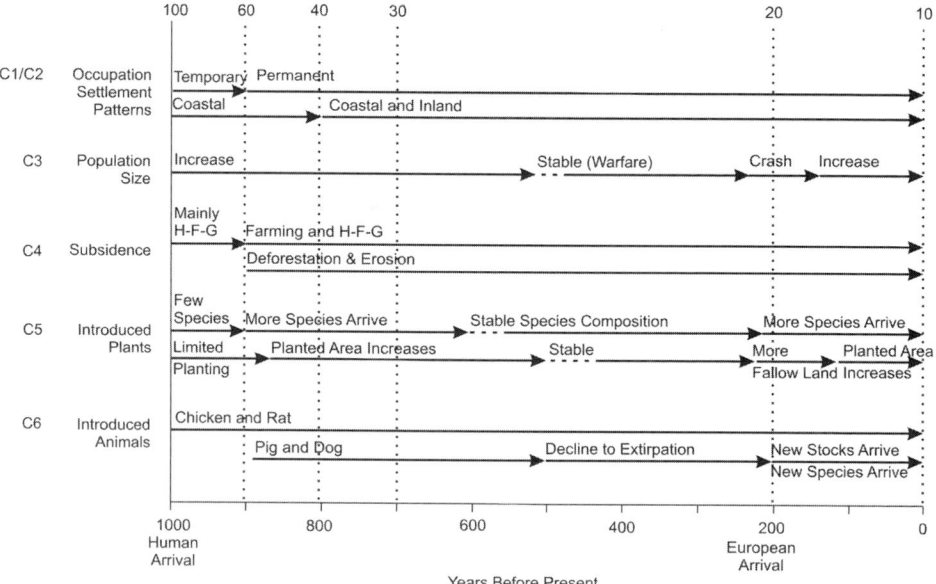

FIGURE 15.7. Hypothetical example of how cultural factors (C) affected the number of avian extinctions on Pacific oceanic islands, based on data from East Polynesia. H-F-G are hunter-fisher-gatherers. The horizontal scale (top) shows the percentage of original landbird species remaining (redrawn from Steadman & Martin 2003, fig. 4).

occupation layers. Figure 15.7 shows how endemic landbirds may have declined from the time of the first visits of the Polynesians to the present day. It shows 40 per cent extinct between the initial visits and the establishment of permanent inland settlements about 900 years ago, a further 20 per cent gone by 800 BP, and only 20 per cent only of native species surviving until the first Europeans arrived 200 years ago. The pattern was probably broadly similar on virtually all of the Polynesian islands, and it has parallels on islands all over the globe: the earliest cultural levels of the early site include the local, often endemic, avifauna, which declines in later levels as the birds themselves diminished in number.

Among the candidates for a possible former Western Palaearctic species which became extinct in the Holocene is a second crane. Milne-Edwards and later Harrison postulated the existence of a crane, *Grus primigenia*, as large as the sarus crane of eastern Asia (Milne-Edwards 1875; Harrison & Cowles 1977; von den Driesch 1999; Stewart 2007). The skeletal remains of some Pleistocene and some Early Holocene cranes were much larger than those of the common crane today. Remains from Les Eyzies and La Madeleine were larger than red-crowned (Manchurian) and sarus cranes, neither of which in any case is found in the Western Palaearctic. Remains

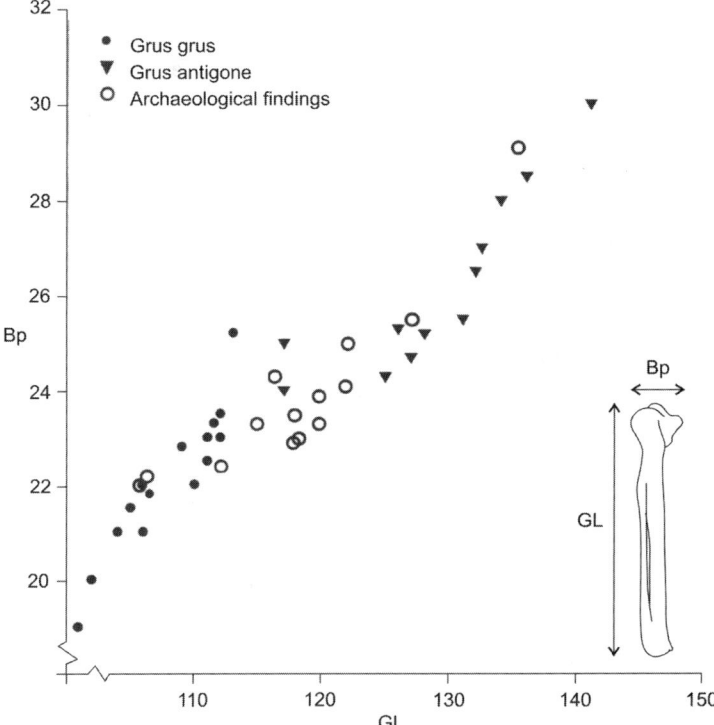

FIGURE 15.8. Size of the carpometacarpus of crane, *Grus grus*, from Late Pleistocene and Holocene Europe (GL = greatest length and Bp = proximal breadth; from von den Driesch 1999).

of very large cranes have been found on sites in Europe up to the Roman period. When the specimens from all over Europe were compared, however, the results (Figure 15.8) cast some doubt on the existence of a species separate from the common crane because the measurements fall into a single size group (with one outlier), implying that a single species is involved. Von den Driesch considered that the larger birds were generally earlier and that the crane declined in size in the Holocene; Stewart interpreted the wide size range as evidence for a larger Western European population. Remains of cranes from Malta were also larger than the common crane, but it is thought inherently unlikely that a population could have become isolated on Malta for long enough to develop into a different species (Alcover et al. 1992). If we are dealing with a single species which became smaller over time, the cause cannot simply be climate change, because large individuals survived until the end of the first millennium BC. The size reduction in the Western population probably resulted from a decline in suitable habitats (Stewart 2007, 104).

DISCUSSION AND CONCLUSIONS

For birds, climate change on its own has wiped out few or no species in the past 20,000 years. Humans have been responsible for most extinctions, either directly or indirectly. The extinction of the large flightless birds at the direct hand of humans has been most dramatic, but they represent only a small percentage of the total of avian extinctions. The small- and medium-sized birds on islands fell victim to introduced ground predators and the destruction of endemic forest as well as direct predation. The process of extinction is visible archaeologically in New Zealand, on many of the Polynesian islands, and on other oceanic islands not discussed here. The initial decline in the population of the great auk can also been seen on successive archaeological sites, but the passenger pigeon's demise happened too rapidly for a decline to be evident in fossil deposits.

Bird remains from both natural and anthropogenic sites are a valuable tool for those who study climate change in the past, because birds are sensitive indicators of the environment. However, it is important to be alert to the possibility that some may have had slightly different habitat preferences in the past. Morales (1993b) made the point that 'this plasticity casts some doubts on the apparently sensible ecological classifications of avifaunas made by different authors'. We have to be alert to the possibility that non-analogue faunas existed in the Pleistocene era, at least on the shores of the Mediterranean.

Bird remains are especially useful for interpreting climatic fluctuations in the Pleistocene, as remains have survived well in caves. The range of contexts in which bird remains are found is greatly increased in the Holocene, but most sites are anthropogenic so they have a bias towards large birds and birds which can be caught easily (Chapter 10). The fact that ducks are the most frequent species in so many Early Holocene inland sites in temperate and boreal regions reflects human hunting preferences as well as the fact that the wetlands developed over America and Eurasia. On coastal sites seabirds rather than ducks were selected, and other species ignored.

Archaeological as well as palaeontological sites are an important resource for the study of past changes in avian distribution. Up to now ornithologists have been slow to use such records in spite of the fact that, as we have seen, archaeology can give time depth to studies of past distributions (Vigne et al. 1991). The greatest potential for advances in understanding historical biogeography and past extinctions lie in collaborative research by ornithologists, zooarchaeologists and archaeologists, as exemplified by some of the research in Polynesia.

16

Conclusions and Outstanding Questions

In this book I have described many cultures where birds were important for subsistence, for feathers, and for the symbolic roles which people assigned to them. Why, then, are bird remains uncommon on so many prehistoric and later sites, especially in Europe?

WHY ARE BIRD REMAINS SCARCE?

One reason for the scarcity of bird bones is taphonomic, relating to the small size of the birds and of their bones. In towns and other complex sites, rubbish was often cleared away from where it was first generated and redeposited in dumps elsewhere (Figure 16.1). We find bones of larger domestic mammals in these reworked rubbish dumps, but less often find the small pieces of bone from birds, fish, and young mammals such as lambs and piglets (Serjeantson in press-b). It is only in well-protected environments such as pits, wells, and cisterns that bird bones survive as well as those of mammals. Where deposits are not sieved, all but the largest elements of chickens and larger birds are likely to be overlooked. Small- and medium-sized birds may be missed entirely where deposits are not sieved, as discussed in Chapter 5.

However, on many sites the absence of bird remains is real. This is partly economic. As we saw in Chapter 10, for hunters, the energetic return is less than with medium and large mammals: hunting birds and other small game was less economic in terms of the input of calories for the expenditure of energy. Preparing the equipment (snares, nets, bow, and arrow), catching birds, and plucking them preparatory to cooking and consumption, were more labour intensive than catching a large mammal and preparing and cooking it. This is also the reason why large birds were preferred as food to small birds, and why very small birds were often ignored. But even if

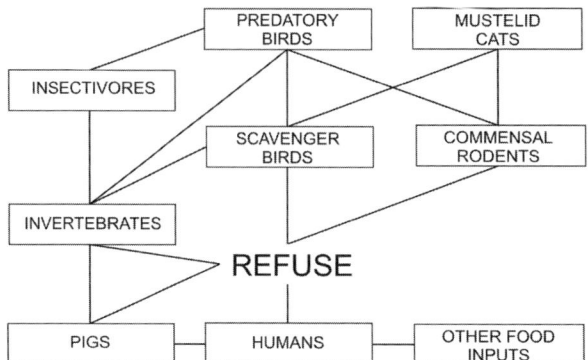

FIGURE 16.1. Pathways by which animal remains, including birds, become incorporated into settlement refuse (after O'Connor 2000).

birds were not caught for food everywhere, they were caught for their feathers and were then often eaten. An early anthropologist who worked among the Tlingit of the Pacific Northwest described how birds were a minor food resource compared with the fish, sea mammals, and land mammals: they caught many of the birds because they wanted to use the feathers, but they did then eat them (Oberg 1980).

Surprisingly, there is very little evidence that birds were caught at all on inland sites in the British Isles and elsewhere in Europe in later prehistoric times. It is possible there that birds and eggs were not just uneconomic to catch and process but were actually avoided, as fish seems to have been (Serjeantson et al. 1994). Except when people are starving – and sometimes even then – food consumption is closely linked to culture and tradition; there are ritualised aspects in what is eaten and how (Barker & Grant 1999). The scarcity of birds on later prehistoric farming settlements other than in marginal environments may reflect a taboo on their consumption. If so, the few remains present are best explained as collected for feathers or for tools.

ANCIENT BIRD BONES AND ENVIRONMENTAL CONSERVATION

Whatever their anthropological significance, bird remains are a resource for conservation of the environment today. When the Bird Working Group of the International Council for Archaeozoology was founded in 1993, Morales foresaw that the information on past distributions of birds which has been gained from zooarchaeological research 'might prove invaluable for programs of conservation in the future' (Morales 1993b). This is already proving to be the case. There is now a large body of evidence for birds in England in the past based on the abundant records from archaeological assemblages (Yalden & McCarthy 2004; Yalden & Albarella 2008). For one species in particular, the white-tailed sea eagle, there is enough evidence for its former abundance in the British Isles to suggest that the current reintroduction programme is appropriate and probably has a good chance of success (Yalden 2007). In Canada, the bird remains from excavated coastal shell middens on the shores of the Straits of Georgia have been compared with present distributions and abundance and form a basis for future conservation decisions for the region (Hobson & Driver 1989).

Bird conservation is at the forefront of ecological concern today in the developed world. In its modern form, conservation started in the nineteenth century in Massachusetts, Germany, and Holland, but the protection of breeding birds has a longer history. We saw in Chapter 7 how farmers in Norway used to regulate the collection of eggs from the nests of eider ducks. In the Orkney Islands each sea cliff or rock which held a breeding colony of seabirds was in the private ownership of a local farmer who limited his catch. St Kilda preserved a more primitive arrangement, in which the seabird nesting cliffs were assigned by lot each year to individuals or family groups in the same way as arable fields were allotted in the Outer Hebrides. Numbers taken from offshore islands with breeding colonies were limited: islands were visited once a year only (Serjeantson 2001b). King James the Second of Scotland in 1457 legislated against the slaughter of 'pertrykes, pluvars, wilde dukes and sik lik fowlys' (partridges, plovers, wild ducks and suchlike fowls) in the breeding season, the first recorded reference to conservation (Fisher 1966, 136), though it was done to preserve the birds for hunting rather than with wholly altruistic motives.

We saw in Chapter 10 how remains with medullary bone are rare in assemblages from farming sites. Were female breeding birds avoided as a conservation strategy? A more cynical interpretation is that birds in general were neglected at this time because there were other sources of food available in early summer. The decline in the face of predation of the birds on the Polynesian and other islands (see Chapter 15) suggests that the first colonisers had no notion that it might be a good idea to conserve the species which presented themselves so abundantly. Conservation may have been a hard won concept.

The timidity of most birds in the presence of humans today is a behavioural adaptation which may only have evolved quite recently in palaeontological terms, as humans did not begin to capture birds systematically until about 40,000 years ago. It is possible that waterfowl and seabirds were more confiding in the presence of humans at the beginning of the Holocene than they are now. The flocks of waterfowl which proliferated on the wetlands of northern Europe at this time must have been relatively unaccustomed to predation. They may well have been less wary of humans and easier to catch then than they are today. This may help to explain the abundance and also variety of species in some Mesolithic sites (Chapter 10). Humans have adapted with unprecedented rapidity in the past 40,000 years, but birds too have had to adapt to new human behaviours.

Chapter 1 raised the question of whether the analysis of bird bones from archaeological sites was the province of palaeontologists or zooarchaeologists. With the focus of the former mainly in evolution and extinction and former distributions of birds, collections of bones from settlements of historic periods – many of which are dominated by chicken bones – lack appeal. These are usually the province of zooarchaeologists, but even these occasionally contain significant finds of unusual species; see, for instance, the pygmy cormorant from medieval Oxford (Cowles 1981) and the gadfly petrel remains found on three Scottish sites (Serjeantson 2005a). Continued dialogue between the two disciplines is very necessary.

UNRESOLVED QUESTIONS OF METHODOLOGY

At various points in this book, I have indicated where bird remains raise questions which are still unresolved. They relate not only to the history of wildfowling and the domestication of birds but also include some key practical questions of identification, taphonomy, and interpretation.

Identification

The survey of the literature on identification and the results of DNA analysis of ancient bird bones show that zooarchaeologists do well to err on the side of conservatism in assigning elements to species. If the species listed in the assemblage are to have palaeontological significance, the identification to species must be reliable. Fortunately for the anthropological study of the past, however, it is possible to interpret human activity even where remains have been identified to family or a higher category (Chapter 4). Many researchers use a hierarchy from 'certain' to 'probable' and from species to family identification.

Physical and Chemical Analysis

The study of ancient DNA has a short history so far as birds are concerned. Up to now with wild birds it has been applied to the remains of geese from England and albatrosses from shell middens around the shores of Japan and Korea (Chapter 4).

Despite the fact that morphometrical study suggested that three albatross species were possibly present, all were shown to be the short-tailed albatross. Analyses of ancient DNA are also in progress on the chicken and turkey, as discussed in Chapters 11 and 12. DNA analysis can confirm identification of species and the position of the specimen in the spectrum of breeds and types. Stable isotope analysis has the potential for indicating whether a bird was resident or migratory (Grupe & Mekota 2005), so it will be valuable for studies of past distributions and for seasonal wildfowling. Radiocarbon dating can now be carried out on a single bone, something which is going to transform our knowledge of the spread of the domestic chicken in the next ten years. It is surprising how many people have uncritically listed the presence of chicken in contexts where no domestic chickens should be. Now, any chicken bone apparently earlier than the main body of records from an area can be radiocarbon dated. (At this point, nine times out of ten, the archaeological project manager discovers that after all there was a possible contamination from deposits of a later period.) Chicken remains from early sites in the Americas have quite rightly received attention and have revealed pre-Columbian contact between the Pacific islands and South America (Storey et al. 2007). DNA and other chemical and physical techniques may be too expensive in time and equipment to be used routinely, but they are going to be used increasingly to interpret domestication and past distributions.

Taphonomy

It is particularly important with bird remains to distinguish those discarded or deposited by people from non-anthropogenic material (Chapter 5). The most secure indication that a bird was eaten is when bone fragments are found in coprolites, as at Lovelock Cave, Nevada (Chapter 6), but this is rare. Otherwise, the distinction can be quite tricky with birds; this is not only the case with caves but even applies to hunting camps, rural settlements, and towns. The pathways by which refuse, including bird remains, enter archaeological deposits are shown schematically in Figure 16.1. Many of the agents which contribute to the formation of the deposit, including cats, scavenging birds, pigs, and rodents, as well as humans, are likely to disturb deposits as well as to add to them.

Element Survival

When one is investigating just how people were involved with the bird whose remains have been excavated, the most unambiguous data available are the relative numbers

Table 16.1. *Summary of the anatomical elements of birds which give the best information on identification, ageing, sex distinctions, butchery, and other uses. See also Table 4.10.*

Element	Age	Sex	Metrical analysis	Other
Skull				Identification, symbolism
Coracoid			Medium	Butchery
Sternum	High			
Humerus			High	Butchery, bone tools
Ulna			High	Butchery, bone tools
Radius				Bone tools
Carpometacarpus	High		High	Feather collection
Major digit of wing				Feather collection
Synsacrum	High			Butchery
Femur		Medullary bone	High	
Tibiotarsus	High	Medullary bone	High	Butchery
Tarsometatarsus	High	Spur in galliformes	High	
Ungual phalanx				Symbolism (raptors)

Note: See also Table 4.9 in Chapter 4. 'High', 'Medium' refer to usefulness of information.

of the different elements, especially the relative abundance of wing and leg bones (Chapter 5 and Chapter 6). Though this is a straightforward quantification to produce, the interpretation is not straightforward. There is a relationship between the relative robusticity of the wing and leg bones and their survival in the archaeological and palaeontological records, but whether it relates to size or to structural density or to some other measure is not yet clear. Study after study has shown the main wing elements, that is, humerus and ulna, survive better than the main leg bones, that is, femur and tibiotarsus, in waterfowl and seabirds; in species which live mainly or exclusively on the ground, however, the leg bones survive better than the wing. Any interpretations of human activity such as cooking, feather use, or transport of wings or body parts has to start from this basis.

Any subselection of elements to identify and record will depend on the research aims of the project. We have seen in earlier chapters how elements other than the main wing and leg bones can be informative for some interpretations. For instance, the scapula, sternum, and synsacrum give information on age and sex (Chapter 3). The wing digits and even foot phalanges can reveal feather collection. Cut marks on certain elements from the body such as the furcula and scapula and synsacrum are diagnostic of meat consumption (Chapter 6), while those on other parts of the body may indicate food preparation, food consumption, feather removal, bone cleaning for tool use, or a combination of any of these (Table 16.1).

Curation

Important specimens may well be re-examined in the future, not only to re-identify material but to carry out radiocarbon dating or DNA analysis. If this is to be possible, it is important for bones to be retained and returned to the appropriate museum or store for curation. In Chapter 14 we saw how some remains of what turned out to be ritual burials of scarlet and military macaws and parrots in Pueblo settlements in the American Southwest are now lost. Without the possibility of re-examining these bones, we shall never know whether the birds involved were local or had been imported from civilisations to the south. The obligation to curate material appropriately is important for all classes of excavated material, but with bird remains there are often just a few small bones which become separated from the remainder of the faunal material; storing these securely is a heavy responsibility shared by the zooarchaeologist or palaeontologist and the excavator.

OUTSTANDING QUESTIONS ABOUT BIRD DOMESTICATION

Questions about the earliest domestication of the chicken and each of the other domestic birds remain unanswered. The insignificance with which the domestic chicken – let alone other domestic birds – has been treated in the past compared with the attention given to cattle, pigs, sheep, and camelids has meant that their early history has been terribly neglected. Up to now it has admittedly been difficult for researchers to confirm the date and identification of possible early records, but, as we have seen, this is no longer the case. So far as chicken husbandry is concerned, the answer to the question 'Which came first, the chicken or the egg?' is unambiguous. At least in Western Asia and Europe, the chicken was initially introduced and kept for sacrifice and for cockfighting (Chapter 13) rather than for meat or eggs. Only later did people begin to keep chickens on a large scale and eat the meat and eggs regularly. The questions of how soon the laying season extended to take in much of the year and how soon people learned the technique of castrating male birds to fatten them are still unresolved.

BIRDS IN HUMAN PREHISTORY

Early hominids may have scavenged birds and their eggs from time to time, but catching birds for feathers, food, and raw material for tools started in a systematic way only in the Upper Palaeolithic period in Western Asia and Europe. There, it coincided with the appearance of fully modern humans. It is from this time that the earliest musical instruments, bird bone flutes, were first made, a very early reflection of the development of human appreciation of music. At this time too, people began to use feathers for decoration (Chapter 8). Evidence for a contribution of bird remains to dance came later, with tantalising evidence from the crane wing bones from Catal Höyük discussed in Chapter 14. Upper Palaeolithic art occasionally depicts birds as well as mammals: ptarmigan at Isturitz (Clark 1952, fig. 7), an owl in Chauvet Cave, and the great auk at Grotte Cosquer and possibly elsewhere (Clottes et al. 1997; D'Errico 1994). Birds were therefore integral to the early development of the aesthetic sense in humans.

Birds with other small game contributed to the change to broad spectrum foraging which took place from the Late Glacial onwards (Simmons & Nadel 1998; Stiner et al. 2000). Birds were a major resource only on uninhabited islands at the time that they were first occupied, but – as Graham Clark pointed out – they were an important minor resource for some hunter-gatherers, especially in high latitudes. Very often birds met a need in a season when food was otherwise sparse. Some farming communities focussed on food production to the extent that birds were ignored, but others, especially those in areas where cultivation was marginal or domestic animals were few, continued to catch and eat wild birds.

Obtaining feathers for use and especially for decoration has been an important reason for catching birds at all periods (Chapter 8). Feathers were probably one of the first items of trade at the time of initial contacts between hunter-gatherers and farmers (Bogucki 1999). In Central and South America, feathers were not just adornment but were used as expressions of hierarchy, power, and status. Feathers of turkeys, scarlet macaws, and some other species were among the most important trade items in the American Southwest and also in the Pacific Northwest, and in the case of turkeys and macaws, the birds too were also traded for ritual use. As with chicken remains, the presence of certain species can be important evidence for prehistoric trade and contact.

In complex societies, birds were also important, though not necessarily for subsistence. They were brought into service as symbols of wealth and power. Rulers have had their own menageries of wild animals, including exotic birds, at least since Babylonian and Egyptian times (Chapter 14). Even in medieval Europe wildfowl were a means of displaying status (Sykes 2004). Hawking was restricted to the nobility because hawks were so expensive to procure and train (Chapter 13), and the wildfowl which they caught were as important for show at the banquets as for food.

The survey of birds in the past in the preceding chapters has brought together research from all over the world. Conclusions reached in one region on topics such as the role of birds for food, the selection of species and elements for tools, and the symbolic significance of birds can be seen to be valid much more widely. By bringing together research from every continent and from the Palaeolithic to historic times, I have been able to offer some provisional conclusions on many of the subjects discussed, but I hope that they will be no more than a springboard for much future research.

APPENDIX 1

List of Scientific and English Names of Species Referred to in the Text

The scientific and English names here are taken from *The Howard and Moore Complete Checklist of the Birds of the World* (Dickinson 2003). As well as providing a standard for the scientific names, this publication reflects the standardisation of the English names of common birds which has taken place over the past twenty years. Many of the revised English names are not yet in general use and have not been used in this book, so both the old and new names are listed here. Scientific names have also changed – and continue to change – as research on cladistics and especially on relationships revealed by DNA are published. Here I have quoted the scientific name used in the original publication as well as the up-to-date version. Names of extinct species have been taken from the literature cited.

African collared dove, *Streptopelia roseogrisea*
Alpine chough, *Pyrrhocorax pyrrhocorax*
American coot, *Fulica americana*
Andean condor, *Vultur gryphus*
Arctic tern, *Sterna paradisaea*
Atlantic puffin, *Fratercula arctica*
Audouin's gull, *Larus audouinii*
Azure-winged magpie, *Cyanopica cyanus*
Bald eagle, *Haliaeetus leucocephalus*
Barbary dove, *Streptopelia 'risoria'*
Barn owl, *Tyto alba*
Barred buttonquail, *Turnix suscitator*
Bean goose, *Anser fabalis*
Bearded vulture or lammergeier, *Gypaetus barbatus*
Bee hummingbird, *Mellisuga helenae*
Bewick's swan, *Cygnus columbianus bewickii*

Bittern – see Eurasian bittern
Black francolin, *Francolinus francolinus*
Black grouse – see Eurasian black grouse
Black guillemot, *Cepphus grylle*
Black vulture – see Cinereous vulture
Black-billed magpie, *Pica hudsonia*
Blackbird – see Eurasian blackbird
Black-chested buzzard-eagle, *Geranoetus melanoleucus*
Black-footed albatross, *Phoebastria nigripes*
Black-legged kittiwake, *Rissa tridactyla*
Bobwhite – see Northern bobwhite
Brent goose or brant, *Branta bernicla*
Brunnich's guillemot or thick-billed murre, *Uria lomvia*
Budgerigar, *Melopsittacus undulates*
Buzzard – see Eurasian buzzard
California turkey, *Meleagris californica*
Canada goose, *Branta canadensis*
Cape eagle-owl, *Bubo capensis*
Cape gannet, *Morus capensis*
Capercaillie – see Western capercaillie
Carrion crow, *Corvus corone*
Cassowary – see Southern cassowary
Chukar partridge, *Alectoris chukar*
Cinereous vulture, *Aegypius monachus*
Collared dove, *Streptopelia decaocto*
Common coot, *Fulica atra*
Common crane, *Grus grus*
Common eider, *Somateria mollissima*
Common loon or great northern diver, *Gavia immer*
Common magpie, *Pica pica*
Common murre – see Guillemot
Common nightingale, *Luscinia megarhynchos*
Common pheasant, *Phasianus colchicus*
Common pochard, *Aythya ferina*
Common quail, *Coturnix coturnix*
Common redshank, *Tringa totanus*
Common scoter, *Melanitta nigra*
Common snipe, *Gallinago gallinago*
Common swift, *Apus apus*

Common or green-winged teal, *Anas crecca*
Coot – see Common coot
Corn bunting, *Emberiza (Miliaria) calandra*
Cormorant – see Great cormorant
Crag martin – see Eurasian crag martin
Crane – see Common crane
Curlew – see Eurasian curlew
Dalmatian pelican, *Pelecanus crispus*
Dodo, *Raphus cucullatus*
Double-crested cormorant, *Phalacrocorax auritus*
Double-spurred francolin, *Francolinus bicalcaratus*
Eagle owl – see Eurasian eagle-owl
Egyptian goose, *Alopochen aegyptiaca*
Eider – see Common eider
Elephant bird, *Aepyornis maximus*
Emu, *Dromaius novaehollandiae*
Eurasian bittern, *Botaurus stellaris*
Eurasian black grouse, *Lyrurus (Tetrao) tetrix*
Eurasian blackbird, *Turdus merula*
Eurasian buzzard, *Buteo buteo*
Eurasian crag martin, *Ptyonoprogne (Hirundo) rupestris*
Eurasian curlew, *Numenius arquata*
Eurasian eagle-owl, *Bubo bubo*
Eurasian griffon, *Gyps fulvus*
Eurasian jackdaw, *Corvus monedula*
Eurasian oystercatcher, *Haematopus ostralegus*
Eurasian sparrowhawk, *Accipiter nisus*
Eurasian spoonbill, *Platalea leucorodia*
Eurasian stone curlew, *Burhinus oedicnemus*
Eurasian wigeon, *Anas penelope*
Eurasian woodcock, *Scolopax rusticola*
European goldfinch, *Carduelis carduelis*
European honey buzzard, *Pernis apivorus*
European robin, *Erithacus rubecula*
European shag, *Phalacrocorax aristotelis*
European starling, *Sturnus vulgaris*
European turtle dove, *Streptopelia turtur*
European white stork, *Ciconia ciconia*
Finsch's duck, *Chenonetta finschii*

Flightless cormorant, *Phalacrocorax harrisi*
Fork-tailed storm petrel, *Oceanodroma furcata*
Francolin – see Black francolin
Friendly fantail, *Rhipidura albolimbata*
Fulmar – see Northern fulmar
Gadfly petrels, *Pterodroma* spp.
Gannet – see Northern gannet
Garganey, *Anas querquedula*
Glaucous gull, *Larus hyperboreus*
Golden eagle, *Aquila chrysaetos*
Golden-fronted woodpecker, *Melanerpes aurifrons*
Goldfinch – see European goldfinch
Goosander, *Mergus merganser*
Goshawk – see Northern goshawk
Great auk, *Pinguinus impennis*
Great black-backed gull, *Larus marinus*
Great bustard, *Otis tarda*
Great cormorant, *Phalacrocorax carbo*
Great crested grebe, *Podiceps cristatus*
Great curassow, *Crax rubra*
Great grey shrike, *Lanius excubitor*
Great northern diver – see Common loon
Great skua, *Stercorarius (Catharacta) skua*
Great tinamou, *Tinamus major*
Great white egret, *Egretta alba*
Great woodswallow, *Artamus maximus*
Greater flamingo, *Phoenicopterus ruber*
Greater prairie chicken, *Tympanuchus cupido*
Greater rhea, *Rhea americana*
Greater sage grouse, *Centrocercus urophasianus*
Greater spotted eagle, *Aquila clanga*
Greater white-fronted goose, *Anser albifrons*
Great-tailed grackle (Teozanatl), *Quiscalus mexicanus*
Green peafowl, *Pavo muticus*
Grey heron, *Ardea cinerea*
Grey partridge, *Perdix perdix*
Greylag goose, *Anser anser*
Griffon vulture – see Eurasian griffon

Grouse – see Willow grouse and Rock ptarmigan
Guillemot or common murre, *Urial aalge*
Guineafowl – see Helmeted guineafowl
Gyrfalcon, *Falco rusticolus*
Haast's eagle, *Harpagornis moorei*
Hawai'i mamo, *Drepanis pacifica*
Heath hen, *Tympanuchus cupido*
Helmeted guineafowl, *Numida meleagris*
Heron – see Grey heron
Herring gull, *Larus argentatus*
Honey buzzard – see European honey buzzard
Horned puffin, *Fratercula corniculata*
House martin – see Northern house martin
House sparrow, *Passer domesticus*
I'iwi, *Vestiaria coccinea*
Iceland gull, *Larus glaucoides*
Indian peafowl, *Pavo cristatus*
Indian white-backed vulture, *Gyps bengalensis*
Jackass penguin, *Spheniscus demersus*
Jackdaw – see Eurasian jackdaw
Kaka, *Nestor meridionalis*
Kakapo, *Strigops habroptila*
Kelp goose, *Chloëphaga hybrida*
King cormorant, *Phalacrocorax albiventer*
King vulture, *Sarcorhamphus papa*
Kittiwake – see Black-legged kittiwake
Lanner falcon, *Falco biarmicus*
Laughing falcon, *Herpetotheres cachinnans*
Laysan albatross, *Phoebastria immutabilis*
Leach's storm petrel, *Oceanodroma leucorhoa*
Least auklet, *Aethia pusilla*
Lesser black-backed gull, *Larus fuscus*
Lesser rhea, *Pterocnemia (Rhea) pennata*
Little auk, *Alle alle*
Little bustard, *Tetrax (Otis) tetrax*
Little egret, *Egretta garzetta*
Little grebe, *Tachybaptus ruficollis*
Long-eared owl, *Asio otus*

Long-tailed duck, *Clangula hyemalis*
Magellanic penguin, *Spheniscus magellanicus*
Magellanic steamer duck, *Tachyeres pteneres*
Magpie – see Common magpie
Mallard, *Anas platyrhynchos*
Manx shearwater, *Puffinus puffinus*
Marabou, *Leptoptilus crumeniferus*
Military macaw, *Ara militaris*
Mollymawk – see Shy albatross
Muscovy duck, *Cairina moschata*
Mute swan, *Cygnus olor*
New Zealand pigeon, *Hemiphaga novaeseelandiae*
Nightingale – see Common nightingale
Norfolk Island parakeet, *Cyanoramphus cookii*
North American robin, *Turdus migratorius*
Northern bobwhite, *Colinus virginianus*
Northern flicker, *Colaptes auratus*
Northern fulmar, *Fulmarus glacialis*
Northern gannet, *Morus bassanus*
Northern goshawk, *Accipiter gentilis*
Northern house martin, *Delichon urbica*
Northern pintail, *Anas acuta*
Ocellated turkey, *Meleagris ocellata*
O'o, *Moho braccatus*
Osprey, *Pandion haliaetus*
Ostrich, *Struthio camelus*
Oystercatcher – see Eurasian oystercatcher
Passenger pigeon, *Ectopistes migratorius*
Peacock – see Indian peafowl
Pelican – see Dalmatian pelican
Peregrine falcon, *Falco peregrinus*
Pheasant – see Common pheasant
Pied bushchat, *Saxicola caprata*
Pink-footed goose, *Anser brachyrhynchus*
Pintail – see Northern pintail
Pochard – see Common pochard
Prairie falcon, *Falco mexicanus*
Prairie hen – see Greater prairie chicken

Ptarmigan – see Rock ptarmigan
Puffin – see Atlantic puffin
Purple gallinule – see Purple swamphen
Purple swamphen, *Porphyrio porphyrio*
Pygmy cormorant, *Phalacrocorax pygmeus*
Quail – see Common quail
Raven, *Corvus corax*
Razorbill, *Alca torda*
Reed bunting, *Emberiza schoeniclus*
Red grouse – see Willow grouse
Red junglefowl, *Gallus gallus*
Red kite, *Milvus milvus*
Redshank – see Common redshank
Red-billed chough, *Pyrrhocorax pyrrhocorax*
Red-breasted merganser, *Mergus serrator*
Red-crowned crane, *Grus japonensis*
Red-crowned parakeet, *Cyanoramphus novaezelandiae*
Red-necked grebe, *Podiceps grisegena*
Red-tailed hawk, *Buteo jamaicensis*
Red-throated diver, *Gavia stellata*
Resplendent quetzal, *Pharomachrus mocinno*
Rhea – see Greater rhea and Lesser rhea
Rock dove, *Columba livia*
Rock partridge, *Alectoris graeca*
Rock ptarmigan, *Lagopus muta*
Rock sparrow, *Petronia petronia*
Rook, *Corvus frugilegus*
Ruffed grouse, *Bonasa umbellus*
Sacred ibis, *Threskiornis aethiopicus*
Sage grouse, *Centrocercus* sp.
Saker falcon, *Falco cherrug*
Sandhill crane, *Grus canadensis*
Sarus crane, *Grus antigone*
Scarlet macaw, *Ara macao*
Shag – see European shag
Sharp-shinned hawk, *Accipiter striatus*
Sheldgeese, *Chloephaga* species
Short-eared owl, *Asio flammeus*

Short-tailed albatross, *Phoebastria albatrus*
Shy albatross, *Thalassarche cauta*
Snipe – see Common snipe
Snow goose, *Anser (Chen) caerulescens*
Snowy owl, *Nyctea (Bubo) scandiaca*
Song thrush, *Turdus philomelos*
Sooty shearwater, *Puffinus griseus*
Sooty tern, *Sterna fuscata*
Southern cassowary, *Casuarius casuarius*
Sparrowhawk – see Eurasian sparrowhawk
Spectacled eider, *Somateria fischeri*
Spoonbill – see Eurasian spoonbill
Spotted eagle-owl – see Cape eagle-owl
Starling – see European starling
Steamer duck – see Magellanic steamer duck
Stock dove, *Columba oenas*
Stork – see European white stork
Swan goose, *Anser cygnoides*
Swift – see Common swift
Takahe, *Porphyrio mantelli/hochstetteri*
Tasmanian emu, *Dromaius novaehollandiae diemenensis*
Tawny owl, *Strix aluco*
Teal – see Common teal
Thick-billed parrot, *Rhynchopsitta pachyrhyncha*
Tufted duck, *Aythya fuligula*
Tufted puffin, *Fratercula cirrhata*
Tui or Parson bird, *Prosthemadera novaeseelandiae*
Turkey, *Meleagris gallopavo*
Turkey-vulture, *Cathartes aura*
Turtle dove – see European turtle dove
Twite, *Carduelis flavirostris*
Velvet or white-winged scoter, *Melanitta fusca*
Western capercaillie, *Tetrao urogallus*
White pelican, *Pelecanus onocrotalus*
White-fronted goose – see Greater white-fronted goose
White-fronted tern, *Sterna striata*
White-rumped vulture – see Indian white-backed vulture
White-tailed ptarmigan, *Lagopus leucurus*

White-tailed sea eagle, *Haliaeetus albicilla*
Whooper swan, *Cygnus cygnus*
Whooping crane, *Grus americana*
Wigeon – see Eurasian wigeon
Willow (Red) grouse, *Lagopus lagopus*
Wood swallow – see Great woodswallow
Woodcock – see Eurasian woodcock
Woodpigeon, *Columba palumbus*
Yelkouan shearwater, *Puffinus yelkouan*
Yellow-crowned parakeet, *Cyanoramphus auriceps*

APPENDIX 2

Illustrations and Definitions of Bone Zones

DEFINITIONS OF ZONES

Humerus

1. proximal end, including head
2. proximal end, including fossa
3. proximal shaft, including deltoid crest
4. proximal end, ventral, including bicipital crest
5. distal shaft, dorsal
6. distal shaft, ventral
7. distal end, including dorsal epicondyle
8. distal end, including ventral epicondyle

Coracoid

1. articular facet
2. acrocoracoid process
3. proximal shaft, including scapular facet
4. proximal shaft, including procoracoid process
5. distal shaft, dorsal
6. distal shaft, ventral
7. sterno-coracoidal process
8. sternal facet

Scapula

    1 acromion
    2 glenoid facet
3+4 blade, proximal
5+6 blade, distal
7+8 blade, distal

Ulna

1 proximal articular end, including dorsal cotyla
2 proximal end, including prominence for anterior articular ligament
3 proximal shaft, including depression for brachialis
4 proximal shaft, including quill knobs
5 distal shaft, dorsal
6 distal shaft, ventral
7 distal end, including dorsal condyle
8 distal end, including ventral condyle

Radius

1+2 proximal articular end
3+4 proximal shaft
5+6 distal shaft
  7 distal end, including ligamental prominence
  8 distal end, ventral

Carpometacarpus

1 proximal end, including extensor process
2 proximal end, including carpal trochlea
3 major metacarpal, proximal shaft
4 minor metacarpal, proximal shaft
5 major metacarpal, distal shaft
6 minor metacarpal, distal shaft

7 distal end, including facet for major digit
8 distal end, including facet for minor digit

Furcula

1+2 interclavicle
3 body, proximal, left
4 body, proximal, right
5 body, distal, left
6 body, distal, right
7 extremity, distal, left
8 extremity, distal, right

Sternum

1 left coracoidal groove
2 right coracoidal groove
3 rostrum
4 apex of keel
5 left rib facets
6 right rib facets
7 pars hepatica, left
8 pars hepatica, right

Pelvis

1 left ilium
2 right ilium
3 left acetabular region
4 right acetabular region
5 left pubis
6 right pubis
7 left ischium
8 right ischium

Synsacrum

1+2 synsacral thoracic vertebrae
3+4 synsacral lumbar vertebrae
5+6 synsacral sacral vertebrae
7+8 synsacral caudal vertebrae

Femur

1 femoral head
2 trochanter
3 shaft, proximal medial
4 shaft, proximal lateral
5 shaft, distal medial
6 shaft, distal lateral
7 distal end, medial condyle
8 distal end, lateral condyle

Tibiotarsus

1 cranial cnemial crest
2 proximal articular surface
3 shaft, proximal medial
4 shaft, proximal including fibular crest
5+6 shaft, distal
7 distal articular end, including internal condyle
8 distal articular end, including external condyle

Tarsometatarsus

1 proximal articular end, including medial cotyle
2 proximal articular end, including lateral cotyle
3 proximal shaft, medial
4 proximal shaft, lateral

5 distal shaft, including facet for first metatarsal
6 distal shaft, lateral
7 trochlea for metatarsal II
8 trochlea for metatarsal IV

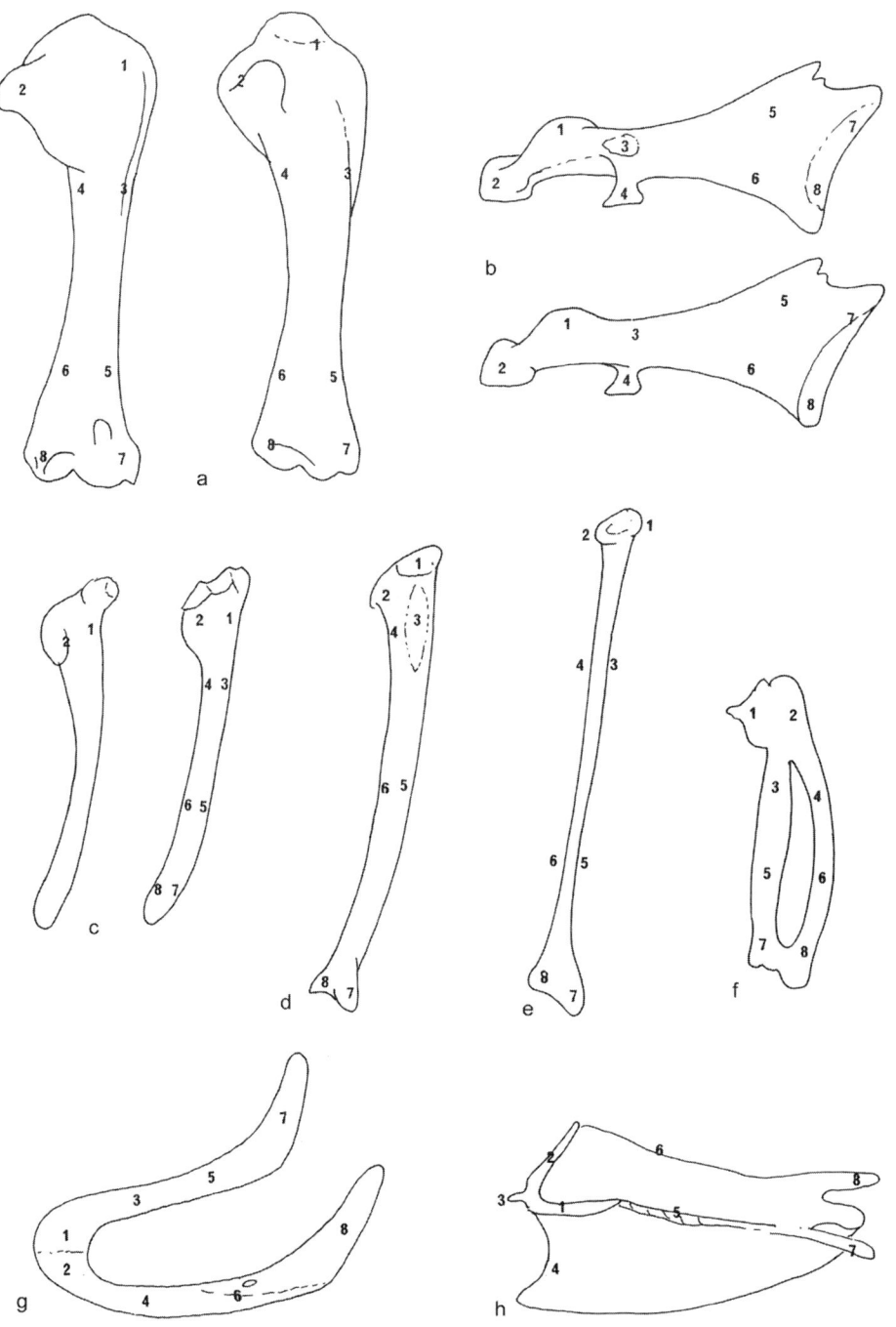

APPENDIX FIGURE 1. Illustration of bone zones on a, the humerus, b, the coracoid, c, the scapula, d, the ulna, e, the radius, f, the carpometacarpus, g, the furcula, and h, the sternum (Cohen & Serjeantson 1996, fig. 8).

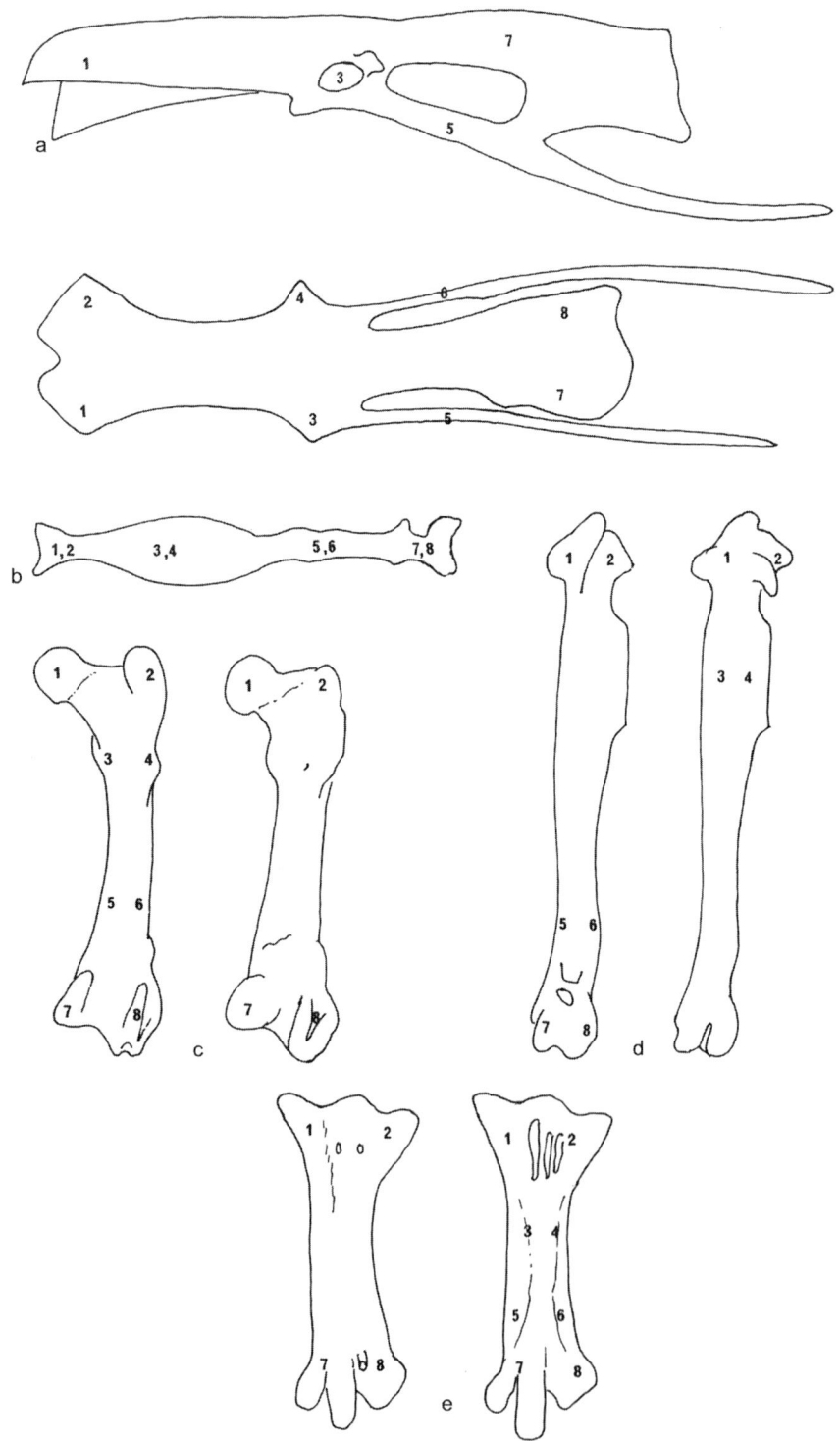

APPENDIX FIGURE 2. Illustration of bone zones on a, the pelvis, b, the synsacrum, c, the femur, d, the tibiotarsus, and e, the tarsometatarsus (Cohen & Serjeantson 1996, fig. 9).

APPENDIX 3

Organisations and Internet Resources

http://www.alexandriaarchive.org/icaz/workbird.htm. (2 January 2008)
International Council for Archaeozoology (ICAZ) Bird Working Group. Forum for zooarchaeologists who work with bird remains. This site has a facility for posting pictures of mystery bones.

http://www2.nrm.se/ve/birds/sape/litt001.html.en (3 January 2008)
SAPE – Society for Avian Palaeontology and Evolution. International scientific society dedicated to the study of the evolution of birds; includes a list of avian palaeontological literature.

http://www.aou.org/checklist/index.php3 (3 January 2008)
American Ornithologist's Union (AOU) checklist of birds of North America. AOU publishes *The Auk*, *Handbook of North American Birds*, Ornithological Monographs, and *Ornithological Newsletter*. Full text of the 1998 book *The AOU Check-list of North American Birds*, 7th edition, is accessible online. National Museum of Natural History, Smithsonian Institution, Washington DC, 20560.

http://animaldiversity.ummz.umich.edu/site/accounts/information/Aves.html
(2 January 2008)
University of Michigan Museum of Zoology Animal Diversity Web, an online database of animal natural history, distribution, classification, and conservation biology; includes a list of scientific names for Aves taxonomy (family and below) from *The Howard and Moore Complete Checklist of the Birds of the World*; also illustrations and photographs of specimens, including skulls.

http://mvz.berkeley.edu/Bird_Collection.html (19 January 2009)
Website for the University of California Vertebrate Zoology collection. The MVZ bird collection, which is one of the largest in the United States, houses over 181,000

catalogued specimens, including 174 holotype and 2 syntypes. The majority of specimens are study skins, but the collection also contains over 21,000 skeletal specimens and 3,200 fluid-preserved specimens.

http://www.zoonomen.net/avtax/frame.html (3 January 2008)
Checklist with Sibley-Ahlquist taxonomy. Peterson, Alan P. (Editor). 1999. Zoological Nomenclature Resource (Zoonomen).

http://web.telia.com/~u11502098/pleistocene.pdf (2 January 2008)
Supplement to *Pleistocene Birds of the Palaearctic: a catalogue*. Publications of the Nuttall Ornithological Club No. 27, Cambridge, Mass. 1998, ix + 720 pp. The supplementary catalogue is updated on this internet site from time to time.

http://www.flmnh.ufl.edu/research_collections.htm (20 July 2008)
Searchable database of the skins and skeletons in the Florida Museum of Natural History. The website also publishes the museum's ethical collection policy.

http://www.skullsite.com (3 January 2008)
Dutch internet site with information on the skulls and anatomy of birds from the Western Palaearctic and other areas of the world, hosted by the Experimental Zoology Group, Wageningen University, The Netherlands; includes advice on cleaning specimens and an irresistible quiz on recognizing bird skulls.

http://www.nhm.ac.uk/research-curation/departments/zoology/bird-group (3 January 2008)
Natural History Museum London, Bird Group. Introduction to the collections, library and archives. Database of bird type specimens.

http://www.toninton.de/english/1knochen.html (3 January 2008)
German internet site devoted to musical instruments; includes bird bone flutes with examples of music played on the flutes.

http://www.jiscmail.ac.uk/lists/zooarch.html (3 January 2008)
ZOOARCH: an email discussion list and newsgroup for the analysis of animal bones from archaeological sites.

http://www.racm.nl/content/xml_racm/boneinfo-00.xml.asp (3 January 2008)
BONEINFO: Dutch internet site with meta-information for archaeozoology which gives access to the literature of the Netherlands, including the grey literature.

http://www.archeozoo.org (3 January 2008)
Archéozoo: French internet site for the archaeozoological community created by the Unité Mixte de Recherche (UMR 5197) as an open forum for the exchange of information relevant to zooarchaeology. Readers can post pictures of mystery bones.

http://www.ethnozootechnie.asso.educagri.fr (3 January 2008)
Ethnozootechnie: French journal and internet site set up as a forum for the social sciences, natural sciences, and animal husbandry; promotes interdisciplinary approach to problems of animal husbandry.

http://ads.ahds.ac.uk/catalogue/collections/blurbs/348.cfm (2 January 2008)
ABMAP – Animal Bone Metrical Archive Project: a database of measurements of bones of domestic animals from more than 100 archaeological assemblages from excavations in southern Britain. The birds included are domestic fowl and goose. The assemblages are from all periods from the Neolithic to the eighteenth century AD, with most from later periods. The database gives zooarchaeologists the opportunity to find data with which to compare their own individual bone or assemblage and to research size change.

BIBLIOGRAPHY

Akishinonomiya, F., T. Miyake, S.-I. Sumi, M. Takada, S. Ohno, & N. Kondo, 1994. One subspecies of the Red Junglefowl (*Gallus Gallus Gallus*) suffices as the matriarchic ancestor of all domestic breeds. *Proceedings of the National Academy of Sciences*, 91, 12,505–12,509.

Albarella, U., 1997a. Birds of urban Italy. *Urban Nature*, 3, 76.

Albarella, U., 1997b. Crane and vulture at an Italian Bronze Age site. Special issue: Subsistence and symbol. Papers from the International Council for Archaeozoology Bird Group meeting, 1995, *International Journal of Osteoarchaeology*, 7(4), 346–349.

Albarella, U., 1997c. Size, power, wool and veal: zooarchaeological evidence for late medieval innovations, in *Environment and Subsistence in Medieval Europe*, eds. G. D. Boe & F. Verhaeghe. Papers of the Medieval Europe Brugge 1997 conference, Vol. 9. Zellik: I.A.P., 19–30.

Albarella, U., 2005. Alternate fortunes? The role of domestic ducks and geese from Roman to Medieval times in Britain, in *Feathers, Grit and Symbolism: Birds and Humans in the Ancient, Old and New worlds*, eds. G. Grupe & J. Peters. Proceedings of the 5th meeting of the ICAZ Bird Working Group, Munich, 26–28 July, 2004, Documenta Archaeobiologiae 3. Rahden: Verlag Marie Leidorf, 249–258.

Albarella, U. & R. Thomas, 2002. They dined on crane: bird consumption, wild fowling and status in medieval England. Proceedings of the 4th meeting of the ICAZ Bird Working Group, Krakow, Poland, 11–15 September, 2001, *Acta Zoologica Cracoviensia*, 45, 23–38.

Alcover, J. A., F. Florit, C. Mourer-Chauviré, & P. D. M. Weesie, 1992. The avifaunas of the isolated Mediterranean islands during the Middle and Late Pleistocene. Science Series 36. Los Angeles: Los Angeles County Museum, 273–283.

Alerstam, T., A. Hederström, & S. Åkesson, 2003. Long-distance migration: evolution and determinants. *Oikos*, 103, 247–260.

Altuna, J., A. Eastham, K. Mariezkurrena, A. Spiess, & L. Straus, 1991. Magdalenian and Azilian hunting at the abri Dufaure, SW France. *Archaeozoologia*, IV(2), 87–108.

Anderson, A. J. (ed.), 1979. *Birds of a Feather. Osteological and Archaeological Papers from the South Pacific in Honour of R. J. Scarlett*. International Series 62. Oxford: BAR.

Anderson, A. J., 1984. The extinction of moa in Southern New Zealand, in *Quaternary Extinctions: a prehistoric revolution*, eds. P. S. Martin & R. G. Klein. Tucson: The University of Arizona Press, 728–740.

Anderson, A. J., 1988. Prehistoric fowling in the Nothofagus forest of southern New Zealand. *Archaeozoologia*, II(1/2), 201–208.

Anderson, A. J., 1989a. Mechanics of overkill in the extinction of New Zealand moas. *Journal of Archaeological Science*, 16, 137–151.

Anderson, A. J., 1989b. *Prodigious Birds: Moas and Moa-Hunting in Prehistoric New Zealand*. Cambridge: Cambridge University Press.

Anderson, A. J., 1996. Origins of procellariidae hunting in the Southwest Pacific. *International Journal of Osteoarchaeology*, 6, 403–410.

Anderson, A. J., 2000. Differential reliability of 14C AMS ages of *Rattus exulans* bone gelatin in South Pacific prehistory. *Journal of the Royal Society of New Zealand*, 30(3), 243–261.

Anderson, A. J., 2001. No meat on that beautiful shore. *International Journal of Osteoarchaeology. Special Issue: Zooarchaeology of Oceanic Coasts and Islands*, 11(1–2), 14–23.

Anderson, A. J., 2005. Subpolar settlement in South Polynesia. *Antiquity*, 79, 791–800.

Anderson, A. J., H. Martinsson-Wallin, & K. Stothert, 2007. Ecuadorian sailing rafts and oceanic landfalls, in *Vastly Ingenious: Papers on Pacific Material Culture*, eds. A. J. Anderson, K. Green, & B. F. Leach. Dunedin: University of Otago Press.

Anderson, A. J. & R. McGovern-Wilson, 1991. *Beech Forest Hunters: The Archaeology of Maori Rockshelter Sites on Lee Island, Lake Te Anau, in Southern New Zealand*. Monograph 18. Auckland: New Zealand Archaeological Association.

Anderson-Mackenzie, J., D. Hulmes, & B. H. Thorp, 1997. Degenerative joint disease in poultry – differences in composition and morphology of articular cartilage are associated with strain susceptibility. *Research in Veterinary Science*, 63, 29–33.

Andrews, C. W., 1917. Report on the remains of birds found at the Glastonbury Lake-Village, in *The Glastonbury Lake Village*, eds. A. Bulleid & H. S. G. Gray. Glastonbury: Antiquarian Society, 631–637.

Andrews, P., 1990. *Owls, Caves and Fossils*. London: Natural History Museum.

Armour-Chelu, M., 1988. Taphonomic and cultural information from an assemblage of Neolithic bird bones from Orkney, in *The Exploitation of Wetlands*. British Series 186, eds. P. Murphy & C. French. Oxford: BAR, 69–76.

Atkinson, C. T., R. J. Dusek, K. L. Woods, & W. M. Iko, 2000. Pathogenicity of avian malaria in experimentally-infected Hawaii Amakihi. *Journal of Wildlife Diseases*, 36(2), 197–204.

Audoin-Rouzeau, F. & J. Pichon, 1992. Dindon. *Ethnozootechnie. Le Dindon*, 49, 63–70.

Auxiette, G., 1995. L'évolution de rituel funeraire à travers les offrands animales des nécropoles Gauloises de Bucy-le-Long (450/100 avant J.-C.). *Anthropozoologica*, 21, 245–252.

Avery, G., 1983. Late Holocene avian remains from Wortel, Walvis Bay, SWA/Namibia, and some observations on seasonality and Topnaar Hottentot prehistory. *Madoqua*, 14(1), 63–70.

Avery, G. & L. G. Underhill, 1986. Seasonal exploitation of seabirds by Late Holocene coastal foragers: analysis of modern and archaeological data from the Western Cape, South Africa. *Journal of Archaeological Science*, 13, 339–360.

Ayres, K., A. Locker, & D. Serjeantson, 2003. Mammal, bird and fish remains and oysters. Phases 2f-4a: The Medieval Abbey: Food consumption and production, in *Aelfric's Abbey: Excavations at Eynsham Abbey, Oxfordshire, 1989–1992*. Thames Valley Landscapes Volume 16, eds. A. Hardy, A. Dodd, & G. Keevill. Oxford: Oxford University School of Archaeology/Oxford Archaeology, 360–406.

Bacher, A., 1967. *Vergleichend morphologische Untersuchungen an Einzelknochen des postkranialen Skeletts in Mitteleuropa vorkommender Schwäne und Gänse*. Munich: Institut für Paläoanatomie, Domestikationsforschung und Geschichte der Tiermedizin der Universität München.

Badam, G. L., 1984. Holocene faunal material from India with special reference to domesticated animals, in *Animals and Archaeology 3: Early Herders and their Flocks*. International Series 202, eds. J. Clutton-Brock & C. Grigson. Oxford: BAR, 339–353.

Baird, R. F., 1989. Fossil bird assemblages from Australian caves: Precise indicators of late Quaternary environments? *Palaeogeography, Palaeoclimatology, Palaeoecology*, 69(3–4), 241–244.

Bakels, C. & J. T. Zeiler, 2005. The fruits of the land: Neolithic subsistence, in *The Prehistory of the Netherlands*, eds. L. P. Louwe Kooijmans, P. W. van den Broeke, H. Fokkens, & A. L. van Gijn. Amsterdam: Amsterdam University Press, 311–335.

Baker, J. & D. Brothwell, 1980. *Animal Diseases in Archaeology*. London: Academic Press.

Baldwin, J. R., 1974. Sea bird fowling in Scotland and Faroe. *Folk Life*, 12, 60–130.

Baldwin, J. R., 2005. Seabirds, subsistence and coastal communities: an overview of cultural traditions in the British Isles, in *Traditions of Seabird Fowling in the North Atlantic Region*, ed. J. Randall. Stornoway: The Islands Book Trust, 12–36.

Barclay, A., D. Serjeantson, & J. Wallis, 1999. Worked bone and antler, in *Excavations at Barrow Hills, Radley, Oxfordshire. Volume 1. The Neolithic and Bronze Age monument complex*. Thames Valley Landscapes Volume 11, eds. A. Barclay & C. Halpin. Oxford: Oxford University School of Archaeology/Oxford Archaeology, 74–76.

Barker, G. & A. Grant, 1999. Food and Farming, in *Companion Encyclopedia of Archaeology* (vol. II), ed. G. Barker. London: Routledge, 546.

Barnes, I. & K. Dobney, 2000. DNA-based identification of goose species from two archaeological sites in Lincolnshire. *Journal of Archaeological Science*, 27, 91–100.

Barnes, I., K. Dobney, & P. W. Young, 1998. The molecular palaeoecology of geese: identification of archaeological goose remains using ancient DNA analysis. *International Journal of Osteoarchaeology*, 8(4), 280–287.

Barnes, S., 2005. *How to Be a Bad Birdwatcher*. London: Short Books.

Baumel, J. J., 1979. *Handbook of Avian Anatomy: Nomina Anatomica Avium*. Cambridge, MA: Nuttall Ornithological Club.

Baumel, J. J., A. S. King, J. E. Breazile, H. E. Evans, & J. C. Vanden Berge (eds.), 1993. *Handbook of Avian Anatomy: Nomina Anatomica Avium* (2nd ed.). Cambridge, MA: Nuttall Ornithological Club.

Baumel, J. J. & L. M. Witmer, 1993. Chapter 4. Nomenclature, in *Handbook of Avian Anatomy: Nomina Anatomica Avium* (2nd ed.), eds. J. J. Baumel, A. S. King, J. E. Breazile, H. E. Evans, & J. C. Vanden Berge. Cambridge, MA: Nuttall Ornithological Club, 45–132.

Baxter, I. L., 1993. Eagles in Anglo-Saxon and Norse poems. *Circaea*, 10(2), 78–81.

Beatty, J., 1992. *Sula. Seabird-hunters of Lewis.* London: Michael Joseph.

Becker, C., 2005a. Birds, mice, and slaughter refuse from an Islamic mosque in Syria – a puzzling mixture at a peculiar location, in *Feathers, Grit and Symbolism: Birds and Humans in the Ancient, Old and New worlds*, eds. G. Grupe & J. Peters. Proceedings of the 5th meeting of the ICAZ Bird Working Group, Munich, 26–28 July, 2004, Documenta Archaeobiologiae 3. Rahden: Verlag Marie Leidorf, 272–280.

Becker, C., 2005b. The sound of music over ar-Raqqa – on a rare find of a flute from an Islamic glassworks. *Revue de Paléobiologie*, 10, 327–336.

Behrensmeyer, A. K., 1978. Taphonomic and ecologic information from bone weathering. *Paleobiology*, 4, 150–162.

Bellairs, A. D. A. & C. R. Jenkin, 1960. The skeleton of birds, in *Biology and Comparative Physiology of Birds*, ed. A. J. Marshall. London: Academic Press.

Bellwood, P., 2005. *First Farmers: The Origins of Agricultural Societies.* Carlton, Victoria: Blackwell.

Benecke, N., 1993. On the utilization of the domestic fowl in Central Europe from the Iron age up to the Middle Ages. *Archaeofauna. Archaeornithology: Birds and the Archaeological Record*, 2, 21–31.

Benecke, N., 1994. *Der Mensch und seine Haustiere.* Stuttgart: Theiss.

Bennet, A. C. & R. L. Lyman, 1991. Archaeology of Whale Cove (35LNC60), in *Prehistory of the Oregon Coast*, ed. R. L. Lyman. New York: Academic Press.

Bergman, C. A., 1993. The development of the bow in Western Europe: a technological and functional perspective. *Archaeological Papers of the American Anthropological Association*, 4(1), 95–105.

Bickhart, K. J., 1984. A field experiment in avian taphonomy. *Journal of Vertebrate Palaeontology*, 4, 525–535.

Biltz, R. M. & E. D. Pellegrino, 1965. Avian osteopetrotic bone. *Journal of Bone and Joint Surgery*, 47A, 1365–1377.

Binford, L. R., 1981. *Bones: Ancient Men and Modern Myths.* New York: Academic Press.

Birkhead, T., 1993. *Great Auk Islands: A Field Biologist in the Arctic.* London: Poyser.

Blench, R. & K. C. MacDonald, 2000. Chickens, in *The Cambridge World History of Food* (vol. 1), eds. K. F. Kiple & K. C. Ornelas. Cambridge: Cambridge University Press, 496–499.

Blondel, J. & C. Mourer-Chauviré, 1998. Evolution and history of the western Palaearctic avifauna. *Tree*, 13(12), 488–492.

Blount, W. P., 1947. *Diseases of poultry, with specialist chapters on poultry husbandry.* Baltimore: Williams & Wilkins.

Bochenski, Z. M. (ed.), 2002. Proceedings of the 4th meeting of the ICAZ Bird Working Group, Krakow, Poland, 11–15 September, 2001, *Acta Zoologica Cracoviensia*, 45.

Bochenski, Z. M., 2005. Owls, diurnal raptors and humans: signatures on avian bones, in *Biosphere to Lithosphere*, ed. T. O'Connor. Oxford: Oxbow, 31–45.

Bochenski, Z. M. & K. E. Campbell, 2005. The identification of turkey remains to species – a metrical approach, in *Feathers, Grit and Symbolism: Birds and Humans in the Ancient, Old and New worlds*, eds. G. Grupe & J. Peters. Proceedings of the 5th meeting of the ICAZ Bird Working Group, Munich, 26–28 July, 2004, Documenta Archaeobiologiae 3. Rahden: Verlag Marie Leidorf, 19–26.

Bochenski, Z. M. & K. E. Campbell, 2006. *The extinct California turkey*, Meleagris californica, *from Rancho La Brea: comparative osteology and systematics*, in Contributions in Science 509. Los Angeles: Los Angeles Natural History Museum.

Bochenski, Z. M., K. Huhtala, P. Jussila, E. Pulliainen, R. Tornberg, & P. S. Tunkkari, 1998. Damage to bird bones in pellets of Gyrfalcon *Falco rusticolus*. *Journal of Archaeological Science*, 25, 425–433.

Bochenski, Z. M. & T. Tomek, 1995. How many comparative skeletons do we need to identify a bird bone? *Courier Forschungsinstitut Senckenberg*, 181, 357–361.

Bochenski, Z. M. & T. Tomek, 1997. Preservation of bird bones: erosion versus digestion by owls. Special issue: Subsistence and symbol. Papers from the International Council for Archaeozoology Bird Group meeting, 1995, *International Journal of Osteoarchaeology*, 7(4), 372–387.

Boessneck, J., 1991. Riesige Hausgänse aus der Spätzeit des Alten Ägypten. *Archiv für Geflügelkunde*, 55, 105–110.

Boessneck, J. & A. von den Driesch, 1973. *Die jungpleistozänen Tierknochenfunde aus der Brillenhöhle*. Stuttgart: Müller and Graff.

Boessneck, J. & A. von den Driesch, 1979. *Eketorp. Befestigung und Siedlung auf Oland/Schweden. Die Fauna*. Stockholm: Almqvist and Wiksell.

Boessneck, J. & A. von den Driesch, 1982. *Studien an subfossilen Tierknochen aus Ägypten*. Munich: Institut für Paläoanatomie, Domestikationsforschung und Geschichte der Tiermedizin der Universität München.

Boessneck, J. & A. von den Driesch, 1988. *Die Tierwelt des alten Ägypten untersucht anhand kulturgeschichtlicher und zoologischer Quellen*. Munich: Beck.

Boev, Z., 1993. Archaeo-ornithological and synanthropisation of birds: a case study for Bulgaria. *Archaeofauna*, 2, 145–153.

Boev, Z., 1995. On the appearance of the domestic fowl (*Gallus gallus* domestica) in Bulgaria and Balkan Peninsula and the question of domestication of junglefowls (Genus Gallus Brisson, 1760) in southeast Europe. *Historia Naturalis Bulgarica*, 5, 37–49.

Boev, Z., 1996. The Holocene avifauna of Bulgaria (A review of the ornitho-archaeological studies). *Historia Naturalis Bulgarica*, 6, 59–81.

Bogucki, P., 1979. Neolithic bird remains from Brzesc Kujawski, Poland. *Ossa*, 3(7), 33–40.

Bogucki, P., 1999. Foragers and farmers, in *Companion Encyclopedia of Archaeology* (vol. 2), ed. G. Barker. London: Routledge, 839–869.

Boisseau, S. & D. Yalden, 1998. The former status of the Crane *Grus grus* in Britain. *Ibis*, 140, 482–500.

Boissier, A., 1984. Un habitat et un mode de vie traditionnel, in *Notes et monographies techniques 16*. CNRS 2nd Fish Osteoarchaeology meeting, ed. N. Desse-Berset. Valbonne: CNRS, 195–200.

Bökönyi, S. & L. Bartosiewicz, 1983. Testing the utility of quantitative methods in sex determination of hen (*Gallus gallus* L.) bones. *Zoologischer Anzeiger, Jena*, 210(3/4), 204–212.

Bond, J. M., 1996. Burnt offerings: animal bone in Anglo-Saxon cremations. *World Archaeology*, 28(1), 76–88.

Bond, J. M. & T. P. O'Connor, 1999. *Bones from Medieval deposits at 16–22 Coppergate and other sites in York. The Archaeology of York. The animal bones, 15/5*, York: Council for British Archaeology.

Bond, J. M. & F. L. Worley, 2006. Companions in death: the roles of animals in Anglo-Saxon and Viking cremation rituals in Britain, in *Social Archaeology of Funerary Remains*, eds. R. Gowland & C. Knusel. Oxford: Oxbow, 89–98.

Borson, N., F. Berdan, E. Strak, J. States, & P. J. Wettstein, 1998. Origins of an Anasazi Scarlet Macaw feather artifact. *American Antiquity*, 63(1), 131–142.

Bottema, S., 1975. The use of gastroliths in archaeology, in *Archaeozoological Studies*, ed. A. T. Clason. Amsterdam: North-Holland Publishing Company, 397–406.

Bottema, S., 1989. Some observations on modern domestication processes, in *The Walking Larder: Patterns of Domestication, Pastoralism and Predation*. One World Archaeology 2. London: Unwin Hyman.

Bourdillon, J., 1998. The faunal remains, in *The Lost Manor of Hextalls, Little Pickle, Bletchingley*, ed. R. Poulton. Kingston: Surrey County Archaeological Unit, 139–174.

Bourne, W. R. P., 1981. The birds and animals consumed when Henry VIII entertained the King of France and the Count of Flanders at Calais in 1532. *Archives of Natural History*, 10(2), 331–333.

Bovy, K. M., 2002. Differential avian skeletal part distribution: explaining the abundance of wings. *Journal of Archaeological Science*, 29, 965–978.

Boyer, P., 1999. The eggshell, in *Roman and Medieval Occupation in Causeway Lane, Leicester. Excavations 1980 and 1991*. Leicester Archaeology Monographs No. 5, eds. A. Connor & R. Buckley. Leicester: Leicester City Museum Service, 329–333.

Brain, C. K., 1976. Some principles in the interpretation of bone accumulations associated with man, in *Human Origins: Louis Leakey and the East African Evidence*, eds. G. L. Isaac & E. McCown. Berkeley, CA: Benjamin, 97–116.

Bramwell, D., 1960. Report on a collection of bird bones from the 1929 excavations at Soldier's Hole, Cheddar. *Proceedings of the Somersetshire Archaeological and Natural History Society*, 104, 87–90.

Bramwell, D., 1977. Bird bone, in *Kings Lynn Excavations, 1963–1970*, eds. H. Clarke & A. Carter. London: Society for Medieval Archaeology, 399–409.

Bramwell, D., D. W. Yalden, & P. E. Yalden, 1987. Black grouse as the prey of the golden eagle at an archaeological site. *Journal of Archaeological Science*, 14, 195–200.

Bratrein, H. D., 2005. Sea-bird fowling in northern Norway, in *Traditions of Seabird Fowling in the North Atlantic Region*, ed. J. Randall. Stornoway: The Islands Book Trust, 181–193.

Brisbin, I. L., 1995. Conservation of the wild ancestors of domestic animals. *Conservation Biology*, 9(5), 1327–1328.

Brisbin, I. L. J., 1993. The Carolina bantam chicken – an experimental approach to life in the feral state. *American Minor Breeds Conservancy News*, 10(1), 1, 4–5.

Brooke, M., 1990. *The Manx Shearwater.* London: Poyser.

Brothwell, D., 1993. Avian osteopathology and its evaluation. *Archaeofauna. Archaeornithology: Birds and the Archaeological Record*, 2, 33–43.

Brothwell, D., 1997. Interpreting the immature chicken bones from the Romano-British ritual complex on West Hill, Uley. Special issue: Subsistence and symbol. Papers from the International Council for Archaeozoology Bird Group meeting, 1995, *International Journal of Osteoarchaeology*, 7(4), 330–332.

Brothwell, D., 2002. Ancient avian osteopetrosis: the current state of knowledge. Proceedings of the 4th meeting of the ICAZ Bird Working Group, Krakow, Poland, 11–15 September, 2001, *Acta Zoologica Cracoviensia*, 45, 315–318.

Broughton, J. M., D. Mullins & T. Ekker, 2007. Avian resource depression or intertaxonomic variation in bone density? A test with San Francisco Bay avifaunas. *Journal of Archaeological Science*, 34, 374–391.

Broughton, J. M., D. Rampton & K. Holanda, 2002. A test of an osteologically based age determination technique in the Double-crested Cormorant *Phalacrocorax auritus. Ibis*, 144, 143–146.

Brown, L., 1976. *British Birds of Prey. New Naturalist 60.* London: Collins.

Brown, L. D. & C. Heron, 2005. Presence or absence: a preliminary study into the detection of fish oils in ceramics, in *The Zooarchaeology of Milk and Fats*, eds. J. Mulville & A. Outram. Oxford: Oxbow, 67–76.

Brown, R., J. Ferguson, M. Lawrence, & D. Lees, 1999. *Tracks and Signs of the Birds of Britain and Europe.* London: Helm.

Bulmer, R., 1979. Tameness and mystical associations of wild birds, in *Birds of a Feather. Osteological and Archaeological Papers from the South Pacific in Honour of R. J. Scarlett.* International Series 62, ed. A. J. Anderson. Oxford: BAR, 67–74.

Burke, A., 2001. Patterns of animal exploitation at Leptiminus: faunal remains from the East Baths and from the cemetery (site 10). *Journal of Roman Archaeology*, (Supplement 41), 442–456.

Canby, J. V., 2002. Falconry (hawking) in Hittite lands. *Journal of Near Eastern Studies*, 61(3), 161–201.

Carter, G. F., 1971. Pre-Columbian chickens in America, in *Man Across the Sea: Problems of Pre-Columbian Contacts*, eds. C. L. Riley, J. C. Kelley, C. W. Pennington, & R. L. Rands. Austin: University of Texas Press, 178–218.

Cassoli, P. F. & A. Tagliacozzo, 1997. Butchering and cooking of birds in the Palaeolithic site of Grotta Romanelli, Italy. Special issue: Subsistence and symbol: Papers from the International Council for Archaeozoology Bird Group meeting, 1995, *International Journal of Osteoarchaeology*, 7(4), 303–320.

Causey, D., D. G. Corbett, C. Lefèvre, D. L. West, A. B. Savinetsky, N. K. Kisleva, & B. F. Khassanov, 2005. The palaeoenvironment of humans and marine birds of the

Aleutian Islands: three millennia of change. *Fisheries Oceanography*, 14(Supplement 1), 259–276.

Causey, D. & C. Lefèvre, 2007. Diagnostic osteology and analysis of the mid- to late Holocene dynamics of shags and cormorants in Tierra del Fuego. *International Journal of Osteoarchaeology*, 17, 119–137.

Ceron-Carrasco, R., 1994. Feathers from deposit F23 in the stone-lined pit (F22), in *Excavations at Pluscarden Priory, Moray*, ed. F. McCormick. Edinburgh: Society of Antiquaries of Scotland, 414.

Chami, F. A., 2004. Implementation of the Swedish-sponsored archaeological project on the coast of East Africa and its deep interior. in *Arkeologi och antik historia: Afrikansk och jämförande arkeologi: ULD-symposium*. Uppsala, Sweden: Uppsala University; http://www.arkeoligi.uu.se/afr/symposium/abstracts/chami.htm.

Cherryson, A., 2002. The identification of archaeological evidence for hawking in Medieval England. Proceedings of the 4th meeting of the ICAZ Bird Working Group, Krakow, Poland, 11–15 September, 2001, *Acta Zoologica Cracoviensia*, 45, 307–314.

Christensen, A. F., 2000. The fifteenth- and twentieth-century colonization of the Basin of Mexico by the Great-tailed grackle (*Quiscalus mexicanus*). *Global Ecology & Biogeography*, 9, 415–420.

Chun, M. S., 2005. Ung Kol Pang, a 14th century Korean treatise on falconry, in *Feathers, Grit and Symbolism: Birds and Humans in the Ancient, Old and New worlds*, eds. G. Grupe & J. Peters. Proceedings of the 5th meeting of the ICAZ Bird Working Group, Munich, 26–28 July, 2004, Documenta Archaeobiologiae 3. Rahden: Verlag Marie Leidorf, 287–294.

Clark, J. G. D., 1948. Fowling in prehistoric Europe. *Antiquity*, 22, 116–130.

Clark, J. G. D., 1952. *Prehistoric Europe: The Economic Basis*. Cambridge: Cambridge University Press.

Clark, J. G. D., 1961. *World Prehistory: A New Outline*. Cambridge: Cambridge University Press.

Clason, A. T., 1967. *Animals and Man in Holland's Past*. Groningen: J. B. Wolters.

Clason, A. T. & D. Brinkhuisen, 1993. Bergschenhoek, in *Skeletons in Her Cupboard. Festschrift for Juliet Clutton-Brock*, eds. A. T. Clason, S. Payne, & P. Uerpmann. Oxford: Oxbow, 61–73.

Clason, A. T. & A. Prummel, 1979. Bird remains from the Netherlands, in *Archaeozoology*, ed. M. Kubasiewicz. Szczecin, Poland: Agricultural Academy, 233–242.

Clavel, B., 2001. L'animal dans l'alimentation médiévale et moderne en France du Nord (XIIe–XVIIe siècles). *Revue Archéologique de Picardie. Numéro spécial*, 19, 108–111.

Clavel, B., M. C. Marinval-Vigne, S. Leptetz, & J.-H. Yvinec, 1997. Evolution de la taille et de la morphologie du coq au cours de périodes historiques en France du Nord. Le Coq. *Ethnozootechnie*, 58, 3–12.

Clayton, G. A., 1984a. Common duck, in *Evolution of Domesticated Animals*, ed. I. L. Mason. London: Longman, 334–339.

Clayton, G. A., 1984b. Muscovy duck, in *Evolution of Domesticated Animals*, ed. I. L. Mason. London: Longman, 340–344.

Clottes, J., J. Courtin, J. Collina-Girard, J. Arnold, & H. Valladas, 1997. News from Cosquer Cave. *Antiquity*, 71, 321–326.

Clutton-Brock, J., 1981a. *Domesticated Animals From Early Times*, London: Heinemann/British Museum (Natural History).

Clutton-Brock, J., 1981b. Nomenclature of the domestic mammals, in *Domesticated Animals From Early Times*, ed. J. Clutton-Brock. London: Heinemann/British Museum (Natural History), 194–197.

Cohen, A. & D. Serjeantson, 1996. *A Manual for the Identification of Bird Bones From Archaeological Sites*. London: Archetype Press.

Cole, R. K. & R. E. Austic, 1980. Hereditary uricemia and articular gout in chickens. *Poultry Science*, 59, 951–975.

Columella, L. J. M., 1941. *Columella De Re Rustica V-IX*. London: Heinemann.

Cook, M. E., 2000. Skeletal deformities and their causes: introduction. *Poultry Science*, 79, 982–984.

Cook, T. & R. E. M. Pilcher, 1982. *The History of the Borough Fen Decoy*. Ely: Providence Press.

Cooper, J., 2007. A tomb wader: X-raying the birds of the gods. *Bulletin of the British Ornithologists' Club*, 125(2), 162.

Cooper, J. H., 2005. Pigeons and pelagics: interpreting the Late Pleistocene avifaunas of the continental 'island' of Gibraltar. Proceedings of the international symposium, Insular Vertebrate Evolution: The Palaeontological Approach, Mallorca, Spain, 16–19 September, 2003, *Monografies de la Societat d'Historia Natural de les Balears*, 12, 101–112.

Corke, E., S. Davis, & S. Payne, 1998. The organisation of a zoo-archaeological reference collection of bird bones. *Environmental Archaeology*, 2, 67–69.

Corona-M., E., 2005. Archaeozoology and the role of birds in the traditional medicine of pre-Hispanic Mexico, in *Feathers, Grit and Symbolism: Birds and Humans in the Ancient, Old and New worlds*, eds. G. Grupe & J. Peters. Proceedings of the 5th meeting of the ICAZ Bird Working Group, Munich, 26–28 July, 2004, Documenta Archaeobiologiae 3. Rahden: Verlag Marie Leidorf, 295–302.

Corona-M., E., 2002. The pleistocene bird record of Mexico. Proceedings of the 4th meeting of the ICAZ Bird Working Group, Krakow, Poland, 11–15 September, 2001, *Acta Zoologica Cracoviensia*, 45, 293–306.

Cosgrove, R., 1995. *The Illusion of Riches: Scale, Resolution and Explanation in Tasmanian Pleistocene Human Behaviour*. International Series 608. Oxford: BAR.

Cowles, G. S., 1981. The first evidence of Demoiselle Crane (*Anthropoides virgo*) and Pygmy Cormorant (*Phalacrocorax pygmaeus*) in Britain. *Bulletin of the British Ornithologists' Club*, 101(4), 383–385.

Coy, J., 1982. The role of wild vertebrate fauna in urban economies in Wessex, in *Environmental Archaeology in the Urban Context*, eds. A. R. Hall & H. K. Kenward. London: Council for British Archaeology, 107–116.

Coy, J., 1983. Birds as food in prehistoric and historic Wessex, in *Animals in Archaeology: 2. Shell Middens, Fishes and Birds*. International Series 183, eds. C. Grigson & J. Clutton-Brock. Oxford: BAR, 181–195.

Coy, J., 1984. The bird bones, in *Danebury* (vol. 2), ed. B. Cunliffe. London: CBA, 527–531.

Coy, J., 1989. The provision of fowls and fish for towns, in *Diet and Crafts in Towns: The Evidence of Animal Remains From the Roman to the Post-Medieval Periods*. British Series 199, eds. D. Serjeantson & T. Waldron. Oxford: BAR, 25–40.

Cracraft, J., F. K. Barker, & A. Cibois, 2003. Avian higher-level phylogenetics and the Howard and Moore checklist of birds, in *The Howard and Moore Complete Checklist of the Birds of the World*, ed. E. C. Dickinson. Princeton, NJ: Princeton University Press, 16–21.

Cramp, S. (ed.), 1977. *Handbook of the Birds of Europe, the Middle East and North Africa* (vol. 1). Oxford: Oxford University Press.

Cramp, S. (ed.), 1980. *Handbook of the Birds of Europe, the Middle East and North Africa. The birds of the Western Palearctic* (vol. II). Oxford: University Press.

Crawford, R. D., 1984a. Domestic fowl, in *Evolution of Domesticated Animals*, ed. I. L. Mason. London: Longman, 298–311.

Crawford, R. D., 1984b. Goose, in *Evolution of Domesticated Animals*, ed. I. L. Mason. London: Longman, 345–349.

Crawford, R. D., 1984c. Turkey, in *Evolution of Domesticated Animals*, ed. I. L. Mason. London: Longman, 325–334.

Creel, D. & C. R. McKusick, 1994. Prehistoric macaws and parrots in the Mimbres area, New Mexico. *American Antiquity*, 59(3), 510–524.

Crockford, S., G. Frederick, & R. Wigen, 1997. A humerus story: albatross element distribution from two Northwest coast sites, North America. Special issue: Subsistence and symbol. Papers from the International Council for Archaeozoology Bird Group meeting, 1995, *International Journal of Osteoarchaeology*, 7(4), 287–291.

Crowe, A., 2001. *Which New Zealand bird?* Auckland: Penguin Books.

Cruz, I., 2005. La representación de partes esqueléticas de aves. Patrones naturales e interpretación arqueológica. *Archaeofauna*, 14, 69–81.

Cruz, I., 2008. Avian and mammalian bone taphonomy in southern continental Patagonia: A comparative approach. *Quaternary International*, 180, 30–37.

Csapo, E., 1993a. Deep ambivalence: notes on a Greek cockfight (Part I). *Phoenix*, 47(1), 1–28.

Csapo, E., 1993b. Deep ambivalence: notes on a Greek cockfight (Part II-IV). *Phoenix*, 47(2), 115–124.

Cupere, B. de, W. Van Neer, H. Monchot, E. Rijmenants, M. Udrescu, & M. Waelkens, 2005. Ancient breeds of domestic fowl (*Gallus gallus* f. domestica) distinguished on the basis of traditional observations combined with mixture analysis. *Journal of Archaeological Science*, 32, 1587–1597.

Darwent, C. M., 2004. The highs and lows of High Arctic mammals: temporal change and regional variability in Paleoeskimo subsistence, in *Colonisation, Migration and Marginal Areas*, eds. M. Mondini, S. Munoz, & S. Wickler. Oxford: Oxbow, 62–73.

Darwin, C. R., 1868. *The Variation of Animals and Plants Under Domestication* (vol. 1). London: John Murray.

Darwin, C. R., 1897. *Journal of Researches Into the Natural History and Geology of the Countries Visited During the Voyage of HMS 'Beagle' Round the World* (rev. ed.). London: John Murray.

Davis, P. G., 1997. The bioerosion of bird bones. Special issue: Subsistence and symbol. Papers from the International Council for Archaeozoology Bird Group meeting, 1995, *International Journal of Osteoarchaeology*, 7(4), 388–401.

Davis, P. G. & D. E. G. Briggs, 1995. Fossilization of feathers. *Geology*, 23(9), 783–786.

Davis, S. J. M., 1989. Animal remains from the Iron Age cemetery, in *Verulamium, the King Harry Lane Site*. English Heritage Archaeology Report 12, eds. I. M. Stead & V. Rigby. London: English Heritage, 250–259.

Davis, S. J. M., 1992. A rapid method for recording information about mammal bones from archaeological sites. Ancient Monuments Laboratory Reports 19/92. London: English Heritage.

Davis, S. & S. Payne, 1992. 101 ways to deal with a dead hedgehog: notes on the preparation of disarticulated skeletons for zoo-archaeological use. *Circaea*, 8[1992 for 1990(2)], 95–104.

Davis, T. N., 1980. Gizzard stones. *Alaska Science Forum, November 3rd 1980*, Article 439, 1.

Dawson, E. W., 1969. Bird remains in archaeology, in *Science in Archaeology* (2nd ed.), eds. D. Brothwell & E. S. Higgs. London: Thames and Hudson, 359–375.

deFrance, S. D., 2005. Late Pleistocene marine birds from southern Peru: distinguishing human capture from El Niño-induced windfall. *Journal of Archaeological Science*, 32, 1131–1146.

DePuydt, R. T., 1994. Cultural implications of avifaunal remains recovered from the Ozette site, in *Ozette Archaeological Project Research Reports, Volume II, Fauna*, ed. S. R. Samuels. Seattle: Department of Anthropology, Washington State University, Pullman, and National Park Service, Seattle.

D'Errico, F., 1994. Birds of the Grotte Cosquer: the Great Auk and Palaeolithic prehistory. *Antiquity*, 68, 39–47.

D'Errico, F., C. Henshilwood, G. Lawson, M. Vanhaeren, A.-M. Tillier, M. Soressi, F. Bresson, B. Maureille, A. Nowell, J. Lakarra, L. Backwell, & M. Julien, 2003. Archaeological evidence for the emergence of language, symbolism and music – an alternative multidisciplinary perspective. *Journal of World Prehistory*, 17(1), 1–70.

Dewar, R. E., 1984. Extinctions in Madagascar: The loss of the subfossil fauna, in *Quaternary Extinctions: A Prehistoric Revolution*, eds. P. S. Martin & R. G. Klein. Tucson: The University of Arizona Press, 574–593.

Diamond, J., 1984. Historic extinctions: a Rosetta stone for understanding prehistoric extinctions, in *Quaternary Extinctions: A Prehistoric Revolution*, eds. P. S. Martin & R. G. Klein. Tucson: The University of Arizona Press, 824–862.

Diamond, J., 2002. *The Rise and Fall of the Third Chimpanzee*. London: Vintage Press.

Dickinson, E. C., 2003. *The Howard and Moore Complete Checklist of the Birds of the World.* (3rd ed.). Princeton, NJ: Princeton University Press.

Diez Fernandez-Lomana, C., A. Sanchez Marco, & V. Moreno Lara, 1995. Grupos avicaptores del Tardiglaciar: Las aves de Berroberria. *Munibe*, 47, 3–22.

Dirrigl, F. J. Jr, 2001. Bone mineral density of wild turkey (*Meleagris gallopavo*): skeletal elements and its effect on differential survivorship. *Journal of Archaeological Science*, 28, 817–832.

Dirrigl, F. J. Jr, 2002. Differential identifiability between chosen North American gallinaceous skeletons and the effect of differential survivorship. Proceedings of the 4th meeting of the ICAZ Bird Working Group, Krakow, Poland, 11–15 September, 2001, *Acta Zoologica Cracoviensia*, 45, 357–367.

Dirrigl, F. J. Jr, 2004. Dual-energy X-ray absorptiometry of birds: an examination of excised skeletal specimens. *Journal of Veterinary Medicine*, A51, 313–319.

Dobney, K. & D. Jaques, 2002. Avian signatures for identity and status in Anglo-Saxon England. Proceedings of the 4th meeting of the ICAZ Bird Working Group, Krakow, Poland, 11–15 September, 2001, *Acta Zoologica Cracoviensia*, 45, 7–21.

Dohner, J. V., 2001. *The Encyclopedia of Historic and Endangered Livestock and Poultry Breeds*. New Haven, CT: Yale University Press.

Dove, C. J., 1997. Quantification of microscopic feather characters used in the identification of North American plovers. *The Condor*, 99, 47–57.

Dove, C. J., 1998. Feather evidence helps clarify locality of anthropological artifacts in the Museum of Mankind. *Pacific Studies*, 21(3), 73–85.

Dove, C. J., 1999. Feather identification and a new electronic system for reporting US Air Force bird strikes. Proceedings of the first USA/Canada joint annual meeting of the Bird Strike Committee, Vancouver, BC, 1999; http://digitalcommons.unl.edu/birdstrike1999/13.

Dove, C. J., P. G. Hare, & M. Heacker, 2005. Identification of ancient feather fragments found in melting Alpine Ice patches in Southern Yukon. *Arctic*, 58(1), 38–43.

Dove, C. J. & S. Peurach, 2002. Microscopic analysis of feather and hair fragments associated with human mummified remains from Kagamil Island, Alaska, in *To the Aleutians and Beyond: The Anthropology of William S Laughlin*. Ethnographical series 20, eds. B. Frohlich, A. B. Harper, & R. Gilberg. Copenhagen: Department of Ethnography, National Museum of Denmark, 51–61.

Driver, J., 1982. Medullary bone as an indicator of sex in bird remains from archaeological sites, in *Ageing and Sexing Animal Bones from Archaeological Sites*. British Series 109, eds. B. Wilson, C. Grigson, & S. Payne. Oxford: BAR, 251–254.

Driver, J., 1999. Raven skeletons from Palaeoindian contexts, Charlie Lake Cave, British Columbia. *American Antiquity*, 64(2), 289–298.

Driver, J. C., 1992. Identification, classification and zooarchaeology. *Circaea*, 9 [1992 for 1991(1)], 35–47.

Driver, J. C. & K. A. Hobson, 1992. A 10,500-year sequence of bird remains from the southern Boreal forest region of Western Canada. *Arctic*, 45(2), 105–10.

Duff, S. R., 1984. The morphology of degenerative hip disease in male breeding turkeys. *Journal of Comparative Pathology*, 94, 127–139.

Duff, S. R., 1990. Diseases of the musculoskeletal system, in *Poultry diseases*, ed. F. T. W. Jordan. London: Baillière Tindall, 254–283.

Duff, S. R. & B. H. Thorp, 1985. Patterns of physiological bone torsion in the pelvic appendicular skeletons of domestic fowl. *Research in Veterinary Science*, 39, 307–312.

Eastham, A., 1971. The bird bones, in *Excavations at Fishbourne, 1961–1969*, ed. B. Cunliffe. London: Society of Antiquaries, 388–393.

Eastham, A., 1977. Birds, in *Excavations at Portchester Castle: Vol 3: Medieval: The Inner Bailey*, ed. B. Cunliffe. London: Society of Antiquaries, 233–239.

Eastham, A., 1985. The Magdalenian avifauna at Erralla cave. *Munibe*, 37, 59–80.

Eastham, A., 1997. The potential of bird remains for environmental reconstruction. Special issue: Subsistence and symbol. Papers from the International Council for Archaeozoology Bird Group meeting, 1995, *International Journal of Osteoarchaeology*, 7(4), 422–429.

Eastham, A., 2001. Choughs, man and a shared environment: a study of chough bones from Upper Pleistocene sites in south west Europe, in *Animals and Man in the Past: Essays in Honor of Dr. A.T. Clason*, eds. H. Buitenhuis & W. Prummel. Groningen: ARC-Publicatie, 178–191.

Eastham, A. & M. Eastham, 1995. Palaeolithic images and the Great Auk. *Antiquity*, 69, 1023–1025.

Eastham, A. & I. A. Gwynn, 1997. Archaeology and the electron microscope: eggshell and neural network analysis of images in the Neolithic. *Anthropozoologica*, 25, 85–94.

Eda, M., Y. Baba, H. Koike, & H. Higuchi, 2006. Do temporal size differences influence species identification of archaeological albatross remains when using modern reference samples? *Journal of Archaeological Science*, 33(3), 349–359.

Eda, M., H. Koike, F. Sato, & H. Higuchi, 2005. Why were so many albatross remains found in northern Japan?, in *Feathers, Grit and Symbolism: Birds and Humans in the Ancient, Old and New Worlds*, eds. G. Grupe & J. Peters. Proceedings of the 5th meeting of the ICAZ Bird Working Group, Munich, 26–28 July, 2004, Documenta Archaeobiologiae 3. Rahden: Verlag Marie Leidorf, 131–140.

Edwards, H. M., 2000. Nutrition and skeletal problems in poultry. *Poultry Science*, 79, 1018–1023.

Elston, D. A., A. W. Illius, & I. T. Gordon, 1996. Assessment of preference among a range of options using log ratio analysis. *Ecology*, 77(8), 2538–2548.

Emery, K. F., 2004. In search of assemblage comparability: methods in Maya zooarchaeology, in *Maya Zooarchaeology: New Directions in Theory and Method*. Monograph 51, ed. K. F. Emery. Los Angeles: Cotsen Institute of Archaeology, University of California, Los Angeles, 28–30.

Emslie, S. D., 1981. Birds and prehistoric agriculture: The New Mexican pueblos. *Human Ecology*, 9(3), 305–329.

Enghoff, I. B., 2003. *Hunting, Fishing and Animal Husbandry at The Farm Beneath the Sand, Western Greenland*. Man and Society 28. Copenhagen: Danish Polar Centre.

English Heritage, 1991. *Management of Archaeological Projects*. London: English Heritage.

Erbersdorbler, K., 1968. *Vergleichend morphologische Untersuchungen an Einzelknochen des postkranialen Skeletts in Mitteleuropa vorkommender mittelgrosser Hühnervögel*. Munich:

Institut für Paläoanatomie, Domestikationsforschung und Geschichte der Tiermedizin der Universität München.

Ericson, P., 1987. Interpretations of archaeological bird remains: a taphonomic approach. *Journal of Archaeological Science*, 14, 65–75.

Ericson, P. & T. Tyrberg, 2004. *The Early History of the Swedish Avifauna. A Review of the Subfossil Record and Early Written Sources*. Stockholm: Kungl. Vitterhets Historie och Antikvitets Akademien.

Ericson, P. G. P., T. Tyrberg, A. S. Kjellberg, L. Jonsson, & I. Ullen, 1997. The earliest record of House Sparrows (*Passer domesticus*) in Northern Europe. *Journal of Archaeological Science*, 24(2), 183–190.

Erritzoe, J., 2005. *House of Bird Research*; http://www.birdresearch.dk/gb/gbmenu.htm; 6 May 2006.

Esser, E. & M. Verhagen, 2001. The white stork (*Ciconia ciconia*) in an archaeological and historical perspective, in *Animal and Man in the Past: Essays in Honor of Dr. A.T. Clason*, eds. H. Buitenhus & W. Prummel. Groningen: ARC-Publicatie, 291–307.

Estevez, J., L. Mameli, & N. Goodall, 2002. An expert system to help taxonomic classification in avian archaeology: a first attempt with bird species from Tierra del Fuego. Proceedings of the 4th meeting of the ICAZ Bird Working Group, Krakow, Poland, 11–15 September, 2001, *Acta Zoologica Cracoviensia*, 45, 383–391.

Estevez, J., E. Piana, A. Schiavini, & N. Juan-Muns, 2001. Archaeological analysis of shell middens in the Beagle Channel, Tierra del Fuego Island. *International Journal of Osteoarchaeology. Special Issue: Zooarchaeology of Oceanic Coasts and Islands*, 11(1–2), 24–33.

Evans, C. & D. Serjeantson, 1988. The backwater economy of a fen-edge community in the Iron Age: the Upper Delphs, Haddenham. *Antiquity*, 62, 360–370.

Feduccia, A., 1999. *The Origin and Evolution of Birds*. New Haven, CT: Yale University Press.

Fenton, A., 1978. *The Northern Isles*. Edinburgh: John Donald.

Fick, O. K. W., 1974. *Vergleichend morphologische Untersuchungen an Einzelknochen europäischer Taubenarten*. Munich: Institut für Paläoanatomie, Domestikationsforschung und Geschichte der Tiermedizin der Universität München.

Fishel, R. L., 1997. Medicine birds and Mill Creek-Middle Mississippian interaction. The contents of Feature 8 at the Phipps Site (13CK21). *American Antiquity*, 62(3), 538–553.

Fisher, J., 1947. *The Birds of Britain*. London: Collins.

Fisher, J., 1966. *The Shell Bird Book*. London: Ebury Press.

Fisher, J. & R. T. Peterson, 1964. *The World of Birds*. London: MacDonald.

Fitzgerald, G. R., 1991. Pleistocene ducks of the Old Crow Basin, Yukon Territory, Canada. *Canadian Journal of Earth Sciences*, 28, 1561–1571.

Fok, K. W., C. M. Wade, & D. T. Parkin, 2002. Inferring the phylogeny of disjunct populations of the azure-winged magpie *Cyanopica cyanus* from mitochondrial control region sequences. *Proceedings of the Royal Society of London. Biological Sciences*, 269(1501), 1671–1679.

Fraser, J. G., 1963. *The Golden Bough* (abridged. ed.). London: Macmillan.

Fuller, D. Q., 2006. Agricultural origins and frontiers in South Asia: a working synthesis. *Journal of World Prehistory*, 20, 1–86.

Fuller, E., 1999. *The Great Auk*. Southborough, Kent: Erroll Fuller.

Gade, D. W., 2000. Muscovy ducks, in *The Cambridge World History of Food* (vol. 1), eds. K. F. Kiple & K. C. Ornelas. Cambridge: Cambridge University Press, 559–561.

Gál, E., 2005a. New data on bird bone artefacts from Hungary and Romania, in *From Hooves to Horns, from Mollusc to Mammoth*, eds. H. Luik, A. M. Choyke, C. Batey, & L. Lōugas. Tallinn, Estonia: Muinasaja Teadus, 325–338.

Gál, E., 2005b. New evidence of fowling and poultry keeping in Pannonia, Dacia and Moesia during the period of the Roman Empire. *Documenta Archaeobiologiae*, 3, 303–318.

Gál, E., 2006a. Bird bone double pipe from the Avar cemetery of Szegr-Szőlőkalja., in *Das awarenzeitliche Gräberfeld in Szegr-Szőlőkalja*. Monographia Archaeologica 2, eds. L. Bende & G. Lőrinczy. Szeged, Hungary: A Móra Ferenc Múzeum Évkönyve, 145–147.

Gál, E., 2006b. The role of archaeo-ornithology in environmental and animal history studies, in *Archaeological and Cultural Heritage Preservation within the Light of New Technologies*, eds. E. Jerem, Z. Mester, & R. Benczes. Budapest: Archaeolingua, 49–61.

Gál, E., 2007. *Fowling in Lowlands. Neolithic and Chalcolithic Bird Exploitation in South-East Romania and the Great Hungarian Plain*. Budapest: Archaeolingua.

Gala, M., J.-P. Raynal, & A. Tagliacozzo, 2005. Bird remains from the Mousterian levels of Baume-Vallée (Haute Loire, France): preliminary results, in *Feathers, Grit and Symbolism: Birds and Humans in the Ancient, Old and New Worlds*, eds. G. Grupe & J. Peters. Proceedings of the 5th meeting of the ICAZ Bird Working Group, Munich, 26–28 July, 2004, Documenta Archaeobiologiae 3. Rahden: Verlag Marie Leidorf, 141–145.

Garcia Petit, L., 2002. La migration du coq: de l'Extrême Orient à la Mediterranée, in *Mouvements ou Déplacements de Populations Animales en Méditerranée au cours de l'Holocène*. International Series 1017, ed. A. Gardeisen. Oxford: BAR, 73–80.

Garcia Petit, L., 2005. Recent studies on prehistoric to medieval bird bone remains from Catalonia and Southeast France, in *Feathers, Grit and Symbolism: Birds and Humans in the Ancient, Old and New Worlds*, eds. G. Grupe & J. Peters. Proceedings of the 5th meeting of the ICAZ Bird Working Group, Munich, 26–28 July, 2004, Documenta Archaeobiologiae 3. Rahden: Verlag Marie Leidorf, 147–163.

Gaskell, J., 2004. Remarks on the terminology used to describe developmental behaviour among the auks (Alcidae), with particular reference to that of the Great Auk *Pinguinis impennis*. *Ibis*, 146, 231–240.

Gautier, A., 1987. Taphonomic groups: how and why? *Archaeozoologia*, I(2), 47–52.

Geertz, C., 1993. Deep play: notes on the Balinese cockfight, in *The Interpretation of Cultures*, ed. C. Geertz. New York: Fontana Press, 412–453.

Getty, R., 1975. *Sisson & Grossman's The Anatomy of the Domestic Animals*. London: Saunders.

Giardina, M. A., 2006. Anatomia economica de Rheidae. *Intersecciones en Antropologia*, 7, 263–276.

Gilbert, B. M., L. D. Martin, & H. G. Savage, 1981. *Avian Osteology*. Laramie, WY: B. Miles Gilbert.

Gill, B. J., 2000. Morphometrics of moa eggshell fragments (Aves: Dinornithiformes) from Late Holocene dune-sands of the Karikari Peninsula, New Zealand. *Journal of the Royal Society of New Zealand*, 30(2), 131–145.

Glue, D., 1977. Feeding ecology of the Short-eared Owl in Britain and Ireland. *British Trust for Ornithology*, 24(2), 70–78.

Glue, D. E., 1972. Bird prey taken by British owls. *Bird Study*, 19(2), 91–95.

Godula, G., J. Wrobel, & T. Tomek, 2002. Avian artefacts in the collections of the Archaeological Museum in Krakow. Proceedings of the 4th meeting of the ICAZ Bird Working Group, Krakow, Poland, 11–15 September, 2001, *Acta Zoologica Cracoviensia*, 45, 393–404.

Goody, J., 1982. *Cooking, Cuisine and Class*. Cambridge: Cambridge University Press.

Gotfredsen, A. B., 1997. Seabird exploitation on coastal Inuit sites, west and southeast Greenland. Special issue: Subsistence and symbol. Papers from the International Council for Archaeozoology Bird Group meeting, 1995, *International Journal of Osteoarchaeology*, 7(4), 271–286.

Gotfredsen, A. B., 2002. Former occurrences of geese (Genera *Anser* and *Branta*) in ancient West Greenland: morphological and biometric approaches. Proceedings of the 4th meeting of the ICAZ Bird Working Group, Krakow, Poland, 11–15 September, 2001, *Acta Zoologica Cracoviensia*, 45, 179–204.

Gould, S. J., 1980. A quahog is a quahog, in *The Panda's Thumb*, ed. S. J. Gould. London: Penguin Books, 170–177.

Gourichon, L., 2002. Bird remains from Jerf el Ahmar, a PPNA site in Northern Syria with special reference to the Griffon Vulture (*Gyps fulvus*), in *Archaeozoology of the Near East*, eds. H. Buitenhuis, A. Choyke, M. Mashkour, & A. H. al-Shiyab. Groningen: ARC-Publicatie, 138–152.

Gourichon, L., 2004. *Faune et saisonnalité: l'organisation temporelle des activités de subsistence dans l'Epipaléolithique et Néolithique précéramique du Levant nord, Syrie. Thèse.* Lyon, France: L'Université Lumière Lyon 2.

Grahame, I., 1984. Peafowl, in *Evolution of Domesticated Animals*, ed. I. L. Mason. London: Longman, 315–318.

Grant, A., 1988. Animal resources, in *The Countryside of Medieval England*, eds. G. G. Astill & A. Grant. Oxford: Blackwell, 149–187.

Grant, A., 1991. Economic of symbolic? Animals and ritual behaviour, in *Sacred and Profane*. Monograph 32, eds. P. Garwood, D. Jennings, R. Skeates, & J. Toms. Oxford: Oxford University Committee for Archaeology, 109–114.

Gray, R., 1871. *The Birds of the West of Scotland*. Oxford: Oxford University Press.

Grayson, D. K., 1977. A review of the evidence for early Holocene Turkeys in the Northern Great Basin. *American Antiquity*, 42(1), 110–114.

Grayson, D. K., 1981. A critical view of the use of archaeological vertebrates in paleoecological reconstructions. *Journal of Ethnobiology*, 1, 28–38.

Greenfield, H., 1999. The origins of metallurgy: distinguishing stone from metal cut-marks on bones from archaeological sites. *Journal of Archaeological Science*, 26, 797–808.

Grieve, S., 1885. *The Great Auk or Garefowl – Its History, Archaeology and Remains*. London: Thomas C. Jack.

Grigson, C., 1978. Towards a blueprint for animal bone reports in archaeology, in *Research Problems in Zooarchaeology*, eds. D. Brothwell, K. D. Thomas, & J. Clutton-Brock. London: Institute of Archaeology, 121–128.

Grigson, C., 1981. Mammals and man on Oronsay: some preliminary hypotheses concerning Mesolithic ecology in the Inner Hebrides, in *Environmental Aspects of Coasts and Islands*. International Series 94, eds. D. Brothwell & G. Dimbleby. Oxford: BAR, 163–180.

Grigson, C., 1986. Bird-foraging patterns in the Mesolithic, in *The Mesolithic in Europe. Papers Presented at the Third International Symposium*, ed. C. Bonsall. Edinburgh: John Donald.

Grupe, G. & A.-M. Mekota, 2005. Stable isotope analysis of archaeological avian bones, in *Feathers, Grit and Symbolism: Birds and Humans in the Ancient, Old and New Worlds*, eds. G. Grupe & J. Peters. Proceedings of the 5th meeting of the ICAZ Bird Working Group, Munich, 26–28 July, 2004, Documenta Archaeobiologiae 3. Rahden: Verlag Marie Leidorf, 57–67.

Guminski, W., 2005. Bird for dinner: Stone Age hunters of Dudka and Szczepanki, Masurian Lakeland, NE-Poland. *Acta Archaeologica*, 76(2), 111–147.

Gurney, J. H., 1921. *Annals of Ornithology* (reprinted 1972). Chicheley: Paul Minet.

Habermehl, K.-H., 1975. *Die Altersbestimmung bei Haus- und Labortieren*. Berlin: Paul Parey.

Hagen, A., 1995. *A Second Handbook of Anglo-Saxon Food and Drink: Production and Distribution*. Norfolk: Anglo-Saxon Books.

Hahn, J. & S. Munzel, 1995. Knochenflöten aus den Aurignacien des Geissenklösterle bei Blaubeuren, Alb-Donau-Kreis. *Fundberichte aus Baden-Württemberg Landesdenkmalamt Baden-Wurttemberg. Stuttgart*, 20, 1–12.

Hall, S., 1992. Scottish island survivors. *The Ark*, May, 174–176.

Hamilton-Dyer, S., 1993. The animal bone, in J. D. Zienkiewicz, Excavations in the *Scamnum Tribunorum* at Caerleon: The Legionary Museum Site 1983–5. *Britannia*, 24, 132–136.

Hamilton-Dyer, S., 1997. The domestic fowl and other birds from the Roman site of Mons Claudianus, Egypt. Special issue: Subsistence and symbol. Papers from the International Council for Archaeozoology Bird Group meeting, 1995, *International Journal of Osteoarchaeology*, 7(4), 326–329.

Hamilton-Dyer, S., 1998. Roman Egypt – provisioning the settlement in the Eastern Desert, with particular reference to the quarry settlement of Mons Claudianus, in *Life on the Edge: Human Settlement and Marginality*, eds. C. M. Mills & G. Coles. Oxford: Oxbow, 121–126.

Hamlet, M. P. & H. I. Fisher, 1967. Air sacs of respiratory origin in some procellariform birds. *The Condor*, 69, 586–595.

Hangay, G. & M. Dingley, 1985. *Biological Museum Methods*. Sydney: Academic Press.

Hansell, J., 1998. *The Pigeon in History*. Bath: Millstream Books.

Hargrave, L. L., 1970. *Mexican Macaws: Comparative Osteology and Survey of the Remains from the Southwest*. Anthropological papers 20, Tucson: University of Arizona.

Hargrave, L. L. & S. D. Emslie, 1980. Passenger Pigeon bones from archaeological sites in New Mexico, in *Papers in Avian Paleontology Honoring Hildegarde Howard*. Contributions in Science 330, ed. K. E. Campbell. Los Angeles: Los Angeles County Museum.

Harrison, C. J. O., 1980. A re-examination of British Devensian and earlier Holocene bird bones in the British Museum (Natural History). *Journal of Archaeological Science*, 7(1), 53–68.

Harrison, C. J. O., 1987. Pleistocene and prehistoric birds of South-West Britain. *Proceedings of the University of Bristol Spelaeological Society*, 18(1), 81–104.

Harrison, C. J. O., 1988. Bird bones from Soldier's Hole, Cheddar, Somerset. *Proceedings of the University of Bristol Spelaeological Society*, 18(2), 258–264.

Harrison, C. J. O., 1989. Bird remains from Gough's Old Cave, Cheddar, Somerset. *Proceedings of the University of Bristol Spelaeological Society*, 18(3), 409–411.

Harrison, C. J. O. & G. S. Cowles, 1977. The extinct large cranes of the North West Palaearctic. *Journal of Archaeological Science*, 4, 15–17.

Harrison, C. J. O. & D. Reid-Henry, 1988. *The History of the Birds of Britain*. London: Collins/Witherby.

Harrison, C. J. O. & J. R. Stewart, 1999. Avifauna, in *Boxgrove: A Middle Pleistocene Hominid Site at Eartham Quarry, Boxgrove, West Sussex*. Archaeological Report 17, eds. M. B. Roberts & S. A. Parfitt. London: English Heritage, 187–196.

Harting, J. E., 1978. *The Ornithology of Shakespeare*.Woking, Surrey: Gresham.

Harvey, B., 1993. *Living and Dying in England 1100–1540: The Monastic Experience*. Oxford: Clarendon Press.

Harvey, B. F., 2006. Monastic pittances in the Middle Ages, in *Food in Medieval England: Diet and Nutrition*, eds. C. M. Woolgar, D. Serjeantson, & T. Waldron. Oxford: Oxford University Press, 215–227.

Harvey, E. B., H. E. Kaiser, & L. E. Rosenberg, 1921. *Atlas of the Domestic Turkey* (Meleagris gallopavo). *Myology and Osteology*. Washington, DC: U.S. Atomic Energy Commission, Division of Biology and Medicine.

Haskins, C. H., 1921. The 'De Arte Venandi' of the Emperor Frederick II. *The English Historical Review*, 36(143), 334–355.

Hawes, R. O., 1984. Pigeons, in *Evolution of Domesticated Animals*, ed. I. L. Mason. London: Longman, 351–356.

Helmer, D., L. Gourichon, & D. Storder, 2004. À l'aube de la domestication animale. Imaginaire et symbolisme animal dans les premières sociétés néolithiques du nord du Proche-Orient. *Anthropozoologica*, 39, 143–163.

Hernandez Carrasquilla, F., 1992. Some comments on the introduction of domestic fowl in Iberia. *Archaeofauna*, 1, 45–53.

Hernandez, F., M. Martin, & J. C. Rando, 1993. Estudio osteologico comparado de dos subspecies de *Corvus corax* (Aves: Passeriformes). *Archaeofauna. Archaeornithology: Birds and the Archaeological Record*, 2, 181–190.

Higgins, J., 1999. Tunel: A case study of avian zooarchaeology and taphonomy. *Journal of Archaeological Science*, 26(12), 1449–1457.

Higgs, E., 1973. Palaeoeconomy, in *Palaeoeconomy*. Cambridge: Cambridge University Press, 1–7.
Hill, J. D., 1996. The identification of ritual deposits of animal bones. A general perspective from a specific study of 'special animal deposits' from the southern English Iron Age, in *Ritual Treatment of Human and Animal Remains*, eds. S. Anderson & K. Boyle. Oxford: Oxbow, 17–32.
Hobson, K. A. & J. C. Driver, 1989. Archaeological evidence for use of the Strait of Georgia by marine birds, in *The Ecology and Status of Marine and Shoreline Birds in the Strait of Georgia, British Columbia.* Special publication, eds. K. Vermeer & R. W. Butler. Ottawa: Canadian Wildlife Service, 168–173.
Hochmuth, M., N. Benecke, & M. Wittmeyer, 2005. Cocks and song birds for *Isis Panthea* and *Mater Magna*: the bird remains from a sanctuary in *Mogontiacum*/Mainz, in *Feathers, Grit and Symbolism: Birds and Humans in the Ancient, Old and New Worlds*, eds. G. Grupe & J. Peters. Proceedings of the 5th meeting of the ICAZ Bird Working Group, Munich, 26–28 July, 2004, Documenta Archaeobiologiae 3. Rahden: Verlag Marie Leidorf, 319–328.
Hogg, D. A., 1980. A comparative evaluation of methods for identification of pneumatization in the avian skeleton. *Ibis*, 122, 359–363.
Hojlund, F., 1983. The maussolleion sacrifice. *American Journal of Archaeology*, 87(2), 145–152.
Holdaway, R. N., 1991. Bird skin and feathers, in *Beech Forest Hunters: The Archaeology of Maori Rockshelter Sites on Lee Island, Lake Te Anau, in Southern New Zealand.* Monograph 18, eds. A. J. Anderson & R. McGovern-Wilson. Auckland: New Zealand Archaeological Association, 67–71.
Holdaway, R. N., 2002. Late Holocene extinction of Finsch's duck (*Chenonetta finschii*), an endemic, possibly flightless, New Zealand duck. *Journal of the Royal Society of New Zealand*, 32(4), 629–651.
Holdaway, R. N. & C. Jacomb, 2000. Rapid extinction of the moas (Aves: Dinornithiformes): model, test and implications. *Science*, 287(24 March), 2250–2253.
Holz, P. H., 2003. Coracoid fractures in wild birds: repair and outcomes. *Australian Veterinary Journal*, 81, 469–471.
Hooper, W. D. & H. B. Ash, 1935. *Cato and Varro on Agriculture*. London: Loeb.
Hornell, J., 1946. The role of birds in ancient navigation. *Antiquity*, 20, 142–149.
Horniman Museum, 2006. *Amazon to Caribbean: Early People of the Rainforest*. London: Horniman Museum.
Houlihan, P. F. & S. M. Goodman, 1986. *The Birds of Ancient Egypt*. Warminster: Aris and Phillips.
Howard, H., 1929. The avifauna of Emeryville Shellmound. *University of California Publications in Zoology*, 32 (2), 301–394.
Hoyo, J., A. Elliot, & J. Sargental, 1992. *Handbook of the Birds of the World*. Barcelona: Lynx.
Huckleberry, G., C. Beck, G. T. Jones, A. Holmes, M. Cannon, S. D. Livingston, & J. M. Broughton, 2001. Terminal Pleistocene/Early Holocene environmental change at the Sunshine Locality, North-central Nevada, U.S.A. *Quaternary Research*, 55, 303–312.
Hull, R., 2001. *Scottish Birds: Culture and Tradition*. Edinburgh: Mercat Press.

Humber, R. D., 1966. *Game Cock and Countryman.* London: Cassel.

Ikram, S., 2005. Divine creatures: animal mummies, in *Divine Creatures: Animal Mummies in Ancient Egypt*, ed. S. Ikram. Cairo: The American University in Cairo, 1–15.

Ingold, T., 1986a. Hunting, sacrifice and the domestication of animals, in *The Appropriation of Nature: Essays on Human Ecology*, ed. T. Ingold. Manchester: Manchester University Press, 243–275.

Ingold, T., 1986b. The significance of storage in hunting societies, in *The Appropriation of Nature: Essays on Human Ecology*, ed. T. Ingold. Manchester: Manchester University Press, 199–221.

Jennison, G., 1937. *Animals for Show and Pleasure in Ancient Rome.* Manchester: Manchester University Press.

Jensen, E. L. & C. L. Miller, 2001. Staphylococcus infections in broiler breeders. *AviaTech*, 1, 1–6.

Jett, S. C., 1991. Further information on the geography of the blowgun and its implications for early transoceanic contacts. *Annals of the Association of American Geographers*, 81(1), 89–102.

Jochim, M. A., 1976. *Hunter-Gatherer Subsistence and Settlement: A Predictive Model.* New York: Academic Press.

Johnston, R. E., 2000. Pigeons, in *The Cambridge World History of Food* (vol. 1), eds. K. F. Kiple & K. C. Ornelas. Cambridge: Cambridge University Press, 561–565.

Jolie, E. A. & E. M. Hattori, 2005. The spread of coiled basketry in the prehistoric Great Basin, in *Unraveling the Boundary: Perishable Technologies Across and Between the Prehistoric Great Basin and the Southwest*, eds. E. A. Jolie & M. E. McBrinn. Utah: http:/www.perishabletechnology.com/downloads/Jolie_Hattori_2005_SAA.pdf.

Jones, A., 1998. Where eagles dare: Landscape, animals and the Neolithic of Orkney. *Journal of Material Culture*, 3(3), 301–324.

Kandel, A. W., 2004. Modification of ostrich eggs by carnivores and its bearing on the interpretation of archaeological and paleontological finds. *Journal of Archaeological Science*, 31, 377–391.

Kandel, A. W., 2005. Production sequences of ostrich eggshell beads and settlement dynamics in the Geelbeck Dunes of the Western Cape, South Africa. *Journal of Archaeological Science*, 32, 1711–1721.

Kear, J., 1990. *Man and Wildfowl.* London: Collins.

Kearton, R., 1902. *With Nature and a Camera.* London: Cassell.

Keepax, C. A., 1981. Avian egg-shell from archaeological sites. *Journal of Archaeological Science*, 8, 315–335.

King, A., 2005. Animal remains from temples in Roman Britain. *Britannia*, 36, 329–369.

King, A. S. & J. McLelland, 1984. *Outlines of Avian Anatomy.* London: Baillière Tindall.

Kitchener, A., 1993. Justice at last for the dodo. *New Scientist* (28 August).

Kitchener, A., 2007. The fossil record of birds in Scotland, in *The Birds of Scotland*, eds. R. W. Forrester, I. J. Andrews, C. J. McInerny, R. D. Murray, R. Y. McGowan, B. Zonfrillo, M. W. Betts, D. C. Jardine, & D. S. Grundy. Aberlady: Scottish Ornithological Club, 19–25.

Klein, R. G. & K. Cruz-Uribe, 1984. *The Analysis of Animal Bones from Archaeological Sites*. Chicago: University Press.

Klingender, F. D., 1971. *Animals in Art and Thought to the End of the Middle Ages*. Cambridge, MA: MIT Press.

Klomp, N. I. & R. W. Furness, 1992. A technique which may allow accurate determination of the age of adult birds. *Ibis*, 134, 245–249.

Koch, T. & E. Rossa, 1973. *Anatomy of the Chicken and Domestic Birds*, trans. B. H. Skold & L. de Vries. Ames: Iowa State University Press.

Kock, N. D., R. A. Kock, J. Wambua, G. J. Kamau, & K. Mohan, 1999. Mycobacterium avium-related epizootic in free-ranging lesser flamingos in Kenya. *Journal of Wildlife Diseases*, 35, 297–300.

Krim, A. J., 1992. On "Geography of the blow-gun and early transoceanic context" by Jett. *Annals of the Association of American Geographers*, 82(2), 315.

Kurtz, D. C. & J. Boardman, 1971. *Greek Burial Customs*. London: Thames and Hudson.

LaBianca, O. S. & A. von den Driesch, 1995. Birds, reptiles and amphibians, in *Hesban 13. Faunal Remains: Taphonomical and Zooarchaeological Studies of the Animal Remains from Tell Hesban and Vicinity*, eds. O. S. LaBianca & A. von den Driesch. Berrien Springs, MI: Andrews University Press, 131–168.

Lagae, E., 2005. Un traité inédit d'autourserie et de fauconnerie en moyen français. *Anthropozoologica*, 40, 81–97.

Lamblard, J.-M., 1975. Les étapes de la domestication de la pintade *Numida meleagris* Linné, in *L'homme et l'animal. Premier colloque d'ethnozoologie*, ed. R. Pujol. Paris: Institut International d'Ethnosciences, 421–430.

Lansang, A. J., 1973. *Cockfighting University: Past and Present Outline of our National Pastime*, Manila, Philippines: n.p.

Lapena, M., D. Paton, F. Hernandez, F. de Lope, & A. Juarranz, 1993. Two examples showing contradictory results by using skeletochronology in birds. *Archaeofauna. Archaeornithology: Birds and the Archaeological Record*, 2, 175–179.

Laroulandie, V., 1998. Etudes archéozoologique et taphonomique des lagopèdes des saules de la grotte Magdalenienne des Eglises (Ariège). *Anthropozoologica*, 28, 45–54.

Laroulandie, V., 2000. *Taphonomie et archéozoologie des oiseaux en grotte: Applications aux sites Paléolithiques du Bois-Ragot (Vienne), de Combe Saunière (Dordogne) et de la Vache (Ariège)*. Bordeaux: Université de Bordeaux I.

Laroulandie, V., 2001. Les traces liées à la boucherie, à la cuisson et à la consommation d'oiseaux. Apport de l'expérimentation, in *Préhistoire et approche expérimentale*, eds. L. Bourgignon, I. Ortega, & M.-C. Frère-Sautot. Montagnac: Editions Monique Mergoil, 97–108.

Laroulandie, V., 2002. Damage to pigeon long bones in pellets of the eagle owl *Bubo bubo* and food remains of peregrine falcon *Falco peregrinus*: zooarchaeological implications. Proceedings of the 4th meeting of the ICAZ Bird Working Group, Krakow, Poland, 11–15 September, 2001, *Acta Zoologica Cracoviensia*, 45, 331–339.

Laroulandie, V., 2003. Exploitation des oiseaux au Magdalénien en France: état des lieux, in *Mode de vie au Magdalénien/Magdalenian lifeways*, eds. S. Costamagno & V. Laroulandie. Oxford: BAR, 129–138.

Laroulandie, V., 2004. Exploitation du Harfang au Magdalenien final: l'exemple du Bois-Ragot (Gouex, Vienne). XXVe Congres Préhistorique de France, in *Approches fonctionelles en Préhistoire*. Nanterre: Congres Préhistorique de France, 387–396.

Laroulandie, V., 2005a. Bird exploitation pattern: the case of Ptarmigan *Lagopus* sp. in the Upper Magdalenian site of La Vache (Ariège, France), in *Feathers, Grit and Symbolism: Birds and Humans in the Ancient, Old and New Worlds*, eds. G. Grupe & J. Peters. Proceedings of the 5th meeting of the ICAZ Bird Working Group, Munich, 26–28 July, 2004, Documenta Archaeobiologiae 3. Rahden: Verlag Marie Leidorf, 165–178.

Laroulandie, V., 2005b. Anthropogenic versus non-anthropogenic bird bone assemblages: new criteria for their distinction, in *Biosphere to Lithosphere*, ed. T. O'Connor. Oxford: Oxbow, 25–30.

Laroulandie, V., 2007. Cent trente ans d'études des relations entre l'homme et l'oiseau dans le Paléolithique français: le regard d'une archéozoologue, in *Congrès du Centenaire: Un siècle de construction du discours scientifique en Préhistoire*. vol. 2, 'Des idées d'hier...'. XXVIe congrès préhistorique de France – Avignon, 21–25 septembre 2004. Société préhistorique française, 25–30.

Laubin, R. & G. Laubin, 1980. *American Indian Archery*, Norman: University of Oklahoma Press.

Lauwerier, R. C. G. M., 1986. A meal for the dead. *Palaeohistoria*, 25, 188–193.

Lauwerier, R. C. G. M., 1993a. Bird remains in Roman graves. *Archaeofauna*, 2, 75–82.

Lauwerier, R. C. G. M., 1993b. Twenty-eight bird briskets in a pot; Roman preserved food from Nijmegen. *Archaeofauna. Archaeornithology: Birds and the Archaeological Record*, 2, 15–19.

Lauwerier, R. C. G. M., 2002. Animals as food for the soul, in *Bones and the Man*, eds. K. Dobney & T. P. O'Connor. Oxford: Oxbow.

Lauwerier, R. C. G. M., 2004. The economic and non-economic animal, in *Behaviour Behind Bones: The Zooarchaeology of Ritual, Religion, Status and Identity*, ed. S. J. O'Day. Oxford: Oxbow, 66–72.

Leach, B., 1979. Maximizing minimum numbers: avian remains from the Washpool midden site, in *Birds of a Feather. Osteological and Archaeological Papers From the South Pacific in Honour of R. J. Scarlett*. International Series 62, ed. A. Anderson. Oxford: BAR, 103–121.

Leaf, H., 2007. Medieval bone flutes in England, in *Breaking and Shaping Beastly Bodies*, ed. A. Pluskowski. Oxford: Oxbow, 11–17.

Lecuyer, J. & R. Pujol, 1975. L'oie plumassiere du Poitou, utilisation des peaux et des plumes, in *L'homme et l'animal. Premier colloque d'ethnozoologie*, ed. R. Pujol. Paris: Institut International d'Ethnosciences, 206–216.

Lee, R. B., 1968. What hunters do for a living, or how to make out on scarce resources, in *Man the Hunter*, eds. R. B. Lee & I. DeVore. Chicago: Aldine, 30–48.

Lefèvre, C., 1988. Choix des espèces aviaires par les indiens 'canoeros' de Patagonie. Approche ethno-archeologique. *Anthropozoologica*, numéro special: L'animal dans l'alimentation humaine: les critères de choix, 35–39.

Lefèvre, C., 1993. Exploitation par l'homme de l'avifaune marine en milieu insulaire. Exemples de la Patagonie australe, des îles Aléoutiennes et de l'Atlantique nord, in *Exploitation des animaux sauvages à travers le temps. IV colloque international de l'homme et l'animal*, eds. J. Desse & F. Audoin-Rouzeau. Juan les Pins: APCDA, 115–123.

Lefèvre, C., 1997. Seabird fowling in Southern Patagonia: a contribution to understanding the nomadic round of the Canoeros Indians. Special issue: Subsistence and symbol. Papers from the International Council for Archaeozoology Bird Group meeting, 1995, *International Journal of Osteoarchaeology*, 7(4), 260–270.

Lefèvre, C., D. G. Corbett, D. West & D. Siegel-Causey, 1997. A zooarchaeological study at Buldir Island, western Aleutians, Alaska. *Arctic Anthropology*, 34(2), 118–131.

Lefèvre, C., S. Lepetz & D. Legoupil, 2003. Chasseurs terrestres, chasseurs marins? L'exploitation des ressources animales dans le locus 1, in *Cazadores-recolectores de Ponsonby (Patagonia austral) y su paleoambiente desde VI al III milenio A.C.*, Magallania. Tirada especial (Documentos), Vol. 31, ed. D. Legoupil. Punta Arenas, Chile: Universidad de Magallanes, 63–116.

Lefèvre, C. & M. C. Marinval-Vigne, 1992. Histoire culturelle du dindon dans le nouveau monde. *Ethnozootechnie*, 49(Le Dindon), 25–46.

Lefèvre, C. & E. Pasquet, 1994. Les modifications post-mortem chez les oiseaux: l'exemple de l'avifaune holocène de Patagonie australe. Outillage peu elaboré en os et en bois de cervides, IV. *Artefacts*, 9, 217–229.

Lefèvre, C. & D. Siegel-Causey, 1993. First report on bird remains from Buldir Island, Aleutian Islands, Alaska. *Archaeofauna. Archaeornithology: Birds and the Archaeological Record*, 2, 83–96.

Legge, A. J., 1993. A method for the preparation of very small animal skeletons. *Circaea*, 10(2), 81.

Legge, A. J. & P. Rowley-Conwy, 1988. *Star Carr Revisited*. London: London University Centre for Extra-Mural Studies, Birkbeck College.

Lentacker, A., A. Ervynck, & W. Van Neer, 2004. Gastronomy or religion? the animal remains from the *Mithraeum* at Tienen (Belgium), in *Behaviour Behind Bones: The Zooarchaeology of Ritual, Religion, Status and Identity*, eds. S. Jones O'Day, W. Van Neer, & A. Ervynck. Oxford: Oxbow, 77–94.

Lentacker, A. & W. Van Neer, 1996. Bird remains from two sites on the Red Sea Coast and some observations on medullary bone. *International Journal of Osteoarchaeology*, 6(5), 489–497.

Levitan, B., 1993. Vertebrate remains, in *The Uley shrines: excavation of a ritual complex on West Hill, Uley, Gloucestershire: 1977–9*, eds. A. Woodward & P. Leach. London: English Heritage in association with British Museum Press, 257–262.

Lieberman, P., 2007. The evolution of human speech. *Current Anthropology*, 48, 39–66.

Lignereux, Y. & J. Peters, 1999. Elements for the retrospective diagnosis of tuberculosis on animal bones from archaeological sites, in *Tuberculosis Past and Present*, eds. P. Palfi, O. Dutour, J. Deak, & I. Hutas. Budapest: Golden Book Publisher, 337–348.

Lignereux, Y., J. Peters, A. Bubién-Waluszewska, & P. Sillières, 1995. Sacrifices d'oiseaux en l'honneur d'Isis au 1er siècle après Jésus-Christ à Bélo, en Bétique (Bolonia, Cadix, Andalousie). *Revue de Médecine Vétérinaire*, 146(8–9), 575–582.

Limet, H., 1994. Le chat, les poules et les autres: le relais mesopotamien vers l'Occident, in *Des animaux introduits par l'homme dans la faune d'Europe*, ed. L. Bodson. Liège: University of Liège, 39–54.

Liu, Y.-P., G.-S. Wu, Y.-G. Yao, Y.-W. Miao, G. Liukhart, M. Baig, A. Beja-Pereira, Z.-L. Ding, M. G. Palanichamy, & Y.-P. Zhang, 2006. Multiple maternal origins of chickens: out of the Asian jungles. *Molecular Phylogenetics and Evolution*, 38(1), 12–19.

Livingston, S. D., 1989. The taphonomic interpretation of avian skeletal part frequencies. *Journal of Archaeological Science*, 16, 537–147.

Lockerby, L., 1959. From moa hunter to classic Maori in southern New Zealand, in *Anthropology in the South Seas*, eds. J. D. Freeman & W. R. Geddes. New Plymouth: Avery, 75–110.

Lothrop, S. K., 1928. *The Indians of Tierra del Fuego. An account of the Ona, Yaghan, Alacaluf and Haush Natives of the Fuegian Archipelago* (reprinted 2002). Buenos Aires: Zagier and Urruty.

Louchart, A. & R. Soave, 2002. Changement d'ampleur de l'exploitation des oiseaux entre le Magdalénien et l'Azilien: l'exemple du Taï 2 (Drome). *Quaternaire*, 13(3–4), 297–312.

Louwe Kooijmans, L. P., 2001. *Hardinxveld-Giessendam De Bruin, Een Kampplaats uit het Laat-Mesolithicum en het Begin van de Swifterbant-cultur (5500-4450 v. Chr)*. ROB Rapportage Archeologische Monumentzorg, 88. Amersfoort, the Netherlands: ROB.

Love, J., 2005. Seabird resources and fowling in Scotland, in *Traditions of Seabird Fowling in the North Atlantic Region*, ed. J. Randall. Stornoway: The Islands Book Trust, 54–77.

Luff, R. M., 1982. *A Zooarchaeological Study of the Roman North-western Provinces*. International Series 137. Oxford: BAR.

Luff, R. M., 2000. Ducks, in *The Cambridge World History of Food.* (vol. 1), eds. K. F. Kiple & K. C. Ornelas. Cambridge: Cambridge University Press, 517–524.

Luff, R. M., 2001. New light on ancient Egyptian fishing and fowling, in *Animal and Man in the Past: Essays in Honor of Dr A. T. Clason*, eds. H. Buitenhus & W. Prummel. Groningen: ARC-Publicatie, 357–363.

Lyman, R. L., 1994. *Vertebrate Taphonomy*. Cambridge: Cambridge University Press.

Lyman, R. L., 2008. *Quantitative Paleozoology*. Cambridge: Cambridge University Press.

Lyon, P. J., 1991. Feathers are for flying, in *The Gift of Birds: Featherwork of Native South American Peoples*, eds. R. E. Reina & K. M. Kensinger. Philadelphia: University Museum of Archaeology and Anthropology, 70–77.

MacDonald, K. C., 1992. The domestic chicken (*Gallus gallus*) in Sub-Saharan Africa: a background to its introduction and its osteological differentiation from indigenous fowls (*Numidinae* and *Francolinus* sp.). *Journal of Archaeological Science*, 19, 303–318.

MacDonald, K. C., 1993. Chickens in Africa: the importance of Qasr Ibrim. *Antiquity*, 67, 584–590.
MacDonald, K. C., 1995. Why chickens? The centrality of the domestic fowl in West African ritual and magic In *The Symbolic Role of Animals in Archaeology* (eds.) K. Ryan & P. J. Crabtree. Philadelphia: MASCA. University of Pennsylvania Museum, 50–56.
MacDonald, K. C., 2003. The domestic chicken in the Tylos burials of Bahrain. *Arabian Archaeology and Epigraphy*, 14, 194–195.
MacDonald, R. H., K. C. MacDonald, & K. Ryan, 1993. Domestic geese from Medieval Dublin. *Archaeofauna*, 2, 205–218.
MacGregor, A., 1985. *Bone, Antler, Ivory and Horn: The Technology of Skeletal Materials Since the Roman Period*. Beckenham: Croom Helm.
MacGregor, A., 1995. Swan rolls and beak markings. Ancient practice and a new discovery. *Anthropozoologica*, 22, 39–68.
Mackinder, A. & K. Reilly, 2000. *A Romano-British Cemetery on Watling Street. Excavations at 165 Great Dover Street, Southwark, London*. London: MOLAS/Surrey Archaeological Society.
MacPherson, H. A., 1897. *A History of Fowling*. Edinburgh: Douglas.
Makowiecki, D. & A. B. Gotfredsen, 2002. Bird remains of Medieval and Post-Medieval coastal sites at the Southern Baltic Sea, Poland. Proceedings of the 4th meeting of the ICAZ Bird Working Group, Krakow, Poland, 11–15 September, 2001, *Acta Zoologica Cracoviensia*, 45, 65–84.
Mallye, J. B., D. Cochard, & V. Laroulandie, 2008. Accumulation osseuse en périphérie de terriers de petits carnivores: les stigmates de prédation. Actes de la Table Ronde 'Taphonomie: des référentiels aux ensembles fossiles' 23–25 Novembre 2005, Toulouse. *Annales de Paléontologie*, 94, 187–208.
Maltby, J. M., 1979. *Faunal Studies on Urban Sites: The Animal Bones From Exeter 1971–1975*. Huddersfield: H. Charlesworth.
Maltby, M., 1993. Animal bones, in *Excavations at the Old Methodist Chapel and Greyhound Yard, Dorchester*, eds. P. J. Woodward, S. M. Davies, & A. H. Graham. Dorchester: Dorset Natural History and Archaeological Society, 315–340.
Maltby, M., 1997. Domestic fowl on Romano-British sites: inter-site comparisons of abundance. Special issue: Subsistence and symbol. Papers from the International Council for Archaeozoology Bird Group meeting, 1995, *International Journal of Osteoarchaeology*, 7(4), 402–414.
Maltby, M., In press. *Feeding a Roman Town*. Winchester Excavations Volume 4, Winchester: Winchester Museum Service.
Mameli, L., 2002. Bird management in America's extreme south during the 19th century. Proceedings of the 4th meeting of the ICAZ Bird Working Group, Krakow, Poland, 11–15 September, 2001, *Acta Zoologica Cracoviensia*, 45, 151–165.
Mameli, L. & J. Estevez, 2004. *Etnoarqueozoologia de aves: el ejemplo del extremo sur americano*. Treballs d'etnoarqueologia, 5, Madrid: Consejo superior de investigaciones cientificas.
Mannermaa, K., 2003. Birds in Finnish prehistory. *Fennoscandia Archaeologica*, XX, 3–39.

Mannermaa, K. & L. Lougas, 2005. Birds in the subsistence and cultures in four major Baltic Sea Islands during the Neolithic, in *Feathers, Grit and Symbolism: Birds and Humans in the Ancient, Old and New Worlds*, eds. G. Grupe & J. Peters. Proceedings of the 5th meeting of the ICAZ Bird Working Group, Munich, 26–28 July, 2004, Documenta Archaeobiologiae 3. Rahden: Verlag Marie Leidorf, 179–199.

Mannermaa, K. & J. Stora, 2006. Stone Age exploitation of birds on the Island of Gotland, Baltic Sea: a taphonomic study of the avifauna on the Neolithic site of Ajvide. *International Journal of Osteoarchaeology*, 16(5), 429–452.

Martin, P. S., 1984. Prehistoric overkill: the global model, in *Quaternary Extinctions: A Prehistoric Revolution*, eds. P. S. Martin & R. G. Klein. Tucson: The University of Arizona Press, 354–403.

Martinez-Lira, P., E. Corona-M., J. Arroyo-Cabrales, & J. P. Carpenter, 2005. Bird bundles from La Playa, Sonora, Mexico, in *Feathers, Grit and Symbolism: Birds and Humans in the Ancient, Old and New Worlds*, eds. G. Grupe & J. Peters. Proceedings of the 5th meeting of the ICAZ Bird Working Group, Munich, 26–28 July, 2004, Documenta Archaeobiologiae 3. Rahden: Verlag Marie Leidorf, 201–206.

Martinsson-Wallin, H. & S. Crockford, 2001. Early settlement of Rapa Nui (Easter Island). *Asian Perspectives*, 40(2), 244–278.

Mason, I. L. (ed.), 1984. *Evolution of Domesticated Animals*. London: Longman.

Masseti, M., 1997. Representation of birds in Minoan Art. Special issue: Subsistence and symbol. Papers from the International Council for Archaeozoology Bird Group meeting, 1995, *International Journal of Osteoarchaeology*, 7(4), 354–363.

Masson, M., 2004. Faunal exploitation from the Preclassic to the Postclassic Periods at four Maya settlements in Northern Belize, in *Maya Zooarchaeology: New Directions in Theory and Method*. Monograph 51, ed. K. F. Emery. Los Angeles: Cotsen Institute of Archaeology, University of California, Los Angeles, 97–122.

Maxfield, V. A. & D. P. S. Peacock, 2001. *Mons Claudianus. Survey and Excavation*, vol. 2. Cairo: Institut française d'archéologie orientale.

McGovern-Wilson, R., 2005. Feathers flying in paradise: the taking of birds for their feathers in prehistoric Polynesia, in *Feathers, Grit and Symbolism: Birds and Humans in the Ancient, Old and New Worlds*, eds. G. Grupe & J. Peters. Proceedings of the 5th meeting of the ICAZ Bird Working Group, Munich, 26–28 July, 2004, Documenta Archaeobiologiae 3. Rahden: Verlag Marie Leidorf, 207–222.

McGovern, T., S. Perdikaris, Á. Einarsson, & J. Sidell, 2006. Coastal connections, local fishing, and sustainable egg harvesting: patterns of Viking Age inland wild resource use in Mývatn District, Northern Iceland. *Environmental Archaeology*, 11(1), 187–206.

McKusick, C. R., 1980. Three groups of turkeys from southwestern archaeological sites, in *Papers in Avian Paleontology Honoring Hildegarde Howard*. Contributions in Science 330, ed. K. E. Campbell. Los Angeles: Los Angeles County Museum, 225–235.

Megaw, J. V. S., 1960. Penny whistles and prehistory. *Antiquity*, 34, 6–13.

Meldgaard, M., 1988. The Great Auk, *Pinguinus impennis* (L) in Greenland. *Historical Biology*, 1, 145–178.

Méniel, P., 1995. Découp et mise en place des animaux dans la nécropole de Lamadelaine (Luxembourg, 1er siècle avant notre ère). *Anthropozoologica*, 21, 267–282.

Mert, N., 1991. A biochemical investigation of chicken gout observed in the Marmara region of Turkey. *Advances in Experimental Medicine and Biology*, 309A, 251–254.

Messinger, N. G., 1965. Methods used for identification of feather remains from Wetherill Mesa, in *Contributions of the Wetherill Mesa Archaeological Project*. Memoir No. 19, ed. D. Osborne. Salt Lake City: Society for American Archaeology, 206–215.

Mikhailov, K. E., 1997. *Avian Eggshells: An Atlas of Scanning Electron Micrographs*. Occasional Publications No. 3. Tring, Hertfordshire: British Ornithologists' Club.

Milberg, P. & T. Tyrberg, 1993. Naive birds and noble savages: a review of man-caused prehistoric extinctions of island birds. *Ecography*, 16, 229–250.

Milne-Edwards, A., 1867–1871. *Recherches anatomiques et paléontologiques pour servir a l'histoire des oiseaux fossiles de la France*. Paris: Victor Masson.

Milne-Edwards, A., 1875. Observations on the birds whose bones have been found in the caves of the south-west of France, in *Reliquiae Aquitanicae; Being Contributions to the Archaeology and Palaeontology of Perigord and the Adjoining Provinces of Southern France*, eds. E. Lartet & H. Christie. London: Williams and Norgate, 226–247.

Minnis, P. E., M. E. Whalen, J. H. Kelley, & J. D. Stewart, 1993. Prehistoric Macaw breeding in the North American southwest. *American Antiquity*, 58(2), 270–276.

Mohl, U., 1978. Aggersund-bopladsen zoologisk belyst. Svanejagt som årsag til bosættelse? (Zoological analysis of the Aggersund settlement: a special purpose camp for hunting swans?). *KUML. Arbog for Jysk Arkaeologisk selskab*, 72–74.

Mongin, P. & M. Plouzeau, 1984. Guinea-fowl, in *Evolution of Domesticated Animals*, ed. I. L. Mason. London: Longman, 322–324.

Monroe, B. L. & C. G. Sibley, 1997. *A World Checklist of Birds*. New Haven, CT: Yale University Press.

Morales, A. (ed.), 1993a. *Archaeornithology: Birds and the Archaeological Record*. Proceedings of the first meeting of the ICAZ Bird Working Group, Madrid, Spain, 7–10 October, 1991, *Archaeofauna*, 2.

Morales, A., 1993b. Ornithoarchaeology: the various aspects of the classification of bird remains from archaeological sites. *Archaeofauna. Archaeornithology: Birds and the Archaeological Record*, 2, 1–13.

Moreno-Garcia, M., C. Pimenta, & M. Gros, 2005. Musical vultures in the Iberian Peninsula: sounds through their wings, in *Feathers, Grit and Symbolism: Birds and Humans in the Ancient, Old and New Worlds*, eds. G. Grupe & J. Peters. Proceedings of the 5th meeting of the ICAZ Bird Working Group, Munich, 26–28 July, 2004, Documenta Archaeobiologiae 3. Rahden: Verlag Marie Leidorf, 329–348.

Mourer-Chauviré, C., 1979. La chasse aux oiseaux pendant la Préhistoire. *La Recherche*, 10(106), 1202–1210.

Mourer-Chauviré, C., 1983. Les oiseaux dans les habitats Paléolithiques: gibier des hommes ou proies des rapaces?, in *Animals and Archaeology: 2. Shell Middens, Fishes and Birds*. International Series 183, eds. C. Grigson & J. Clutton-Brock. Oxford: BAR, 111–124.

Mozino, J. M., 1991. *Noticias de Nutka*, trans. I. H.W. Engstrand. Vancouver, BC: Douglas & McIntyre.

Mudie, R., 1835. *The Feathered Tribes of the British Islands.* London: n.p.

Muir, R. J. & J. Driver, 2004. Identifying ritual use of animals in the northern American Southwest, in *Behaviour Behind Bones: The Zooarchaeology of Ritual, Religion, Status and Identity*, eds. S. Jones O'Day, W. Van Neer, & A. Ervynck. Oxford: Oxbow, 128–143.

Mulkeen, S. & T. P. O'Connor, 1997. Raptors in towns: towards an ecological model. Special issue: Subsistence and symbol. Papers from the International Council for Archaeozoology Bird Group meeting, 1995, *International Journal of Osteoarchaeology*, 7(4), 440–449.

Munzel, S. C., 1987. *Umingmak: A Muskox-Hunting site on Banks Island: Archaeozoological Analysis of Area ID.* Tubingen: Archaeologia Venatoria.

Murnane, R. D. & M. M. Garner, 1987. Visceral gout in a rough legged hawk (*Buteo lagopus*). *Journal of Wildlife Diseases*, 23, 515–517.

Murphy, P., 1985. Avian eggshell, in *Excavations in Norwich 1971–1978 Part II*. Report No. 26, eds. M. Atkin, A. Carter, & D. H. Evans. Norwich: East Anglian Archaeology, 68.

Murphy, P., 1990. *Baldock, Hertfordshire. Land Molluscs, Carbonised Cereals and Crop Weeds, Charcoal, Avian Eggshell and Coprolites From Prehistoric and Roman Contexts.* Ancient Monuments Laboratory Report 123/90. London: English Heritage.

Murphy, P., U. Albarella, M. Germany & A. Locker, 2000. Production, imports and status: biological remains from a Late Roman farm at Great Holts Farm, Boreham, Essex, UK. *Environmental Archaeology*, 5, 35–48.

Murray, E., F. McCormick, & G. Plunkett, 2004. The food economies of Atlantic island monasteries: the documentary and archaeo-environmental evidence. *Environmental Archaeology*, 9, 179–188.

Mutalib, A., B. Miguel, T. Brown & W. Maslin, 1996. Distribution of arthritis and osteomyelitis in turkeys with green liver discoloration. *Avian Diseases*, 40, 661–664.

Nagaoka, L., 2001. Using diversity indices to measure changes in prey choice at the Shag River Mouth site, Southern New Zealand. *International Journal of Osteoarchaeology. Special Issue: Zooarchaeology of Oceanic Coasts and Islands*, 11(1–2), 101–111.

Nelson, B., 1980. *Seabirds: Their Biology and Ecology.* London: Hamlyn.

Nelson, R. K., 1969. *Hunters of the Northern Ice.* Chicago: Chicago University Press.

Nelson, R. K., 1983. *Make Prayers to the Raven.* Chicago: Chicago University Press.

Newton, I., 1979. *Population Ecology of Raptors.* Berkhamstead: Poyser.

Nicholson, R. A., 1996. Bone degradation, burial medium and species representation: debunking the myths, an experiment-based approach. *Journal of Archaeological Science*, 23, 513–533.

Noli, D. & G. Avery, 1988. Protein poisoning. *Journal of Archaeological Science*, 15, 398–401.

Northcote, E. M., 1980. Some Cambridgeshire Neolithic to Bronze Age birds and their presence or absence in England in the Late-glacial and Early Flandrian. *Journal of Archaeological Science*, 7, 379–383.

Northcote, E. M., 1981. Size differences between limb bones of recent and subfossil Mute Swans *Cygnus olor. Journal of Archaeological Science*, 8, 89–98.

Northcote, E. M., 1983. Morphology of Mute Swans (*Cygnus Olor*) in relation to domestication, in *Animals and Archaeology: 2. Shell Middens, Fishes and Birds*. International Series 183, eds. C. Grigson & J. Clutton-Brock. Oxford: BAR, 173–179.

O'Brian, P., 1987. *Joseph Banks. A Life*. London: Collins.

O'Connor, R. J., 1984. *The Growth and Development of Birds*. London: Wiley.

O'Connor, T. P., 1982. *Animal Bones from Flaxengate, Lincoln c. 870–1500*. London: Council for British Archaeology.

O'Connor, T. P., 1988. *Bones from the General Accident Site, Tanner Row. The Archaeology of York. The Animal Bones, 15/2*. York: York Archaeological Trust/Council for British Archaeology.

O'Connor, T. P., 1993. Birds and the scavenger niche. *Archaeofauna. Archaeornithology: Birds and the Archaeological Record*, 2, 155–162.

O'Connor, T. P., 1997. Another look at animal domestication. *Antiquity*, 71, 271.

O'Connor, T. P., 1998. Environmental archaeology: a matter of definition. *Environmental Archaeology*, 2, 1–6.

O'Connor, T. P., 2000. *The Archaeology of Animal Bones*. Gloucester: Sutton.

O'Connor, T. P., 2003. *The Analysis of Urban Animal Bone Assemblages: A Handbook for Archaeologists. The Archaeology of York 19/2*. York: Council for British Archaeology.

O'Connor, T. P., 2005. Biosphere to lithosphere: an introduction, in *Biosphere to Lithosphere: New Studies in Vertebrate Eaphonomy*, ed. T. P. O'Connor. Oxford: Oxbow, 1–3.

Oakes, J. & T. Stone, 1990. *Coats of Eider*. Winnipeg: Aboriginal Issues Press.

Oberg, K., 1980. *The Social Economy of the Tlingit Indians*. Vancouver, BC: Douglas & McIntyre.

Oggins, R. S., 2004. *The Kings and their Hawks: Falconry in Medieval England*. New Haven, CT: Yale University Press.

Ogilvie, M. A., 1984. Swan, in *Evolution of Domesticated Animals*, ed. I. L. Mason. London: Longman, 349–351.

Oliver, J. S., & R. W. Graham, 1994. A catastrophic kill of ice-trapped coots: time-averaged versus scavenger-specific disarticulation patterns. *Paleobiology*, 20, 229–244.

Olsen, S. J., 1968. The osteology of the wild turkey, in *Fish, Amphibian and Reptile Remains from Archaeological Sites*, ed. S. J. Olsen. Papers. of the Peabody Museum of Archaeology and Ethnology, Vol. 56, No. 2. Cambridge, MA: Harvard University, 107–135.

Olsen, S. J., 1979. *Osteology for the Archaeologist*. Papers of the Peabody Museum of Archaeology and Ethnology, Vol. 56. No. 4. *North American Birds: Skulls and Mandibles*. No. 5. *North American Birds: Postcranial Skeletons*. Cambridge, MA: Harvard University.

Olsen, S. J., 2000. Turkeys, in *The Cambridge World History of Food* (vol. 1), eds. K. F. Kiple & K. C. Ornelas. Cambridge: Cambridge University Press, 578–583.

Olson, S. L., 2003. Development and use of avian skeleton collections. *Bulletin of the British Ornithologists' Club*, 123A, 26–34.

O'Reilly, D. J. W., A. von den Driesch, & V. Voeun, 2006. Archaeology and archaeozoology of Phum Snay: a Late Prehistoric Cemetery in Northwestern Cambodia. *Asian Perspectives*, 45(2), 188–211.

Owen, R., 1879. *Memoirs on the Extinct Wingless Birds of New Zealand: With an Appendix on Those of England, Australia, Newfoundland, Mauritius and Rodriguez.* London: John van Voorst.

Pachur, H.-J. & J. Peters, 2001. The position of the Murzuq Sand Sea in the palaeodrainage system of the Eastern Sahara. *Palaeoecology of Africa*, 27, 259–290.

Parker, A. J., 1988. The birds of Roman Britain. *Oxford Journal of Archaeology*, 7(2), 197–226.

Parkin, R. A., P. Rowley-Conwy, & D. Serjeantson, 1986. Late Palaeolithic exploitation of horse and red deer at Gough's Cave, Cheddar, Somerset. *Proceedings of the University of Bristol Spelaeological Society*, 17(3), 311–330.

Parmalee, P. W., 1980. Utilization of birds by the Archaic and Fremont cultural groups of Utah, in *Papers in Avian Paleontology Honoring Hildegarde Howard.* Contributions in Science 330, ed. K. E. Campbell. Los Angeles: Los Angeles County Museum, 237–250.

Paul, A. A. & D. A. T. Southgate, 1978. *McCance and Widdowson's The Composition of Foods.* London: Her Majesty's Stationery Office.

Pavlović, A. & D. C. Nieweg, 2007. Archeologisch onderzoek Vijverhof (Valkhuis), gemeente Den Haag. Den Haag: Gemeente Den Haag, afd. Archeologie Dienst Stadsbeheer.

Pawankar, S. J. & P. K. Thomas, 1997. Fauna and subsistence pattern in the Chalcolithic culture of Western India, with special reference to Imagaon. *Anthropozoologica*, 25–26, 737–746.

Pearson, R. & A. Underhill, 1987. The Chinese Neolithic: recent trends in research. *American Anthropologist, New Series*, 89(4), 807–822.

Pegge, S., 1775. A memoir on cock-fighting; wherein the antiquity of it, as a pastime, is examined and stated. *Archaeologia*, 3, 132–150.

Penney, D. W. & G. C. Longfish, 1994. *Native American Art.* New York: Hugh Hunter Levin.

Peters, J., 1997a. Hahn oder Kapaun? Zur Kastration von Hähnen in der Antike (Rooster or capon? On the castration of cocks in antique times). *Archiv für Geflügelkunde*, 61(1), 1–8.

Peters, J., 1997b. Zum Stand der Hühnerhaltung in der Antike. *Beiträge zur archäozoologische und prähistorische Anthropologie* 1, 42–58.

Peters, J. & G. Grupe (eds.), 2005. *Feathers, Grit and Symbolism: Birds and Humans in the Ancient, Old and New Worlds.* Proceedings of the 5th meeting of the ICAZ Bird Working Group, Munich, 26–28 July, 2004, Documenta Archaeobiologiae 3. Rahden: Verlag Marie Leidorf.

Peters, J. & K. Schmidt, 2004. Animals in the symbolic world of Pre-Pottery Neolithic Göbekli Tepe, south-eastern Turkey: a preliminary assessment. *Anthropozoologica*, 39, 179–218.

Peters, J., A. von den Driesch, N. Pöllath, & K. Schmidt, 2005. Birds in the megalithic art of Pre-Pottery Neolithic Göbekli Tepe, Southeast Turkey, in *Feathers, Grit and Symbolism: Birds and Humans in the Ancient, Old and New Worlds*, eds. G. Grupe & J. Peters. Proceedings of the 5th meeting of the ICAZ Bird Working Group, Munich, 26–28 July, 2004, Documenta Archaeobiologiae 3. Rahden: Verlag Marie Leidorf, 223–234.

Petersen, E. B. & C. Meiklejohn, 2003. Three cremations and a funeral: aspects of burial practice in Mesolithic Vedbæk, in *Mesolithic on the Move*, eds. L. Larsson, H. Kindgren, K. Knutsson, D. Loeffler, & A. Åkerlund. Oxford: Oxbow, 485–493.

Peterson, A. & I. L. Brisbin, 1999. Genetic endangerment of wild red Junglefowl *Gallus gallus*? *Bird Conservation International*, 9, 387–394.

Pichon, J., 1988. Les oiseaux, gibiers de choix au proche-orient. *Anthropozoologica*, numéro special: L'animal dans l'alimentation humaine: les critères de choix, 41–49.

Pichon, J., 1991. Les oiseaux au Natoufien, avifaune et sedentarité, in *The Natufian Culture in the Levant*. International Monographs in Prehistory. Archaeological Series 1, eds. O. Bar-Yosef & F. R. Valla. Ann Arbor: University of Michigan, 371–380.

Pieper, H., 1982. Probleme der Artbestimmung an Knochen des Extremitätenskelettes sowie Bemerkungen zur systematischen Gliederung der Gattung *Aythya* (Aves: Anatidae). *Schriften der Archäologisch – Zoologischen Arbeitsgruppe, Schleswig-Kiel*, 6, 63–89.

Pike-Tay, A., L. Bartosiewicz, E. Gál, & A. Whittle, 2004. Body part representation and seasonality: sheep/goat, bird and fish remains from Early Neolithic Ecsegfalva 23, SE Hungary. *Journal of Taphonomy*, 2(4), 221–246.

Pimentel, D. & M. Pimentel, 1979. *Food, Energy and Society*. London: Edward Arnold.

Pinkley, J. M., 1965. The Pueblos and the turkey: who domesticated whom? *American Antiquity*, 31, 70–72.

Pitts, M., 2006. Flight of the eagles. *British Archaeology*, 86; http://www.britarch.ac.uk/ba/ba86/news.shtml; January 8, 2008.

Pollard, J., 1977. *Birds in Greek Life and Myth*. London: Thames and Hudson.

Poole, K., In press. Bird introductions, in *Extinctions and Invasions: The Social History of British Fauna*, eds. T. P. O'Connor & N. J. Sykes. Oxford: Oxbow.

Poplin, F., 2000. Sur le polissage des oefs d'autruche en archéologie, in *Archaeozoology of the Near East IV*, eds. M. Mashkour, A. M. Choyke, H. Buitenhuis, & F. Poplin. Groningen: ARC-Publicatie, 32.

Poulos, P. W., S. Reiland, & S. E. Olsson, 1978. Skeletal lesions in the broiler, with special reference to dyschondroplasia (osteochondrosis). Pathology, frequency and clinical significance in two strains of birds on high and low energy feed. *Acta Radiologica*, 358, 229–275.

Powell, A., 1995–1996. Appendix 1: Bird bones and cremations. In 'The house of Amarantus at Pompeii (I, 9, 11–12): An interim report on survey and excavations in 1995–96', pp. 77–113, by M. Fulford and A. Wallace-Hadrill. *Rivista di Studi Pompeiani*, 7, 102–105.

Powell, A., D. Serjeantson, & P. Smith, 2001. Food consumption and disposal: the animal remains, in *St Gregory's Priory, Northgate, Canterbury: Excavations 1988–1991*, eds. M. Hicks & A. Hicks. Canterbury: Canterbury Archaeological Trust, 289–333.

Pressman, J. F., 1991. Feathers of blood and fire. The mythological origins of avian coloration, in *The Gift of Birds: Featherwork of Native South American Peoples*, eds. R. E. Reina & K. M. Kensinger. Philadelphia: University Museum of Archaeology and Anthropology, 78–91.

Prummel, W., 1987. Poultry and fowling at the Roman castellum Velsen 1. *Palaeohistoria*, 29, 183–201.

Prummel, W., 1993. Birds from four coastal sites in the Netherlands. *Archaeofauna*, 2, 97–105.

Prummel, W., 1997. Evidence of hawking (falconry) from bird and mammal bones. Special issue: Subsistence and symbol. Papers from the International Council for Archaeozoology Bird Group meeting, 1995, *International Journal of Osteoarchaeology*, 7(4), 333–338.

Prummel, W., 2005. The avifauna of the Hellenistic town of New Halos, Thessaly, Greece, in *Feathers, Grit and Symbolism: Birds and Humans in the Ancient, Old and New Worlds*, eds. G. Grupe & J. Peters. Proceedings of the 5th meeting of the ICAZ Bird Working Group, Munich, 26–28 July, 2004, Documenta Archaeobiologiae 3. Rahden: Verlag Marie Leidorf, 350–360.

Prummel, W. & J. T. Zeiler, 2002. Bird remains from 17th century whaling stations on Spitsbergen (Svalbard). Proceedings of the 4th meeting of the ICAZ Bird Working Group, Krakow, Poland, 11–15 September, 2001, *Acta Zoologica Cracoviensia*, 45, 205–213.

Rae, A. & B. Wills, 2002. Love a duck: the conservation of feathered skins, in *The Conservation of Fur, Feather and Skin*, ed. M. M. Wright. London: Archetype, 43–61.

Rainey, F., 1939. *Archaeology in Central Alaska*. Anthropological Papers of the American Museum of Natural History 36, 4. New York: American Museum of Natural History.

Randall, J. (ed.), 2005. *Traditions of Seabird Fowling in the North Atlantic Region*. Stornoway: The Islands Book Trust.

Rea, A., 1980. Late Pleistocene and Holocene Turkeys in the Southwest, in *Papers in Avian Paleontology Honoring Hildegarde Howard*. Contributions in Science 330, ed. K. E. Campbell. Los Angeles: Los Angeles County Museum, 209–224.

Recchi, A. & A. Gopher, 2002. Birds and humans in the Holocene: the case of Qumran Cave 24 (Dead Sea, Israel). Proceedings of the 4th meeting of the ICAZ Bird Working Group, Krakow, Poland, 11–15 September, 2001, *Acta Zoologica Cracoviensia*, 45, 139–150.

Reeves, C., 1995. *Pleasures and Pastimes in Medieval England*. Stroud: Sutton.

Reichstein, H. & H. Pieper, 1986. *Untersuchungen an Skelettresten von Vögeln aus Haithabu. Ausgrabung 1966–1969*. Neumünster: Wachholz.

Reiland, S., S. E. Olsson, P. W. Poulos, & K. Elwinger, 1978. Normal and pathologic skeletal development in broiler and leghorn chickens. A comparative investigation. *Acta Radiologica*, 358, 277–298.

Reina, R. E., 1991. Feather objects in culture, in *The Gift of Birds: Featherwork of Native South American Peoples*, eds. R. E. Reina & K. M. Kensinger. Philadelphia: University Museum of Archaeology and Anthropology, xiii–xvii.

Reina, R. E. & J. F. Pressman, 1991. Harvesting feathers, in *The Gift of Birds: Featherwork of Native South American Peoples*, eds. R. E. Reina & K. M. Kensinger. Philadelphia: University Museum of Archaeology and Anthropology, 110–115.

Reis, K. R. & D. W. Steadman, 1999. Archaeology of Trants, Montserrat. Part 5. Prehistoric avifauna. *Annals of Carnegie Museum*, 68(4), 275–287.

Reitz, E. J., 1986. Vertebrate fauna from Locus 39, Puerto Real, Haiti. *Journal of Field Archaeology*, 13(3), 317–328.

Reitz, E. J. & E. S. Wing, 1999. *Zooarchaeology*. Cambridge: Cambridge University Press.

Rich, P. V., 1980. Preliminary report on the fossil avian remains from late Tertiary sediments at Langebaanweg (Cape Province), South Africa. *South African Journal of Science*, 76, 166–170.

Ricklefs, R. E., 1968. Patterns of growth in birds. *Ibis*, 110, 419–451.

Ricklefs, R. E., 1973. Patterns of growth in birds. II. Growth rate and mode of development. *Ibis*, 115, 177–201.

Riddell, W. H., 1943. The domestic goose. *Antiquity*, 17, 148–155.

Ritchie, J., 1920. *The Influence of Man on Animal Life in Scotland.* Cambridge: Cambridge University Press.

Robert, I. & J.-D. Vigne, 2002. Bearded vulture *Gypaetus barbatus* contributions to the constitution of two different bird assemblages: modern reference data and an archaeological example in Corsica. Proceedings of the 4th meeting of the ICAZ Bird Working Group, Krakow, Poland, 11–15 September, 2001, *Acta Zoologica Cracoviensia*, 45, 319–329.

Rockwell, R. F., B. M. Pezzanite, & P. Matulonis, 2003. Developmental abnormalities in wild populations of birds: examples from lesser snow goose (*Chen caerulescens caerulescens*). *American Museum Novitates*, 400, 1–14.

Rodriguez Loredo de March, C., 1993. La chasse de rapaces diurnes pour l'obention de plumes dans le site inca de 'Potrero-Chaquiago' (Argentina), in *Exploitation des animaux sauvages à travers le temps. IV colloque international de l'homme et l'animal*, eds. J. Desse & F. Audoin-Rouzeau. Juan les Pins: APCDA, 517–521.

Ross, A., 1974. *Pagan Celtic Britain.* London: Sphere.

Rothschild, B. M. & R. Panza, 2006. Osteoarthritis is for the birds. *Clinical Rheumatology*, 25, 645–647.

Rothschild, B. M. & F. R. Ruhli, 2007. Comparative frequencies of osseous macroscopic pathology and first report of gout in captive and wild-caught ratites. *Journal of Veterinary Medicine*, A54, 265–269.

Routledge, K., 1917. The bird cult of Easter Island. *Folklore*, 28(4), 337–355.

Rowley-Conwy, P., 1989. Bird bones from the temple at Qasr Ibrim. *Archéologie du Nil Moyen*, 3, 35–38.

Russell, N. & K. J. McGowan, 2003. Dance of the cranes: crane symbolism at Catal Höyük and beyond. *Antiquity*, 77, 445–455.

Sadler, P., 1990. Faunal remains, in *Faccombe Netherton: Excavation of a Saxon and Medieval Manorial Complex II*, ed. J. R. Fairbrother. London: British Museum, 462–508.

Sadler, P., 1991. The use of tarsometatarsi in sexing and ageing domestic fowl (*Gallus gallus* L.), and recognising five toed breeds in archaeological material. *Circaea*, 8(1), 41–48.

Sanchez Marco, A., 2004. Avian zoogeographical patterns during the Quaternary in the Mediterranean Region and palaeoclimatic interpretation. *Ardeola*, 51(1), 91–132.

Satterthwait, L., 1986. Aboriginal Australian net hunting. *Mankind*, 16(1), 31–47.

Schaeuffelhut, S., H. Tello, & H. Schneider, 2002. Cleaning of feathers from the Ethnological Museum, Berlin, in *The Conservation of Fur, Feather and Skin*, ed. M. M. Wright. London: Archetype, 62–68.

Schäfer, W., 1972. *Ecology and Paleoecology of Marine Environments.* Edinburgh: Oliver and Boyd.

Scheinson, V. G., 1990–1992. El sistema de produccion de los instrumentos oseos y el momento del contacto: un puente sobre aguas turbulentas. *Relaciones de la Sociedad Argentina de Antropologia*, XVIII(1990–1992), 121–138.

Schmiz, A., 1971. Honey buzzards at Falsterbö. *Birds*, November/December Issue, 300.

Schorger, A. W., 1962. Introduction of the Domestic Pigeon. *The Auk*, 69, 467–8.

Schorger, A. W., 1966. *The Wild Turkey: Its History and Domestication.* Norman: University of Oklahoma Press.

Schulting, R., A. Tresset, & C. Dupont, 2004. From harvesting the sea to stock rearing along the Atlantic facade of North-West Europe. *Environmental Archaeology,* 9, 143–154.

Scott, G. R., 1957. *The History of Cockfighting.* London: Charles Skilton.

Serjeantson, D., 1988. Archaeological and ethnographic evidence for seabird exploitation in Scotland. *Archaeozoologia,* II(1/2), 209–224.

Serjeantson, D., 1991. The bird bones, in *Danebury: An Iron Age Hillfort in Hampshire* (vol. 5), eds. B. Cunliffe & C. Poole. London: CBA, 479–481.

Serjeantson, D. (ed.) 1997. Subsistence and symbol. Papers from the International Council for Archaeozoology Bird Group meeting, 1995, *International Journal of Osteoarchaeology,* 7(4).

Serjeantson, D., 1998. Birds: a seasonal resource. *Environmental Archaeology. Special Issue: Seasonality,* 3, 23–33.

Serjeantson, D., 2000a. Bird bones, in *Excavations at Carisbrooke Castle, Isle of Wight, 1921–1996,* ed. C. Young. Salisbury: Wessex Archaeology, 182–185.

Serjeantson, D., 2000b. Bird bones, in *Late Iron Age and Roman Silchester: Excavations on the Site of the Forum Basilica 1977, 1980–86.* Britannia Monograph Series 15, eds. M. Fulford & J. Timby. London: Society for the Promotion of Roman Studies, 484–500.

Serjeantson, D., 2000c. Good to eat *and* good to think with: classifying animals from complex sites, in *Animal Bones, Human Societies,* ed. P. Rowley-Conwy. Oxford: Oxbow, 179–189.

Serjeantson, D., 2001a. A Dainty Dish: consumption of small birds in late medieval England, in *Animal and Man in the Past: Essays in Honor of Dr. A.T. Clason,* eds. H. Buitenhus & W. Prummel. Groningen: ARC-Publicatie, 263–274.

Serjeantson, D., 2001b. The Great Auk and the Gannet: a prehistoric perspective on the extinction of the great auk. *International Journal of Osteoarchaeology. Special Issue: Zooarchaeology of Oceanic Coasts and Islands,* 11(1–2), 43–55.

Serjeantson, D., 2002. Goose husbandry in medieval England, and the problem of ageing goose bones. Proceedings of the 4th meeting of the ICAZ Bird Working Group, Krakow, Poland, 11–15 September, 2001, *Acta Zoologica Cracoviensia,* 45, 39–54.

Serjeantson, D., 2005a. Archaeological records of a gadfly petrel *Pterodroma* sp. from Scotland in the first millennium AD, in *Feathers, Grit and Symbolism: Birds and Humans in the Ancient, Old and New Worlds,* eds G. Grupe & J. Peters. Proceedings of the 5th meeting of the ICAZ Bird Working Group, Munich, 26–28 July, 2004, Documenta Archaeobiologiae 3. Rahden: Verlag Marie Leidorf, 235–246.

Serjeantson, D., 2005b. 'Science is Measurement'; ABMAP, a database of domestic animal bone measurements. *Environmental Archaeology,* 10(1), 95–101.

Serjeantson, D., 2006a. Animal bones, in *Marshland Communities and Cultural Landscapes from the Bronze Age to the Present Day. The Haddenham project* (vol. 2), ed. C. Evans. Cambridge: McDonald Institute, 213–246.

Serjeantson, D., 2006b. Birds as food and markers of status, in *Food in Medieval England: Diet and Nutrition,* eds. C. M. Woolgar, D. Serjeantson, & T. Waldron. Oxford: Oxford University Press, 131–147.

Serjeantson, D., 2007a. The bird bones, in *Excavations at Pool, Sanday, Orkney*, ed. J. Hunter. Kirkwall: Orcadian Press.

Serjeantson, D., 2007b. Bird bones, in *Excavations at Tofts Ness, Sanday, Orkney*, ed. S. Dockrill. Kirkwall: Orcadian Press.

Serjeantson, D., In press-a. Bird bones, in *Excavations in the Sanctuary of Poseidon on Kalaureia*, ed. B. Wells. Stockholm: Swedish Institute of Athens.

Serjeantson, D., In press-b. Food, craft and status: the animal and plant remains in the wider context, in *Food, Craft and Status in Medieval Winchester: The Plant and Animal Remains From the Suburbs and City Defences*. Winchester Excavations Volume 10, eds. D. Serjeantson & H. Rees. Winchester: Winchester Museums.

Serjeantson, D., In press-c. Extinct birds, in *Extinctions and Invasions: A Social History of British Fauna*, eds. N. J. Sykes & T. P. O'Connor. Oxford: Oxbow.

Serjeantson, D., B. Irving, & S. Hamilton-Dyer, 1993. Bird bone taphonomy from the inside out: the evidence of gull predation on the Manx shearwater *Puffinus puffinus*. *Archaeofauna*, 2, 191–204.

Serjeantson, D. & P. Smith, In press. Medieval and Post-Medieval Animal Bone from the Northern and Eastern Suburbs and the City Defences, in *Food, Craft and Status in Medieval Winchester: The Plant and Animal Remains From the Suburbs and City Defences*. Winchester Excavations Volume 10, eds. D. Serjeantson & H. Rees. Winchester: Winchester Museums.

Serjeantson, D., S. Wales, & J. Evans, 1994. Fish in later prehistoric Britain, in Special issue: Archaeo-Ichthyological Studies. Papers Presented at the 6th meeting of the I.C.A.Z. Fish Remains Working Group, ed. D. Heinrich. *Offa 51*. Neumunster: Wachholz, 332–339.

Serjeantson, R. W., 2001. The passions and animal language, 1540–1700. *Journal of the History of Ideas*, 62, 425–444.

Shaw, F. J., 1980. *The Northern and Western Islands of Scotland: Their Economy and Society in the Seventeenth Century*. Edinburgh: John Donald.

Sibley, E., 1794. *An Universal System of Natural History* (vol. 5). London: Champante and Whitrow.

Sidell, E. J., 1993. A methodology for the identification of avian eggshell from archaeological sites. *Archaeofauna. Archaeornithology: Birds and the Archaeological Record*, 2, 45–51.

Sidell, J., 1997. The eggshell, in *Excavations at the Priory and Hospital of St Mary Spital, London*. MoLAS Monograph 1, eds. C. Thomas, B. Sloane, & C. Philpotts. London: Museum of London.

Sidell, J., 2006. Eggshell, in *Marshland Communities and Cultural Landscape: The Haddenham Project* (vol. 2), ed. C. Evans. Cambridge: McDonald Institute, 233–234.

Sillitoe, P., 1988. From head-dresses to head-messages: the art of self-decoration in the highlands of Papua New Guinea. *Man. New Series*, 23(2), 298–318.

Simmons, T. & D. Nadel, 1998. The avifauna of the Early Epipalaeolithic site of Ohalo II (19 400 years BP), Israel: species diversity, habitat and seasonality. *International Journal of Osteoarchaeology*, 8, 79–96.

Simms, E., 1979. *The Public Life of the Street Pigeon*. London: Hutchinson.

Simoons, F. J., 1994. *Eat Not This Flesh: Food Avoidances From Prehistory to the Present*. Madison: Wisconsin University Press.

Sinclair, J., 1978. *The Statistical Account of Scotland 1791–1799* (facsimile edition). Wakefield: EP Publishing.

Smith, D. A., 2005. Garden game: shifting cultivation, indigenous hunting and wildlife ecology in Western Panama. *Human Ecology*, 33, 505–537.

Smith, R. E., 1982. Avian osteopetrosis. *Current Topics in Microbiology and Immunology*, 101, 75–94.

Snow, D. W. & C. M. Perrins, 1998. *The Birds of the Western Palearctic. Volume 1: Non-passerines*. Oxford: Oxford University Press.

Sokoloff, L., 1963. Degenerative joint disease in birds. *Laboratory Investigation*, 12, 531–537.

Solecki, R. L., 1977. Predatory bird rituals at Zawi Chemi Shanidar. *Sumer*, 33, 42–47.

Sparkes, B. A., 1997. Painted birds at Pompeii. Special issue: Subsistence and symbol. Papers from the International Council for Archaeozoology Bird Group meeting, 1995, *International Journal of Osteoarchaeology*, 7(4), 350–353.

Speller, K. & D. Yang, 2006. Investigating the role of wild and domestic turkeys in the Southwestern USA through ancient DNA analysis. Conference presentation, 27 August 2006. ICAZ International Conference, Mexico City.

Spenneman, D. H. R. & S. Colley, 1989. Fire in a pit: the effects of burning on faunal remains. *Archaeozoologia*, III(1/2), 51–64.

Stahl, P. W., 2005. An exploratory osteological study of the Muscovy Duck (*Cairina moschata*) (Aves: Anatidae) with implications for neotropical archaeology. *Journal of Archaeological Science*, 32(6), 915–29.

Stahl, P. W., 2006. New evidence for pre-Columbian Muscovy Duck *Cairina moschata* from Ecuador. *Ibis*, 148, 657–663.

Starck, J. M., 1994. Quantitive design of the skeleton in bird hatchlings: does tissue compartmentalization limit posthatching growth rates? *Journal of Morphology*, 222, 113–131.

Steadman, D. W., 1980. A review of the osteology and palaeontology of turkeys (Aves: Meleagridinae), in *Papers in Avian Paleontology Honoring Hildegarde Howard*. Contributions in Science 330, ed. K. E. Campbell. Los Angeles: Los Angeles County Museum, 131–207.

Steadman, D. W. & P. V. Kirch, 1990. Prehistoric extinction of birds on Mangaia, Cook Islands, Polynesia. *Proceedings of the National Academy of Sciences*, 87, 9605–9609.

Steadman, D. W. & P. Martin, 2003. The Late Quaternary extinction and future resurrection of birds on Pacific islands. *Earth-Science Reviews*, 61, 133–147.

Steadman, D. W., A. Plourde & D. V. Burley, 2002. Prehistoric butchery and consumption of birds in the Kingdom of Tonga, South Pacific. *Journal of Archaeological Science*, 29, 571–584.

Steadman, D. W. & B. Rolett, 1996. A chronostratigraphic analysis of landbird extinction on Tahuata, Marquesas Islands. *Journal of Archaeological Science*, 23, 81–94.

Stephenson, R., 1991. Post-medieval ceramic bird pots from excavations in Greater London. *London Archaeologist*, 6(12), 320–321.

Stewart, H., 1977. *Indian Fishing: Early Methods on the Northwest Coast*. Vancouver, BC: Douglas & McIntyre.

Stewart, H., 1996. *Stone, Bone, Antler and Shell: Artifacts of the North-west Coast*. Vancouver, BC: Douglas & McIntyre.

Stewart, J. R., 2002. Seabirds from coastal and non-coastal, archaeological and "natural" Pleistocene deposits. Proceedings of the 4th meeting of the ICAZ Bird Working Group, Krakow, Poland, 11–15 September, 2001. *Acta Zoologica Cracoviensia*, 45, 167–178.

Stewart, J. R., 2007. *An Evolutionary Study of Some Archaeologically Significant Avian Taxa in the Quaternary of the Western Palaearctic.* International Series 1653, Oxford: BAR

Stewart, J. R. & F. Hernandez Carrasquilla, 1997. The identification of extant European bird remains: a review of the literature. Special issue: Subsistence and symbol. Papers from the International Council for Archaeozoology Bird Group meeting, 1995, *International Journal of Osteoarchaeolgy*, 7(4), 364–371.

Stiner, M. C., N. D. Munro & T. A. Surovell, 2000. The tortoise and the hare. Small-game use, the broad-spectrum revolution, and paleolithic demography. *Current Anthropology*, 41(1), 39–73.

Stone, D. J., 2006. The consumption and supply of birds in Late Medieval England, in *Food in Medieval England: Diet and Nutrition*, eds. C. M. Woolgar, D. Serjeantson, & T. Waldron. Oxford: Oxford University Press, 148–161.

Stora, N., 1968. *Massfångst av Sjöfågel i Nordeurasien: En Etnologisk Undersökning av Fångstmetoderna.* Åbo: Åbo Akademie.

Storey, A. A., T. Ladefoged & E. A. Matisoo-Smith, 2008. Counting your chickens: density and distribution of chicken remains in archaeological sites of Oceania. *International Journal of Osteoarchaeology*, 18(3), 240–261.

Storey, A. A., J. M. Ramirez, D. Quiroz, D. V. Burley, D. J. Addison, R. Walter, A. J. Anderson, T. L. Hunt, J. S. Athens, L. Huynen, & E. A. Matisoo-Smith, 2007. Radiocarbon and DNA evidence for a pre-Columbian introduction of Polynesian chickens to Chile. *Proceedings of the National Academy of Sciences*, 104(25), 10,335–10,339.

Strott, N., 2005. Histomorphometric examination on different poultry species, in *Feathers, Grit and Symbolism: Birds and Humans in the Ancient, Old and New Worlds*, eds. G. Grupe & J. Peters. Proceedings of the 5th meeting of the ICAZ Bird Working Group, Munich, 26–28 July, 2004, Documenta Archaeobiologiae 3. Rahden: Verlag Marie Leidorf, 83–94.

Strutt, J., 1810. *Glig Gamena Angel Theoth: Or the Sports and Pastimes of the People of England* (2nd ed.). London: White.

Studer, J., 1992. Selective hunting or unintentional trapping? *Archaeozoologia*, V(1), 79–85.

Studer, J., 1996. La faune romaine tardive d'Ez Zantur, à Pétra, in *Petra, Ez Zantur I. Ergebnisse der Schweizerisch Liechtensteinischen Ausgrabungen 1988, 1992. Terra Archaeologica II*, ed. R. A. Stucky. Mainz: Stiftung für Archäologische Forschungen im Ausland, 359–375.

Sykes, N. J., 2004. The dynamics of status symbols: wildfowl exploitation in England AD 410–1450. *The Archaeological Journal*, 161, 82–105.

Sykes, N. J., 2007. *The Norman Conquest: A Zooarchaeological Perspective.* International Series 1656, Oxford: BAR.

Tagliacozzo, A. & M. Gala, 2002. Exploitation of Anseriformes at two Upper Palaeolithic sites in southern Italy: Grotta Romanelli (Lecce, Apulia) and Grotta del Santuario della

Madonna a Praia a Mare (Cosenza, Calabria). Proceedings of the 4th meeting of the ICAZ Bird Working Group, Krakow, Poland, 11–15 September, 2001, *Acta Zoologica Cracoviensia*, 45, 117–131.

Taylor, T. G., 1962. Calcium absorbtion and metabolism in the laying hen, in *Nutrition of Pigs and Poultry*, eds. J. T. Morgan & D. Lewis. London: Butterworths, 148–157.

Taylor, T. G., K. Simkiss, & D. A. Stringer, 1971. The skeleton: its structure and metabolism, in *Physiology and Biochemistry of the Domestic Fowl* (vol. 2), eds. D. J. Bell & B. M. Freeman. London: Academic Press, 621–640.

Tchernov, E., 1993. Exploitation of birds during the Natufian and early neolithic of the southern Levant. *Archaeofauna. Archaeornithology: Birds and the Archaeological Record*, 2, 121–143.

Tell, L. A., L. Woods, & R. L. Cromie, 2001. Mycobacteriosis in birds. *Revue Scientifique et Technique*, 20, 180–203.

Thom, V. A., 1986. *Birds in Scotland*. Waterhouses, Staffordshire: T. and A. D. Poyser.

Thomas, P. K., P. P. Joglekar, Y. Matsushima, S. J. Pawankar, & A. Deshpande, 1997. Subsistence based on animals in the Harappan culture of Gujarat, India. *Anthropozoologica*, 25–26, 767–776.

Thorp, B. H., 1994. Skeletal disorders in the fowl – a review. *Avian Pathology*, 232, 203–236.

Ticehurst, N. F., 1957. *The Mute Swan in England: Its History, and the Ancient Custom of Swan Keeping*. London: Cleaver-Hume.

Tomek, T. & Z. Bochenski, 2000. *The Comparative Osteology of European Corvids (Aves: Corvidae), With a Key to the Identification of Their Skeletal Elements*. Krakow: Institute of Systematics and Evolution of Animals.

Tomek, T. & Z. Bochenski, 2002. Bird scraps from a Greek table: the case of Klisoura Cave. Proceedings of the 4th meeting of the ICAZ Bird Working Group, Krakow, Poland, 11–15 September, 2001, *Acta Zoologica Cracoviensia*, 45, 133–138.

Toynbee, J. M. C., 1973. *Animals in Roman Life and Art*. London: Thames and Hudson.

Trapani, J., 1998. Hydrodynamic sorting of avian skeletal remains. *Journal of Archaeological Science*, 25, 477–487.

Traxler, B., G. Brem, M. Muller, & R. Achmann, 2000. Polymorphic DNA microsatellites in the domestic pigeon, *Columba livia* var. *domestica*. *Molecular Ecology*, 9, 366–368.

Tuck, J. A., 1971. An Archaic cemetery at Port au Choix, Newfoundland. *American Antiquity*, 36(3), 343–358.

Turvey, S. T., O. R. Green, & R. N. Holdaway, 2005. Cortical growth marks reveal extended juvenile development in New Zealand moa. *Nature (London)*, 435, 940–943.

Tyrberg, T., 1995. Palaeobiogeography of the genus *Lagopus* in the West Palearctic. *Courier Forschungsinstitut Senckenberg, Frankfurt*, 181, 275–291.

Tyrberg, T., 1998. *Pleistocene Birds of the Palearctic: A Catalogue*. Publication No. 27. Cambridge, MA: Nuttall Ornithological Club.

Tyrberg, T., 2002. The archaeological record of domesticated and tamed birds in Sweden. Proceedings of the 4th meeting of the ICAZ Bird Working Group, Krakow, Poland, 11–15 September, 2001, *Acta Zoologica Cracoviensia*, 45, 215–231.

Ubelekar, D. H. & W. R. Wedel, 1975. Bird bones, burials and bundles in Plains archaeology. *American Antiquity*, 40(4), 444–452.

Ugan, A. S., 2005. Does size matter? Body size, mass collecting, and their implications for understanding prehistoric foraging behaviour. *American Antiquity*, 70(1), 75–89.

Underhill, A. P., 1997. Current issues in Chinese Neolithic archaeology. *Journal of World Prehistory*, 11(2), 103–160.

Van Neer, W. & H. Bocoum, 1991. Etude archéozoologique de Tulel-Fobo, site protohistorique (IVe–Xe siècle) de la moyenne vallée du Fleuve Sénégal (République du Sénégal). *Archaeozoologia*, IV(1), 93–114.

Van Neer, W. & A. Ervynck, 1999. The faunal remains, in *Report of the 1997 Excavations at Berenike and the Survey of the Egyptian Eastern Desert, Including Excavation at Shenshef*. Leiden: C.N.W.S.

Van Neer, W., K. Noyen, B. De Cupere, & I. Beuls, 2002. On the use of endosteal layers and medullary bone from domestic fowl in archaeozoological studies. *Journal of Archaeological Science*, 29, 123–134.

Ventura, C., 2003. The Jakaltek Maya blowgun in mythological and historical context. *Ancient Mesoamerica*, 14(2), 257–268.

Vigne, J.-D., C. Lefèvre, J.-C. Thibault, & I. Guyot, 1991. Contribution archéozoologique a l'histoire récente des oiseaux marin de l'île Lavezzi (Corse – XIV–XX siècles). *Alauda*, 59(1), 11–21.

Vigne, J., S. Bailon, & J. Cuisin, 1997. Biostratigraphy of amphibians, reptiles, birds and mammals in Corsica and the role of man in the Holocene faunal turnover. *Anthropozoologica*, 25–26, 587–604.

Vilette, P., 1983. Avifaunes du Pléistocène final et de l'Holocène dans le sud de la France et en Catalogne. *Atacina Carcassonne*, 11, 1–90.

Villari, P., 1991. The faunal remains in the Bothros at Eolo (Lipari). *Archaeozoologia*, IV(2), 109–126.

Vita-Finzi, C. & E. S. Higgs, 1970. Prehistoric economy in the Mount Carmel area of Palestine: site catchment analysis. *Proceedings of the Prehistoric Society*, 36, 1–37.

Voitkevich, A. A., 1966. *The Feathers and Plumage of Birds*. London: Sidgwick and Jackson.

von den Driesch, A., 1976. *A Guide to the Measurement of Animal Bones from Archaeological Sites*, Cambridge, MA: Harvard Peabody Museum.

von den Driesch, A., 1999. The crane, *Grus grus*, in prehistoric Europe and its relation to the Pleistocene crane, *Grus primigenia*, in *Archäologie in Eurasien 6*, ed. N. Benecke. Rahden:. Verlag Marie Leidorf, 201–207.

von den Driesch, A., 2005. Würmzeitliche Avifauna aus der Sesselfelsgrotte, Altmühltal, in *Feathers, Grit and Symbolism: Birds and Humans in the Ancient, Old and New Worlds*, eds. G. Grupe & J. Peters. Proceedings of the 5th meeting of the ICAZ Bird Working Group, Munich, 26–28 July, 2004, Documenta Archaeobiologiae 3. Rahden: Verlag Marie Leidorf, 27–42.

von den Driesch, A. & I. Baumgartner, 1997. Die spätantiken Tierreste aus der Kobbat Bent el Rey in Karthago. *Archeozoologia*, IX, 155–172.

von den Driesch, A., D. Kessler, F. Steinmann, V. Berteaux & J. Peters, 2005. Mummified, Deified and Buried at Hermopolis Magna – The Sacred Birds from Tuna el-Gebel, Middle Egypt. *Egypt and the Levant*, 15, 203–244.

von den Driesch, A. & N. Pöllath, 2000. Tierknochen aus dem Mithrastempel von Künzing, Lkr. Deggendorf, in *Vorträge des 18 Niederbayerischen Archäologentages*, ed. K. Schmotz. Rahden: Verlag Marie Leidorf, 145–162.

Walker, R. B. & P. W. Parmalee, 2004. A noteworthy cache of goose humeri from Late Paleoindian levels at Dust Cave, Northwestern Alabama. *Journal of Alabama Archaeology*, 50(1), 18–35.

Wall, S. M., 1980. The animal bones from the excavation of the Hospital of St Mary of Ospringe. *Archaeologia Cantiana*, 96, 227–266.

Warren, D. C., 1937. *Physiologic and genetic studies of crooked keels in chickens.* Technical Bulletin 44 of the Agricultural Experiment Station, Kansas State College of Agriculture and Applied Science. Manhattan: Kansas State College Press.

Washko, R. M., H. Hoefer, T. E. Kiehn, D. Armstrong, G. Dorsinville, & T. R. Frieden, 1998. *Mycobacterium tuberculosis* infection in a green-winged macaw (*Ara chloroptera*): report with public health implications. *Journal of Clinical Microbiology*, 36, 1101–1102.

Watson, W., 1969. Early animal domestication in China, in *The Domestication and Exploitation of Plants and Animals*, eds. P. Ucko & G. W. Dimbleby. London: Duckworth, 393–395.

Weigelt, J., 1989. *Recent Vertebrate Carcasses and their Paleobiological Implications.* Chicago: University of Chicago.

Weisler, M. I., 1995. Henderson Island prehistory: colonization and extinction on a remote Polynesian island. *Biological Journal of the Linnean Society*, 56, 377–404.

Weisler, M. I., 2001. Life on the edge: prehistoric settlement and economy on Utrok Atoll, northwest Marshall islands. *Archaeology in Oceania*, 36(3), 109–133.

Weisler, M. I. & R. H. Gargett, 1993. Pacific island avian extinctions: the taphonomy of human predation. *Archaeology in Oceania*, 28, 85–93.

West, B., 1982. Spur development: recognising caponised fowl in archaeological material, in *Ageing and Sexing Animal Bones from Archaeological Sites*. British Series 109, eds. B. Wilson, C. Grigson, & S. Payne. Oxford: BAR, 255–261.

West, B., 1985a. Chicken legs revisited. *Circaea*, 3(1), 11–14.

West, B., 1985b. Poultry-fanciers' section. *Circaea*, 3(2), 131.

West, B. & B.-X. Zhou, 1988. Did chickens go north? New evidence for domestication. *Journal of Archaeological Science*, 15(5), 515–554.

Whittow, G. C., 2000. *Sturkie's Avian Physiology* (5th ed.). New York: Academic Press.

Whitehead, C. C., 2004. Overview of bone biology in the egg-laying hen. *Poultry Science*, 83, 193–199.

Whitehead, C. C. & R. H. Fleming, 2000. Osteoporosis in cage layers. *Poultry Science*, 78, 1033–1041.

Wigen, R. & B. Stucki, 1988. Taphonomy and stratigraphy in the interpretation of economic patterns at Hoka River Rockshelter. *Research in Economic Anthropology*, Supplement 3. *Prehistoric Economies of the Pacific Northwest Coast*, 87–146.

Wijngaarden-Bakker, L. H. Van, 1997. The selection of bird bones for artefact production at Dutch Neolithic sites. Special issue: Subsistence and symbol. Papers from the International Council for Archaeozoology Bird Group meeting, 1995, *International Journal of Osteoarchaeology*, 7(4), 339–345.

Wijngaarden-Bakker, L. H. Van, 2002. Winter in a wetland. The bird remains from a Late Mesolithic camp site at Polderweg, municipality of Hardinxveld-Giessendam. Proceedings of the 4th meeting of the ICAZ Bird Working Group, Krakow, Poland, 11–15 September, 2001, *Acta Zoologica Cracoviensia*, 45, 55–64.

Williamson, K., 1948. *The Atlantic Islands: A Study of the Faeroe Life and Scene*, London: Collins.

Wings, O., 2004. *Identification, Distribution, and Function of Gastroliths in Dinosaurs and Extant Birds With Emphasis on Ostriches* (Struthio camelus), Bonn: Dissertation zur Erlangung des Doktorgrades (Dr. rer. nat.) der Mathematisch-Naturwissenschaftlichen Fakultät der Rheinischen Friedrich-Wilhelms-Universität.

Woelfle, E., 1967. *Vergleichend morphologische Untersuchungen an Einzelknochen des postkranialen Skelettes in Mitteleuropa verkommender Enten, Halbgänse und Sager*, Munich: Institut für Paläoanatomie, Domestikationsforschung und Geschichte der Tiermedizin der Universität München.

Wood-Gush, D. G. M., 1958. A history of the domestic chicken from Antiquity to the 19th century. *Edinburgh: Agricultural Research Council Poultry Research Centre*, 9, 321–326.

Wood, H. B., 1941. Fractures among birds. *Bird-Banding*, 12, 68–72.

Woolgar, C. M., D. Serjeantson, & T. Waldron, 2006a. Conclusion, in *Food in Medieval England: Diet and Nutrition*, eds. C. M. Woolgar, D. Serjeantson, & T. Waldron. Oxford: Oxford University Press, 267–280.

Woolgar, C. M., D. Serjeantson, & T. Waldron, 2006b. Introduction, in *Food in Medieval England: Diet and Nutrition*, eds. C. M. Woolgar, D. Serjeantson, & T. Waldron. Oxford: Oxford University Press, 1–8.

Worthy, T. & R. Holdaway, 2002. *The Lost World of the Moa: Prehistoric Life of New Zealand*, Bloomington: Indiana University Press.

Yalden, D., & U. Albarella, 2008. *The History of Birds in Britain*. Oxford: Oxford University Press.

Yalden, D. W., 2007. The older history of the White-tailed eagle in Britain. *British Birds*, 100, 471–480.

Yalden, D. W. & R. I. McCarthy, 2004. The archaeological record of birds in Britain and Ireland compared: extinctions or failures to arrive? *Environmental Archaeology*, 9, 123–126.

Yalden, D. W. & P. A. Morris, 1990. *The Analysis of Owl Pellets*. London: The Mammal Society.

Yapp, B., 1981. *Birds in Medieval Manuscripts*. London: British Library.

Young, J. Z., 1950. *The Life of Vertebrates*. Oxford: Oxford University Press.

Lepetz, S. & J.-H. Yvinec, 2002. Présence d'espèces animales d'origine méditerranéenne en France du nord aux périodes romaine et médiévale: actions anthropiques et mouvements naturels, in *Mouvements ou Déplacements de Populations Animales en Méditerranée au cours de l'Holocène*. International Series 1017, ed. A. Gardeisen. Oxford: BAR, 33–42.

Zeiler, J. T., 2006. Birds, in *Schipluiden: A Neolithic Settlement on the Dutch North Sea Coast c. 3500 cal BC. Analecta Praehistoria Leidensia*, eds. L. P. Louwe Kooijmans & P. F. B. Jongste. Leiden: Faculty of Archaeology, Leiden University, 421–442.

Zeiler, J. T. & A. T. Clason, 1993. Fowling in the Dutch Neolithic at inland and coastal sites. *Archaeofauna. Archaeornithology: Birds and the Archaeological Record*, 2, 67–74.

Zeuner, F. E., 1963. *A History of Domesticated Animals*. London: Hutchinson.

Zhang, J., X. Xiao, & Y. K. Lee, 2004. The early development of music. Analysis of the Jiahu bone flutes. *Antiquity*, 77, 31–44, 769–778.

Zhilin, M. G. & A. A. Karhu, 2002. Exploitation of birds in the early Mesolithic of Central Russia. Proceedings of the 4th meeting of the ICAZ Bird Working Group, Krakow, Poland, 11–15 September, 2001, *Acta Zoologica Cracoviensia*, 45, 109–116.

INDEX

Aartswoud, 210, 211, 213, 217
Abri Dufaure, 221, 225, 257
Abydos, 245
Acheulian culture, 261
Africa, 3, 9, 72, 165, 180, 261, 280, 285, 311, 333. *See also* North Africa, South Africa, West Africa
African collared dove, 304
African goose. *See* Chinese goose
age class, 45–47, 240, 267
ageing, 35–38, 45, 398. *See also* fusion, porosity
    bone length, 43, 44, 46, 61
    incremental lines, 40–43
    line of arrested growth (LAG), 40, 42
Aggersund, 200, 257, 449
agricultural clearance, 315, 365, 374, 377, 385
agriculture, 252, 265, 300, 306, 376, 381, 383
    marginal, 230, 263, 400
Ain Mallaha, 372
Ainu, 206, 336
Ajvide, 51, 154, 221, 259
Alabama, 211
Alaska, 14, 195, 210, 226, 246, 363
Aldrovandi, 274, 303
Aleutian Islands, 204, 214, 216, 226, 231, 252, 445
Alligator site, 198
Alpine chough. *See* choughs
altricial species, 11, 12, 38
Amaknak, 214, 216, 217
Amazon Basin, 273, 332

American coot, 106, 108, 122, 147, 403
American Ornithologist's Union, 419
American Southwest, 177, 189, 193, 289, 291, 292, 312, 333, 345, 399, 400, 450
amulet, 200, 201, 226, 227, 229, 359. *See also* talisman
analogue fauna, 369
Anasazi, 289, 292
Anatolia, 271, 320, 337, 354, 359. *See also* Turkey
ancient DNA, 34, 285, 292, 314, 396, 399
    albatross, 69
    chicken, 69, 268, 273
    grey geese, 69, 296–297
    turkey, 291
Andean condor, 9, 403
Anglo-Saxon period, 225, 297, 299, 344, 364
Animal Bone Metrical Archive Project, 71, 421
Antarctica, 14, 252, 266
anthropogenic assemblage, 156
    recognising, 100, 104, 130–131
Apalle Cave, 376, 377
Apicius, 341, 343
Aquincum, 342, 351
Arabia, 316, 325
archaeological project manager, 84, 343, 397
Arctic, 14, 122, 168, 204, 205, 209, 235, 241, 253, 254, 258, 266, 426, 432, 434
arctic tern, 14, 167, 403
Argentina, 92, 200, 302

Aridos, 261
Arizona, 178, 193, 194, 345
arrow, 209, 210, 213, 215, 241, 242, 246–247. *See also* bow and arrow
arthritis, 55, 58, 60
Asia, 3, 199, 272, 280, 285, 292, 304, 316, 317, 320, 325, 334, 380, 385, 390. *See also* Southeast Asia, Western Asia
assessment, 83
Assiniboine Indians, 356
Atlantic Ocean, 2, 168, 381, 382, 384
Atlantic puffin. *See* puffins
Auckland Islands, 252
Audouin's gull, 379, 403
Aurignac Cave, 218
Aurignacian period, 218, 262, 376. *See also* Upper Palaeolithic
Australia, 63, 177, 183, 241, 244, 245, 250, 368, 371, 372
avian distribution, 5, 288, 392. *See also* range change, 34, 64, 263, 270, 365, 368, 374, 379, 380. *See also* agricultural clearance, colonisation, drainage, forest clearance
past, 5, 36, 64, 365, 394, 396
aviary, 314, 332
awl, 210–214, 223, 224. *See also* bird bone point
cache with burial, 211
axial skeleton, 22–26
Ayalán, 302
Azilian. *See* Epipalaeolithic period
Aztecs, 193, 377
azure-winged magpie, 380, 403

Babylonian period, 306, 310, 331, 400
Bahrain, 344
Balatonboglár, 222, 223
bald eagle, 117, 186, 187, 376, 403
Baldock, 179
Balkans, 284, 369
Baltic Region, 155, 250, 251, 256, 259, 263
Baltic Sea, 15, 51, 154
Banks Island, 258
Banks, Joseph, 204
banquet, 265, 400. *See also* feast

barbary dove, 304, 403
Barchin del Hoyo, 271
barn owl, 121, 366, 368, 403
barred buttonquail, 38, 403
Barrow Hills, Radley, 210
Basketmaker culture, 289, 291
basketry, 185, 193, 245
bead
  bird bone, 209, 210, 217, 221–222, 225
  manufacture, 222
  ostrich eggshell, 180, 181
Beagle Channel, 90, 92, 255
beak, 5, 186, 200, 223, 358
  decoration, 226
  mark, 117–119, 128, 131, 147
  pin, 215
bean goose, 257, 262, 403
bearded vulture, 116, 358, 376, 403
bee hummingbird, 9, 403
Belcher Island, 204, 205
Bélo, Temple of Isis, 351
Berenike, 51–53, 272, 283
Bergschenhoek, 152, 210, 249
Beverley, 200
Bewick's swan, 152, 210, 249, 403
Biggleswade, 322
bioerosion, 109, 110, 112–114, 120
biomass, 89, 92, 253
bird bone pipe. *See* flute
bird bone point, 211, 213, 215, 223
bird bone structure, 17–18, 34, 113
bird bone tool, 2, 7, 69, 130, 362, 366, 394, 398, 401
  manufacture, 132, 213, 223, 224, 228
  raw material, 164, 202, 212, 229, 239, 263, 399
  species selected, 209–212
bird bone tube, 210, 211, 215–217, 221, 222
  offcut, 217
bird burial, 336, 348–349
  buzzard, 360
  duck mummy, 333
  eagle, 348
  hawk, 323
  macaw, 201, 347, 348

raven, 360, 361, 364
turkey, 289, 349
bird capture. *See* fowling methods
bird lime, 248
bird mummy, 348
   duck, 333
   falcon, 353
   goose, 352
   sacred ibis, 45, 353–354
bird pot, 378
Bird Working Group, 6, 394, 419
birdsong, 1, 316, 332. *See also* voice
birdwatcher, 1
bite mark, 147. *See also* chewing, gnawing
bittern, 32, 265, 318, 404, 405
black grouse, 71, 126, 164, 264, 404
   identification, 71
black guillemot, 167, 404
Black Mesa, 178
Black Sea, 271
black vulture, 9, 200, 212, 219, 221, 404. *See also* vultures
black-billed magpie, 371, 404
blackbird, 66, 332, 404
black-chested buzzard-eagle, 200, 404
black-footed albatross, 69, 404
blind. *See* hide
blowgun, 238, 248, 273
bobwhite, 73, 404
body weight, 12, 13, 38, 82, 93–95, 210, 231, 232, 265, 318
Bois-Ragot, 55, 137–140, 145, 202, 203, 226, 228
bolas, 241
Bolivia, 302
bone density. *See* density
bone mineral, 160, 161
bone survival. *See* survival
bone weight, 93, 94. *See also* quantification
bone zone, 48, 79, 81, 89, 155. *See* Appendix 2
Book of St Albans, 317, 318
bothros, 342
bow and arrow, 188, 238, 246, 248, 331, 393
Bow River Museum, Calgary, 226
Boxgrove, 81, 261

breeding colony, 107, 165, 168, 236–238, 241, 243, 379, 381, 384
   ownership, 395
brent goose, 14, 232, 262, 404
Brillenhöhle, 72
Brisson, Mathurin Jacques, 5
Britain, 64, 106, 177, 265, 295, 311, 325, 329, 331, 367, 376
British Camp, San Juan Islands, 157, 158
British Columbia, 187, 384, 395
British Isles, 68, 167, 168, 256, 257, 272, 321, 369, 376, 379, 380, 394, 395
broad spectrum, 261, 262, 400
Bruniquel Cave, 100
Brunnich's guillemot, 41, 253, 404
Brzesc Kujawski, 225, 234
Bucy-le-Long, 344
budgerigar, 38, 244, 404
Buglé people, 243, 256
Buldir Island, 231, 252
Bulgaria, 64, 377
burning, 130, 131, 143, 149–153, 163, 180, 203, 206, 350, 351, 357, 358. *See also* charring, calcination
   eggshell, 177
   experimental, 151
   incidence, 162
   recording, 81
burrow, 105, 106, 237, 241, 244, 246
butchery, 34, 37, 77, 103, 153, 223, 398
   experimental, 132, 133, 142, 146, 163
   mark, 99, 163, 185. *See also* cut mark, chop mark
   primary, 142, 143, 207
   secondary, 142, 143
butchery site, 150
buzzard, 200, 203, 317, 318, 336, 359, 374, 404
by-catch, 246

Caerleon Roman fort, 331
cage, 199, 313, 336
cage bird, 287, 314, 332, 333
cage stone, 313
calcination, 150, 343

calcium, 36, 49, 55, 170
California turkey, 54, 404
Californian Indians, 203, 336
calories, 233, 234, 393. *See also* quantification
Canada, 14, 199, 203–205, 306, 395. *See also* British Columbia, Yukon
Canada goose, 51, 73, 161, 212, 258, 404
Canoe Indians, 237, 240, 243
Canyon de Chelley, 289
Canyon Del Muerto, 194
cape, 199, 203. *See also* cloak
Cape eagle-owl, 240, 354, 404
Cape gannet, 239, 240, 404
capercaillie, 115, 404
Capitularum de Villis, 301
capon, 43, 55, 95, 268, 274, 281, 282, 301
caponisation, 48, 275–279
capture methods. *See* fowling methods
carcass processing, 79, 132, 140, 142, 143, 145, 153, 154, 233, 398
Caribbean Islands, 290, 302, 382
Carisbrooke Castle, 52, 88, 90, 140, 141, 154, 164, 284, 340
Carpathian Basin, 218
carrion crow, 27, 28, 66, 76, 78, 404
cartilage, 17, 21, 25, 37, 38, 58, 113
Casas Grandes, 248, 313
Cashinahua peoples, 185
Caspian Sea, 271
cassowary, 9, 165, 404
Castle Acre Priory, 179
Castle Hedingham, 322
Castle Mall, Norwich, 298
castration. *See* caponisation
Caucasus region, 271, 369
Causeway Lane, Leicester, 173, 175
Central America, 72, 85, 288, 289, 311, 313, 325
Centro Austral de Investigaciones Científicas, Argentina, 68
Chaco Canyon, 178
Charlie Lake Cave, 361, 384
charm, 185. *See also* talisman
charring, 150–153, 163, 289

Chauvet Cave, 400
Cheddar Caves, 104
chewing, 123
  herbivore, 122
  human, 130, 131, 146–149, 163
chicken, 1, 95, 267, 268, 283, 284, 288, 341, 397. *See also* cockfighting
  age at death, 45–47, 279, 281. *See also* ageing
  DNA, 397
  domestication, 2, 5, 267–270, 283, 399
  early history, 269–270
  eggs. *See* egg production
  feathers, 194
  identification, 71
  in grave, 340
  meat production, 265, 268, 270, 281–282, 285
  pathology, 36, 61
  plumage, 268, 273, 279
  ritual importance, 362. *See also* grave goods, sacrifice
  sexing, 35, 275–276
  size, 279–280
  wild ancestor. *See* red junglefowl
  with cremation, 342
chicken breeds, 39, 48, 49, 55, 270, 271, 273, 275, 277–281, 284, 326, 332
chicken dispersal, 270
  Africa, 272
  Americas, 273
  Asia, 270, 271
  Britain, 93, 272
  Egypt, 271
  Europe, 271–272
  Polynesia, 272, 284
children, 168, 178, 195, 201, 204, 231, 345, 347
Chile, 243, 273
China, 217, 269, 292, 293, 320, 380
  chickens, 1, 268, 270, 271, 274, 283, 326
  ducks, 300
Chinese goose, 292, 293
chisel, 18, 223. *See also* bird bone point

chop mark, 131, 140–142, 144, 163, 343
  incidence, 143
choughs, 9, 104, 264, 375
chukar, 123, 124, 162, 201, 221, 232, 404
cinereous vulture. *See* black vulture
cistern, 178, 393
cladistics, 4, 403
Clark, Graham, 3, 5, 241, 265, 400
classical world, 265, 269, 325, 343, 355
classical writer, 245, 270. *See also individual authors*
classification, 419
  archaeological material, 84
  ecological, 392
  folk taxonomy, 4, 364
  Linnean, 4
claw, 5, 32, 186, 201, 204, 225, 226
  in grave, 225
  mark, 117, 119
  perforated, 225
  talisman, 225
climate, 369, 373
  change, 1, 2, 4, 253, 263, 367, 369, 371, 372, 379, 380, 384, 391, 392
cloak, 185–187, 194
clothing, 138, 193, 194, 197, 199, 204, 205, 213, 221, 226, 228, 229, 348
club, 237, 238, 241
clutch, 10, 12, 165, 168, 281, 305, 310
cock, 35, 43, 49, 150, 268, 273–275, 279, 328, 351, 362
  crow, 362
cockerel, 268, 274. *See also* cock
cockfighting, 268, 271, 273, 280, 316, 325, 334, 338, 362
  breed, 273, 326, 330
  history, 325–327
  morality, 325, 330
  symbolism, 326, 330
cockpit, 327–328
collared dove, 76, 404
colonisation
  avian, 305, 307, 377
  human, 2, 239, 251, 365, 378, 381, 383, 384
Colorado, 193, 290

colour, 1, 9, 62, 185, 186, 200, 364. *See also* feather colour
Columella, 270, 274, 279, 282, 293, 298, 309, 311, 330
Combe Saunière, 145
commensal species, 300, 305, 306, 360, 374, 376
commensalism, 302, 375
common crane, 20, 24, 65, 106, 162, 201, 232, 257, 265, 379, 404. *See also* cranes
  bone used for tool, 210, 211, 213, 221
  engraving, 337
  feathers, 207
  immature, 39, 41
  size, 390, 391
  wing, 355
common duck, 174, 288, 299
  history, 300–301
  identification, 74
  plumage, 300
  size, 74
common loon, 203, 257. *See also* loons
common murre. *See* guillemot
common scoter, 367, 404
companion animal, 55, 57, 59, 310, 316, 332–334, 348, 352
  burial, 345
  cremation, 344
complex society, 265, 266
confiding behaviour, 237, 251, 383, 384, 387, 395
Connley Caves, 53
conservation
  birds, 35, 259, 395
  environment, 394
  feathers, 193
consumption, 83, 144, 248, 261, 265, 298
  mark of rank, 265, 281, 294
  ritual, 394
  seasonal, 282, 297, 298
Cook Islands, 387–389
cooking, 99, 128, 130, 150, 152, 155, 163, 182, 343, 393, 398
  boiling, 213
  experimental, 151

470 INDEX

cooking (*cont.*)
   in oven, 150, 252
   open fire, 138, 143, 151, 152
   stewing, 138
coot, 94, 244, 245, 256, 404. *See also*
   American coot
Coppergate, York, 329
coprolites, 147, 156, 397
cormorant, 5, 30, 167, 216, 221, 236, 314, 406
corn bunting, 235, 405
Corsica, 85, 101, 376–379
Corsican owl, 379
cortex, 18, 40, 41, 50, 52, 160
Costa Rica, 290
Cozumel Island, 288
crag martin, 100, 405
crane dance, 354, 364
cranes, 1, 231, 247, 318, 332, 338, 358. *See also*
   common crane
cremation, 130, 340, 344, 345
   bird bone with, 150, 348
   eggshell with, 179
   food offering, 343
   hawk with, 323
Cretaceous era, 4
Crimea, 271
crooked keel, 56
crop. *See* gizzard
curation
   bird bone assemblage, 399
   feathers, 207
   skeleton collection, 67
curlew, 215, 405
cut mark, 5, 130, 134–163, 205, 212, 256, 354, 355, 361, 398
   feather removal, 138, 202–203, 207
   filleting, 132–134, 355
   incidence, 134–136, 139, 162
   location, 133, 135, 137, 140
   recording, 132, 155
   skinning, 132, 204, 207, 359
   skull, 138, 356, 359
   striated, 131–133, 137, 223
   wing removal, 132, 203, 207

Dalmatian pelican, 105, 379, 405. *See also*
   pelicans
dance, 335, 364, 400
Danebury hillfort, 376
Danube delta, 379
Darwin, Charles, 5, 165, 241, 268, 304, 305
De Arte Venandi, 321
decoration, 184, 224
   claw, 225
   feathers, 9, 184, 185, 193, 197, 228, 289
   on bird bone, 229
   on bird bone point, 213, 215
   on phalanx, 226
   phalanx, 227
   skull, 226
   wing, 185, 201, 348
decoy
   bird, 249, 319
   whistle, 248
   pond, 249, 250
defleshing, 131, 137. *See also* cut mark
   by raptors, 116, 118
Deggendorf, Temple of Mithras, 95
Denmark, 188, 200, 257, 263, 345
density, 79, 100, 110, 121, 130, 156, 158–161, 164, 398
depiction
   bird-man, 338, 339
   cock, 269, 270, 326, 330
   common crane, 337, 355
   ducks, 301
   Egyptian goose, 292
   great auk, 5
   greylag goose, 293
   griffon vulture, 359
   hawk, 354
   macaw, 313
   mallard, 301
   ostrich, 331
   owl, 400
   pigeon, 308
   ptarmigan, 400
   rock dove, 306
   turkey, 289, 290

diagnostic zone. *See* bone zone
digestion mark, 118–121, 128, 131
disarticulation. *See also* dismembering
    in water, 111
    natural, 106–109, 114, 240
disease, 35, 36, 55, 59, 104, 316, 381, 388
dismembering, 132–134, 144, 145, 212, 340, 355. *See also* carcass processing
    overextension, 144, 145, 149
disposal, 102, 130, 150, 153, 307, 323, 394, 397
    differential, 153–155, 207, 351
distribution
    avian. *See* avian distribution
    skeletal element. *See* survival
divers, 215. *See also* loons
divination, 337, 362
divine animal, 336
DNA analysis, 4, 66, 69, 97, 273, 297, 305, 403. *See also* ancient DNA
dodo, 8, 232, 237, 383, 384, 405
domestic duck. *See* common duck, mallard, Muscovy duck
domestic goose, 124, 143, 144, 295. *See also* swan goose, greylag
    ageing, 40
    breeds, 189, 294
    feathers, 189, 190, 198, 200
    history, 294
    identification, 297
    immature, 283, 293, 297, 298
    meat production, 295, 298
    pathology, 57
    plumage, 297
    size, 73, 294, 296
domestic peafowl. *See* peacock
domestic pigeon, 5, 288, 301, 304–310, 316. *See also* rock dove
    ageing, 39
    breeds, 332
    domestication process, 305, 306
    history, 305
    identification, 69
    immature, 35, 61, 105, 308, 309
    meat production, 298
    plumage, 306
    racing, 331
    size, 75, 308
    spread to Europe, 304, 307
domestic turkey, 32, 177, 234, 288, 290. *See also* turkey
    ageing, 44
    eggshell, 289
    history, 289–290
    identification, 73
    plumage, 290, 291
    size, 291
    spread to Europe, 290
    wild ancestor, 289
domestication, 2, 9, 169, 267, 287, 288, 314–315. *See also individual species*
Dorchester, 284, 301, 307, 329
double-crested cormorant, 19, 41, 148, 161, 405
double-spurred francolin, 32, 405
dovecot, 3, 105, 305–309
down. *See* feather
drainage, 106, 256, 374, 380
dream-catcher, 185
Dryas period, 371, 372
Dudka, 257
Dunstable, 364
Dust Cave, 211

eagle owl, 115, 117, 118, 125, 225, 317, 374, 405
eagles, 20, 152, 186, 317, 376
    feathers, 199, 335
    phalanges, 225, 356
    prey, 13, 116, 126
    ritual importance, 336, 337
Easter Island, 265, 338, 339
eburnation, 58, 60
economic value. *See* energetic return
Ecuador, 302, 303
egg production, 36, 165, 169, 178, 183, 268, 270, 281–283, 285

eggs, 10, 12, 165–169. *See also* clutch
   collecting, 165–169
   consumption, 1, 167
   development, 49
   in grave, 178
   symbolic value, 178
   weight, 13
   whole, 178, 179, 182
eggshell, 3, 36, 177
   bead. *See* ostrich eggshell
   colour, 171, 177
   curvature, 176
   flask. *See* ostrich eggshell
   hatched, 182
   identification, 170–172, 175–177, 181
   non-anthropogenic, 182
   quantification, 176
   recovery, 170
   structure, 170–173
   survival, 169, 177
   thickness, 172–177
Egypt, 182, 269, 271, 281, 292, 294, 305, 308, 311, 314, 331, 352, 362, 373, 377, 400
   catacombs, 348, 352, 353
   Roman sites, 176, 178, 183, 194, 269
   temples, 201, 245, 351, 354
   tombs, 194, 293, 333, 344
Egyptian goose, 292, 344, 405
eider, 51, 167, 189, 199, 204, 205, 221, 253, 344, 395, 404, 405
Eketorp, 280, 296, 301
El-Amarna, 293, 294, 307
element
   presence or absence, 100, 124, 130, 155–156, 163
   survival. *See* survival
element distribution. *See* survival
elephant bird, 165, 382, 383, 405
el-Maskhuta, 294
Emeryville shellmound, 5, 17, 151, 161, 258
Emperor Frederick II, 306, 311, 321, 332
emu, 9, 183, 231, 232, 405
endemic fauna, 101
endemic species, 194, 252, 379–381, 383, 385, 388, 390

endosteal layer, 17, 40, 41, 43, 50
energetic return, 169, 231, 233, 235, 239, 265, 393, 394
English Heritage, 67
engraved bone, 215, 219, 220, 228
environment, 3, 136, 266, 365
   change, 1, 2, 365, 367, 370, 371, 379
   marginal, 149, 394
   past, 85, 97, 115, 369, 373
   reconstruction, 85, 365, 366, 372, 374
environmental indicator, 367, 368, 371, 373, 374, 392
Epipalaeolithic period, 262–264, 377
Eralla Cave, 225
Erg of Murzuq, 373
erosion, 115, 121, 213, 221. *See also* bioerosion, digestion mark
Ertebølle, 87
Estonia, 345, 437
Eurasian stone curlew, 221, 405
European robin, 4, 405
excavator, 7, 34, 100, 101, 399
exchange. *See* trade
excrement, 3, 289, 308, 309, 313
Exeter, 281, 301
extinction, 5, 101, 365, 366, 380–382, 386, 390, 392, 396
   habitat destruction, 385
   other causes. *See* agricultural clearance, drainage, forest clearance
   overkill, 381–385
   role of climate, 380
   role of competitors, 388
   role of disease, 388
   role of predators, 387
Eynsham Abbey, 52, 82, 83, 170, 176, 182, 281, 284

Faccombe Netherton, 308, 323
falconry. *See* hawking
Falsterbö, 15, 236
Farm Beneath the Sand, 201, 202
Faroe Islands, 167, 168, 206, 237, 245, 246, 253

fat, 95, 116, 118, 206, 233–234, 260
    beneath the skin, 15, 138, 204, 205
    body, 93, 300
    within bone, 19, 116, 147, 149
    young birds, 12, 238
fattening
    capon, 95, 268, 282, 399
    duck, 300, 301
    goose, 297
    ostrich, 331
    swan, 334
fear of birds, 339, 362
feast, 102, 281, 282, 298, 336, 349, 351
feather
    colour, 186–187, 193, 194
    contour, 189, 191
    down, 189, 198
    filoplume, 189
    flight, 28, 184, 189, 192, 196, 237
    identification, 193
    impression, 195
    micromorphology, 193
    primary, 188, 191, 192, 196, 201, 207
    structure, 189
    tail, 23, 187, 189, 192, 195, 198
    taphonomy, 197, 198
    wing, 185, 189, 190, 199, 200, 202
feather bundle, 193, 194, 196
feather fan, 194
feather removal, 140, 143, 145, 163, 185, 199, 233, 398. *See also* cut mark
feathered skin, 5, 138, 184, 185, 194, 203–206, 288, 336, 355–357, 363
feathers, 184, 201, 231, 394
    decoration, 187, 194
    mark of rank, 207, 208
    ritual, 194
    survival, 184, 193–196
    symbolic value, 184–186, 189
    taphonomy, 197
    warmth, 184, 189
feather-string, 197
    robe with burial, 194
Feddersen-Wierde, 299
Fenlands, 41, 102, 105, 168, 195, 256, 379

feral species, 84
    chicken, 305, 375
    duck, 375
    guineafowl, 312
    Muscovy duck, 302, 303
    mute swan, 334, 375
    pigeon, 75, 304, 305, 375, 378
    turkey, 375
fetish. *See* talisman
Finland, 195, 215
Finsch's duck, 386, 387, 405
Fishbourne Roman villa, 301
fishhook, 209, 223, 224
fishing, 13, 246, 253, 263, 338
fledgling, 10, 12, 13, 46, 107, 237, 309
fletching, 184, 185, 193, 194, 197, 207. *See also* arrow
flightless cormorant, 8, 383, 405
flightlessness, 8, 9, 18, 158, 261, 381, 384
Flixborough, 296, 297
flocking, 12, 15, 231, 235–237, 243, 244, 248, 257, 265, 395
Florida, 114, 375
Florida Museum of Natural History, 65, 66, 420
flute, 2, 209, 212, 217–222, 229, 244, 400, 420
    decorated, 218
    elements used, 217
food avoidance, 169, 265, 266, 282, 289, 317, 339, 394
food preparation. *See* carcass processing
food preservation
    birds, 143, 253, 259–260
    eggs, 168
food processing. *See* carcass processing
food resource, 149, 236, 250–251, 266
    eggs, 165
    major, 235, 250–255, 266, 400
    minor, 250, 251, 254–256, 266, 394, 400
    primary, 250, 251, 254
    rare, 250, 256, 266
    supplementary, 51, 250, 256, 263, 265
forest clearance, 374, 377, 385, 392
fork-tailed storm petrel, 231, 406
Foula, 122

Foveaux Straits, 236, 237, 260
fowling. *See also* food resource
   generalised, 87
   intensive, 250, 251
   occasional, 250, 251, 256, 261, 264
   prehistory, 260, 335, 395
   specialised, 86, 250, 253, 255, 261–264
   unspecialised, 251
fowling methods, 238, 265. *See also individual methods*
fracture
   dry, 148, 154
   fresh, 120, 154
   healed, 36, 57, 342
   in live bird, 58, 60
   spiral, 142, 146, 228
fragmentation, 100, 121, 128, 131, 154, 348
   recording, 79
francolin, 30, 162, 201, 232, 332
   fighting, 325
Fremont period, 234
friendly fantail, 339, 406
Ft Berthold, 356
fulmar, 41, 167, 168, 206, 253, 406
funeral meal, 340, 348, 349
fusion, 36, 38–41, 46, 47, 279
   of spur, 39, 47, 274, 275, 277

gadfly petrel, 396, 406
Galapagos Islands, 8, 383
Galaz Ruin, 349
galliformes identification, 71
Gallo-Roman period, 276, 277, 279, 283
Ganj Dareh, 123, 124
gannet, 36, 37, 86, 87, 167, 168, 216, 232, 233, 236, 238, 240, 253, 366, 406
garganey, 74, 406
garment, 185, 186, 195, 203, 226, 336. *See also* clothing
gastrolith. *See* gizzard stone
Geelbek Dunes, 179

Geissenklosterle, 218
gender role. *See* men, women
Germany, 6, 263, 290, 362, 395
   Medieval, 296, 323
   Palaeolithic, 218, 246, 261
   Roman, 94, 95, 312, 351
Gibraltar, 15, 351, 366–368, 370, 372, 374, 380
gift
   feathers, 186
   live bird, 313
gift exchange, 188, 284
gizzard, 32, 33, 352
gizzard stone, 3, 14, 32–34, 357
glaucous gull, 45, 148, 406
Glenaray, 33
gnawing, 99, 124, 128, 131, 159, 162, 163, 361. *See also* chewing
   carnivore, 123, 124, 130, 147, 179
   rodent, 123, 124
Göbekli Tepe, 337, 355, 359
Gokstad ship, 195, 311
golden eagle, 125, 126, 406
golden-fronted woodpecker, 187, 406
goldfinch, 332, 406
goosander, 246, 256, 406
goshawk, 318, 323, 324, 406
   in grave, 323
Gotland, 51, 154, 221
Grasshopper Ruin, 345
grave goods, 340–344, 358
   birds, 344–345
   chicken, 340, 342, 344
   crane wing, 345
   domestic goose, 294
   eggs, 178–179
   food, 341, 343, 344, 348
   hawk, 346
   hen, 344
   raptor, 345
   scarlet macaw, 333, 345
   turkey, 345
   votive, 343
   wing, 345

Gravettian period, 133, 218, 219, 221. *See also* Upper Palaeolithic
grease, 67, 206, 213. *See also* fat
great auk, 9, 141, 142, 167, 204, 241, 258, 261, 263, 400, 406
    beak necklace, 226
    extinction, 2, 168, 237, 339, 384, 385, 392
Great Basin, 371, 372, 374
great black-backed gull, 106, 107, 118, 119, 149, 167, 236, 406
great bustard, 53, 152, 232, 261, 262, 264, 372, 406
great crested grebe, 66, 373, 406
great curassow, 243, 406
great grey shrike, 319, 406
great northern diver. *See* common loon
great skua, 41, 174, 406
great tinamou, 243, 406
great white egret, 199, 406
greater flamingo, 171, 332
greater spotted eagle, 225, 354, 406
great-tailed grackle, 187, 377, 406
Greece, 167, 186, 270, 284, 300, 306, 310, 311, 326, 330, 349
    Classical, 299, 311, 320
    Hellenistic, 47, 49, 178
    Palaeolithic, 152, 261
Greek colonies, 307
green peafowl, 310, 406
Greenland, 14, 45, 73, 147, 148, 195, 201, 202, 236, 238, 253, 258, 264
grey heron, 20, 406. *See also* heron
grey partridge, 133, 143, 261, 324, 406
greylag goose, 31, 132, 134, 210, 232, 287, 288, 292–293, 295, 406
    immature, 198
griffon vulture, 200, 201, 205, 212, 217, 221, 227, 359, 406
Grotta della Madonna, 134, 136, 138, 155
Grotta Romanelli, 132–134, 136, 145, 152, 155, 261, 262
Grotte Cosquer, 4, 400
Grotte de Bourouilla, 148
Grotte de la Madeleine, 390

grouse, 99, 115, 120, 130, 134, 145, 147, 243, 244, 259, 263, 380, 406. *See also* ptarmigan, willow grouse
    identification, 71, 72
Grus primigenia, 390
Guatemala, 289
guillemot, 11, 27, 51, 86, 87, 173, 177, 245, 247, 406
guineafowl, 174, 288, 311–312, 315, 407
    eggshell, 179
    identification, 72
    in Europe, 312
    plumage, 311
    skull, 311
Gulf of California, 357
Gulf of Georgia, 157, 212
gun, 237, 248, 325
Gürcütepe, 359
Guyana, 185
Gwennap, 327
gyrfalcon, 115, 120, 127, 196, 317, 318, 323, 407
    in grave, 323

Haast's eagle, 9, 118, 119, 252, 407
Haddenham, 39, 41, 102, 103, 107, 123, 177, 195, 256
Haida Gwaii, 186, 187
Haithabu, 280, 296
Haiti, 312, 322
Halikarnassos, 178, 182
Hamanaka, 202
Hamwic, 53, 140
Hanamiai, 252
Harappa, 311
harbinger
    of death, 340
    of the season, 1, 338
hatchling, 10, 11, 37, 46, 61, 268
Hauterive-Champréveyres, 256
Haversian canal, 17, 69
Havnø, 237
Hawai'i mamo, 187, 407
Hawaii, 105, 147, 186, 212, 375

hawking, 239, 316–325, 345
  bell, 320–322
  capture of hawk, 317
  equipment, 320, 321
  evidence from pathology, 323
  history, 316, 320–321
  mark of rank, 316, 317, 321, 325, 400
  predominance of females, 324
  prey, 317, 324
  species used, 317, 318
  training, 36, 319
Hawksburn, 142, 150
Hayonim, 221, 262, 372, 376
Hazendonk, 210, 234
headdress, 185, 186, 203
heath hen, 388, 407
Hebrides, 5, 142, 168, 189, 233, 253, 395
hen, 49, 95, 268, 274, 275, 344, 362. *See also* chicken
Hermopolis Magna. *See* Tuna el-Gebel
heron, 265, 318, 374, 407. *See also* grey heron
herring gull, 26, 28, 108, 149, 167, 232, 236, 407
Herschel Island, 255
Hextalls, 61, 102, 308
hide, 248, 319
Hittites, 320, 322
Hogup Cave, 193
Holocene era, 64, 239, 263, 365, 369, 373–374, 376, 379, 381, 384, 390, 392, 395
hominid, 238, 399
Honduras, 289
honey buzzard, 236, 260, 407
Honeycomb Hill Cave, 105
Hopi people, 336, 349
horned puffin, 407. *See also* puffins
Horniman Museum, London, 185
Hornish, 142
house martin, 41, 42, 407
House of Amarantus, Pompeii, 146, 350
house sparrow, 376–378, 407
Howard, Hildegarde, 5, 21, 87, 151
human speech, 184, 229, 335
  imitation, 198, 332, 363
Humboldt Current, 254

Humboldt, Nevada, 84, 156
Hungary, 64, 178, 220–223, 276, 342, 351
hunting, 385. *See also* fowling, hawking
  crane, 331
  ostrich, 331

I'iwi, 187, 407
Iceland, 14, 34, 144, 166, 167, 177, 237, 253, 264, 323, 384, 407
Iceland gull, 92, 148, 253, 407
identification, 2, 8, 21, 34, 63–64, 66–68, 76, 78–80, 84, 97, 98, 358, 366, 396–399. *See also* eggshell, feather
  corvids, 76, 78
  ducks, 74, 75
  geese, 73, 295, 296
  grouse, 71, 72
  guide, 67–68, 97
  micromorphology, 69
  pigeons, 74, 76
  process, 64–65
  swans, 75, 77
Illaunloughan monastery, 265
Illinois, 108, 122, 211
Inca culture, 200, 265
Indian peafowl, 310, 407, 408. *See also* peacock
Indian subcontinent, 1, 268–272, 284, 310, 311, 326, 358
International Council for Archaeozoology, 6, 70, 394, 419
introduced species
  avian, 377, 380. *See also individual domesticates*
  competitor, 388
  predator, 122, 381, 387, 392
intrusive material, 84, 182, 270, 348, 397
Inuit, 45, 168, 199, 205, 206, 226, 236, 260
Invercargill Museum, 243
Iowa, 356
Iran, 123, 124, 270. *See also* Persia
Ireland, 241, 265, 272, 305, 367

Isbister, 360
Isis, 351
Islamic era, 218, 220, 221
Israel, 262
Isturitz, 218, 219, 221, 400
Italy, 132, 133, 183, 208, 262, 271, 290, 303, 312, 369

jackass penguin, 239, 240, 258, 407
jackdaw, 104, 182, 333, 378, 407
Japan, 69, 202, 211, 239, 320, 336, 380, 396
Jenne-jeno, 273
Jordan, 35, 217, 323, 385

Kagamil Island, 195, 204, 226
kaka, 194, 197, 199, 203, 243, 332, 407
kakapo, 194, 407
Kalaureia, 47, 49, 178
Kamchatka, 168, 226, 237, 241
kelp goose, 203, 407
keratin, 21, 32, 38, 47, 184
king cormorant, 240, 407
King Harry Lane, St Albans, 150
king vulture, 186, 407
King's Rock, 224
Kings Lynn, 296
kinky back, 56
kittiwake, 45, 148, 168, 258, 404, 407
kiva, 289, 361
Klasies River Mouth, 261
Klintsø, 258
Klisoura Cave, 152, 261
knife, 138, 204
    flint, 138
    metal, 138, 140
Korea, 320, 322, 380, 396
Korucutepe, 271
Krakow Archaeological Museum, 217
k-resource, 250
Kunda culture, 263
Künzing, Temple of Mithras, 94, 351
Kuriles people, 199, 226

La Colombière, 185
La Grotte des Eglises, 130

La Playa, 357
La Starza, 208
La Vache, 72, 133, 134, 136, 144, 145, 147, 151, 253
Lacomb-Tayac, 100
Laguna de On, 93
Lake Mývatn, 167
Lamadeleine, 343
Langebaaweg, 110
lanner falcon, 323, 407
Lapita culture, 272
Lattera, 271
laughing falcon, 186, 407
Lavender Canyon, 194
Lavezzi, 101, 379
Laysan albatross, 69, 407
Lazaret, 261
Leach's storm petrel, 231, 407
least auklet, 231, 407
Lee Island, 194, 197, 199, 203
leg elements, 29–32, 125, 156
Les Eyzies, 209, 213, 390
lesser black-backed gull, 149, 167, 236, 407
ligament, 29, 38, 58, 67, 109, 113, 132, 133, 145, 202, 413
Lincoln, 57, 61, 296, 297
Links of Noltland, 81, 120
Lipari, 342
little auk, 366, 407
little bustard, 134, 152, 232, 262, 372, 407
little egret, 314, 407
little grebe, 374, 407
long-eared owl, 121, 367, 407
long-tailed duck, 371, 407
loons, 20, 29, 30
Lovelock Cave, 101, 147, 156, 157, 249, 397
Lower Palaeolithic, 81, 261
Lung Shan, 269
lure, 238, 317, 319, 321
Luxemburg, 343

Madagascar, 312, 383
Magdalenian period, 130, 133, 134, 137, 202, 218, 225, 228, 253, 257, 259, 263, 264. *See also* Upper Palaeolithic

Magellanic penguin, 237, 238, 241, 407
magpie, 332, 408
Malaysia, 311
Mali, 273
mallard, 25, 27, 74, 123, 136, 156, 232, 234, 256, 299–301, 315, 373, 408
Malta, 391
Mamluk period, 329
manx shearwater, 12, 31, 106, 107, 119, 237, 265, 366, 408
Maori, 167, 199, 234, 332
Maple Bank, 158, 212
marabou, 9, 70, 408
Marquesas Islands, 101, 252
marrow, 17–19, 50, 59, 67, 114, 122, 142, 147, 148, 162, 163, 233, 356
mass capture, 233, 235
Massachusetts, 331, 395
Mauritius, 8, 383, 385
Mayan civilisation, 93, 248
medicine bundle, 2, 203, 355–358, 366
Medio culture, 198, 313
medullary bone, 36, 48–53, 62, 258, 259, 298, 344, 395
    formation, 50, 367
    incidence, 51, 52, 169, 182, 282, 284
Meiendorf, 246
men, 168, 186, 204, 265, 317, 326, 330, 344, 345
Merriam's turkey, 291
Mértola, 220
Mesoamerica. See Central America
Mesolithic period, 152, 155, 224, 241, 242, 246, 250, 251, 257, 396
    Denmark, 86, 87, 200, 201, 237, 247, 250
Mesopotamia, 269, 293, 305, 331
messenger
    of the ancestors, 339
    of the gods, 339, 344, 363
Mexico, 4, 64, 186, 187, 248, 288, 289, 302, 312, 356, 357, 377
midden, 88, 90, 154, 156, 175, 177, 182, 366, 379
    coastal, 116, 154, 231, 240, 252, 395
    kitchen, 155, 257
    shell, 94, 156, 240, 254, 258, 396. See also shellmound

Middle Palaeolithic, 127, 261, 262
Middle Stone Age, 179
migration, 11, 14–15, 34, 192, 235, 236, 297, 319, 370, 371
Migration period, 53, 322
military macaw, 313, 347, 399, 408
Milne-Edwards, Alphonse, 5, 99, 131, 213, 390
Mimbres, 201, 289, 313, 345, 347, 348
Mitchell site, 356
Mithraism, 94, 351, 363
moa, 5, 9, 18, 37, 68, 104, 105, 231, 237, 245, 252
    bone, 6, 22, 25, 26, 42, 118, 119, 142, 150
    bone tool, 18, 212, 223, 224, 366
    eggshell, 172, 176, 179, 180
    extinction, 2, 382–384
    gizzard stone, 33
Mobridge site, 345, 356
Moche culture, 302
modern human, 229, 238, 335, 400
Modoc Rock Shelter, 211
Mogollon culture, 177
Mohenjo-Daro, 269
mollymawk, 214, 408
Moloka'i, 105, 212
Mons Claudianus, 176, 178, 194, 272
Monte Verde, 243
Morin, 148
moulting, 12, 50, 192, 197, 204
Mug House Ruin, 289
Mullerup, 258
muscle attachment, 67, 132, 134, 140
Muscovy duck, 288, 299, 302–304, 315, 408
    domestication, 302
    spread, 303
Muséum national d'Histoire naturelle, 65
music, 2, 229, 335, 400, 420
mute swan, 22–24, 26–28, 30, 33, 75, 84, 93, 94, 177, 232, 288, 314, 408
muttonbird, 236, 237, 252, 260. See also sooty shearwater

Natufian period, 221, 306, 372, 376
natural accumulation, 5, 7, 100, 104–105, 110, 131, 154, 156, 176, 212, 240, 365, 366, 392
    eggshell, 179

natural damage, 115. *See also* water sorting, weathering, bioerosion
Natural History Museum, 5, 65, 420
Nea Halos, 271, 306, 308
needle, 204, 206, 209, 210, 212, 213, 216
 manufacture, 214, 216
nestling, 10, 35, 45, 46, 240, 258
net, 156, 233, 235, 238, 244–250, 263, 266, 316, 319, 324, 393
Netherlands, 64, 244, 249, 319, 379
 Medieval, 150, 217, 322, 348
 Mesolithic, 152
 Neolithic, 88, 91, 210, 211, 215, 234, 264
 Roman, 260, 275, 277
Nevada, 101, 156, 371
Nevali Cori, 359
New Guinea, 4, 184, 185, 339, 358
New Mexico, 193, 289, 345, 347, 377
New Zealand, 9, 64, 88, 105, 184, 187, 189, 194, 199, 214, 217, 223, 241, 272, 381, 386. *See also* moa
New Zealand pigeon, 199, 408
Newfoundland, 214, 226, 384
Nicaragua, 289
nightingale, 332, 404, 408
Nijmegen, 154, 260, 340, 341
Nipisat, 45, 50, 73, 238, 258, 259
Niue, 273
non-analogue fauna, 369–370
non-anthropogenic
 assemblage, 182, 365, 397. *See also* natural accumulation
 species, 84, 371, 373
Norfolk Island parakeet, 389, 408
Norman period, 176, 299, 314
Normanton barrow, 218
Norse period, 253, 363. *See also* Viking period
North Africa, 178, 257, 306, 321, 331, 334, 371, 385
North American robin, 4, 408
North Dakota, 356
Northampton, 295
northern flicker, 185, 196, 408
Norway, 167, 168, 195, 199, 311, 323, 395

Norwich, 200, 281, 283, 333
notarium, 23, 24, 38, 39
notch
 beak mark, 119
 cut mark, 131
 dismembering, 144, 145
Nuchanulth, 186, 187, 241
Nunamira Cave, 177
Nunamiut, 167, 241, 256, 363
nutrient foramen, 19, 221
nutritional value, 230, 233, 234, 266

ocellated turkey, 287, 408
offering
 eggs, 178, 182
 food, 179, 344
 votive, 352, 354, 358, 364
Ohalo, 261
oil, 184, 206
Ølby Ling, 86
Old Crow Basin, 369
Oldenburg Castle, 53, 324
Omaha Indians, 188
Ona Indians, 203, 241, 244
o'o, 187
Oosterbeintum, 348
optimal foraging, 230
Oregon, 53, 214
Orkney, 116, 175
 archaeology, 81, 116, 141, 148, 175, 216, 236, 360, 384, 385
 ethnography, 166–168, 235, 243, 245, 247, 395
Orkrusset, 148
ornament
 bird, 301, 310, 316, 332–334
 bone, 138, 204, 221, 348, 362
ornithology, 3, 10, 15, 64, 368
osprey, 13, 408
ossification, 11, 38, 46, 47
osteoarthritis. *See* arthritis
osteon, 17, 69
osteopetrosis, 60–62
osteophyte, 58
osteoporosis, 55, 57, 62

ostrich, 9, 22, 32, 33, 194, 206, 231, 232, 288, 314, 373, 385, 408
   eggshell, 165, 179–181, 183
   eggshell bead, 180, 181
   eggshell flask, 181
Otford Castle, 172
overkill, 381–385
Owen, Richard, 5, 6
owls, 118, 126–128, 339, 345. *See also* pellet
   prey, 87, 115, 366
   ritual importance, 337, 362
   skeletal anatomy, 25, 29, 30
Oxford, 328, 329, 396
oystercatcher, 167, 408
Ozette, 210, 212

Pacific Northwest, 147, 157, 164, 167, 186, 200, 210, 212, 214, 216, 241, 376, 394, 400
Pailón, 302
Palaeoeskimo period, 253
palaeontology, 3, 5, 6, 34, 104, 365, 396
Paleo-Indian period, 211, 361, 371
Palliser Bay, 88, 199
Panama, 243, 302
papillae ulnare. *See* quill knob
parka, 204
parrots, 1, 12, 25, 29, 30, 32, 189, 198, 199, 207, 244, 313, 332, 333, 387
passenger pigeon, 51, 384, 392, 408
passerines, 11, 12, 20, 82, 100, 101, 111, 117, 361, 366
   food remains, 102, 153, 233, 261
   identification, 26, 29, 63
   raptor prey, 116
Patagonia, 5, 45, 78, 148, 158, 203, 234, 235, 237, 238, 240, 241, 243, 244, 254, 255
Paternoster, 240, 258
peacock, 9, 140, 141, 192, 198, 288, 310–311, 314–316, 332, 334, 408
   in grave, 195
pectoral girdle, 23, 26
peeling, 131, 144, 145, 163
pelicans, 13, 25, 30, 36, 123
pellet, 84, 104, 117, 118, 121, 126, 127, 129, 156, 387

eagle owl, 125
gyrfalcon, 119, 120
owl, 81, 116, 117, 120, 125, 128, 376
peregrine falcon, 25, 117, 118, 125, 126, 317–319, 323, 354, 408
   in grave, 323
periosteal layer, 17, 40, 41, 43, 50
periosteal new bone, 59, 60
Persia, 271, 310, 320, 326. *See also* Iran
Peru, 109, 138, 185, 239, 302
pet. *See* companion animal
Petersfels, 261
pheasant, 11, 20, 30, 31, 64, 71, 192, 195, 233, 234, 270, 285, 288, 314, 318, 404, 408
   identification, 71
Philippines, 325–327
Phipps Mill Creek, 356
Phoenician settlement, 271
Phum Snay, 271
pied bushchat, 339, 408
pin, 209, 213, 215
pink-footed goose, 34, 297, 408
pintail, 176, 373, 408
pitfall, 245, 368
Plains Indians, 2, 185, 186
pleasure, 265, 308, 316, 332
Pleistocene era, 4, 14, 261, 369, 371, 376, 379, 380, 390
   avian distribution, 377
   cave assemblage, 72, 130, 306, 365, 367, 370
Pliocene era, 4
plucking, 132, 163, 188, 197, 204, 233, 393
   by raptors, 116, 197
   live bird, 197–199, 246, 293. *See also* secondary product
plumage, 10, 35, 192, 303, 314, 332, 349, 358, 364, 375
Pluscarden Priory, 195, 197
pneumatic foramen, 19, 20, 26, 28, 73
pneumatisation, 18, 20, 21, 160, 218
pochard, 94, 244, 404, 408
Poland, 111, 225, 257
Polderweg, 257, 374
polish, 213, 219, 221, 223, 225, 228
Polynesia, 101, 147, 184, 186, 189, 207

chickens, 286
extinctions, 5, 252, 387, 388, 390, 392, 395
Polynesian colonists, 2, 237, 252, 384
Pompeii, 123, 124, 146, 349, 352
Ponsonby, 254, 255
Pool, 141, 216
porosity, 36, 37, 39, 40, 45, 46, 56, 61, 159
Port au Choix, 214, 226
Portchester Castle, 301
Portugal, 219, 220, 371
Post-Medieval, 61, 248, 279, 297, 304, 311, 334
Potrero-Chaquiago, 200
Pottery Mound site, 377
Pounawea, 214, 224
prairie falcon, 356, 408
prairie hen, 73, 408
precocial species, 11, 12, 38
pre-Columbian era, 199, 273, 285, 286, 288, 303, 397
Pre-Pottery Neolithic, 74, 123, 200, 201, 221, 222, 235, 236, 306, 337, 359
preservation. *See* food preservation, survival
prey selection, 115, 369
    carnivore, 121, 122
    human, 98, 231, 250
    raptors, 115–116
protein, 231, 233, 267, 308
    bird meat, 233, 234
    egg, 169
ptarmigan, 71, 99, 115, 130, 134, 136, 144, 151, 177, 246, 253, 262, 264, 318, 369, 370, 409. *See also* grouse
Pueblo, 178, 182, 194, 198, 289, 291, 292, 313, 348, 360, 399
puffins, 144, 167, 168, 237, 243, 245–247
pullet, 56, 95, 268
purple gallinule, 332, 409
pygmy cormorant, 396, 409
pyre, 150, 342, 348

Qajaa, 148
Qasr Ibrim, 201, 354
Qoormoq, 148
quail, 174, 261, 329, 332, 373, 404, 409
    fighting, 325

quantification, 83, 85, 92, 93, 98
    bone weight, 88, 91, 93–95, 97
    kilocalories, 94, 96, 98
    log ratio, 86, 87
    meat weight, 89, 94–97
    minimum number of elements, 88, 90, 95
    minimum number of individuals, 85, 87–88, 92, 95
    number of identified specimens, 85, 92, 95
Quebrada Tacahuay, 138, 153, 239, 254, 263
quill, 188, 189. *See also* feather
quill knob, 28, 219
Qujialing, 269
Qumran Cave, 153, 222, 225, 306

racing, 331
radiocarbon dating, xxiv, 285, 366, 397, 399
Rancho La Brea, 5, 53, 87, 105, 366
range, 1, 13, 131, 229, 284, 375, 379
    contraction, 64, 292, 367, 370, 378–380, 384–386, 389
    expansion, 55, 64
Rapa Nui. *See* Easter Island
raptors
    ritual importance, 362
Raqqa, 221
ratites, 8, 18, 23, 88, 162, 165, 191, 252
raven, 1, 62, 76, 226, 332, 337, 345, 349, 356, 359, 361, 376, 378, 409
    beliefs about, 363
    ritual importance, 363–364
razorbill, 5, 51, 167, 245, 409
recipe, 233, 311, 341, 343
recording, 98, 398. *See also* bone zone
    age class, 46, 61
    elements, 78, 83
    size class, 81–84
    unidentifiable fragments, 82, 83
recovery, 21, 79, 83, 100, 128, 272, 393. *See also* sieving
    hand, 83, 102, 103
    sampling, 102, 103
red grouse. *See* willow grouse

red junglefowl, 165, 268–270, 273, 280, 281, 284, 409
red kite, 378, 409
red-billed chough. *See also* choughs
red-breasted merganser, 48, 257, 409
red-crowned crane, 217, 390, 409
red-crowned parakeet, 88, 200, 409
red-necked grebe, 66, 409
redshank, 41, 318, 404, 409
red-tailed hawk, 357, 409
red-throated diver, 374, 409
reed bunting, 374, 409
reference collection, 420
    eggshell, 175, 183
    feathered skins, 65, 193, 420
    skeletons, 6, 65–67, 84, 97, 420
refugium, 369, 380
Regensburg cemetery, 179
resplendent quetzal, 187, 409
rheas, 158, 165, 241, 409
ritual
    deposit, 176, 182, 225
    item, 2, 198, 203, 216, 228, 358
    meal, 342
    refuse, 360, 361
robe. *See also* cloak
rock dove, 9, 111, 115, 153, 156, 237, 271, 304–308, 314, 409
    identification, 75
rock partridge, 261, 409
rock sparrow, 100, 409
Roman Empire, 183, 233, 301, 340, 341, 344, 351
Romania, 225, 270
Romano-British period, 173, 175, 179, 301, 307, 314, 321, 327, 331, 364, 376
    chickens, 43–45, 92, 272, 277, 281, 329
Rome, 290, 293, 308, 311, 320, 326, 330, 332, 338, 349
rook, 66, 76, 78, 94, 318, 409
roost, 104, 116, 125, 127, 128, 164, 237, 361, 366
rooster. *See* cock
root etching, 111
r-resource, 250

ruffed grouse, 73, 409
Russia, 241, 242, 332

Saarburg, 312
sacred ibis, 2, 36, 45, 46, 314, 409
sacrifice, 150, 349–352
    chicken, 43, 272, 349–352, 362
    cock, 342, 350
    macaw, 349
    partridge, 342
sacrificial bird, 265, 268, 284, 293, 299, 305, 308, 314, 332, 336
Sagalassos, 51, 53, 277, 278, 280
sage grouse, 51, 53, 409
saker falcon, 353, 409
Samos, Temple of Hera, 310
Sancton, 344
Sand Canyon Pueblo, 290, 360, 361
sandhill crane, 211, 361, 409
Saqqara, 353
sarus crane, 390, 409
scanning electron microscopy, 131, 163, 171, 173, 175
scarlet macaw, 2, 265, 287–289, 312–314, 345, 362, 399, 400, 409
    burial, 347
    feathers, 189, 193, 198, 201
scavenging, 104, 108, 109, 114, 115, 126, 397
    birds, 13, 107, 323, 359, 376, 378
    carnivore, 122, 179
    herbivore, 122
    human, 7, 212, 239–240, 263
    raven, 363
    vulture, 116, 362
Schipluiden, 88, 91, 101, 264
Schleswig, 296
Scotland, 5, 34, 64, 167, 168, 195, 236–238, 240, 263, 272, 293, 336, 384, 395
scrape mark, 137, 138, 203, 207, 212, 215, 217, 222, 223, 226. *See also* cut mark
screening. *See* sieving
season of capture, 257. *See also* breeding colony, moulting
    autumn, 257, 260, 366

breeding, 258, 259
moult, 12, 237, 241
spring, 236, 254, 255, 257, 259, 266
summer, 240, 253, 254, 258, 266
winter, 15, 86, 235, 254, 257, 266, 366
season of occupation. *See* seasonal indicator, season of capture
seasonal indicator, 15, 204, 256
eggshell, 168
immature birds, 258
medullary bone, 258–259
migrant, 257
secondary product, 97, 315
eggs. *See* egg collecting, egg production
feathers, 197–199
sedentism, 124, 270, 305, 376
Senegal, 311
Sesselfelsgrotte, 127
sex distinctions, 398. *See* sexual dimorphism, medullary bone, spur
sexual dimorphism, 36, 43, 49, 53–55, 65, 71, 73–75, 280, 291, 302, 304, 317
shag, 5, 41, 167, 232, 237, 379, 409
Shag Mouth, 179, 180, 252
sharp-shinned hawk, 371, 409
Sheepen, 364
sheldgeese, 78, 409
shellmound, 5, 155, 156, 160, 161, 239
Shetland Islands, 167
Shijiahe, 269
short-eared owl, 51, 116, 121, 196, 264, 367, 409
short-tailed albatross, 69, 211, 397, 409
shrine, 349, 355, 364
Siberia, 14, 198, 292
Sicily, 317, 321, 342
sieving, 82, 83, 100, 102, 103, 128, 393
bulk, 101
mesh size, 101, 103
Sigtuna, 49
Silchester, 45, 52, 284, 329
sinew, 138, 184, 195, 196, 204–206, 214, 216, 243, 244, 246. *See also* tendon
Sioux Indians, 188
Skara Brae, 175
Skedemose, 272

skeletal malformation, 55, 56
skeletal maturation, 10, 17, 29, 35, 36
skeleton
number of bones, 92
skin, 2, 113, 184, 204, 213, 234, 355. *See also* feathered skin
Skomer Island, 107
skull elements, 21–22
sky burial, 358–360
sling, 241
Slovakia, 362
Smyrna, 326
snare, 238, 243–246, 263, 393
snipe, 93, 94, 231, 232, 318, 404, 410
snow goose, 22, 211, 258, 410
snowy owl, 32, 55, 115, 120, 137–140, 145, 202, 203, 225, 226, 228, 380, 410
Society for Avian Palaeontology and Evolution (SAPE), 419
socket primordium. *See* spur scar
Solymár, 178
song thrush, 66, 154, 232, 260, 410
songbirds, 146, 233, 352. *See also* passerines
sooty shearwater, 214, 234, 255, 410
sooty tern, 167, 338, 410
sorting, 103
South Africa, 45, 110, 179, 181, 239, 240, 261
South Dakota, 345, 356
Southeast Asia, 248, 268, 272, 273, 288, 300, 302, 303, 310, 375
Southern Britain, 43, 102, 283, 284, 301, 326, 360, 379, 421
Southwark Roman cemetery, 342
Spain, 212, 219, 261, 271, 367, 369, 377, 380
sparrowhawk, 125, 321, 323, 324, 374, 405, 410
in grave, 323
spear, 241, 248, 331
special animal deposit, 360
spectacled eider, 258, 410
speech. *See* human speech
Spong Hill, 225, 344
spoonbill, 222, 410
sport, 265, 316

spotted eagle-owl. *See* Cape eagle-owl
spur, 30, 35, 274
    artificial, 326–329
    development, 38, 43, 47, 48
    modification, 274, 326, 328, 329
    on hen, 49, 281
    shield, 47, 49
spur scar, 47–49, 274–276, 278, 279
St Albans Abbey, 53
St Gregory's Priory, 52, 79, 102, 142, 143, 146, 153, 284
St Kilda, 167, 168, 188, 206, 215, 243, 253, 260, 265, 339, 395
stable isotope analysis, 397
stalking horse, 248
Star Carr, 257
starling, 100, 104, 306, 332, 378, 410
steamer duck, 45, 78, 243, 254, 258, 410
stick, 240, 241, 246. *See also* club
stock dove, 76, 410
    identification, 75
stork, 217, 257, 373, 378, 410
storm petrels, 206
Sumeria, 326
survival
    bird bone, 21, 105, 107, 109, 162, 272, 393
    bird bone tool, 213, 229
    element, 79, 97, 98, 107, 108, 124–128, 131, 156–158, 161–164, 227, 240, 397–398
sustainable harvesting
    eggs, 168
    wild birds, 253, 395
swan goose, 287, 288, 292, 410
Sweden, 49, 236, 243, 260, 263, 272, 299, 301, 321, 322, 345, 346, 376, 377
swift, 100, 101, 104, 410
Swifterbant, 210, 234
synanthropic species, 75, 374, 375–378
    farmers, 376
    hunters, 375
    towns, 378
Syria, 74, 75, 100, 123, 200, 201, 218, 236, 269–271, 359
syrinx, 21, 48

taboo, 336. *See also* food avoidance
Tahuata, 101, 272
Taï, 134–136, 155, 263, 264
takahe, 388, 410
talisman, 224, 226, 348, 356–358, 366
    beak, 226
tamed bird, 198, 287
    goose, 293
    jackdaw, 333
    mallard, 300
    mute swan, 333
    ostrich, 314, 331
    pheasant, 314
    sacred ibis, 182
    swan, 168
taming, 267, 325
Tamula, 345
Tangatatau Rockshelter, 387–389
Tasmanian emu, 177, 410
tawny owl, 30, 31, 340, 367, 410
taxonomy, 4, 34, 85, 419, 420
Te Papa Tongarewa, Museum of New Zealand, 187
teal, 74, 84, 94, 156, 232
Tell Hesban, 35, 217, 225, 323, 329, 385
Tell Mureybet, 74, 75, 123, 235
Tell Sweyhat, 271
tendon, 29, 32, 67, 113, 132
terminology
    bird names, xxiii, 403
    directional, 21
    skeletal elements, 5, 15, 16, 32
Tertiary era, 110
Thailand, 268, 271
thick-billed murre. *See* Brunnich's guillemot
thick-billed parrot, 313, 345, 347, 348, 410
Thorsbjerg, 188
Thule culture, 253
Tibet, 358
Tibocoaia Cave, 225
Tienen, 351
Tikopia Island, 252
Tlatilo, 289
Tlingit people, 167, 394

Tofts Ness, 116, 121, 148, 149, 236
Tokerau, 176
Tonga, 252
Torre della Curia, Genoa, 312
totem animal, 226, 336
trabecular bone, 18, 19, 160
trade, 289
    bone tool, 158
    eggs, 167
    feathers, 188, 189, 199, 200, 288, 400
    live birds, 289, 311, 312
    oil, 206
    wild birds, 250, 259, 260, 265, 366
    wings, 212
trap, 245, 316, 319, 324
    natural, 105, 237, 368
trapping, 229, 231, 243, 244
tufted duck, 244, 410
tufted puffin, 410. *See also* puffins
    with burial, 226
tui, 200, 332
Tularosa Cave, 177, 289
Tuna el-Gebel, 45, 46, 354
Túnel, 90, 92, 94, 96, 160, 209, 212, 226, 228
turkey
    corral, 177, 289
    feathers, 188, 193, 203, 207, 289, 291
    identification, 72
    sexing, 53
    size, 74
    spur, 43
    wild, 51, 53, 72, 232, 287, 291
Turkey, 51, 178, 270, 277, 278, 284. *See also* Anatolia
turkey vulture, 186, 356, 361, 410
turtle dove, 74, 410
Tutankhamen's tomb, 194
Twann, 245, 256
twite, 235, 410

Ukraine, 270
Uley, Temple of Mercury, 43, 44, 351
Umingmak, 258

University of California Museum of Vertebrate Zoology, 65, 419
University of Kansas Natural History Museum, 65
University of Michigan Museum of Zoology, 65, 419
University of Southampton, 6, 92
Upper Palaeolithic, 188, 205, 257, 400
    art, 226, 229
    bird bone objects, 209, 218, 225
    butchery, 134, 136
    cooking, 153
    feathers, 184
    fowling, 130, 231, 243, 246, 261, 263
Utah, 193, 234, 313, 385
utility index, 98

Vancouver Island, 158, 255
Varro, 270, 274, 293, 294, 310, 311
Vaufrey, 104
Vedbaek, 226, 247, 345
Velsen, 275, 277, 278, 280, 295, 301, 311, 329, 331
velvet scoter, 237, 367, 410
vertebrae, 22, 23, 79, 81, 109
veterinary science, 15, 21, 48, 61
Viking period, 2, 49, 177, 195, 202, 216, 344
villa, 93, 272, 301, 311, 321
Vimose, 188
Visegrad, 220
Visigothic period, 219
vision, 1, 186
voice, 1, 2, 316, 339, 363
vultures, 207
    ritual importance, 337, 359, 362

Wadi Kubbaniya, 257
Wageningen University, 66, 420
Wairau Bar, 176, 179
WaiWai people, 185, 339
Walbrook, Temple of Mithras, 351
Wales, 107, 327
Warring States period, 301

Washington State, 158, 210
water sorting, 100, 109–110
waterlogged conditions, 107, 177, 195, 210
Watmough Bay, 157
wear, 215, 217, 218, 220, 221, 226, 228. *See also* polish
weathering, 104, 109–112, 119, 120, 128
  experimental, 111
  stages, 112, 113
weight. *See* body weight
West Africa, 272, 303, 304, 311, 338, 362
West Indies, 72, 311. *See also* Caribbean Islands
Western Asia, 3, 183, 263, 265, 270, 271, 285, 288, 292, 306, 362, 385, 399, 400
Western Cape, 179–181, 239, 240, 258
Whale Cove, 214
Whalen Farm, 157
whistle, 209, 217, 218, 248. *See also* flute
white pelican, 379, 410
white-fronted goose, 26, 132, 134, 262, 406, 410
white-fronted tern, 167, 410
white-rumped vulture, 358, 410
white-tailed ptarmigan, 195, 196, 198, 410
white-tailed sea eagle, 26, 201, 202, 210, 211, 359, 363, 366, 376, 378, 395, 410
whooper swan, 34, 54, 55, 75, 200, 210, 218, 257, 411
whooping crane, 411
  in burial, 356
wigeon, 132, 134, 411
wildfowling. *See* fowling

willow grouse, 27, 71, 232, 234, 264, 318, 369, 370, 411. *See also* grouse
  identification, 71
Winchester, 52, 61, 200, 203, 296, 298, 323, 340
wing, 185, 200, 201, 345, 354, 356
  crane, 355
  fan, 349
  in grave, 201
  temple furniture, 201
wing elements, 26–29, 125, 146, 156, 158, 159, 164, 192, 202, 207, 398
wing removal, 79, 140, 142, 145, 146, 163, 199, 352. *See also* cut mark
women, 168, 186, 204, 216, 231, 317, 330, 344, 345
Wood Quay, Dublin, 123, 124, 142, 144
wood swallow, 358
woodcock, 15, 94, 243, 344, 374, 411
woodpigeon, 24, 76, 232, 308, 318, 411
  identification, 74
wreck, 35, 105, 366

Yámana, 204, 228
Yanomamo, 332
yelkouan shearwater, 379, 411
Yellow Jacket Pueblo, 290
yellow-crowned parakeet, 88, 200
Yerba Buena shellmound, 161
York, 57, 277, 281, 329
Yoruba region, 362
Yukon, 195–198, 369
Yuquot, 212